Principles of
Social Psychology

Principles of
Social Psychology

Kelly G. Shaver
The College of William and Mary

Winthrop Publishers, Inc.
Cambridge, Massachusetts

Library of Congress Cataloging in Publication Data

Shaver, Kelly G
  Principles of social psychology.

  Includes bibliographies and index.
  1. Social psychology. I. Title.
HM251.S465   301.1   76-46598
ISBN 0-87626-696-0

© 1977 by Winthrop Publishers, Inc.
17 Dunster Street, Cambridge, Massachusetts 02138

10 9 8 7 6 5 4 3 2 1

Text design by Sandra Rigney
Cover design by Melanson Associates

To my Mother and Father
and again,
to Carole

Contents

Social Perception: The Other Person as a Stimulus Object   91
Chapter Three

Preface

The field of social psychology encompasses theory, research, and practical application, and no introductory textbook can do justice to all three concerns. As the title *Principles of Social Psychology* suggests, I have chosen to emphasize conceptual ideas rather than the natural social relevance of the discipline. The understanding of social behavior and the solution of social problems are important goals for social psychology, and they are goals I support. My emphasis upon theory reflects my belief that concepts need to be taught, whereas practical applications will readily suggest themselves to people who know the concepts.

As much as possible, I have tried to write a book that would *teach* the concepts of social psychology. The structure of the book progresses from internal processes of social perception and attitude formation to interpersonal phenomena of social influence and group behavior; all the chapters were written in the order in which they appear. Throughout this development of the book, however, the level of theoretical analysis remains the same. I have applied the mid-range theories of social psychology both to social perception and to group processes, rather than shifting from a psychological approach on the one hand to a sociological approach on the other. Through extensive cross-referencing of concepts I have sought to show some of the history and progression of social psychology, to integrate various aspects of the discipline, and to aid instructors who would prefer to take the chapters in a different order.

But organization alone is not enough. To simplify the reader's learning task, chapters open with outlines of the topics to be presented and close with summaries and lists of suggested additional readings. Important concepts are printed in color and included in a glossary at the end of the book. Although a particular theory's usefulness may be mentioned at several different locations, a thorough description of the theory will be found in a single place. No attempt has been made to catalogue all the research in social psychology; studies that are described were chosen for their historical or explanatory value, and principles are often illustrated with everyday examples. Even with these aids to learning, the study of social psychology remains conceptually challenging and this book reflects some of that challenge.

With two exceptions, chapters in the book were intended to be roughly equivalent in length. First, the chapter on research methods (Chapter Two) is significantly longer than average in order to permit comparisons among methods in a single chapter. This chapter may also prove the most difficult, especially for students with little previous exposure to psychological research. As a consequence, some instructors may wish to consider the chapter in two parts—non-experimental methods and experimental methods. Second, the chapter on reinforcement and social exchange (Chapter Nine) is significantly shorter than average. It deals with theories—social learning, exchange, equity—that have applications to a variety of topics in interpersonal behavior, so it stands alone rather than being grafted onto a particular topic. Because of its more exclusive concentration on theory, it may well require as much time as the longer topical chapters.

This book reflects my view of social psychology, but that viewpoint and my way of communicating it bear the imprint of a number of teachers and friends whose contributions I wish to acknowledge. As an undergraduate student I was introduced to social psychology by Jack Brehm, and I was to benefit from his advice during my graduate education as well. As a graduate student I learned a great deal about teaching from Bert Forrin. Ezra Stotland impressed upon me the social relevance of social psychology, and his commitment to practical applications still serves as an excellent example. John Thibaut stimulated my interest in interpersonal processes, and his requirement for a weekly paragraph taught me to be concise. To Ladd Wheeler I owe many of my attitudes about the profession of social psychology, as well as what I know about social comparison theory. My greatest debt is to Ned Jones, whose willing guidance contributed so much to my graduate education, whose heavy blue pencil dramatically improved my writing, and whose friendship I continue to enjoy.

Although I bear the responsibility for whatever weaknesses are in the book, a number of people deserve mention for their participation in its completion. My thanks first to Paul O'Connell of Winthrop Publishers for giving me the opportunity to write this book, and for his ideas, encouragement, and support during its preparation. Mark Snyder, David Lundgren, Robert A. Baron, William Ickes, Alice H.

Eagly, Ronald P. Abeles, Robert E. Kleck, and Donnah Canavan-Gumpert graciously reviewed and commented on various portions of the manuscript. A special note of thanks goes to Barbara Sonnenschein of Winthrop, whose perceptive and judicious copy-editing contributed a great deal to the readability of the book. I am grateful to my students at William and Mary for their suggestions about early drafts of the book, and to my colleagues for their goodwill and encouragement along the way. Finally, I could not have done the book at all without the help of my wife, Carole, who read the entire manuscript as it was written and rewritten, suggested major organizational changes that improved several chapters, insisted upon an epilogue, and continually forced me to be clear. She also typed the entire manuscript, helped me proofread galleys and pages, kept our daughter Vicky out of my study, and provided the support I needed to complete such a sustained project.

K. G. S.

Acknowledgments

Table 1-1: Copyright 1963 by the American Psychological Association. Reprinted by permission.

Figure 2-1: From H. L. Ross and D. T. Campbell, The Connecticut speed crackdown: A study of the effects of legal change. In H. L. Ross (Ed.), *Perspectives on the Social Order*. New York: McGraw-Hill, 1968. Copyright 1968 by McGraw-Hill. Reprinted with permission of the author and the publisher.

Figure 2-2: Copyright 1969 by the American Psychological Association. Reprinted by permission.

Table 2-3: Copyright 1969 by the American Psychological Association. Reprinted by permission.

Figure 3-2: From E. T. Hall, Proxemics. *Current Anthropology*, 1968, 9, 83–95. Copyright 1968 by the Wenner-Gren Foundation for Anthropological Research, Inc. Reprinted by permission of the author and The University of Chicago Press, publisher.

Figure 3-4: Copyright 1952 by the American Psychological Association. Reprinted by permission.

Figure 4-4: Adapted from H. H. Kelley, Attribution Theory in Social Psychology, from *Nebraska Symposium on Motivation, 1967*, edited by D. Levine, by permission of University of Nebraska Press. Copyright 1967 by the University of Nebraska Press.

Table 5-1: Data copyright 1951, 1969, 1971 by the American Psychological Association. Adapted by permission of the publisher and the authors.

Box, p. 178: From Angus Campbell, *White Attitudes toward Black People*. Copyright © August 1971 by the Institute of Social Research. All rights reserved. Reprinted by permission of the author and the Institute for Social Research of the University of Michigan.

Table 5-3: From L. L. Thurstone (Ed.), *The Measurement of Social Attitudes*. Copyright 1932 The University of Chicago. Reprinted by permission of The University of Chicago Press, publisher.

Figure 11-5: Copyright 1960 by the American Psychological Association. Reprinted by permission.

Table 11-1: Reprinted by permission of Silver Burdett Company.

Figure 12-1: Copyright 1946 John Wiley & Sons. Adapted by permission of the publisher.

Table 12-2: Copyright 1970 Academic Press. Adapted with permission of the author and publisher.

Figure 13-1: Leavitt material copyright 1960 by the American Psychological Association. Reprinted by permission.

While the decisive answers social psychology presently has to offer
are limited, the questions it asks are fascinating.

Social Psychology: What It Is and What It Is Not

Chapter One

Even more than in the year before, Amory neglected his work, not deliberately but lazily and through a multitude of other interests. Co-ordinate geometry and the melancholy hexameters of Corneille and Racine held forth small allurements, and even psychology, which he had eagerly awaited, proved to be a dull subject full of muscular reactions and biological phrases rather than the study of personality and influence. That was a noon class, and it always sent him dozing.

F. Scott Fitzgerald
This Side of Paradise

As it happens, Amory might well have been surprised even by social psychology, although social influence is one of the major topics in any social psychology course. Why? Because he would have expected a different balance between research and theory on the one hand and practical application on the other. Never mind about theories of social power and experimental research on interpersonal influence, teach me how to maintain my independence. Never mind about models of social exchange, just tell me why people like each other. Never mind about theories of social perception and attribution, just show me how to read and understand people's thoughts and motives.

Fitzgerald's character was describing psychology as it was taught just prior to the 1920s, but the problem of student expectations is as important today as it was then. Courses in English are not all grammar and composition, courses in history are not all names and dates from past centuries, and courses in social psychology are not all solutions to social problems. This is not to say that there is no social relevance in social psychology; one of the reasons social psychologists build theories and do research is their hope that the knowledge gained will be of social benefit. It is just that the *transition* between accumulated knowledge and social policy is not as direct, nor as immediate, as many beginning students might expect it to be. Indeed, if only facts are considered, the knowledge-action transition can become more difficult, rather than less difficult, as our information about the problem increases.

At the most basic level, it is simpler to make a decision on the basis of our own values and biases than it is to consider any information whatsoever: "My mind is made up, don't confuse me with the facts." For example, let us examine the social problem of welfare. Perhaps the simplest solution is to assert that people's dependence upon government assistance is not really a *social* problem at all, but rather an individual problem. If we assume that anyone who wants to work can get a job, then the only cause for being on welfare is personal laziness, and this line of reasoning leads to the conclusion that all welfare should be terminated. After all, why should those of us who work and pay our taxes be required to support people who are too lazy to find work for themselves? There, my mind is made up. But what are the facts?

Suppose we learned that at least 35 percent of welfare money goes to disabled persons and to children under the age of twelve. Can we believe these figures and still argue that only laziness is involved? Most probably not. So now our decision becomes more complicated. Provide assistance to children and disabled people, but not to any able-bodied adults. But suppose an additional 10 percent of money goes to people whose education and training are so meager that it is virtually impossible for them to obtain employment in today's tech-nological society? What about the amount that goes to well-trained people who have been laid off their jobs because of the state of the national economy? Or the amount that goes to the mothers of all of those children in homes where the father is absent? If we force the women to work, who will look after the children? Simple, put the kids into day care centers. But what if there are not nearly enough day care centers? Notice that the facts have not only complicated our thinking about welfare, they have identified at least four other prob-lems—education, unemployment, father absence and lack of day care facilities—which ought to be considered at the same time. Our social policy decision has been complicated by these new aspects of the problem, and we realize that our decision must take these additional factors into account.

The relationship between accumulated knowledge and social action would be made even less strong should we discover that some of our newly acquired information contradicts what we thought we already knew for sure. Suppose I want to convince you that your taxes should be raised (we will assume that you would initially oppose such a raise). Let us further suppose that I thought the best way to accomplish this change in attitude would be to have you make a public statement to the effect that everyone's taxes (obviously includ-ing your own) should be increased. Now what would happen if I offered to pay you to make such a statement? For a good many years we would simply have assumed that the more money I paid you, the more you would change your attitude in favor of what I wanted you to say, just as any reinforcement or incentive theory would predict. But an experiment by Festinger and Carlsmith (1959) obtained just the opposite results. The more subjects were paid to advocate publicly a position counter to their own position, the *less* they changed their attitudes in the direction they advocated. We shall return to a more detailed discussion of this study and subsequent research in Chapter Six. For now, however, it is sufficient to note that Festinger and Carlsmith's results appear to contradict a well-established principle. So now if you were to approach me and say, "All right, you are the social psychologist; you tell me whether I can get people to want higher taxes more by paying them a lot of money to advocate a tax increase, or by paying them practically nothing for advocating an increase," I would have to answer that it would depend upon the circumstances. You would think (correctly) that I had not been of much help.

We have seen that the simple accumulation of facts, by revealing new aspects of a problem, reducing the chances for free exercise of bias, and suggesting alternative possible outcomes of a decision can actually reduce the certainty with which social policy decisions are made. In the practice of their profession, social psychologists deal with this uncertainty in three principal ways: gathering the data, building theories, and qualifying their conclusions. First, they gather whatever data they believe to be relevant to the problems that interest them. A social psychologist interested in attitude change would attempt to determine the conditions under which increasing the payment would lead to greater attitude change and the conditions under which increasing the payment would actually reduce the attitude change. Does the payment have to be money, or will some other reward work in the same way? How does the strength of your attitude before the experiment change the results? Will the nature of the audience of your public advocacy make any difference in the amount of your attitude change? These data and others are necessary for a full understanding of the issue.

The second way that social psychologists deal with uncertainty is by devising theories to account for particular results. The prediction that attitude change will vary as a direct function of payment is a derivation from traditional reinforcement theory. The prediction that Festinger and Carlsmith actually confirmed was a derivation from a different sort of theory, to be discussed more fully in Chapter Six. The organization of various social facts into theories has three primary advantages for the social psychologist: simplification, determination of explanatory value, and prediction to novel situations.

First, a theory simplifies the task of cataloguing a large number of different phenomena. Without any organizing theories, I would have to remember all of the single bits of experimental and anecdotal data that social psychology has accumulated. With theories available to guide me, I can better recall where certain data can be found, and more importantly I can know what "facts" can safely be ignored. It isn't necessary for me to remember the evidence in favor of a thoroughly discredited theory. If social facts were all listed in a large mail-order catalog, theories would serve as the index, the sort of index that tells which lines of merchandise have been discontinued.

The second advantage of having theories is that they, unlike isolated facts, can be compared to each other to determine their explanatory value. Facts tell you what is the case, and theories try to explain why those particular facts occur as they do. The explanatory value of a theory depends upon the number of isolated facts it appears to explain and on the number of different situations in which it applies (in both cases more is better). Does one theory account for more of the available data than another, and does it seem to apply to more different situations? If so, then it is a better candidate for reducing the uncertainty generated by all of those previously conflicting facts.

The third advantage of building theories is that they allow predictions to be made for novel situations. Once again, facts tell you only what is the case now, not what is likely to be the case in the future. And just as theories can be compared to determine their relative explanatory value, they can be compared to determine their relative predictive value. The more often a theory generates predictions that bear out, the more confident we can be about it and the more we can rely upon it to reduce the uncertainty inherent in facts alone.

The gathering of data and the building of theory lead naturally to the third way in which social psychologists attempt to deal with the ambiguity of social phenomena—qualification of conclusions. In the case of attitude change following public advocacy of a position inconsistent with an initial opinion, we have seen that the social psychologist's answer to the policy maker is not "Pay more" or "Pay less," but "It depends." Any social psychologist will quickly point out that "It depends" is *not* equivalent to "I don't know." It is not that we have learned nothing from our observations of human social behavior, but rather that we are completely certain of very little. We have a large number of theories about aspects of social behavior, and we can make predictions fairly confidently from many of these theories, but we have not yet discovered The Truth. When we conduct theory-testing research, we try to build the strongest case possible for our position, but the limitations and qualifications are always there (even if they are only apparent to other professional social psychologists).

So that is how we conduct our professional lives—we gather data, build theories, and qualify our conclusions. How do we try to teach social psychology to our students? We know what many of your expectations are. And we may believe that you, like Amory, will be surprised when we tell you about research and theory rather than about "personality and influence." But because of the importance of actually gathering data relevant to social issues and policies, we have a responsibility to teach you how research should be conducted, and to base our own conclusions on empirical evidence as firmly as possible. Because of the increased explanatory and predictive value that they offer, we have an obligation to tell you about currently respected theories. Every teacher of social psychology, and every social psychology textbook, must try to accomplish these goals in a way that will maintain your interest. We must carefully balance what we think you need to know against what you expect to learn. The relative weight given to each of these needs is a major dimension on which social psychology textbooks can be separated, and this book will emphasize the former. We are confident that this can be done without losing your interest, because we believe that although the decisive answers social psychology presently has to offer are limited, the questions it asks are fascinating.

THE BEGINNINGS OF SOCIAL PSYCHOLOGY

One reason that social psychology has, at present, few decisive answers to offer is that by almost any standards it is still a young and growing discipline. Certainly it is true that people have been observing social behavior, and trying to understand it, since before our distant ancestors left the caves, and the philosophical underpinnings of much of social psychology can be traced to Aristotle, Hobbes (1651), Locke (1690), Hume (1739), Kant (1781), Bentham (1789), and Comte (1830, 1852). But the first experimental research in social psychology was performed by Triplett and reported in 1897. The era of modern social psychology is usually traced to the publication in 1908 of the first two textbooks to bear that title, one by a psychologist named William McDougall and one by a sociologist named Edward Ross (Allport, 1954; Sahakian, 1974).

Each of these books helped to establish social psychology as an independent discipline, but each is more important for its historical role than for any lasting theoretical contribution. McDougall attributed nearly all social behavior to the operation of a set of *instincts*, such as self-assertion, curiosity, and gregariousness. Use of a single explanatory principle is today regarded as overly simplistic, but it was characteristic of the time: other such principles included pleasure-pain, power, imitation, sympathy, and suggestion. It is not surprising that Ross's treatment of social psychology was as sociological as McDougall's was psychological. Ross concentrated on interpersonal processes such as imitation, crowd behavior, and mob mind. In many ways these topics are more closely related to the concerns of present-day social psychology than was McDougall's instinct theory, but while Ross's approach was group-oriented, present theories concentrate on the individual.

Although there have been significant advances in theory since the time of McDougall and Ross, it is the changes in research—in conceptual complexity, experimental sophistication, and sheer volume—that have been truly dramatic. Well over 90 percent of all the research done in social psychology has been conducted within the last twenty-five years. The first compilation of data and theory was Murchison's *Handbook of Social Psychology*, published in 1935, which consisted of four hundred pages devoted to twelve topics. In 1954 a second *Handbook* was published, edited by Lindzey, which included over a thousand pages and more than double the number of topics. The most recent *Handbook* (Lindzey and Aronson, 1969) consists of five volumes with nearly four thousand pages devoted to forty-five topics. The first American journal devoted in part to social psychology was the *Journal of Abnormal and Social Psychology*, first published in 1922 as an outgrowth of the *Journal of Abnormal Psychology*. Journals often reflect the tenor of their times, and this particular combination resulted from the belief of the journal's founder, Morton Prince, that certain aspects of psychopathology could be linked to social behavior (Sahakian, 1974). In 1965, reflecting a different time, the *Journal* reverted to its old title, and the portion devoted to social psychology became the *Journal of Personality and Social Psychology*. At about this same period, other journals devoted in whole or in large part to research in social psychology came into being, with the result that now more than a dozen accept contributions from social psychologists. Some of these journals (and the dates of their founding) include the *Journal of Social Psychology* (1930), the *Journal of Experimental Social Psychology* (1966), the *Journal of Applied Social Psychology* (1971), the *Journal of Social Issues* (1945), *Representative Research in Social Psychology* (1970), and the *Personality and Social Psychology Bulletin* (1974).

The First Experiment

It is, of course, contemporary research, theory, and applications with which this textbook is primarily concerned. Nevertheless, there are a few classic studies, illustrating the breadth of research in social psychology, which deserve brief mention here. Triplett's (1897) study of the effects of pacemaking and competition upon performance is important not only because it was the first ever reported, but also because it successfully combined field and laboratory research addressed to the same conceptual issue. It began with Triplett's observation that people riding bicycles seemed to ride faster when there were other cyclists nearby than when potential competitors were not available. Triplett then asked cyclists to complete a 25-mile course under one of three experimental conditions: unpaced but against time, paced by another cyclist without actual competition, and paced with competition. Riders in the unpaced condition, racing only against the clock, covered the course at an average speed of some 24 miles per hour (those of you who ride bicycles will understand that even this level is quite a lot of work just for an experiment). In the paced-against-time condition (another cyclist present, but no competition) the average speed went up to slightly over 31 miles per hour, an increase of nearly 30 percent! Adding competition raised the average speed an additional 5 percent to 32.6 miles per hour. Triplett replicated these findings in the laboratory, using such tasks as counting, jumping up and down, and cranking fishing reels, and concluded that simultaneous participation by more than one person in various activities "serves to liberate latent energy not ordinarily available" (1897, p. 533). In a recent paper Zajonc (1965) suggests some alternative interpretations for similar social facilitation effects, but Triplett's ingenuity and methodological sophistication were an excellent example for his time.

Study of Ongoing Social Processes

Despite Triplett's good beginning, it was another thirty years before experimental social psychology really took hold. This occurred in 1936, when Sherif reported a series of experiments which demonstrated that an *ongoing social process*—the development of social norms—could be subjected to the same kind of experimental scrutiny previously directed only toward the outcome of a process (such as the *effects* of pacemaking and competition). The experimental task that Sherif employed was a perceptual illusion known as the *autokinetic effect*. If you are asked to sit in a completely darkened room and to look continuously at a pinpoint of light, pretty soon you will think that the point of light is moving. It isn't, of course, and the source of the perceived movement is generally agreed to be the result of your eye movements. For Sherif's purposes, however, what was important was that (a) perceived movement does occur; (b) over a long series of trials subjects will report a relatively stable amount of movement; (c) there are substantial individual differences in these personal distributions of amounts of movement; and (d) there is no objective or absolute frame of reference that can be used to establish a "correct" amount of movement. In other words, almost all of the conditions were conducive to the operation of social influence processes.

Sherif's experimental question was this: how will an individual's judgments of the movement when viewing the light alone compare with his or her judgments when viewing the light in the presence of other people? Will the individual judgments of a group remain disparate, or will they converge into a *common norm* for the group? And how will an individual's later judgments made alone be affected by a previously established group norm? To answer these questions subjects were asked to make three separate sets of 100 judgments each. The first set of judgments was made when each subject was alone in the experimental room, and these judgments showed wide variation across individuals in the degree to which the autokinetic effect was reported. During the second phase of the experiment, several subjects at a time reported their perceptions out loud, with the result that there was a *convergence* of the individual judgments about a common norm for the group. In the third stage of the experiment, the subjects were once again separated and run as individuals. And interestingly enough, these reports showed almost no individual differences—the subjects had come to agree on a common norm for movement in the second phase of the experiment, and they carried this norm with them as a frame of reference in the third stage. This experiment served not only to establish the efficacy of the experimental method in social psychology, it also served as a theoretical foundation for later work in social comparison theory (Festinger, 1954; to be discussed in Chapter Eight) and social influence processes (Chapter Twelve).

The Social Psychology of Research

So far we have seen early examples of two of the major goals of research in social psychology—combination of laboratory and field methods directed toward a single conceptual issue, and experimental study of an ongoing social process. Our next example was the first demonstration (quite by accident) that the research process itself is a social psychological phenomenon. This fact has come to be represented in a number of different concepts (to be discussed in Chapter Two) such as experimenter expectancy (Rosenthal, 1966), evaluation apprehension (Rosenberg, 1965), and demand characteristics (Orne, 1962), but the first indication of its influence was in an extensive series of field experiments reported by Roethlisberger and Dickson (1939).

These experiments were designed to assess the effects of various working conditions upon the output of workers who were assembling electrical components at the Hawthorne Works of the Western Electric Company. Roethlisberger, a professor at the Harvard Graduate School of Business, and Dickson, a member of Western Electric's research department, and their colleagues began by studying the effects of differences in illumination in the work area. Following proper experimental procedure, they separated the workers into two groups: an experimental group which received varying intensities of illumination, and a control group which received a constant intensity of illumination of the work area. To the investigator's surprise, there was an increase in output in *both* groups. Then the researchers tried other variations in illumination, even including telling the experimental group that there would be a change and not actually changing the intensity. Still the output increased. The only decline was observed when the level of illumination was lowered to an amount equivalent to moonlight! The studies continued for a period of five years (changing numerous conditions other than illumination and using different sets of workers in the plant) with remarkably consistent findings. Almost no matter what experimental conditions were imposed, there were increases in output, and these increases typically were maintained even when all experimental conditions were removed. The investigators had obviously influenced the subjects' behavior merely by studying that behavior, and this phenomenon has become known as the *Hawthorne effect*. The fact that being a subject in research alters your natural pattern of behavior is one of the most interesting and perplexing problems still facing contemporary social psychology.

Theory and Application

For our purposes Roethlisberger and Dickson's work is noteworthy primarily because of the Hawthorne effect, but at the time their research helped to establish the idea that the methods of social psychology could be brought to bear upon important problems in the "real world" outside the laboratory.

This interaction between social psychological methods and theory and practical applications of social importance is best represented in the work of Kurt Lewin. Not only was he an astute observer of social behavior, he also returned to the real world to test the theories developed on the basis of these observations, firmly believing that "there is nothing so practical as a good theory" (1951, p. 169). Nowhere is this relationship between theory and practical application better illustrated than in Lewin's 1947 studies of the effects of group discussion and consensus upon attitude and behavior change. Lewin's extensive field theory of human behavior led him to conclude that even well-established social attitudes are not permanently fixed. On the contrary, they are *dynamic* entities, maintained in part by the social consensus they receive from other people. Consequently, variations in the social climate can produce lasting attitude change by first *unfreezing* the existing attitude, then *changing* it, and finally solidifying the change by *refreezing* the attitude at its new position.

During the Second World War Lewin had the opportunity to test these theoretical notions when he and his associates became involved in a project to change the eating habits of families in order to conserve meats needed for the troops. The subjects were Red Cross volunteers, in groups of thirteen to seventeen, and the purpose of the program was to increase the home use of beef hearts, sweetbreads, and kidneys. There were two experimental conditions—lecture and group decision— and half of the subjects were assigned to each condition. In the Lecture condition the groups heard an interesting lecture linking nutrition problems to the necessity of conserving meat for the war effort, emphasizing the nutritional content of the three meats, and presenting sample recipes along with detailed instructions on preparation of the meats (suggesting ways of minimizing their unattractive characteristics). The lecturer recounted her success in preparing these "delicious dishes" for her own family. In the Group Decision condition there were a few introductory remarks about the nutritional value of the meats, and about the war effort, and then a discussion was started to involve the subjects in the process of deciding whether to serve the dishes. These group discussions concentrated on the obstacles against using beef hearts, sweetbreads, and kidneys (such as the smell during cooking and objections of the family), and the same remedies and recipes were distributed as in the Lecture condition. At the end of the meeting, the subjects in the Group Decision condition were asked to indicate by a show of hands just how many people intended to try one of the meats during the following week.

A later interview with all of the groups showed that among the Lecture groups only 3 percent of the individuals actually served the recommended meats, but among the Group Decision groups 32 percent of the individuals did so. There are, of course, several possible explanations. Perhaps the group decision produces greater involvement, perhaps the public commitment of agreeing to try a previously unattractive food creates an obligation to do so, perhaps the thought of having to return to a group where some consensus has already been established creates social pressure to join in that consensus. Subsequent research with different subjects and different foodstuffs served to rule out some artifacts in the first study and to narrow the possible explanations to group decision and public commitment, but a later study by Bennett (1955) suggested that these might not be as important as the process of discussion and the degree of perceived consensus. Despite the qualifications of results that now appear to be necessary,

Lewin's methodological contributions can be seen in contemporary studies of group problem solving (Kelley and Thibaut, 1969) and choice shifts in group discussion (Kogan and Wallach, 1965; Cartwright, 1971), and his theoretical ideas are reflected in the later conceptual formulations of his students. Finally, Lewin's emphasis on the practical applications of social psychological theory has made a strong imprint on the later development of the discipline.

In the examples cited here we have tried to trace some of the early developments in research in social psychology. These studies are important for reasons other than their historical value. They illustrate the essential elements of the research process, and they help to define the domain of social psychology. Researchers still try to combine laboratory and field investigation, to apply experimental methods to ongoing social processes, to avoid the confounding that can arise from the necessarily social nature of the data-gathering process, and to find practical applications for their conclusions. The examples also show social psychology's emphasis on the individual person, suggesting that behavior must be understood by looking both at the social situation and at whatever unique characteristics the person brings into that situation. Let us keep these considerations in mind as we turn to a more precise definition of the field of social psychology.

CONSTRUCTING A DEFINITION OF SOCIAL PSYCHOLOGY

Just what is the field of social psychology? At first, it involves interest in social behavior. We want to know why two eyewitnesses to an accident can give completely different accounts of the reasons for its occurrence. We want to learn why people come to hold certain attitudes, and to discover how attitudes can be changed. We want to determine when a person's needs and motives will affect his or her behavior toward others. Why do people help each other; and what are the social roots of human aggression? Why do our friends like us, and why do some people remain unfriendly? How do people influence each other; and what effects does group membership have on a person's actions? To one degree or another, we are all interested in social behavior, but interest alone is not enough. As we shall see in the next section, the conclusions of social psychology often differ markedly from the predictions that would be made by interested individuals. These differences arise because social psychology applies the *scientific method* to the study of social behavior, as illustrated in the historical examples, while interested individuals typically do not do so.

The accumulation of scientific data differs from the satisfaction of individual curiosity primarily in terms of the methods employed.

But how can social psychology be distinguished from other disciplines—such as psychology and sociology—that also employ scientific methods in the study of human behavior? The answer to this question lies in the *level of analysis* of the field. Social psychology chooses to focus on the meaningful social behaviors of an individual person. Both a person's social milieu (physical and social surroundings) and unique personal characteristics are thought to influence the person's behavior, and this behavior is described in socially meaningful terms that most closely correspond to those of everyday language. In contrast to this emphasis on the socially meaningful actions of an individual person, general experimental psychology is concerned with *portions* of the individual's behavior (physiological processes, learning, sensation, and perception), while sociology is concerned with the *structural* elements (social roles, formal organizations, social institutions) that are thought to remain essentially unchanged no matter who the particular individuals are.

Consider, for example, the ways in which each discipline might describe a family dinner. Depending upon his or her specialty within the discipline, a general experimental psychologist might study the eye-hand coordination necessary to bring the food from the plate to the mouth, the subjective experiences corresponding to the taste and smell of the meal, or perhaps the learning processes involved in getting the children to eat their spinach. For the sociologist, again depending upon his or her specialty within the discipline, the most interesting data might be the degree to which the role of "pleasant and conversant spouse" conflicts with the role of "supervising parent," the importance of an evening meal in the daily contact between members of a nuclear family, or the larger social function of the meal for the particular social class or ethnic group of people involved. The social psychologist might wonder whether the family would conduct itself the same way with invited guests present as it does when eating alone, whether suggestions to the children have more impact when delivered with good food than when delivered at other times, or how a parent's unpleasant interchange with his or her boss during the afternoon might affect enjoyment of the meal and communication with other members of the group.

Notice that the experimental psychologist concentrates on the sensory, perceptual, and learning processes of individuals, allowing for some differences between people but virtually ignoring the social nature of the setting in which these processes are observed. The sociologist concentrates on the social significance of the gathering— role strain, maintenance of a social institution (the family), and cultural

or demographic variations—virtually ignoring the personal characteristics of the particular individuals involved. For the social psychologist, however, it is the *interaction* between individual characteristics and social situation that is of paramount importance. Tasting
food ought to be relatively constant across situations, and role strain
ought to be relatively constant across individual people, but "having
dinner" involves both the situation and the person. It can now be seen
that the field of social psychology may be most clearly identified if we
define it as the scientific study of the personal and situational factors
that affect individual social behavior. Having suggested the limits of
the discipline by this definition, we can now expand upon the distinction between scientific social psychology and the naive social
psychology of the individual person.

IMPLICIT THEORIES OF SOCIAL PSYCHOLOGY

Usually when you begin to study an unfamiliar academic discipline,
you quickly become aware of how little you know. Neither your past
experience nor your everyday language can be brought to bear upon
what you must try to learn. When the physics professor speaks of
wave propagation, cascading, and hyperons; when the chemistry instructor talks of atomic weights, organic compounds, and complex
molecules; or even when the clinical psychologist discusses contingency management, schizophrenic withdrawal, and lithium therapy,
you try to take very careful notes so that you won't miss anything.
You feel sufficiently uncertain of your background in the area that you
find it difficult to formulate intelligent questions to ask, and you
wouldn't dream of actually contradicting the professor on the basis of
your personal experience. You recognize your limitations, and you
realize that you must learn a new language—the technical jargon of
the discipline.

What happens when you study social psychology? To begin with,
all of your past social experience seems to be relevant. You have engaged in social perception, you have formed friendships, you have
dealt with people who had power over you, and you have exercised
influence over others. You have changed attitudes, developed a self-
concept, and joined groups. Moreover, you have a fairly good idea of
the functional *relationships* between elements of your social world.
You know what circumstances, and what individual characteristics, are
most likely to lead to one sort of behavior as opposed to another. You
know that you behave differently when you are with your parents than
when you are with your friends (that the situation and your role in-

fluence your behavior). You know that there are some people whose attitudes can be changed by simply providing them with information that contradicts their beliefs, but that there are others who will not be changed unless you appeal to their baser instincts (logical versus emotional persuasive appeals). You know that in any group, some people seem to become leaders while others remain followers (emergent leadership). In the course of accumulating all this inter-personal experience, you have developed what can best be described as an *implicit theory of social psychology:* a haphazard collection of ideas about what situations, and what personal characteristics, are associated with particular kinds of social behavior.

This implicit theory of social psychology is derived from your own personal experience, and because it has subjective validity for you, you are likely to believe that it is "correct" in some more objective sense. You have observed regularities in the social behavior of people around you, and you may even have verified your own experiences by comparing them with those of your friends or acquaintances. Since there are few things subjectively more real than your own experience, it is difficult for you to understand that other people might view the same situations in entirely different ways. You may underestimate the extent to which your implicit theory of social psychology might just represent your unique viewpoint; what is real for you must surely gen-eralize to other people as well. As a result, you are likely to compare new information (say, from your social psychology professor) to your implicit theory. When the new information agrees with your theory, you might be tempted to accuse social psychologists of "studying the obvious," wasting a lot of valuable research time just to generate find-ings that are apparent to anyone who has the requisite common sense. In short, you might consider the research results *trivial* and not worth bothering with. On the other hand, should the new information contra-dict your implicit theory of social psychology, you might dismiss it as an anomaly or error. You might regard such a *counterintuitive* finding with a good deal of suspicion, because of the overwhelming reality of your own experience. In either case you would be making a mistake, as can be illustrated by two examples.

Common Sense and Inconsistency

First, let us consider a finding that you might think trivial. A large number of observational and experimental studies (e.g., Ajzen, 1974; Byrne, 1971; Kaplan and Anderson, 1973; Newcomb, 1961) has found a positive relationship between attitude similarity and interpersonal attraction, although there is some theoretical disagreement about the reasons for that relationship (we shall return to this discussion in

Chapter Ten). In short, the more you think that my attitudes are similar to yours, the more you will like me. If you were to compare this finding to your implicit theory of social psychology, you would probably answer, "Of course the more similar we are the more I will like you. That conclusion is so trivial that it can even be found in proverbs: 'Birds of a feather flock together.' Why did I need a lot of expensive social psychology research to tell me that?"

To answer this question we need to take a closer look at one of the characteristics of any implicit theory—its potential for inconsistency. Because your implicit theory of social psychology is so real for you, you do not look for its inconsistencies, and because it is not publicly recorded, it would be difficult for you to find them even if you did choose to look. So when you say that a positive relationship between similarity of attitudes and interpersonal attraction can even be explained by a proverb, you conveniently forget an alternative proverb: "Opposites attract." Now suppose that I had begun this example by telling you that a number of studies suggest that people whose personalities and needs are *complementary* will be attracted to each other (Beier, Rossi, and Garfield, 1961; Cattell and Nesselroade, 1961; Kerckhoff and Davis, 1962; Levinger, 1964; and Winch, 1958). In the absence of any other information, you would most probably conclude, "Of course, opposites attract."

The lesson to be learned here is that your implicit theory of social psychology does *not* suggest, as the research findings of scientific social psychology do, the circumstances or *limiting conditions* under which each similarity-attraction relationship might be found. It turns out that a positive relationship (greater similarity leading to greater attraction) seems to be the rule, with a negative relationship (greater difference leading to greater attraction) the exception, limited primarily to personality differences among certain engaged or married couples (Berscheid and Walster, 1969; Kerckhoff and Davis, 1962). Your implicit theory of social psychology can only interpret relationships that are obtained, without the capacity to distinguish between conflicting explanations. In contrast, the formal theory and research of scientific social psychology can be used to suggest the limiting conditions for apparently contradictory findings. The question "Which relationship is correct?" becomes "What are the circumstances under which one relationship might obtain, and what are the circumstances under which the other relationship might occur?"

Counterintuitive Findings: Milgram's Experiment

If reliance on an implicit theory of social psychology is a forgiveable mistake when the problem appears trivial, it can be a serious blunder when actual results of research would not agree with expectations. As an example let us consider the experiment by Milgram (1963) dealing with destructive obedience. Milgram tried to study, in the experimental laboratory, some of the factors that might be involved in "following orders" to the extent of causing serious harm to other persons. He argued that the systematic murder practiced during World War II, while perhaps conceived by a single person, "could only be carried out on a massive scale if a very large number of persons had obeyed orders" (1963, p. 371). The first question, of course, deals with the likelihood that people will actually engage in destructive obedience. Was the Nazi experience based on a combination of the times and some unique flaw in the German national character (your implicit theory of social psychology might well suggest that it was), or could a laboratory analog be constructed? Could anyone (including your own presumably moral fellow Americans) be induced to follow the orders of an experimenter, even though doing so might endanger the health (or perhaps life) of an innocent person?

To investigate these questions Milgram devised an experiment in which a naive subject was asked to administer electric shocks of increasing intensity to another person as part of a purported study of the effects of punishment for errors in paired associate learning. The subject was given the task of teaching a list of paired associate words, such as blue-girl, nice-day, and fat-neck, to another subject (who was, in fact, a confederate of the experimenter). Every time that the learner made an error, he was to receive an electric shock of increasing intensity. These shocks were to be delivered by the teacher (the naive subject) using an authentic-looking shock generator which contained a single row of thirty toggle switches, each one representing a 15-volt increment over the one immediately to its left. The shock scale thus ran from a low of 15 volts to a high of 450 volts, and each toggle switch was marked by the appropriate number of volts. In addition to these numerical designations, groups of four switches were also labeled (from left to right) as follows: Slight Shock, Moderate Shock, Strong Shock, Very Strong Shock, Intense Shock, Extreme Intensity Shock, and Danger: Severe Shock. The last two switches were simply marked XXX. Whenever a switch was depressed, a pilot light went on, an electric buzzing was heard, a blue light labeled "voltage energizer" flashed on, and a needle on a large voltmeter moved quickly to the right. Just to ensure credibility, each subject was given a sample shock of 45 volts, using the third switch from the left (which was actually wired to a 45-volt battery housed inside the shock generator).

As part of the initial instructions, both the naive subject and the experimental confederate drew slips from a bowl to determine which one of them would be the teacher and who would be the learner. Both slips had the word "teacher" printed on them, and the confederate simply announced that his slip said "learner." After a description of the learning task, the experimenter took the learner (the confederate) into an adjoining experimental room, asking the subject to accompany them so that he could see the remainder of the experimental set-up. Once in the adjoining room, the learner was seated in a chair and asked to take off his coat and roll up his sleeve. Electrode paste was then applied to his wrist "to avoid blisters and burns," and his arm was strapped to the chair in such a was that his wrist was firmly placed on an electrode plate ostensibly connected to the shock generator. At this point the learner reported that he had recently been diagnosed as having a mild heart condition. He stated that it was nothing to worry about, but wondered how serious the shocks might be. The experimenter assured him that "although the shocks may be quite painful, they should produce no lasting physiological damage." Finally, the experimenter took the subject back to the other room, seated him in front of the shock generator, and had him begin teaching the lists of word pairs.

The major dependent variable in this experiment was the point at which the subject adamantly refused to continue. This could happen before the first shock was administered, at any point during the sequence, or not at all. If the subject continued until the highest voltage level was reached, he would have had to administer that level for several successive errors before the experimenter terminated the procedure. What sort of results would your implicit theory of social psychology predict? Would anyone continue to the end? If not, when would the majority of people terminate their participation? Let me be even more specific, and ask you the kind of question that Milgram asked some senior psychology majors and a number of his professional colleagues: Of one hundred American males of diverse occupations, ranging in age from twenty to fifty, what percentage would continue until the highest shock level had been reached? None of the estimates was higher than 3 percent, with the most pessimistic student predicting that three out of a hundred subjects would continue to increase the shock level until the highest level was reached. These estimates probably correspond fairly well to the estimate that you might have made. To return to the language that we have used above, it is at least *counterintuitive*, even frightening, to believe that large numbers of subjects would continue to administer ever-increasing shocks to a middle-aged man with a possible heart condition long after he has screamed in protest, pounded on the wall, and then fallen silent.

Indeed, if we were to rely upon our implicit theories of social psychology, we might never perform this experiment in the first place. We might look at the experimental conditions and conclude that so few people would ever begin the series of shocks, much less continue to administer them, that it would be very difficult to obtain useful data.

After all, it would be impossible to discover situational factors or individual characteristics that contribute to compliance with the experimenter's demands if no subjects actually follow his orders. Our implicit theories of social psychology would suggest that destructive obedience should occur only under the most extreme circumstances: People whose own lives are threatened might willingly inflict pain upon others; the compelling horror of war might lead to atrocities; occasional psychopaths might find satisfaction in others' discomfort. But we would fervently hope that it would be impossible to construct a laboratory analog of these situations, even one which is by comparison relatively moderate.

Sadly, we would be mistaken. The actual distribution of breakoff points obtained in Milgram's experiment is shown in Table 1-1. A total of forty subjects participated in the study that we have described, and 65 percent (twenty-six of the forty subjects) obeyed the experimenter right up to the bitter end. Only fourteen subjects defied the experimenter at all, and none of these subjects did so until after the learner fell silent at the 300-volt level.

How Could It Happen?

This experiment raises several important issues. First, we must wonder why so many subjects disregarded their better judgment and followed the experimenter's orders. He had no real power over them; they had been told at the beginning of the study that they could keep the payment they received for particpating, regardless of what happened in the experiment; and it was clear from their behavior that they were in serious conflict during the experiment. Why, then, did so many continue? Perhaps they had faith in the experimenter's competence and in the reputation of the university (Yale) where the study was conducted, believing that neither would permit serious harm to come to any participants in an experiment. Perhaps they believed that what they were doing was for the "good of science," a long-term goal that might justify some short-range suffering. Or perhaps they simply acted without reflection on the possible consequences of their behavior. It is important to note that none of these possibilities diminishes the force of the conclusions. In real life situations requiring the obedient execution of orders, the source of those orders is most often a legitimate authority, making its demands on the basis of a larger "principle," often without adequate time for reflection and discussion of the possible consequences. We shall return to these issues in Chapter Twelve, when we consider social influence and conformity in more detail.

TABLE 1-1
Distribution of the breakoff points in the Milgram (1963) study
of destructive obedience

VERBAL DESIGNATION AND VOLTAGE INDICATION	NUMBER OF SUBJECTS FOR WHOM THIS WAS MAXIMUM SHOCK
Slight shock	
15	0
30	0
45	0
60	0
Moderate shock	
75	0
90	0
105	0
120	0
Strong shock	
135	0
150	0
165	0
180	0
Very strong shock	
195	0
210	0
225	0
240	0
Intense shock	
255	0
270	0
285	0
300	5
Extreme intensity shock	
315	4
330	2
345	1
360	1
Danger: severe shock	
375	1
390	0
405	0
420	0
XXX	
435	0
450	26

Reprinted from Milgram (1963), p. 373.

A Question of Ethics

A second set of issues raised by the Milgram experiment deals not so much with the results themselves as with the methods used to obtain those results. The experiment combined two of the most ethically questionable elements of some research in social psychology: powerful deception of the subjects and a procedure that virtually guarantees that the subjects will learn something negative about themselves in the course of their participation. Among other things, the subjects were misled into believing (1) that the learner was simply another subject, (2) that there was real possibility of harm to him, and (3) that they had actually caused serious harm to come to him. It is clear from the reports of observers who watched the subjects performing their task that administering the shocks was a traumatic experience. In the words of one observer, "I observed a mature and initially poised businessman enter the laboratory smiling and confident. Within 20 minutes he was reduced to a twitching, stuttering wreck, who was rapidly approaching a point of nervous collapse . . ." (p. 376). One must wonder whether the debriefing given each subject (including an explanation of the study and a friendly reconciliation with the learner) was sufficient to counteract both the stress of the moment and the impact of the realization that "I am the kind of person who will obediently follow orders, even though it might cause serious harm to another person." We shall return to further consideration of these issues in Chapter Two, in a discussion of the ethical responsibilities of the social psychologist.

Implicit Theories Are Not Enough

The final lesson to be learned from the Milgram experiment is the discovery that our implicit theories of social psychology can be inadequate in predicting what people will actually do. Certainly it is true that our implicit theories contain provisions for man's well-documented inhumanity to man (and, as the My Lai massacre illustrated, Americans take part in atrocities just as do other national groups). But because these provisions suggest the necessity of extreme conditions, they do not prepare us for the possibility that people from all walks of life who are simply participating in an experiment will, with relatively little external justification or pressure, obediently follow orders that conflict with their moral and ethical values. What Milgram's experiment teaches us as human beings is that we should be conscious of the relationship between our ethical principles and our behavior not only in extreme circumstances, but always. What it teaches us as students of social psychology is that we must not rely solely upon our implicit theories: if we seek thorough understanding and accurate prediction, we must perform the necessary research.

PLAN OF THE BOOK

In our attempt to show how scientific social psychology addresses the fundamental questions about the causes of social behavior, we will begin with processes and products that are essentially internal to the individual and end with the interchange found among members of a social group. Chapters Three through Eight consider social perception, attitude organization and change, and the social self; Chapters Nine through Eleven examine the ways in which an individual's motives might affect his or her behavior toward other people (altruism, attraction, competition, and aggression), and Chapters Twelve and Thirteen discuss the person's participation in social groups (social influence and group processes). Thus we move from *intra*personal processes to *inter*personal ones, from smaller units of behavior to larger ones. Although we have found such an organization helpful, some instructors may choose to consider the material in a quite different order, so throughout the book the level of theoretical analysis remains constant: the mid-range theories of social psychology are applied both to social perception and to group dynamics. We have not used more "psychological" theories on the one hand and more "sociological" theories on the other.

Since any scientific theories of social psychology differ from implicit theories primarily in their emphasis upon research, a thorough grounding in methodology is a valuable prelude to the remainder of this book. Chapter Two begins with a discussion of operational definitions and replication, two of the elements of scientific procedure that distinguish it from the individual's methods of acquiring social knowledge. After considering the problem of validity in research procedures, the chapter turns to discussion of the major research methods —archival research, observational methods, and experimental techniques. Discussion of other procedures, such as correlational techniques and attitude measurement, will be postponed until the appropriate content areas are considered (Chapters Four and Five respectively). The research chapter concludes with a discussion of the ethical responsibilities of the researcher.

Much of our knowledge about the social world is obtained through processes of social perception. Chapter Three begins with similarities and differences between the perception of physical objects and the perception of other persons, suggesting that these processes differ not only in degree but also in kind. Next it covers the basic verbal and nonverbal ingredients of impression formation, illustrating how these might be combined into a coherent whole, and suggesting how stimulus persons might manage the impressions they convey. Completing the coverage of social perception, Chapter Four takes the viewpoint of the perceiver. Rather than being an utterly faithful processor of information, the perceiver is an active participant in the perceptual endeavor, interpreting social behavior in terms of his or her experience and desires. The attribution processes that perceivers employ to enhance their understanding of social behavior can be compared to some of the experimental procedures of scientific social psychology, even to the extent that the perceiver's values, like the investigator's values, may affect the outcome.

Remaining on the level of internal phenomena, Chapter Five describes the affective, cognitive, and behavioral components of attitudes. The particular attitude considered is racism, and there is evidence that this attitude involves stereotyping, value judgments, and emotions as well as overt behavioral discrimination. Various techniques of attitude measurement—Thurstone scaling, Likert scaling, and semantic differential scaling—are presented, and some of the advantages and disadvantages of each method are discussed.

The ways in which social attitudes might be organized are considered in Chapter Six. One of these makes an analogy to a syllogism, suggesting that the belief component and the evaluative component might serve as premises leading to the attitudinal conclusion. The dynamic relationships among attitudes are often thought to be governed by a principle of cognitive consistency, which holds that inconsistency can serve as a motivation for attitude change. Three theories of cognitive consistency—balance theory, congruity theory, and dissonance theory—are discussed, and some of the research flowing from dissonance theory is presented to illustrate the cumulative nature of knowledge and theory in social psychology. Chapter Seven concludes the discussion of attitude change, distinguishing first between real change and apparent change. Sources of resistance to influence attempts and sources of facilitation of change are considered, including the characteristics of the persuasive communication, the relationship of the communication to the attitudinal position held by the recipient, and the recipient's participation in the process of attitude change.

Our concentration upon primarily internal processes concludes in Chapter Eight with discussion of the social self. An individual's self-concept includes both properties (such as values, attitudes, and possessions) and processes (social perception, the capacity for self-evaluation and self-regard). The social self is influenced to a significant degree by comparison with other people, and this comparison can affect emotional states, a more enduring self-concept, and self-esteem. Needs for maintenance and enhancement of self-esteem can energize a variety of interpersonal behaviors, many of which will be considered in later chapters.

Even as our focus shifts to interpersonal behavior, we remain concerned with the personal and situational factors that affect social action. Chapter Nine is an overview of several theories of social behavior—social learning theory, exchange theory, equity theory—all based in one way or another on the principle of reinforcement. People usually try to maximize their rewards in social interaction, and the continuation of an interaction may depend upon each participant's belief that his or her outcomes are positive and comparable to the rewards achieved by the other participants. Beginning with positive aspects of interpersonal behavior, Chapter Ten considers altruism, helping behavior, and attraction between people. The fact that helping behavior can be characterized in a variety of ways—by reference to the actor's intention, or to the benefits received by the recipient, or to the demands of the situation—helps illustrate some of the difficulties encountered in the attempt to describe behavior with the precision necessary for sound research and theory. The study of interpersonal attraction provides another example of the need for empirical research to establish the limiting conditions of predictions that would be made from implicit theories of social psychology.

A different side of human interaction—competition and aggression—is dealt with in Chapter Eleven. In both of these cases the description of the action in positive or negative terms may depend as much upon the viewpoint of the observer as upon the nature of the action itself. Competition may be affected by the characteristics of the game situation, by the potential for communication between participants, and by internal factors such as achievement motivation. The existence of aggression has been attributed to instinctive drives and to frustration, but much of the research evidence suggests that social learning plays an important role in the instigation to, and expression of, aggressive behavior. This chapter concludes with a discussion of the specific question of televised violence.

In the final chapters we consider the mutual influence that occurs in social interaction. Chapter Twelve first distinguishes between power and influence, then discusses the sources of social power, the potential for resistance, and the difference between compliance and acceptance. The influence of one individual over another is illustrated by studies of obedience, and the influence of a group over an individual is demonstrated in research on conformity. Even in a relationship between a powerful majority and a less powerful minority there is some mutual contingency in interaction, and this contingency may contribute to social change. Chapter Thirteen builds upon the potential for influence held by social groups, showing how communication within the group, the nature of the group's leadership, and the process of group decision making can affect the achievement of group and individual goals. In the extreme, pressures toward uniformity of opinion within a group may cause the group to lose touch with social reality, producing one bad decision after another.

The book concludes with an Epilogue that reviews the approach and findings of scientific social psychology, recapitulating how they apply to everyday concerns. Social psychology cannot make your moral decisions and value judgments for you, but its research and theory can help identify the effects of various policy decisions. And because social problems affect the behavior of individuals, the approach of scientific social psychology may offer constructive suggestions for social change.

Suggested Additional Readings

ALLPORT, G. W. The historical background of modern social psychology. In G. Lindzey and E. Aronson (Eds.) *Handbook of social psychology.* (2nd ed.) Vol. 1. Reading, Mass.: Addison-Wesley, 1969. Pp. 1–80. This revision of Allport's chapter on the history of social psychology found in the 1954 *Handbook* traces the philosophical antecedents of contemporary social psychology. It traces the development of the field from the "simple and sovereign theories" of human behavior—hedonism, power, sympathy, and imitation—to the mid-range theories and experimental methods more prevalent today.

SAHAKIAN, W. S. *Systematic social psychology.* New York: Chandler, 1974. This detailed and interesting book begins with a discussion of social psychology in antiquity, then considers the contributions to social psychology made by nearly all of the major theoreticians, researchers, and methodologists from 1908 to the late 1950s. Highly recommended.

SHAW, M. E., and COSTANZO, P. R. *Theories of social psychology.* New York: McGraw-Hill, 1970. This comprehensive review of theories in social psychology presents the mid-range theories of modern social psychology and contains evaluative comments about the contribution and importance of various theoretical models. Thorough but difficult.

Evidence that is expected or desired may be observed when it does not really exist, and disconfirming evidence may be overlooked.

Research Methods in Social Psychology

Chapter Two

Explaining social behavior is both a major interest of individuals and the principal task of scientific social psychology, but the different methods used by the two often lead to quite different conclusions. In the course of their experience people develop implicit theories of social psychology: they observe and categorize social behavior, noting what they believe to be recurrent relationships between behavior and various situations and personal characteristics. But these observations are necessarily limited by the individual's own viewpoint. The relevant data are gathered haphazardly, remembered and interpreted privately in light of preexisting ideas. Evidence that is expected or desired may be observed when it does not really exist, and disconfirming evidence may be overlooked.

In contrast, social psychologists develop formal theories of social behavior based on data gathered *systematically*. Research procedures are standardized and reported so that they may be repeated by other investigators, attempts are made to minimize or eliminate bias in the research process, and conclusions are drawn publicly so that they may be verified (or rejected) by later research. As the results of Milgram's (1963) experiment so dramatically demonstrated in Chapter One, the conclusions drawn from the informal question "What do I think people will do?" can differ substantially from those based on the research question "What will people *actually* do?"

The purpose of this chapter is to illustrate some of the methods that social psychologists employ in their attempts to answer this fundamental question. We begin with the problem of definition and the need for replication of research findings, and then consider particular methods. Throughout the chapter examples will be drawn from the research literature to illustrate important concepts and methods. In addition, to provide greater continuity across the various research procedures, we will take a specific social behavior that needs explanation —cheating in college—and show how each research method might be applied to that behavior.

DEFINITIONS, OPERATIONS, AND REPLICATION

Suppose that you are a social psychologist. You are teaching at a college or university, the time for final examinations is fast approaching, and you happen to be discussing with some of your colleagues the need for imposing tight security on the departmental office during preparation of examinations. You all agree that it is a sad commentary on the state of academic affairs, and one of your colleagues says, "All right, you are the social psychologist, why don't you tell us why students cheat?" You might be tempted to give a quick answer, such as "To get better grades," or "Because there is such a small chance of getting caught," or even (if you have grown very cynical) "Why not? Doesn't everyone?" These answers suggest quite different possible explanations, and help to illustrate that the example generalizes quite well to other situations—preparation of fraudulent income tax returns, unethical business or political practices, white-collar crime. In conceptual terms, the rationale provided by the first answer is an instrumental one. Dishonesty is seen as the means toward a desired end. The second answer assumes that people's natural evil tendencies can be prevented from affecting their behavior only if the punishment for transgression is swift and sure. That sort of viewpoint should have a familiar ring to anyone who has listened to the justifications given for most of our criminal laws. The third answer suggests that morality ought to be defined not in terms of any universal principles, but only in terms of the most frequent behavior, and, further, that to be moral is to put yourself at a disadvantage when compared to those others who are behaving dishonestly. That these three rationales for behavior occur so frequently suggests that while our example of college cheating is, itself, limited in scope, its assumptions about human nature will be relevant for a wide variety of other situations.

Now, what else can be said about the answers to the question? Although any one of your responses might have been correct, it is important to notice that you have not answered *as a social psychologist*. You have not gathered the relevant data and then based your conclusions on those data. You have answered with guesses based on your own implicit theory of social psychology, and though this implicit theory may be a rich source of *hypotheses*, it may be much less helpful as a source of conclusions. Instead of responding with a quick answer, you should have asked a few questions of your own. In the first place, you need to know what your colleague *means* by the word "cheat." Does this category of "cheating behavior" include the actions of a student who looks at another's paper during an examination as well as the actions of a student who steals the examination in advance? What about a student who has someone else take the test in his or her place? Does cheating also include purchasing a term paper? Bringing an electronic calculator to a mathematics exam? Getting special tutoring from the laboratory assistant? Asking questions in class that are almost certain to appear on the test? But wait a minute. At least this last possibility sounds more like "being a good student" than it sounds like "cheating." As a matter of fact, obtaining extra tutoring also

sounds more like responsible behavior than like cheating. And bringing an electronic calculator may be unfair to the students who cannot
afford one, but is it really cheating?

The crucial point is that, although there might be rather widespread agreement that some of these practices are "cheating" and
some are not, certainty can be achieved only with a proper definition.
The abstract concept of cheating must be reduced to an agreed-upon
set of observable behaviors. Let us say that you and I had agreed to
compare the level of cheating at our two institutions. Suppose that I
included bringing a calculator among the behaviors I referred to as
cheating, but you excluded that particular action. We would most
probably find that there was more cheating at my school than at yours,
but that difference would be a *spurious* one based on a difference in
definition, rather than a real one based on the different persons and
situations involved. One of the principal goals of scientific social psychology is that findings obtained in one setting be *replicable*, or
repeatable, in other settings. In practice, this is often difficult to accomplish even with agreement on the set of behaviors under study;
without such agreement the goal is unattainable.

The Difficulty of Replicating Findings

One of the reasons that replicability is difficult to achieve in
practice is that the process of measuring a social behavior exerts influence over the behavior being measured. This problem of intrusion
of the measurement procedure into the ongoing phenomena under
study will be discussed more fully in a later section. Although the
problem exists for any scientific enterprise, its effects are more pronounced in the social sciences, and most troublesome in social psychology. Why? Because of social psychology's interest in the behavior
of the individual person. The physical sciences deal with matter incapable of intentional action, so observer effects are limited to those
(usually slight) changes brought about by the presence of the measuring devices. Biologists and psychologists who work with animals
certainly affect the behavior of their subjects, but few people would
argue that the animals choose to behave one way or another depending upon what they believe their experimenters desire. Finally, the
other disciplines dealing with human behavior concern themselves
either with large systems (economics, political science) or groups
(sociology) unlikely to respond to the observer in a consistent manner,
or with smaller portions of behavior (experimental psychology) less
likely to be influenced by observation. If you know that I am studying
your income and spending habits, you cannot do much to change your

income and you cannot alter your fixed expenses for food and shelter, so only a small portion of the behavior I am interested in is under your direct and immediate control. Similarly, if I study your voting habits, you are restricted, in America at least, to five basic choices— Democrat, Republican, an occasional independent or splinter-party candidate, write-in, or no vote at all. If I observe your interaction with a group of your friends, your initial self-consciousness at my presence will fade, and the momentum developed in the group will probably restrict your chances to respond only to me. If, however, we are alone together, and I ask you to tell me your attitude toward, say, abortion, your answer may be determined as much by my presence and by the way I ask the question as by your *true* feelings on the matter. This problem has implications not only for the ways in which research is conducted (the social psychology of the social psychological experiment, discussed later in this chapter), but also for the initial definition of the behavior to be studied.

Let us return to the cheating example. We have already seen the necessity of constructing a behavioral definition of the concept so that different researchers will be studying the same set of behavior. But is that enough? Suppose that you and I have agreed to exclude from the category of cheating behavior everything but "looking at other students' papers during an examination." Now if I take all my measurements during midterm exams in small classes where the professor remains in the room, and you make all of your observations from the projection booth of a large lecture hall during final examinations conducted without proctors, the amounts of cheating that we observe will almost certainly be different. But is the difference a function of the character of the two schools and their students, or is it attributable to the differences in time and method of measurement? It is clear that for the data from the two settings to be strictly comparable, we must change our behavioral definition of the concept into an **operational definition**: a definition stated in terms of the operations performed to measure the behavior of interest.

Empirical Replication

Strict comparability between two or more settings is particularly important only when the goal of the research is the documentation of the existence or prevalance of a phenomenon. If the conclusions to be drawn are of the form "There is more cheating at University A than at University B," then we must be very certain that the behaviors included in the definition and the operations used to measure cheating in the two cases are as similar as we can possibly make them. If we conduct such a comparison we will have performed what is known as an **empirical replication**: research in which the procedures for the second study (or subsequent studies) are as nearly identical as possible to those employed in the first study (or preceding studies). There will, of course, still be some differences—place, time, subjects, researchers—but the procedures followed are the same.

Empirical replications are most useful in permitting us to compare data gathered from different populations, or at different times and places, but even here we must not forget the social psychology of research. Suppose, for example, we conduct an experiment with one group of subjects and then repeat the same study in the same setting with a different group of subjects, but obtain different results. If there is no evidence to suggest that the time variable affected the outcome, then we might be tempted to conclude with some confidence that the subject populations differ. After all, the procedures were exactly the same, weren't they? The problem is that identical behavior on the part of the experimenter might be differently perceived by varying subject populations, with the result that from the subject's viewpoint the procedures were quite different. Consider a specific example: I am investigating the responses of different subject groups to frustration arising out of failure to complete a task, and I am not very sensitive to some of the implications of the language that I employ. Just before I ask the subjects to attempt the task (at which I am confident they will fail) I say, "All right, boys, now please read the instructions for this task." Since I do want to be a careful experimenter, I make sure that I say these exact words to all of my subjects, half of whom are black, and half of whom are white. Finally let us assume that I find a higher level of aggression as a response to the frustration of failure among the black subjects than among the white subjects.

The procedures were exactly the same (from my view) so the results can be attributed to a difference in the base rate of aggression between the two races of subjects. Or can they? Most probably not. I have failed to recognize that the word *boy* has a meaning to my black subjects that it does not have to my white subjects, and that rather than being a neutral term, it is one that might well produce an aggressive response. My white subjects have only the frustration of failure, but my black subjects also suffer the frustration of being referred to by a term they consider quite derogatory. It is thus impossible for anyone to tell from this experiment alone whether there is *really* a racial difference, or whether the obtained difference is merely due to a difference in the meaning to the subjects of what appears to the experimenter to be an "identical" procedure. In passing it should be noted that exactly this sort of problem is at the heart of the controversy over presumed racial differences in intelligence. If one assumes that the intelligence test administered constitutes "the same procedure" whether the subject is black or white, then any differences in average scores are attributed to racial differences. If, however, one assumes that because of a different cultural background the language involved in standardized tests is in an important sense *not* the same procedure, then any differences in scores cannot reliably be attributed to discrepancies in the presumed intellectual ability of the two races.

Conceptual Replication

Now let us return to the cheating example. We have discovered that empirical replications might provide us with information about the relative frequency of cheating at different universities, and if those empirical replications are carefully performed and interpreted, they might even suggest some of the characteristics involved in the production of different overall levels of cheating across the two subject populations. But remember that the task of scientific social psychology is to discover the situational, as well as personal, factors that are involved in social behavior. To achieve this alternative goal, strict comparability of the empirical replication may not be necessary—or even desirable. In many cases, the generality of research findings can be increased by using different procedures in different circumstances.

Suppose that we wanted to determine whether there was more cheating on final examinations than on midterm examinations (presumably because of the greater pressure created by the final exam). You would measure the incidence of cheating at both examination times at your university, and I would observe the incidence of cheating at both times at my university. Each one of us would, of course, have to use the same operational definition of cheating for the final examination that was used for the midterm, but we might increase the generality of our results by using *different* operational definitions in the two universities. If you observed the large lecture class from the projection booth (where you would not be seen) and I observed several small classes from the rear of the room, we would, as indicated earlier, probably discover a larger amount of cheating at your university. But now the absolute level of cheating is not our primary concern; instead, we are interested in the *change* in cheating from the midterm to the final. The level of cheating observed at midterm would be the base rate for each set of research circumstances (your university or mine, large or small classes, presence or absence of supervisory figures, and obvious presence or apparent absence of an observer). The level of cheating observed at the final examination would then be expressed as a function of the base rate found during midterms, and the differences between the two measurements obtained at one university would be compared to the differences obtained at the other. What we have conducted is an elementary conceptual replication: we have both tested the same concept—change in cheating behavior—but we have used quite different operations to do so.

Now let's assume that we discover that (a) there are overall differences in absolute amount of cheating, with your university having a higher incidence than mine, and (b) in each university there is about twice as much cheating on the final as there was on the midterm exam. We do not even attempt to interpret the overall differences in levels of cheating, because we know that they might have been produced as much by the different measurement techniques as by any intrinsic characteristics of the students. We do compare the two *rates* of increase, find them to be the same, and conclude that final examinations will produce about twice as much cheating as will midterms. We are more confident of this conclusion based on entirely different procedures than we would be of results obtained using an empirical replication technique. Since about all that was constant was the examinations, we feel quite comfortable attributing the results of the research to those examinations. In general, then, we achieve a higher degree of confidence from a successful conceptual replication than from a successful empirical replication.

An Illustration: Status and Compliance

An excellent example of the theoretical gains to be made from conceptual replication is an experiment conducted by Thibaut and Riecken (1955). These investigators wanted to determine how the social status an individual possesses affects the perceptions that other people have about the causes for his or her compliance with an influence attempt. Suppose, for example, that I ask you to do a favor for me, and you agree to do so. Thibaut and Riecken hypothesized that if I think you have high social status, I will attribute your assistance to *internal* causes—your pleasant disposition or your desire to be helpful. If, on the other hand, I think you have low social status, then I will attribute your compliance to *external* forces such as the persuasiveness of my request. These conceptual hypotheses were tested by two different sets of operations, using two different subject populations.

At each of the locations (the University of North Carolina and Harvard University), the subjects were introduced to two experimental confederates who were trained to play specific roles. After the introductions the subject made an initial rating of the two confederates (who were ostensibly just other subjects in the experiment), and then the experimental task began. This task had been designed so that the subject would have to make repeated requests for help from each of the two confederates, and, eventually, both complied with the requests. Finally, the subject made a second evaluation of each confederate and indicated what he thought to be the reasons for compliance with his requests. The conceptual variables involved were, of course, the same at the two locations. But the ways in which these conceptual variables were operationalized differed, and these differences are summarized in Table 2-1. Discrepancies in status were

TABLE 2-1
Summary of the operational definitions of conceptual variables in the Thibaut and Riecken (1955) study of the perception of social causality

CONCEPTUAL VARIABLE	OPERATIONAL DEFINITION OF THE VARIABLE	
	NORTH CAROLINA EXPERIMENT	HARVARD EXPERIMENT
High Status	A recent Ph.D. who has just joined the UNC instructional staff.	The graduate of a well-known preparatory school and of an Ivy League university (where he had been editor of the daily newspaper). Veteran of Navy combat service with command responsibilities. Presently enrolled in Harvard Law School.
Low Status	An Army veteran who had just completed his first year of undergraduate school.	A freshman at a nearby but low-prestige college. He had attended public high school in a drab mill town, and his only "leadership experience" was serving as secretary for his high-school camera club.
Influence Attempt	Use prepared messages to try to convince confederates to participate in a Red Cross blood drive.	Use prepared messages to try to convince confederates to share a special dictionary necessary for the completion of original crossword puzzles.
Compliance	No intermediate responses by confederates permitted. At conclusion of message-sending, both confederates said they had been influenced to donate blood.	Intermediate responses of reluctance to relinquish the dictionary. After later messages both confederates sent their dictionaries to the subject.

created either by a combination of academic achievement and professional position (North Carolina), or by a combination of academic
achievement, social position, and leadership experience (Harvard).
The experimental tasks were different, with North Carolina subjects
believing that they were serving as the "communicator" in a study of
persuasive communication, while the Harvard subjects believed that
they were creating original crossword puzzles as part of a study of
differences between individual and group productivity. The vehicle
for the influence attempt was the same in both cases (prepared messages), but the aims of the messages were different, as were the operational definitions of compliance (with no intermediate responses
possible at North Carolina, with intermediate reluctance expressed
at Harvard).

Perceived locus of causality for compliance with the request was
measured at North Carolina by a postexperimental interview question:
"Suppose that you had to decide that one of the members of the
audience said 'yes' because you forced him to and the other said 'yes'
because he just naturally wanted to anyway. Which one would you
say you forced, and which one would you say just wanted to anyway?"
(1955, p. 120). A similar question was asked at Harvard to determine
the perceived reasons for compliance by both the high status and low
status confederates. There were some differences in the perceived
status of the confederates at the two universities (not surprisingly,
the status manipulation was more effective at Harvard), but with this
qualification the results generally supported the predictions. Locus of
causality for action was perceived as internal for the high status confederate, but as external for the low status confederate. The results
from the two locations are all the more convincing when considered
together, because of the substantial differences in the way the conceptual variables were operationalized at the two universities.

Problems With Conceptual Replications

Conceptual replications, however, are not without their draw-
backs. Just as we stand to gain more if we are successful, we also
stand to lose more if we fail. If we conduct a careful empirical replication and the results found with one subject population (or in one
location) differ from those found in a different setting, we begin to
wonder whether the early results were somehow unique to that time,
place, and group of people. If we attempt a conceptual replication—
changing many of the procedures at the same time we change location
and subjects—we cannot be sure that a failure to obtain similar results
is not due merely to the change in methods. Worse yet, the more

aspects of the procedure we change, the less certain we can be about *which* procedural difference might have been the culprit.

To return to the cheating example, consider only one of the possible failures to replicate: compared to its level at midterm, cheating doubles in your university but remains at the same low level in mine. Perhaps this is because the presence of an observer is sufficiently threatening that only the most desperate students will risk being caught either at midterm or during the final. Or, perhaps the greater group solidarity engendered by small classes establishes implicit norms against cheating (again, violated only by the most desperate). Or, perhaps the students at my school have more rigid superegos, while the students at your school believe in a situationally based set of ethical principles that permits cheating if the stakes are high enough. The problem with an unsuccessful conceptual replication is that we simply cannot tell (from any of the data available) which of these possibilities, or others we have not mentioned, actually produced the difference in results.

What is the solution? The best research strategy should combine elements of both empirical and conceptual replication. As Campbell and Fiske (1959) have argued, the concepts of social psychology are sufficiently complex so that no single operation can serve as a complete definition. As a consequence, sound research procedure would require what Campbell and Fiske (1959) have called **multiple operationism**: the use of different operations, in varied contexts, to measure any particular concept. Assuming that we could agree that cheating involved stealing exams, using crib notes, having others take the tests, copying from another's paper, and a limited number of other specific behaviors, then different parts of our research study (or different studies conducted by other investigators) ought to try varied means for measuring only a few of these behaviors at any one time. This is the essence of conceptual replication, and such a research strategy would, if successful, permit us to learn a great deal about the nature of cheating.

In addition, to guard against the possibility of learning nothing, our ideal research plan should also include at least some conditions that permit exact comparison across different research settings. As Aronson and Carlsmith (1968) point out, one of the reasons for a failure in conceptual replication might well be a lack of skill on the part of the investigator. I might discover a lower level of cheating in my university not because my students are more moral than yours, but only because I am not as observant as you are. In order to rule out differential competence as an explanation for failure of a conceptual replication, you and I should arrange our study so that *both* of us include large and small classes, sometimes using hidden observers and sometimes using obvious observers, sometimes having proctors present and sometimes having no proctors. Even more importantly, I should conduct half of the research done at your school, and you should conduct half of the research done at mine. In short, we should perform the research in a way that will permit us to determine whether I can "reproduce your results" at the same time that I am obtaining my own (different) findings under different conditions. This is most important if you and I are having a theoretical argument in which I suggest that your findings are the result of some artifact in the procedure (e.g., your hiding in the projection booth during the mid-term examination is a dishonest sort of behavior that, if widely reported among the large lecture class, will encourage increased dishonesty on the students' part during the final). But reproducibility is also valuable across situations and subjects even if you and I agree on the theoretical ideas involved.

It should be emphasized here that a healthy combination of conceptual and empirical replication, with all the proper controls and with enough auxiliary data to permit alternative explanations to be ruled out, very seldom (if ever) occurs in actual practice. Even with unlimited time, money, subjects, and assistants, such goals would be difficult to achieve within the framework of a single research study. Notice how complicated our cheating experiment began to sound—and we were considering only a few of the possible operational definitions of that concept. But time, money, subjects, and assistants are limited; in many cases they can best be described as meager. As a result, researchers must find ways to compromise on the joint goals of empirical and conceptual replication. They must depend upon lengthy programs of research rather than single large studies which might answer more of the questions, and they must judiciously select from among the available methods those few most appropriate to their needs.

VALIDITY OF THE RESEARCH METHOD

As noted before, the task of scientific social psychology (as compared to the naive social psychology of the individual) is to discover how people actually behave in social situations. This task imposes two responsibilities upon the social psychologist—the elimination of measurement artifacts, and the demonstration that research findings will generalize to the real social world. Both of these responsibilities must be met in order to ensure the validity of the research (Campbell, 1957), and we shall consider them in turn.

Internal Validity: Meaningful Differences

First the researcher must be certain that the findings he or she obtains reflect real differences of psychological importance, rather than mere artifacts of the research procedure. For example, suppose that you and I were observing the level of cheating on examinations at our two universities. We have agreed to use the same size classes, to do the research during the same semester, and to define cheating as "looking at another's paper during the examination." But we have carelessly forgotten to agree on just where in the room the observer will be stationed. As a result, I observe from the projection booth, while you observe from the rear of the room. Let us say that the planned comparison was the overall level of cheating (your university has a very strict honor code, mine does not). Further assume that our results indicate a lower level of cheating at your university. Is your university's honor code that much more effective in preventing cheating? Perhaps so, but perhaps the difference is that your students knew you were there, while mine thought no one was watching. By observing from different vantage points, we have introduced a measurement artifact into the research. We can't be certain that the obtained difference is of psychological importance, since it may be just a spurious difference. The more a researcher can be confident that the findings represent real differences (the more carefully artifacts have been eliminated), the greater the internal validity of the research will be. Internal validity thus reflects the degree of control inherent in the research. The better the controls against artifacts, the more likely it is that obtained differences represent true psychological differences.

External Validity: Results that Generalize

But even true psychological differences assume social importance only if they generalize beyond the observational setting or laboratory in which they were obtained. The extent to which a finding will generalize to other subject samples, to other times, and to other settings is the external validity of the finding. If you and I had successfully guarded against measurement artifacts (thus achieving high internal validity) and had still obtained differences in the level of cheating found at our two universities, we might still wonder how far those results could be generalized. Is it the case that all colleges with strict honor codes have less cheating than do colleges without such strict codes? Or to phrase the question in conceptual terms, does the greater threat of punishment deter cheating? To answer this question adequately, we would have to study cheating on tasks other than tests, to examine the effects of punishments other than those specified by honor codes, and to demonstrate comparable differences across more than two universities. If this comparison across time, methods, and subjects sounds familiar, it is because the process of conceptual replication is one of the principal means of establishing the external validity of a particular set of results. The more different ways we test a theoretical proposition, provided the results remain the same, the more confident we become of the external validity of our original test of the conceptual idea.

In addition to conceptual replication, there are other ways that the researcher can enhance the external validity of the findings. The first of these is to ensure that the subjects used for the research are representative of the population to which the results are to be generalized. How easily can the results of our cheating studies be generalized to the broader issue of income tax fraud, or unethical business practices? Do these also increase with increasing pressure? The question of representativeness is more complex than it would first appear, since some phenomena of interest to social psychology are likely to generalize more easily than others. For example, if we want to determine how various descriptive adjectives are combined into a complete impression of a stimulus person (this work is discussed in detail in Chapter Three), then the fact that our experiments are conducted using college sophomores may not be much of a threat to the external validity of the findings. There is no a priori reason to believe that these basic processes of impression formation would be substantially different in other subjects, just so long as all the subjects shared the same fundamental language. In other words, the results should be externally valid for any speakers of the language spoken by the actual subjects.

In contrast, if we are attempting to study the convictions and acquittals made by juries through simulation with college sophomores, we face an almost insurmountable problem in attempting to assure external validity. Here it is easy to see that college sophomores are not representative of the class of potential real jurors (usually composed of registered voters), but even the most careful subject selection cannot guarantee representativeness of *experience*: our experimental juries will almost always be just that. No matter how "real" we make our simulation of jury process, it will still be true that no defendant's fate or freedom rests on the decision that is made. And this crucial difference in experience will limit the external validity of findings from studies of simulated juries. This limit to external validity does not, of course, render the findings from studies of simulated juries any less real (in the internal validity sense of their having psychological importance), and it does not put an end to such research. It does mean that experimenters need to be cautious in generalizing their findings.

How can researchers include the two aspects of representativeness—similarity between the subjects used and the target population in both social characteristics and relevant experience—in their designs? If the circumstances were always ideal this would be only a minor inconvenience: potential subjects would be randomly chosen from a complete listing of all members of the target population; all potential subjects would take part; and the research would be completely concealed as part of the subject's everyday life.

Unfortunately for the social psychologist, the real conditions that are usually found in research settings never even remotely approach this set of ideal circumstances. Very seldom is the entire target population known, so the various sampling techniques can only approximate the pure random sample described in the example. Ethical and methodological considerations either prevent the use of subjects who do not know they are participating in research or limit the kinds of research questions that can be asked. Subjects refuse to participate, refuse to give permission for their data to be included in the analysis, make responses that are not interpretable, or do not make observable responses at all. As a consequence, research in social psychology cannot be judged by comparing what was actually done to a set of absolute standards. What can be expected is that the investigator will take the precautions necessary to rule out what Webb, Campbell, Schwartz, and Sechrest (1966) call plausible rival hypotheses: potential explanations of the data that are derived either from an alternative theoretical position or from the presence of artifacts in the research procedure. We now consider one such artifact—the experience of being a research subject—in greater detail.

REACTIVITY IN SOCIAL PSYCHOLOGICAL RESEARCH

In most cases, the people who serve as subjects in social psychological research are aware that they are not merely behaving, they are creating data. Because social psychology is interested in the behavior of the individual person, its findings are most likely to be affected by the subjects' knowledge that their behavior is being recorded for later analysis. The extent to which the resulting data are distorted by the unique features of "participating in research" is referred to as the reactivity of the measurement technique. This potential source of error is present almost no matter what research method is employed. Several sources of reactive bias have been identified (Webb, Campbell, Schwartz, and Sechrest, 1966), and for our purposes these may be grouped into two general categories: problems arising from awareness of being tested, and problems arising from response sets.

The Awareness of Being Tested

Although you may be a willing, cooperative, and well-intentioned participant in my research, you are still "behaving like a subject" rather than "behaving naturally." This problem arises whether the research is conducted in an experimental laboratory or in the subjects' normal surroundings, and it can take on quite substantial proportions. Webb and colleagues cite an incident in which a number of graduate students were sent to a South Side Chicago street which intersected an informal racial boundary. The students were to observe the numbers of blacks and whites in stores, bars, restaurants, and theaters to determine how these proportions might change as one moved from the predominantly white end of the street to the predominantly black end. The observers were simply to make counts, not to question any people on the street. As research goes, this should have been relatively innocuous, yet two merchants were sufficiently upset that they placed repeated calls to the university to determine whether the observers were performing an official function or casing their places of business in preparation for a later robbery. The problem is that if the observers had this much effect on the merchants, it is difficult to deny that their presence also affected the behavior of the passersby who were being counted.

If behaving like a subject is a problem in field observation, it is even more troublesome in the experimental laboratory. In what was to be a test of the power of hypnosis, Orne (1962) reports a series of pilot studies designed to create an experimental task that nonhypnotized subjects would quickly refuse to continue. (Once such a task had been discovered, Orne would have asked subjects under hypnosis to perform the task, predicting that they would continue for much longer durations.) In one of these pilot experiments subjects were asked to sum pairs of adjacent numbers on sheets filled with rows of random digits. To finish even a single sheet would require 224 additions, and the subject was presented with a pile of nearly 2000 such sheets. After the initial instructions, the experimenter removed the subject's watch, and told the subject to begin working, saying that he would "return eventually." After as much as *five and one-half hours,* the experimenter gave up and returned to stop the subject.

Thinking that the subjects might have found some rationale for this absurd task, Orne then tried to make its meaninglessness even more clear for a second group of pilot subjects. They were given the same addition task, but now upon completion of each page of additions the subject was to receive further instructions by turning over the top card in a large stack of index cards. Every card in this stack instructed the subject to tear the sheet of additions just completed into not less than thirty-two pieces. Surprisingly, subjects persisted in this task for several hours without objection! Postexperimental interviews revealed that even in this situation, subjects attributed meaning to their performance, often believing it to have been an endurance test.

As Orne points out, "Just about any request which could conceivably be asked of the subject by a reputable investigator is legitimized by the quasi-magical phrase, 'This is part of an experiment,' and the shared assumption that a legitimate purpose will be served by the subject's behavior" (1962, p. 777). Participation in a psychological experiment can be seen as problem-solving behavior. In order to be helpful (to confirm the experimenter's hypothesis), the subject must first discover what that hypothesis is. To make this decision, the subject presumably relies on what Orne (1959) calls the demand characteristics of the experimental situation: the sum total of the cues which convey an experimental hypothesis to the subject. It must be emphasized that this need not be the *experimenter's* hypothesis, but only one that the subject considers plausible in the circumstances. Indeed, it is just this difference that provides one rationale for the use of deception in experimental research: If the experimental cover story can suggest a plausible alternative hypothesis, the subject's behavior relevant to that hypothesis may be biased, but the behavior relevant to the true hypothesis may be much more natural. If, for example, I could convince you that I was conducting cross-cultural research on handwriting styles under stress, you might be more likely to "behave naturally" (i.e., cheat if that were your predilection) than if you thought I was investigating the personality characteristics of people who cheat.

Response Sets

Unfortunately for the social psychologist, the problems created by awareness (especially demand characteristics) are not the only reactive effects present in research. A second important problem is the response set: a general tendency to respond in a specified way, regardless of the particular circumstances or information content. For example, when people are asked to answer interview questions, they will more frequently agree with a statement than they will disagree with the statement's opposite (Sletto, 1937). This tendency is referred to as the acquiescence response set. Although there is some evidence (Rorer, 1965) that it may not apply to virtually any content, acquiescence does affect measures of importance to social psychologists (Campbell, Siegman, and Rees, 1967). Both for this reason and because the correction is so simple—word half of the items in a positive direction, half in a negative direction—acquiescence is most often reduced to negligible proportions.

Other response sets, such as social desirability (Edwards, 1957; Crowne and Marlowe, 1964), are more difficult to deal with. People hold private beliefs that do not always agree with those widely approved in society, and investigators often find most interesting the basically "undesirable" behaviors—cheating, aggression, the raw exercise of even legitimate power. For either or both of these reasons the researcher runs the risk of obtaining from the subject not true feelings or behavior, but an opinion or behavior the subject believes will meet with the investigator's approval. To complicate the issue still further, social desirability may well be defined by the subjects in terms of the subculture represented by the particular interviewer or experimenter, rather than in terms of society as a whole. For example, if in my study of academic cheating I employ interviewers who boast about their own exploits (such as "boosting" cars and "ripping off" large department stores) before asking the questions of respondents, I am likely to get an overestimate of the cheating that actually occurs. In response to the social desirability demands of the interview situation, the subjects have had to prove that they, too, are in a position to take risks. Their "socially desirable" answers may thus overrepresent the existence of a behavior considered in a broader context to be socially disapproved.

How Can Reactivity Be Minimized?

What can the social psychologist do to reduce or eliminate these reactive effects? There is no simple answer, but there are several research methods of possible usefulness. First, the investigator can employ what Crano and Brewer (1973) have called unvoluntary subjects. These are subjects who are exposed either to controlled observational settings, or to experimental treatments, in the course of their everyday behavior. Their actions in the controlled setting are recorded, and wherever physically possible the subjects are then contacted, informed that they have just participated in research, and given the opportunity to exclude their data from any subsequent analysis (in lieu of obtaining their advance consent to serve as subjects). A second possibility is the use of unobtrusive measures such as physical traces (Webb et al., 1966). For example, the most popular exhibit at a children's zoo might well be determined by measures of erosion (how often the grass needs to be reseeded) or by measures of accretion (how many popsicle sticks litter the ground in front of the exhibit). A third possibility is the use of archival data—written records of all kinds, previously gathered for some purpose other than the research at hand. As Webb et al. (1966) point out, these archival data include everything from sales receipts, government vital statistics, and private letters to tombstone sizes. Finally, if it is impossible to keep the subjects from realizing that they are participating in research, the investigator may contrive the situation in such a manner as to mislead the subjects about the true purpose of the study. As we shall see in later sections of this chapter, none of these methods is entirely without problems, but each can contribute to a reduction in reactivity, a basic goal of any social psychologist who hopes that his or her findings will generalize beyond the population of experimental subjects.

Try to keep the issues of conceptual replication, internal validity, and external validity, and the problem of measurement reactivity, in mind as we turn to kinds of research methods in social psychology. For purposes of comparison the methods are grouped into three major categories: archival research, observational research, and experimental research. At the risk of some oversimplification, the three groups of methods can be seen as representing different points on the dimensions of reactivity and validity.

First, they reflect, in the order presented, an increasing intrusion by the researcher into the social behavior being observed. In the archival methods the subjects are seldom identified, and their behavior is measured only after it has occurred. In the observational methods the focus is on behavior happening at the time, but the researcher extends his or her control (when it is exerted at all) only to selected elements of the situation. In contrast, a subject in an experiment is aware of being a subject and is placed in a situation in which nearly all aspects of the situation are under the experimenter's explicit control.

Second, the methods are presented in what may best be described as an increasing ratio of internal to external validity. Archival methods are moderate in external validity (generalizing well to the sample they represent, but somewhat less well to the larger population), but they are low in internal validity, since many plausible rival hypotheses exist for any differences that might be found. Observational methods may be confounded by the presence of the researcher, but this presence permits accumulation of data necessary to rule out alternative explanations. The experimental methods permit strong conclusions about the effects of treatments within the experiment (high internal validity), but they may sacrifice a substantial amount of generalizability in the bargain. It is ironic that the information most useful for theory testing should be derived from a methodology that is the furthest removed from everyday experience.

ARCHIVAL METHODS: HISTORY AS SOCIAL PSYCHOLOGY

The ongoing, continuing records of a society are its archives, and although they are usually maintained for other purposes, many of these records can be put to effective use by social psychologists. When you hear the term archival methods you are likely to think of gnome-like researchers with thick glasses, pouring over dusty manuscripts deep in the catacombs of large libraries. Although there may once have been a grain of truth in this stereotype, it does not do justice either to the sources of archival data or to the imaginative uses to which such data can be put. Let us consider an example that may change your impression a bit.

In its November 1974 issue, *Esquire* magazine reported a list of the ninety-two "most publicized persons in the world." The claim is an exaggeration, but the method for constructing the list is interesting. The editors of *Esquire* began by arbitrarily restricting the duration of the project to the first six months of 1974, and six publications were chosen as sources—the *New York Times, Women's Wear Daily*, the *National Star*, and *Time, Newsweek*, and *People* magazines. A scoring system was devised that gave differential weight to being mentioned (as opposed to being photographed) in the relevant section or location of each publication. The then Secretary of State Henry Kissinger received the highest score (39), closely followed by Senator Edward Kennedy (36) and Jacqueline Onassis (32). The scoring system is shown in Table 2-2. Although this "Great Celebrity Ball" was obviously done with tongue in cheek, using a highly restricted (and arbitrarily selected) set of sources, it does help counter the stodgy, dusty image of archival research.

TABLE 2-2
*Archival sources, locations, kinds of citations, and points awarded
in the* Esquire *celebrity scoring system*

SOURCE	SECTION OR LOCATION	CITATION	POINTS
New York Times	Notes on People	Mention	1
		Picture	2
Women's Wear Daily	Eye & Eye View	Picture	1
National Star	Front Page	Mention	2
		Picture	3
Time	People	Mention	1
	People	Picture	2
	Cover	Picture	3
Newsweek	Newsmakers	Mention	1
	Newsmakers	Picture	2
	Cover	Picture	3
People	Cover	Mention	2
		Picture	3

Data from *Esquire* magazine, November 1974.

An Illustration: A Speeding Crackdown

A society's public documents and legal records, in addition to its
mass media, are an excellent source of archival data of significance to
social psychologists. A study by Ross and Campbell (1968) on the
effects of a Connecticut crackdown on speeders illustrates both the
principles of archival research and some of the problems in interpretation that need to be guarded against. In 1955 the traffic death toll in
Connecticut was 324 (a level that turned out to be an all-time high for
the decade), and in an attempt to reduce this fatality level the governor, Abraham Ribicoff, began an unprecedented program of enforcement in December, 1955. Anyone caught speeding in Connecticut
would have his or her operator's license suspended for thirty days for
a first offense, with longer suspensions for repeated offenders.

The program was most vigorously pursued during the first six
months of 1956, with suspensions for speeding rising to 5,398 from
231 in the comparable period of 1955. As the figures were released
during the year, the governor praised the program's effectiveness, concluding at the end of 1956 (when the final fatality figure for the year

was 284) that "with the saving of forty lives in 1956, a reduction of 12.3% from the 1955 motor vehicle death toll, we can say that the program is definitely worthwhile" (p. 31). But was the program really effective, or did it just appear to be so?

It must be kept in mind that while archival data have external validity, they can still suffer from a lack of internal validity: if the samples chosen for comparison happen to be selective or biased, any conclusions drawn will be faulty. The celebrities mentioned in the *Esquire* example were most frequently cited in the sources chosen, but who was most frequently mentioned in similar publications? Certainly 284 fatalities is a reduction from 324, but what happened in previous years and in neighboring states? If the crackdown were really causing the reduction in fatalities, then Connecticut's drop in deaths should have been greater than the drop (if there was one) in New Jersey, Massachusetts, New York, and Rhode Island. In addition to the problem of selective sampling, archival research must guard against change in the base rate over time. If, for example, we counted the number of deaths in the world (without accounting for the increase in population), we could conclude that in a certain number of years there would be nobody left (because the absolute number of deaths is increasing). Rather than using absolute numbers for comparison, most raw figures obtained in archival research should be transformed into what Webb et al. (1966) call index numbers: numbers corrected for base rate.

Applying these corrections for base rate and for sampling trends, Ross and Campbell arrived at a much different conclusion about the effectiveness of the Connecticut speed crackdown. They first converted the fatality figures into deaths per 100 million miles traveled in the state, taking into account that there would most probably be more miles driven in every succeeding year. Then they extended the sample by plotting similar mileage death rates for all of the years between 1951 and 1959. The result of this comparison is shown in Figure 2-1 and indicates the difficulty of drawing comparisons from a restricted sample of archival data. From 1951 through 1955 the mileage death rate is unstable, taking a large jump upward in 1955. From 1956 onward, the rate rather steadily decreases, even though the major thrust of the enforcement program occurred in 1956 alone. When it is seen in the context of earlier and later years, the apparently dramatic shift from 1955 to 1956 loses much of its impact. In fairness to Governor Ribicoff, it should be pointed out that in 1956 he could not be expected to know what the mileage death rates would be in later years. But the preceding instability of the rate should have led him to be more cautious in his interpretation of the 1955–1956 change.

FIGURE 2-1
*Connecticut traffic fatalities from 1951 to 1959, plotted in terms
of deaths per 100 million miles driven. (Adapted from Ross and
Campbell, 1968)*

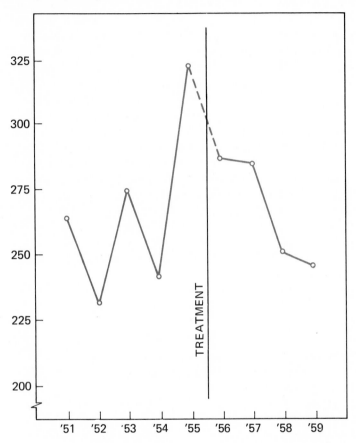

This example illustrates the need for extreme care in selecting the
particular comparisons to be made in archival research. Not only must
the data be transformed into index numbers, taking account of the base
rate of the phenomenon being measured, but the segments of the
archival record from which these data are taken must be chosen in a
manner that will minimize bias. The time periods and particular
sources that are chosen for study in archival research correspond to
the subjects chosen for participation in other forms of research; consequently, the best solution (wherever practicable) is random sampling from among the various periods and sources available.

Threats to Internal Validity

Even when researchers are careful in their sampling of archival data and in the use of index numbers, there are still two major threats to the validity of archival research. The first of these is what Webb et al. (1966) call selective deposit: the possibility that some records will be established more fully than others, either because of deliberate administrative action or because of contemporary social custom. One example that Webb and co-workers cite is the study of Roman life expectancy conducted by Durand (1960) in which the principal data were tombstone inscriptions. Durand noted that one possible source of error in his data was that wives who outlived their husbands were probably less likely to have had tombstones than were wives who died before their husbands did. This would have been an inadvertent selective deposit, but if we consider our college cheating example, we see that any selective deposit that occurs would more probably be the result of deliberate suppression by administrative officers concerned with their college's public image. As a result, an important datum might be whether or not the university maintains such records. We might find, for example, that most universities seem to report a relatively constant (though small) proportion of students disciplined or expelled for cheating. In contrast, there might be some other colleges that go for periods of years without a single report of cheating, and then all in one year expel a large number of students. Under these circumstances it is less plausible to argue that the moral fiber of the students has suddenly changed than to suggest that the problem suddenly became so large that it could no longer be kept quiet. The administrative tendency toward selective deposit was simply overwhelmed.

A second threat to the internal validity of archival research is the related problem of selective survival: the possibility that some records will not last as long as others, either because of natural decay or because of deliberate destruction. It is, for example, unlikely that future historians will ever achieve anything approaching complete access to lists of Central Intelligence Agency undercover operatives. Such lists are routinely destroyed to preserve both the life of the present agents and the cover of future ones. A university that maintains its disciplinary records among stacks of other materials in the basement of the administration building will be less likely to have complete records many years from now than will a university that computerizes its records. However they have been maintained, the records of a university that has maintained a fairly stable size (and location) for many years will be more complete than the records of a university whose administrative offices have been moved several times a year.

The problems of selective deposit and selective survival illustrate some of the difficulties that can be encountered in archival research. One final limitation should be noted: Many times the hypotheses of interest to researchers cannot be evaluated by reference to archival data, because the relevant data are not available. We have no way of learning what the motives of a student expelled for cheating might have been. We could obtain fragmentary records on the socioeconomic status of students expelled for cheating, and we might make guesses based on this evidence of the necessity for passing courses in order to maintain scholarship aid, but detailed psychological profiles of the students' motives do not exist.

Archival data can be used to suggest changes in a phenomenon over time, to establish its incidence in various locations, and to discover social conditions correlated with its occurrence. These data have the advantage of high external validity—there is no researcher standing around with a clipboard, no experimenter directing the subjects' behavior—and can be quite helpful in the generation of hypotheses for testing. But there can be serious limitations in internal validity. We have seen that social customs and deliberate actions may affect which data are recorded; records may be carelessly maintained or destroyed; the data to test many hypotheses simply do not exist. Paradoxically, both the principal advantages and the major disadvantages of the method arise from the fact that the data were originally collected for purposes *other than* social psychological research.

OBSERVATIONAL METHODS: THE HERE AND NOW OF BEHAVIOR IN PUBLIC PLACES

It is a simple matter to specify the limits of both archival and experimental research, but a precise definition of observational methods is much more difficult to establish, because this category is usually considered to include everything in between the archives and the experimental laboratory. We have seen that archival research consists of the selection and interpretation by social psychologists of data originally recorded in the past for some purpose other than research. Although we may not immediately think of cover photographs from weekly tabloids, collections of personal letters, or tombstone sizes and arrangements as data, they can be used in this way, and they do represent *past* action. In contrast, observational methods are used for the direct collection of *present* data. Since this contemporary data collection is almost always performed by the social psychologists who have identified the conceptual hypotheses to be tested, and who will interpret the data in terms of those hypotheses, the behavior to be observed can be chosen with these goals in mind. There is no need to adapt records collected for another purpose to suit the hypothesis of interest (or, more importantly, to limit the hypotheses to those that can be tested using the data known to be available).

If observational techniques can be distinguished from archival research by their focus on contemporary behavior, they can be distinguished from experimental methods primarily by the subject's awareness of the research. With the exception of participant observation—in which the observer is usually present with the people being observed, recording impressions or the data of interest as unobtrusively as possible—the subject in an observational study does not *know* that he or she is the object of the research. The subject does not enter into an explicit contract with the experimenter to "participate in an experiment," and can never be certain whether the events happening are natural occurrences or contrived manipulations. True, the subject may become suspicious—is that fragile-looking elderly woman struggling with a large suitcase someone's grandmother or someone's experimental confederate? But suspicion is not the same as certainty, and the remaining element of doubt is sufficient to make the subject's reactions more natural.

There are four commonly employed observational techniques: simple observation, participant observation, natural experiments, and field experiments. The first two are more nearly "observational" in character, while the latter two are analogs to the experimental procedures of the laboratory. In simple observation, the researcher is concealed and records the subject's behavior without any interference in the situation. Assessing the level of cheating on an exam from a hidden position such as the projection booth is an example of this sort of observation. At the next level of interference in the natural setting is participant observation. Here the researcher may be concealed (we could have a "plant" in the class who would appear to be taking the test while really recording the behavior of the other students) or visible. Obviously, if the observer's presence is known to the subjects, the fact that observation is taking place will affect their behavior. And this is particularly true if the actions that would be taken in the observer's absence would be socially undesirable, potentially embarrassing, or illegal. What are proctors of examinations for, if not to reduce cheating by their ability to observe its occurrence?

Concealed Participant Observation: The Doomsday Believers

To preclude the inhibiting effects of the observer's presence, social psychologists have resorted to surreptitious observation by someone who appears to be a full participant in the ongoing behavior. This was the case in the classic study of a "doomsday" religious group reported by Festinger, Riecken, and Schachter (1956). Through newspaper accounts, these investigators became aware of a small group of believers who were preparing for the end of the world. The leader of this group called "The Seekers" (who was given the fictitious name of Marian Keech) had been receiving messages in the form of automatic writing from a planet called Clarion. The messages warned that on a specific day a cataclysmic flood would destroy the city in which she lived, and would spread to create an inland sea from the Arctic Circle to the Gulf of Mexico. In return for their heroic efforts to warn the general public about the impending disaster, Mrs. Keech and her followers were to be saved from the flood by being taken aboard a flying saucer dispatched from planet Clarion. To prepare for their salvation most of the believers sold their possessions, left (or were dismissed from) their jobs, and held meetings to determine how they would greet their rescuers from Clarion.

For Festinger, Riecken, and Schachter the Seekers provided a perfect opportunity for a field test of some theoretical principles about the behaviors that might follow the disconfirmation of an expectancy. They reasoned that a person who is committed to a belief or expectation that turns out to be erroneous will be unable to accept the disconfirmation for what it is, and will instead interpret it in a manner consistent with the original belief. To bolster that erroneous interpretation, the person will try to convince other people of its validity. But because the Seekers refused to grant press interviews that would have helped them publicize their cause, it was highly unlikely that they would have permitted themselves to be used as sources of data. So the investigators elected to *join* the group under false pretenses and to conduct their observations from the inside. They participated in the group's meetings and were on hand when the fateful hour for the rescue came—and went. Four hours after the scheduled time for the rescue, Mrs. Keech received another message, and this one stated that the flood had been averted by heavenly intervention, largely in response to the preparations and faith of the group. This message rekindled the group's lagging belief, led to a dramatic increase in the attempts by members to recruit new converts, and in both of these ways confirmed the researchers' predictions.

This study illustrated both some of the possibilities of covert participant observation and some of its difficulties. In order to maintain a "cover," the researcher runs the risk of spuriously enhancing the phenomenon under study. In the words of Festinger, Riecken, and Schachter:

> There is little doubt that the addition of four new people to a fairly small group within ten days had an effect on the state of conviction among the existing members, especially since the four seem to have appeared when public apathy to the belief systems was great [1956, p. 240].

Thus the observer may contribute to the strength of the group's view of the world, even while being careful to avoid becoming an advocate for the group's position. This possibility is greatest in a group with restrictive admission policies, since in such a group mere passive agreement may not be sufficient. The researcher who has infiltrated a juvenile gang may well have to begin stealing cars right along with everyone else.

In addition to the methodological problems, concealed participant observation raises serious ethical questions. Whatever else he or she may be doing, the researcher is violating the right to privacy of the group. The behavior under study would not typically be open to the public (or the researcher would have settled for simple observation), but even if it were public, some ethical questions would remain. For example, people will participate in demonstrations, engage in public displays of affection, or confide their personal secrets to strangers in ways that they would not if they thought that they were contributing to a permanent record by which they could be later identified. Most observational researchers deal with these ethical and methodological problems by selecting a method of *partial* concealment, in which the presence of the researcher is made obvious to the subjects, but the specific behavior to be assessed is not revealed. For example, when Chesler and Schmuck (1963) conducted a study of a superpatriot discussion group, they identified themselves as graduate students in educational research, but they did not explicitly state the sorts of analyses that were intended for the observational data collected. Partial concealment preserves some of the advantages of observational methods while putting the subjects on notice that their privacy is being invaded.

Natural Experiments

Up to this point we have been discussing the ways in which observational methods may be employed to collect behavioral data of interest. Now we turn to consideration of ways in which the observational setting can be manipulated to produce the desired behaviors (or at least to produce the opportunity for the desired behaviors to occur). In the natural experiment this manipulation is provided by the environment. As it happens, we have already seen, in the Festinger, Riecken, and Schachter (1956) study, an illustration of the natural experiment. True, the behavior was examined through the use of concealed participant observation, but the conceptual variable—disconfirmation of expectancy—was manipulated by the natural environment. From the researcher's point of view this particular study had an important advantage not often found in other natural experiments, a precise date (and even hour) on which the manipulation would take place. It is much more typical for a researcher to make observations before the fact and then wait months for the natural manipulation (an airplane crash, a criminal indictment, an earthquake, a riot) to occur.

If ideal conditions could be maintained, natural experiments might be the social psychologist's dream. The manipulations performed by the environment (election results, changes in laws, catastrophic accidents, natural disasters) are significantly more powerful and involving than any which could in good conscience be employed in an experimental laboratory. As a result, they hold the potential for extremely high internal validity. In addition, since the subjects are "real people" behaving naturally in familiar surroundings where their actions can be recorded unobtrusively, the potential for high external validity is also great. But such ideal conditions are almost never realized. If natural manipulations are powerful, they are also unpredictable. They may occur so quickly that a researcher does not have adequate time for preparation (e.g., to administer premeasures), or they may take so long to happen that any changes obtained would be hopelessly confounded by other intervening events. It is virtually impossible to ensure internal validity if you cannot control the occurrence of the manipulation.

Field Experiments

To enhance internal validity while preserving the external validity inherent in research performed in natural settings (with unsuspecting or "unvoluntary" subjects), many social psychologists have turned to field experiments. Although these research methods closely resemble the experimental methods of the laboratory, the fact that the subjects are unaware justifies considering these methods under the general rubric of observational techniques. The setting is altered enough to produce the manipulation, but not so much that the subjects become suspicious; behavioral responses to the manipulation are recorded, but as unobtrusively as possible. An excellent example of this method is provided by a study of bystander response to an apparent emergency situation conducted in the New York subway system by Piliavin, Rodin, and Piliavin (1969).

This experiment was designed to determine what effects the race of a supposed "victim" (black or white) and the supposed reason for his problem (drunk or ill) would have on the help he received. There were other conditions involving the behavior of a model, but for now we will consider only the four possible conditions arising from variations in the victim's appearance. The experimental team consisted of four persons—the victim, the model, and two observers—and the research was conducted on the old subway cars of the Eighth Avenue A and D trains, since these trains make no stops between 59th and 125th Streets, and the cars have a seating arrangement (shown in Figure 2-2) of two-person seats. The four members of the team entered the car from different doors, with the victim and the model standing next to the pole in the "critical" end area of the car while the two observers took the seats indicated in the "adjacent area." Between 59th and 125th there was a period of approximately 7.5 minutes during which any passengers in the critical area were a captive audience for the experiment. About a minute after the train passed the first station, the victim staggered and collapsed on the floor, remaining in that position either until someone helped him, or until the train stopped (when the model helped him out the door). The victim was a black or white male between the ages of twenty-six and thirty-five, and was casually dressed. In the drunk condition he smelled of liquor and carried a pint bottle tightly wrapped in a paper bag; in the ill condition he appeared sober and walked with a cane. The observers

FIGURE 2-2
Diagram of the critical and adjacent areas of the subway car, showing locations of victim, model, and observers. (Adapted from Piliavin, Rodin, and Piliavin, 1969)

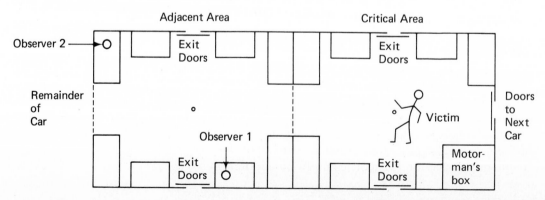

recorded data as unobtrusively as possible for the entire duration
of the ride, and all four team members disembarked at the station,
waited until other passengers had left the platform, and then went
to another platform to repeat the experiment on a train going in the
other direction.

There were eighty-four such trials conducted with no intervention
by the model, and these were performed before an audience that
averaged forty-three people in the entire car, with an average of 8.5
people in the critical area. The percentage of trials on which the
victim received help was truly impressive, as the data in Table 2-3
indicate. Only the black drunk received help on less than 100 percent
of the trials, and in a majority of cases help was rendered by more
than one other passenger. Men were more likely to help than were
women, although, as the authors point out, the sort of intervention
called for—lifting the victim, or at least dragging him to a seat—
would be more difficult for a woman to accomplish. In addition, there
was a tendency for passengers to help a victim of their own race more
than they helped a victim of the other race. We shall return to these
results, and some later research by Piliavin and Piliavin (1972), in
Chapter Ten, but for now it is sufficient to note the degree of control
over a natural setting that can be exerted by a carefully executed
field experiment. Admittedly, there are few natural settings that
provide the kind of captive audience found on a subway, but even in
public places with free access the setting can be controlled enough to
eliminate some of the immense variation that would otherwise occur.

TABLE 2-3
*Percentage of trials on which help was rendered in each condition
of victim race and state of health*

RACE OF VICTIM:	BLACK		WHITE	
HEALTH CONDITION:	CANE	DRUNK	CANE	DRUNK
Number of trials conducted	8	11	54	11
Percentage on which there was help given the victim	100	73	100	100

Adapted from Piliavin, Rodin, and Piliavin (1969)

Comparisons of Methods

The observational methods that we have discussed can be compared to each other (and to experimental and archival research) on a
number of dimensions, and these can be summarized as in Table 2-4.
At the beginning of this section it was suggested that observational
methods could be distinguished from archival research on the basis of

TABLE 2-4

Comparison of archival, observational, and laboratory experimental research methods

| DIMENSIONS | ARCHIVAL RESEARCH | OBSERVATIONAL METHODS | | | | | LABORATORY EXPERIMENTS |
| | | SIMPLE OBSERVATION | PARTICIPANT OBSERVATION | | NATURAL EXPERIMENTS | FIELD EXPERIMENTS | |
			CONCEALED	NONCONCEALED			
When are the data collected?	Past	Present	Present	Present	Present	Present	Present
Are the subjects aware?	No	No	No	Yes	No	No	Yes
What is the degree of control?	None	None	Low	Low	Low	High	High
How intrusive is the measurement?	Low	Low	Low	Moderate	Low	Low	High
What is the typical internal validity?	Low	Low	Moderate	Moderate	Moderate	Moderate	High
What is the typical external validity?	Moderate	High	High	Moderate	High	High	Low
How great are the ethical problems?	Low	Low	High	Low	Low	Moderate	Moderate

58

their use of contemporary, rather than historical, data. In addition, with the exception of nonconcealed participant observation, the observational methods can be differentiated from the experimental methods by the fact that the subject is unaware of participating in research.

The degree of *control over the setting* possible in observational methods can range from zero (simple observation) to a high amount (a field experiment in a restricted setting). This increasing control carries with it two principal advantages, the first of which deals with the relative frequency of occurrence of behaviors of interest to observers. It has been suggested (Webb et al., 1966; Weick, 1968) that there may be an inverse relationship between the importance of a particular behavior and the natural frequency of its occurrence: socially significant events happen only occasionally. By increasing the control over the setting, a researcher can devise situations that will produce the behavior of interest more frequently and at a predictable time. No doubt a frequent traveler on the New York subway system would be exposed to occasional fallen victims, but providing one's own victim greatly improves the efficiency of the research.

The second advantage to be gained from increased control over the setting is an increase in the internal validity of the research (as Table 2-4 indicates). An immense number of factors other than the variable of interest can influence behavior in a natural setting, so if the researcher can alter the setting to eliminate some alternative explanations for the actions observed, while maintaining the natural character of the situation, the gain can be substantial. A restricted setting like the subway is ideal for this purpose, but other settings can be altered as well. For example, if you were interested in people's reactions to a lost wallet, you would drop your experimental wallet on a narrow sidewalk that you had further narrowed by a small pile of sand and a barricade, rather than planting the wallet in the middle of a large plaza where most passersby would not even notice it. You would have maintained the natural quality of the setting but would have altered it enough to argue against "did not notice" as a reason for a failure to stop and examine the wallet. Of course, as Table 2-4 indicates, even a field experiment cannot match the degree of control (and, accordingly, the degree of internal validity) possible in a laboratory experiment.

Observational methods can also be compared to each other, and to the other research methods, in terms of the *degree of intrusiveness* of the measurement process. In the simple observational study when the observer is effectively concealed, there should be no contamination of natural behavior. As a result, the simple observational study is high in external validity. In natural experiments and field experiments the researcher may be "out in the open," but surreptitious recording of data can still minimize the reactive effects of being observed, especially if the experimental manipulation is powerful enough to capture

and hold the subject's attention. The presence of the researcher is a
more serious problem in participant observation, regardless of
whether the observation is covert or obvious. In concealed studies
the observer may, as noted before, contribute to the effect by the
actions he or she takes to establish and maintain a cover. In nonconcealed participant observation the observer's presence is likely
to distort the subject's natural reactions. Since there is some contamination in each case, you may wonder why we suggest (Table 2-4)
that the external validity of concealed participant observation is
higher. The reason is that the subjects' awareness that their behavior
is under scrutiny is presumed to be a more damaging sort of contamination. Real people in natural settings may normally have their
behavior affected by others in the group who have different motives
for being there, but they do not usually consider themselves engaged
in the act of "being a subject."

Because of the large variations possible in the researcher's amount
of control over the setting and possible intrusion into the measurement
process, the observational methods range from being as unobtrusive
as archival research to being nearly as contrived and potentially reactive as laboratory experiments. In addition, they present all possible
levels of ethical difficulty, from the low level found in most methods,
to the moderate level found in field experiments (subjects cannot
always be contacted to be told they have been subjects), to the serious
problems associated with concealed participant observation. In choosing an observational method, one must balance the need to be certain
that the differences obtained reflect the psychological processes of
interest (internal validity) against the need to ensure that these differences will generalize beyond the particular setting and subjects
involved (external validity). As control over the setting and precision
of measurement increase the internal validity will increase, but the
external validity may well decrease. Finally, both the need for precision and the need for generalizability must be balanced against the
possibility that the methods used might raise ethical difficulties. For
all these reasons, confidence in a particular result will be enhanced
through conceptual replication in a variety of settings.

EXPERIMENTAL METHODS: THEORY TESTING
IN THE LABORATORY

If the archival methods tell us how things were, and the observational
methods tell us how things are, the experimental methods attempt to
tell us *why* things are the way they appear to be. Let us return to our

cheating example to look more closely at the sort of information provided by each of the methods. Through careful analysis of the academic records of a selected sample of universities, we may have found some interesting regularities in the rates of expulsion for cheating. For example, we may have learned that the rates of expulsion fluctuate over the years, increasing during wartime or economic crisis, but decreasing at other times. More importantly, we may have discovered that the increases during wartime contain an extremely high proportion of male students, while the increases during recession contain about equal proportions of males and females. We have identified a *correlation* between expulsions and social conditions: more expulsions are found in the presence of war and recession than in their absence. It is important to emphasize that a correlation between two variables does *not* necessarily imply that the two are *causally* related. Certainly we would not argue that expulsions cause wars and recession, and the data we have available give us no more confidence in concluding the reverse.

What the data do permit is a speculation about the relationship between social conditions and cheating that can be tested in later research. Since wars and recessions apparently do not produce equal amounts of cheating by males and females, we know that something else must intervene between the social conditions and the cheating, and we might guess that this *intervening variable* is pressure to succeed. In wartime a male student who flunks out of school will almost certainly end up in the armed forces, but a female student would not have been expected to do so. In contrast, during a recession, both males and females need all the education they can obtain to make themselves employable. So pressure to succeed in school could be equal for male and female students during recession, but higher for males during wartime.

Selecting a Hypothesis

We have examined the correlation between social conditions and level of cheating, and have offered a post hoc speculation that this correlation might be accounted for in terms of a conceptual variable called pressure to succeed. But because we recognize the danger of selective deposit and survival, and because we know that post hoc reasoning is not a sufficient explanation, we decide to see whether the correlation between pressure and level of cheating will also be found in data that we collect ourselves. Not wanting to cause a war or a recession simply for the purpose of doing research, we choose a conceptual replication such as the natural experiment offered in various testing procedures. The concept of pressure to succeed is retained, but now that pressure is introduced by a factor like the importance of an examination: students taking a final examination which accounts for 80 percent of their grade should be under more pressure on that exam than would be students taking an exam that accounted for only 40 percent of their grade. Suppose that we selected two such classes at our university and found (through some form of concealed observation) that, as expected, there was a higher level of cheating in the 80 percent class than in the 40 percent class. Have we isolated pressure to succeed as the cause of cheating? No. We have only uncovered another sort of correlation between our dependent variable (the behavior of interest to the researcher—in this case the level of cheating) and the circumstances that might lead to pressure to succeed. We cannot be certain, because the circumstances might well lead to other intervening variables, such as dislike for the class, that could produce the same results without any pressure at all. This is a less parsimonious explanation, because it cannot account for the previously obtained correlation between social conditions and level of cheating, but it cannot be ruled out completely. The classes were different in content and instructor, the teaching styles were different (indicated by the choice of weight for the final examination), and the students who selected those courses presumably did so on the basis of some information about these differences.

Can we find more conclusive evidence if we intervene in the situation and conduct a field experiment? Probably so. We could rule out differences in instructor's reputation and course content by using two sections of our own course in social psychology. We would simply flip a coin at the beginning of the term to decide which class would get a final examination worth 40 percent, and which would have a final worth 80 percent. Although this manipulation of the exam is more satisfactory than our earlier methods, it still leaves something to be desired, this time because of our own multiple motives in the situation. We are not merely conducting research, we are also trying to do an effective job of teaching, and we are concerned about avoiding disastrous student evaluations of our courses. As a result, we are likely to find that the final examination is not the only thing that differs between the two classes. At best, we could successfully rule out only the content and instructor variables, still having to base our belief that the results were due to pressure on the *inference* that the different exams produce different levels of pressure to succeed (and little else). At worst, our behavior might interact with the exam weight (feeling sorry for the 80 percent group, we would do all we could to relieve their anxiety) so that the results would be hopelessly confounded. Even in the field experiment there are too many other variables unrelated to the conceptual variable of interest. Certainly our manipulation caused a number of intervening events, one or more of which led to differential levels of cheating. But our conclusions must be guarded in direct proportion to the *number* of such events that our manipulation might have produced. Not surprisingly, the procedures of the laboratory experiment permit us to keep the number of these other possibilities to an absolute minimum.

A clear test of a hypothesis requires conditions that will not only lead to confirmation of the hypothesis if it is "true," but will also lead to disconfirmation if the hypothesis is false. Consider the hypothesis "Increasing the pressure to succeed will increase the likelihood of cheating." Suppose that after we have conducted our field experiment we discover no difference between the 80 percent final examination group and the 40 percent final examination group. Is that because the hypothesis is wrong? Or is it because some flaw in our design obscured the truth? If our predictions are not confirmed, do we discard the theories that gave rise to them, or do we wonder about confounding in our methods? Philosophers of science (notably Popper, 1959) argue that theories should be stated in terms that will give them falsifiability: in principle at least, we should be able to find cases in which a theory *does not apply*. The same should be true of our research methods. When we claim to be testing theories, rather than simply gathering information, our methods must be so precise that negative results will reflect on the theory, rather than on the procedures. And this sort of control is extremely difficult to achieve outside the experimental laboratory. Both because of its limitation of alternative explanations of positive results, and because of its power in the interpretation of negative results, the laboratory experiment has become the method of choice for theory testing. We now look more carefully at the elements of a laboratory experiment in social psychology.

Experimental and Control Groups

One of the best ways to identify some of the unique features of laboratory experiments in social psychology is to compare their procedures with laboratory experiments in *other* areas of psychology. In its simplest form, the psychological experiment consists of two conditions or treatment groups: an *experimental* group in which some variable of conceptual interest, called the independent variable, is manipulated, and a *control* group in which there is no experimental treatment.

As an example of this sort of design, suppose that you were interested in the effects of reward on learning. To avoid differential experience among your subjects, you might choose to have them learn lists of nonsense syllables, and you might manipulate the reward (the independent variable) by offering to pay subjects in the experimental group if they correctly learn several of the lists. You would construct the lists, probably of consonant-vowel-consonant (CVC) trigrams such as CAX, JIK, or TUD, and you would place each list on a memory drum (a piece of apparatus that displays each word individually at a standard rate of exposure). A subject arriving at your laboratory would be assigned at random to either the experimental (reward) or control (no reward) condition, perhaps by flipping a coin. Any subject in the control condition would simply be told that the task was to learn as many of the lists as possible, and then he or she would be given a standard number of trials on each list. Any subject who was assigned to the experimental condition would be told everything that control subjects were told, and *in addition* would be informed that he or she would be paid a dollar for every list correctly learned. The subjects, both control and experimental, would then be given the lists to learn, and the dependent variable would be the average number, or proportion, of lists correctly learned by the subjects in each of the two groups.

Suppose that the experimental group learned an average of eight out of ten lists (or to put it in statistical terms, the experimental group's mean score was 8.00). Now suppose that the control group's mean score was only 5.00, or a *mean difference* of 3.00. You would then perform an appropriate statistical test on the group scores to determine whether this mean difference of 3.00 was the result of chance factors, or whether it was due to your experimental manipulation. Psychologists usually consider an experimental outcome to be the product of a manipulation if the odds are less than one in twenty that the outcome could have occurred by chance. In other words, if you were to repeat the experiment twenty times, and if a mean difference between the two groups of 3.00 or more would occur on only one of these twenty times by chance, then we would say that your manipulation produced a statistically significant difference between the two groups. As a result, you could conclude that reward does increase performance on a learning task.

The Factorial Design

The laboratory experiment in social psychology also involves experimental manipulations, and its results are also evaluated by statistical tests, but it often differs from the simple two-group model in several ways. The typical differences are (a) the inclusion of more than one conceptual variable, (b) the absence of a traditional control group, and (c) the consequent necessity for extra precautions against experimenter effects. Let us consider the first two of these issues in the context of a hypothetical experiment on cheating (experimenter effects will be discussed in a later section). Recall that our archival research uncovered differences between the levels of cheating by males and females, and suggested that these differences might be attributable to differential social pressure to succeed. Our observational research further confirmed the importance of pressure to succeed as a contributor to cheating, but it failed to rule out completely some other potential contributors, such as dislike for the task. The principal advantage of the laboratory experiment is that it permits us to examine the *causal* influence of more than one variable at a time. Social situations are so complex that a conceptual variable may operate in one way under one set of circumstances (one time, place, subject population, or situation) but in an entirely different way in other circumstances. To try to do justice to this complexity, it is important to include more than a single dimension in a social psychological experiment.

An Illustration: Two × Two = Four

For example, is it always true that increases in the pressure to succeed will lead to increased cheating, or is it possible that there are other circumstances, such as strong liking for the task, that will prevent almost all cheating? These questions can best be answered in what is known as a **factorial experiment**: an experiment in which there are systematic variations in more than one conceptual variable or *factor* (such as pressure to succeed or liking for the task) at a time. The design of such a factorial experiment is presented in Table 2-5, with Factor A (Pressure to Succeed) having two *levels* or variations (high and low), and with Factor B (Liking for the Task) also having two levels (high and low). In conducting such an experiment you might select a task for the subjects to perform that would permit them to cheat if they wanted to (such as having them score their own papers). You might also vary the nature of that task so that for some of the subjects it would be dull and boring, but for others it would be exciting and attractive, in order to manipulate liking for the task. In addition, to manipulate pressure to succeed, you might tell some of the subjects that they would be paid for their participation in the experiment no matter how well they did on the task, but would tell others that they would be paid only if they performed to some high level of competence. As a result, any individual subject would receive one of the four possible treatment combinations (two levels of pressure crossed with two levels of liking): Unconditional Pay for a Dull Task, Un-

TABLE 2-5

Factorial design of a hypothetical experiment to determine the effects of pressure to succeed and liking for the task on level of cheating

FACTOR A: PRESSURE TO SUCCEED	FACTOR B: LIKING FOR THE TASK	
	Level 1: Low Liking	*Level 2: High Liking*
Level 1: Low Pressure	Dull Task Unconditional Pay	Attractive Task Unconditional Pay
Level 2: High Pressure	Dull Task Conditional Pay	Attractive Task Conditional Pay

conditional Pay for an Attractive Task, Conditional Pay for a Dull Task, or Conditional Pay for an Attractive Task.

What Happened to the Control Group?

One of the first things you notice about an experiment of this sort is that there is no control group, at least in the traditional sense of a group in which there is no experimental treatment whatsoever. Why not? One reason of major importance is that when the variables of experimental interest are social variables, it is very difficult to argue that a "no treatment" situation is possible. High pressure to succeed cannot be contrasted with a total absence of pressure, because at the very least subjects will bring a certain amount of desire to succeed with them into laboratory. In a similar way, high liking for the task cannot be contrasted with a total absence of emotional reactions to the task, because in the absence of any direction from the experimenter, the subjects will simply form their own emotional impressions of the task. Consequently, high liking for the task must be contrasted not with "neutral," but rather with a manipulated dislike for the task. This illustrates that in most cases of research in social psychology a true control (no manipulation whatsoever) group would in reality become an "individual differences" group. Each subject's performance in that group would be determined by whatever unique personal dispositions the subject brought into the experimental laboratory.

Analysis of Variance Describes the Results

If there is no control group, how are we to determine the effects of the manipulations we performed? As it happens, there is a statistical procedure called *analysis of variance* that is appropriate for factorial designs. This technique can be used to identify the effects of each factor acting alone, as well as the effects of the two factors acting in combination. For example, suppose that we had run ten subjects in each of the four treatment combinations of our experimental design. Each subject had been given the opportunity to score his or her answers on twenty-five problems, and we can simply count the number of times that each subject altered an answer in order to get the problem correct. Then we obtain the mean score for instances of cheating by averaging across the subjects in each treatment combination.

MAIN EFFECTS. Now suppose we had believed that pressure to succeed would lead to cheating regardless of whether the task was attractive or dull. In the language of analysis of variance, we would have predicted a main effect for pressure to succeed, and the mean scores shown in Table 2-6 would represent such a main effect. Notice that the mean scores in both Low Pressure (Unconditional Payment) conditions are low—leading to a low total in the margin—while the mean scores in both High Pressure (Conditional Payment) conditions are high, leading to a high marginal total. The main effect for pressure to succeed is derived from a comparison of these *marginal totals*, summing over the two levels of Liking for the Task.

As a second possibility, suppose that we had believed that liking for the task was the major influence on cheating, and that pressure to succeed really had nothing to do with the level of cheating. Then we would have predicted a main effect for Liking for the Task, and mean scores representing this main effect are shown in Table 2-7. Within the two Low Liking (Dull Task) conditions there is a high degree of cheating regardless of the level of pressure to succeed, but within the two High Liking (Attractive Task) conditions there is a low level of cheating, and again this does not vary with the level of pressure to succeed. As a result, the marginal total for the Dull Task (summing

TABLE 2-6

Main effect for pressure to succeed (fictitious experiment on the effects of pressure and liking for task on level of cheating)

	LIKING FOR TASK		Marginal Total
PRESSURE	Low (Dull Task)	High (Attractive Task)	
Low (Unconditional Payment)	5	5	10⎤ Main
High (Conditional Payment)	15	15	30⎦ effect
Marginal Total	20	20	

TABLE 2-7

Main effect for liking for task (fictitious experiment on the effects of
pressure and liking for task on level of cheating)

| | LIKING FOR TASK | | Marginal Total |
PRESSURE	Low (Dull Task)	High (Attractive Task)	
Low (Unconditional Payment)	15	5	20
High (Conditional Payment)	15	5	20
Marginal Total	30	10	
	Main effect		

across both levels of pressure) is much higher than the marginal total
for the Attractive Task. There is no difference between the marginal
totals for the two Pressure to Succeed rows. These results would indicate that only Liking for the Task affects the level of cheating,
with pressure to succeed contributing virtually nothing to the outcome
of the experiment.

In a factorial design when the results show only a main effect for
one of the factors, we conclude that the other factor made no difference in the findings and might have been omitted entirely from the
experiment. This does *not* mean that we have wasted our time by including the second factor. Indeed, we have learned that it made no
difference precisely by including it! If we had simply conducted one
two-group design, varying only the two levels of one factor (either
Pressure to Succeed or Liking for the Task), we would not have had
the opportunity to learn that the other factor would not affect the outcome. If we had varied only Pressure to Succeed, we would then have
had to conduct a second two-group experiment, varying Liking for the
Task. But the various main effects are not the only possible outcomes.

THE INTERACTION. The final possible outcome of a factorial experiment is an interaction between the two conceptual variables. One
such interaction is shown in Table 2-8, and it indicates that the level
of cheating is *jointly determined by both conceptual variables*. First
you will notice that the marginal totals for Unconditional Payment are
identical to the marginal totals for Conditional Payment, indicating
that no overall differences are produced by Pressure to Succeed. In
addition, the marginal totals for Dull Task are identical to the marginal
totals for Attractive Task, indicating that Liking for the Task produced
no overall differences either. But the mean scores for the four cells
(treatment combinations) *do* differ, with the level of cheating being
high in the Unconditional-Dull and the Conditional-Attractive conditions, but low in the Unconditional-Attractive and Conditional-Dull
conditions. Not surprisingly, these results are much more difficult to

TABLE 2-8

Interaction between pressure and liking (fictitious experiment on the effects of pressure and liking for task on level of cheating)

	LIKING FOR TASK		Marginal Total
PRESSURE	*Low (Dull Task)*	*High (Attractive Task)*	
Low (Unconditional Payment)	20 ⎯⎯⎯⎯ *Interaction* ⎯ ⎯ ⎯ 10		30
High (Conditional Payment)	10 ⎯ ⎯ ⎯ 20		30
Marginal Total	30	30	

interpret than are the main effect findings we discussed earlier. When the pressure on the subject is low, there is more cheating on a dull task than on an attractive one, suggesting that perhaps the subjects cheat to relieve the boredom inherent in the dull task. In contrast, when the motivation to succeed is high (the Conditional Payment conditions), there is enough interest in the task to prevent cheating from boredom (the low level of cheating in the Conditional-Dull condition). However, when the additional incentive of an attractive task is added to the incentive provided by conditional payment (the Conditional-Attractive condition), the level of cheating increases. These findings suggest that when the subject's motivation is very low there will be cheating (to relieve boredom), that when motivation is increased to some intermediate level cheating will decrease, but that when the motivation is very high cheating will once again increase (but now because of an intense desire to succeed). If the results had turned out this way we most probably would have concluded that there are at least two different reasons for the level of cheating observed—taking chances to make life more interesting, and taking chances to ensure success. Which one of these possibilities actually occurs will be jointly determined by the attractiveness of the task and the person's motivation to perform well on that task.

This contribution of both conceptual variables to the outcome illustrates the unique value of the factorial design: *only if two (or more) conceptual variables are manipulated within the context of the same experiment can possible interactions between variables be observed.* Separate manipulations in different experiments can produce results that are mathematically equivalent to the main effects of a factorial design, but separate experiments cannot permit us to discover the interactions between variables that more closely approximate the conditions in the world outside the laboratory. Precisely because the experimental procedures and setting are so unrepresentative of the complexity of everyday life, the social psychologist should make sure that some of the conceptual complexity of that world is preserved by the use of factorial experiments.

Operationalization

Once the investigator has decided upon an experimental design—the number of conceptual variables to be included, and the levels of each variable—those variables must be turned into operations that can be replicated by other researchers. For example, let us consider the conceptual variable of pressure to succeed, employed in our cheating experiment. Although we used conditional versus unconditional payment as the manipulation of pressure to succeed, that is not the only operation which could have been employed. As a second possibility, we might have created differences in pressure to succeed by making the task relevant to the subjects' self-esteem. In the low pressure condition we could describe the task as an indirect and unreliable measure of intelligence, and we could have pointed out that the reason for its unreliability is that so many other factors are involved in the performance of such a task. In contrast, in the high pressure condition we could have asserted that the task is a very direct and reliable, though nonverbal, test of intelligence and we could have enhanced this pressure by telling the subject that although there are some individual differences, nearly 90 percent of his or her peers have successfully completed the task.

In most cases there will be several possible operationalizations of a conceptual variable, and which one will actually be employed in the experiment depends on a number of considerations. First, a manipulation is chosen that will be appropriate with the *other* conceptual variables included in the research. In our cheating experiment we hope to manipulate both the pressure to succeed and the attractiveness of the task, so we must choose a manipulation of pressure that is *independent* of the manipulation of attractiveness. This requirement rules out a manipulation of pressure in terms of intelligence testing, because to say that the task is either unreliable or accurate is also to affect the attractiveness manipulation. An otherwise dull task that serves as an accurate measure of intelligence has some redeeming value, but an otherwise dull task which doesn't measure anything of importance will be perceived as even more worthless. In short, our manipulation of pressure to succeed must not contain any explicit or implicit statements about the intrinsic value of the task itself, and both payment and timing satisfy this criterion.

After the inappropriate operations have been ruled out, the researcher may evaluate the remaining ones to determine which of them offers the greatest potential difference between conditions while at the same time permitting the subjects to be treated in as similar a manner as possible. If we were to use timing as the manipulation of pressure to succeed, we might not mention time to the low pressure group but might emphasize its importance to the high pressure group. This would probably produce a large difference in pressure, but it has the disadvantage of having one group (the low pressure group) totally ignorant of timing. In contrast, if we use payment as the manipulation of pressure, we can inform both groups of subjects that they will be paid, we can pay them the same amount of money, and the entire manipulation can be contained in a simple phrase: "whether or not" as opposed to "only if" you complete the task. This operationalization of pressure to succeed will, we hope, lead to large differences in perceived pressure, even though the instructions given to the subjects are almost identical.

The Pretest

But how can we be sure that the instructions actually create the differences we intend them to produce? We can guess, based on our experience as people and as experimenters, but a better way is to *pretest* the manipulations on a sample of subjects who are similar to the subjects who will be used in the actual experiment. For example, if your experiment will be conducted with juvenile delinquents, pretesting of the manipulations should also be conducted with a sample of delinquents. In order to determine how much pressure to succeed is actually generated by our payment manipulation, we might deliver the instructions to a pretest sample and then simply ask them to describe their feelings toward the task, including how much pressure they feel to complete the task successfully. We would do this both for the high pressure groups (Conditional Payment) and for the low pressure groups (Unconditional Payment) and would then perform an appropriate statistical test to determine whether there is a significant difference in the perceived pressure to succeed.

To assess the liking for the task, we would use a different sample of subjects, split that sample into two groups, and have one group perform the task we have designed to be dull and boring, while the other group performs the task we have designed to be interesting and attractive. Then we would have the two groups evaluate their experience with the tasks, including a measure of the subjects' liking for the two tasks. An appropriate statistical test would then tell us whether there was a significant difference in liking for the task. It is important to emphasize that *in neither one of these pretests have we collected information on the dependent variable*—level of cheating—to be used in the final experiment. We must make whatever corrections are necessary to produce the conceptual variations we seek without knowing what changes those corrections in manipulation are likely to make in the level of the final dependent variable. Otherwise we would simply be doing the experiment twice—once to see that it will work, and once to collect the data.

If the opportunities for pretesting are limited, or if the manipulations are quite familiar ones, an alternative procedure is to measure the perceptions of the operations that are held by the subjects run in the final experiment. We might have sufficient reason to believe that a conditional payment of five dollars will create pressure to succeed so that we believe pretesting on that question is unnecessary. Similarly, we might believe that the difference in attractiveness between an intricate Chinese block puzzle and an insultingly simple jigsaw puzzle is obvious enough without pretesting. Under these circumstances we could just conduct the experiment, collect the data on the dependent variable (observe or record the level of cheating), and then assess the subjects' opinions of the task and the instructions. The same scales that would have been used in pretesting to establish the level of perceived pressure to succeed and to measure liking for the task can be used in the context of the experimental sessions as *checks on the manipulations*.

The differences between pretesting and obtaining checks on the manipulations are the time of administration (before the experiment as opposed to during the experiment) and the subjects involved (similar subjects or the "real" experimental subjects). Obtaining checks on the manipulations during or immediately after the experiment has the advantage of saving time and subjects used, but it also has a disadvantage. The subjects' judgments about the strength of the independent variables may be colored by their performances in terms of the dependent variable. For example, in the High Pressure conditions, a person who actually did cheat may assert that he or she felt an irresistible pressure to do so. This may be more of a rationalization for his or her actions than a statement of the actual force of the manipulation. Given the complexity of most social psychological variables, either pretesting or other verification of the manipulations is usually necessary, and which method is chosen will depend on the balance between these advantages and disadvantages.

Selection of Subjects

After the investigator has operationalized and pretested the conceptual variables of interest, he or she is prepared to proceed with the job of conducting the experiment or, as it is often called, "running the subjects." But who are the subjects to be, and how will they be induced to take part in the research? These questions are very important to the external validity of the research, but unfortunately the answers are often unsatisfactory.

We have noted earlier that the laboratory experiment, by virtue of its degree of abstraction and the experimenter's control over the situation, typically produces results with high internal validity but low external validity. As a consequence, the laboratory experiment is an excellent vehicle for conducting tests of theoretical propositions, but is a poor choice for determining whether the results of those tests will apply to the complex situations found in everyday life. This is not meant to suggest that nothing the experimenter does will increase the external validity of the research. On the contrary, use of a factorial design, rather than a design in which only a single isolated variable is tested, is a first step in this direction. A second step could be the inclusion of a broad and representative sample of subjects, but this step is too seldom taken.

In the early days of social psychology and other behavioral sciences, McNemar (1946) observed that "the existing science of human behavior is largely the science of the behavior of [college] sophomores" (p. 333). Since then, the picture has deteriorated. As Rosenthal and Rosnow (1969) point out, the *presently* existing science of human behavior "may be largely the science of those sophomores who both (a) enroll in psychology courses and (b) volunteer to participate in behavioral research" (pp. 59–60). If the college sophomore is an unrepresentative subject, the *volunteer* from an introductory psychology course is even more unrepresentative. An interest in psychology and behavioral science leads to an increased willingness to volunteer for psychological research (Ora, 1966), and the volunteer tends to be more likely to confirm the experimenter's hypothesis than the nonvolunteer (Rosenthal and Rosnow, 1969). In their review of the research on volunteering, Rosenthal and Rosnow (1969) identify other characteristics of volunteers that have direct implications for research in social psychology. Compared to nonvolunteers, volunteers tend to be better educated, more intelligent, higher in need for approval, less authoritarian; and somewhat more sociable, unconventional, and arousal-seeking. In addition, when the task is a standard one, females tend to be more likely to volunteer than are males, with the reverse being true for unusual tasks (sex interview, sensory deprivation, electric shock).

Reliance on college subjects or, more particularly, students in introductory psychology classes becomes even more detrimental to the external validity of research if subjects participate in more than a single experiment. During the course of a semester, such a student becomes more sophisticated about the subject matter and about the nature of experimental design and control. (Virtually anyone who attempts to perform a replication of the Milgram [1963] destructive obedience research will find that the subjects know exactly what is happening.) A subject who has been deceived in an earlier experience with research may alter his or her behavior in subsequent studies (Silverman, Schulman, and Wiesenthal, 1970), and rumor mills being what they are, subjects typically overestimate the occurrence of deception in research (Oksner and Shaver, 1973).

Why then do experimenters rely so heavily upon students enrolled in introductory psychology classes? The two principal reasons are cost (usually none, or a very small amount) and convenience. Introductory psychology students can be required to take part in a certain number of experiments as part of the course, creating a ready pool for the research to be done. Usually in such cases the students are given their choice among several different research projects, but anyone who has run subjects who show up at the laboratory with rampant indifference—"All right, to fulfill my contract I will give you my head for an hour, just don't bother me"—has to wonder about the quality of the data obtained. Consider the alternatives. An investigator conscientiously attempting to obtain a widely representative group of subjects would have to place advertisements in the local papers, or call people randomly selected from the telephone directory, or send recruiters out house-to-house. As it is, all that is necessary is to post a sign-up sheet. Moreover, "real-world people" would have to be paid to donate their time (as would students who were not pressured by course requirements), and they would have to be scheduled by a secretary and reminded of their time to come. The costs of research in social psychology (both those of paying subjects and those of paying for administrative support) would increase dramatically. Despite these problems, social psychologists will almost certainly be forced to move in the direction of more representative subject populations, perhaps through increased use of observation and field experiments, if they are to continue asserting that their research findings have validity outside the laboratory.

Running the Experiment

Regardless of the identity of the subjects, certain features of the experimental procedure should be relatively constant, and these relate to both the internal and the external validity of the research. First, the subjects must be *randomly assigned* to the experimental conditions— by flipping coins, writing the treatments on index cards and shuffling the cards together, or (most frequently) by using a table of random numbers. Why is true random assignment (as opposed to some systematic or haphazard assignment determined by the experimenter) so important? Look closely at the sequence of events in a social psychology experiment. With the exception of a small number of studies in attitude change, there is never any measurement of the dependent variable *before* the experimental treatments are administered: the subjects are recruited, arrive at the laboratory, are assigned to experimental conditions, are given the instructions or manipulations, and only then are data on the dependent variable (e.g., level of cheating on a task) collected. To be certain that the differences obtained between experimental conditions are due entirely to those conditions, the very first thing that we must be sure of is that the subject groups *began* the experiment with no differences on the dependent variable. In the cheating example an alternative explanation for our findings might have been that more innate cheaters were somehow placed in the Unconditional-Dull and Conditional-Attractive conditions. The only way to argue against this interpretation (since we did not even attempt to measure level of cheating before the experiment) is to assign subjects randomly to treatment conditions and presume that this random assignment will cancel out any relevant individual differences between the subjects. This presumption will occasionally be in error, but without random assignment it cannot even be made.

A second feature common to all laboratory experiments in social psychology is the delivery of the experimental manipulations, and Crano and Brewer (1973) have identified three major ways in which this can be accomplished: *social, environmental,* and *instructional* manipulations. In most cases the experimental procedure will include elements of all three methods, but meaningful distinctions can be drawn among them. Social manipulations require the actual behavior of a person other than the subject (usually an experimental accomplice, or confederate). An excellent example of *social* manipulation is contained in an experiment by Schachter and Singer (1962) which was designed to determine whether different emotional labels could be placed on the same underlying physiological arousal. This experiment will be discussed in more detail in Chapter Eight, but for now it is sufficient to say that some of the subjects in the study were given injections of epinephrine (adrenalin) which they thought were simply an experimental vitamin supplement. Then they were asked to sit in a room with another participant (an experimental confederate) and complete a series of questionnaires. After a few minutes (long enough for the onset of the effects of the injection—increase in heart rate, sensation of warmth and flushing—to be felt), the confederate began to be-

have either in an angry fashion, pounding his fist on the table and
making negative comments about the research, or in an euphoric
manner. The dependent variable was the subject's self-assessment of
his emotional state, and Schachter and Singer found that subjects who
had no appropriate label for their physiological arousal simply described themselves in terms of the behavior of the confederate. Thus
the manipulation, provision of a label for emotional arousal, was accomplished through the social behavior of the confederate.

An example of *environmental* manipulation of the independent
variable is the so-called Prisoner's Dilemma game (Luce and Raiffa,
1957) used in research on cooperation and competition. This research
will be discussed more thoroughly in Chapter Eleven; here it is
enough to say that the subject is led to believe that he or she is playing a game with a real opponent. There are repeated trials of the game,
and on each trial the subject and the "opponent" can make either of
two choices, a "cooperative" one or a "competitive" one. If both participants make a cooperative choice, then each will receive a certain
number of points; if both make a competitive choice, both lose a prescribed number of points; and if one makes a cooperative choice while
the other makes the competitive choice, the one who cooperated
loses, while the one who competed *wins*. Some of the interesting
questions that can be asked deal with the relationship between the
strategy of the subject and the apparent strategy of the opponent. For
example, will subjects take advantage of unconditionally cooperative
opponents, or will they cooperate? Will a subject try to retaliate against
an unconditionally uncooperative opponent? These questions can be
answered clearly only if the experimenter has control over the apparent behavior of the opponent, so the subject's choices are made using
an electric apparatus that records those choices and indicates to the
subject the choice of the opponent (who is ostensibly located in a
different experimental room). In fact, there is no real opponent. The
experimenter simply conveys a programmed series of choices to the
subject and observes the subject's responses to those choices. Thus
the subject's behavior is affected by the opponent's presumed choices,
and whether these choices appear cooperative or competitive is conveyed to the subject through the environment rather than through the
actual behavior of a live person.

The third method involves an *instructional* manipulation given by
the experimenter to the subject. Not only is this the most common of
the three methods, it is difficult to imagine a laboratory experiment in
social psychology without any setting instructions whatsoever. Verbal
instructions may be used in conjunction with other types, or they may
stand alone. Why did the behavioral manipulation of emotional state
"take" on Schachter and Singer's subjects? Because they had been led

to believe, through prior verbal instructions, that the purported vitamin injection would not have physiological effects anything like the ones experienced. In the absence of an appropriate verbal label, the subjects took their cues from the behavior of the confederate. Why does the environmental manipulation in the Prisoner's Dilemma game affect the subject's strategy? Because previous verbal instructions have led the subject to believe that he or she is playing against a *real* opponent. In our cheating experiment, the manipulation of Pressure to Succeed was accomplished entirely with verbal instructions—subjects were told either that they would be paid for participation regardless of their success with the puzzle, or they were told that payment would be contingent upon their success. In contrast, the manipulation of Liking for the Task was a wholly environmental one—based on the intrinsic attractiveness of the task.

Problems in Experimentation

Maintaining Experimental Realism

Whatever sort of manipulations are used, the experimenter must construct a situation that will permit the highest possible internal and external validity. How can this be done in an admittedly artificial setting in which subjects know that their behavior is under both control and observation? Aronson and Carlsmith (1968) suggest that the internal validity of the laboratory experiment can be enhanced if the research can be made high in **experimental realism**—psychological impact on the subject. A subject thrust into a powerful and dramatic situation is likely to become so involved in it that he or she forgets to "behave like a subject." Of the research that we have mentioned so far, Milgram's (1963) obedience research is certainly the highest in experimental realism. There is little doubt that the subjects found this an extremely involving, if frightening, experience. Both the subjects who refused to go to the end of the scale and those who continued to obey showed a great deal of conflict over their decisions. The distinct absence of an "as if" quality to the research enhanced its internal validity.

But the gain in internal validity arising from experimental realism is achieved at some real cost to the subject, and this, too, is illustrated by Milgram's work. Who can say for certain that a manipulation with a high degree of experimental realism will not leave long-lasting psychological damage? When does a manipulation change from being involving to being traumatic? If you can truly succeed in making the subject forget that "this is only an experiment," have you removed one of the defenses against the realization that he or she is the sort of person who will cause harm to others? Milgram did conduct follow-up interviews with his subjects in an attempt to determine whether there were any residual negative effects of having participated in the experiment, and he found that 84 percent of the subjects thought the research worthwhile and stated that they would be willing to take part in similar research in the future. But what really does this tell us? It is not likely that a subject who felt severely upset by the experiment would tell that to the person responsible for conducting it. And even if the subjects were expressing what they believed to be their true feelings, those feelings are exactly what cognitive dissonance theory (Chapter Six) would predict. Just as Mrs. Keech and the Seekers had to justify their beliefs by recruiting new members to the group after doomsday failed to come, so Milgram's subjects may have been justifying their participation (and their actions) by inflating the scientific value of the research.

A second issue related to the impact of the study is the use of *deception* to construct a situation that will not only have impact, but will also permit measurement of the desired dependent variables. What is the best way to make the experimental setting real to the subject? And how can the researcher prevent the subject from behaving according to what he or she thinks the experimenter expects? Many social psychologists would suggest deception as the best answer to both questions. It is understandably difficult to obtain aggressive responses from subjects by greeting them with, "Hello. This is an experiment to determine what conditions will lead you to administer painful electric shock to a fellow human being." The same is true for other antisocial responses or, for that matter, for positive social actions as well. If I told subjects that I was investigating the relationship between dependency and helping, and then presented them with a small child who had apparently become separated from its parents, do you think any subjects would fail to help? In the case of any dependent variable with social desirability overtones (of either a positive or negative sort), deception by the experimenter may be required to elicit truth from the subject. Whenever deception is employed, it is the experimenter's responsibility to reveal that deception at the conclusion of the experiment. If the behavior elicited by experimental deception is positive, it is easy to send the subject away from the research feeling good. When deception is employed to elicit a negative behavior, the experimenter is confronted not only with the necessity to explain the use of deception, but also with the problem of dealing with the disagreeable self-knowledge that the subject has acquired through participation in the research.

Maintaining Mundane Realism

The external validity of the research can be enhanced and some problems arising from deception can be mitigated if the experiment possesses a second sort of realism, what Aronson and Carlsmith (1968) call mundane realism. In contrast to experimental realism (impact), mundane realism refers to the correspondence between the experimental task and the actions a subject might perform in everyday life outside the laboratory. Milgram's research, for example, is extremely *low* in mundane realism (at least for anyone outside of combat units of the armed forces). Very few of us are ever asked, outside a laboratory, to administer what may best be described as torture to other people. As a consequence, we can remain satisfied with ourselves, and never be confronted with the possibility of having to learn just how far we will go in following orders. In contrast to Milgram's research, our cheating experiment is lower in experimental realism, but higher in mundane realism. Its dependent variable—level of cheating—is also socially undesirable, but that is the sort of behavior we might perform in the real world of our everyday lives. Because our experiment is lower in experimental realism, not every subject who participates will cheat; because of its high mundane realism, our experiment may not reveal anything new to those who do cheat. Certainly we should not estimate the proportion of dishonest people from the level of cheating in our experimental situation, but people who have been caught cheating on our task are not going to be as devastated as they would be to learn the degree to which they might follow destructive orders. There is virtually no chance that a subject would make the latter discovery in the course of life outside the laboratory. And consequently, when the negative information comes as a result of a task with low mundane realism, the experimenter has a greater responsibility to protect the self-esteem of the subjects.

The Subject's Desire to Perform Well

Throughout this chapter we have noted the importance, and the difficulty, of ensuring that the subjects in social psychological research behave naturally rather than behaving "as subjects." Although this problem is found with some of the observational methods, it is particularly acute in laboratory experiments, so it is in this context that we will consider bias in more detail. Whether a volunteer or a nonvolunteer, the experimental subject probably approaches the task with mixed feelings. He or she may be taking part to earn money, to help advance psychological science, to obtain course credit, to kill time between classes, or to be amused by seeing what nonsense the psychologists are interested in now. In addition to these various motivations to participate, the subject may feel some reluctance. The psychologist's business is to learn about people, and the subject may wonder what his or her behavior in the experiment will reveal. The subject's concern over attaining a positive evaluation from the experimenter is known as **evaluation apprehension** (Rosenberg, 1965). Rosenberg has noted that if any cues to the behavior of "the average subject" are available in the experimental situation, the actual subject will try to respond in what he or she considers to be the "typical" manner. This response bias must certainly be corrected for the social desirability of the response—you may not cheat in our experiment even if I have informed you indirectly that most people do cheat— but precautions should be taken to avoid indicating to any one subject what "most subjects do" (unless such a comparison is an intentional part of a manipulation).

In addition to introducing a bias toward "typical" responding, the subject's apprehension about what the experimenter is learning contributes to his or her susceptibility to the *demand characteristics* of the research (Orne, 1962). As we noted earlier in this chapter, the demand characteristics of an experiment are the sum total of the cues that convey an experimental hypothesis to a subject. Perhaps because of concern about being evaluated, the subject approaches participating in an experiment in a problem-solving frame of mind. Just what is it that the experimenter is studying? The hypotheses that a subject develops to answer this question, if combined with a desire to be a "good subject," can produce dramatic differences in behavior.

If subjects look upon the experiment as a problem-solving situation, and if their behavior is dramatically affected by their perceptions of whether they have correctly solved the problem, how can the careful experimenter control or eliminate this source of confounding of results? Orne (1969) suggests several different methods. The first of these is a detailed postexperimental interview in which the experimenter makes it clear to the subject that he or she is sincerely interested in the subject's hypotheses about the "true purpose" of the research. All too often the subject and experimenter share what Orne (1959) called a "pact of ignorance": each knows that if the subject has correctly divined the hypotheses, the experimenter's data will be useless. In that case, both the subject's time and the experimenter's effort will have been wasted, so each tends not to probe or reveal to excess. From the standpoint of the discipline, of course, the occasional need to discard data is much less of a problem than is building theory on demand characteristics rather than social variables, so the postexperimental interview is an important component of any experiment. Other procedures are the "nonexperiment," in which subjects are asked to behave as if they were subjects and their responses are compared with those of real subjects; and the use of simulator-subjects, who take part in the actual experiment but have been preinstructed by a different experimenter to pretend the experimental treatment affected them (even though they have been warned about it in advance). These two last controls for demand characteristics are costly in terms of subjects and experimenter time, and so they tend to be used infrequently. A full postexperimental interview is thus the most practical method of determining the subject's stake in the research.

The Experimenter's Desire to Perform Well

If evaluation apprehension and demand characteristics are products of the subject's interest in the research, then the set of potential biases known as *experimenter effects* (Rosenthal, 1966) reflects the fact that the researcher also has a stake in the outcome of the experiment. The most obvious experimenter effects are the infrequent intentional distortions of research data that, when discovered, destroy the career of the researcher, arouse suspicion toward the discipline involved, and provide evidence that dishonesty can be found in any profession. More subtle are the interpreter effects that arise from an overreliance on a tenuous theory (the scientific version of "My mind is made up, don't confuse me with the facts"), the biosocial effects based on the race, sex, and appearance of the experimenter (the problem of using white experimenters to test the intelligence of children in an inner-city black neighborhood), and the effects of the experimenter's expectancy regarding just how the research is likely to (or should) turn out. This last potential source of bias is the least available to public scrutiny, and it is the experimenter effect that has received the most thorough study.

Experimenter expectancy is a problem in social psychological research, but it is not an unexpected problem. We noted earlier that an investigator's values will influence his or her choice of problems for study (e.g., will they be prosocial behaviors or antisocial ones, problems of one segment of society versus problems of another), the choice of methodology (observation or experimentation, deception or some alternative, college or noncollege subjects), and to some extent the particular hypotheses proposed. Research in social psychology is seldom conducted as a "fishing expedition" by people who have no interest in the outcome. Rather it is conducted on limited problems by interested experimenters who have theoretical or practical goals toward which the research is directed. Thus it is not surprising, nor even undesirable, that experimenters have definite ideas about what their research might show. Expectancy effects only become troublesome when the experimenter inadvertently communicates them to the subject. In this case, the experimenter's expectation becomes a *self-fulfilling prophecy* (Merton, 1957): it is communicated to the subject who (possibly because of a desire to be helpful, or a fear of being evaluated) behaves according to the expectancy even though he or she otherwise might not do so. Thus the problem for the researcher is not to deny having any notion of how the research will turn out, but rather to make certain that this expectancy is not communicated to the subject.

In his extensive work on experimenter expectancy, Rosenthal has employed variations upon a standard experimental procedure illustrated by an early study of Rosenthal and Fode (1963b). In this study ten experimenters were drawn from an advanced course in experimental social psychology. These experimenters were either graduate students or advanced undergraduate students, and all had previously been involved in conducting research in social psychology. The experimenters were told that their task was to replicate some "well-established" findings in person perception. Each experimenter was assigned a group of approximately twenty undergraduate students as subjects and was to show a series of ten photographs to each subject individually. The subjects were to rate the photographs on the degree of success or failure shown by the persons in the pictures. These photographs had been selected so that they would, on the average, show neither success nor failure, but half of the experimenters were led to expect ratings of success, and the other half to expect ratings of failure. The experimenters then ran their subjects, and the data showed that those who had expected ratings of success found ratings significantly more in that direction than did experimenters who had expected ratings of failure. In short, even these relatively sophisticated experimenters generated findings in accordance with their expectations.

Well over a hundred similar experiments have been conducted with human subjects, in topic areas as diverse as psychophysical judgments, laboratory interviews, person perception and impression formation, reaction time, and inkblot tests, although there has been some criticism of much of this work (Barber and Silver, 1968). In addition, experiments such as another by Rosenthal and Fode (1963a) have demonstrated expectancy effects with animal subjects. They found that student experimenters who expected their white rats to be "maze-bright" obtained better performance in maze learning than did experimenters who had been told that their animals were "maze-dull." If experimenter expectancy can play an important role in a highly controlled experimental setting, imagine its possible influence in a less structured situation. Consider, for example, the educational system. Have you ever had the experience of taking a course with several examinations and having your course grade turn out to be the same as the grade on your first exam, almost no matter how well or poorly you think you have done on the others? Have some of your friends become known as "A" students to such a degree that their subsequent grades seem as much determined by their previous reputation as by their present level of effort? To put it in more practical terms, should students insist on blind grading of examinations?

A number of studies by Rosenthal and his associates (Rosenthal and Jacobsen, 1968; Conn, Edwards, Rosenthal, and Crowne, 1968) suggest that the answer to this question should be yes. In the Rosenthal and Jacobsen (1968) experiment, children in an elementary school were given an intelligence test described to their teachers as a test of intellectual "blooming." Within each of eighteen classrooms, 20 percent of the students were chosen at random to constitute the experimental group. Their teachers were told that these children's scores on the intelligence blooming test indicated that they might show dramatic gains in intelligence during the remainder of the academic year. Eight months later the same intelligence test was administered again, and in both total IQ and reasoning IQ the experimental group children showed important gains over members of the control group. Keep in mind that these dramatic gains were achieved with standardized intelligence tests which were not even scored by the teachers!

Keeping The Experimenter Blind to the Conditions

Contamination of research data by experimenter expectancy effects could best be avoided by trying to keep the experimenters as *blind* as possible to the experimental hypotheses, or the experimental conditions. At first, this sounds like an impossible task. But it can be done more easily than it would first appear. For one thing, these experiments are often actually conducted by graduate or undergraduate students who may be kept at least somewhat in the dark about the specific predictions of the research. As a second general possibility, in a factorial experiment each set of conditions can be introduced by a different experimenter. Another possibility is to give general instructions to the subjects and let them choose slips of paper that accomplish the condition assignments. For example, in our laboratory study of cheating, the experimenter could describe *both* the puzzles to be employed, and also state that some subjects would be paid for their participation on a conditional basis while others would be paid on an unconditional basis. After answering any questions that the subject might have, the experimenter could direct the subject to draw a single card from each of two stacks. One stack would contain cards reading "Conditional" or "Unconditional," with a reiteration of just what is meant by each of these descriptions; the other stack would contain cards reading "Puzzle A" or "Puzzle B," directing the subject to begin work on whichever puzzle was specified. Although the experimenter could be present in the room (to make sure the subject performed as directed), he or she would be totally blind as to the payment condition and could remain blind as to the puzzle chosen until a box containing the puzzle was actually opened.

Such procedures would virtually eliminate the possibility of experimenter bias, but the researcher might have to balance this advantage against the potential disadvantages of confounding from other sources. For example, to deliver the instructions in such a manner might actually *increase* the demand characteristics by informing the subject of all of the experimental conditions. When I am to be paid whether I complete a task or not, will my behavior be the same when I mistakenly believe that all subjects are being paid as when I correctly believe that some will not be paid unless they are successful? Delivery of the instructions by card drawing may also decrease both the experimental realism and the mundane realism of the research. How involving can it be to obtain your final instructions from an index card, and how often does that occur in real life? These other problems are raised not to suggest that we ignore experimenter expectancy effects, but rather to indicate the complexity of the task facing the experimental social psychologist. The laboratory experiment is the most powerful conceptual tool available for testing social psychological theory, but it is a tool that must be well understood and carefully designed.

CONCLUDING NOTE: ETHICS AND RESEARCH IN SOCIAL PSYCHOLOGY

A great many of the procedures that are *methodologically* desirable raise ethical questions that must be considered by the social psychologist. One of the most widely debated procedures is the use of deception—to generate experimental realism, to permit study of behavior with high loadings of social desirability, and to provide a convincing rationale for the introduction of manipulations. In a survey of social psychological research, Stricker (1967) found that subjects were intentionally misled about some aspect of the research in nearly 25 percent of the 390 studies reviewed. The response among social psychologists to this use of deception predictably ranges from those who encourage its use to those who would do away with it entirely.

The former position is illustrated by Freedman (1969), who, although concerned about the ethical issues involved, argues that the methodological advantages of deception justify its continued use in research. He correctly notes that social psychologists should be studying what people *actually* do, rather than what they think they might do (the problem of counterintuitive findings) and argues that deception is sometimes necessary to achieve this end. Taking an even stronger position, McGuire (1969) argues that since the accumulation of useful knowledge requires research, social psychologists who do no research at all are more morally reprehensible than those who do research involving deception.

In contrast to this position, Kelman (1968) asserts that deception in the laboratory contributes to, and further reinforces, an unfortunate and growing trend toward considering people as no more than manipulable objects. Similarly, Seeman (1969) has argued that deception research is characterized by unreality (what seems true to the subject is not really the case) and distrust, and has suggested that these conditions may not only be unethical, but also may lead to the development of psychopathology.

Whether to employ deception in social psychological research is, ultimately, a decision that each investigator must make individually. But it is not a decision to be taken lightly. Just as researchers have a responsibility to their colleagues to report all the data collected (not just those that support the hypothesis), and just as they have a responsibility to consumers of research (people who might make decisions affecting social policy on the basis of the findings) to conduct research as free as possible from artifacts, they also have an obligation to the subjects who provide the data they gather. Before undertaking research involving deception or other ethically questionable procedures, researchers must examine their own motives and ask themselves a number of important questions.

Is deception (or any ethically questionable procedure) the *only appropriate method* for studying the behavior of interest? How much *risk to the subject* is involved? For example, will a deception be relatively minor, or will it establish a situation (like Milgram's experiments) that could be quite damaging to the subject's self-esteem? In a field experiment, will the manipulations cause subjects to do something illegal or potentially dangerous, or will it leave them with an erroneous view of the world that will alter their future behavior? Can there be a **debriefing** that is thorough enough to remove or reduce any residual effects of the manipulation? Will the subjects understand the reasons they had to be deceived? Will they be informed of the true purpose of the experiment, and will they be given the opportunity to consent to have their responses included in any data to be analyzed? Will their anonymity be protected? And finally, is the *potential benefit* of the research (to society, in the accumulation of knowledge) great enough to justify whatever risks there are to the participants in the research? For example, is the primary goal of the study to train future researchers in the technique, or is the purpose to increase scientific knowledge of human behavior?

These are the sorts of questions that must be asked before research is conducted. They apply most specifically to cases in which the researcher intends to employ ethically questionable procedures, but they should also be considered when the only risk is that we might waste the subject's time. Most importantly, these questions illustrate the complexity of the issues involved in social psychological research, and they testify to the fact that no matter how experimentally sophisticated such research may become, it can never be value-free.

Summary

One of the principal goals of scientific social psychology is to develop theories about individual social behavior that will hold in many different sets of circumstances. We must be able not only to repeat research findings when exactly the same procedures are used (**empirical replication**) (p. 32), but also to test our theoretical ideas successfully in a number of different ways (**conceptual replication**) (p. 34). As a first step toward this goal, we must construct **operational definitions** (p. 31) of the conceptual variables of interest and publicly report the operations so that they (or variations on them) can be used by other researchers. In conducting our research we must try to ensure that the differences we find in our research have both **internal validity** (p. 39)—reflect real psychological differences rather than measurement artifacts—and **external validity** (p. 39)—will generalize to the real world outside the confines of any particular research procedure.

A major threat to both internal and external validity is that a subject who is aware of participating in research may be "behaving like a subject" rather than behaving "naturally." If subjects are aware of the psychological nature of the research, they may wonder what of their secrets are revealed by their actions, and as a result of this **evaluation apprehension** (p. 80) may behave in a socially desirable fashion, particularly if they suspect that the researcher is interested in behavior with loadings (positive or negative) on social desirability. Subjects try to understand the researcher's purpose or hypothesis, and they use the **demand characteristics** (p. 43) of the research to make these guesses. Although subject response biases can be reduced, and quasi-controls can be employed to measure the extent of demand characteristics, these sources of invalidity cannot be completely removed.

The major research methods include archival research, observational methods, and experimental research. The continuing records of a society are its **archives** (p. 46), and although they are maintained for other purposes, many of these can be used as sources of social psychological data. In using archival data, the researcher must guard against three sources of invalidity: the possibility that by oversight or intention items were originally **selectively deposited** (p. 50), the possibility that certain sorts of records are better maintained than others **selective survival** (p. 50), and the possibility that atypical cases might be drawn through selective sampling (p. 48) by the investigator.

The observational methods include **simple observation** (p. 52), **participant observation** (p. 52), **natural experiments** (p. 55) and **field experiments** (p. 55). The principal advantage of these methods is their high degree of external validity, derived from the study of subjects who are behaving naturally in settings which are familiar to them. To increase the frequency of behaviors for observation, to study unusual situations, and to enhance the internal validity of the research, the observer can increase **control** (p. 59) over the setting. And even in highly controlled settings, the essential "natural" quality of the situation can be maintained through full or partial **concealment** (p. 53) of the observers. Although control over the setting enhances the validity of observational methods, it raises ethical problems of concealment and invasion of privacy.

Experimental methods (p. 60) are most valuable for testing particular social psychological theories because of their high degree of internal validity, which permits negative results to be used in the **falsification** (p. 63) of theories. Many experiments in social psychology employ **factorial** *designs* (p. 65) to determine whether the variables manipulated **interact** (p. 68) to influence social behavior. The stages in a social psychology experiment typically include operationalization of the independent variables, **pretesting** (p. 71) of the manipulations, selection of the research subjects (who, unfortunately, tend to be college student volunteers) (p. 73), **conducting** (p. 74) the experiment, and **debriefing** (p. 85) the subjects. Although the experiment can be constructed to have **experimental realism** (p. 77) (impact on the subject) and **mundane realism** (p. 79) (similarity to events that might occur in the world outside the laboratory), substantial problems may still arise from the subject's knowledge that he or she is participating in research. In addition to the problems of *evaluation apprehension* and *demand characteristics*, laboratory experiments can also be biased by the experimenter's expectancy (p. 81) unless the research is conducted with the experimenter blind (p. 83) to at least some of the experimental conditions.

Research methods in social psychology can be compared on several dimensions, including the reactivity of the measurement technique, the degree of control over the setting, the internal validity, the external validity, and the ethical problems associated with each method. Unfortunately, a great many of the procedures that are methodologically desirable raise important ethical questions. Before beginning any research project the investigator must balance the potential risk (p. 85) to the subject against the potential benefit (p. 86) to be gained from conducting the research. The serious ethical questions raised by various research procedures eloquently indicate that despite methodological sophistication, research in social psychology can never be truly value-free.

Suggested Additional Readings

ARONSON, E., and CARLSMITH, J. M. Experimentation in social psychology. In G. Lindzey and E. Aronson (Eds.) *Handbook of social psychology.* (2nd ed.), Vol. 2. Reading, Mass.: Addison-Wesley, 1968. Pp. 1-79. A thorough discussion of problems of validity in experimental methods, including detailed instructions on how to conduct experiments in social psychology. Favors deception as a means of increasing the internal validity and realism of the research.

COOK, S., KIMBLE, G., HICKS, L., McGUIRE, W. J., SCHOGGEN, P., and SMITH, M. B. *Ethical principles in the conduct of research with human participants.* Washington, D.C.: American Psychological Association, 1973. This report of the APA ad hoc committee on ethical standards for research with human subjects presents summaries of incidents, ethical guidelines, and procedures for implementing those guidelines.

CRANO, W. D., and BREWER, M. B. *Principles for research in social psychology.* New York: McGraw-Hill, 1973. An excellent introduction to laboratory and field methods of research in social psychology. Includes strategies of research design, methods of interviewing, attitude scale construction, and experimentation as well as various procedures for data analysis. Less difficult reading than Aronson and Carlsmith.

ROSENTHAL, R., and ROSNOW, R. L. *Artifact in behavioral research*. New York: Academic Press, 1969. A collection of lengthy chapters on the volunteer subject, pretest sensitization, experimenter expectancy, demand characteristics, evaluation apprehension, and subject suspiciousness. These papers were written by experts in the field for advanced students and professionals, so they are extensive, and more difficult than Crano and Brewer's treatment of the same topics.

WEBB, E. J., CAMPBELL, D. T., SCHWARTZ, R. D., and SECHREST, L. *Unobtrusive measures: Nonreactive research in the social sciences*. Chicago: Rand McNally, 1966. A thorough but nontechnical discussion of the ways to obtain measures of human behavior—through archival and observational methods—with only minimal awareness by the subjects.

WINER, B. J. *Statistical principles in experimental design*. New York: McGraw-Hill, 1962. Strictly for those of you who plan to conduct experiments using factorial designs. Its primary advantage is a clear explanation of computational procedures for experiments in which there are different numbers of subjects in the various treatment combinations. These can be found for both two-factor (pp. 228–244) and three-factor (pp. 248–258) designs.

Social perception begins with a person in the external world and ends with the perceiver's organized impression of that person.

Social Perception:
The Other Person as a Stimulus Object

Chapter Three

What does it mean to say that someone is an attractive person? As we shall see in Chapter Ten, that judgment involves more than a physical description; it also includes strength of character, disposition, personality, and other aspects of the person that are not so readily observable. Suppose for a moment that we limited the judgment to physical appearance, or restricted it even more to include only facial features. If we asked a hundred people to tell us how attractive a particular individual's facial features were, would we obtain unanimity in the judgments? Probably not. The people making the judgment (we will call them the *perceivers*) might well agree on the components necessary for a face—two eyes, a nose, a mouth, a chin, two cheeks, a forehead (and perhaps two ears)—but there could be disagreement about which particular combinations of these are attractive, and which are not. And this is only considering the standard equipment. If the optional extras such as hair color and length, presence or absence of moustaches or beards on males, and presence or absence of make-up on females were included, the amount of disagreement would increase. Now if we were to ask perceivers to make a more inclusive evaluation of attractiveness, considering elements of personality and disposition as well as facial features, our perceivers might no longer agree even on the components that were necessary. Should attractiveness include a pleasing personality, or is beauty only skin deep? Does the overall attractiveness of a physically appealing and socially charming, but totally immoral, person differ from the attractiveness of a less appealing, brusque, but completely honest person? More importantly, how do we make judgments regarding the personal characteristics that we cannot directly observe? When will such judgments be made? What will make them accurate? How will they affect our subsequent behavior? All these questions are involved in the process of social perception.

As noted in Chapter One, many of our objectives as human beings engaged in day-to-day social interaction correspond to the goals of scientific social psychology: the explanation and prediction of individual social behavior. Our individual explanations and predictions are contained in our implicit theories of social psychology, just as the scientific explanations are contained in the accepted theories of social psychology. And just as the scientific method is the basic source of information for formal theory, *social perception is the basic source of information for an individual's implicit theory.* Your judgments of the physical attractiveness of other people involve social perception. Whether you are persuaded by a communicator who is trying to change your attitudes will depend to no small degree upon your perception of the person's motives. Your own self-concept may be determined in part by what other people think of you (their social perceptions) and how you come to learn of their opinions (your social perception). Whether you decide to help a person in an emergency may depend upon your assessment of the situation. What a group wants you to do, and its success in directing your behavior, both may depend on your judgment of the group's objectives and power over you. The list could go on, but the point is this: virtually all your own social behavior will be based on your *perception* of the social world around you. For this reason, a thorough understanding of social perception is an essential beginning for the study of social psychology. In this chapter we begin with the object of much of your attention—the other person —and with consideration of the setting in which social perception occurs. In Chapter Four we examine more closely the process of social perception and the contribution to the process that you make as a perceiver.

PERSON PERCEPTION AND OBJECT PERCEPTION: A DIFFERENCE IN DEGREE OR A DIFFERENCE IN KIND?

Percepts: The Representations of Objects and People

Before turning to the complexities of social perception, we should review some of the elements and principles of the perception of inanimate objects. Whether the stimulus for perception is a person or an inanimate object, the internal representation of that stimulus is called a **percept**, defined by Allport (1955) as "a phenomenological experience of the object, that is to say, the way some object or situation appears to the [perceiver] . . ." (p. 23).

Let us examine some of the implications of this definition. First, the fact that a percept is a phenomenological experience of an object implies that your knowledge and understanding of the object are obtained through your senses, rather than through thought or intuition. You can remember a tree, a mountain, or a river in its absence, but you can only perceive it through sight, smell, touch, hearing, or taste. A second implication of the definition is that there does exist an objectively real world of things and people outside the perceiver, not merely a fantasy world of inner experience. It should be noted that this assumes away some important philosophical problems, since a great deal of philosophical inquiry has been addressed to the question of whether there can be a logical proof of the existence of an external world outside the self. Our inattention as psychologists to these problems of importance to philosophers can perhaps best be justified by pointing out that whether or not the external world really exists, people behave as though it did, so our task as social psychologists is to describe the individual social behavior that occurs within the context of such widely shared assumptions. As a result, theories of social perception, like the people to whom they are applied, assume the existence of a world outside the mind of the perceiver.

A final implication of the definition is that the perceptual process involves more than a literal translation of the incoming sensation. A series of musical tones with a specific pitch and loudness is perceived as a melody. A vertical wooden post with crosspieces at its top will be perceived as a telephone pole whether the perceiver is standing next to the pole or is looking at it from a block away. An "eyewitness account" of a crime will tell us something about the objective circumstances, and something about the perceiver as well. To say that a percept is the perceiver's experience, the way the object or situation *appears* to that person, is to leave open the possibility for two different kinds of deviation from the stimulus array: the perceiver may reach the proper perceptual conclusion even though there is a change in the sensory representation of the incoming stimulus (the case of the telephone pole); or the perceiver may reach an improper conclusion by adding to, or subtracting from, an unchanging but ambiguous stimulus (the case of erroneous eyewitness testimony).

Veridicality: Agreement Between Percept and Reality

Both kinds of deviation from the stimulus array assume not only that a real world of objects and people exists outside the perceiver's mind, but also that the true nature of those objects can be ascertained, at least in principle. Obtaining the true description of the telephone pole—height, circumference at various points, composition—is a relatively simple matter. All we need do is have a number of observers make the necessary measurements and compare their findings. Most probably there will be a very high degree of agreement among these observers about the characteristics of the telephone pole, and we can then assume that this consensus reflects the "true nature" of the object. We then compare your percept of the object with the consensus of the observers, and your percept is said to be veridical (Allport, 1955) if it agrees completely with the objective reality of their description. The more closely your phenomenological experience parallels objective reality, the more veridical your percept is said to be.

The determination of veridicality is much more difficult in the case of the social perception of the eyewitness than in the judgment of the telephone pole. For one thing, the pole obligingly stays in one place and submits without protest to the repeated measurements taken by the observers. The same is not true either for a person or for a situation. A second difference is that the telephone pole does not arouse any particular emotion, either in you or in the observers, that might interfere with the perceptual judgments being made. In contrast, the prosecuting attorney has one view of the scene of the crime, the defendant has an entirely different view (and a substantial stake in having that view prevail), the defense attorney may have a viewpoint slightly different from that of the defendant, and the eyewitness may not agree completely with any of the others. So even if the conditions for observation were optimal, each perceiver's motives and vantage point could have produced different perceptions of the events. In summary, when the stimulus is a person or a social situation, it is much more difficult to establish the objective standard against which an individual's percept can be compared to determine whether the percept is veridical.

The Principle of Organization

Some students of perception, such as Gibson (1950), maintained that perceivers are passive and objective encoders of stimulus information. The mechanical card reader of a computer provides an excellent example of this model of perception. The card reader has limits (there are only eighty columns on a card that can contain information, only a single card can be read at a time, and only so many cards can be read per minute) that correspond to the limits of human attention and "channel capacity." But within these limits of the system (the mechanical system of the card reader and the physiological system of the human perceiver) information is thought to be objectively processed. The card reader must be told where to find the information on the card, but it will not miss anything it is told to read, and as anyone with such experience can tell you, it will not correct the mistakes you made in punching the card. In other words, the information that gets transmitted into the processing unit of the computer will be an utterly faithful representation of the stimulus input. Nothing will be added, and nothing will be taken away.

Although the view of people as objective information-processors was consistent with the behaviorism popular at the time, it was a view that could not prevail against some of the compelling demonstrations of the Gestalt psychologists (such as Koffka, 1935; and Köhler, 1929). The first of these demonstrations was contained in Wertheimer's (1912) studies of apparent movement, and involved what is known as the **phi phenomenon**. Suppose that you were one of the subjects in this experiment. You would be seated in front of a piece of apparatus consisting of a five-foot-long rectangular box containing two lights that can be flashed on and off. The interval between the time that one light goes off and the time that the other comes on can be precisely regulated by a special timing device. The box is placed on a table so that its length is in a horizontal plane, and the lights are placed at either end of the box. Then the experimenter asks you to report "how things appear" to you as the lights flash on and off. At first the time between the two flashes is very short (approximately 1/30 of a second), and what you perceive is two lights, one at each end of the box, flashing on and off simultaneously. If the time interval between the two is lengthened to approximately 1/5 of a second, you will still perceive two lights, but now they will appear to be flashing in succession. At an interval between these two times (the optimum interval is approximately 1/16 of a second) you will report seeing a *single* light moving the length of the box from one light to the other. And at a slightly longer interval (approximately 1/10 of a second) you may report an eerie experience of "pure movement" that follows the same path as the visual movement, but is somehow different from that visual movement. This experience of *phi movement*, as well as the perception of a single light moving from one point to the other, is a *perceptual* phenomenon that is not produced by the physical stimulation alone (successively flashing lights). The next time you see a lighted advertising sign or theater marquee whose message seems to be moving from one side to the other—commercial applications of the phi phenomenon— you will know just how compelling this demonstration can be.

Demonstrations such as the phi phenomenon were performed by the Gestalt psychologists to support their contention that the process of perception involves not simply the faithful encoding of external stimulation, but rather requires the active *organization* of that stimulation into a meaningful whole unit or gestalt. A large number of specific variations on this principle of organization have been formulated; some of the better known are proximity, similarity, and closure. For example, if several lines are drawn on a page at varying distances from each other, the lines that are close together will be perceived as a unit separated from other units on the page. This illustrates the principle of proximity. The principle of similarity comes into play if a large number of dots are scattered on a page, most of them of one color and a few in a contrasting color. The latter will be perceived as a unit, either as a connected line or as the outline of the space they appear to enclose. Finally, if I briefly show you a picture of a circle with a small gap in it and ask you to report exactly what you see, you will answer "a circle" in a tone of voice that suggests that you thought the question silly. In your perceptual organization of the stimulus you have closed the gap. It is because of the perceiver's active contribution to the perceptual process that even in the perception of objects "the whole is greater than the sum of its parts." And, as we shall see more completely in Chapter Four, the perceiver's contribution to the process is vastly greater in the case of social perception.

The Lens Model of Social Perception

The process of perception begins with an object in the external world and ends with a phenomenological experience of that object, a meaningful whole organized by the perceiver. In an early model of the perceptual process, Brunswik (1934) likened the process of perception to the focusing of light by a lens, and this "lens model" is diagrammed in Figure 3-1. The model was originally proposed to account for object perception, but Heider (1958) has shown that it can readily be adapted to social perception. As a consequence, the lens model can serve as the first point of comparison between object perception and social perception.

A Chain of Interpretation in Perception

The physical objects and social entities in the external world are referred to as **distal stimuli**, to indicate that they are remote from the perceiver and can be experienced only through the senses. After some appropriate kind of *mediation*—light waves, sound waves, physical

FIGURE 3-1
Brunswik's (1934) lens model of perception. (Reprinted from Shaver, 1975)

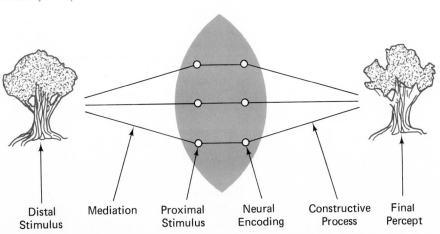

| Distal Stimulus | Mediation | Proximal Stimulus | Neural Encoding | Constructive Process | Final Percept |

contact—a distal stimulus will become represented at the perceiver's peripheral sense organs. The light waves produce an identifiable pattern on the rods and cones of the retina of the eye, the sound waves stimulate a particular pattern of response by various elements of the inner ear, and the physical contact gives rise to a certain pattern of response from receptors in the skin that are sensitive to temperature and pressure. In each case the resulting pattern of stimulation of receptors is called the **proximal stimulus**, and is the local and immediate representation of the distal object. It is generally agreed that the proximal stimulus is a less than perfect reproduction of the distal stimulus (see Allport, 1955). Some information is almost necessarily lost, either through selective attention on the part of the perceiver, or through limitations in the information processing capability of the central nervous system. Just as the computer card reader can only deal with one card at a time, the human information processing system— sense organs and central nervous system—can accept and encode only a limited amount of information at any particular moment. A complex stimulus can easily overwhelm the capacity of the perceiver's senses, with the result that only a fraction of the available information becomes represented in the proximal stimulus.

But even the proximal stimulus must undergo further modification before it results in a final percept. As Figure 3-1 shows, the neural encoding of the proximal stimulus (parallel lines in the lens) occurs in a relatively faithful manner, with little loss of information, but the encoded stimulus then encounters the interior face of the lens. The encoded stimulus is then evaluated against a background of whatever *other* neural activity is occurring at the same time—from organic states such as hunger or thirst, from muscle feedback, from the general cognitive activity of the brain—and it is in the context of this existing activity that the final step in perception occurs. Although the precise neural mechanisms are not clear, the field of activity can include not only present stimulation, but also memories of past events and expectations for the future. Thus the interpretation of the encoded proximal stimulus can best be considered to be what Heider (1958) calls a **constructive process**, an active interpretation of sensory input with other ongoing activity. It is through the operation of this constructive process that such perceptual phenomena as constancies, organization, and *phi* are thought to occur. The constructive process is the sum total of the perceiver's contribution to the process of perception.

To illustrate the model, suppose that you are listening to recorded music with a group of friends. The sound is available to all of you, as indicated by the lines diverging from the distal stimulus, and it is up to each of you to act as a lens for this sensory experience, focusing it into an individual percept of the music. Just as information is lost between distal stimulus and proximal stimulus, still other changes occur in the final transformation by the constructive process. You may be concentrating on the sheer loudness of the music, one of your friends may be more attuned to the rhythm, and another may be listening primarily to the lyrics. As a result, *the percept may differ for each one of you, even though the proximal stimulation is the same.*

Three Comparisons Between Object Perception and Social Perception

The lens model provides the first opportunity for a comparison between the perception of inanimate objects and the perception of people, and if we begin at the distal end of the process the first differ-ence we discover may be in the *nature of the mediation.* Recall that in the case of object perception, mediation typically consists of phys-ical entities—light waves, sound waves, temperatures, pressures, and so forth. In contrast, when the distal stimulus is a social situation or another person, the perceiver's proximal stimulus may not even be derived through firsthand contact with the distal stimulus. Your prox-imal stimulus of me may well be completely based on a verbal de-scription of me made to you by someone who knows us both. Or, even one step further removed, you have social impressions of people, such as government figures and celebrities, for whom the proximal stimulus is an anonymous report of the person in the media. This possibility of mediation by third parties will, of course, increase the likelihood that the proximal stimulus will not be a completely accurate reflection of the distal object. Now the third party's needs, and his or her attitudes toward the stimulus person, are interposed between the distal object and the proximal stimulus, and these attitudes are bound to affect the quality of the mediation.

There is an additional possibility for error in mediation of social perception that is largely absent in the mediation of object perception, and this error can occur even when the observation is firsthand. In the perception of inanimate objects (or of animals presumed incapable of intentional action), "what you see is what you get." An oak tree is simply an oak tree, not an elm tree in disguise; a dog chasing a cat is not doing so in order to prove its masculinity, or to impress other dogs that might be observing, or even to teach the cat a lesson. There are few hidden meanings in the appearance of inanimate objects, and there are no hidden motives in the behavior of infrahuman animals. This does not assume that the motives behind animal behavior will always be obvious to us, only that the animals will make few active attempts to conceal their motives. But if the object of our perception (the distal stimulus) is the *motive* behind the behavior of a person (presumably as revealed by the actions of the person), difficulty in interpretation can easily arise.

When you are perceiving another person, you are as interested in the person's reasons for acting as you are in the actions themselves. In this case the actions can be considered to be part of the mediation between you and the distal stimulus—the reason for acting. If the actions of the stimulus person reflect the distal stimulus unequivocally, those actions would be, in Heider's (1958) terms, synonymous mediation for the underlying disposition. The action is a synonym for the disposition. If a person is observed dashing into a burning building at considerable personal risk in order to save people trapped inside, that action rather unequivocally reflects motives of altruism and helpfulness. On the other hand, if the actions of the stimulus person could reflect any number of possible motives, there is said to be ambiguous mediation. A person who is observed helping his or her employer build an addition onto the employer's house might have any of several motives for doing so. The employee might truly be helpful, might simply be trying to be ingratiating in order to obtain a raise, or might be gaining experience for some intended additions to his or her own home. And as the mediation becomes more ambiguous, the certainty of the proximal stimulus will decrease. Because the stimulus person's reasons for acting are hidden and must be inferred (we will consider the inference processes in greater detail in Chapter Four), the mediation for social perception may be less than perfect even though the observation has been firsthand.

A second difference between social perception and object perception is in the greater *complexity of the stimulus*, and this is first reflected in the proximal stimulus. Regardless of the faithfulness of the mediation, it is extremely difficult for us to sense all the potentially relevant dimensions of another person. In the case of object perception, the important qualities of the object are its physical properties—size, weight, color, possibility for movement, and so forth—and there is a relatively limited number of such properties which must be considered. Because the set of properties is limited, most of them can be accepted by the sense organs without overloading the channel capacity of those organs. And even if some aspects of a physical stimulus must be ignored to prevent overloading, the *proportion* of available information actually processed into the proximal stimulus will remain high. In contrast, when the distal stimulus is a person, even a complete physical description might overload the senses, and this description would fail to consider the large number of possible reasons for acting. Thus, when our senses establish a proximal stimulus of a person, the proportion of information available that is actually considered will be much lower than in the case of object perception. We simplify our perceptual worlds whether the distal stimuli are persons or objects, but this simplification is more costly when the distal stimulus is a person.

Assuming that the proximal stimulus of a person is faithfully encoded into neural transmission, the final difference between the perception of objects and the perception of people will be in *the part played by the constructive process*. Our expectations about the behavior of people are more extensive than our expectations about the behavior of objects; the fact that the other person is capable of intentional action that might benefit or harm us will influence our impressions, and the greater complexity of the stimulus person will lead to a greater need for interpretation. For all these reasons, the constructive process will assume greater importance in the perception of persons than in the perception of objects. And since this is an internal process rather than a representation of external stimulation, it is more prone to error. Unfortunately, it is also more difficult to assess the extent of such errors in social perception, because of the lack of a readily available objective standard against which the veridicality of a social perception can be evaluated. Because a social perception cannot be judged against a physical standard, veridicality must be determined by comparisons among a number of perceivers in the sometimes naive hope that their viewpoints and biases will cancel each other out.

Social Perception as Categorization

Criterial Attributes and Stereotyping

We have noted that when the distal stimulus is a person rather than an object, the proximal stimulus will represent a smaller proportion of the available information. Once it has been encoded, this proximal stimulus is subject to even further modification through a constructive process heavily influenced by the perceiver's own needs, motives, and expectations. This interpretation of the stimulus by the perceiver can, as Bruner (1957) suggests, best be characterized as an act of *categorization:* through experience the perceiver learns what stimulus elements are reliably associated with each other and learns to combine these into meaningful categories. Perception (especially person perception) is seen as a problem-solving task in which the perceiver tries to decide whether the stimulus person possesses attributes that would place him or her in any of several appropriate categories. Once the assignment has been made, the perceiver responds to the stimulus person more as a representative of a social category than as a completely unique human being.

In making the category assignment, some attributes of the stimulus person are obviously more relevant than others. For example, in the 1950s a person's hair length was almost always a good indication of the person's sex: males had short hair and females had long hair. But hair length is not what Bruner would call a **criterial attribute**: a necessary attribute that helps define the boundaries of the category. The criterial attributes for the determination of gender are, of course, the sexual organs, but these are most often hidden from the casual perceiver. So perceivers search for other identifying attributes, like hair length, and are occasionally reminded (to their embarrassment) that such attributes are not criterial. Some social categories are defined by a single criterial attribute—FBI agent, Democrat, and Lion are categories defined by membership in a formal organization—while other categories have multiple criterial attributes. For example, the category of "statesman" has behavioral criterial attributes as well as formal criterial attributes. A statesman must be a government leader, but not all government leaders are statesmen.

Given the complexity of social stimuli, and the extensive participation of the perceiver in constructing the final percept, some degree of categorization in social perception is inevitable. But at the same time, an overreliance on categorization can obscure individual characteristics and lead to *stereotyping*, the belief that every individual who can be placed in a social category possesses *all* the traits ever associated with that category (Lippmann, 1922). Consider for a moment the social category "housewife." The criterial attributes of this category usually include being female (although the emergence of the term *househusband* suggests that this attribute may become less criterial), being married (this, too, may change in time), and having no job outside the home. It is important to notice that while these are the only truly criterial attributes, they are not the only attributes ever found among members of the category. Housewives often have children, sometimes drive station wagons, and occasionally become so wrapped up in their home lives that they lose interest in anything else. Indeed, it is possible that in the experience of a particular perceiver these additional attributes form part of the "typical instance" of the category.

The perceptually justifiable process of categorization becomes potentially dangerous stereotyping when the perceiver assumes that each new instance of the category possesses all of the attributes (those that are criterial and those that are not) associated with his or her typical instance of the category. In your own experience it may be true that every housewife you have met has also driven a station wagon (the typical instance), but you can see that it would be a mistake for you to assume that any woman driving a station wagon will necessarily be a housewife (as defined by the truly criterial attributes).

The Prior Entry Effect

Stereotyping is a perceptual error based on experience with a category of stimulus persons, but there are other possibilities for error in the organization of that experience. In all but the most rigid perceivers, the process of categorization is an interchange between the cognitive category and the new information that is received. When a perceiver is confronted by a social stimulus or situation that is novel to that person, he or she has difficulty distinguishing between the truly criterial attributes and other attributes that may be unique to the particular instance. Take the large lecture class as an example. First we must presume that you have had no experience in lecture classes in high school, so that although you may have some general expectations about how a lecture class is conducted, you do not know for certain what attributes of the situation are criterial. On the first day of classes, you walk into your lecture section of introductory psychology. You take a reading list from a table near the door, find a seat in the auditorium, and begin talking quietly to the other students sitting near you. The time for the class to begin comes, but still there is no professor. Finally, after what seems like an interminable five minutes, a strange-looking fellow saunters down to the front of the room, opens a folder containing several sheets of paper, and spreads them out on the table. Then he opens a small bag, removes a microphone with a long cord, straps the microphone around his neck, and inserts the plug into a socket in the lectern. He then announces over the public address system in the room that he is Dr. Cykolog, that the course is Psychology 101, that there will be a midterm examination and a final examination, and that 25 percent of the people in the class will probably flunk. Without so much as a pause for the class's collective gasp, he begins lecturing by reading almost verbatim from his notes. He stops talking when the bell rings to end the period, packs up his papers and microphone, and quickly departs through a back door.

Since this is your first day of college classes, you have several perceptual categories to form—lecture class, nonlecture class, grade expectations, college professor, professor of psychology, and a number of others. Now you face the problem of trying to distinguish among these possibilities. Will all of your lecture classes be so big? Will the professors always use microphones and insist upon being called "Doctor"? Will that matter at all if they never permit time for questions (or are you not supposed to ask questions in a lecture course)? Will the professor always be late; will it always be a male; how will professors typically be dressed? And will all of the lecture classes be so darn boring (especially when the subject matter ought to be intrinsically interesting)?

In your attempt to answer all these questions, you must distinguish between the attributes of the lecture method (independent of the subject and the professor), attributes of the discipline (psychology), and attributes of the particular professor. But it will take time and experience with other classes and teachers to make these distinctions. As a result, at the very beginning of your college career every category will be heavily influenced by this one class experience. To take one specific perception, you may decide that "dull" is a criterial attribute of the lecture method. After all, what else could make an inherently interesting subject boring? Should you later take a lecture course that was highly lively and interesting, you would see it as an *exception* to your characterization of the lecture method. You have experienced what Jones and Gerard (1967) call the **prior entry effect**: the early information encountered will contribute more to the formation of the category than later contradictory information will contribute to change in the category. If the first lecture you encountered had been interesting, that would have formed your impression, and the later dull lecture would have been seen as the exception. In truth, whether a lecture is dull or interesting is probably not a criterial attribute of the *method*, but rather of the subject matter or the professor. But your early information created the category, and that existing category shaped the later input.

The prior entry effect screens out relevant information (if there is wide variation in the interest value of lectures, then shouldn't interest value be an attribute of something other than the method?), and adds to the information given (you may assume that all professors want to be addressed as "Doctor," even though they don't say so). In part because of the cognitive prior entry effect, the attitudes and values you form during the early development of your categories will be highly resistant to later change. This problem, like the problem of stereotyping, will reappear in the later discussions of attitude formation and change (Chapters Six and Seven). And, because of the greater complexity of social stimuli, each problem is of more concern in social perception than in the perception of inanimate objects.

DESCRIPTION OF THE STIMULUS
IN PERSON PERCEPTION

During the constructive process in person perception, perceptual categories are actively formed from the diverse attributes of the stimulus person or situation. The process is subject to the overcategorization errors of stereotyping and prior entry, and in assessing the influence of such errors it is important to know how elements of the stimulus situation are combined into the final impression held by the perceiver. Does the order in which a perceiver considers various elements of a single stimulus person affect the final impression? Are some aspects of the stimulus person or situation more important than others in organizing the resulting perception? In short, how does the way in which the stimulus is described affect the perceiver's impression?

The Order of Presentation

Suppose that I described a hypothetical stimulus person to you, and I asked you to write a more inclusive description of that person from the information given you. If I tell you that the stimulus person is "envious, stubborn, critical, impulsive, industrious, and intelligent," how "happy and sociable" will you believe the person to be? What if I give you the same description, but simply *reverse* the order of the adjectives? Will changing the order affect your impression? In one of the first laboratory studies of impression formation, Asch (1946) tried to answer just such questions. His subjects were instructed to form an integrated impression of a stimulus person from limited information provided to them. Half the subjects received the adjectives in the order given here, while half received the reverse order. Asch found that subjects receiving the order beginning with "intelligent" were more likely than the other subjects to see the stimulus person as "happy," "humorous," "sociable," and "restrained."

This apparently greater influence of early information was called the primacy effect, and it was explained in terms of word meaning. You will notice that the adjective list contains words that differ widely in desirability—"intelligent" as opposed to "envious," for example. Asch argued that the early words in the series established an evaluative direction, and that the later words were considered in light of this evaluation. In other words, the connotative meaning of the word *critical* may be different when it is interpreted as an attribute of an intelligent person than when it is interpreted as an attribute of an envious person. It is almost as though the perceiver makes a snap judgment on the basis of the first word in the series and then integrates the remainder of the description into the impression established by that word.

An alternative to Asch's suggestion of meaning change as the explanation for primacy effects is the notion that the early words are simply given more weight in the impression, as in the case of the prior entry effect for categories. Suppose, for example, that you were given the same list of adjectives, but were instructed to refrain from forming your impression until you had heard the entire series. This procedure should equalize the weight given to each adjective but should not affect shifts in meaning, since each succeeding adjective will still be heard against the context of the ones which have preceded it. Using the same list of adjectives, Luchins (1957) performed this experiment and found that the primacy effect disappeared. In a similar approach to the problem, Anderson and Hubert (1963) used the same list but asked subjects to recall all the adjectives before making their judgments about the stimulus person. Their results showed dissipation of the primacy effects in this recall condition, indicating that the primacy effect occurs because the perceiver places less weight on the adjectives late in the series.

The Organizing Influence: Central Traits

In the description of a social stimulus, then, the order of presentation of the elements does seem to make a difference. What about the nature of the individual elements? Again we can begin to answer this question by referring to the classic work of Asch (1946). Just as Asch's Gestalt view of impression formation led him to postulate meaning change as the explanation for primacy, it also suggested to him that some adjectives might exert an *organizing* influence upon those presented with them. A person attempting to form an integrated impression of a stimulus person from a list of descriptive adjectives might consider some of these adjectives or traits more important, or more central, than others. In exactly the same way that the partially closed circle exerts an organizing influence, leading the perceiver to ignore the small gap in its circumference, these central traits might be more powerful than others in organizing the perceiver's impression of the stimulus person. To test this idea Asch presented a second group of subjects with a list of traits—"intelligent, skillfull, industrious, warm, determined, practical, and cautious"—describing a hypothetical stimulus person. Half of these subjects received the list exactly as it appears, and half received a list with the word *cold* substituted for the word *warm* in the series. All subjects then wrote a brief paragraph describing the person, and completed a series of rating scales describing the person. The results showed that the warm-cold variable did produce substantial differences in the final impressions of the stimulus person. The "warm" stimulus person was more likely to be seen by subjects as generous, happy, and humane, while the "cold" stimulus person was thought to be ungenerous, humorless, unhappy, and ruthless. It also appeared that the difference was not simply a matter of a positive description versus a negative description, because both stimulus persons were described by subjects as curious, important, honest, and strong—all positive characteristics.

In an important extension of this study, Kelley (1950) showed that the warm-cold variable could influence behavior toward a live stimulus person. Students in three sections of an introductory psychology course were told that there would be a guest instructor for an upcoming session and were then given a brief, written biographical note describing the guest. In fact, there were two different descriptions passed out in each course, one describing the guest as "a rather warm person," the other describing him as "a rather cold person." The guest then entered, and after a brief introduction by the professor led the class discussion for twenty minutes. During the discussion the professor (experimenter) recorded which students initiated discussion with the guest. After the twenty minutes had passed, all students were asked to rate the guest instructor on a series of adjective rating scales. Scores on these scales replicated the warm-cold personal differences found by Asch (1946), and, more importantly, the behavioral data showed that most of the discussion had been initiated by students who were told that the instructor was warm. Although some later experiments cast doubt on word-meaning-change as the sole explanation for the operation of central traits (Wishner, 1960), it appears that there are adjectives (such as warm-cold) which do exert substantial organizing influence upon the impressions formed of other people.

NONVERBAL MEDIATORS IN PERSON PERCEPTION

Until now we have been speaking of the stimulus in person perception as it might be described by a third party. The stimulus for both the order effects (primacy) and the combinatorial effects (central traits) is a list of descriptive adjectives. Although such lists form the core of traditional impression-formation experiments, and generalize pretty well to real third-party descriptions, they play a much less important role in firsthand observation. Only a well-schooled Boy Scout is likely to rattle off a series of descriptive adjectives—kind, cheerful, reverent, brave, and so forth—if you ask for a self description. Most people will begin with a single trait or trait cluster, and elaborate upon that trait before moving on to others. In fact, research with the Twenty Statements Test (Kuhn and McPartland, 1954; Gordon, 1968) shows that a person's initial responses are primarily social categories. In the Twenty Statements Test the subject is asked to make a total of twenty self-descriptive statements and is limited to a time period of twelve minutes. The first few self-descriptions are typically such social categories as race, sex, name, age, and religion rather than descriptive adjectives. This may be because these characteristics are central to the self-concept (Kuhn and McPartland, 1954) but it may also be because these relatively "public" qualities are less embarrassing (and less revealing) to report than descriptive adjectives would be.

More importantly, even these self-descriptions have to be elicited by rather direct questions from the perceiver, and perceivers do not usually form impressions by asking the stimulus person for a self-description. It is much more likely that the perceiver will simply observe the stimulus person's overt behavior and try to reach conclusions about the person on the basis of that behavior. The stimulus person's actions may be *communicative*—the product of an active attempt to convey a message to the perceiver—or they may simply be *expressive* of his or her emotional state. Communicative nonverbal behaviors, like verbal statements, are presumed to be under the stimulus person's conscious control, while expressive actions are not designed for the perceiver's benefit. But both sorts of nonverbal behavior will enter into the perceiver's impression.

Personal Space

As unobtrusively as you can, take a look at other people's behavior in a crowded elevator. You will probably discover that as people enter the elevator they move to the rear, turn around to face the front, and carefully direct their eyes either straight ahead or at the lighted panel showing which floors have been chosen. If you dare, turn to another passenger and try to begin a meaningful conversation. Soon you will begin to feel a sort of oppressive silence, and you will probably stop talking. Why should everyone be so hostile toward a little conversation, and why is it that everyone carefully avoids looking directly at anyone else (until they all look daggers at you)? One reason is that in a crowded elevator, everyone's *personal space* is being violated, and there are certain implicit norms for behavior under these circumstances (which you have had the bad manners to break).

The Study of Social Distances

The social implications of various physical distances were first fully documented by Hall (1959), who coined the term **proxemics** to refer to the study of these distances. Hall identified four levels of personal distance, each with a *close phase* and a *far phase*, and catalogued the social behaviors that are most prevalent (and appropriate) at each of these distances. These distances and behaviors are summarized in Figure 3-2, which shows how some of the distances are set by body position. The far phase of *public distance* (more than 25 feet) is found most typically in the case of public figures, or in an interaction between a speaker and members of the audience, and is usually characterized by status differences between the observers and the stimulus person (*Senator* Snodgrass, *Dr.* Cykolog). Only one-way conversation is really possible, and even then the speaker's voice must be amplified. It isn't just the number of other students in the class that inhibits your asking questions in a large lecture; it is also the distance between you and the lecturer. In the close phase of public distance (from 10 to 25 feet), it is possible to carry on a conversation, but only if both participants use formal and syntactically correct speech, and if both raise their voices slightly. Again, status differences between the participants at this distance are common.

At the far phase of *social distance* (7 to 10 feet), conversation can be sustained with eye contact between the participants, and only with mutual consent. Status differences begin to blur, but the voice must still be raised slightly, and there is often some formal relationship between the two parties. This distance is a common one between receptionists and visitors to an office, since it is close enough for the receptionist to initiate enough conversation to determine who the visitor is, what his or her purpose is, and to give whatever directions are necessary, but it is still far enough away that the visitor will not begin an informal conversation that would take the receptionist away from other duties. In the close phase of social distance (4 to 7 feet), the usual social behavior is informal business, with no status or dominance differences. This phase encompasses a great deal of informal social interaction by acquaintances, colleagues, and casual friends.

A little closer to the person we find the far phase of *personal distance* (30 to 48 inches). This distance marks the boundary of a "bubble" around the person known as **personal space**: the area that the person considers his or her own. At this distance there can be touching of two parties, but only by mutual consent since the two people are

FIGURE 3-2

How various phases of social distance are set. (Adapted from Hall, 1968, p. 93)

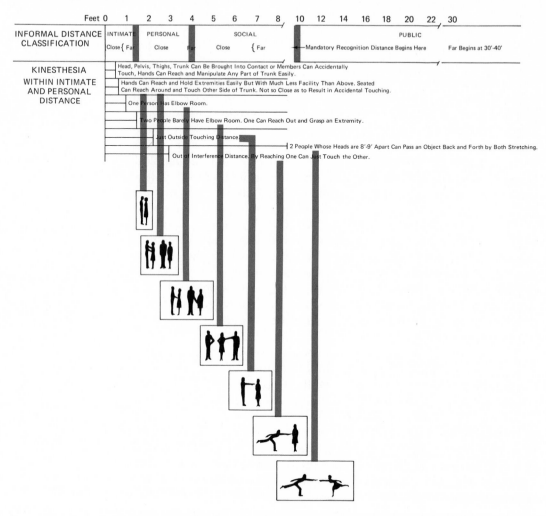

"arm's length" apart. The personal space bubble is not a perfect circle around the person, but tends to be egg-shaped—greater at the rear and in front than at either side. It is permissible for good friends of the same sex to converse at this distance, but for most Americans, intrusion into personal space must be accompanied by such friendship, or must be explained by the circumstances, such as a crowded room during a cocktail party. Europeans tolerate closer personal distance than do Americans. The close phase of personal distance has, in American culture at least, a certain sort of meaning for the relationship between the persons involved, and so does their bodily orientation within that distance. Such a distance is appropriate for a husband and wife, or for close friends of opposite sexes, but it is inappropriate for casual acquaintances, or for most situations involving persons of the same sex.

Finally, the last phase in Hall's scheme is what he calls (not surprisingly) *intimate distance* (zero to 18 inches). And now we discover why people in the elevator reacted as they did. In a crowded elevator (as opposed to a crowded party) the people are likely to be complete strangers, they are likely to be in bodily contact, and as a result of these two factors they are likely to be quite uncomfortable. The interpersonal distances they are forced to maintain by the situation are ones usually reserved for lovers. The behaviors appropriate for the distance are inappropriate for the level of acquaintance, and to try to ease the discomfort people try to *ignore* the personal space. Each person carefully faces forward (so that no two people are facing each other), and each watches the floor designations (which for most people are outside personal space). These norms very clearly define the situation in a way that minimizes psychological (if not physical) contact and permits each person to maintain the illusion that his or her personal space has not been violated. Since conversation at intimate distance is usually a prelude to lovemaking, in the crowded elevator you are perceived as invading the privacy of any person you talk to and as forcing the other passengers to invade your privacy by observing. No wonder everyone hopes that the next stop will be your floor.

What Does Interpersonal Distance Tell the Perceiver?

From the standpoint of a perceiver making an assessment of a stimulus person, proxemic information can be useful in at least two respects. First, if a stimulus person is regularly observed interacting with a small number of people, the person's spatial relationships to those people can be of value to the perceiver. For example, if a man is frequently observed in the company of his wife, and if for most of this time he places a distance of several feet between them, the perceiver may begin to wonder about the quality of their relationship. The perceiver would become even more suspicious if he should notice that the stimulus person seems quite comfortable at a closer distance when in the company of other women. Despite his verbal protestations to the contrary, the person's physical distance from his wife is likely to be interpreted as a manifestation of psychological distance.

The second sort of information that can be obtained through proxemics comes not from the stimulus person's relationship to specific other people, but rather from the person's personal space requirements regardless of who is in the immediate vicinity. People differ in the size of their personal space "bubbles," and these differences can have psychologically important consequences. For example, research by Kinzel (1970) has shown that inmates in federal prisons who have a history of personal violence have larger personal space requirements than do nonviolent prisoners. Certainly being in prison would make you more conscious of your personal space, but the researchers suggest the assaultive prisoners' violent behavior might be a product of what they perceive to be a violation of their personal space. What would be social distance for most people might be perceived by them as a more intimate distance. While most people might respond to a violation of personal space by backing up, the assaultive prisoner might have responded aggressively. To continue this line of reasoning, it might be possible to infer certain personality dispositions from personal space requirements. For example, the smaller a person's proxemic area, the more open and (quite literally) approachable we might expect him or her to be. At the present state of research in the area, these ideas receive most of their support from anecdotal, rather than experimental, evidence, but they are interesting avenues that could be explored.

Spatial Arrangement

In addition to proxemic area, the orientation of the stimulus person in a specified space can be of value to the perceiver. Why is it that a group of chairs arranged in a circle seems more informal and congenial than the same group of chairs arranged in several rows? How can privacy be maintained in a confined space with only minimal potential for change of the surroundings? What clues to character are contained in seating choice? These and similar questions are the subject matter of a growing interest in the field of spatial arrangement, largely based on the pioneering research of Sommer (1969). Although this work has implications for the placement of furniture, architectural design (especially of institutions such as schools, mental hospitals, and prisons), and interpersonal phenomena such as the level of intimacy that can be attained by a small group, we will concentrate on the influence of spatial arrangement on person perception.

The degree to which perceivers seem to be sensitive to spatial cues must often be inferred from the behavior of stimulus persons, rather than obtained directly from the perceivers themselves. This can be illustrated by Sommer's (1969) research with library table arrangements. Suppose that you need to study for an important examination, and have chosen to do so in the college library because your living quarters are simply too hectic for you to be able to concentrate. But libraries have social uses other than their main academic purpose—they are centrally located places where numerous social encounters can be arranged, and where new acquaintances can be made in an unpressured situation. How are you going to make it clear to others that your purpose is the academic one, and that you truly want to be left alone? Sommer suggests that there are two defensive positions—the *retreat* position and the *active defense* position—that can be adopted to ensure privacy, and he argues that they reflect different degrees of commitment to privacy.

Combining techniques of field observation in libraries with laboratory analogues of those situations, Sommer found that there was a good consensus among subjects about the difference between the two strategies. He devised a set of diagrams (shown in Figure 3-3) showing rectangular tables with either three, four, or five chairs per side. The situation was described as a library room, and the subjects were asked to select the position they would occupy in order either to sit "as far as possible from the distraction of other people" (the retreat instructions), or to sit in such a manner as "to have the table to yourself" (the *active defense* instructions). With the retreat instructions, the overwhelming choice was the end chair on either side. In contrast, when the instructions emphasized active defense, the almost unanimous choice was the middle seat on either side. What is most interesting about these choices for our purposes is that they are communicative behaviors that assume a common spatial language between the defender and potential encroachers on the territory. It may not be a conscious choice; the person who sits at the middle of the table has his or her personal space extending to both sides, and if the "bubbles" are not to touch, a person who approached might have to sit some-

FIGURE 3-3
Diagrams of library tables used in the Sommer (1969) studies of spatial arrangement.

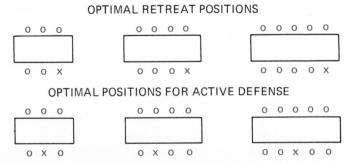

where else just to maintain an appropriate distance, without thinking of the stimulus person's purposes. But it does have the effect of protecting privacy.

Not only can the stimulus person's public behavior carry meaning to the perceiver, but the modifications of his or her own domain can serve as cues to the person's social status and attitudes. Professors whose doors are always open are more likely to be seen as receptive than are those whose office doors are closed. In most large corporations, people must be in executive positions before they are permitted to have enclosed, private offices, and only the most senior executives are permitted the embellishments of paintings on the walls and rugs on the floors. An extreme example of the relationship between possessions and status is provided by the Paris peace talks convened in an attempt to bring an end to the Vietnam conflict. The very first issue on the agenda was the shape of the table to be used in the later negotiations, and this issue took an incredible time to resolve. Why? Consider the implications of some of the alternatives.

Perhaps the most obvious choice would be a long rectangular table, with the two sides (North Vietnamese and their allies, South Vietnamese and their allies) facing each other across the table. This arrangement was unsatisfactory because it did not take into account that there were several interested parties, and that in many instances the interests of groups usually thought to be allies might conflict. On the other hand, a large circular table would have the effect of giving equal status, and equal part in the discussion, to virtually every government or organization involved, regardless of its role in the conflict or its resolution. Eventually the decision was made to use a round table (King Arthur must have been right), but the fact that extensive deliberations were necessary to reach the decision indicates the important effects of features of the physical environment on social behavior. And an individual's use of those physical features—degree of rearrangement, choice of seating position, readiness to decorate with graffiti—can reveal something of the person's intentions and character.

Kinesic Cues

We have considered how a perceiver's impression might be influenced by the manner in which a stimulus person is described, by the person's use of interpersonal space, and by his or her location in and modifications of that space. Now we turn to the stimulus person's overt behavior. With the growth of various self-awareness techniques, there has been a renewed interest within social psychology in nonverbal aspects of behavior. If your parents patted you on the head when you were a little child, it was probably because the top of your head was as low as they could reach without bending over. If they continue to pat you on the head when you are eighteen, that action may well be interpreted as an indication that they still consider you a child. All the body movements readily perceptible to the perceiver can be considered **kinesic cues**. Broadly conceived, this category includes both communicative and expressive movements; not only posture, gestures, and tactile communication, but also more specific elements such as facial cues.

It is surprising that until recently there has been so little study of body language in its own right (Weitz, 1974), particularly since our verbal language incorporates so many kinesic descriptions. We describe a person we think timid by saying that "he has no backbone" or that "she will not stand up for her rights," implying a correlation between posture and personal courage. The relationship between physical state and emotional condition, fundamental to the study of psychosomatic medicine, appears in our language not only for expressive emotions like anger ("pounding on the table") but also for more private ones like anxiety ("tied in knots") and apprehension ("butterflies in the stomach"). We recognize the importance of eye contact: in an extensive program of research Exline (1972) has found greater visual contact between persons attracted to each other, confirming our belief that lovers "gaze into each other's souls." But extended visual contact among people unacquainted with each other can be aversive ("staring him down"). For example, Ellsworth, Carlsmith, and Henson (1972) found that pedestrians who were stared at would cross an intersection faster than would those who were not stared at. And, finally, nonverbal cues have a universal quality not obtained in spoken communication—"A smile is a smile in any language."

What sorts of impressions can be conveyed by body position and movement? Let us suppose that you are attending a party at a friend's house, but that outside of your friend you know virtually no one there. You would like to make some new acquaintances, and since you neither want to interrupt an intimate group nor be lost in a large one, you settle on a group of three people. Specifically, let us assume that there are two potential choices, each group composed of one person of your sex and two people of the opposite sex. One of these groups is near the corner of the room, with two of its members facing the wall and only one facing out toward the room, while the other group is arranged in a loose semicircle, sitting on the floor near a coffee table in the center of the room. The fact that they are sitting, and arranged in an open spatial pattern, suggests that they are more approachable. This influence of posture on the perceiver's impression was demonstrated in a study by Mehrabian (1968), who found that seated females whose arms were resting on their laps and whose legs were not crossed were seen as more "pleasant" than seated females whose legs were crossed and whose arms were folded.

Even if the posture of the seated group is not a firm indication of its approachability, other kinesic cues may support your judgment. You may have noticed animated gestures of arms and hands, relatively steady eye contact, and a good deal of smiling. From this information you would guess that the three people would be informal rather than formal (it is difficult to be formal when slouched on the floor), interested in their conversation (a conspicuous absence of furtive glances around to see who has just come in the door), but not intimately engrossed in each other (their eyes are not riveted together, and their gestures are animated). You might not ordinarily be able to verbalize all of this information, but you would surely be surprised to arrive at the group and discover that they were arguing about politics.

Why is it that kinesic cues have such high apparent validity? Perhaps the best answer is the one suggested by Goffman (1959) and later elaborated in the work of Ekman and his associates (e.g., Ekman, 1965; Ekman and Friesen, 1969): body language is less likely to be susceptible to conscious control by the stimulus person. Words can be carefully chosen to obscure the truth (an occasional Freudian slip notwithstanding), but bodily position and movements are much less easily staged. Some excellent mimes can create almost any emotional expression simply by their bodily movements, but the intentional gestures that the rest of us try look just as staged as they are. Consequently, when there is a discrepancy between the verbal message and the nonverbal cues, the latter tend to take precedence. This discrepancy between the verbal message and the nonverbal message has been described by Ekman (1965) as nonverbal leakage, and it can contribute substantially to the accuracy of the perceiver's impression.

Unfortunately, this use of nonverbal cues can have both positive and negative effects. On the positive side, our legal system is constructed to take advantage of nonverbal leakage in its attempt to reach the truth. Witnesses in trials cannot simply submit written statements, they must be examined in person and subjected to cross-examination by the opposing side's attorneys. The jury is specifically instructed to observe each witness's "demeanor" in order to make a judgment about how credible the witness's testimony is. In contrast, the possibility for harm from conflicting verbal and nonverbal messages is represented in the clinical literature by the *"double-bind"* hypothesis of the origin of childhood schizophrenia (Bateson, Jackson, Haley, and Weakland, 1956). The parent who tells the child, "I love you," while holding the child stiffly away in a manner that says, "You disgust me," is putting the child in a double bind. If the child responds to the verbal message, he or she will be rebuffed; if the child responds to the nonverbal message, the parent will wonder indignantly, "How can you say that about me?" The situation is further complicated by the greater validity of the nonverbal message. Any attempt on the child's part to correct the situation would be met with, "How can you think that when I *said* how much I love you?" Not surprisingly, the child receiving a double-bind message is confused, and Bateson and associates argue that the childhood schizophrenic's characteristic withdrawal from social interaction is just an adaptive response to intolerable emotional inconsistency.

Facial Cues

Recognition of Emotion

Even though facial expressions are one sort of kinesic cue, they deserve special treatment because of their importance in the communication of emotion (Ekman, 1972; Tomkins, 1962, 1963). Let us return to your friend's party. You initially guessed that the three people sitting on the floor would be interesting and approachable from their spatial behavior, but that impression had to be confirmed by the facial cues of eye contact and smiling. More importantly, when you join the group you will study their faces carefully, trying to read from their expressions what effect you are having upon them. At first just an approving smile will be enough reassurance, but as time goes on it will become imperative to distinguish between a bored, but polite smile, and a smile of real approval that confirms your worth as a person. Once again, it is assumed that the perceiver and the stimulus person share a common nonverbal language. This is not to say that there are no individual differences in sensitivity to facial cues—no doubt at some point you have been trapped in a conversation with someone so persistent that no amount of looking away, or staring through the person, or smiling inappropriately would get the point across. But then, such a person might not be sensitive to subtle linguistic cues, either.

How can you tell from a person's face what emotion he or she is experiencing? Or, to put it another way, if you are confident that you hold the winning hand in a high stakes poker game, what can you do to produce a "poker face" that won't give you away? Recognition of facial emotion is a classic problem in person perception, and sophistication in study of the problem has accompanied the increasing application of mathematical scaling models and cross-cultural comparisons. In the usual case, subjects are shown still photographs of a single stimulus person (usually a trained actor) who has been asked to illustrate a whole range of emotions through facial expressions. These photographs are presented in a random order to each subject, and the subject is to guess the emotion expressed in each one. The subject's accuracy is measured by comparing his or her guesses with the actual emotion thought to be expressed.

Early studies of recognition of emotion (Feleky, 1924) found only minimal accuracy on numerous emotional expressions, but as Woodworth (1938) pointed out, these studies failed to distinguish between errors made on simple judgments and errors made on difficult judgments. In other words, if you had made an error on "anger," that mistake would have been given the same weight as a mistake on "contemplation." Woodworth examined the data from several earlier studies and concluded that emotions could be ordered into a continuum of categories: (1) love, happiness, and mirth, (2) surprise, (3) fear and suffering, (4) anger and determination, (5) disgust, and (6) contempt. Using this revised coding scheme, Woodworth found an average accuracy of nearly 80 percent and found that very seldom did the judges make errors of more than one category step. Some years (and a good deal of intervening research) later, Schlosberg (1952) found that for several sets of stimulus materials judges frequently tended to confuse Category (1), honest happiness, with Category (6), haughty and derisive laughter. On this basis Schlosberg concluded that Woodworth's scale was best represented as a circle (shown in Figure 3-4) whose two major dimensions were evaluation (*pleasant-unpleasant*) and involvement (*attention-rejection*). These two dimensions were thought to describe the quality of an emotion, while a third dimension (not represented on the diagram, but best conceived of as an elevation above the page), called *activation level,* described the intensity of the emotional experience. Recent applications of *factor analysis,* the mathematical scaling procedure originally developed by Thurstone (1947), have shown that a complete description of the judgments of faces may require as many as five dimensions—pleasantness (corresponding to Schlosberg's evaluative dimension), interest value (involvement), intensity of emotional expression (activation level), social evaluation by the perceiver, and surprise (Frijda, 1969).

Components of Facial Emotion

While some researchers have been attempting to characterize the dimensions of facial emotion, others have been more concerned with the specific facial components that enter into the perceiver's judgment, and with the substantial cross-cultural reliability in such judgments. For example, while Schlosberg might describe "happiness" as high pleasantness, high activation, and neither attention nor

FIGURE 3-4
Schlosberg's circular classification of facial emotional expressions.
(Reprinted from Schlosberg, 1952, p. 232)

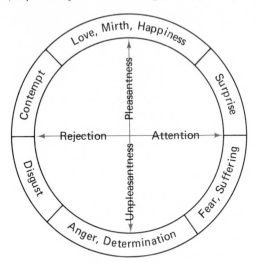

rejection, Ekman and his associates would point out that whatever
its dimensional characteristics, happiness is one of the emotions
that seems to be interpreted the same way across cultures (Ekman,
Friesen, and Tomkins, 1971). Other emotions with similar meanings across cultures include sadness, anger, fear, surprise, and disgust
(Ekman, 1968; Ekman and Friesen, 1971; Izard, 1968, 1970).

In an attempt to understand which components of the face contribute to this cross-cultural reliability in the judgment of emotion,
Ekman, Friesen, and Tomkins (1971) developed what they call the
facial affect scoring technique (FAST). In the FAST system the
face is divided into three separate areas: eyebrows-forehead, eyelids-
bridge of nose, and lower face (consisting of cheek-nose-mouth-chin-
jaw). These divisions were chosen primarily for their potential for independent movement (you can raise your eyebrows without moving
your mouth, but not without wrinkling your forehead).

To score an emotion using the FAST system, the facial photograph representing the emotion would be split into the three divisions, and each component would be compared to the relevant
FAST item-components. In other words, if you were shown the eyes
from a facial photograph, you would compare those eyes with the
eyes for each of the six emotions included in the FAST manual: are
these "surprise" eyes, or are they "anger" eyes, or are they some
other sort of eyes? Next you would make the same sort of comparison
judgment for the brow-forehead segment of the photograph, and then

for the lower face segment. Finally your judgments about each segment would be compared with the emotion represented in the whole
facial photograph to see how accurately you were able to estimate
the emotion from each of the three segments.

In a first study of the validity of the FAST system, Ekman,
Friesen, and Tomkins (1971) found that subjects trained in the FAST
scoring system could predict the true emotion represented in the
whole facial photograph with substantial accuracy. There were some
interesting discrepancies—happiness was correctly identified from the
lower face 100 percent of the time, but the lower face produced
no successful identifications of sadness—but on the whole the predictions for all emotions save fear were extremely good. What is
perhaps most interesting about this program of research is that the
FAST system is based on a formalization of the researchers' intuitions
about which elements of the face ought to reveal which emotions.
Although the validation study was accomplished with posed photographs rather than with spontaneously occurring "live" facial emotions, the success of the system does suggest how perceivers might
use different elements of the face to distinguish reliably between
different expressed emotions.

That perceivers can judge emotion from facial expression has
two consequences of interest to us. First, the relatively high reliability of the judgments reinforces the notion of a shared (even
cross-cultural) nonverbal language, and suggests that facial expressions are an essential element in the process of person perception.
Second, the fact that judgments of facial emotion are not perfect
(either in the dimensional studies or in the FAST system) illustrates
the importance of the surrounding context (a point also noted by
Ekman, Friesen, and Ellsworth, 1972). In any live performance there
will be much more information available—the nature of the situational context, the proxemic and kinesic cues, the verbal and
paralinguistic behavior—so the perceiver's impression is likely to be
even more accurate. What this means for you poker players is that
rather than trying to conceal your true feelings with a "poker" face,
you might be more successful in confounding your opponents by
expressing a random assortment of emotions which have no predictable relationship to your true feelings.

Paralinguistic Cues

In this description of the stimulus for person perception we have
begun our analysis away from the verbal behavior of the stimulus person and have moved steadily closer to that behavior—from the

descriptions given by others, through the stimulus person's use of space and kinesic cues, to his or her facial expressions. Now we turn to *how* the person says what is said, the cues to perception derived from the **paralinguistic** features of verbal behavior. These have been characterized by Mahl (1957) as including four dimensions: *vocal* (loudness, pitch), *temporal* (rate of speaking, duration of speech segments), *verbal-stylistic* (dialect, vocabulary peculiarities), and *interaction* (behavior in a conversation such as a tendency to interrupt or dominate). The latter two are perhaps the most noticeable to an untrained observer, and so we will begin our discussion with them.

Let's look first at the use and abuse of dialect. One of the first things that you notice about an unfamiliar person's speech is whether or not he or she speaks with an identifiable dialect. Among the more recognizable ones are the clipped and crisp speech of the New Englander, the accent of the Brooklyn New Yorker, and the twang of a southern drawl. But do these speech characteristics tell the perceiver anything more than the probable origin of the speaker? Hollywood television and movie producers certainly seem to think so. For example, think of the last movie or television show you saw in which the hero was having difficulty with a small-town sheriff. If the sheriff was characterized as a little dull, as willing to bend the law to accommodate the local townspeople, and as openly hostile to people from the city, he probably also spoke with an identifiable southern drawl. Even though Labov (1970) has shown that the basic features of various nonstandard dialects of English are structurally and functionally similar, perceivers still believe in stereotyped views of people, based in part on their dialect.

Not only the speaker's dialect, but also his or her control over the linguistic interaction will influence the perceiver's impression. What do you think of a person who "won't let you get a word in edgewise"? You consider such a person domineering, overbearing, and egocentric—more interested in the sound of his or her own voice than in actually communicating. You make an inference about the stimulus person's personality characteristics from verbal assertiveness, and from the person's failure to heed your desire to speak. But how do you indicate your desire to be heard? Duncan and Niederehe (1974) suggest that there are at least four specific cues employed by a listener to indicate that the listener wants to take a turn at speaking. These make up the **speaker state signal,** and include (1) a shift away in head direction, from pointing directly toward the speaker to pointing in some modified direction; (2) an audible inhalation of breath, as a preparation for beginning to speak; (3) the initiation of a gesticulation (defined so as to include both hand movements away from the body and tensing of the hands, such as making a fist); and (4) paralinguistic overloudness.

This last cue needs a little elaboration. In any continued conversation both the speaker and the listener are actively participating. The speaker is talking, and the listener is indicating attention and interest by emitting what Yngve (1970) calls *back-channel behaviors*. These back-channel behaviors include head movements such as nods and shakes, and verbalizations such as "m-hm," "yeah," and even short sentences such as "That's right." Ordinarily the back-channel verbalizations are relatively low in intensity and serve the expressive function of indicating that the listener is paying attention, being sympathetic, or agreeing with what the speaker is saying. But if a back-channel verbalization is overloud, it can serve the communicative purpose of indicating a desire to speak: the "That's right" spoken softly implies agreement, the loud "That's right" may well mean "That's right *but . . .*" Given the nature of the cues that form the speaker state signal, it is not surprising that you infer egocentrism, lack of interpersonal sensitivity, and dominance from the actions of a speaker who refuses to yield.

If a speaker's pattern of interaction can be a clue to personality, the pitch and loudness of the speech can suggest emotional state. Calm and controlled speech may be firm, but every child knows that a shouting parent means business. And, since the development of the voice spectrometer (Hargreaves and Starkweather, 1963), an instrument that makes a record of the power, pitch, and overtones of a voice, more detailed analysis of the vocal content of speech is possible. An individual's "voiceprint" may reveal emotional state for the same reasons that body language may do so—we are not trained in the use of our voices, and that is a dimension of our behavior to which we are not consciously sensitive. As a result, while we may control what we say (the *semantic content*) of our speech, and how loudly we say it, we usually do not try to control other features of our voices such as the pitch. Perceivers' sensitivity to these characteristics of speech is illustrated by the work of Soskin and Kauffman (1961), in which judges could infer the emotional state of a speaker even when the semantic content of the speech was filtered out. There is still enough animal in us that we can identify a growl even when the semantic content of the hostile remark is removed.

Finally, the temporal characteristics of a person's speech can help to reinforce the impressions gained from interaction, stylistic, and vocal cues. If we are talking about something we know well, we speak quickly and without hesitation, but if we "hem and haw" it will be clear that we are uncertain. On the other hand, police may doubt the alibi of a criminal suspect if the story is produced too quickly after the question is asked. It is as though the answer were planned in advance, and we wonder why the suspect thought we would ask about that particular time period. The relationship between temporal patterning and emotional state, for example, is illustrated by the work of Kanfer (1959, 1960). He showed that words per minute spoken by female psychiatric patients declined when the topic of discussion was shifted from their present state to their relationships with men. In contrast, there were no words per minute differences between content areas for normals. Although there is little research dealing with perceivers' ability to distinguish among various temporal patterns, the differences that Kanfer found are just the sort we might expect, and the anecdotal evidence suggests that we can make relatively reliable inferences at least about the speaker's certainty from the temporal characteristics of what he or she says.

THE STIMULUS AS PERSON: SELF-PRESENTATION

Until now we have been considering the stimulus person as a stimulus rather than as a behaving person, ignoring or discounting the person's conscious control over the image that he or she puts forward. We have looked at the verbal descriptions given by third parties, without considering how these people might have come to have the impressions they relate to the perceiver. And we have seen that the sort of terms used, and the manner in which they appear, can influence the perceiver's impression. We then turned to the stimulus person's nonverbal behavior to see how use of space, gestures, and manner of speaking might contribute to our perception of the person. Implicit in the consideration of nonverbal behavior, and explicit in the idea of nonverbal leakage, is the presumption that it will reveal the stimulus person's *true* emotions, attitudes, and personality because nonverbal behaviors are typically not under conscious control. Indeed, recent research by Ekman and Friesen (1974) suggests that even conscious control of facial and body cues may not prevent the detection of deception. To conclude this chapter we shift our attention to the behavior that *is* under conscious control—the stimulus person's self-presentation.

Perhaps the most important difference between stimulus persons and stimulus objects is that the stimulus persons are not just inactive collections of attributes. They are thinking and feeling beings actively engaged in what Goffman (1959) calls *self-presentation*, the creation and maintenance of a public self. In Goffman's view, an en-

counter between two or more people involves a mutually agreed-
upon set of rules that prescribes what behaviors are appropriate for
the situation. Of course there are different expectations for different
roles and circumstances. You don't behave the same way with your
parents that you do with your close friends, but in all cases some
of the same rules can be seen to apply. Each person brings to the
encounter what Goffman calls a *line*, a complete pattern of verbal
and nonverbal acts through which is communicated one's view of the
situation and the participants (especially oneself). It is important to
note that because this line can differ from situation to situation,
it cannot be equated with the person's entire repertoire of behaviors.
Rather, it is the subset of the repertoire that the stimulus person
believes appropriate for the circumstances.

A central element of the person's line is called the *face*, defined
as the positive social value that the person claims for himself or herself in the interaction. If all the information contributed by participants in the encounter is consistent with the stimulus person's
positive social value, the person is said to be "maintaining face." In
contrast, if information provided either by the person or by others
disconfirms the person's self-worth, then the person is said to be
"out of face." And although Goffman doesn't specifically say so, the
process is comparable to the situation described in everyday language
as "losing face."

One of the most important rules of interaction is that such encounters involve *mutual commitment*. Each participant's face becomes a property of the group, and all participants do what they can
(within reason) to maintain each other's face. If you don't believe
this, just try telling someone straight out, with no euphemisms, why
you think he or she is perhaps the most obnoxious person you have
ever met. Perhaps one of the most upsetting features of the student
radicals of the sixties, at least as far as many older people were
concerned, was their tendency to describe policies they disapproved
of not with sophisticated derogatory terms, but with profanity. They
were somehow not playing the game properly, not letting other
participants "save face."

The maintenance of face is not the goal of interaction, but rather
is a necessary condition for its continuation. When you are conversing
with close friends, your primary goal is not self-aggrandizement, but
rather the conduct of a relationship in which all of you can express
your true feelings, exchange ideas, and only occasionally pat each
other on the back. If any "incidents" occur that threaten the face of a
participant, however, a corrective process called *face-work* will be
initiated to preserve the interaction.

Goffman's ritual analysis of interaction serves to illustrate two aspects of the crucial difference between a stimulus object and stimulus person: properties are selected by the person for presentation, and observation is a social behavior. When the stimulus for perception is an object, even an animate though infrahuman one, nearly all of its properties are accessible to the perceiver. True, the mediating conditions may preclude full knowledge (it is difficult to tell the color of an object in the dark), but those conditions are not under the active control of the object itself. In contrast, when the stimulus is a person, there is an active selection of *which* verbal and non-verbal behaviors to reveal, and that choice depends on the situation. Second, person perception is an interpersonal phenomenon, governed by the same kinds of rules and expectations that regulate other forms of social interaction. What behaviors the stimulus person chooses to emit can have implications for the perceiver, and the impressions the perceiver forms can in the same way affect the stimulus person. The social nature of person perception thus places restrictions and expectations upon both participants.

Summary

Virtually all of people's social behavior will be affected by their perception of the social world around them. In social perception, as in object perception, a perceiver's phenomenal experience, the **percept**, (p. 93) is not a perfect representation of the objects, or **distal stimuli**, (p. 97) in the world, although its **veridicality** (p. 94) can be determined through appropriate comparisons. One reason that the percept and distal stimulus may differ is that the perceiver *organizes* his or her impressions.

Although social perception and object perception can both be described by a *lens model*, there are some important differences between the two. First, social perception may be *mediated* either through the reports of other people or through potentially ambiguous behaviors on the part of the stimulus person. Second, the stimulus person is so much more complex than a stimulus object that social perception is more likely to involve simplification through categorization according to the **criterial attributes** (p. 102) of the stimulus person. This process of categorization may produce errors such as *stereotyping* (p. 102) and the **prior entry effect** (p. 104).

The description of the stimulus in social perception has often taken the form of lists of descriptive adjectives, and some of these adjectives appear to be more central (p. 106) than others. In addition, the presentation of the adjectives may, unless controlled, produce primacy effects (p. 105). In firsthand observation, of course, descriptive adjectives play a much less important role than such nonverbal mediators of impressions as personal space (p. 109), spatial arrangements, the body language of kinesic cues (p. 115), and the paralinguistic cues (p. 121) which accompany speech. These nonverbal cues can be used as clues to deception in the verbal communications of stimulus persons, and if the discrepant communication is from parent to child the resulting double-bind can have serious consequences for the emotional well-being of the child. Among the kinesic cues, the expressions of the face are perhaps the most important, and over the years a number of different systems have been devised to measure the recognition of facial emotion. Recent developments suggest that nonverbal signals serve not only to mediate social impressions, but also to regulate interaction through such mechanisms as speaker state (p. 121) signals. Finally it must be remembered that the stimulus for social perception, the person, utilizes his or her entire repertoire of verbal and nonverbal behaviors in a purposeful *self-presentation* (p. 123) that may or may not reveal the person's true nature.

Suggested Additional Readings

ALLPORT, F. W. *Theories of perception and the concept of structure.* New York: Wiley, 1955. An extensive, scholarly discussion of the classic theories of object and social perception. Difficult reading, but well worth the effort if you wish to learn where perceptual theories fit in the larger context of psychological tradition.

HASTORF, A. H., Schneider, D. J., and Polefka, J. *Person perception.* Reading, Mass.: Addison-Wesley, 1970. A short and clearly written introduction to person perception, including recognition of emotion, interpersonal accuracy, and a section on attribution.

TAGUIRI, R. Person perception. In G. Lindzey and E. Aronson (Eds.) *Handbook of social psychology.* (2nd ed.) Vol. 3. Reading, Mass.: Addison-Wesley, 1969. An extensive review of research on the problems of interpersonal accuracy, personality judgment, and the process of social perception. Much more difficult than Hastorf, Schneider, and Polefka.

WEITZ, S. (Ed.) *Nonverbal communication.* New York: Oxford University Press, 1974. An excellent collection of papers dealing with facial expression, paralanguage, body movement and gestures, spatial behavior, and multichannel communication. The integrative commentary at the beginning of each section is particularly helpful.

People's social behavior is determined by social reality as seen
through their own not-always-rose-colored glasses.

Photo by Paul Seder

The Perceiver's Contribution to Social Perception

Chapter Four

The process of social perception is fundamental to the study of social psychology, because most theoretical explanations of behavior assume that individuals are responding to the social world as it appears to them. In the preceding chapter we focused our attention on a principal element of that social world—another person—and discovered that people are complex stimuli whose verbal and nonverbal behavior must be evaluated in order to form an impression. We base our judgments of people in part upon what they say, in part upon what they do, and in part upon what other people say about them. We look for discrepancies between words and deeds in an attempt to separate "truth" from self-presentation. In short, we actively *interpret* the complex information that we receive. In many cases this constructive process of interpretation enhances the veridicality of our social perceptions, but in some instances our own motives as perceivers can decrease the accuracy of our impressions. Complete discussion of the process of social perception must include not only the stimulus information available to the perceiver, but also the perceiver's use of that information. It is to these interpretive processes that we now turn.

ACCURACY IN THE JUDGMENT OF OTHERS

Let us begin with perceivers at their interpretive best, and consider some of the factors that contribute to the substantial accuracy of our everyday social perception. We form impressions of the people we meet, guess about their backgrounds and interests, and evaluate their intentions toward us. And for the most part, these judgments are correct. We seldom become involved with people who turn out to be completely different from the first impression we form. There are exceptions—"But he didn't look like a criminal"—and these can be based, as we will see later on, as much on our motivation as on a misleading self-presentation by the stimulus person. But when we have sufficient time to make the judgment we can usually differentiate true praise from ingratiation, tell who will keep our secrets and who will not, and distinguish the person who really believes in honor and justice from the hypocrite who merely talks about them.

Possible Sources of Accuracy

What sorts of factors contribute to such accuracy in person perception? Intuitively we might identify several possibilities. Suppose that you were asked to choose a person who would be a good room-

mate for you. First we might expect that your accuracy in such a judgment would increase with your *experience*. When you first arrive at
college, you are uncertain of your own potential study habits, your
interpersonal relationship with your new roommate, and the amount of
adjustment that will be necessary to adapt to this relatively unfamiliar
life style. But after a term or two, you know which of your personal
habits are likely to get on a roommate's nerves and vice versa, you
know how much mutual self-disclosure you would consider desirable,
and you know what proportion of your time you can afford to spend
just talking as opposed to studying. In the terms of social perception
theory, your experience has given you a better idea of the behavior to
be predicted, or the *criterion*. You now know what behavioral qualities
a "good roommate" for you should have.

As a second possibility, since the accurate assessment of other
people involves some cognitive work, we might expect that the more
intelligent you were, the more accurate your interpersonal perception
would be. You need to be able to formulate precise questions to ask
potential roommates, to recall your own experiences, and to learn
from the mistakes of others. It just seems reasonable that these
abilities should be related to more general intellectual capability.
Finally, you ought to be sensitive to the other person's needs and
emotions, so that you can put yourself into his or her shoes. After
all, how well the two of you get along will depend in part on
whether your future roommate can tolerate you. Your ability to place
yourself in the other's position is what Mead (1934) referred to as
"taking the role of the other," and we shall consider this process in
more detail in Chapter Eight. The ability to experience another
person's emotional state has been proposed as a operational definition
of empathy (Stotland, Sherman, and Shaver, 1971), and we shall return
to this concept during the discussion of helping behavior (Chapter
Ten). We would expect that both your empathy for another person
and your ability to put yourself in his or her place would increase
with your *similarity* to the stimulus person.

Early Research on Accuracy

Thus our intuitive theories of social psychology would suggest that
experience, intelligence, empathy, ability to take the role of the
other, and personal similarity would all be involved in determining
the accuracy of your interpersonal judgment. How could we apply the
methods of scientific social psychology to test these presumptions?
In the early work on accuracy in interpersonal judgment, investigators
simply asked subjects to describe themselves, close friends, and
strangers on a number of rating scales, and then compared these

descriptions to the ratings made by the stimulus persons (the friends or strangers). For example, in one of the first studies Vernon (1933) had subjects take a number of personality tests, rate themselves on a variety of dimensions, evaluate other people whom they knew well (who were also participating in the research), and make judgments about strangers from verbal descriptions and handwriting samples. In this way Vernon could obtain three different measures of accuracy: (1) the degree to which subjects' self-ratings corresponded to the ratings made of them by others and to the actual personality test scores (accuracy in self-rating), (2) the degree to which subjects' ratings of their friends corresponded to both the friends' self-ratings and personality tests of the friends (accuracy in judging friends), and (3) the degree to which the subjects' ratings of the strangers corresponded to the personality test scores previously achieved by these stimulus persons (accuracy in judging strangers).

In each case the accuracy score was determined by the numerical discrepancy between the subject's rating of the stimulus person and the stimulus person's self-description (either the personality test score or the self-rating). For example, if you said that the trait "dominance" was very much like your friend (a scale score of 5), but your friend said that dominance was only moderately like him (a scale score of 4), the numerical discrepancy between the two would be a difference of 1 point. Whether the difference is a +1 or a −1 would depend on the direction of the difference, but on the grounds that only the discrepancy (not its direction) was important, the absolute difference would simply be squared. The final estimate of your success as a judge of character would be the sum of the squared differences for each trait assessed. So, on a test that contained ten items, your veridicality could vary from a *high* of 0 (no differences between your rating and the criterion rating on any of the ten items) to a low accuracy of 160 (a difference of four points on each of the ten items, with each of these differences squared). This total squared discrepancy score was known as D^2, and the lower the value of D^2, the greater your accuracy in social perception.

It is important to note that in these early studies both your rating and the criterion (whether it was a personality test or the stimulus person's self-rating) were simply taken at face value, leading Cline (1964) to characterize this era of research as "naive empiricism in social perception." There was no consideration of the fallibility or error in the personality tests employed, even though no personality test is completely reliable or valid. There was no correction for possible self-presentation biases on the part of the stimulus persons, although many of the descriptive adjectives were so heavily loaded on social desirability (e.g., generosity, apathy, submissiveness) that we might suspect less than accurate reports. And finally, there was inappropriate comparison between the subject's self-ratings and the stimulus person's self-ratings (the problem of similarity, to which we shall return later).

What Sort of Accuracy?

The methodological problems inherent in early research on judgmental accuracy were first noted extensively by Cronbach (1955). As so often happens in social psychology, Cronbach's critique demonstrated that before valid answers could be obtained regarding accuracy in social perception, better and more sophisticated questions would have to be asked. Specifically, Cronbach noted that the D^2 statistic was a "global measure" of accuracy that should really be separated into four relatively independent components. One of these deals with the perceiver's willingness to use the extremes of the scale of judgment (elevation), one deals with the ability to place stimulus persons in the proper rank order even though the absolute judgment of each might be incorrect (differential elevation), and a third represents the perceiver's sensitivity to the distribution of traits in the larger population (stereotype accuracy). Only the fourth component, **differential accuracy**, reflects the perceiver's ability to estimate correctly how much of a particular trait is possessed by a particular stimulus person. The other three components of the D^2 score can contribute to the apparent accuracy of a perceiver, but they do not represent ability to make absolute judgments of the degree of a trait possessed by a particular stimulus person. Thus, Cronbach argued that only differential accuracy should be considered a "pure" accuracy score, and later researchers have pointed out methodological difficulties even with differential accuracy (Cline, 1964; Taguiri, 1969).

In addition to suggesting that three of the components of D^2 were of little use in describing the perceiver's social acuity, Cronbach (1955) also suggested that similarity between the perceiver and the stimulus person could spuriously increase the perceiver's apparent accuracy. If you have no information about the traits of a stimulus person, you might guess that the person would be at least somewhat similar to yourself. Suppose that you are given a personality test to measure your "assertiveness" and that the same test is also given to a friend of yours. Now you are asked to judge how assertive your friend is, and you make the judgment partly on what you know of your friend's behavior, and partly on your own degree of assertiveness (as you know it).

The researcher would then have three separate scores available for analysis: your own assertiveness score from the test—we will call this score *(a)*, your friend's score on the test *(b)*, and your estimate of your friend's score on the test *(c)*. Using these three scores, we can define three different variables. The first variable is *accuracy* (in the sense of Cronbach's differential accuracy), and it is defined by the extent to which $c = b$. If you estimate correctly, you are said to be accurate. The second variable is the *real similarity* between you and your friend, defined by the extent to which $a = b$. The third variable, called *assumed similarity* by Cronbach (1955), is defined by the extent to which $a = c$. The problem is this: if your estimate of your friend's score is largely based on projection from your own level of assertiveness, then *your apparent accuracy will increase as the real similarity between you and your friend increases.* Even if you were a terrible judge of character (and had to rely entirely upon projection from your own traits), you would appear to be extremely accurate when you were judging people quite similar to you. Procedures have been developed by Hatch (1962) and Taft (1966) to deal with this assumed similarity problem, but they add further complexity to the measurement of judgmental accuracy and are of somewhat limited usefulness outside the confines of the experimental situation.

Do Cronbach's criticisms help us to answer our original question? Are there certain personality characteristics which are reliably associated with accuracy in judgment, or is it impossible to obtain valid accuracy scores? In his extensive review, Cline (1964) concludes that a completely satisfactory technique for measuring the accuracy of interpersonal judgment is still to be found, and this conclusion is reinforced by Warr and Knapper (1968) and Taguiri (1969). But because investigators interested in the problem of accuracy have developed a number of different methods to assess accuracy, not all studies suffer from the *same* methodological difficulties. In the best tradition of conceptual replication (see Chapter Two), research by one investigator will not be perfect, but will correct the deficiencies in research by others. As a result, Allport (1961) could conclude that even though there seems to be no generalized "ability to judge others," certain personality traits do contribute to greater accuracy. These include *breadth of personal experience, intelligence, self-insight, social skill and adjustment, and cognitive complexity* (the last to be discussed more fully in a later section of this chapter). And Taguiri (1969) asserts that "Allport may well be correct, on the whole, in his summation" (p. 413), while noting that "different types of persons may be accurate, depending upon the form of interpersonal judgment and the type of object [stimulus] person involved" (p. 413).

Although there have been further studies of the characteristics of good judges (e.g., Christenson, 1970, 1974; Edwards and Mc-Williams, 1974; Hjelle, 1969), most of the recent interest in interpersonal perception has concentrated on the *process* rather than the *outcome*. Rather than trying to catalog all the personality traits that might make one an excellent judge of others, researchers have sought to discover more about the way in which *any* perceiver (not just an extremely accurate one) processes the information received about other people. We noted in Chapter Three that this process of social perception involves an active contribution by the perceiver to the final percept, and suggested that the perceiver's role could be likened to the role of a lens in focusing light (Brunswik, 1934). Information received from distal stimuli is focused by a constructive process (Heider, 1958) that occurs against a background, or field, of other stimulation present at the time. Because of the complexity of social stimuli, the constructive process most probably involves categorization of the stimulus person according to his or her apparent criterial attributes (Bruner, 1957). In short, the perceiver actively interprets the social world. We now consider some of the consequences of this activity, and then conclude the chapter with a discussion of models of impression formation and attribution processes.

THE PERCEIVER'S INVOLVEMENT: A SOURCE OF ERROR IN PERCEPTION

In earlier chapters we have compared the social perception processes of an individual with the research methods of scientific social psychology. There are substantial differences in methodology, but there are some conceptual similarities between scientific social psychology and individual social perception. The object of each is the understanding of human social behavior, a goal which, if achieved, would permit the explanation of past behavior and the prediction of future action. Each involves the observation of social behavior, and each seeks to interpret observed behavior in terms of existing information. Finally, each process is subject to error. Just as scientific procedures may be adversely affected by the experimenter's expectancy, the social perception of an individual may be distorted by the perceiver's expectancy. Just as the experimenter's personality and values influence the choice of research topics and procedures, the individual's personality and values may bias social perception. These sources of bias in scientific social psychology were considered

in Chapter Two, and now we look more closely at the potential
for error in social perception.

Effects of Personal Dispositions

Authoritarianism

In 1950 a group of researchers at the University of California at
Berkeley published a massive study of what they called the
authoritarian personality (Adorno, Frenkel-Brunswik, Levinson, and
Sanford, 1950). This study had taken nearly ten years to complete,
and had involved attitude scaling, sociological analysis, and clinical
interviews. The best-known product of the study was an attitude scale
for the measurement of fascistic tendencies, known as the F scale
(or sometimes the California F scale). Both this particular scale and
the overall approach of the research study have been criticized on
a number of methodological grounds (e.g., Christie and Cook, 1958;
Christie and Jahoda, 1954; Deutsch and Krauss, 1965; Hyman and
Sheatsley, 1954). But there is enough confirmation that authoritarianism is related to social behavior (e.g., Kirscht and Dillehay,
1967; Martin and Westie, 1959; Wrightsman, 1965) to warrant our
consideration of its possible effects upon social perception.

Authoritarianism is regarded as a personality syndrome — a collection of separate traits — including rigid adherence to conventional
values, concern for power and toughness in interpersonal relationships, and a tendency to shift responsibility for events with negative
consequences away from the self and to project their causes onto
forces beyond individual control. If there is any validity at all to the
hypothesized nature of this personality syndrome, authoritarianism
should be an important determinant of social perception, and a
number of studies suggest that it is. For example, in his extensive
study of the development of friendship, Newcomb (1961) predicted
that authoritarians would be less accurate in their judgments of others
than would nonauthoritarians. Early in the study, before the subjects
had time to make acquaintances, the authoritarians and nonauthoritarians were equally inaccurate. As time passed, however, the nonauthoritarians became more accurate, while the authoritarians erroneously projected their own attitudes onto others. One explanation for
the greater sensitivity of the nonauthoritarians is that they are less
likely to conceive of the social world in terms of a few limited
(and rigid) categories. This possibility is suggested by the finding
of Steiner and Johnson (1963) that highly authoritarian people are
less likely than low authoritarians to believe that "good people" can

possess both good and bad attributes. It is apparent from these findings that a personality disposition such as authoritarianism can, indeed, distort an individual's social perception by affecting its accuracy and its complexity.

Cognitive Complexity

The most comprehensive examination of the effects of personality dispositions on social perception is the work of George Kelly (1955, 1963), which deals specifically with the issue of cognitive complexity, the presumed sophistication of the cognitive categories used to describe the social world. Like Bruner (1957) and Heider (1958), Kelly views people as perceptual problem solvers: the perceiver is thought to approach each social situation with an hypothesis about it, and then to compare that hypothesis with the reality of the situation. Kelly calls these hypotheses personal constructs, and shows how they are interrelated into a consistent scheme. Although the elements which compose these personal constructs are the same across perceivers, no two complete sets of personal constructs are ever identical.

The personal constructs that a perceiver holds are thought to determine the way in which he or she views the world, and Kelly has developed a method for measuring the constructs that are used. This is the Role Construct Repertory (or "Rep") Test, which asks subjects to compare the occupants of various role positions (e.g., boss, subordinate, person you dislike, friend, parent, spouse). The roles are presented in triads, and you are asked to tell how two members of each triad are like each other but different from the third member. For example, how are "parent" and "boss" like each other but different from "friend"? Your answers to this test reveal a number of features about your social perception, such as *which* constructs you choose (examples might be likability, equality, power), *how many* different constructs you employ, and the *relative frequency* of each construct used. One of the most fruitful differences identified through use of the Rep Test (or variants on the theme by other investigators such as Bieri, 1961; Harvey, Hunt, and Schroder, 1961) was the dimension of cognitive complexity. Although this dimension is typically defined simply in terms of the total number of constructs used by the subject, it has been shown to be related to various aspects of social perception. For example, Bieri (1961) found that cognitively complex subjects showed a greater facility than did cognitively simple subjects in forming an integrated impression of a stimulus person from conflicting descriptive traits. Obviously, the dimension of cognitive complexity would then affect a person's performance in Asch's (1946) traditional studies of impression formation from trait descriptions, and it may account for Steiner and Johnson's (1963) findings with high authoritarians. In other words, the fact that highly authoritarian people seem to be cognitively simpler than low authoritarians (illustrated by their relative insensitivity to others' characteristics) may account for their social perception inaccuracy as much as do their fears and projection.

We have chosen the examples of authoritarianism and cognitive complexity to illustrate the fact that a person's enduring personality characteristics can distort social perception. But these are by no means the only examples. Other relatively enduring influences on social perception would be the level of the perceiver's *dogmatism* or closed-mindedness (Rokeach, 1960), locus of control (Rotter, 1966), and Machiavellianism (Christie and Geis, 1970). We shall return to the last characteristic in Chapter Eleven; here it is sufficient to note that any of the three can affect social perception. A dogmatic person is not likely to look beyond the surface of another's apparent characteristics to see what the person is really like ("my mind is made up—don't confuse me with the facts"). A perceiver who believes that he or she has personal control over important events (a belief in *internal control*) will view another's actions in more personal terms than will a perceiver who believes that the environment, or fate, is the force behind events (a belief in *external control*). Finally, a person high in Machiavellianism is more likely to see other people simply as objects to be manipulated. In these and other ways, a perceiver's personality can adversely affect his or her judgment of other people.

Effects of Motivation

The perceiver's more transient motivation and personal needs, as well as relatively stable personality dispositions, can affect his or her opinion of a stimulus person. Remember that the perception of another person is a *constructive* process which occurs in the context of the other stimulation (the *field*) present at the same time. How the perceiver feels, what he or she thinks about the world, and his or her temporary motives should all be represented in this field and should, therefore, affect the veridicality of the perceiver's social perception. This distortion would most probably not occur for all stimuli, but only for those relevant to the temporary activity in the field.

Although there have been numerous studies that illustrate the interaction between motivation and perception, perhaps the most influential and controversial group is the series of experiments that in the 1940s constituted a "New Look" in perception. In his comprehensive review of this research, Allport (1955) grouped these studies into six broad categories, according to the presumed source of the motivational influence: (1) bodily needs (Levine, Chein, and Murphy, 1942); (2) reward and punishment (Proshansky and Murphy, 1942; Schafer and Murphy, 1943); (3) the personal values of the perceiver (Postman, Bruner, and McGinnies, 1948); (4) the monetary value of the stimulus object (Ashley, Harper, and Runyon, 1951; Bruner and Goodman, 1947; Bruner and Postman, 1948; Lambert, Solomon, and Watson, 1949); (5) the personality characteristics of the perceiver (Cattell and Wenig, 1952; Thurstone, 1944); and (6) the potentially threatening nature of the perceptual judgment to be made (McGinnies, 1949). There were important methodological critiques of most of these experiments, and Allport (1955) correctly concludes that the evidence for these particular propositions is only partially favorable. As a consequence, we shall consider in detail only the sixth category, because of its impact on the study of motivated distortion of perception.

The fundamental idea in this category is that threat from the stimulus (situation or person) can influence the perceiver's judgment in such a way that even the perceiver will be unaware that the influence has taken place. Without knowing it, the perceiver will protect himself or herself against the threatening aspects of the stimulus, engaging in perceptual defense. According to Allport (1955), perceptual defense presented the most formidable theoretical difficulties posed by any of the New Look studies at the same time that it was "the winner of all honors for revolutionary outlook" (p. 321). Although people were just becoming accustomed to the psychoanalytic mechanisms of repression, wish-fulfillment, projection, and rationalization —all of which produce distortions in cognition and/or perception— the idea that such motivational influences could affect college students looking at words in a tachistoscope was difficult to grasp.

Suppose that you had been a subject in this revolutionary experiment. You would have arrived at the experimental laboratory, and after some introductory remarks by the experimenter you would have been seated at a tachistoscope, a piece of apparatus which presents visual stimuli with precise controls for level of illumination and duration of display. Then you would have looked into the screen of the tachistoscope, where a series of words would have been presented, one at a time. The first time that each word was presented, it would have been for such a short time that you would not have been able to identify what it was (you were supposed to guess, even if you were not sure). Gradually the presentation duration would have been increased by the experimenter until you correctly identified the word presented. The duration of exposure necessary for you to make a correct report would have been your score for that word.

What the subjects in this experiment were *not* told was that some of the words in the list were neutral ones (such as *apple, child,* and *danced*), while others were critical ones (such as *bitch, whore,* and *raped*). By today's standards these certainly do not seem like "critical" words that subjects would hesitate to report, but that was a different time. McGinnies (1949) found that greater exposure times were required for the correct report of critical words; that the pre-recognition guesses of those words were nonsense, while the pre-recognition guesses of the neutral words were structurally similar to the real word; and that a physiological measure of arousal during prerecognition showed greater arousal for the critical words than for the neutral ones. From these results McGinnies concluded that the critical words were threatening, and that to defend against this threat *the perceivers had tried not to perceive them* (hence the name perceptual defense).

As critics of perceptual defense were quick to point out (e.g., Hochberg and Gleitman, 1950; Howes and Solomon, 1950), the idea has a certain homunculus quality to it: for perceptual defense to operate as McGinnies suggested it did, there would have to be a little miniperceiver in your head who perceived things before you did and screened out what he thought was going to be threatening to you. Particularly when considered with some of the methodological problems in McGinnies's experiment, such as lack of control for the frequency of occurrence of the critical words in natural language (as opposed to written material), the preperception screening explanation was generally unconvincing. Much more plausible was the idea that there was delay not in *perceiving* the critical words, but rather in *reporting* them to the experimenter. From what we know of evaluation apprehension (Rosenberg, 1965) we can well imagine that the subjects were reluctant to report potentially embarrassing words until they were certain of them. There is still some disagreement about the prevalence of motivated distortions in perception, and the mechanisms involved in these distortions remain unclear, but the basic idea that motivation can influence perception is well accepted today (Eriksen and Eriksen, 1971). Particularly as the stimulus situation becomes more ambiguous and as the perceiver's motivation increases, social perception may be increasingly affected by motivational factors. We shall return to this interaction between perception and motivation in the last section of the chapter.

Effects of Expectations

Implicit Personality Theory

We have seen that because of the perceiver's active participation in social perception, the resulting percept can be affected by the perceiver's relatively enduring personality dispositions and by his or her more temporary personal needs and motives. A final major source of perceiver inaccuracy is the set of expectations that the perceiver holds about the behavior and personality traits of other people. For example, what personality traits are thought to go together? Will a gentle, kind person also be thought sincere? And what is the nature of the relationship among these traits? Is the relationship reflexive—if an unpredictable person is considered dangerous, will a dangerous person be considered unpredictable?—or is the relationship not reflexive (with dangerousness not necessarily implying unpredictability)? This set of expectations about which personality traits will be mutually associated is referred to as the perceiver's *implicit personality theory* (Bruner and Taguiri, 1954).

The perceiver's implicit theory of personality differs from what we have called an "implicit theory of social psychology" because it is primarily concerned with the covariation among personality traits, rather than with the covariation between social behavior and the personal/situational determinants of that behavior. More importantly, a perceiver's implicit theory of personality should be distinguished from a set of personal constructs as described by Kelly (1955, 1963). The implicit personality theory represents the perceiver's view of which traits covary in *other* people, while personal constructs represent what these traits mean *to the perceiver*. For an individual perceiver to report that kindness, gentleness, and sincerity are correlated with each other (his or her implicit personality theory) does not tell us what the perceiver *means* by any of those adjectives (his or her personal constructs). A particular adjective is defined (in personal construct terms) more by its *opposite* than by the other adjectives with which it is associated. For example, a perceiver who says that the opposite of sincerity is "glibness" uses the word in a manner different from the perceiver who says that its opposite is "untrustworthiness."

Measurement of Implicit Personality Theory

Suppose that you were interested in measuring the implicit personality theories held by some of your friends. Your first task would be to obtain from your friends a list of trait covariations, and your second

task would be to interpret those covariations in terms of some accepted scaling methods. The list of covariations to be interpreted
could be constructed in any of several ways, depending upon your
research goal. If you wanted to see what your friends *had in common,* you might choose a *correlational* method (Wishner, 1960), a
trait implication method (Bruner, Shapiro, and Taguiri, 1958), or a
peer-nomination method (Norman, 1963; Passini and Norman, 1966).
If, on the other hand, you were primarily interested in the unique
characteristics of one individual's implicit personality theory, you
might employ one of the *naturalistic,* or free-response methods
(Hastorf, Richardson, and Dornbusch, 1958; Rosenberg and Sedlak,
1972). Let us briefly consider what is involved in the general methods.
(For a more thorough discussion of measurement techniques the
reader is referred to Hastorf, Schneider, and Polefka, 1970; Rosenberg
and Sedlak, 1972; and Warr and Knapper, 1968.)

CORRELATIONAL METHODS FOR INDIVIDUAL PERCEIVERS. Beginning with the *correlational* method, you would provide each of your
friends with the same list of stimulus persons (people all your friends
would be equally acquainted with, such as some of your mutual acquaintances, some of your college professors, or even some public
figures whom all of you know only by reputation). Then you would
ask each of your friends to rate each stimulus person on a series of
rating scales such as the following:

good	:	7	:	6	:	5	:	4	:	3	:	2	:	1	:	bad
weak	:	1	:	2	:	3	:	4	:	5	:	6	:	7	:	strong

A similar seven-point scale would be provided for every adjective pair
you chose to include. Each of your subjects would be instructed to
place a mark on each scale in the division that best represents his or
her estimate of the stimulus person. Every scale consists of a pair of
bipolar adjectives (which are presumably psychological antonyms),
and the scale follows the format of the **semantic differential** (Osgood,
Suci, and Tannenbaum, 1957). The semantic differential is a method
designed to permit the measurement of the connotative meaning of
any stimulus, whether that stimulus is a concrete object, a person,
or an abstract concept such as "freedom." The semantic differential
will be described more fully in Chapter Five; for now it is sufficient
to point out that the subject's placement of a mark will correspond to
a numerical score for the adjective pair. Although these numbers do
not usually appear on the forms actually given to subjects, they are
typically arranged as shown in the example, with higher numbers
indicating more of the positively valued element of the adjective
pair.

When each of your subjects has completed the task, you will have a rating on each scale for every stimulus person, for each subject. An example is shown in Table 4-1, which includes the ratings on two dimensions for each of four hypothetical stimulus persons—a politician, a professor, an acquaintance of yours, and a friend of yours—made by each of five subjects. A variety of scores can be computed from these forty ratings, depending upon your particular interest. The first thing you might wonder is whether the two rating dimensions covary for a *single* subject; in the proper statistical terms, are the rating dimensions *correlated* with each other? Look first at the ratings made by Subject #1. As this person's rating on the dimension of good-bad increases across stimulus persons, the rating of strong-weak also increases. In fact, for this subject the two ratings are identical, and represent a *perfect positive correlation* between the two sets of scores. If we compute the statistical measure of this association, the correlation coefficient (represented by the symbol r), we find that the value of $r = +1.00$ (as shown in Table 4-1).

In the case of Subject #2, the correlation is positive (the scores vary in the same direction, with one set increasing as the other increases) and quite high ($r = +.95$), but the correlation is not a perfect one. Subject #3 has scores on the good-bad dimension that are *independent of* the scores on the strong-weak dimension, since the correlation between his two sets of scores is zero. As we shall see in Chapter Five, this is the more typical case with the two dimensions used in the example: Osgood, Suci, and Tannenbaum (1957) have shown that in the ratings of most concepts the *evaluative* dimension (good-bad) is relatively independent of the *potency* dimension (strong-weak), and this independence probably holds fairly well for the judgment of stimulus persons. Finally, the scores for Subject #4 and Subject #5 show that the correlation between two variables can be a *negative* one, with the numerical scores on one variable decreasing as the numerical scores on the other variable increase. Once again, these negative correlations can have different values for r, this time ranging from zero to -1.00 (a perfect negative correlation).

To return to the issue of implicit personality theory, we might say that Subjects #1 and #2 share an implicit personality theory which states that goodness and strength are positively correlated: the "better" a person is, the more likely the person is also to be "strong." In contrast, Subjects #4 and #5 share an opposite implicit personality theory. For both of these subjects it is "better" to be "weak." And finally, in Subject #3's implicit personality theory strength and goodness are independent.

It is important to point out that a correlation between two personality ratings (or any two variables) tells us only that the two vari-

TABLE 4-1
Trait ratings on two dimensions for four hypothetical stimulus persons

SUBJECT AND DIMENSION	HYPOTHETICAL STIMULUS PERSONS				SUBJECT'S MEAN RATING	CORRELATION BETWEEN DIMENSIONS
	POLITICIAN	PROFESSOR	ACQUAINTANCE	FRIEND		
Subject #1						
good-bad	1	3	5	7	4.0	
strong-weak	1	3	5	7	4.0	+1.00
Subject #2						
good-bad	1	2	5	6	3.5	
strong-weak	4	5	6	7	5.5	+ .95
Subject #3						
good-bad	1	2	6	7	4.0	
strong-weak	5	3	3	5	4.0	0.00
Subject #4						
good-bad	1	2	3	4	2.5	
strong-weak	6	4	3	1	3.5	− .96
Subject #5						
good-bad	1	3	5	7	4.0	
strong-weak	7	5	3	1	4.0	−1.00
Mean Rating for Each Stimulus Person (M)						
good-bad	1.0	2.4	4.8	6.2		
strong-weak	4.6	4.0	4.0	4.2		+ .05

ables are associated. It does not identify the cause of the association. For example, there are three logically possible causes of the positive correlations found for Subjects #1 and #2. First, the perceiver's rating of strength might have been caused by his or her view of goodness (a psychological implication that could be characterized as "right makes might"). A second possibility is the reverse—a stimulus person's goodness is determined by strength ("might makes right"). The third possibility is that both the rating of strength and the rating of goodness are the product of the perceiver's ideas about *something else* not measured by these two particular ratings. Because there are these three possible reasons for the association between any two variables, *we cannot infer causality from correlation.*

CORRELATIONAL METHODS FOR PERCEIVERS IN GENERAL. We have seen that the data in Table 4-1 can be used to assess the implicit personality theories of individual perceivers. A second question that can be dealt with using those data is the broader one, "To what extent do the implicit personality theories of people in general suggest a relationship between strength and goodness?" To answer this question you would combine the ratings made by all of your subjects, in effect (though not in actual statistical procedure) *averaging* the ratings on each dimension across your five subjects.

To give you an indication of what this overall correlation would show, the mean scores on both rating dimensions appear at the bottom of Table 4-1. These scores, averaged over subjects, show that the evaluation of stimulus persons on the good-bad dimension increases from the Politician to the Friend, while the estimate of strength does not vary greatly from one stimulus person to another. And, not surprisingly, the overall correlation coefficient is virtually zero ($r = +.05$). From this overall lack of correlation we conclude that there is no generally shared implicit personality theory regarding the relationship between strength and goodness. Of course, in our example the absence of an overall correlation is the result of the positive correlations of subjects #1 and #2 canceling out the negative correlations of Subjects #4 and #5. This is an unusual situation, since in most cases in which there is no overall correlation, individual subjects also show no significant correlations. Despite the unusual quality of the individual subject correlations in our example, it is still fair to conclude that there is no generally shared expectation about the relationship between strength and goodness.

In the usual study of implicit personality theory, researchers include many more than two rating dimensions, from a minimum of 15 or 20 to a maximum of more than 100. In such cases there would be a separate correlation coefficient for *every possible pair* of rating dimensions, and each of these correlation coefficients would have a value anywhere between +1.00 and −1.00. The complete set of correlations form what is known as a correlation matrix, and such a matrix is shown in Table 4-2 for some of the adjectives used by Asch (1946). The correlations in this matrix are hypothetical and were chosen to illustrate the "centrality" of the warm-cold variable. You will notice that typically only the correlations in the upper half of the table are printed, because those in the lower half would be the same (e.g., the correlation between warm-intelligent is identical to the correlation between intelligent-warm). In addition, since the correlation of every variable with itself must be +1.00 (as illustrated by warm-warm), these values usually are omitted as well. If warm-cold is a central organizing trait, then the average correlation between warm and other variables should be higher than the average correlations among the remainder of the variables, and the scores in the table were chosen with this in mind. Indeed, the analysis by Wishner (1960) suggests that average intercorrelation might be a useful measure of the centrality of a trait.

THE TRAIT IMPLICATION METHOD. The trait intercorrelations that form the basis for the study of general implicit personality theory are usually obtained through correlational procedures, but they can also be gathered through the trait implication method of assessment (Bruner, Shapiro, and Taguiri, 1958). In this method, instead of presenting your subjects with a set of particular stimulus persons—politician, professor, acquaintance, and friend—you would just use an unidentified "person." And instead of asking your subjects to rate that person on a series of scales, you would attempt a direct measure of the subject's belief that the presence of one trait *implies* the presence of another. For example, you would say to the subject, "A person is 'good.' To what extent is such a person also likely to be 'strong'?" What you have done is increase the structure inherent in the subject's task. You have provided what Warr and Knapper (1968) call a *cue trait*, and have asked for the extent to which that cue trait implies the presence of a particular *response trait*.

The trait implication method provides somewhat more precise information than does the correlational method, because it permits measurement of the direction of causality. Remember that a correlation between two traits may be the result of one "causing" the other, the other "causing" the one, or both being "caused" by some third (and unidentified) aspect of the perceiver's implicit personality theory. The trait implication method permits the researcher to distinguish among these possibilities. For example, Warr and Knapper (1968) have found that a cue trait of "cynicism" will imply (among other things) a response trait of "precision," but that the reverse is *not*

TABLE 4-2
Hypothetical intercorrelations between adjectives used in Asch's (1946) study of central organizing traits

	WARM	INTELLIGENT	INDUSTRIOUS	PRACTICAL	DETERMINED	CAUTIOUS
WARM	+1.00	.75	.50	.50	.35	.40
INTELLIGENT		—	.40	.50	.30	.10
INDUSTRIOUS			—	.35	.35	.10
PRACTICAL				—	.65	.05
DETERMINED					—	.25
CAUTIOUS						—

true. In short, your knowledge that a person is cynical may cause you to evaluate that person as precise, but your knowledge that a person is precise tells you nothing about whether the person is also cynical. For this reason, the trait implication method is preferable if you are interested in the *structural* relationships among elements of an implicit personality theory.

THE PEER NOMINATION METHOD. The third method for measuring a generalized implicit personality theory is the peer nomination method, and this procedure was used by Passini and Norman (1966) in their demonstration of just how generalized some aspects of implicit personality theory can be. Peer nomination proceeds in the opposite direction from methods we have considered so far: the subjects are given the rating dimensions (e.g., good-bad, weak-strong, active-passive) and are asked to *nominate* stimulus persons who represent each pole of each dimension. For instance, in a group of six subjects, each subject would be asked to identify secretly to the experimenter one-third of the group (two persons, excluding that subject) who best represented the "active" end of the scale, and another two who best represented the "passive" end of the scale. This nomination procedure would be followed for every one of the rating dimensions to be included.

Thus, for a dimension like active-passive, the subject's task would simply be to decide who were the two "most active" people and who were the two "least active" people in the group. You can imagine that this would be a relatively easy task, especially for people who knew each other well—no complicated rating scales, just a dichotomous judgment. In fact, such a judgment might not be too difficult even for people who did not know each other well as long as they had had some previous interaction with each other. Before beginning their study, Passini and Norman reviewed previous research using the peer nomination technique (e.g., Norman, 1963; Tupes and Christal, 1958). They noted that factor analyses of the ratings obtained in these studies showed a remarkable consistency across studies, even though the participants in one study had been acquainted for as long as three years, while the participants in another had been acquainted only for as short a period as three days. In either case a factor analysis revealed five major clusters of ratings: extroversion (talkativeness, openness), agreeableness, conscientiousness, emotional stability, and degree of culture (refined, artistically sensitive, polished).

From this similarity of factor structure Passini and Norman concluded that the important variable was not the *length* of interaction, but rather the *fact* of interaction. To test this idea they performed a peer nomination study using students on the first day of an experimental psychology class before the students had had the opportunity for any interaction with each other whatsoever. They predicted that under these circumstances the regularity in the ratings would disappear. The results were a surprise. The same five-factor structure was found in these unacquainted subjects. Apparently the peer nomination procedure measures the *implicit personality theories* of the raters rather than the true characteristics of the stimulus persons, and this generalized implicit personality theory includes the five factors.

The expectations for others' behavior represented by a perceiver's implicit personality theory can adversely affect the accuracy of interpersonal judgment in at least two major ways. First, to the extent that perceivers share the sort of implicit personality theory discovered by Passini and Norman, they may overlook other aspects of the stimulus person's behavior. Indeed, the fact that a perceiver with as much as three years' experience evaluates a stimulus person similarly to a perceiver with no prior experience with the stimulus person indicates that there is little increase in interpersonal sensitivity over time. Second, to the extent that the perceiver's implicit personality theory is a unique record of his or her own experience and values rather than a set of shared judgments, the perceiver may not view the social situation in the same terms that others (the stimulus person, for example) do. In both of these cases, what the perceiver reports to us may tell us as much about the perceiver as it does about the stimulus person.

When the potential for inaccuracy in social perception that arises from implicit personality theories is combined with the potential for error based on the perceiver's personality and motivation, it is a bit surprising that social perception is as accurate as it appears to be. We now conclude the chapter by discussing models that describe how the perceiver might integrate into a complete impression all the information received about a stimulus person, and how the perceiver might try to understand the stimulus person's motives and reasons for acting.

COGNITIVE THEORIES OF SOCIAL PERCEPTION

If we have learned nothing else from our study of accuracy and error in social perception, we have learned that the process is at least as much *cognitive* as it is *perceptual.* The perceiver constructs social perceptions out of the stimulus information given, categorizes stimulus persons according to their criterial attributes, and interprets social behavior and social situations. Interpersonal accuracy increases with the perceiver's intelligence, cognitive complexity, experience, and empathic ability—all of which affect cognitive processing ability to a much greater extent than they improve sight, hearing, touch, or the efficiency of the central nervous system. But perceivers are not always accurate. As a result of an active interpretation of the social world, the perceiver may make certain kinds of errors. What perceivers look for in other people will be determined in no small degree by their implicit personality theories; what they see will be affected by their own personality traits; and their interpretations of particular social situations may be influenced by their temporary needs or motivational states. But even these errors in social perception reflect the cognitive nature of the process, giving further testimony to the view that social perception is much more than sensation. Thus it is not surprising that the major contemporary models of social perception—information integration theory and attribution theory—are fundamentally cognitive in nature. Although there have been recent attempts to integrate the two theoretical positions (Anderson, 1974), we shall consider the two separately because of important differences in their focus. Information integration theory deals primarily with the way in which a perceiver combines bits of information about a stimulus person into a unified impression of the person, so its major focus is the beginning of the constructive process. In contrast, attribution theory attempts to explain how the perceiver gives meaning to an impression by searching for the *causes* of the stimulus person's behavior.

Information Integration Theory: Formation of Impressions

Ever since Asch's (1946) pioneering study of the formation of social impressions from descriptive adjectives, social psychologists have tried to specify just how these adjectives might be combined by the perceivers. Are some traits more central than others, and if so, how could that difference be represented? Does the order of presentation of the adjectives produce differences in the final impression (such as primacy effects), and how could those differences be accounted for? How can the process of impression formation be described, and can its final product be related to the perceiver's future behavior toward the stimulus person? One recent development that may hold an answer to many of these questions is the program of research by Anderson and his associates (e.g., Anderson, 1965, 1968, 1974; Anderson and Barrios, 1961; Anderson and Hubert, 1963; Kaplan and Anderson, 1973; Leon, Oden, and Anderson, 1973) on an information integration theory of impression formation.

The Mathematical Model

The core of information integration theory is a mathematical model of the impression formation process, and this mathematical model describes how descriptive adjectives might be *integrated* into a final impression of a stimulus person. Suppose that we reconsider Asch's original descriptive adjectives—warm (or cold), intelligent, skillful, practical, cautious—and ask how these might be combined into a final impression. We have already seen, from Asch's work and from the later work of Kelley (1950), that the perceiver's final impression differs depending upon whether we use the word "warm" or the word "cold." The entire group of adjectives presented to the subject is called the *set*, and each adjective is an *element* of that set. An important distinction can be drawn between possible models of impression formation on the basis of the way these elements are thought to combine.

If, as Asch (1946) suggested, the central trait alters the final impression by changing the meaning of every other element in the set, then the most appropriate model would be one which specified a *multiplicative* relationship between elements of the set:

$$\text{Impression} = \frac{\text{Positivity of}}{\text{Central Trait}} \times \frac{\text{Positivity of Every}}{\text{Other Element}}$$

For example, "cautious" multiplied by "warm" might appear to the perceiver to be twice as positive as "cautious" multiplied by "cold." This multiplicative relationship would, of course, have to hold for every element of the adjective set. If, on the other hand, changing the central trait alters the final impression without necessarily changing the meaning of every other element in the set, then a different sort of model would be more appropriate. One such alternative would be a linear model which predicts a final impression determined by the addition of stimulus elements:

$$\text{Impression} = \text{Sum of the Elements}$$

For example, the noncentral elements might be added together (intelligent + skillful + practical + cautious) to create a sum representing the impression, and this sum would then be either dramatically increased by adding "warm" or dramatically decreased by subtracting "cold."

As this example indicates, however, simple addition of elements is not a complete description of the process. How can we take into account the dramatic effect of the central trait (either warm or cold) on the overall impression and the smaller individual effects of the other elements? We can provide for this discrepancy by building into the model the possibility that the perceiver might give different weights to the different stimulus elements. In other words, we can consider each descriptive adjective to have *two* characteristics: first, the adjective will have a *scale value* (a numerical score indicating the adjective's positivity or likableness), and second, it will have its own *weight* (some estimate of its contribution to the perceiver's impression). Intuitively it is simplest to think of an adjective's weight as representing the proportion that the adjective contributes to the final impression, and this can be accomplished by requiring that the weights sum to 1.00. Considering both the element's scale value and its weight, and requiring that the sum of the weights be 1.00, the linear model of information integration holds that the

$$\text{Impression} = \sum s_i W_i$$

where s_i = scale value of the *i*th adjective in the set and W_i = a normalized weight for the *i*th adjective, created by dividing the weight for the adjective, w_i, by the sum of all of the weights.

Application of the Model

Table 4-3 shows how the adjectives from Asch's research could be combined into a final impression of the stimulus person, using arbitrary scale values and weights for the purposes of illustration. The table contains two sets of adjectives, one with the central element "warm," the other with the central element "cold." To represent the power of each of these elements relative to the power of the other elements, the weights of the central trait words are shown as being much greater than the weights of the other adjectives. We can see from this example that substantial differences between the likableness of the two stimulus persons could be produced without having to

TABLE 4-3

Computation of a perceiver's final impression of a stimulus person, using a weighted average model with arbitrary scale values and element weights

STIMULUS ELEMENT (ADJECTIVE)	SCALE VALUE (s_i)	ELEMENT WEIGHT (W_i)	VALUE × WEIGHT $(s_i W_i)$
Set 1: With "warm"			
Warm	6.0	.60	3.60
Intelligent	5.0	.10	.50
Skillful	5.0	.10	.50
Practical	4.0	.10	.40
Cautious	3.0	.10	.30
		Likableness of Final Impression =	5.30
Set 2: With "cold"			
Cold	1.0	.60	.60
Intelligent	5.0	.10	.50
Skillful	5.0	.10	.50
Practical	4.0	.10	.40
Cautious	3.0	.10	.30
		Likableness of Final Impression =	2.30

assume that the central traits change the meaning of the other elements of the stimulus set.

Although the data in Table 4-3 were specifically chosen to illustrate the computation of a predicted impression through the method of weighted averaging, they may not be too far off the mark as a representation of the phenomenon of central traits as well. Perceivers do seem to make impression judgments that correspond to predictions from the weighted averaging formula in Anderson's information integration theory (Anderson, 1974; Hendrick, 1968; Rosenberg, 1968). Furthermore, they do make judgments that involve differential weights in situations as diverse as personality impression formation (Anderson and Jacobson, 1965) and moral evaluation (Leon, Oden, and Anderson, 1973). The latter study showed, for example, that in comparative judgments of criminal offenses, more serious crimes (homicide, rape, and kidnapping) have more extreme scale values than less serious crimes (vagrancy, forgery, bootlegging), and carry more weight as well. And differential weighted averaging is all that is necessary to explain the phenomenon of central organizing traits.

Let us reconsider the questions that began this section. We have seen that central traits could be represented by the weighted averaging linear model of impression formation. The same is true for primacy effects (Anderson and Hubert, 1963), and for the opposite *recency* effects. Certainly the perceived "likableness" of a stimulus person (the typical dependent variable in weighted-averaging studies of impression formation) should be related to the perceiver's behavior toward the stimulus person, so the weighted-averaging model of information integration theory would seem to be applicable here as well.

Lest you conclude that weighted averaging is the only possible explanation for the phenomena of impression formation, a few words of caution are in order. First, there are other models of the process, and there is some controversy over the relative explanatory power of the weighted-averaging formulation as compared to these other models (e.g., Fishbein and Hunter, 1964; Hodges, 1973). Second, there is some disagreement about the degree to which the dependent variable, likableness of the stimulus person, is related to such presumably relevant behavior as interpersonal attraction (e.g., Byrne, Clore, Griffitt, Lamberth, and Mitchell, 1973). Third, there is the more general question of the degree to which a formed impression will be predictive of actual behavior (Rodin, 1972). And finally, the weighted-averaging model is just that—a *model* of the process that has not been observed directly, but rather has been confirmed because of agreement between its predictions and the perceiver's actual impressions. This is not unusual in research on social perception, but it does leave open the possibility that some other model not yet considered will provide an even more convincing explanation. Despite these difficulties, the weighted-averaging model of information integration is the best presently available explanation of how the perceiver might combine the social stimulus information available. We now leave the topic of impression formation to consider what the perceiver might do with impressions once they are formed.

Attribution Theory: The Search for the Causes of Behavior

Just as the information integration theory describes how a perceiver combines information from the social world, attribution theory describes how this knowledge is interpreted. Attribution processes are the cognitive processes through which perceivers interpret the actions of other people (and in some cases their own actions as well). We are not content merely to observe other people; we try to *explain* their past behavior and *predict* their future actions. If we have formed the impression that a stimulus person is "hostile," we do not stop with that impression. We also wonder *why* the person is hostile, and wonder what consequences that hostility might have for us.

Three Stages of Attribution

Whenever we search for the causes of another person's actions, we are engaging in social attribution. Like impression formation, attribution usually occurs too quickly for us to observe it directly, so the theoretical models of attribution typically must be tested indirectly. There is, however, an example of attribution extended through time which, although of limited usefulness in testing theory, does help greatly in our intuitive understanding of the process. This example is a criminal trial, in which a jury (the perceiver) evaluates the *behavior* of a defendant (the stimulus person), and the *circumstances* in which that behavior occurred in order to decide whether to attribute the criminal action either to the defendant (attribution to a personal disposition) or to the circumstances beyond the defendant's control (attribution to the environment or situation). Since the jury's task is extended in time, sometimes over a period of months, we can use it to illustrate the attribution process.

Suppose we sit in the courtroom and observe the trial of a person accused of murdering an acquaintance by shooting the victim with a pistol. As Shaver (1975) has pointed out, there are three basic stages in the attribution process (as shown in Figure 4-1). The first of these is the *observation of action*, either firsthand or through the reports of intermediaries who observed the action themselves. The latter mediation by other people (the witnesses to the shooting) cannot be considered a perfectly accurate representation of the incident, since the witnesses (as perceivers themselves) will be interpreting the action through the filter of their own personalities, expectations, and personal motives. It should be noted that the legal system has, in this instance, not kept pace with the findings of social psychology, because "eyewitness testimony" remains an extremely strong form of evidence, despite experimental evidence against its validity (Buckhout, 1974). In any case, before there can be an attribution, there must be *some* observation that can provide information to the perceiver.

The second stage of the attribution process is the *judgment of intention.* The perceiver must decide that an action was intentionally produced before a valid (veridical) attribution can be made. Involuntary reflexes, routine performances of habitual behavior, and accidental occurrences should not tell us much about the stimulus person's reasons for his or her behavior. If the jury wonders why the defendant shot the victim, and the defense convincingly maintains that the shooting was an *accident,* there will be an acquittal on the charge of murder (but perhaps a conviction for involuntary manslaughter) because an accidental occurrence is by definition an occurrence that was not intended. And, as an unintended occurrence, the accident reveals nothing to us about the defendant's motives. This is not to rule out attribution in the case of what Heider (1958) referred to as *unconscious intentions*—reasons for acting that may be apparent to observers but not consciously recognized by the actor. Indeed, it is because the actions arising from unconscious intentions do *not* appear

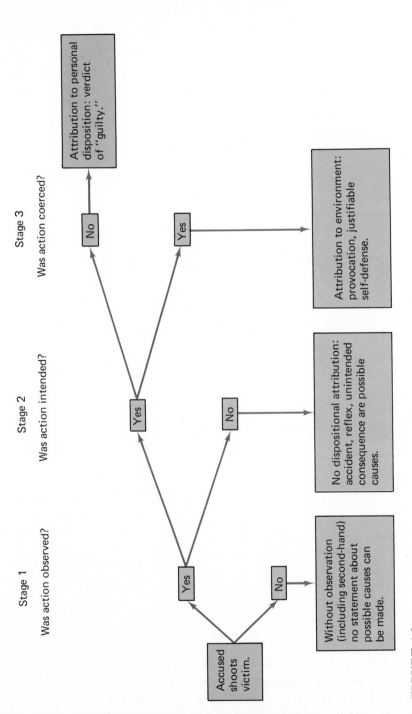

Stage 1

Was action observed?

Stage 2

Was action intended?

Stage 3

Was action coerced?

FIGURE 4-1
Stages of the attribution process. (Adapted from Shaver, 1975)

accidental that perceivers can use those actions as the basis of attributions.

The final link in the chain is the *making of a dispositional attribution*. Having observed the action (or had it reported), and having decided that the action was intentionally produced, the perceiver must now determine what underlying **personal disposition** (a relatively enduring personality or motivational characteristic of the actor) could have led to the intentional action. In the most fundamental sense it is this final judgment that provides an answer to the question "Why?" For our jury there are several possibilities. Assuming that the report of the incident has been shown to be reliable, and that the prosecution has convincingly ruled out an accidental release of the trigger, the jury still has some decisions to make. Did the defendant intentionally pull the trigger because of the threats of a *third* person? If so, this could provide a justification for the action that would relieve the defendant of personal responsibility for the action. (Such a defense of "following orders" was common in the Nuremberg trials of Nazi war criminals, and was also an element in the defense of Lt. William Calley for the My Lai massacre during the Vietnam war.) Did the defendant pull the trigger intentionally but in the heat of rage (what in legal terminology is an "irresistible impulse"), also relieving the defendant of full blame? Or did the defendant not know the difference between right and wrong at the time of the incident (the defense of "temporary insanity," or "diminished responsibility")? In attribution theory terms, the jury must rule out *environmental coercion* and other circumstances presumably beyond the defendant's control, in order to reach a verdict of guilty of murder (an attribution of full personal responsibility).

Theories of Attribution

Most of the social attributions we make do not carry the consequences that accompany the attributions made by juries, and most are made so quickly that the elements of the process are never in full view. But perceivers do make attributions of causality (McArthur, 1972), of ability (Jones, Rock, Shaver, Goethals, and Ward, 1968; Thompson, 1972), of responsibility (Shaw and Sulzer, 1964; Walster, 1966), of emotional state (Nisbett and Valins, 1972), and of motivation (Weiner, 1974), to mention a few. Three major theories—by Heider (1958), Jones and Davis (1965), and Kelley (1967, 1971, 1973)—and a number of theoretical ideas dealing with aspects of the attribution process attempt to account for this aspect of the perceiver's social perception. Our goal here is to summarize the three major theories very briefly, and to present some research that illustrates the attribution approach to social perception. For a more complete discussion of the three theories the reader is referred to Shaver (1975), and for a more thorough review of attribution research to Jones, Kanouse, Kelley, Nisbett, Valins, and Weiner (1972).

"NAIVE" PSYCHOLOGY. Present interest in attribution processes and theory began with the comprehensive and fruitful work of Heider (1958). Trained in the tradition of Gestalt psychology, with its emphasis upon the subjective experience (phenomenology) of the subject, Heider tried to construct a naive psychology of attribution that would explain how we, as ordinary perceivers, try to identify the causes of human action. Shaver (1975) has noted that in Heider's model the perceiver plays a role analogous to that of a *philosopher* who tries to identify the factors that would be logically necessary for action to occur. The actions of a stimulus person are taken at face value, and the perceiver deduces what factors must have been present in order for the action to have occurred. For example, consider the action "building a brick wall." For this action to be successfully completed, the actor must have had the *intention* to build the wall (nobody does that sort of thing by accident), must have *exerted* energy to complete the action (laying bricks is not such an easy task that it "accomplishes itself"), and the actor's *ability* must have been sufficient to overcome the inherent *task difficulty*. This last necessity involves a relationship between an element of personal force (ability) and an element of environmental force (task difficulty): if personal force exceeds the opposing environmental force, the actor *can* accomplish the task, but an actor who does not possess the requisite ability cannot succeed no matter how hard he or she may try.

The relationships among the various factors logically necessary for the production of action can be diagramed as shown in Figure 4-2. The components can be grouped under the general headings of *personal force* and *environmental force*, with personal force first subdivided into ability and the general motivational component Heider calls *trying*. As noted earlier, ability combines with task difficulty to determine the possibility of action, the state Heider refers to as *can*. The general motivational factor of trying is subdivided into the components of intention and exertion, and these (in the presence of *can*) lead to the final action. The degree to which the actor is held responsible for the occurrence of the action will depend on the relative contributions of personal and environmental forces to the final outcome (Shaw and Sulzer, 1964).

CORRESPONDENCE OF INFERENCE. If Heider's ideal perceiver can be considered to be a philosopher, analyzing the actor's behavior to determine the factors logically necessary for that behavior to occur,

FIGURE 4-2
The personal and environmental components of action. (Adapted from Shaver, 1975)

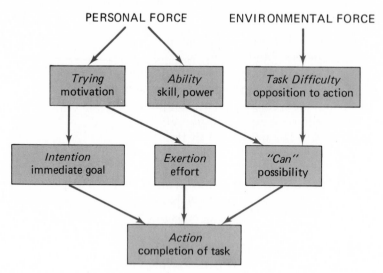

the ideal perceiver in Jones and Davis's (1965) correspondent inference theory can be thought of as an *information processor*. Jones and Davis extend Heider's ideas by suggesting that the perceiver takes into account what the actor *might have done*, as well as what he or she actually did. All behavior is conceived of as involving choices by the actor, even if the choice is between action and inaction, and the choices an actor makes can reveal his or her personal dispositions. For example, let us suppose that you have two choices right now: continuing to read your assignment in this book or beginning to read a bestselling novel.

Each of those choices has certain *effects* for you: continuing to read this book will have the effects of finishing your assignment, tiring your eyes, and perhaps boring you a bit. On the other hand, beginning a bestselling novel will have the effects of making you sound well read in your informal conversations with your friends, tiring your eyes, and holding your attention and interest. Notice that one of these effects (tiring your eyes) is common to both choices. Jones and Davis suggest that this common effect is of no attributional value: an effect you produce by either action tells us nothing about why you choose between the two actions. On the other hand, each choice has two noncommon effects, effects not produced by the other action. If you read this book you might be bored (a negative effect), but you would finish your assignment (a positive effect). If you choose to read the novel you would be interested (a positive effect) and you would sound well read to your friends (another positive effect).

Jones and Davis argue that the number of noncommon effects produced by a choice, and the *assumed desirability* of those noncommon effects, can be used by the perceiver to understand the actor's reasons for making one choice as opposed to another. More importantly, the number of noncommon effects and the desirability of those effects influence the perceiver's *certainty* about the attribution he or she makes. The nature of this influence is shown in Figure 4-3. When the number of noncommon effects is large (when there are a great many different effects produced by an action), any attribution by the perceiver is going to be ambiguous, as indicated by the first row of the figure. In contrast, when the number of noncommon effects is low, we can be relatively certain of the reasons for the choice, as indicated by the second row. When the noncommon effects are highly desirable, they tell us only that any person placed in the situation would respond in the same manner. Highly desirable effects (an environmental influence on behavior) do not reveal anything of interest about the personal dispositions of the actor, as indicated by the "trivial" in the first column of the figure. On the other hand, when the assumed desirability of the effects is *low*, we assume that the person made that particular choice because of some interesting *personal* disposition.

The conjunction of low number of noncommon effects and low desirability of those effects is the condition Jones and Davis refer to as high correspondence of inference. This means that the perceiver's inference about the actor is most likely to correspond to the underlying personal disposition that actually prompted the choice by the actor. High correspondence is a measure of the perceiver's certainty about the causal role of the personal disposition and is most likely to be obtained when the actor's behavior disagrees with what most people would have done in the situation (Jones, Davis, and Gergen, 1961;

FIGURE 4-3
The determination of correspondence of inference from the number and assumed desirability of the noncommon effects of action. (Adapted from Jones and Davis, 1965, p. 229)

| | | Assumed Desirability of Effects | |
		High	Low
Number of Noncommon Effects	High	Trivial ambiguity	Intriguing ambiguity
	Low	Trivial clarity	High correspondence

Messick and Reeder, 1974). Specific tests of the informational value of noncommon effects (Newtson, 1974) and assumed desirability (Ajzen, 1971) have produced results consistent with the correspondent inference model, as have other studies more generally related to the idea of correspondence (Jones and Harris, 1967; Jones, Worchel, Goethals, and Grumet, 1971; Snyder and Jones, 1974).

THE PRINCIPLE OF COVARIATION. The third major theory of attribution is that of Harold Kelley (1967, 1971, 1973)—not to be confused with the personal construct theory of George Kelly (1955, 1963). Like correspondent inference theory, Kelley's attribution theory borrows heavily from Heider's (1958) original work in the area, but where Jones and Davis concentrate on the link between an intentional action and the actor's underlying personal dispositions, Kelley concentrates on the distinction between attribution to the actor and attribution to the environment. Kelley's theory embodies the analogy we have repeatedly made between social perception and social psychological research: his ideal perceiver can be likened to a *social scientist* conducting a series of perceptual experiments. The fundamental principle in Kelley's theory is that of covariation: an effect will be attributed to the presumed cause which is present when the effect is present and absent when the effect is also absent.

Suppose, for example, that you have an internal feeling of pleasure when you see a new film with a group of friends right after your last examination of the term. To what will you attribute this feeling of pleasure? Specifically, will you attribute your reaction to the film (what Kelley calls the *entity*), or will you attribute your reaction to the circumstances of good friends and the end of an exam period (referred to as the *time* and *modality*) under which the film was seen? Just as the social psychologist will attempt to verify a particular theory by testing it under a variety of conditions, Kelley argues that the perceiver will sample various entities and times, and compare his or her reactions with the reactions of other persons in order to arrive at an attribution. The theory can be summarized in terms of the three-dimensional model shown in Figure 4-4. One dimension is the dimension of Entities, in this case representing the particular film in question (New Film) and several other films you have seen previously (Other Film #1, Other Film #2). The second dimension (Time/Modality) represents the particular circumstances under which it is possible to see films (After Exam, During Vacation at Home, On Television). The third dimension of the model (Persons) includes both you (Self) and others with whom you can compare reactions (Friend, Acquaintance).

What attributional criteria are involved in an attribution of your pleasure to the particular entity as opposed to something else? Kelley

FIGURE 4-4
Attributional data table representing an attribution of
likability (L) to an entity (New Film) by all observers under
all circumstances. (Adapted from Kelley, 1967)

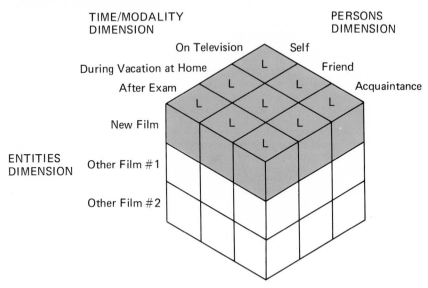

suggests that at first your reaction to the particular entity must be *distinctive.* If you are a "film nut," liking virtually all the films you see (bad ones as well as good ones), your reaction to this particular film is not distinctive. But if there are some films you do not enjoy, and if your reaction to this one is somehow special, then the criterion of distinctiveness has been met, and you can move on to another dimension.

The second attributional question you ask yourself is, "Was it just because exams were finally over, or would I feel the same way about the film under different circumstances?" If your reaction to the film were the same when you saw it at home during vacation, or later when you saw it again on television, Kelley would say that your reaction was *consistent* across circumstances, and the fact of this consistency would increase your certainty that the attribution of pleasure should be made to the film.

Finally, just to check the possibility that your feelings might be unique for some reason, you could compare your reaction to the film with the reactions of other persons. If a close friend and even a casual acquaintance also liked the film, the attributional criterion of *consensus* has been met, and you can conclude with some assurance that your reaction is *attributable* to the film. Your distinctive reaction has been the same over different circumstances, and a similar reaction has been felt by other people. As Figure 4-4 shows, there is a virtual "slice" of liking (L) for the film. Although the principles of Kelley's theory have not yet been thoroughly tested, presently available studies (e.g., Kelley and Stahelski, 1970; McArthur, 1972) suggest that the theory may provide a good model of the attribution process.

The process of attribution is basically a rational attempt by the perceiver to make sense out of his or her social world, and out of the actions of other people. Whether the perceiver is thought of as a philosopher, an information processor, or a social scientist, his or her basic task remains the explanation and prediction of social behavior. It should be emphasized that although these distinctions about the ideal perceiver illustrate differences in theoretical focus, they do not represent fundamental theoretical incompatibility. As Shaver (1975) has noted, each of the later theories borrows heavily from Heider, and the most comprehensive attribution theory would necessarily include elements of all three approaches. A thorough understanding of attribution requires consideration of situational variation and consensus, study of the elements of action, and knowledge of the process of inference.

Distortion in Attribution

Finally, it should be noted that even the fundamentally rational process of attribution can be affected by the perceiver's personality, expectations, and personal motives. For example, Sosis (1974) found that subjects who scored on the internal end of Rotter's (1966) Internal-External Locus of Control scale attributed more responsibility to an automobile driver who caused a serious accident than did subjects who scored on the external end of the scale. Apparently, if you believe that you have control over the important events in your own life, you expect others to have the same degree of control over theirs. In the area of expectancies for others' behavior, Jones, Worchel, Goethals, and Grumet (1971) found that if subjects were told that a stimulus person favored individual autonomy in life style (leading to an expectation that the stimulus person would be for decriminalization of marijuana) and then read an essay on marijuana laws ostensibly written by the stimulus person, their attributions of his true attitude were more extreme when the essay agreed with their expectancies than when it did not.

Among the personal motives that can distort rational attribution are a **need to believe in a just world** (Lerner, 1966; Lerner and Matthews, 1967) in which people get what they deserve and deserve what they get. Lerner and Matthews found that subjects would derogate a victim who was suffering through no fault of her own, making their evaluations of her personal worth correspond to the negative experiences she was having. A related attributional distortion is a self-protective tendency called **defensive attribution** (Shaver, 1970), which leads to a denial of responsibility for actions with negative consequences. This defensive attribution occurs when the perceiver believes both that he or she might sometime be in circumstances like those affecting the stimulus person, and that he or she is personally similar to that person (and hence would make the same mistakes). To protect himself or herself from the implication of future blame in a similar situation the perceiver relieves the stimulus person of responsibility for the mishap (Chaikin and Darley, 1973; Shaver, 1970; Sorrentino and Boutilier, 1974).

Thus we see that attribution, like other processes of social perception, can be affected by the active involvement of the perceiver. Under most circumstances perceivers are accurate in their impressions of others, and logical in their interpretations of behavior. But the fact that social perception is a cognitive process undertaken by a perceiver who has a distinctive personality, a particular implicit theory of the personality of others, and a unique set of personal motives can sometimes lead to distortion and error. It will be valuable in subsequent chapters to remember that individuals' social behavior is determined by social reality as seen through their own not-always-rose-colored glasses.

Summary

The perceiver is an active participant in the process of social perception, and at best can be quite accurate. This accuracy increases with increasing breadth of personal experience, intelligence, self-insight, social skill and adjustment, and cognitive complexity. But judgmental accuracy is extremely difficult to measure, and traditional methods for obtaining estimates of accuracy were really measuring four basic components: elevation, differential elevation, stereotype accuracy, and **differential accuracy** (p. 133). In addition, the perceiver's very involvement can produce various sorts of error and distortion in social perception. These include enduring personal dispositions such as **authoritarianism** (p. 136), dogmatism (p. 138), **locus of control** (p. 138), and **Machiavellianism** (p. 138), and ways of looking at the world through individualized sets of **personal constructs** (p. 137). Not only the perceiver's stable dispositions, but also motivation and *implicit personality theory* (p. 141), can affect the veridicality of his or her social perception.

Most of the recent research on social perception has concentrated more on describing the process (p. 135) as it presumably occurs than on describing the accuracy of the outcome. The way that a perceiver combines bits of information about a stimulus person into a unified impression can be described by the weighted-averaging model of information integration theory (p. 150). The way that the perceiver interprets the behavior of others can be described by models of the attribution process (p. 153), which requires the observation of action, the judgment of intention, and the making of dispositional attributions. These attributions may involve judgments about the relative contributions to action of *personal force* (p. 157) and *environmental force* (p. 157); judgments of the number and *assumed desirability* (p. 159) of the noncommon effects (p. 158) of action; and estimates of the covariation (p. 160) between effects and potential causes.

Suggested Additional Readings

ANDERSON, N. H. Cognitive algebra: Integration theory applied to social attribution. In L. Berkowitz (Ed.) *Advances in experimental social psychology.* Vol. 7. New York: Academic Press, 1974. Pp. 1–102. An extensive review of information integration theory and its applications to various sorts of social judgments. After an opening discussion of both averaging and multiplicative models, this paper shows how information integration theory can be applied to judgments of personality, of causality for success and failure, and moral judgment.

CLINE, V. B. Interpersonal perception. In B. A. Maher (Ed.) *Progress in experimental personality research.* Vol. 1. New York: Academic Press, 1964. Pp. 221-284. A thorough review of the problem of obtaining a valid measurement of the accuracy with which people form impressions of each other. In addition to a detailed discussion of Cronbach's critique, this paper notes other sorts of errors that can plague accuracy research, and presents the author's own model of interpersonal judgment.

HEIDER, F. *The psychology of interpersonal relations.* New York: Wiley, 1958. This scholarly work is the foundation for present attribution theory. As any number of subsequent experimental studies have demonstrated, this "naive psychology" of perception, motivation, desire, and duty is common sense at its sophisticated best. It is difficult reading, but will reward the reader who has enough time to appreciate its depth.

JONES, E. E., KANOUSE, D. E., KELLEY, H. H., NISBETT, R. E., VALINS, S., and WEINER, B. *Attribution: Perceiving the causes of behavior.* Morristown, N. J.: General Learning Press, 1972. A collection of chapters by experts in attribution written primarily for advanced students and other professionals. Topics include order effects, self-perception, differences between the attributions of actors and observers, the role of attributions in emotional disorder, language and attribution, attributions of causality and for success and failure.

ROSENBERG, S., and SEDLAK, A. Structural representations of implicit personality theory. In L. Berkowitz (Ed.) *Advances in experimental social psychology.* Vol. 6. New York: Academic Press, 1972. Pp. 235–297. An innovative application of multidimensional scaling methods to the study of a perennial problem in social perception. After a brief introduction to scaling methods and interpretation, the authors describe their naturalistic method for obtaining a measure of implicit personality theory, and illustrate the value of the method for analyzing written materials as well as free-response trait ratings made by subjects. Very technical material.

SHAVER, K. G. *An introduction to attribution processes.* Cambridge, Mass.: Winthrop, 1975. This book outlines the essential elements of attribution, presents and compares the three major theories, and suggests some interpersonal consequences of the attributions we make. Much less difficult than either the Jones et al. volume or the theoretical papers of Jones and Davis, Kelley, and Heider.

Why should there be such emotion tied up with racial attitudes?

United Press International Photo

The Components and Measurement of Attitudes

Chapter Five

The Three Components of Attitudes

How do you feel about military spending? Do you think that marijuana ought to be legalized or be prohibited as a health hazard? If the local school board informed you that your child would have to be bused out of your neighborhood to attend school across town, what would you do? All these questions, and a great many more of social importance, involve your attitudes toward various social objects (people, issues, institutions). If there is a single concept that has dominated social psychology through most of its existence, that concept is the social attitude. Although there have been a number of definitions of the concept through the years (see reviews by McGuire, 1969; Shaw and Wright, 1967), most of these definitions can be summarized by saying that an attitude is an *organized predisposition to respond in a favorable or unfavorable manner toward a specified class of social objects.*

This definition is derived from the one originally suggested by Allport (1935), and it implies that there are at least three separate components of an attitude: a *cognitive* component, an *affective* component, and a *behavioral* component. As we noted in Chapter Three, a person's social world is organized into a set of cognitive categories, and there is at least one such category for every class of social objects of importance to the person. But the cognitive component of an attitude is more than the category representing the class of objects; it also includes the person's beliefs about the objects. For example, consider the attitude object "folk singer." The criterial attributes for membership in this category might be stated as making a living from singing a particular sort of lyrics with a minimum of accompaniment, but the cognitive component of your attitude toward any folk singer would also include your *noncriterial beliefs* about that performer. How does he or she stand on the issues of the day? How much does he or she make in royalties from records? What is he or she like as a person? These and other beliefs about folk singers will certainly influence your attitude, even though they do not serve as criterial attributes for the category.

If the cognitive component of an attitude is the sum total of all you believe about the attitude object, the affective component is the sum total of your feelings about the object. Your values, your emotions, and your experience will all lead you to *evaluate* aspects of your social world in positive or negative terms, and this evaluation will be of paramount importance in your attitudes. Do you feel that the folk singer's positions on important issues are good ones or bad ones? Do you feel that his or her royalties on record sales are exorbitant, fair, or insufficient? Would you like the singer as a person? It is these evaluative judgments that predispose you to act in a generally favorable or generally unfavorable manner toward the attitude object, and many social psychologists would consider evaluation to be the essential component of an attitude (e.g., Fishbein and Ajzen, 1975).

Finally, the social attitude contains a *behavioral* component—the "predisposition to respond"—which reflects both the beliefs about the attitude object and the evaluative judgments made of the object. If your overall evaluation of folk singers is positive (given what you believe to be true about them), we would expect you to engage in actions, such as attending concerts and buying records, that would be consistent with this evaluative judgment. In contrast, if your attitude is a negative one, then we would expect you to refrain from these favorable actions, and perhaps to take some unfavorable actions. It should be emphasized that the behavioral component of an attitude is regarded only as a general *predisposition* to engage in favorable or unfavorable actions, not as a set of specific behaviors that can be expected to occur under any circumstances. As we shall see later in this chapter, there are environmental constraints that may keep people from acting in accordance with their expressed attitudes.

To illustrate the attitudinal components more fully we shall use a single example: the attitude of racial bias. The discussion will be limited to the biases of whites against blacks, but not because this is the only form of bias present in contemporary society. There is also discrimination against other ethnic minorities; against women, the elderly, and the poor; and against a variety of groups whose life styles differ from the norm. We choose to concentrate on racism because this problem has received the greatest amount of attention from social psychologists, because of its pervasiveness and extensive social consequences, and because it serves as a model for other forms of discrimination (as suggested by terms like "sexism" and "ageism"). You might keep some of these parallels in mind throughout the discussion of racism.

Racial bias is usually referred to in any of several ways—as discrimination, stereotyping, prejudice, or racism—and it is important to distinguish among these terms. Social psychologists have traditionally used the word "stereotyping" to refer to the cognitive processes involved in assigning characteristics to members of an object group, and we shall continue this usage. Thus in terms of the three components of an attitude, stereotyping may be thought of as part of the cognitive component of a racially biased attitude. It has also been customary to refer to the racially biased behavior of an individual or group as discrimination, and we shall use this term in the same way. Again in terms of the three components of a racially biased attitude, the predisposition toward discrimination would be the behavioral component.

We begin to get into trouble, however, when we try to find a term for the affective component of racial bias, and for the attitude as a whole. Social psychologists have traditionally used the word *prejudice* to represent the entire attitude (Allport, 1954; J. M. Jones, 1972; Wrightsman, 1972), but for several reasons we prefer to use the term *racism* instead. The first reason is a psychological one. As J. M. Jones, a black social psychologist, points out, "Few people would call someone who commented that a talented black individual is 'a credit to his race' a prejudiced person. Yet most black people consider that comment insulting rather than complimentary, and view its speaker as a racist. The comment seems to be based on the assumption that the talented person is *unusual* among his race—unusual in the sense that he is talented" (1972, p. 127). In short, racism is psychologically more inclusive a term than is prejudice, and the overall evaluation should be described by terms that are as inclusive as possible. In addition, the term *racism* generalizes to the actions of groups and institutions much more appropriately than does the term prejudice. Prejudice is usually defined to include a strongly negative emotional reaction to the object group (Allport, 1958; J. M. Jones, 1972), and it is difficult to describe the policies of an institution as "emotional." Indeed, the evaluative connotation of the term *prejudice* suggests that it would be an ideal label for the *affective component* of a racially biased attitude.

For these reasons, we shall use *racism* to refer to the overall attitude of racial bias. The attitude has the potential components of stereotyping, of prejudice, and of discrimination, and we shall discuss each component in some detail. For a more complete picture of the psychological processes involved in the development and maintenance of white racism than it is possible for us to draw in this limited space, the reader is referred to the classic study of prejudice by Allport (1954, 1958), or to more recent analyses by J. M. Jones (1972), R. L. Jones (1972), and Loye (1971).

THE COGNITIVE COMPONENT: STEREOTYPING AND ITS MEASUREMENT

The Elements of Stereotyping

As we noted earlier, the definition of an attitude includes a cognitive component that has many of the features of a *cognitive category* (Chapter Three), because it refers to a "specified class of social objects," and because it is presumed to be an "organized" way of representing those objects. In the case of the attitude of racism, the class of social objects is "black people," or in the terminology of an earlier day, "Negroes." The thought processes involved in the organization of the category embody nearly all of the errors in categorization and social perception outlined in Chapters Three and Four. Indeed, Allport has described the process as "faulty and inflexible generalization" (1958, p. 10). The generalization is inflexible because it is not altered by new, contradictory information; the category has been formed with such an overwhelming *prior entry effect* that disconfirmations of early biases have virtually no effect on the shape of the category. Not only is the generalization inflexible, it is also faulty, because it includes much surplus material that is not *criterial* to the formation of the cognitive category.

Research on Stereotyping

The problem of deciding exactly what information is criterial to the category "black people" deserves further comment, because these decisions are reflected in the well-known stereotypes about black people that are still held by many white perceivers. The first empirical study of stereotyping was performed by Katz and Braly (1933), and their study established a method that has since been used by a large number of other researchers. The subjects were 100 male undergraduate students at Princeton, and each subject was asked to describe ten national or ethnic groups—Americans, Chinese, English, Germans, Irish, Italians, Japanese, Jews, Negroes, and Turks—using a list of eighty-four descriptive adjectives. The subject's task was to select (for each national or ethnic group) those adjectives he believed to be "most characteristic" of members of the group. Exactly the same procedure was repeated at Princeton (with different numbers of subjects) eighteen years later by Gilbert (1951), and again eighteen years after that by Karlins, Coffman, and Walters (1969), and a similar procedure has been common in studies of stereotyping conducted by researchers in other locations (see Brigham, 1973; Ehrlich and Rinehart, 1965; and Jones and Ashmore, 1973 for critical reviews of the method).

The five traits most frequently ascribed to black people by Katz and Braly's subjects were "superstitious," "lazy," "happy-go-lucky," "ignorant," and "musical." The percentage of Katz and Braly's subjects who considered each of these traits to be most characteristic of Negroes is shown in the first column of Table 5-1. The second column of the table shows the percentages obtained by Gilbert (1951), and the third column presents the percentages found by Karlins et al. (1969).

TABLE 5-1
Several measures of stereotyping in the judgment of Negroes

TRAIT NAME	PERCENTAGE OF SUBJECTS ASSIGNING EACH TRAIT			KARLINS ET AL. FAVORABILITY SCORE	"CHARACTERISTICNESS" RANK SIGALL & PAGE (1971)	
	KATZ & BRALY (1933)	GILBERT (1951)	KARLINS, COFFMAN, & WALTERS (1969)		PIPELINE	RATING
Superstitious	84	41	13	−.84	14	14
Lazy	75	31	26	−1.12	9	19
Happy-go-lucky	38	17	27	.45	5	16
Ignorant	38	17	27	−1.37	9	12
Musical	26	33	47	.90	2	1
Number of Subjects, Range of Favorability, or Number of Ranks	100	333	150	+2 to −2	22	22

Adapted from Karlins, Coffman, and Walters (1969) and from Sigall and Page (1971).

Just looking at these percentages across the three studies, it would appear that the social stereotypes ascribed to blacks have faded a great deal over the intervening years. Of the five original traits, the percentage endorsement declines through time for four traits, with only the trait "musical" showing an increase in percentage endorsement from 1933 to 1969.

Can we safely conclude that there is less ethnic stereotyping now than there was in Katz and Braly's day? Unfortunately we cannot, at least not without some additional information. For one thing, present stereotypes might merely involve traits other than those measured by researchers. There is some evidence against this idea, in that Karlins et al. report (as did Gilbert) that their subjects showed resistance when asked to make the necessary judgments, often complaining that it was unfair to categorize people on the basis of their national or racial identification. We have all had our "consciousness raised" about the importance of treating each other as individual human beings, rather than responding to each other simply as instances of some social category. To put it in terms of one of the response biases discussed in Chapter Two, we have all become sensitive to the social desirability constraints upon such matters as ethnic and racial judgments.

The apparent fading in social stereotypes across the three studies might have been more the result of an unwillingness to *report* the existence of prejudices to the experimenter than of an actual decline in the extent of prejudice felt by the subjects. Some other data gathered by Karlins et al. suggest that social desirability might play an important role in the changes. In addition to making the ratings of national and racial groups, the subjects in the Karlins study were also asked to judge the "favorableness" of each of the 84 adjectives on a five-point scale (+2 to −2). The resulting ratings for the original five most important traits are shown in the fourth column of Table 5-1, and although the correlation between favorability score and percentage endorsement is not perfect, it is interesting to notice that only the most favorable adjective (musical) *increases* in percent endorsement through the years. It is probably no more correct to describe blacks as musical than to describe them as superstitious, but it is much less socially desirable to do the latter. Is there any way to separate real change from socially desirable responding? Let us consider this problem in more detail.

Change, Social Desirability, and Attitude Measurement

The problem of socially desirable responding is particularly salient in the study of racial attitudes, but it confounds responses in other attitude areas as well. Any time that an attitude issue is highly controversial, people may answer a researcher's questions in a socially desirable manner for at least two reasons: they believe that their answers will be accepted at face value, and they want this "truth" to reflect positively upon them. Whether this is the product of a general desire for positive self-presentation or is specific to the research setting (like evaluation apprehension), it can lead to a consistent overestimation of the positivity of many social attitudes. Social psychologists have developed a variety of techniques for dealing with social desirability, and some of these have had a good degree of success. For example, the attitude questions can be phrased in a **forced-choice** format (as are the items in the scale of Machiavellianism to be discussed more fully in Chapter Twelve). This format forces the subject to indicate a response by choosing between two items matched for social desirability, only one of which is relevant to the attitude under investigation. It doesn't matter whether the social desirability of the pair is high, moderate, or low; as long as the two choices are equally socially desirable, the subject's response will reflect his or her feelings about the attitude object rather than a desire for a positive self-presentation. As another possibility the attitude researcher might employ *unobtrusive measures*, inferring the respondents' attitudes from their public behavior. These measures were discussed in more detail in Chapter Two, but as examples a researcher might infer people's attitudes toward members of a minority group by how close to members of the minority group such people are willing to stand, or how they react to a forced contact with the group.

These measures, and other traditional ones, generally assume that a direct measurement of attitude cannot be accomplished without some contamination from social desirability. But what if we could convince people that we could accurately measure their *real* attitudes (rather than their verbal reports) by some sophisticated physiological procedure? Since these physiological processes are much less susceptible to conscious control, the respondent would have no reason for engaging in a positive self-presentation. Should the subject still try to self-present, we would not only learn his or her true attitude, we would also discover that an attempt was being made to conceal it from us. If we could convince people that we have such an accurate measure of their physiological processes, then we ought to obtain verbal reports that would be free of social desirability response biases. This line of reasoning is the basis for a method of attitude measurement developed by Jones and Sigall (1971) called the *bogus pipeline* (to the subject's true emotions and attitudes).

The Bogus Pipeline

A subject whose attitudes are to be measured using the bogus pipeline is brought into the laboratory and seated before an array of electrical apparatus that is described as a small laboratory computer. The subject is asked to indicate his or her attitudes by using both arms to turn what looks like a small steering wheel, thereby moving a pointer on the attitude scale. While the subject grips this steering wheel (which is locked in a stationary position), electrodes which lead to the computer are attached to his or her arms. Then the experimenter explains that the apparatus is similar to a lie detector, with the difference that the present equipment permits measurement of both the direction and intensity of a judgment. This information is presumably gained through a variant of **electromyography**, a procedure for measuring the electrical potentials generated by implicit muscle movements. The experimenter claims that through sophisticated analysis of these implicit muscle movements the computer can accurately estimate in what direction, and how far, the subjects *would* turn the steering wheel if it were not locked in its position in the center of the scale.

Some demonstration trials are conducted based on an attitude questionnaire about some noncontroversial—and therefore presumably honestly answered—issues administered in a different setting well in advance of the experimental session. In all these trials an experimental confederate in an adjacent room actually controls the "readings" shown by the computer so that they correspond to the subject's answers on the earlier questionnaire, even when the subject is explicitly instructed to try to "fool" the machine. After this "calibration" of the apparatus to convince the subject of its effectiveness, the experimenter is ready to assess the attitudes or emotions of interest. The subject's task with these items of interest is to "predict" what the machine will show, and it is assumed that these predictions will be almost entirely free of distortion from social desirability.

To try to distinguish real change in social stereotypes from socially desirable responding, Sigall and Page (1971) used the bogus pipeline in a variant of the Katz and Braly ethnic stereotype procedure. Sigall and Page asked their subjects to state how "characteristic" of an ethnic (target) group was each one of twenty-two descriptive adjectives, including the ones shown in Table 5-1 (p. 172). Unlike previous stereotyping studies, there were only two target groups to be evaluated: Americans and Negroes. Each target group was judged by a different set of subjects, half of whom were run under full bogus pipeline conditions (the Pipeline group) and half of whom simply used the steering wheel to make normal ratings (the Rating group). Thus half the subjects thought the experimenter could directly monitor the physiological concomitants of their attitudes, while the other half of the subjects did not think the experimenter had any insight into their covert responses.

The extent to which social desirability might influence stereotyping can be estimated by comparing the ratings of Negroes made under the Pipeline and Rating conditions. For the five original traits these ratings are shown in the last two columns of Table 5-1. For purposes of comparison with earlier research, the scale values obtained by Sigall and Page have been transformed in the table into their rank order among the twenty-two descriptive adjectives used. Thus we see that "musical" was considered most "characteristic" (a rank of 1) by the Rating group, and was thought to be the second-most characteristic trait by the Pipeline group. With this sole exception for the trait "musical," the ranks of the adjectives shown were never higher in the Rating condition than in the Pipeline condition. In short, the Pipeline subjects appeared to be using the components of the original stereotyped view of black people to a greater extent than did the Rating subjects. It should be emphasized that the extensive procedural differences between the bogus pipeline method and the traditional measures of stereotyping preclude exact comparisons. And, as we shall see in a moment, there are some problems of validity unique to the pipeline method.

Problems with the Pipeline

Is the bogus pipeline the solution to the problem of socially desirable responding on attitude issues? Probably not, as critics of the method (e.g., Ostrom, 1973) have pointed out, for a variety of reasons. First of all, the bogus pipeline procedure is perhaps the height of deception by the experimenter in the attempt to ensure honest responses from subjects. Not only does the cover story have the immediate effect of suggesting to the subject that his or her inner-most feelings are soon to become public, it has the long-term effect (after the debriefing) of increasing the subject's suspicions in all future research. Second, the pipeline procedure may be differentially effective depending upon the previous experimental sophistication of the subjects, although it is difficult to predict in advance just what difference sophistication might make. Of course, subjects who had previously heard about the technique would not accept the experimenter's explanations, even with the bogus calibration procedure. On the other hand, sophisticated subjects who did believe the procedures might be aware of the unconscious determinants of actions and attitudes, and overestimate their "predictions" in a *negative* direction to be sure that the later readings from the pipeline showed them to be self-effacing. Third, a detailed comparison of the results for Sigall and Page's experiment with the results for the Karlins et al. (1969) survey, including findings not presented in Table 5-1, indicates

that the Pipeline condition may be more comparable to other procedures than it would first appear (Ostrom, 1973).

Thus the evidence for "faking" provided by the differences in
ranks across Pipeline and Rating conditions must be interpreted with
caution. There is probably more stereotyping than the Karlins et al.
study would indicate, but there is probably not as much faking as
the Sigall and Page results might suggest. Finally, the bogus pipeline is much less practical than many other measures of attitudes.
Subjects can be run only one at a time, and the experimental
procedure requires a great deal of "overhead"—a long introduction
and the use of a confederate—for the data that are ultimately collected.
For all of these reasons, the bogus pipeline's performance in obtaining attitude measures uncontaminated by social desirability has been
less impressive than we might have expected it to be. Its further
refinement might hold some promise, but for now a clear solution to
the problem of socially desirable responding remains elusive.

All the stereotype research reported here was conducted with
college students, who for a variety of social and psychological reasons
are likely to engage in less stereotyping than is the general population. But there has been a corresponding shift in the attitudes of a
majority of white people, as indicated by changes in laws pertaining
to civil rights on local, state, and national levels; by the dramatic
increase in the number of appointed and elected black officials; and
by the results of numerous opinion surveys through the years (e.g.,
Campbell, 1971). This is not to say that white people no longer possess
racial stereotypes—only to suggest that there is less stereotyping now
than in Katz and Braly's day. As the next two sections of this chapter
indicate, complete eradication of racism will require more than a
simple change in white people's beliefs about black people.

THE AFFECTIVE COMPONENT:
EVALUATION, EMOTION, AND PREJUDICE

Let us return for a moment to the definition of an attitude. We have
seen that attitudes encompass the process of cognitive categorization,
and that errors in this process can produce stereotypic beliefs about
the people toward whom the attitude is directed. But there is more to
an attitude than the cognitive category constructed to represent the
social objects of the attitude. As a predisposition to respond "in a
favorable or unfavorable manner," an attitude also includes an
evaluative judgment. For racial and ethnic attitudes, as well as for

others, the affective component includes both the general impression of favorability or unfavorability toward the attitude objects, and the specific feelings that give the attitude its affective tone, some of which can be quite emotional.

The Presence of Emotion

Some of the specific feelings that might accompany ethnic attitudes have been identified by Harding, Kutner, Proshansky, and Chein (1969): "On the positive side they include such feelings as admiration, sympathy, and 'closeness' or identification; on the negative side they include contempt, fear, envy, and 'distance' or alienation" (p. 4).

The extremes that are possible in these feelings can be illustrated by excerpts from an interview that was part of an extensive project to assess white and black attitudes (Campbell, 1971). The largest single study in this project was a survey of 2945 white and 2814 black residents of fifteen major American cities. The survey was conducted in early 1968, and many of its questions dealt with the riots that occurred in several inner-city ghettoes during the summers of 1966 and 1967. As one way of summarizing the contrasts present in the attitudes of white people toward these disturbances (and black people in general), Campbell presents the verbatim answers of two respondents to several of the interview questions. One of these sets of answers is shown below; it indicates quite dramatically the intense emotions that can accompany racial bias.

What do you think was the main cause of these disturbances?
"Nigger agitators. Martin Luther King and Rap Brown, and that black bastard [Stokely] Carmichael."

Have the disturbances helped or hurt the cause of Negro rights?
"Hurt. Whites are starting to wise up what a danger these people can be. They are going to be tough from now on. People are fed up with giving in and giving them everything their little black hearts want."

What do you think the city government could do to keep a disturbance from breaking out here?
"Ship them all back to Africa. Lock up all the agitators and show them we mean business."

(From Campbell, 1971, p. 2)

Admittedly this person's responses were chosen by Campbell to represent an extreme viewpoint, but at least in terms of the affective component they are not completely atypical. The strong emotion present in these responses has been obtained in less prejudiced subjects as well, as several investigators have noted (Porier and Lott, 1967; Rankin and Campbell, 1955; Vidulich and Krevanick, 1966: Westie and DeFleur, 1959). These studies have compared the emotional reactions to black people exhibited by ethnically biased and unbiased subjects, and the general method can be illustrated by the work of Porier and Lott (1967).

This experiment was a conceptual replication of the earlier study by Rankin and Campbell (1955), in which there had been greater emotional reaction to black experimental assistants by prejudiced white subjects than by nonprejudiced white subjects. The study by Porier and Lott (1967) was described to subjects (white male undergraduates at a "border state" university) as an investigation of emotional reactions to various stimulus words (in the tradition of the perceptual defense research described in Chapter Four). When each subject arrived at the laboratory for testing, he was met by a white experimenter who explained the ostensible purpose of the study and then attached two sets of electrodes to the subject's hands. The subject was told that both sets of electrodes measured galvanic skin response (GSR), a measure of emotionality which involves conducting a minute electrical current along the surface of the skin. When there is moisture on the surface of the hand (sweating palms indicate emotional arousal), this minute current flows more easily than when the palms are dry, so changes in skin resistance are indicative of changes in emotional arousal.

One set of electrodes was the GSR apparatus as described, but the other set of electrodes was a dummy set placed on the subject only to provide a rationale for physical contact between the white subject and the black experimental assistants. The stimulus word lists were tape-recorded, and there were four blank spaces on the tapes during which an experimental assistant came into the room to "adjust" the dummy set of electrodes. On two of these occasions the experimental assistant making the adjustment was black, and on the other two occasions the experimental assistant was white. So that a subject's responses could be described in terms of the experimental assistant's race rather than in terms of the individual characteristics of any particular assistant, each subject was exposed to two different white assistants and to two different black assistants during his experimental session.

A major dependent variable was, of course, the subject's GSR response during the time that the assistant (white or black) was

"adjusting" the dummy electrodes. To determine the relative emotionality aroused by the two races of assistants, each subject's GSR
response to the two white assistants was subtracted from his GSR
response to the two black assistants. The result would be a measure of
GSR *bias,* with positive numbers indicating a higher level of emotionality in the presence of the black assistants. If all the subjects had
been ethnically biased, they all would have had positive GSR bias
scores (as did thirty-six of Rankin and Campbell's forty subjects). As
it turned out, however, thirty-two of Porier and Lott's subjects had
positive scores, while twenty-eight had negative scores (greater
emotionality in the presence of the *white* assistants), approximating
the fifty-fifty split that would be expected by chance. Porier and Lott
concluded that this important difference between their findings and
the twelve-year-earlier results of Rankin and Campbell was primarily
due to procedural differences, such as using a number of different
experimental assistants (Rankin and Campbell had used only one of
each race). But it is also possible that the difference involves some
fading in the emotional component of racism parallel to the fading in
cognitive stereotyping discussed earlier.

Even in the absence of overall GSR bias, it was possible to
examine the relationship between this measure of emotionality and
ethnic attitudes. A week or more before the experimental sessions
several questionnaire measures of ethnic attitudes, including the
California Ethnocentrism Scale (or "E" Scale), had been administered
to students in all the classes from which subjects for the experiment
were later to be drawn. The E Scale is a general measure of attitudes
toward blacks and other minorities, and if there really is an emotional
component to the attitude of racism, there should have been a positive
correlation between a subject's E Scale score and his or her GSR bias
score. In other words, the greater an individual's ethnic prejudice, the
more emotionally he or she should have reacted to the presence of
the black experimental assistants. The results confirmed this hypothesis and replicated the second finding of Rankin and Campbell:
subjects with higher E Scale scores also had higher (more positive)
GSR bias scores.

Sources of Emotion in Racial Attitudes

Both the interview excerpts from the survey research and the
studies of physiological arousal indicate that there is a strong emotional
tone in the evaluative component of the attitude of racism. This
will come as no surprise to you, since you probably have been ex-

posed to examples of such emotion in your own experience. You have listened to people argue that "if blacks move into the neighborhood the property values will go down," and you may have wondered why even if this were true it should matter to people who previously had no intention of selling their house. You have heard objections to the busing of school children on grounds that the bus ride takes time without adding to the child's education, only to discover that when the schools have been integrated these same people withdraw their children to send them to private schools that are farther away. You may have heard employers who admit that most of their workers receive virtually all their training on the job lament the fact that there are "no blacks qualified" for vacancies. Each of these arguments has an emotional quality to it that seems to be of greater importance to the speaker than is rational consideration of the problem. Why should there be such emotion (usually of a negative sort) tied up with racial attitudes? There is no single answer to this question. Rather there are a number of contributing factors: *socialization* by parents and culture, *belief congruence* (both actual and assumed), and *direct competition* and the *frustration* it can engender.

Socialization

There is little doubt that parental attitudes play an important role in the development of emotions connected with racism. A young child is entirely dependent upon his or her parents, and the fact of this dependence can produce high degrees of conformity in beliefs, attitudes, and values (if not always behavior). In an extended discussion of socialization processes, Jones and Gerard (1967) distinguish between **effect dependence** (the fact that nearly all the child's rewards and punishments are mediated by the parents) and **information dependence** (the fact that a child's knowledge about the social world is derived largely from the information provided by the parents). Both sorts of dependence can be involved in the development of prejudice. For example, an early study of the socialization of racial attitudes in white children in rural Tennessee (Horowitz and Horowitz, 1938) found direct physical punishment being administered for playing with black children. No doubt parents who wish to instill racial prejudice have become less direct in their methods since then, but it is probably not lost on their children that the parents ultimately control all the rewards and punishments. Saying that it is "not nice" to play with children of another race may be just as effective as administering physical punishment. In fact, there is a good deal of research to suggest that threatened withdrawal of love is even more successful in producing internalized values than is physical punishment (Aronson and Carlsmith, 1963; Bandura and Walters, 1963; Glueck and Glueck, 1950; Whiting and Child, 1953).

Not only do parents have control over the outcomes their children obtain, they are in addition the children's principal source of social information. This control is virtually exclusive during the first two or three years of life, but then other socializing influences (preschools, television, peers) enter the picture. It is important to remember, however, that parents exert a great deal of control over *which* other influences are present. Does the child attend a preschool that is integrated, or one that is not? Are the television programs the children are permitted to watch sensitive to the issue of race ("Sesame Street," "The Electric Company"), or are they all white ("Batman," "Superman")? Are friendships with children from other racial and economic groups encouraged or discouraged? Not until a child enters the public schools does a parent's control over the social information available diminish appreciably, and even then the parent remains a prime source of information. Given this background, it is not surprising that a majority of college students in one study reported that their ethnic attitudes were influenced by the attitudes of their parents (Allport and Kramer, 1946), and that the racial attitudes of adults differ according to region of birth—South, Middle Atlantic, Midwest, New England, or West—with favorability toward blacks increasing in the regions in the order they are presented here (Campbell, 1971).

Belief Congruence

Despite the influence on social attitudes that parents can exert, there are still wide variations in the behavior of adults who had presumably similar socialization experience. For example, although Campbell (1971) found the smallest percentage of favorable attitudes among people who had been raised in the South, that percentage still amounted to 30 percent. It is, of course, possible that these people were raised in families whose region of origin was outside the South or whose attitudes were contrary to those prevailing in the South, but these explanations are not especially convincing. More plausible is the suggestion that socialization provides an overall predisposition which can be diminished or augmented by later influences.

One of these factors is belief congruence (Rokeach, 1960): the degree to which the beliefs of one person agree with the beliefs of another person. Just how is this cognitive-sounding factor translated into emotion? As you will see in the discussion of interpersonal attraction (Chapter Ten), people are attracted to those whose attitudes agree with their own. It would be difficult for you to maintain a friendship with another person if the two of you had broad areas of disagreement on important issues—e.g., religion, politics, sex, morality. By the same token, if all you knew about a person was that his or her attitudes differed from yours, you would probably guess that the two of you would not get along too well. What would happen if the only information you had about a person was that he or she was of a different race? Wouldn't you assume that in many respects his or her attitudes would be different from yours? Certainly blacks and whites differ in their attitudes toward racial issues (Campbell, 1971; J. M. Jones, 1972), and the white person's best guess about other issues is to generalize the differences that exist on racial questions.

Given that whites will probably assume some attitude dissimilarity, and given that dissimilarity *decreases* the likelihood of interpersonal attraction, how are we to determine whether a white person's hesitancy about contact with blacks is based on assumed dissimilarity of beliefs, or on a simple dislike for black people, regardless of their beliefs?

One potential solution to this problem was suggested by Rokeach, Smith, and Evans (1960): obtain evaluations of stimulus persons whose race and beliefs are systematically varied. White undergraduate students in two colleges, one in the South and one in the North, were given descriptions of *pairs* of stimulus persons and asked to indicate how likely it was that they might become friendly with either member of every pair. These pairs of stimulus persons were presented in one of three ways. Either the two stimulus persons were alike in race, but different in belief; alike in belief but different in race; or different in both race and belief. For example, on the belief issue of religion, a "white person who believes in God" would be paired successively with a "white atheist," a "Negro who believes in God," and a "Negro atheist." In addition to the topic of religion, the belief issues included three more unrelated to race (socialized medicine, communism, and labor unions), and four issues related to race (speed of desegregation, integration of fraternities or sororities, integration of housing, and overall racial equality). The subjects were asked to indicate their own positions on all these issues so that the investigators could later determine which stimulus persons held beliefs congruent with the beliefs expressed by the subjects.

The results showed that with race held constant, subjects expressed more liking for stimulus persons whose beliefs were similar to their own. With belief held constant, the white subjects expressed more liking for the white stimulus person than for the black stimulus person. Neither of these results is particularly surprising, and neither squarely addresses the question of whether race or belief is the *more important* determinant of attitudes. This question can be answered by specific comparisons across all eight of the belief issues. If subjects' reactions on the third pair of stimulus persons (where both race and belief are different) were primarily determined by the change in race, then their third-pair scores should have been highly intercorrelated with their second-pair scores (belief constant, race varied). If however, belief congruence was the more important determinant of evaluative reactions, then the third-pair scores should be highly intercorrelated with scores on the first pair (race constant, belief varied).

The intercorrelations across pairs supported the belief congruence hypothesis. Third-pair scores were not at all correlated with the race variations (second pair) but were highly correlated with the belief variations (first pair). These results indicate that belief congruence was more important than race in determining the evaluation of the stimulus person.

It would be tempting to stop with this optimistic conclusion, but as critics of the research (e.g. Triandis, 1961) quickly pointed out, there are at least two ways in which the findings do not generalize well to the real world outside the laboratory. The first problem is that subjects were asked to judge the likelihood that they would become friendly with the stimulus persons. It may well be the case that belief congruence is a prerequisite for friendship, but this fact does not tell us much about the relative importance of race and belief in less intimate social settings. Most real-world contact between blacks and whites is not on the level of intimacy required for friendship, so the results of the experiment may not generalize well to these more distant contacts. To support this criticism, Triandis presented data that showed race greatly to outweigh belief congruence in the prediction of a variety of social distance measures, such as acceptance in a neighborhood, a club, or in marriage.

The second problem with the Rokeach et al. findings is that in this experimental situation, both the stimulus person's race *and* his or her beliefs are thoroughly specified in advance of any evaluation by the subject. In a real social situation, only the individual's race is readily apparent. We have already suggested that in these circumstances perceivers will assume dissimilarity of attitudes, and a number of studies show that this is the case (e.g., Byrne and Wong, 1962; Stein, Hardyck, and Smith, 1965). You may well be comfortable with a person of another race as long as his or her beliefs agree with yours, but if you assume that the person's beliefs are different until proven otherwise, how are you ever going to get close enough to discover that you have been mistaken? In fact, the very persistence of some perceptual and cognitive errors (see Chapter Four) suggests that not even forced contact will necessarily correct the misimpressions held prior to such contact.

The research on belief congruence and assumed dissimilarity

provides the premises for an unfortunate syllogism to describe part of the negative emotion associated with prejudice and racism. The first premise is that belief congruence leads to interpersonal attraction —or, to put it in terms of negative emotions, belief dissimilarity leads to decreased liking. The second premise is that when whites are given information only about a stimulus person's race, they will assume belief similarity to other whites but belief dissimilarity to blacks. And, as Byrne and Wong (1962) demonstrated, this assumed dissimilarity to blacks will be greater for highly prejudiced whites than for nonprejudiced ones. The unfortunate conclusion of this syllogism is that assumed belief dissimilarity will mediate at least part of a white's dislike for black people (the reverse is also true).

Competition and Frustration

If both assumed belief dissimilarity and real belief dissimilarity can help to account for a prejudiced white person's dislike of black people, they do not seem powerful enough to account for the even stronger emotions that are all too often expressed. "I don't think we have anything in common" is not at all the same as "Lock them up to show them we mean business." Nor is real belief dissimilarity sufficient even as a rationalization for the several hundred lynchings that have occurred in America. To the extent that these outbreaks of violence are attributed to individual white people (rather than to organized groups), most overt acts of aggression toward blacks may be considered to be the product of two related factors: competition and frustration. Virtually no experimental evidence exists with which to evaluate their claims, but a number of social psychologists (Allport, 1954; Harding et al., 1969; Pettigrew, 1971) give frustration the primary role.

The original frustration-aggression hypothesis was advanced by Dollard, Doob, Miller, Mowrer, and Sears (1939). It maintained that all aggression is the product of frustration, and that all frustration inevitably causes aggression. As we shall see in Chapter Eleven, this relatively unsophisticated view of aggression has undergone substantial modification. But the essential principle remains intact: aggression is the product of events in the situation, and not the result of any inherent aggressive instincts (see Freud, 1933; Lorenz, 1966; for the alternative viewpoint). Applied to racial violence, the argument goes like this: Life in America has always carried with it some frustration—in interpersonal relations between lovers or spouses, in relations between employees and their bosses, in the virtual certainty that few people's achievements will live up to the goals set by the "American Dream." All of this frustration cries out for release through aggression, as evidenced by our everyday language ("control your-self," "don't take it out on me"), our love of institutionalized violence (everything from football and the roller derby to the size of the military establishment), and our nostalgia about the "good old days when the only law was a fast gun." But ironically, this pent-up aggression usually cannot be directed at the *source* of the frustration.

Inherent in the idea of frustration is the concept of a power differ-ential between the frustrating agent and the person being frustrated. You can't ordinarily tell your boss "where to go," no matter how much you would like to do so. If you push far enough, your lover will leave you; your spouse will sue for divorce. But no matter how far short of the American Dream you fall, you can't stop the advertisers from trying to sell you still more. What must happen? Your aggression will typically be *displaced* onto a convenient person or object with still less power than you have, so that no retaliation is possible. An employee who has been chewed out by the boss will yell at his or her spouse; the spouse will take it out on the children, who will then kick the cat. Everyone is looking for a suitable victim, and for a large number of reasons, black people have filled that role quite well (J. M. Jones, 1972).

Blacks began their history in this country as victims, and their color has made them much more readily identifiable than members of any other minority group. A great deal of the social interaction be-tween whites and blacks has emphasized this role, from the foot-shuffling Step-'n-Fetch-It of early Hollywood movies right through the implicit assumption of many white liberal participants in the civil rights movement in the 1960s that the southern rural blacks could not take care of their own problems without outside help from con-cerned whites. Each of these views of black people may or may not have been an accurate reflection of social reality at its time, but regardless of its accuracy, each contributed to maintenance of the belief that blacks are victims. Recent black pride movements, and discussions of black power (Carmichael and Hamilton, 1967), have as one of their principal targets this view of black-as-victim. Finally, the stereotypic view of blacks as "lazy and ignorant" can serve as justification for the conclusion that these particular victims "deserve what they get." And as Lerner and Matthews (1967) have shown, people derogate victims who appear to be suffering through no fault of their own.

Not only is it possible for whites to perceive blacks as appropriate victims who deserve what they get, but the very same whites who need victims are probably in economic competition with black people and can identify (legitimately, in their eyes) blacks as the source of their troubles. In other words, this is one of the few instances in which even an indirect source of frustration can be the object of direct aggression. The whites who are unemployed, or are unfulfilled in low-prestige occupations, are in direct economic competition with some black people. Those whites who are employed can believe that the government is using their tax money to support with welfare payments black people who don't have the initiative to help themselves. It is impossible to aggress against the government, but black people provide a ready target for the release of frustration. This relationship between economic competition and violence has been thoroughly explored by Brown (1965), who points out that although lynchings in the early 1900s were rationalized on various grounds, there was usually a strong correlation between economic conditions and the outbreak of violence.

None of the contributors to the emotional component of racist attitudes—socialization, belief congruence, or frustration—is presumed to occur in isolation. Socialization and situation combine to produce some of the emotions associated with racial attitudes. These emotions will, in turn, interact with the individual's cognitions about black people, and the result will be a tendency for the person to behave in a prescribed manner toward blacks. Not surprisingly, one of the principal reasons that social psychologists study the affective and cognitive components of attitudes is that better understanding of these processes should enable us to make more accurate predictions of social behavior. But is this faith in the strong relationship between affect-cognition and behavior justified? Unfortunately, as we shall see in the next section, some caution is in order.

THE BEHAVIORAL COMPONENT: DISCRIMINATION OR NOT?

Let us return for the last time to the definition of an attitude. More than anything else, an attitude is supposed to be a predisposition to *behave* in a specified way toward members of the object group. You would expect a strongly prejudiced person to discriminate actively against black people, while you would be surprised to discover discrimination on the part of an egalitarian person. Here your implicit theory of social psychology would agree with the attitude theorists who assume that in the absence of external constraints people will behave in accordance with their beliefs and emotions.

But an attitude is not a behavior, it is a *predisposition* toward behavior; and we must keep this distinction in mind. It is possible for prejudiced people to behave in a nondiscriminatory fashion, and it is also possible for nonprejudiced people to give tacit support to racist institutions. For example, a prejudiced restaurant owner might be forced to serve a black family that had made reservations over the telephone. This example is suggested by research of LaPiere (1934) and Kutner, Wilkins, and Yarrow (1952), although Dillehay (1973) has noted some important limitations in their methods. From the proprietor's viewpoint, the demands of the immediate social situation (a tradition of courtesy to customers, an unwillingness to create a scene over a single small group of people) might have been sufficient to suppress discriminatory behavior. If there had been larger numbers of people involved, or if there had been some reason for the proprietor to think that serving this one group carried strong implications for the future, the response might well have been different. After all, during the civil rights movement of the 1960s numerous restaurants, city recreation areas, and even some public schools closed down entirely rather than integrate their facilities.

In contrast to the discrepancy between attitude and behavior suggested by this example, some research studies have identified conditions under which the correspondence between behavior and attitude is stronger. When the behavior involved is *long-term* rather than short-term, and when it is based on *individual choice* rather than law or social custom, negative racial attitudes tend to be translated into discriminatory actions. Prejudiced people are less likely to develop friendships with blacks than are nonprejudiced people (Williams, 1964; Wilner, Walkley, and Cook, 1952). In addition, prejudiced people are less likely to interact with black co-workers in an employment setting (Hughes and Hughes, 1952; Southall, 1950). Other examples are greater reluctance on the part of prejudiced people to appear with blacks in photographs to be used for public distribution (De Fleur and Westie, 1958; Green, 1969), to participate in discussions about civil rights (Fendrich, 1967), or to develop more positive attitudes through intergroup contact (Cook, 1970). In each of these cases, more highly prejudiced subjects (as identified by their responses to various questionnaire measures of belief and affect) maintained a higher degree of discriminatory behavior than did less prejudiced subjects.

What are we to conclude from all these results? Several reviews of the attitude literature (e.g., Brigham, 1971; Kiesler, Collins, and Miller, 1969; Wicker, 1969) indicate that there is not necessarily a relationship between expressed attitudes and overt behavior. But since an attitude is only defined as a *predisposition* toward behavior, and since attitudes and behavior do correlate to some degree (Fishbein, 1972), it is more appropriate to try to identify the circumstances in which the correlation will (or will not) be found. You will recognize this suggestion as another in the series that for us began in Chapter Three with the issue of accuracy in person perception: in social psychology, as in other disciplines, the first step in the accumulation of scientifically valuable information is the asking of precise and sophisticated questions. Just as it makes more sense to wonder, "Under what conditions will judges be accurate?" than to ask, "What are the characteristics of an accurate judge?" it will also be more useful for us to inquire, "*When* are attitudes correlated with behavior?" than to wonder *whether* any correlation exists. From evidence currently available, it appears that cognition and affect predict behavior best when the situational demands are minimal, when the behavior will be long-term rather than short-term, and when the behavior must be initiated by the individual in question.

We have seen that an attitude is truly a predisposition to behave in a favorable or unfavorable manner toward a specified class of social objects. There are cases in which the individual's beliefs and emotions will be reflected in overt behavior, and there are other times at which behavior will be primarily controlled by elements of the situation. But with the exception of the bogus pipeline technique, our discussion of attitudes has thus far omitted a crucial topic: how are the components of attitudes measured? It is fine to discuss similarities and differences among affect, cognition, and behavior, but without some indication of how these components can be measured—and compared experimentally—the discussion is no more than implicit social psychology. The tripartite division of the person into emotion, cognition, and behavior is as old as Plato, but the methodological tools necessary to isolate these components have become available, even in a limited form, only recently. It is these techniques of attitude measurement and scaling that we now consider.

The Measurement of Attitude Components

GENERAL ISSUES IN ATTITUDE MEASUREMENT

As a predisposition to behave in a favorable or unfavorable manner toward a specified class of social objects, an attitude consists of cognitive, affective, and behavioral components. For the attitude of racism these components are, respectively, stereotyping, prejudice, and discrimination. But before we can accurately describe a person's attitude, we must be able to measure each of these components, and some of the responses involved in such measurement are shown in Figure 5-1. For each component only some of the possible techniques are included, and these were chosen to illustrate two important aspects of attitude measurement. First, attitudes can be measured either by techniques quite specific to the class of attitude objects, or they can be assessed by adapting techniques originally designed for other purposes entirely. Second, each attitude component can be assessed in a variety of different ways, always including as a possibility the *verbal responses* the individual might make—statements of belief, evaluations of the positive or negative characteristics of the attitude object, descriptions of behavioral intentions. Let us consider each of these points in turn.

You will recognize that, for example, the Role Construct Repertory Test, originally developed to measure a perceiver's orientation to the social world, and his or her cognitive complexity, is suggested here as a way to measure the cognitive component of the attitude of racism. In the original Rep test (described more fully in Chapter Four), a subject is presented with sets of triads, such as employer–spouse–friend, and asked to identify as many dimensions as possible on which two of the triads are like each other but different from the third. The more dimensions a subject employs, the more cognitively complex he or she is considered. To estimate the cognitive component of racism, the usual triads could simply be replaced by sets which differed in racial composition. For example, two actor–politician–musician triads could be constructed, one with black stimulus persons and one with white stimulus persons. If a subject then used *fewer* dimensions for the black triad than for the white triad, we could take this as evidence of a greater tendency to stereotype black people in terms of fewer cognitive categories.

Just as attitude researchers may adapt other techniques to the task of attitude measurement, they may also devise methods that are quite specific, not only to attitude measurement, but also to the particular attitude in question. For example, the Katz and Braly (1933) trait assignment method will only be appropriate for attitudes toward national or ethnic groups (or for other groups that are readily identifiable, such as professors, police officers, or "hippies"). This is a serious limitation, because many socially important attitudes, such as those toward "freedom" or "patriotism," are not concerned with recognized groups of people. As we shall see later, the *semantic differential* method of attitude measurement (Osgood, Suci, and Tannenbaum, 1957) can be used for abstract concepts such as these, but the Katz and Braly technique cannot. Another example of a limited

FIGURE 5-1

Attitude components and measurement.

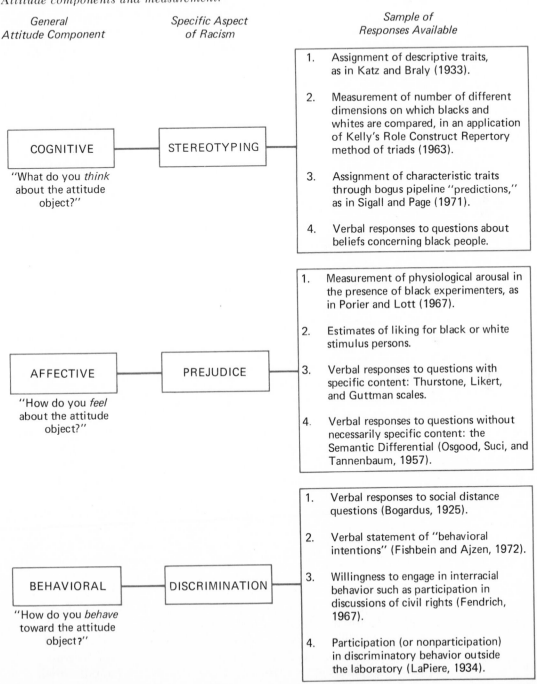

General Attitude Component	*Specific Aspect of Racism*	*Sample of Responses Available*
COGNITIVE "What do you *think* about the attitude object?"	**STEREOTYPING**	1. Assignment of descriptive traits, as in Katz and Braly (1933). 2. Measurement of number of different dimensions on which blacks and whites are compared, in an application of Kelly's Role Construct Repertory method of triads (1963). 3. Assignment of characteristic traits through bogus pipeline "predictions," as in Sigall and Page (1971). 4. Verbal responses to questions about beliefs concerning black people.
AFFECTIVE "How do you *feel* about the attitude object?"	**PREJUDICE**	1. Measurement of physiological arousal in the presence of black experimenters, as in Porier and Lott (1967). 2. Estimates of liking for black or white stimulus persons. 3. Verbal responses to questions with specific content: Thurstone, Likert, and Guttman scales. 4. Verbal responses to questions without necessarily specific content: the Semantic Differential (Osgood, Suci, and Tannenbaum, 1957).
BEHAVIORAL "How do you *behave* toward the attitude object?"	**DISCRIMINATION**	1. Verbal responses to social distance questions (Bogardus, 1925). 2. Verbal statement of "behavioral intentions" (Fishbein and Ajzen, 1972). 3. Willingness to engage in interracial behavior such as participation in discussions of civil rights (Fendrich, 1967). 4. Participation (or nonparticipation) in discriminatory behavior outside the laboratory (LaPiere, 1934).

technique is LaPiere's (1934) comparison between the verbal responses and the actual behavior of restaurant and hotel managers.
This method is primarily suited only to the measurement of attitudes
toward minority groups who are likely to be the victims of
discrimination.

The adaptation of other techniques and the development of
methods specific to the attitude of interest indicate the range of
possibilities available to the attitude researcher. In between these
extremes are a number of measurement techniques that rely upon the
verbal behavior of the respondent, and these methods will be the
principal focus of our discussion. As Figure 5-1 indicates, an individual's verbal responses can be taken as evidence of the cognitive,
affective, or behavioral component of his or her overall attitude. In
each of these cases, however, the attitude measurement is *indirect*,
screened through the respondent's willingness to give an accurate
report. Particularly in the case of an attitude with a high loading (positive or negative) on social desirability, what the respondent tells
us may be as much a function of what he or she wants us to believe
as it is a product of what the person actually feels, thinks, or intends
to do. And as we move from the cognitive component to the affective
component to the behavioral component, the fact that the measurement is indirect becomes more of a problem.

Not only do the social desirability constraints increase from cognition to behavior (we believe that people should be able to *think*
whatever they like, just so long as they don't *behave* in a manner
detrimental to the rights of others), there is an increasing problem
with the relative *appropriateness* of a verbal measure. People are used
to giving verbal descriptions of their thoughts and beliefs, and verbal
indicants of the cognitive component of an attitude are perfectly
acceptable. When the object of interest is affect, rather than cognition,
a verbal description is less satisfactory. It is much more difficult for
people to "put their feelings into words" than it is for them to describe their beliefs. As Schachter (1964) has argued, the subjective
experience of emotion involves both some physiological arousal and a
verbal label for that arousal. A verbal statement corresponds closely
to the cognitive label of the emotional experience, but it is not as
appropriate as a physiologically based measure would be for assessment of the arousal component of the emotional experience.

If a simple verbal description is not entirely appropriate for the
affective component, it is even less desirable as a substitute for actual
behavior. You will remember that in Chapter One we distinguished
between your implicit theory of social psychology and the formal
theories of scientific social psychology by saying that the formal
theories are based not on what we expect people to do, but rather

upon what behaviors they actually perform. We should not retreat from this standard in the measurement of attitudes. Behavior often does not agree with expressed attitudes, behavior can (unlike emotions) easily be observed, and the unique value of the concept of an attitude is that it incorporates both internal processes (cognition and affect) and overt actions. All of these considerations suggest that verbal statements, even of behavioral intentions, are a poor substitute for observed action. As we discuss the various methods of attitude scaling, you should keep in mind that those methods are most appropriate for cognition and evaluation, but are of limited value in the measurement of behavior.

NUMBERS AND SCALES

What does it mean to say that one person has a "stronger" attitude toward an issue than does another person? When is one group's average attitude significantly different from another group's attitude, and how is the fact of statistically significant difference established? How do we decide when an attitude is "positive" rather than "negative"? The answers to all these questions involve comparisions between numerical values, and in order to understand some of the problems in attitude measurement you need to know a little about the various sorts of scales that can be employed to make the comparisons possible.

The Nominal Scale

Suppose, for example, that we want to measure an individual's degree of racism. At the most basic level, we could simply ask, "Are you a racist?" Ruling out uncertain responses ("I don't know," or "What do you mean by that?") and refusals ("What business is it of yours?"), we would be left with two possible answers, "Yes" and "No." If we are attempting to measure the degree of racism, we might be willing to assign a numerical value of zero to the "No" answer, but what value should we give an answer of "Yes"? One, fifty, a hundred, or what? As it happens, numerical values are not justified for this sort of scale. What we have done is to classify our respondents into two groups, but there is no necessary numerical relationship between the two groups. In more formal terms, we have grouped the respondents in terms of a nominal scale: a scale of measurement by which the observations can be classified, but not ordered.

The hypothetical responses of six subjects are shown in the first row of Table 5-2. These responses fall into two categories—"yes" and "no." We could assign numbers to the two groups just for purposes of identification, but these numbers would not indicate anything about the classes other than the fact that they were different. Other examples of the use of nominal scales would be a grouping of subjects into males and females, a grouping of mental patients according to psychiatric diagnosis, or a division of respondents according to their own race. The basic data that are available from classification according to a nominal scale are numbers, percentages, or proportions of subjects who give the different answers possible, or represent the different possible groups.

The Ordinal Scale

At the next highest scale of measurement, the classification scheme we employ would permit the ordering of the groups or individuals involved. Instead of asking whether an individual is a racist, we could try to infer his or her racial attitudes from, for example, political party affiliation. We would ask whether he or she belongs to a number of political parties or organizations such as the National Association for the Advancement of Colored People, the Democratic Party, the Republican Party, the American Independent Party, the John Birch Society, or the Ku Klux Klan. Then we would guess the person's attitudes on the basis of organizational membership. On the average we would expect that a member of the NAACP would have more favorable attitudes toward black people than would a member of the Democratic Party. A Democrat, in turn should hold more positive attitudes than a Republican, who should hold more positive attitudes than a member of the American Independent Party, and so on. In short, given what we believe (perhaps erroneously) about these various groups, we should be able to arrange their members in a logical order of decreasing favorability toward black people.

There would, of course, be exceptions to this order, and we have no way of knowing how much difference there might be between groups. The difference between the average Democrat's views and the average Republican's views might be equal to the difference between a Bircher and a Klansman, or it might be larger, or it might be smaller. We simply have no information on which to base such a judgment. Regardless of the distance between scores, when the data can be rank ordered (usually from the most favorable to the least favorable) they constitute what is known as an ordinal scale of measurement. Such a rank order is indicated in the second row of Table 5-2.

TABLE 5-2

Scales of measurement: hypothetical responses of six subjects to different questions about racial attitudes

SCALE	PERSON A	PERSON B	PERSON C	PERSON D	PERSON E	PERSON F
Nominal Scale "Are you racist?"	No	No	No	No	Yes	Yes
Ordinal Scale Organizational Membership Rank Order	NAACP 1	Dem. 2	Rep. 3	Am. Ind. 4	Birch 5	Klan 6
Interval Scale Attitude Score Transformed Score	80 45	70 35	50 15	25 −10	15 −20	5 −30

At this point a word of caution is necessary. We can assign numbers to the groups that constitute an ordinal scale (as shown by the ranks in the table), but we cannot perform arithmetic operations upon those numbers. The ranks given in the table are patterned after the usual method of ranking, with the most positive score receiving the rank of 1 (just as the person with the best grades in your high school graduating class received the rank of 1). But a rank of 4 does *not* mean that such a person's racial attitudes are the same distance from those of the person who is rank 2 as they are from the person who occupies rank 6. There are methods for determining the statistical significance of differences between sets of ranks, but these do not assume (and consequently do not permit us to conclude) anything about the distances between the ranked objects or people.

The Interval Scale

When the numbers that we assign to identify observations *do* tell us something about the distances between observations (while also providing us with a logical order), those numbers are said to constitute an interval scale of measurement. Most attitude scales strive for this level of measurement, so it is important for us to discuss some of the properties of an interval scale more fully. First, and most fundamental, the intervals between the numbers assigned are presumed to be equal, regardless of the actual unit of measurement. This requirement is most clearly described by an example. Suppose that instead of asking our six respondents what political and social organizations they belong to, we devised an attitude questionnaire to measure racism. This attitude questionnaire would consist of several different *items*—questions or statements relevant to the attitude being measured—and would yield a total score for each subject.

Some hypothetical attitude scores that might be obtained are shown in Table 5-2, in the first row under the designation of "interval scale." You will notice that favorability toward black people, as measured by this attitude questionnaire, does follow the rank order we obtained with the ordinal scale. It would thus appear that the scores do fall into a logical order. But what about the distances between scores? Person B has a score that is 20 points above that of Person C, but only 10 points below the score of Person A, and it doesn't take much arithmetic to observe that these distances are different, not equal. The point is that an interval scale requires equal intervals between the numbers used to form the scale, not between the scores that happen to be achieved by respondents who answer the questions. Thus the difference between the scores of Persons B and C is $70 - 50 = 20$ scale units, and the difference between the scores of Persons D and F is $25 - 5 = 20$ scale units. What the interval scale assumes is that *these identical numerical differences represent identical degrees of psychological difference.* Thus, to meet the assumptions of an interval scale, the B-C difference in favorability of attitudes toward blacks must be psychologically identical to the D-F difference in favorability.

The second property of the interval scale is that it has an *arbitrary zero point*, and this feature makes it quite appropriate for representing psychological variables such as attitudes. Until now we have been speaking of the attitude of "favorability toward black people" as if it were a *unipolar dimension:* a dimension which runs from a minimum value of zero to a maximum value of extreme presence of the variable in question. For example, the amount of sunlight present at any one place is a unipolar dimension, running from a total absence of sunlight (called night) to the maximum of sunlight present at high noon. There can be degrees of sunlight, but not degrees of its absence. If there is an absolute zero point for the dimension called "presence of sunlight," there do not exist absolute zero points for most psychological dimensions. What does it mean to say that a person has a zero attitude toward black people? Does it mean that the person simply doesn't ever think of black people, or that he or she thinks of them but has no opinion one way or the other? Shouldn't an attitudinal dimension have a zero point that represents uncertainty or lack of opinion, rather than a total absence of the attitude? As it happens, most social psychologists would agree that, indeed, attitude dimensions ought to be *bipolar*, running from extremely favorable to extremely unfavorable, with a zero point in the center that represents either uncertainty or neutrality.

To put this in terms of our present example, the attitudes of the NAACP member, the Democrat, and the Republican probably ought to be represented by positive scores (indicating varying degrees of favorability), while the attitudes of the American Independent Party member, the Bircher, and the Klansman most probably ought to be represented by negative scores (indicating varying degrees of unfavorable attitudes). This change in the original scale could be accomplished by subtracting the constant value of 35 from each attitude score.

The resulting *transformed* scores are shown in the last row of Table 5-2, and you can see that this transformation makes no difference in the essential property of the interval scale. The distance between Persons B and C is still 20 scale units ($35 - 15 = 20$) and the difference between Persons D and F is also still 20 units (-10 minus $-30 = 20$), and these identical scale differences are still presumed to represent equal psychological distances. This transformation required the subtraction of a constant, but if it had made psychological sense we could just as easily have added a constant to the scores, multiplied them by a constant, or divided them by a constant, and still have preserved the equality of the intervals. For example, division of each original score by 5 would make the B-C interval 4 units ($14 - 10 = 4$) and the D-F interval also 4 units ($5 - 1 = 4$). In other words, the properties of an interval scale are unchanged by any linear transformation of the scores. A familiar example of such a linear transformation is the changing of a temperature reading from degrees Fahrenheit to degrees Centigrade (with the formula for the transformation being $°C = 5/9 (°F - 32)$. So $0°C$ is the same as $32°F$, shifting the size of the scale units, as well as the location of the zero point, but preserving the relationship between intervals on the scale.

The Ratio Scale

If an interval scale is constructed with an absolute zero point, rather than with an arbitrary one, that scale becomes what is known as a ratio scale. Perhaps the best illustration of a familiar ratio scale is the scale used to measure length (or height). Whether the units of this scale are described in terms of inches and yards or in terms of centimeters and meters, the scale begins from an absolute zero point of no length at all. Because of its absolute zero point, we can legitimately compare the ratios between points on the scale: 6 feet is *twice* as long as 3 feet. We cannot make this kind of statement about interval scale data ($100°$ is not necessarily twice as hot as $50°$; an attitude of 50 is not necessarily twice as favorable as an attitude of 25).

The ratio scale is unchanged by multiplication or division, but its properties are altered by the addition or subtraction of a constant value (add 3 feet to the lengths above and you will see that although $6/3 = 2$, $9/6 \neq 2$). Since attitude scales almost never are ratio scales, we cannot ever be in a position to say that one person's attitude is so many times more or less favorable than another person's attitude. But what we lose in precision we gain in flexibility. Because of its arbitrary zero point, an interval scale can be used to represent a unipolar attitude or a bipolar attitude, and the values obtained can be subjected to whatever linear transformations are psychologically appropriate without changing the essential properties of the scale. Finally, any attitude measures that are interval scales can be subjected to a variety of arithmetic operations and statistical procedures without violating any of the assumptions that underlie these tests.

Keeping the distinctions among nominal, ordinal, interval, and

ratio scales in mind, we now turn to some of the principal methods of
attitude scaling. Perhaps the most widely used scales are those based
on item endorsement (Thurstone scales), those based on summated
agreement (Likert scales), and those involving judgment of the meaning of attitude objects (semantic differential scales). The endorsement
methods can be shown to produce interval scales, the semantic
differential methods can be considered as interval scales, and the
summated agreement scales can (with some additional assumptions)
also be considered to approximate the interval level of measurement.
Readers interested in further discussion of these issues could consult
Hays (1963) for a more detailed treatment of the nature of measurement, and Dawes (1972) for an extensive and rigorous presentation
of additional attitude measurement techniques.

SCALES FOR THE MEASUREMENT OF ATTITUDES

Endorsement Scales: The Equal-Appearing Intervals of Thurstone

As we observed earlier in the chapter, the component analysis
of attitudes into cognition, affect, and behavior has, in principle,
been around for a very long time. The major contribution that social
psychologists have made is to show how those components might be
measured, and the first attempt at attitude measurement was made by
Thurstone (1928). In this influential paper Thurstone asserted that
"attitudes can be measured" and provided a method for constructing
an attitude scale at the interval level of measurement. This method
was expanded and tested, using attitudes toward the church, and the
procedure and results were reported in a book by Thurstone and
Chave in 1929. Their theoretical contribution was a scale of equal-
appearing intervals, made up of attitude statements with known *scale
values* determined by the ratings of judges. Let's consider the procedure in a bit more detail.

Construction of a Thurstone Scale

The first step in the construction of a Thurstone scale is the gathering of attitude and opinion statements from various sources (e.g.,
newspaper editorials on the attitude issue, statements of public
figures on the topic, or statements written by the researchers). These
initial attitude or opinion statements constitute the item pool from
which the statements later to be included in the attitude questionnaire

will be selected. After the item pool has been amassed (usually about one hundred statements), it is presented to a large group of *judges* for the purpose of determining the scale values of the items.

The judges are instructed to sort the attitude statements into eleven piles ranging from most favorable toward the attitude object (11) through no characterization of the attitude object one way or the other (6) to most unfavorable toward the attitude object (1). It should be emphasized that the placement of each statement is to be made on the basis of the apparent favorability *of the statement itself,* not on the basis of the judge's opinion about the attitude object. As we shall see in Chapter Seven, this may be quite difficult for the judges to do, but here we will assume that they can disregard their own opinions. As an example of the sorting technique, consider a scale of attitudes toward war developed by Peterson under Thurstone's direction (reported in Thurstone, 1932).

A number of these items, chosen to represent identical psychological intervals, are shown in Table 5-3. The scale value shown for each of the four attitude statements is the median (midpoint) of the category placements made by the judges for that statement. In other words, regardless of their own position on the attitude object of war, *all* of the judges believed that the statement "War is glorious" was as favorable toward war as a statement could possibly get. In contrast, the scale value for statement B ("We want no more war if it can be avoided without dishonor") is 4.6, indicating that 50 percent of the judges placed the statement in categories .6 of the way through category 4, while the other 50 percent of the judges placed the statement in categories below .6 of the way into category 4. The method assumes that these placements by judges can be made independently of the judges' own attitudes toward war (an issue to which we shall return later in the discussion).

At this point in the construction of our Thurstone scale, we have amassed attitude statements, and have had judges sort those statements into the eleven categories of statement favorability. We have determined the scale value of each statement by finding that point along the continuum of favorability above which, and below which, 50 percent of the category placements have been made. Now how do we reduce this set of one hundred statements (the item pool) to a manageable size? Thurstone (1928) suggested three criteria to guide selection of the final twenty or thirty items to be used as the attitude scale. First, the statements in the final scale should be selected so that they constitute an evenly graded series of scale values. In other words, the final items should cover the whole range of favorability (1–11), and should be approximately equally spaced across that range. The items shown in Table 5-3 would satisfy this criterion. Second, items should

TABLE 5-3
Sample statements from the Thurstone-Peterson scale of attitudes toward war

SCALE VALUE		ATTITUDE STATEMENT
Least Favorable		
1.4	A.	War is a futile struggle resulting in self-destruction.
4.6	B.	We want no more war if it can be avoided without dishonor.
7.8	C.	War is sometimes necessary because right is more important than peace.
11.0	D.	War is glorious.
Most Favorable		

Adapted from Thurstone (1932).

be eliminated if the category judgments show them to be ambiguous. We can measure the ambiguity of an item by determining the *dispersion* of the category judgments: if an item has been placed into nearly all the eleven categories with approximately equal frequency, the category judgments are said to be widely dispersed; if the item has been placed with high frequency into a small number of categories (e.g., two or three, then it is narrowly dispersed. We can compute a statistical measure of the degree of dispersion (the standard deviation) and use this measure to determine in an objective way whether an item is ambiguous. The third criterion is one of irrelevance. If the category judgments appear to have been affected by factors other than the attitude being measured (e.g., the item is out of date, erroneously worded, or obviously distorted by response biases), the item should be discarded.

Use of the Thurstone Scale

After these preliminaries, we finally have an attitude scale suitable for administration to our subjects. The order of the statements in the scale is randomized to avoid order or progression effects arising from beginning with positive (or negative) statements and moving step by step to the other end of the scale. The scale is printed, and is preceded by directions to the subjects, instructing them to agree or disagree with each statement (the scale values of the items are *not* included on the questionnaire the subject receives). To determine a subject's score, the researcher looks at the scale values of all the items the subject has endorsed (agreed with) and determines the *median* (or midpoint) of these scale values. That midpoint is taken as the subject's attitude, and for convenience is usually indicated by the particular item that is closest in scale value to the subject's position. So, for example, a subject whose median score was 8.0 might have his or her position summarized by statement C in Table 5-3, which indicates that war may sometimes be a necessary evil.

Although the Thurstone scaling method does yield data equivalent to an interval scale of measurement (justifying a crucial assumption inherent in any statistical tests that would commonly be performed on such data), it is not without some methodological and conceptual problems. Perhaps the most obvious difficulty is that the procedure is cumbersome. Thurstone (1928) suggests that the item pool consist of at least one hundred statements, and that this pool be sorted by about three hundred judges, with the size of the item pool and the number of judges being designed to produce stable estimates of the scale values and ambiguity of the items. Even though smaller numbers of judges are acceptable (Green, 1954), this procedure still requires a large number of willing judges, a long period of time per judge, a huge number of items constructed by the researcher, and a fast computer to analyze the results (imagine how difficult it was when Thurstone and his associates did their early work without the aid of computers).

Such an expenditure of time and effort is essential for someone interested (as Thurstone was) in thoroughly describing the properties of an attitude scale; it is impractical for a researcher who is simply looking for a dependent variable. Most investigators who would want to determine how a particular pattern of persuasive communications might influence subjects' attitudes toward war, or black people, or some other attitude object are (understandably) reluctant to do such extensive preliminary work.

The second major difficulty with the Thurstone technique is a conceptual one, and it may be part of the reason that so many researchers avoid the eleven-category sorting aspect of the method. This difficulty centers on the assumption that the judges are able to perform their task independent of their own attitudes toward the attitude object. People ought to regard "war is glorious" as an extremely favorable statement, regardless of their own position, and its category scale value of 11.0 suggests that in this case the assumption was justified. But what about less extreme statements? For example, if we asked people to judge the statement "War is sometimes necessary because right is more important than peace" we might find that its category placement would be affected by the judges' own opinions. In some cases these differences of opinion would produce a dispersion of responses great enough to exclude the item, but in many cases the dispersion would be large enough for imprecision without being large enough for rejection of the item.

If people's attitudes are as important a determinant of their behavior as we argue that they are, how can we expect our judges to put their attitudes aside during the judgment task? Not only may the judges have different positions on the meaning of any single statement, the psychological dimension underlying all the statements may also be different for different judges. This point has been made by Sherif and Sherif (1969), who suggest that the way the original eleven-category scale is constructed is equivalent to stretching a rubber ruler, which contains unknown units of different sizes, until eleven categories are formed. The essential problem is that "people do not stretch their acceptances and rejections merely to conform to the objects judged" (p. 368). For this reason, the Thurstone scale may not actually produce equality of *psychological* intervals across individuals even though the numbers that the technique produces do correspond to an interval scale level of measurement.

Summated Agreement: The Likert Scale

Thurstone deserves credit for developing the first scales for the measurement of social attitudes. But for conceptual reasons and practical reasons, the Thurstone scale has been supplanted in contemporary attitude measurement by the Likert scale. In the course of research on liberalism and conservatism, Likert (1932) developed a new method of attitude measurement that differed from the Thurstone technique in two important ways. First, Likert's procedure did not *require* initial category sorting by judges, although judges were recommended for attitude item selection and refinement. Thus a researcher who was quite familiar with the attitude domain in question could simply omit the first step in scale construction. Second, the subject's response alternatives were not restricted to a dichotomous choice of agree-disagree. Instead of this two-choice answer the subject was required to indicate for each attitude item both the direction of his or her response (agree-disagree) and the degree of that choice. Thus, in the original Likert scales there were five response alternatives for every attitude statement: strongly agree, agree, undecided, disagree, and strongly disagree, as shown in Table 5-4. The resulting five-point scale could be represented by numbers ranging from +2 to −2. To find the individual's overall attitude, the researcher would simply add all these numbers together. On a ten-item questionnaire the possible range of the resulting *summated ratings of agreement* would be from a low value (representing consistent strong disagreement) of −20 to a high value (representing consistent strong agreement) of +20.

TABLE 5-4

Adaptation of two items from the Thurstone-Peterson attitudes toward war scale to a five-alternative Likert scale format

ATTITUDE STATEMENT	RESPONSE ALTERNATIVES AND NUMERICAL SCORES	SCALE RANGE
Five-alternative format (with a neutral, or "undecided," point)		
"War is a futile struggle resulting in self-destruction."	SA A U D SD −2 −1 0 +1 +2	(−2 to +2)
"War is glorious."	SA A U D SD +2 +1 0 −1 −2	(+2 to −2)

SA = strong agreement; A = agreement; U = undecided; D = disagreement; SD = strong disagreement. The numerical values are arranged so that higher numbers represent an attitude of greater favorability toward war on the respondent's part.

Construction of a Likert Scale

As is the case with the Thurstone scale, the first task in constructing a Likert scale is to ensure that all the items measure the same underlying attitude continuum. For an attitude dimension unfamiliar to the researcher, the best procedure is to give a large item pool to a large number of judges, and ask the judges to indicate their own attitudes using the five alternatives that will later be used with the subjects. Notice that this is a difference from the Thurstone procedure, in which the judges are forced to use an eleven-point scale to sort the items in a way presumably independent of their own attitudes. After the judges' ratings have been obtained, the items in the pool are subjected to a procedure called item analysis: the scores on each item are intercorrelated with the scores on every other item, and with the total score achieved by each subject. Items which do not correlate with the total score (when that total is adjusted to remove the score for the particular item being compared) do not represent the same attitude dimension and can be discarded. This procedure for item analysis, in conjunction with checks for irrelevance and ambiguity, can be used to reduce the number of items to a size appropriate for the final questionnaire. Unlike the additional requirement of the Thurstone scale, Likert items cannot be distributed across the attitude continuum—the range is provided by the different response alternatives available to the subject.

The Interpretation of Strong Disagreement

Thus, in comparison with the Thurstone method, the Likert scaling technique is less difficult, less costly, and does not assume that the judges can determine a scale value independent of their own attitudes. As a result, it has become generally preferred. But the Likert procedure is not totally without disadvantages. For example, care must be taken in construction of the items to avoid possible misinterpretation of "strong disagreement." Consider the attitude item "Women deserve to have the same employment opportunities that men have." We know what strong agreement with this statement represents. But is strong disagreement reflecting male chauvinism ("I disagree because I believe that women deserve *fewer* opportunities"), or is it reflecting feminism ("I disagree because I think women deserve *greater* opportunities than men")? We have absolutely no way of knowing which of these quite different attitudes led to the strong disagreement. The problem can be alleviated to some extent by writing items that are themselves clearly worded in one direction or the other, such as "Women deserve to have greater employment opportunities than men have." Now the feminist would agree, and the male chauvinist would disagree. But the person who believed in a total lack of discrimination—either against a group or in favor of the group— would also disagree. The best solution for attitude items of this sort is to *let the subjects select the modifiers* instead of forcing them to agree or disagree with a modifier provided by the researcher. The statement could now read as follows:

Women should have employment opportunities which are
____much greater than the ones men have.   (+2)
____greater than the ones men have.   (+1)
____the same as the ones men have.   (0)
____fewer than the ones men have.   (−1)
____much fewer than the ones men have.   (−2)

The subject simply checks the response alternative that represents his or her opinion, and we have a very clear idea of the subject's position on the issue. This is an alternative format used by Likert (1932), and still has the characteristics of the Likert scale.

Elimination of the Neutral Point

There is one other change from the direction-degree five-alternative response format that is often necessary. When an individual is asked to express attitudes about a controversial subject, use of the "undecided" category is likely to be substantially greater than if the attitude issue is a less emotionally involving one. It is not that the subject truly has no attitude, or has truly not made up his or her mind. On the contrary, the subject most probably has decided, but just doesn't want the researcher to know the outcome of the decision. This retreat into the undecided category is especially likely to happen when the respondent knows his or her position is an unpopular one, or when he or she believes that the researcher's own attitude might be the opposite one (the old problems of social desirability response bias and evaluation apprehension, as discussed more completely in Chapter Two). To counteract this tendency to take refuge in the neutral point, many attitude researchers using Likert-type scales simply *eliminate* the neutral point, and often expand the response possibilities accordingly. Now instead of five alternatives, there would be six: *strongly agree, moderately agree, slightly agree, slightly disagree, moderately disagree, strongly disagree*, as shown in Table 5-5. Elimination of the neutral point forces the subject to make his or her position known, but the addition of the "slightly" category on each side of the eliminated neutral point permits the subject to save some face. Such a scale is scored as a *seven*-point scale, since the neutral point is assumed to be part of the underlying continuum even though it is prohibited as a response possibility. The properties of this scale are the same as those of other Likert scales, and it could be argued that the psychological intervals represented by these six alternatives are even more likely to be equivalent than are the intervals contained in the original five-alternative scale.

The Problem of Summation

If some of the problems inherent in the Likert scale can be alleviated with proper modifications, one difficulty in the interpretation of the final score will remain. Consider now a ten-item Likert scale with six response alternatives (to be scored as a seven-point scale). There is only one way to obtain a score of +30, and that is to answer "strongly agree" to all items. Similarly, there is only one way

TABLE 5-5
Adaptation of two items from the Thurstone-Peterson attitudes toward war scale to a six-alternative Likert scale format

ATTITUDE STATEMENT	RESPONSE ALTERNATIVES AND NUMERICAL SCORES						SCALE RANGE
Six-alternative format (without neutral point)							
"War is a futile struggle resulting in self-destruction."	STA −3	MA −2	SLA −1	SLD +1	MD +2	STD +3	(−3 to +3)
"War is glorious."	STA +3	MA +2	SLA +1	SLD −1	MD −2	STD −3	(+3 to −3)

STA = strong agreement; MA = moderate agreement; SLA = slight agreement; SLD = slight disagreement; MD = moderate disagreement; STD = strong disagreement. The numerical values are arranged so that higher numbers represent an attitude of greater favorability toward war on the respondent's part.

to obtain a score of −30, and that is to answer "strongly disagree" on all items. But what about a score of zero? Such a score cannot be achieved by responding "uncertain," since the six-alternative format precludes that response. But it could be achieved by a balanced distribution of responses: five "strong agreements" and five "strong disagreements" (+15 plus −15); or five "slight agreements" and five "slight disagreements" (+5 plus −5). Without looking at their patterns of answers to the questions, we would conclude that these two people with totals of zero had the *same attitude*. But one of the respondents is clearly indifferent to the attitude object and is being forced to answer one way or the other, while the other respondent has very strong, but *conflicting* opinions on the issue. Is it really proper to assume on the basis of a total score that the attitudes of these two individuals are equivalent? Probably not, and the inability of the Likert scale to discriminate between them (without requiring the researcher to evaluate every item for all subjects who have moderate scores) is an important disadvantage of the method.

The Meaning of Attitude Objects: The Semantic Differential

A Multidimensional Method

Part of the difficulty with both the Thurstone scale and the Likert scale is that both of these attitude measurement techniques constrain the respondent to a limited set of possible answers. One has only to administer an attitude scale to hear complaints of, "Why was it worded this way?" or, "What exactly does this mean?" or "What if I don't think that any of these answers are appropriate?" It is hoped that you now understand a little better why Thurstone and Likert scales are constructed as they are, but you can still appreciate the validity of the complaint. Subjects believe that typical attitude scales do not permit them to respond with the complexity their attitudes really contain. One of the primary criteria for the construction of either a Thurstone or a Likert scale is that the statements measure only a single attitude, and an item analysis that removes statements which do not correlate with the total score is the procedure by which this goal is achieved. Unfortunately, all too often the exclusion of un-correlated items produces a scale that measures *only one aspect* of a single attitude. Many of our important social attitudes are multi-dimensional in nature, and it would be desirable to have a technique that could deal with this complexity. The *semantic differential*, origin-ally designed by Osgood and his associates (Osgood, Suci, and Tan-nenbaum, 1957) for the measurement of the connotative meaning of language, is just such a technique.

Construction of a Semantic Differential Scale

Rather than providing the subject with a preselected series of statements with which to agree or disagree, the semantic differential method presents a concept to be evaluated, along with a series of seven-point bipolar rating scales or *dimensions* on which that concept is to be judged. A sample set of dimensions for the concept "war" is shown in Table 5-6, and you will notice that four of the bipolar dimensions—futile-productive, honorable-dishonorable, unnecessary-necessary, humble-glorious—pertain to issues raised by each of the statements from the Thurstone-Peterson Attitudes Toward War scale discussed earlier. Instead of asking the subjects to agree or disagree about the futility of war, the semantic differential technique has them rate the *issue concept* "war" on a scale of futility to productiveness. Instead of including the idea of national honor in a statement, the semantic differential assesses the subject's opinion of that idea by means of an additional rating scale (honorable-dishonorable). This parallel can be extended to nearly all the issues posed in either a Thurstone or Likert scale dealing with the attitude toward war. The rating scales are scored as seven-point scales, and the numbers are arranged so that higher scores represent more favorable evaluations of the concept (the numbers are not usually printed on the forms given to subjects). The subject's task with the semantic differential is certainly more abstract than the task in responding to Thurstone or Likert statements, but it is this greater degree of abstraction that enables the subject to feel that the answers can adequately reflect the complexity of his or her attitudes.

TABLE 5-6
Evaluation of the concept of war through the semantic differential method of attitude assessment

CONCEPT TO BE EVALUATED: "WAR"

Rating Scales to be Used

futile	: −3	: −2	: −1	: 0	: +1	: +2	: +3 :	productive
honorable	: +3	: +2	: +1	: 0	: −1	: −2	: −3 :	dishonorable
good	: +3	: +2	: +1	: 0	: −1	: −2	: −3 :	bad
unnecessary	: −3	: −2	: −1	: 0	: +1	: +2	: +3 :	necessary
active	: +3	: +2	: +1	: 0	: −1	: −2	: −3 :	passive
humble	: −3	: −2	: −1	: 0	: +1	: +2	: +3 :	glorious
strong	: +3	: +2	: +1	: 0	: −1	: −2	: −3 :	weak

Three Dimensions of Attitude Judgments

The other rating scales included in Table 5-6—good-bad, active-passive, and strong-weak—deserve further comment. In a large number of studies in over twenty different cultures, Osgood and his associates found that three fundamental dimensions account for most of the variance in the ratings of most concepts. In these studies subjects were given extensive sets of rating scales to use in their ratings of many different concepts (both issue concepts such as "war" and *person concepts* such as Franklin D. Roosevelt or Winston Churchill or public figures appropriate to the culture). The ratings were then intercorrelated to determine both how an individual rater might use the rating scales to describe different concepts, and how different raters might use the scales to describe the same concept. The resulting intercorrelations were then subjected to a statistical procedure known as **factor analysis** in order to reduce the number of dimensions necessary to describe the ratings. For example, rating scales such as good-bad, valuable-worthless, and beautiful-ugly can typically be accounted for by an underlying factor of *evaluation.* Most of the factor-analytic studies on connotative meaning have found that this evaluative factor and two others—an *activity* factor (represented by the dimension active-passive) and a *potency* factor (represented by the dimension strong-weak)—account for most of the variance in the scores on individual rating scales. In other words, if we know a subject's scores on these three dimensions, we can predict pretty well what his or her ratings would be on a large number of other bipolar dimensions. Of the three factors, the evaluative one seems to be the most important, and it corresponds quite well to the conception of the affective component of an attitude.

Although the semantic differential technique makes some subjects happier about their rating task, it, too, has some disadvantages. One of the major reasons we try to measure people's attitudes toward various social objects is the hope that knowledge of those attitudes will help us to predict social behavior. This hope is based on the premise that what people think and feel about the object will have some implications for the way they behave toward the object. As we discovered earlier in this chapter, the connection between the internal components of cognition and affect and the externally observable behavior is not as strong as we might like, and use of the semantic differential to assess the internal components may weaken the link still further. If an individual indicates by endorsing a Thurstone or Likert scale item that he or she considers the Defense Department budget too high, that response may tell us a great deal about the person's choice of congressional candidates (given that one opposes defense spending while one advocates increasing such spending).

But to know that the same individual considers the concept "defense spending" to be bad, active, and strong (especially since in other circumstances activity and strength have good connotations) leaves us less certain about the individual's probable voting behavior.

At this point in the discussion of scaling methods, you might expect the suggestion that a new attitude measurement technique be devised that would include the advantages of all three methods, while avoiding the disadvantages associated with each. Unfortunately your expectation would overestimate the discipline's ability to solve the problem of attitude measurement. In part because of the importance to scientific social psychology of the concept of an attitude, and in part because of a continuing search for a "perfect" method, investigators have developed a great profusion of attitude measurement techniques, of which the Thurstone, Likert, and semantic differential scales are only the most prominent. But while each of these methods may solve a problem inherent in another technique, each also raises a new problem of its own. The best we can do at present is to know the advantages, disadvantages, and most appropriate applications of each scaling technique, so that the assessment of the particular attitudes of interest will be least affected by the problems inherent in the scaling procedure chosen.

Summary

An **attitude** (p. 168) is an organized predisposition to behave in a favorable or unfavorable way toward a specified class of social objects. As such, it consists of three distinct components: the affective component, the cognitive component, and the behavioral component. The *cognitive component* (p. 170) includes all the individual's beliefs about the attitude object, including both those beliefs that may be accurate and those stereotyped beliefs that may be inaccurate. Studies of racial stereotyping between 1933 and 1969 show that the negative stereotype of black people held by whites has decreased to a significant degree, but research with the bogus pipeline technique (p. 174) indicates that at least some of the apparent fading of social stereotypes may be based on the response bias of social desirability. The *affective component* (p. 177) of an attitude represents the individual's evaluation of the members of the object class. In the attitude of racism, this component (prejudice) can be emotional, and arises from the individual's socialization (p. 181) experiences, from actual and assumed belief congruence (p. 182) with members of the object class, and from the aggression that follows frustration (p. 185) of goals (especially when this frustration is the product of direct competition with members of the object class). The *behavioral component* (p. 187) of an attitude is a general predisposition to action, and in principle it should reflect the individual's beliefs and feelings. In practice, however, actual behavior is determined not only by an individual's attitude, but also by the constraints inherent in the situation. For this reason, behavior does not always correspond to the predictions from affect and cognition; in the case of the attitude of racism, a person who stereotypes black people and who is prejudiced toward them may (under certain circumstances) still fail to discriminate against blacks.

Each of the three attitude components can be measured in a variety of ways, including physiological measurements of affect, observation of behavior, and the verbal responses that an individual might make to a number of rating scales. Some of these attitude measurement techniques have been adapted from other areas of social psychology, some are quite specific to the particular attitude in question, and still others—including the traditional attitude measurement methods—could be employed to assess attitudes toward any class of social objects or social issues. The goal of attitude measurement techniques is to achieve a description of affect, cognition, or behavioral intention that constitutes what is known as an interval scale (p. 196), because that scale's arbitrary zero point and consistency through a linear transformation best represent the presumed psychological characteristics of an attitude. Although the goal of attitude measurement is interval scaling, this goal is not always achieved.

Traditional scales in wide use today for the measurement of social attitudes include the endorsement scales (p. 199), such as the Thurstone scale; the summated agreement scales (p. 203), such as the Likert scale; and the *semantic differential* method (p. 207). The Thurstone scaling method (p. 199) requires an initial sorting of attitude statements by a group of judges to determine the scale value of each statement. Then a selected series of statements (whose scale values are known) is presented to the subjects whose attitudes are being measured. The individual's attitude score is then computed as the median of the scale values of the items the person endorses. The Likert scaling method (p. 203) is procedurally simpler than the Thurstone method and permits a wider latitude of response by the subject. For each statement in a Likert scale, the subject is asked to indicate not only the direction (agree-disagree) of his or her response, but also the degree of commitment to that response (strong, moderate, or slight). The Likert scale is then scored either as a five-point scale or as a seven-point scale (depending upon the format of the scale), and the person's attitude is represented by the sum of his or her scores across all the items in the scale. The *semantic differential* method (p. 207) requires the subject to evaluate the attitude object in terms of a series of bipolar adjectives (p. 197) to determine the connotative meaning (and affective meaning) of the attitude object for the individual. Analyses of semantic differential scores by the method of factor analysis (p. 209) typically reveal three underlying dimensions on which most attitude objects are judged. These three dimensions are the evaluative dimension (p. 209) (which corresponds most closely to the affective component of an attitude), represented by the adjective pair *good-bad*; the activity dimension (p. 209), represented by the adjective pair *active-passive;* and the potency dimension (p. 209), represented by the adjective pair *strong-weak.*

Each of the attitude scaling techniques, as well as others not discussed in the chapter, has its own particular advantages and limitations. It is the attitude researcher's responsibility to remember that any verbal measure of attitudes may be influenced by subjects' natural tendency to present themselves in a favorable light, to recognize the limitations of whatever method of measurement is employed, and to choose whatever method is most appropriate (and least likely to be biased) for the measurement task at hand.

Suggested Additional Readings

DAWES, R. M. *Fundamentals of attitude measurement.* New York: Wiley, 1972. This comprehensive introduction to attitude scaling techniques covers a wide variety of magnitude estimation, proximity estimation, "unfolding," and multidimensional methods, as well as the more traditional rating scale methods described in the present chapter. It is perhaps better as a source of attitude scaling *theory* than as a guide to the construction of simple attitude scales.

JONES, J. M. *Prejudice and racism.* Reading, Mass.: Addison-Wesley, 1972. This book examines the problem of racism in America through a brief review of the history of black people in America and a more extended discussion of the realities of prejudice, discrimination, and racism. It contains an up-to-date review of the components of prejudice originally suggested by Allport (1954), and a discussion of the elements and results of institutional racism as well.

JONES, R. L. (Ed.) *Black psychology.* New York: Harper & Row, 1972. Concentrates on the various psychological effects of being black in white American society. Many of the papers are research studies, but others are based on personal experience. A good overview of the problems created by prejudice and racism.

LOYE, D. *The healing of a nation.* New York: Norton, 1970. This book presents significant events in the history of black people in America, together with a social-psychological analysis of those events. The chapters alternate (history followed by social psychology), and in the course of the book virtually every major theory in social psychology is brought to bear on some aspect of the problem of racism. This book is highly recommended for students interested in the social relevance of social psychological theory.

SHAW, M. E., and WRIGHT, J. M. *Scales for the measurement of attitudes.* New York: McGraw-Hill, 1967. This book begins with a general discussion of attitude scaling and then presents scales developed by researchers interested in social practices; social issues; international issues; abstract concepts; political, religious, and ethnic attitudes; and social institutions. The scale characteristics, reliability and validity data, and actual items used are given for over 175 different attitude scales. Don't make up a scale of your own without looking here to see if someone has already done it for you.

The horizontal and vertical structure of an attitude can become quite complex.

Attitude Organization and the Principle of Cognitive Consistency

Chapter Six

Think for a moment of all the money spent in a year in the attempt to measure and change attitudes. Politicians take extensive opinion polls on controversial issues, advertisers spend millions of dollars trying to sell their products, social psychologists conduct innumerable research projects on attitude formation and change, and in your every-day dealings with other people you try to determine what your friends think about various issues. What justifies all this interest in attitude measurement and change? It is simply the belief that atti-tudes are related to behavior, and that changing attitudes will lead to changes in behavior. The advertiser certainly does not want you only to think highly of a product; he or she wants your attitude to lead to a behavioral choice favorable to it. Although, as we saw in Chapter Five, the relationship between attitudes expressed and overt behavior is less direct than we might at first have believed (with typi-cal correlations between attitudes and behavior averaging about +.50), it is still strong enough to warrant much of the effort devoted to the study of attitude organization and change.

When we speak of attitude change, one of the first questions that comes to mind is, "Why are some attitudes so much more difficult to change than others?" Our intuitive answer to the question might deal with the importance of the attitudes involved, suggesting that un-important or trivial attitudes would be easily changed, but that important attitudes would be very difficult to alter. But what do we mean by importance? Research and theory in scientific social psychology identify two aspects of the importance of an attitude: its *centrality* in the individual's overall attitude structure, and the psychological *function* the attitude serves. The more an attitude is related to other attitudes—that is, the more interconnected it is—the more difficult it will be to change. And the greater the psychological significance of holding a particular attitude, the more difficult it will be to alter that attitude. Before we can address the question of attitude change, we need to examine both attitude organization and attitude function more carefully.

Recall that an attitude is an *organized* predisposition to behave in a favorable or unfavorable manner toward a specified class of social objects. One implication of this organization was discussed in Chapter Five: the affective, cognitive, and behavioral components of an attitude are related to each other, with the first two components com-bining to produce the behavioral predisposition. A second implication of the organized nature of an attitude has not yet been dealt with: attitudes are not organized in isolation from one another; on the contrary, they are interconnected. In short, if we know an individual's attitude on one issue, we can rather reliably predict his or her atti-tudes on related issues. A person who holds a very positive attitude toward big business and its continued prosperity will most probably

favor individual initiative and be opposed to mandatory union benefits, government interference with business, and perhaps even some
social institutions such as the United Nations. Indeed, a scale of
social attitudes developed by Kerlinger (1967) was based on the explicit presumption that these various sorts of attitudes would be
interrelated, and the data Kerlinger collected justify that presumption.

So when we speak of attitude organization, we mean at least two
different things. First, the fact that an attitude is organized within
itself suggests that its cognitive and emotional antecedents are related
to its behavioral consequences. Second, since attitudes do not exist in
isolation, organization refers to the interconnections among various
attitudes. In an ideal world we might hope to develop some sophisticated measurement devices that would enable us to create a map of an
individual's attitude structure, much as a cartographer creates a map
of a highway system. But attitudes, unlike highways, are not directly
observable, so we must construct *models* of attitude organization and
test these models for their explanatory and predictive value. The
particular models of attitude organization to be discussed in this
chapter include a syllogistic model of attitude structure outlined by
Jones and Gerard (1967), a recent information-processing model (Fishbein and Ajzen, 1975), and the cognitive consistency models, including balance (Heider, 1958; Newcomb, 1968), congruity (Osgood and
Tannenbaum, 1955; Tannenbaum, 1968), and dissonance (Aronson,
1968; Festinger, 1957). We begin with the syllogistic model, which
proposes a horizontal and vertical structure to attitudes, and then
consider the information-processing approach. Finally we turn to the
cognitive consistency models, which add a general motivational
principle—the reduction of inconsistency—to their structural descriptions of attitudes.

Logical Models of Attitude Organization

THE SYLLOGISTIC MODEL

The Belief Premise and the Value Premise

The syllogistic theory of attitude structure proposed by Jones and
Gerard (1967) and later elaborated by Bem (1970) provides an explanation of how the cognitive and affective components of an
attitude might combine to produce a behavioral predisposition. The

syllogism is a form of logical reasoning in which two *premises* are related to each other in such a way that they logically imply a *conclusion*. It should be emphasized that not all attitudes are logical representations of the real social world (for example, the attitude of racism). On the contrary, a substantial number of attitudes appear to conform to what Abelson and Rosenberg (1958) have called *psychologic* (reasoning that serves psychological needs, rather than logical necessity). But even here, the syllogism can be a useful model of the derivation of an attitude.

The minor premise, which appears first in an attitude syllogism, is the **belief premise**. Just what is a belief? You will recall from our discussion of cognitive categorization in Chapter Three, and from treatment of the cognitive component of an attitude in Chapter Five, that cognitive categories are formed on the basis of the *criterial,* or defining, attributes of the objects concerned. For example, biological gender is the criterial attribute in the formation of the two cognitive categories male and female. But there are other attributes (appearance, personality characteristics, behavior) which are more or less reliably associated with gender, even though they are not criterial. These attributes constitute our beliefs about "masculine" and "feminine" characteristics. In short, according to Jones and Gerard (1967) a *belief is a statement of the noncriterial attributes of an object.* This definition of a belief in terms of the cognitive process of categorization suggests that the belief premise in an attitude syllogism corresponds quite well to what we have previously called the cognitive component of an attitude.

The major premise, which appears second in an attitude syllogism, is the value or evaluative premise. This **evaluative premise** *states the person's affective or emotional reaction to the characteristic mentioned in the belief premise.* The value contained in this premise is a statement of the positive or negative qualities with which the object is endowed. A positive value motivates the individual to approach or praise the object, but a negative value motivates the person to avoid or denigrate the object. Those objects which have both some positive characteristics and some negative characteristics produce correspondingly ambivalent behavioral predispositions. Just as the belief premise of an attitude syllogism represents the cognitive component of an attitude, the evaluative premise of the syllogism represents the affective component.

The combination of the belief (cognitive) premise with the evaluative (affective) premise produces the attitudinal conclusion. This conclusion is itself a positive or negative evaluation of the attitude object, and it is presumed that such an evaluation will produce the predisposition toward favorable or unfavorable behavior.

Minor Premise (Belief):	*Forests **provide shelter to animals.***
Major Premise (Evaluation):	***Providing shelter to animals** is good.*
Conclusion (Attitude):	*Forests are good.*
Minor Premise (Belief):	*Defense spending **creates jobs.***
Major Premise (Evaluation):	***Creating jobs** is good.*
Conclusion (Attitude):	*Defense spending is good.*

The minor premise in each syllogism is stated first, and this minor premise contains two elements: the subject is the item in question (forests, defense spending), and the predicate is a characterization of that subject (as a shelter for animals) or a statement of the subject's effects (creation of jobs). This predicate of the belief premise is called the *middle term*, because it appears again as the subject of the evaluative premise. The predicate of the major (evaluation) premise is typically a characterization of the middle term (as being either good or bad).

Horizontal Structure

The middle term appears in both premises, and provides the cognitive link between belief and evaluation that is necessary in order for these two premises to imply the attitudinal conclusion. In an important sense, the middle term is the *reason* for the final conclusion, and the fact that this reason disappears from the conclusion strengthens the analogy between the syllogistic model and other views of an attitude. As we learned in Chapter Five, we have only limited success in our attempts to infer a person's attitude from overt behavior. Even when the attitude itself is relatively obvious, the person's reasons for holding the attitude may not be available to us. For example, if we know that an individual has written to a congressional representative asking for an increase in the appropriations to the Defense Department, we would be fairly certain that the writer had a positive attitude toward defense spending. But *why* does the writer favor defense spending? Is it because of a belief that defense spending "creates jobs," or a belief that defense spending "enhances national prestige," or "helps prevent war"? Obviously there are multiple possibilities for the middle terms, so we cannot reliably infer which reason applies just from the demonstrated existence of the attitude. Knowing a person's attitudes is *not* the same thing as knowing why he or she holds those attitudes.

Another way to describe the existence of multiple possibilities for the middle term is to say that the final attitudinal conclusion might be the result of any number of different syllogisms. Consider the following two syllogisms:

Defense spending creates jobs.   *Defense spending prevents war.*
Creating jobs is good.   *Preventing war is good.*
Therefore, *Defense spending is good.*

These two syllogisms differ only in their middle terms (creation of jobs or prevention of war), and both lead to exactly the same attitudinal conclusion: a positive evaluation of defense spending. They are two different reasons for holding the same attitude, although they are relatively independent of each other. Such parallel syllogisms leading to the same attitudinal conclusion form the horizontal structure of the attitude, and the greater the number of such syllogisms, the greater support there is for the attitude. If you think of the attitude as a long iron bar, suspended by a number of ropes with each rope representing a syllogism, the number of different ropes attached to the bar is the measure of the attitude's horizontal structure. The more different ropes there are, the less weight each will have to support.

Vertical Structure

But where did the ideas in each of these horizontally arranged syllogisms come from? Certainly we are not born thinking that defense spending creates jobs and prevents war, so there must be more than these premises to the attitude. Considering the origins of a belief or an evaluation leads us to the idea of the vertical structure of the attitude. Take, for example, the evaluative premise "preventing war is good." This premise might itself be the conclusion of a prior syllogism:

Preventing war can save lives.
Saving lives is good.
Therefore. . .*Preventing war is good.*
Defense spending can prevent war.
Preventing war is good.
Therefore. . .*Defense spending is good.*

In this case, the conclusion of one syllogism has become the evaluative premise of a later syllogism, and this relationship is the basis for the vertical structure of an attitude. To return to the analogy of the attitude as an iron bar, some of the ropes holding it up will be longer than others—will have more extensive vertical structures—and we therefore assume that they will be stronger than the shorter ropes.

A Complex Attitude

The horizontal and vertical structure of an attitude can become quite complex, as indicated by the diagram of a hypothetical attitude toward defense spending shown in Figure 6-1. When you look care-

FIGURE 6-1
The horizontal and vertical structure of an attitude toward defense spending.

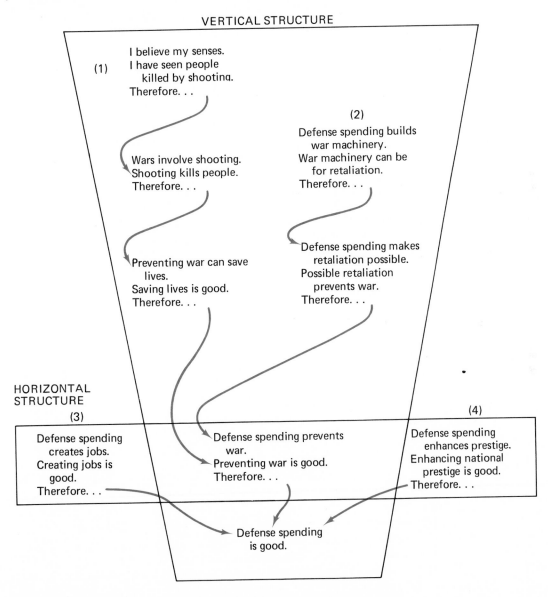

VERTICAL STRUCTURE

(1) I believe my senses.
I have seen people
   killed by shooting.
Therefore. . .

(2)
Defense spending builds
   war machinery.
War machinery can be
   for retaliation.
Therefore. . .

Wars involve shooting.
Shooting kills people.
Therefore. . .

Defense spending makes
   retaliation possible.
Possible retaliation
   prevents war.
Therefore. . .

Preventing war can save
   lives.
Saving lives is good.
Therefore. . .

HORIZONTAL
STRUCTURE
(3)

Defense spending
   creates jobs.
Creating jobs is
   good.
Therefore. . .

Defense spending prevents
   war.
Preventing war is good.
Therefore. . .

(4)
Defense spending
   enhances prestige.
Enhancing national
   prestige is good.
Therefore. . .

Defense spending
   is good.

fully at the syllogisms contained in this diagram, you will see that some of them look a bit different from ones we have considered so far. They *are* different, in two respects. First, at the top of the vertical structure leading to the evaluative premise is a syllogism (identified as number 1) the first premise of which is "I believe my senses."

This premise is what Bem (1970) calls a zero-order belief: a non-conscious faith in the validity of sensory experience. We simply believe what our senses tell us, without questioning the truth value of the information they provide. Not that our perceptions are always veridical. Chapters Three and Four contain enough examples of non-veridical social perception to suggest that we should not accept sensory information as unquestionably valid. Nevertheless, our senses are basically accurate most of the time, so we do not often think about the possibility that they might have been in error. Certainly in the present example the conscious chain of reasoning would begin with "shooting kills people," instead of beginning with the primitive (and nonconscious) syllogism which leads to this conclusion. Thus the complete attitude structure diagramed in Figure 6-1 differs from the separate syllogisms we have presented earlier in that it rests on a primitive belief in the validity of sensory experience.

A second difference that you will notice is that some of the syllogisms in the vertical structure do not appear to have value premises. Take, for example, the "war machinery" syllogism (2). It combines a belief about the origin of war machinery (defense spending) with a belief about the possible use of war machinery (retaliation) to derive a conclusion about the effects of defense spending (increasing the ability to retaliate). This syllogism's conclusion is a *belief*, as are both of its premises. In other words, not all syllogisms are attitudes; only those which contain both a belief premise and an evaluative premise yield a conclusion that is an attitude. The fact that derived beliefs can also be represented as conclusions of syllogisms does not reduce the applicability of the syllogistic model to attitudes; it only implies that an attitude is the result only of a syllogism of a specified form.

Finally, the diagram indicates the presence of the horizontal structure (represented by the parallel syllogisms 3 and 4). Defense spending is good not only because it "prevents war," but also because it "creates jobs," and "enhances national prestige." Although the diagram does not depict them, there is a vertical structure for each of these reasons that corresponds roughly to the vertical structure illustrated for "preventing war." Thus the person's final attitude—defense spending is good—is a *complex* attitude with a large number of horizontal and vertical interconnections.

INFORMATION PROCESSING IN ATTITUDE ORGANIZATION

The syllogistic model indicates the horizontal and vertical structure characteristic of many attitudes, and it suggests that the greater the complexity, the stronger (and more resistant to change) the attitude will be. But as it stands, the syllogistic model considers only the total number of beliefs, not the strength of individual beliefs; the total number of positive and negative evaluations, not the degree of favorability or unfavorability of an attitude toward the object. Is it possible to obtain a more precise description of the structure of a social attitude? Recently developed *information-processing* models of attitude organization (e.g., Fishbein and Ajzen, 1975; Wyer, 1974) indicate how this might be accomplished.

Beliefs, Evaluations, and Behavioral Intentions

Let us consider the model proposed by Fishbein and Ajzen (1975) to account for the manner in which a person processes information about an attitude object. This model follows the traditional tripartite division of an attitude, and many of the terms used in the model are roughly equivalent to the terms we have used throughout our earlier discussion of the components of an attitude. The theory's essential cognitive element is the *belief*, a cognitive link between the attitude object and some characteristic or attribute. It is fair to think of this belief in terms we have used before: a statement of the noncriterial attributes of the attitude object. The affective component in Fishbein and Ajzen's model is called the *evaluation*, and it is a characterization (in positive or negative terms) of each attribute thought to be possessed by the attitude object. Thus this evaluation is virtually identical to the evaluative component in other attitude theories.

The final attitude is a general predisposition to respond in a favorable or unfavorable manner toward the attitude object (the same definition as before), but in addition to this general predisposition. there is a more specific response tendency called the **behavioral intention**. The behavioral intention reflects actions that the person might take toward the attitude object. For example, the question "How do you feel about women in the professions?" is directed toward the general predisposition, while the question "Will you select a female dentist in preference to a male dentist?" deals with a more specific behavioral intention.

With the exception of the behavioral intention, the concepts used in Fishbein and Ajzen's (1975) information-processing theory are nearly the same as those used in other approaches to attitude organization, such as the syllogistic model. But unlike the syllogistic model, the information-processing approach translates these conceptual terms into operational definitions that can easily be measured. To begin with, if a belief is a statement of the characteristics of an attitude object, then **belief strength** can be measured by determining the *subjective probability* that the attitude object actually possesses the characteristic in question. For example, for the belief "Politician X has integrity" belief strength can be assessed by asking the attitude holder to estimate the probability that Politician X really possesses the trait of integrity. Note that this is a subjective estimate on the part of the attitude holder, not an objective assessment of the politician's true characteristics. For some individuals who would agree with the statement "Politician X has integrity," the probability estimate might be low (say, 5 chances in 10), while for others it might be quite high (say, 9 chances in 10). These differences in belief strength would permit us to distinguish between people who otherwise would appear to be similar in their overall beliefs about the attitude object.

The Scaling of an Attitude

As Fishbein and Ajzen point out, it is possible to scale not only a person's belief strength about an attitude object, but also his or her evaluation of the characteristic in question. For example, it is a simple matter to get a subject to tell us how good or bad he or she considers the trait of "integrity," and this is typically accomplished using the semantic differential scale described in Chapter Five. Once the evaluation of the characteristic is obtained, and the subjective probability estimate that the attitude object possesses the characteristic is known, then the overall attitude can be determined. In the information-processing model the attitude (A) toward a stimulus object is determined by the beliefs (b_i) about which characteristics are associated with the object and the evaluations (e_i) of those characteristics, as shown in the formula

$$A = \sum_{i=1}^{n} b_i e_i$$

There are n characteristics associated with the attitude object, and the overall *attitude is determined by multiplying the evaluation of each of these characteristics* (e_i) *by the subjective probability that the attitude object actually possesses that characteristic* (b_i) *and then summing these products.* In one series of experiments, Fishbein and Coombs (1974) asked subjects to estimate *how probable* it was that each of two presidential candidates possessed traits like consistency, mental health, or opportunism, and then to rate each of these characteristics on a *good-bad* semantic differential scale. There were twenty-four belief statements in all, and each subject's attitude was thus the sum of twenty-four products of a belief multiplied by an evaluation. The results of this research indicated that the belief × evaluation model quite closely approximated the measures of attitude obtained through more direct means.

In their presentation of the theory Fishbein and Ajzen (1975) report a number of experimental tests of the information-processing model. They also discuss refinements of the probability estimation technique that attempt to broaden the model to include phenomena of impression formation, attribution, and attitude change, as well as attitude organization. Consideration of these extensions is beyond the scope of this book; for our purposes it is sufficient to note that the information-processing model improves upon the syllogistic conception by showing exactly how beliefs and evaluations may be combined into a final attitude. Each belief × evaluation product can be regarded as one element in the horizontal structure of the attitude. Thus, "Politician X is consistent, and consistency is good"; "Politician X is mentally healthy, and mental health is good"; and "Politician X is not an opportunist, not being an opportunist is good" are three separate belief × evaluation premises leading to the attitudinal conclusion "Politician X is good." The advantage of the information-processing approach is that the subjective probability estimates and the scaled evaluations can be used to produce a numerical estimate of the *strength* of each of these syllogisms and of the overall attitudinal conclusion. And from the attitude researcher's point of view, it is much simpler to get subjects to make these limited sets of probability estimates and evaluative judgments, than to try to get them to list all the syllogisms that might enter into their attitudes.

The Principle of Cognitive Consistency: Relations Among Attitudes

The syllogistic model shows how beliefs and evaluative judgments may combine to produce attitudes, and the information-processing approach provides a metric for measuring the strength of these combinations. But in their emphasis upon the rational processing of attitudinally relevant information, neither of these models supplies an organizing principle that might be used to reconcile what would appear to be conflicting attitudes. Let us reconsider the first two syllogisms mentioned, whose conclusions were "forests are good" and "defense spending is good." We know that these conclusions can serve as the evaluative premises for additional syllogisms, such as:

Senator Smith votes for forests and parks.	Senator Smith votes for defense spending.
Forests are good.	Defense spending is good.
Senator Smith is good.	Senator Smith is good.

In the terms we have used so far, these two syllogisms would simply represent two aspects of the horizontal structure of a favorable attitude toward Senator Smith. But what if the good senator votes for defense spending but *against* forests and parks? The conclusion of one syllogism will then become inconsistent with the conclusion of the other, so the two can no longer be regarded as part of the same horizontal structure. They must be considered different (and conflicting) attitudes toward the same social object (Senator Smith). It is clear that we need some additional explanatory device, and this device is the principle of cognitive consistency.

Notwithstanding the admonition that consistency is the hobgoblin of small minds, the principle of cognitive consistency holds that "the person tends to behave in ways that minimize the internal inconsistency among his interpersonal relations, among his intrapersonal cognitions, or among his beliefs, feelings, and actions" (McGuire, 1966, p. 1). It is important to note that although the principle is usually referred to as one of *cognitive* consistency, it presumably applies not only to cognitions held by a single person, but also to the relationships between those cognitions and various sorts of *interpersonal* behaviors. In addition, the principle of cognitive consistency is both a description of attitude structure (attitudes will be organized in a manner that maintains consistency) and an assertion of a motivational force (reduction of inconsistency) that can guide behavior.

Consistency theory has occupied much of social psychology's interest, and there are six main theoretical positions in the general consistency framework. Only three of these—balance theory, congruity theory, and dissonance theory—will be presented here. Two of the others deal primarily with logical consistency in the structure of thought (McGuire, 1968) and psychological implication (Abelson, 1968), minimizing the motivational aspects of inconsistency. The final theoretical position (Rosenberg, 1968) is really more of an extension of existing theory than it is a distinct alternative. Students who are interested in these additional positions, and in a much more comprehensive and detailed treatment of balance, congruity, and dissonance than is possible here, might want to refer to a scholarly book on cognitive consistency theories edited by Abelson, Aronson, McGuire, Newcomb, Rosenberg, and Tannenbaum (1968), or to a shorter set of position papers edited by Feldman (1966).

Regardless of the particular terms it uses, each of the three major cognitive consistency theories attempts to specify the antecedents and consequences of various *relations between cognitive elements.* A cognitive element can be a belief, a value, an attitude, or the cognitive representation of a behavior. So, respectively, "capitalism is not an appropriate economic system for underdeveloped countries," "justice," "consumer protection is good," and "I am getting soaked standing here in the rain" are all examples of cognitive elements. What sorts of relationships among cognitive elements are possible?

All three of the theories specify variations on three basic possibilities. As a first possibility, two or more cognitive elements may be consistent with each other—a state referred to in balance theory by the term *balance*, in congruity theory by the term *congruence*, and in dissonance theory by the term *consonance*. An example of two consistent cognitive elements would be "I like my wife" and "I am doing something nice for her." The second possibility is that the two cognitive elements might be inconsistent with each other: "I like my wife" but "I am shouting at her." This inconsistency is referred to either as *imbalance* (balance theory), as *incongruity* (congruity theory), or as *dissonance* (dissonance theory). A final possibility recognized by each theory is that the two cognitive elements may have nothing whatsoever to do with each other: "I like my wife" and "Today is February 3." Each of the theories assumes that cognitive consistency is a desired state and that inconsistency is sufficiently unpleasant to serve as a *motive* for change in one or the other of the cognitive elements. So much for what the theories have in common. Let us now take a closer look at some of the differences between them.

BALANCE THEORY

Liking and Unit Formation

Balance theory is primarily an *inter*personal theory of consistency, and its most complete description has been given by Heider (1958). Although some of the concepts involved in balance theory can be seen in Heider's earlier work (1944, 1946), the model presented in his book on interpersonal relations (1958) is the most detailed. The particular interpersonal processes with which balance theory is concerned are what Heider called sentiments—positive and negative feelings between people. What leads people to like, or dislike, each other? One of the answers that Heider suggested (which has since been confirmed in any number of research studies) is that we like those with whom we have some association (members of our families, people who share our attitudes and values, people whom we benefit, and so forth). The tie can be based on kinship, formal organization, similarity, actions, or a number of other possibilities, just so long as the individuals involved form a unit. In other words, unit formation between a person (p) and another (o) will lead to *liking* between p and o. This relationship is designated as follows: $pUo \rightarrow pLo$, where both unit formation (U) and liking (L) are considered to be positive relations.

Just as the positive relationship of unit formation (U) leads to liking (L), the negative relationship of *denial* of unit formation ($\sim$U) leads to disliking ($\sim$L). But as Cartwright and Harary (1956) have noted, there is an added complication, because these two characterizations of unit formation do not exhaust the possibilities. Consider the relations of cooperation and competition as examples. You come to like a person with whom you cooperate to achieve a mutually desired goal ($pUo \rightarrow pLo$). By the same token, you quickly come to dislike a person with whom you are in competition for scarce resources ($p\sim Uo \rightarrow p\sim Lo$). What about a person you meet for the first time, with no thoughts of cooperation or competition? Certainly it would be wrong to assume that there would be an immediate bond formed between the two of you, or to assume that there would be an immediate denial of unit formation. When you meet a person for the first time, you don't know whether the relationship will be positive or negative until you have had at least some opportunity to get acquainted.

Perhaps the best solution, suggested by the breadth of the unit-formation concept and supported by the findings of research on interpersonal attraction (e.g., Darley and Berscheid, 1967; Deutsch and Collins, 1951; Festinger, Schachter, and Back, 1950), is to assume that first encounters ought to be described as instances of *positive* unit-formation. After all, the two of you are together in the same place, you do begin the conversation by discussing topics familiar to you both, and there are some fairly strong social constraints against immediate expressions of dislike.

The Determination of Balance or Imbalance

Thus we see that according to balance theory there are two possible relations between individuals: liking and unit formation. Each of these relations can have either a positive sign (U or L) or a negative sign ($\sim$U or $\sim$L). How do we determine whether a particular relationship is balanced or not? Imagine that each relation (either liking or unit formation) is preceded by the numeral 1, and that this numeral 1 assumes the sign (+ or −) of the relation. Thus both U and L would each be +1, and both $\sim$U and $\sim$L would be represented as

−1. Then simply multiply the numbers together. If the final product carries a positive sign, the relationship is considered balanced; if the product is negative, the relationship is imbalanced. This computational procedure is illustrated in Table 6-1 for a *dyad* (a two-person group). As the table shows, balance is achieved when the signs for both relations are the same. Research by Miller and Geller (1972) indicates that people expect balanced dyadic relationships to be more stable than imbalanced ones, but a recent study by Willis and Burgess (1974) suggests that there may be some important differences between a balanced state based on the liking relation and a balanced state based on the unit formation relation, with the latter being simpler to assess.

It is important to notice that only one of the two balanced states shown in Table 6-1 represents an active association between the two people (pUo with pLo). The other "balanced" state represents both antipathy (p~Lo) and the denial of a relationship (p~Uo). The two states are equally balanced in Heider's system (although Newcomb [1968] differentiates between them), but we would like to think that the former active association is more probable.

The motivational aspect of balance theory predicts that the imbalanced states will be resolved by changing the sign of one of the two relations. Which sign undergoes change may be determined by the ease of change. Suppose that you are employed in a job where one

TABLE 6-1
Computation of balance within a dyad

Numerical Value Attached to Each Relation
  Unit Formation: $U = +1; \sim U = -1$
  Liking: $L = +1; \sim L = -1$

Balanced States	Represented as	Multiplication
1. You like a person with whom you are associated.	pLo and pUo	$+1 \times +1 = +1$
2. You dislike a person with whom you are not associated.	$p\sim Lo$ and $p\sim Uo$	$-1 \times -1 = +1$

Imbalanced States		
1. You dislike a person with whom you are associated.	$p\sim Lo$, but pUo	$-1 \times +1 = -1$
2. You like a person with whom you are not associated.	pLo, but $p\sim Uo$	$+1 \times -1 = -1$

Note: Whenever the product of the multiplication is positive, the state is considered balanced; whenever the product is negative, the state is considered imbalanced.

of your close co-workers is difficult to like (pUo, but $p{\sim}Lo$). Do you change jobs, thereby dissolving the unit that the two of you had formed, or do you learn to like the person for his or her few positive qualities? Obviously the resolution you select will depend upon such things as the other rewards you get from your job, the ease of finding another position, how close your association with the other person must be, and just how objectionable he or she really is.

Degrees of Balance and Imbalance

This example serves to illustrate not only the possible resolutions of a state of imbalance, but also a major disadvantage of the theory as it was originally stated by Heider (1958). The two relations—unit formation and liking—are both *dichotomous* variables: each relation has only two possible values (unit or denial of unit; liking or disliking). Unfortunately, as Cartwright and Harary (1956) have pointed out, the psychological world is not that simple. Your co-worker may not be totally unredeemable but may just have a few upsetting quirks. And the extent to which the job requires that the two of you interact may also vary. You may be part of a production team that must spend the entire day together; you might only have to deal with each other on an occasional, although regular basis; or you might simply work in the same general location. How badly you will need to learn to like the other person, or to look for another job, will thus depend on the *degree* of unit formation and liking as well as upon the *direction* of each relation.

As it was originally proposed by Heider, balance theory did not take into account the possibility of variations in the degree of any liking or unit formation relation, and the all-or-nothing character of these relations has been preserved in some later reformulations of the theory by Newcomb (1968) and Rosenberg (1968). There is no necessary reason this should continue to be the case, and recent extensions of balance theory (Feather, 1966; Wellens and Thistlethwaite, 1971; Wiest, 1965) have specified degrees for each relation. The co-worker example is diagramed in Table 6-2 for varying degrees of liking or disliking, and for differing degrees of unit formation.

Several aspects of the example deserve comment. First, in order to simplify presentation, only positive unit formation is shown in the table. In the social world, of course, there will also be degrees of negative unit formation that would enter into the determination of balance or imbalance. You could leave quickly should you meet the person, move to another town in order to avoid contact, or make public statements dissociating yourself from the person and his or her

TABLE 6-2
Computation of degrees of balance and imbalance in a dyad

Degrees of Unit Formation		*Degrees of Liking*	
Work in same office[a]	$U = +1$	Really a terrific person	$L = +3$
Regular necessary		Generally pleasant	$L = +2$
contact	$U = +2$	Some faults but OK	$L = +1$
Constant interaction	$U = +3$	Slightly unpleasant	$\sim L = -1$
		Generally unpleasant	$\sim L = -2$
		Really an obnoxious	
		person	$\sim L = -3$

Balanced States

  Weak: You work in the same office with a person who has some faults but is generally OK.
$$p[U = +1]o \text{ and } p[L = +1]o$$
$$\text{Balance} = +1 \times +1 = +1$$

  Strong: You have constant interaction with a person who is really terrific.
$$p[U = +3]o \text{ and } p[L = +3]o$$
$$\text{Balance} = +3 \times +3 = +9$$

Imbalanced States

  Weak: You work in the same office with a person whom you consider slightly unpleasant.
$$p[U = +1]o, \text{ but } p[\sim L = -1]o$$
$$\text{Imbalance} = +1 \times -1 = -1$$

  Strong: You must have constant interaction with a really obnoxious person.
$$p[U = +3]o, \text{ but } p[\sim L = -3]o$$
$$\text{Imbalance} = +3 \times -3 = -9$$

[a]Note that for simplicity we will consider here only instances of positive units.

policies. Second, we have arbitrarily chosen to use seven levels of variation in liking/disliking and unit formation to illustrate the point that these relations need not be dichotomous. Other numbers of levels could have been used (e.g., Wellens and Thistlethwaite used five levels) but seven correspond more closely to the semantic differential scaling technique and the Likert attitude measures (discussed in Chapter Five), both of which employ seven-point scales ($+3$ to -3). The advantage of using a seven-point scale to represent degrees of liking and unit formation is that we can simply substitute the Likert scale's adjectives—slightly, moderately, and strongly—for the numerical values of 1, 2, and 3, respectively. The signed numerical value of the unit-formation relation is multiplied by the signed numerical value of the liking/disliking relation, and the *sign* of the product represents either balance or imbalance as before. But in addition, the numerical value of the product now represents the *strength* of the relationship. We should be cautious and assume that the numbers only reach an ordinal level of measurement (as discussed in Chapter Five), but even with this restriction it is obvious that constant

interaction with a wonderful person is a much stronger balanced relationship than is occasional contact with a rather unexciting person.

Scaling the degrees of liking and unit formation not only gives us
more insight into balanced relationships, it also suggests which
element is most likely to be changed if the relationship is imbalanced.
Suppose you have constant interaction with a slightly unpleasant person (a total imbalance of −3). Or, as an alternative, suppose that you
have only occasional contact with a truly obnoxious person (again, a
total imbalance of −3). Even though the total imbalance is the same,
we would expect a resolution of the imbalance in different ways. In
the first case, we would guess that your opinion would change. The
constant interaction is dictated by the requirements of your job, and
the amount of imbalance is not sufficient for you to seek employment
elsewhere. In the second case, it is your opinion of the person that
is more fixed. While you cannot find any redeeming qualities in a
truly obnoxious person, you can arrange your movements at work so
that you seldom run across the person. In each of these cases the
imbalance is resolved through change in the weaker relation. This
sort of prediction will recur in our discussion of congruity theory.

Intrapersonal Balance

Although balance theory was originally formulated in *inter*personal terms, it can also be applied to problems of *intra*personal consistency as well. The internal state, attitude, opinion, or belief, or even
an external object connected with the self, is identified by the term
x, and it, too, is part of liking and unit-formation relations. For example, "I give a televised lecture and am pleased with my performance" might be represented by

$$p[U = +3]x \text{ and } p[L = +3]x$$

where I am person p, the lecture is x, the strength of the unit formation is based on the obvious connection between the televised lecture
and me, and the strength of the liking relation reflects my pleasure
with my performance. Now suppose that instead of being entirely
satisfied with my lecture, I believed that it was not quite up to my
usual standards:

$$p[U = +3]x \text{ but } p[\sim L = -1]x$$

Which of the two relations will be changed? I cannot retract my public
performance—it is there on videotape, ready for instant replay at any
moment—so to remove the imbalance I simply change my private
opinion about my performance.

In this example, change in my internal belief follows directly from the principle that the weaker relation will be the one to change, but what happens if I hated my performance ($\sim$L $= -3$)? The two relations are equally *polarized*, or equally displaced from zero. Even so, we might well expect that the liking relation would be the one to change, because the public unit-formation relation ought to be more difficult to alter. Balance theory, however, does not contain any conceptual distinctions that could be used to justify this assumption. So we are left without a satisfactory answer to the question of which of two equally polarized relations—one public, one private—will be the more likely to change. Just this question has formed the basis for a large amount of research conducted within the framework of cognitive dissonance theory, and we shall return to the problem of inconsistency between word and deed in the course of our discussion of dissonance theory later in the chapter.

Balance in a Triad

The inclusion in the relationship of an object or internal entity, x, represents a broadening of balance theory from its original concern with interpersonal relations to intrapersonal relations. Up until now we have considered relations with only two elements, either two people (p and o) or a single person (p) and an entity (x). The final aspect of balance theory to be considered is the further generalization to a *triad* consisting of two persons (p and o) and an entity (x). This structure is known as the p-o-x triad, and it has received a great deal of research attention. Most of this research demonstrates that p-o-x triads are evaluated as more pleasant when balanced (e.g., Gerard and Fleischer, 1967; Jordan, 1953; Price, Harburg, and Newcomb, 1966; Rodrigues, 1967; Whitney, 1971), although there is still some disagreement about the relative importance of all of the relations in the triad (Crockett, 1974; Fuller, 1974; Newcomb, 1968).

Computation of Balance

The balanced triad is probably best illustrated with a simple example. Suppose that a friend of mine watched me give my lecture on television. Two possible outcomes of this triad (me, my friend, and my lecture) are shown in Figure 6-2. Since these outcomes are considered from my friend's point of view, he is referred to as p. I would be the other person in the triad (o), and my lecture would be the object (x). In the first triad, we see that my friend (p) likes both

FIGURE 6-2
Computation of balance in a triad.

A BALANCED TRIAD

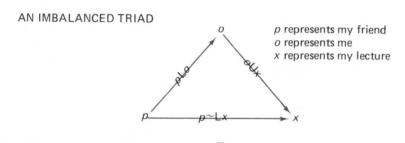

p represents my friend
o represents me
x represents my lecture

My friend likes me and likes the lecture that I presented on television. The sign of each relation is positive, and the multiplication of three positive relations (+1 × +1 × +1 = +1) is positive and, therefore, *balanced*. The direction of the arrows represents the direction of the relation.

AN IMBALANCED TRIAD

p represents my friend
o represents me
x represents my lecture

My friend likes me but dislikes the lecture that I presented on television. Two of the relations have positive signs, but one has a negative sign, and the multiplication of two positives and a negative (+1 × +1 × −1) produces a negative or *imbalanced* product. The direction of the arrows represents the direction of the relation.

me (*o*) and the lecture (*x*) with which I have formed a unit. In the second triad my friend likes me, but dislikes the lecture. The first triad is balanced, because each relation has a positive sign and the multiplication of three positives produces a positive. The second triad is imbalanced, because the product of two positives and a negative is a negative.

Limitations of the Example

As you might guess, the two triads presented in Figure 6-2 over-simplify the relations involved in several ways. First, we have omitted my liking or disliking for the lecture, including in the diagram only the fact that I am connected to it. This makes the diagram less cluttered, but it does so at the cost of assuming I positively value anything

I am connected to. Interestingly enough, purposeful violation of this assumption is one of the interpersonal techniques we employ to distinguish our honest friends from people who simply flatter us because they have something to gain (Jones, 1964). One of the things that true friends ought to do is tell us when we have made fools of ourselves. So if we want to determine how discerning a person is, we might make a statement we know to be preposterous (in balance theory terms, $p\mathrm{U}x$ but $p{\sim}\mathrm{L}x$). By the multiplication rule, the resulting sign of this combination of relations is *negative*. Now suppose that a person compliments me on the statement (places a *positive* evaluation upon it). What must I think of this person, in order for the triad (me, the other person, and my statement) to be balanced? I must evaluate this person *negatively* in order for the final product of the multiplication to be positive (two negatives and one positive). In short, I like my true friends not only because they compliment me when they should, but also because they do *not* tell me how great I am when I do something stupid.

A second way in which the diagram of the triads oversimplifies the situation is that it omits the *degrees* of liking and unit formation that we have discussed before. My friend is characterized as liking me ($p\mathrm{L}o$), but the diagram does not indicate the strength of this liking for me (is it slight, moderate, or strong?). In a similar manner the degree of unit formation between me and my lecture is not specified, nor is the extent to which my friend likes the lecture indicated. If we wished to complicate matters, we could include degrees of liking and unit formation, but balance would still be determined by the *sign* of the multiplicative product, regardless of its strength. And, just as the weaker element in a dyadic relationship would be the one to change, the weakest element in a triadic relationship would be the most probable to change in order to restore balance. In short, adding the degrees of slight, moderate, and strong to the triads would make the diagrams more difficult to follow without changing the underlying principles at all. It is for this reason that they were omitted from Figure 6-2.

Summary of Balance Theory

Let us summarize the balance theory of cognitive consistency. The theory was originally developed to apply to *inter*personal relationships but, as we have seen, it can be generalized to include *intra*-personal phenomena (p. 232) as well. The cognitive elements involved in the theory can be representations of people, events, attitudes, beliefs, emotions, possessions (e.g., you have a unit relationship with the things you own), and all these cognitive elements can be associated with each other in either or both of two ways: the *relations* of liking and unit formation (p. 227). Whether the relationship is a dyadic or a triadic one, balance is determined by the *multiplicative* rule: the signs (positive or negative) of all relations involved in any particular computation are multiplied together, and if the sign of the product is positive, the relationship is balanced (p. 229). If the sign of the product is negative, then the relationship is in an imbalanced state. The amount of imbalance present can be estimated by the *degrees of strength* (p. 230) of the relations involved, and the relation with the least strength is the most probable point of change to restore balance.

CONGRUITY THEORY

Sources and Objects

For a number of reasons the congruity theory of cognitive consistency, developed by Osgood and Tannenbaum (1955), can be regarded as a special case of balance theory. To begin with, the congruity model was originally formulated (according to Tannenbaum, 1968) as a specific explanation for the attitude change that occurs when a *source (S)* is connected to a particular attitude *object (O)*, a narrower goal than that of balance theory. Examples of sources would be newspapers, television commentators, experts in a profession, the person next door, books, your friends, and so forth. In short, sources consist of documents, publications, and people. Attitude objects can include things, people, legislative proposals, social conditions, or in some cases things that would otherwise be considered sources. For example, if a newspaper, such as the *New York Times*, makes an editorial comment about a candidate for Congress, the newspaper is the source and the candidate is the object. But if the candidate takes out an advertisement denouncing the editorial, he or she becomes the source, and the newspaper becomes the object. It is probably simplest to think of *sources* as *the makers of statements about objects*.

All the statements that sources can make about objects are grouped into two classes, according to whether the statement implies a positive connection (known as an associative bond), or a negative connection (a dissociative bond) between the source and the object. These bonds can be equated to the unit-formation relation in balance theory, with the associative bond corresponding to U, and the dissociative bond corresponding to ~U. Thus the dissociative bond is the denial

of a connection, rather than the absence of a connection. Associative
and dissociative bonds can be verbal statements or overt actions. As
in the case of the original formulation of balance theory (Heider,
1958), there is no distinction between degrees of association or
dissociation. For example, if a friend of yours says he thinks a particular musical group is good, he is expressing an associative bond
between himself and the group. The bond would be characterized in
exactly the same way if he had said that the group was "OK," or
"terrific," or had said nothing but had purchased their latest recording.
As long as his description of the group, or his behavior, indicates a
positive connection—regardless of its degree—the congruity model
would say that he has an associative bond with the group.

The final element of congruity theory is the *evaluation* placed by
the person whose attitudes we are considering upon both the source
and the object. This evaluation component of congruity theory was
derived from Osgood's other work on the semantic meaning of concepts (e.g., Osgood, Suci, and Tannenbaum, 1957), so it employed the
same seven-point (+3 to −3) scale used in the semantic differential.
As noted in the discussion of the semantic differential in Chapter
Five, the technique is *content-free*, so it can easily be applied to a
variety of concepts. Congruity theory takes advantage of this methodological capability by assuming that both the sources of statements and
the objects of those statements can be described by their position on
the seven-point evaluative scale.

One possible set of evaluations of sources and objects is presented
in Table 6-3, and from the nature of the evaluations you can see that
the person holding these opinions is a confirmed leftist. The United
States Labor Party, a source, and the issue of government control of
industry, an object, both receive very high evaluations. In contrast,
the source John Birch Society and the object racial segregation both
receive very negative evaluations. It is important to emphasize that

TABLE 6-3
*Possible scale positions of some sources and objects as judged by a
confirmed leftist*

SCALE POSITION	SOURCES	OBJECTS	SCALE POSITION
+3	U. S. Labor Party	Government control of industry	+3
+2	Socialist Party	National health insurance	+2
+1	Democratic Party	Election reform	+1
0	Common Cause		
−1	Republican Party	Continuation of tax loopholes	−1
−2	American Independent Party	Multinational companies	−2
−3	John Birch Society	Racial segregation	−3

all the evaluations shown in the table represent the opinions of the single person whose attitudes are being considered. Other individuals might have quite different rankings of both the sources and the objects listed in the table. Also, for purposes of this example, it is assumed that the evaluations of sources are made purely on partisan grounds, so that Common Cause (an explicitly nonpartisan group) receives a score of 0. In fact, it might be difficult to find an organization engaged in political activity of any kind toward which most people have no evaluative reaction whatsoever. This reality is recognized in the list of objects, though not in the list of sources, by the omission of an element at the zero point on the scale.

Comparisons to Balance Theory

The evaluative dimension in congruity theory corresponds roughly to the liking relation in balance theory, especially if the latter is regarded as having varying degrees of strength, as well as two different directions. But there is an important difference between the two in their respective domains of application: the liking relation in balance theory can be applied to any of the cognitive elements, while the evaluative relation in congruity theory can be applied only to the person's opinion of the source and of the object. There is a similar limitation in congruity theory in the applicability of the associative-dissociative bonds. Both these limitations can best be illustrated by an example, such as the one shown in Figure 6-3.

For purposes of comparison, the figure shows the elements of congruity theory—the *person* whose attitudes are being considered, the *source* of the statement made, and the *object* of that statement—arranged in the form of a balance theory *p-o-x* triad. Suppose that our confirmed leftist learns that the United States Labor Party has advocated government control of industry. The relationship between the leftist and the U. S. Labor Party would be described by congruity theory as an evaluation, and it would be described by balance theory as a liking relation without any expressed unit formation. In the same way, congruity theory would describe the relationship between the leftist and the object, government control of industry, as one of evaluation, while balance theory would describe it as liking without unit formation. Finally, the relationship between the U. S. Labor Party and the issue of government control would be described by congruity theory as an associative bond, and by balance theory as a positive unit (without any stated degree of liking).

Notice the difference in these descriptions. Balance theory has *two* possible relations between each pair of elements in the triad—liking and unit formation—while congruity theory specifies only a

FIGURE 6-3
Comparison of congruity and balance principles in a sample
p-o-x *triad.*

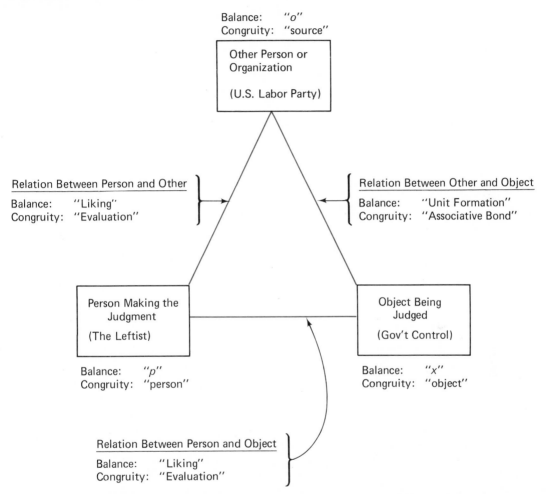

Balance: "o"
Congruity: "source"

Other Person or
Organization

(U.S. Labor Party)

Relation Between Person and Other

Balance: "Liking"
Congruity: "Evaluation"

Relation Between Other and Object

Balance: "Unit Formation"
Congruity: "Associative Bond"

Person Making the
Judgment

(The Leftist)

Object Being
Judged

(Gov't Control)

Balance: "p"
Congruity: "person"

Balance: "x"
Congruity: "object"

Relation Between Person and Object

Balance: "Liking"
Congruity: "Evaluation"

single sort of relation between any two elements. You will remember
that in the original *p-o-x* triad it was possible for *p* to be joined to *o*
either by a relation of unit formation, or by a relation of liking, or by
both. Similar possibilities exist for the relationships between *p* and *x*
and between *o* and *x*. But according to congruity theory, there is only
one possible relation between the source and the object (*o* and *x*), and
that is the relation of association or dissociation. And there is only
one possibility for the relation between the person and the source
(*p* and *o*), or between the person and the object (*p* and *x*): the relation
of evaluation. Congruity theory contains no provision for association or

dissociation between the person and the other two elements, and it contains no provision for an evaluative relation between the source and the object. As a result, congruity theory is most properly considered to be a special case of the more general balance theory.

Resolution of Incongruity

Let us now return to our confirmed leftist, to show how incongruity is created and resolved. Suppose that our leftist learns that the Socialist Party (with a positive scale position of +2) has advocated the continuation of certain tax loopholes (an object with a negative scale position of −1). This associative bond between a source of one sign and an object of the opposite sign will create incongruity, as would an associative bond between two elements of like sign but different scale positions. Both the sign of the source and object and the degree of *polarization* (the scale position) of each will enter into the creation of incongruity. Notice that this is a difference from balance theory. Balance theory (even our modification which includes degrees of balance) defines imbalance *only* in terms of the *signs* of the elements. But to avoid incongruity not only must the signs be the same, the scale positions must also be the same.

By considering both the sign and the scale position, congruity theory has formalized the idea that the weaker of the two elements (the one with a scale position closer to zero) will change more in the resolution of the incongruity. To resolve incongruity, there must be some change in each of the elements involved in the incongruous relationship, and the *change in each element will be proportional to its original scale position.* So for the advocacy of tax loopholes by the Socialist Party, the point of equilibrium after the resolution of incongruity is shown in Figure 6-4. The Socialist Party had an original

FIGURE 6-4
Change in scale positions of Socialist Party and Tax Loopholes necessary to resolve incongruity.

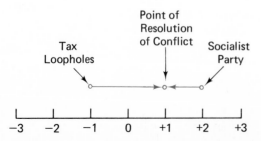

position of +2 (two units away from zero) while the tax loopholes had an original position of −1 (one unit away from zero). Because it was twice as polarized to begin with, the Socialist Party will change only half as much in the resolution of incongruity. It will move one unit toward Tax Loopholes, which will move two units toward the Socialist Party, with the results that both the source and the object will attain a new scale value of +1.

Summary of Congruity Theory

Congruity theory was developed to deal with attitude change on an intrapersonal level, and it is best regarded as a special case of balance theory. The cognitive elements in the theory are grouped into two general categories—*sources* and *objects* (p. 236)—and each element is assigned a scale value on a seven-point scale (+3 to −3). Elements are joined either by *associative bonds* or *dissociative bonds* (p. 236), and incongruity results whenever a source of one sign is joined to an object having the opposite sign, regardless of whether the bond is associative or dissociative. The only determinant of incongruity is *discrepancy in scale position.* The resolution of incongruity will involve a change in scale position of *both* the source and the object, and the distance along the scale that each travels will be *proportional* (p. 240) to its original degree of polarization (more polarization leading to less change in position).

COGNITIVE DISSONANCE THEORY

The theory of cognitive dissonance, originally proposed by Festinger (1957) and later extended by Brehm and Cohen (1962) and Aronson (1969), has generated more research—and more controversy—than any of the other cognitive consistency theories. Dissonance theory's extensive impact on social psychology arises not from its conceptual sophistication (in many respects it is less thoroughly, and less formally, specified than either balance or congruity theory), but from its unique ability among consistency theories to make *nonobvious* predictions. As we have noted throughout this book, the function of theory in social psychology is to formalize and extend our intuitive ideas about human behavior. But much of the time these theoretical formulations appear to be little more than well-specified common sense. Just because a prediction agrees with common sense is no reason not to perform the experimental research, because being able to guess what people ought to do in a particular situation is not the same thing as demonstrating what their actual behavior in that situation is. Although the documentation of human behavior is an important goal of research in social psychology, that task does not generate the excitement that accompanies the discovery of a nonobvious explanation for a wide variety of social behaviors. In this last section of the chapter we consider a common dissonance-arousing experimental technique (forced compliance), the elements of the theory, and some of the research performed to test dissonance theory. Where appropriate in these discussions, we shall also mention some of the criticisms that have been leveled at the theory and at the research flowing from it.

Forced Compliance as an Alternative to Reinforcement

If there is a single, fundamental principle of psychology that seems to apply in the behavior of almost every organism, it is the principle of reinforcement. As you know, the principle of reinforcement states that behavior which leads to rewards is more likely to recur than is behavior which does not lead to positive outcomes. Rewards are supposed to increase the duration of a reinforced behavior, increase the intensity with which the behavior is performed, and decrease the time between occurrences of the reinforced action. The general principle of reinforcement can be seen as an explicit or implicit feature of most psychological theories, including a number of theories in social psychology to be discussed in Chapter Nine.

One of the reasons that cognitive dissonance theory had such an effect was that the first major test of the theory by Festinger and Carlsmith (1959) appeared to contradict the time-honored principle of reinforcement. The purpose of Festinger and Carlsmith's research was to investigate some of the conditions under which an individual's attitude might be changed by inducing the person to behave in a manner that was contrary to his or her existing attitude. Although you will remember from Chapter Five that a person's actions do not always correspond to his or her attitudes, you can still appreciate what a novel idea it was to suggest that people can easily be induced to behave in a fashion directly contradicting their existing attitudes.

Suppose that you had been a subject in the Festinger and Carlsmith experiment. You would have arrived at the experimental laboratory and would have been seated in a small room in front of a table. On this table is the apparatus, an elevated platform with several rows of round holes, each hole containing a round peg. Your task would have been to turn each peg one-quarter turn to the right. When you had finished doing this for the first row, you would continue to the next row, and you would begin all over again as soon as you had completed the last row. This dreadfully dull task would have continued for about twenty minutes. Finally, the experimenter would have told you to stop, and would have explained that the experiment was designed to test the effect of prior instructions on performance of a motor task. Since you were in the control group, you received no instructions, but the next subject to be run (who was now sitting in the waiting room) was supposed to be told that the peg-turning task was interesting and enjoyable. The experimenter then would have continued by telling you (and here comes the manipulation) that the assistant who is supposed to say how enjoyable the task was has not shown up. Rather than dismiss the waiting subject, the experimenter would wonder if you would be willing to give the necessary instructions. In half of the cases the experimenter would have offered to pay you $1 for your help; in the other half, he would have offered you $20. He would say that the choice of whether to help or not is strictly up to you, but that he would be grateful should you decide to help him.

From your perspective, this is an unusual situation, and you decide to help the experimenter out of his predicament. It is difficult to argue that you have a positive attitude toward the task; rather, you agree to help in spite of your negative feelings about the task. What you do not know is that the same request is being made of *every* subject (with a payment of $1 to half the subjects and $20 to the other half). While permitting you to maintain an *illusion of free choice* the experimenter has actually forced you to comply with his request. Not surprisingly, this experimental paradigm is known as the paradigm of *forced compliance*, and it is a common occurrence in research on cognitive dissonance theory.

Counterattitudinal Advocacy and Insufficient Justification

So you have agreed to tell the next subject how interesting and enjoyable you found the peg-turning task. You go out into the waiting room, discover a person sitting there ready to take part in the experiment, and you give your speech about the task. In terms of the theory, what you are doing is engaging in counterattitudinal advocacy. Most probably your own attitude is that the task is boring. Yet you have now told another person (who actually is an accomplice of the experimenter, rather than a real subject) how interesting it is. What will happen to your attitude under these circumstances? The prediction from reinforcement theory is that the more the experimenter has paid you to perform this service, the more your attitude will change in favor of the task. Even with inflation, $20 is still a good payment for a twenty-minute task and a short description of the experiment, so that payment ought to make your real attitude toward the task more positive.

Interestingly enough, the prediction from dissonance theory is just the opposite: there should be more attitude change in the $1 condition than in the $20 condition. The reasoning goes like this. You have a negative attitude toward the task, but despite this negative attitude you have also made a public statement that the task was interesting. Knowledge of these two facts creates *cognitive dissonance:* a negative drive state which arises whenever an individual simultaneously holds two cognitions (ideas, beliefs, opinions, attitudes, representations of behavior) which are inconsistent. Dissonance is unpleasant and must be reduced. You feel uncomfortable having lied about the character of the task, and you begin searching for some justification for your behavior. In the $20 condition, the payment alone constitutes sufficient justification: the cognition "I got paid a bundle for doing it" is so consistent with having described the task as interesting that "I didn't really like the task myself" becomes irrelevant to the issue. But in the $1 condition, the payment is an insufficient justification for the counterattitudinal behavior, so there is dissonance that must be reduced by some other means. What is left? Changing your attitude about the task is the only possibility: "I really wasn't lying, because in retrospect I think that the task did have some useful scientific value, and for that reason alone I feel that it was interesting and enjoyable."

The results of the experiment confirmed Festinger and Carlsmith's predictions on the basis of dissonance theory. After delivering their "instructions" to the waiting subject, each subject was asked to describe his participation in the study. One of the questions on this written evaluation form asked how interesting the task had been, and here the $1 group described the task as significantly *more* interesting than did the subjects in the $20 or control groups (in which there was no delivery of false impressions to a waiting subject). These findings understandably created quite a reaction (e.g., Bem, 1967; Elms, 1967, Janis and Gilmore, 1965; Nuttin, 1966; and Rosenberg, 1965), and we shall return to some of the controversy after a description of dissonance theory.

The Formal Theory

Elements and Relations

As the name of the theory implies, the basic units in cognitive dissonance theory are *cognitive elements*. These can be ideas, attitudes, beliefs, values, representations of past behavior, or expectations about future events. For purposes of comparison it should be noted that the cognitive elements involved in dissonance theory are not as precisely specified as the elements involved in congruity or balance theories. This fact makes the testing of dissonance predictions slightly more difficult but also permits a broader application of the theoretical ideas. There are three possible relationships between these cognitive elements: *consonance*, *dissonance*, and *irrelevance*. Two cognitive elements are said to be in a relationship of consonance if one of the elements *implies* the other. Thus, "It is raining" and "I am carrying my umbrella" are consonant elements, as are "I really enjoy playing tennis" and "I am describing the game in glowing terms to my friends." In both of these pairs of elements, each element implies the other, so each pair is consonant.

In contrast to this pretty cognitive picture, the relation of dissonance exists between two cognitive elements whenever one *implies the opposite of the other*. The cognitions presumably held simultaneously by the subject in Festinger and Carlsmith's (1959) experiment are a perfect illustration of dissonance. It is safe to assume that the subject's attitude is, "I thought that task to be tremendously dull," but his verbal statement, "The task is really quite interesting" is exactly the opposite of what the first element would imply. Festinger (1957) described this relation of dissonance by stating that one element implies the obverse of the other. The difficulty with using this term from formal logic to describe the state of dissonance is that dissonance, like imbalance, deals not so much with formal implication as with psychological expectation. Brehm and Cohen (1962), and later Aronson (1969), point out that dissonance can perhaps best be conceived of as a *violation of expectancy*. We expect that people will behave in accordance with their attitudes (or at least will not behave in direct contradiction of them). When that expectancy is violated, dissonance is created. Brown (1965) has suggested that the essential nature of dissonance can be summarized in the word *but*. "It is raining" *but* "I have not opened my umbrella;" "I am a registered Democrat," *but* "I have just voted Republican;" and "I have prepared for the end of the world" *but* "The world has not ended as planned" are all examples of dissonant pairs of cognitive elements.

Finally, it is possible for cognitive elements to have no psychological implications whatsoever for each other, and these elements are said to be in a relation of *irrelevance*. "I am six feet tall" and "It is usually sunny at the beach in May" are cognitive elements that are irrelevant to each other. How tall I am has no implications for whether or not it will be sunny at the beach, and since I am a person rather than a plant, the amount of sunshine at the beach will not affect my height.

Comparisons to Balance and Congruity Theories

One of the things you will notice about the relations of consonance, dissonance, and irrelevance is that all three are formulated in
terms that are *intrapersonal* in nature. In contrast to both balance and
congruity theory, there are no external objects or persons involved in
any of the relations. There is no Democratic Party as such, only my
recognition that I am a registered Democrat. There is no Republican
Party, only my recognition that I have voted for Republican candidates.
The terms of the other two cognitive consistency theories can be used
to describe the relations between persons and objects, as well as between cognitions, but the terms of cognitive dissonance theory can
be applied only to cognitions. It is true that the propositions used as
elements in dissonance theory can cover much of the same ground,
but the limitation of dissonance to intrapersonal phenomena is still
worth noting.

Another difference between dissonance theory and the other two
consistency theories is that cognitive elements can be considered only
in pairs. Congruity theory deals with the triad composed of the perceiver, the source, and the object; balance theory deals primarily with
dyads (p and o) and triads (p-o-x), but has been generalized by Cartwright and Harary (1956) to apply to even more complex structures
as well. The requirement of dissonance theory that elements be
considered in pairs is not, however, quite as restrictive as it might
seem. Any particular cognitive element can successively be paired
with an unlimited number of others. As a result, one of the contributors to the magnitude of dissonance in any single pair will be the
number of *other* elements that are consonant with, or dissonant with,
the elements in the pair. For example, the cognition "I have voted
Republican" will be more dissonant for a registered Democrat who
had the additional cognitions "I have always voted Democratic,"
"I have done canvassing for Democratic candidates," "I have contributed money to the Democratic Party," and "I have served on my
local Democratic committee" than for a registered Democrat who does
not have these additional dissonant cognitions. By the same token, a
registered Democrat who could think of several cognitions that would
be consonant with his voting Republican, such as "Regardless of party
affiliation, I vote for the best person," and "My views no longer correspond to the platform of the Democratic Party" would reduce the
dissonance arising *from the voting choice.* The addition of cognitions
consonant with the voting choice, however, might have the additional
effect of making the registration dissonant. If I really am that comfortable with the Republican candidates, why should I remain registered
as a Democrat?

The Magnitude of Dissonance

A second determinant of the magnitude of dissonance, in addition to the number of consonant and dissonant cognitions, is the *importance* of each consonant or dissonant relation. Although its operational meaning is not well specified in dissonance theory, the concept of importance has the same effect on the degree of consistency or inconsistency that the scale value of a source or object has in congruity theory, and the same effect that the degree of balance and unit formation would have in balance theory. Simply put, dissonance arising from important issues is more unpleasant, and a greater instigation to attitude change, than is dissonance from unimportant issues. Taking both importance and number of relevant cognitions into account, the magnitude of dissonance can be summarized in the following relation:

$$\text{Magnitude of Dissonance} = \frac{\text{Importance} \times \text{Number of Dissonant Cognitions}}{\text{Importance} \times \text{Number of Consonant Cognitions}}$$

This statement shows that the magnitude of dissonance created by a single element will increase as the number of other cognitions dissonant with the element increases, and as the importance of each of those dissonant cognitions increases. Conversely, the magnitude of dissonance generated by a single element will decrease as the number of consonant cognitions increases and as the importance of those consonant cognitions increases. Because the number of consonant and dissonant elements is not readily available, and because there is no precise definition of "importance," the statement is best left in words, rather than being expressed in symbols or numbers.

You will notice that the estimation of the magnitude of dissonance is much less precise than the estimation of incongruity, and it is also less precise than the procedures for estimation of the magnitude of imbalance. For example, without any specification of the units involved (and dissonance theory does not suggest what those units might be), it is virtually impossible to tell whether the number of dissonant cognitions is more or less influential in producing dissonance than is the importance of those cognitions. We can well imagine that there can be a large amount of dissonance generated by a single extremely important cognition, such as "the world has not ended" for Mrs. Keech and the group of seekers (discussed more fully in Chapter Two). But how many less important cognitions are necessary to create the same amount of dissonance? A few? A hundred? There is no way to know for sure.

This imprecision inherent in the calculation of dissonance has some advantages and some disadvantages. The major advantage is that such imprecision may be a better reflection of social-psychological reality than is, for example, the seven-point scale of congruity theory. As noted in Chapter Five, an interval level of measurement of attitudes is the *goal* toward which attitude scaling techniques are directed. That goal is not always achieved. When the data do not reach the level of an interval scale, a formulation stated in essentially *ordinal* terms, like dissonance theory, might be more appropriate than one that depends on more sophisticated measurement. The principal disadvantage of the dissonance formulation is that without some idea of the units involved, it is difficult to make even ordinal predictions before performing the research of interest.

Certainly Festinger and Carlsmith were able to predict that a payment of $1 would create more dissonance than would a payment of $20. But what about payments between these two figures? Should the magnitude of dissonance increase as the payment decreases, or will there be a "threshold" effect—no dissonance with any payment above a certain amount, but dissonance below that amount? An experiment by Cohen (1962) using several levels of payment for writing an essay counter to one's attitudes ($10, $5, $1, and $.50) suggests that the threshold effect might be the better interpretation. When students were asked to write an essay supporting police intervention in a campus demonstration, the final attitudes toward the police were more positive when the payment was $.50 than when the payment was $1, and the attitudes in the $1 condition were more favorable toward the police than attitudes in the $5 condition. There were, however, no significant differences between a payment of $5, a payment of $10, and a control condition in which there was no payment at all. These results suggest that there may be *both* a gradual change in the amount of dissonance, and a threshold beyond which no dissonance is created.

The Reduction of Dissonance

Although the theory is not entirely clear on the determination of the magnitude of cognitive dissonance, it is quite clear on the motivating properties of dissonance. The state of dissonance is unpleasant and must be reduced. (It is interesting to note that this is essentially a hedonistic principle, just like the principle of reinforcement. "Avoiding pain" is the other side of the "seeking pleasure" coin. Yet dissonance theory has made its mark on social psychology principally because of its apparent contradictions of reinforcement predictions.) In the typical dissonance paradigm, an individual is induced to engage in behavior that disagrees with private opinion. Whether the behavior is counterattitudinal advocacy (Cohen, 1962; Festinger and

Carlsmith, 1959), choice of only one prize from among a selection of attractive alternatives (Brehm, 1956), or undergoing a severe initiation in order to join a group that turns out to be dull (Aronson and Mills, 1959), the cognitive element representing that behavior (called the *behavioral element*) will be dissonant with the cognitive element representing the attitude or opinion (which we shall call the *evaluative element*).

There are four different ways to reduce this dissonance: (1) change the behavioral element, (2) change the evaluative element, (3) add elements consonant with the behavioral element, or (4) change the importance of either the consonant or dissonant elements. The first of these modes of reduction is the least likely. Your behavior is public, and people would think you were strange if you tried to deny that you actually performed actions that all of them observed. In experimental situations, as opposed to real-life situations, changes in importance are also not very likely. In our everyday lives we can (and often do) forget about our inconsistencies, but in the laboratory setting we are constantly reminded of them. Next most probable is the addition of elements consonant with the discrepant behavior, but again the experimental situations are expressly designed to minimize or eliminate this possibility. What is left? Only change in the evaluative element. When the structure of an experiment, or the constraints inherent in social settings outside the laboratory, precludes other modes of dissonance reduction, people will change their private attitudes in order to make those attitudes agree with their overt behavior. Let us now take a closer look at some of the research—and some of the controversy—that has been generated by the cognitive dissonance approach.

An Example of the Evolution of a Concept

In the development of any scientific discipline, refinements in theory go hand in hand with advances in methodology. When theories are relatively crude, simple experiments can be devised to test their differing predictions. But as theories become more complex, and attempt to deal with alternative explanations for the data, new instruments and techniques must be developed that will accommodate the more sophisticated predictions. In social psychology this interplay between competing theories and the development of new methods is best illustrated by some of the research flowing from the theory of cognitive dissonance. This is true not because the theory itself is conceptually sophisticated (balance theory is probably more so), but rather because the large volume of cognitive dissonance research has been interesting and controversial, leading investigators of other persuasions to try to disconfirm dissonance theory.

In many ways the experiment by Festinger and Carlsmith (1959) began the controversy, and it is instructive to examine some of the research based directly or indirectly on that study. Remember that Festinger and Carlsmith found more private attitude change in favor of a boring task when the subjects were paid only $1 to lie about their opinion of the task than when they were paid $20. These results were explained in terms of a principle of insufficient justification: in the $1 condition the external payment provided insufficient justification for engaging in the counterattitudinal behavior (lying to the waiting subject), and this discrepancy created cognitive dissonance that had to be resolved by changing the internal attitude. This, of course, is the explanation given by dissonance theory. But there have been two major alternative explanations: incentive theory and self-perception theory.

Incentive theory is based on the principle of reinforcement, and holds that the more a person is paid to advocate a particular position, the *more* the internal attitude should change in the direction advocated (Elms, 1967; Elms and Janis, 1965; Janis, 1968; Janis and Gilmore, 1965; Rosenberg, 1965, 1968). Festinger and Carlsmith's findings directly contradicted this incentive theory prediction, so the incentive theorists were faced with having to deal with these results. Their first response (Janis and Gilmore, 1965; Rosenberg, 1965) was to suggest that there were *artifacts* in Festinger and Carlsmith's procedure, and in the procedure of other dissonance researchers (Cohen, 1962), which rendered the findings meaningless. We shall discuss this position more fully in a moment.

Self-perception theory (Bem, 1965, 1967, 1972) took a quite different position, agreeing with the results of dissonance studies but disagreeing with the theoretical explanation of those findings. You will recall that a fundamental assumption of any cognitive consistency theory (be it balance, congruity, or dissonance) is that cognitive inconsistency has *motivating* properties. Inconsistency is considered to be unpleasant, and all the consistency theories presume that people will reorganize their cognitive worlds in order to remove that unpleasant inconsistency. Thus a motivational state is thought to intervene between counterattitudinal advocacy and the final expression of private attitudes. It is important to note that there is usually no *direct* measurement of the existence of this internal motivational state in most studies, although research by Brehm, Back, and Bogdanoff (1964), Waterman and Katkin (1967), and Zanna and Cooper (1974) suggests the existence of such an internal motivation. Nevertheless, any dissonance study which contains no direct measurement can be reinterpreted in terms of self-perception theory.

Such a reinterpretation goes like this: even after you have taken part in Festinger and Carlsmith's boring task, your attitude toward that task is vague and uncrystallized. It surely wasn't the most interesting thing you have done, but it wasn't the worst, either. If you now tell another subject (for a payment of $20) that the task was interesting, you will see that action as a product of the external reward, rather than as the result of your internal attitude. If, however, you perform the same services for only $1, the payment is not powerful enough by itself to get you to lie, so you will think your attitude toward the task cannot be all that negative. When the experimenter then asks you to indicate your "true attitude" you observe your behavior in much the same way that another person would observe you, and look for the external variables that might be controlling your actions. In effect, you are asking yourself, "What must my attitude have been, in order for me to describe the task as enjoyable for such a large [small] reward?" Thus the only difference between the dissonance and self-perception explanations is that self-perception does *not* postulate the existence of an internal motivating state.

Some of the experimental research performed in response to the Festinger and Carlsmith (1959) findings is shown in Figure 6-5, and this research is classified according to its theoretical bias (the three horizontal sections of the figure) and according to its place in the controversy (the six stages noted at the top of the figure). The horizontal dotted lines separate the research traditions of incentive, dissonance, and self-perception theory, and the solid lines connecting the various boxes in the figure trace the development of the theory, methods, and research. The diagram begins at the left, with each theory's explanation of Festinger and Carlsmith's findings, and the stages of development in the controversy progress to the right. We shall consider each of these stages in order.

Interpretations of the Results

The findings of more attitude change with a small payment than with a large payment were predicted by dissonance theorists and were explained by the principle of insufficient justification. Self-perception theorists accepted the validity of the findings but suggested a different interpretation, while incentive theorists found it necessary to question the results themselves.

Extensions of the Original Principle

As we noted in Chapter Two, one way to try to verify a conceptual principle is to conduct conceptual replications of the original experiment—changing the experimental situations as much as possible

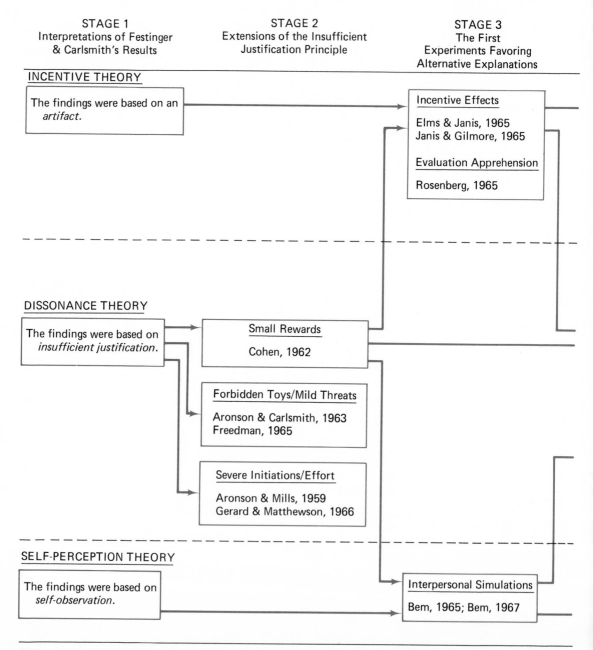

FIGURE 6-5
Experiments and theory traced from Festinger and Carlsmith's $1-$20 experiment.

STAGE 1	STAGE 2	STAGE 3
Interpretations of Festinger & Carlsmith's Results	Extensions of the Insufficient Justification Principle	The First Experiments Favoring Alternative Explanations

INCENTIVE THEORY

The findings were based on an *artifact*.

Incentive Effects

Elms & Janis, 1965
Janis & Gilmore, 1965

Evaluation Apprehension

Rosenberg, 1965

DISSONANCE THEORY

The findings were based on *insufficient justification*.

Small Rewards

Cohen, 1962

Forbidden Toys/Mild Threats

Aronson & Carlsmith, 1963
Freedman, 1965

Severe Initiations/Effort

Aronson & Mills, 1959
Gerard & Matthewson, 1966

SELF-PERCEPTION THEORY

The findings were based on *self-observation*.

Interpersonal Simulations

Bem, 1965; Bem, 1967

while still leaving the theoretical idea intact. Thus the first attempts by dissonance theorists to broaden the principle of insufficient justification included the study described earlier by Cohen (1962) in which subjects were paid varying amounts to write an essay favoring police

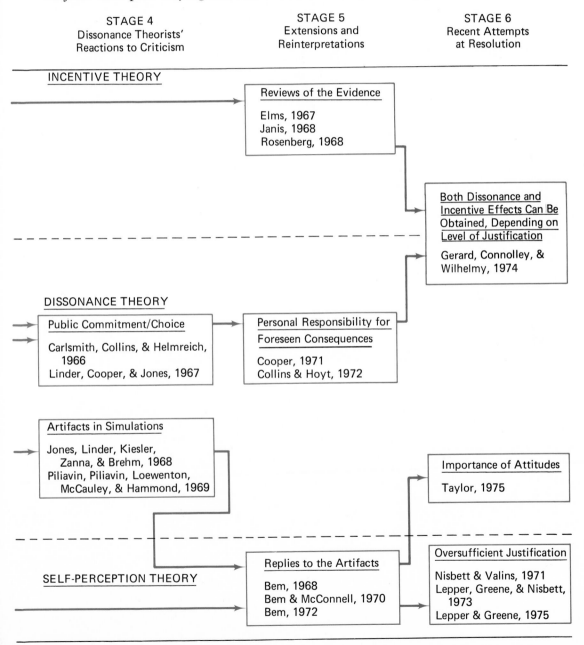

intervention in campus demonstrations, a study by Aronson and Carlsmith (1963), and an experiment by Aronson and Mills (1959). After describing these last two, we shall return to further consideration of the Cohen (1962) experiment.

Just as a behavior performed for insufficient external justification should be valued more highly, a behavior prohibited by an insufficient external justification should be *devalued* ("The only reason I didn't do it was that I didn't *want* to"). This proposition was tested in the Aronson and Carlsmith (1963) experiment, using what has become known as the "forbidden toy" procedure. Preschool children were brought individually into a playroom, where they were permitted free play with any of five very attractive toys. After a few minutes of play, the experimenter used comparisons between pairs of toys to obtain a preference ranking for the five toys, from most preferred to least preferred. The toy that turned out to be the second most liked was left on the table, while the rest of the toys were spread out on the floor. Then the experimenter left the room, saying that he would return in a few minutes, and as he left he delivered the experimental manipulation. In a No Threat condition, he said nothing else and simply took the second-ranked toy with him (the experimenters don't say so, but there were probably a few objections). In a Mild Threat condition, the experimenter left the second-ranked toy on the table, but said that he would be "annoyed" if the child played with it during his absence. In a Severe Threat condition, "annoyed" became "angry," and in addition the experimenter threatened to take all toys and go home if the child disobeyed the prohibition.

All the children were then left alone, and observed for ten minutes. None of the children in either the Mild or Severe Threat conditions actually played with the forbidden toy, and of course the children in the No Threat condition did not have the opportunity to do so. After the ten minutes had elapsed, the experimenter returned and obtained a second set of preference rankings. Dissonance theory predicts that dissonance will be aroused in the Mild Threat condition, because the Mild Threat does not constitute sufficient justification for *not playing* with the forbidden toy, while the Severe Threat does provide one. The dissonance aroused in the Mild Threat condition should lead the child to devalue the forbidden toy: "I am not playing with it because I don't like it." And, as predicted by dissonance theory, only the children who had received the Mild Threat decreased their liking for the forbidden toy. In fact, a majority of children in the Severe Threat condition actually increased their liking of the toy and ranked it first! Later experiments with the "forbidden toy" have found consistent support for the insufficient justification explanation (e.g., Freedman, 1965; Lepper, Zanna, and Abelson, 1970), although some social class differences in responses have been noted (Dembrowski and Pennebaker, 1975), and an alternative view of self-control has recently been suggested (Ebbesen, Bowers, Phillips, and Snyder, 1975).

A second sort of conceptual replication of the insufficient justification principle was performed in an entirely different context. Aronson and Mills (1959) tried to determine the effects of a severe initiation upon a subject's liking for a group. In the context of group discussions on the psychology of sex, female undergraduate students were given a "screening test" to see whether they would be permitted to join an ongoing discussion group. Depending upon the experimental conditions, there were three versions of this screening test. Subjects in the Control condition were simply asked (by the male experimenter) if they could talk freely about sex. Subjects in the Mild Initiation condition were asked if they could talk freely about sex, and in addition they were required to read aloud a list of five sex-related, but innocuous, words. Subjects in the Severe Initiation condition were asked the same initial question, but were then required to read aloud twelve obscene words and two fairly explicit passages describing sexual activity (remember that in the late 1950s, this would have been quite a severe initiation).

After the screening test had been completed, subjects listened to a tape recording of a previous session of the group they were ostensibly to join. This tape was the same for all subjects, and was an extremely boring and worthless discussion of the sexual behavior of animals. After hearing the tape, the subjects evaluated the group discussion and its participants on a series of rating scales. The results showed that those who had received the Severe Initiation made evaluations that were generally more favorable than did subjects in either the Control or Mild Initiation condition. The dull and worthless discussion is, in retrospect, an insufficient justification for the Severe screening test, so to reduce her dissonance the subject must raise her evaluation of the attractiveness of the group. There were several criticisms of the Aronson and Mills experiment, most notably those of Chapanis and Chapanis (1964), but a successful conceptual replication of the initiation study by Gerard and Matthewson (1966) undercut many of the criticisms. It would appear that for the question of initiation severity, as well as for the issue of internalization of prohibitions, insufficient justification is a useful explanatory principle. But what about the topic of counterattitudinal advocacy with which we began? Let's return to that concept and see what the critics did with it.

Experiments Critical of the Dissonance Approach

For their part, the incentive theorists attacked the $20 payment by Festinger and Carlsmith as "inappropriate"—an amount so high that it would have raised the suspicions of even the most trusting subjects. That position was argued best by Rosenberg (1965), who suggested that any experimental subject approaches an encounter with a professional psychologist with a certain amount of evaluation apprehension (the fear, discussed in Chapter Two, that the psychologist will discover his or her emotional weaknesses and immaturities). Evaluation apprehension can contaminate research findings since subjects will presumably be careful to avoid revealing anything damaging about themselves. Given this background, subjects who are (effectively) offered $20 to change their attitudes may resist attitude change to indicate to the experimenter that they cannot be "bought."

To test this idea, Rosenberg repeated the Cohen (1962) experiment with a different issue but arranged to have the dissonance arousal part of the experiment separated from the attitude measurement part. When the subject arrived for the experiment, he found Rosenberg either busily writing or talking to another "student." Rosenberg then explained that he was running late, and as an afterthought suggested that the subject might occupy his time by participating for pay in "another little experiment" unrelated to Rosenberg's own research. When the subjects reported for the "other experiment" (and all but three of them did), they were given Cohen's procedure word for word, except that the university's failure to permit its football team to take part in a postseason game was substituted for the issue of police intervention in a campus disturbance. After each subject had written an essay on why the university was justified (a position no subject had originally agreed with), the "experiment" was concluded and the subject was sent back to Rosenberg's office. There the subject's attitudes on a number of issues (including participation in the postseason game) were assessed and the true nature of the experiment was explained.

The results of this experiment confirmed incentive theory predictions: the more subjects were paid for their counterattitudinal essays, the more likely they were to state that the university had been justified in prohibiting the teams' participation in the postseason game. Thus Rosenberg concluded that with the artifact of evaluation apprehension successfully removed, payment for writing counterattitudinal essays would produce results consistent with incentive theory, rather than results supporting dissonance theory.

Two other experiments by incentive theorists (Elms and Janis, 1965; Janis and Gilmore, 1965) were performed in response to the "inappropriateness" of the $20 payment in Festinger and Carlsmith's original study. In both these experiments there was either a large payment or a small payment, but these payments were offered by either one of two different institutional *sponsors*. When the attitude research had a positively valued sponsor, the *large* payment produced greater attitude change; when the research had apparently shady purposes, the *small* payment produced the greatest change. This was a less direct attack on the question than was Rosenberg's research but it led to the same conclusion: dissonance effects will be obtained for a large payment only when the subjects are suspicious of the experimenter's motives. Thus the incentive theory studies raised some important questions about the validity of Festinger and Carlsmith's, as well as Cohen's, results.

Questions about findings, however, can usually be resolved by further research, so perhaps more threatening to the dissonance position were the reinterpretations made by the self-perception theorists (primarily Bem) of the dissonance studies. You will recall that the self-perception approach accepts the validity of the dissonance findings and simply argues that no internal motivational state is required to account for those findings. To demonstrate this position, Bem (1965) introduced the technique of interpersonal simulation, in which subjects were provided with complete descriptions of Cohen's experiment and were asked to estimate the attitudinal responses that Cohen's subjects would have given under the circumstances. There were three experimental conditions in Bem's study: a Control condition in which there was no mention of any money paid to Cohen's subjects, a $1 condition in which it was stated that Cohen's subjects were paid $1 to write their essays, and a $.50 condition in which the pay Cohen's subjects supposedly received was $.50. These conditions, of course, corresponded to Cohen's actual Control, $1, and $.50 conditions. Bem's prediction was that his *simulating* subjects would make estimates of final attitudes that were the same as the actual attitudes expressed by Cohen's subjects.

The simulation appeared to be a resounding success. Cohen had found significantly more attitude change in the $.50 condition than in the $1 condition, and some evidence that even the $1 condition had changed away from the Control. Bem's simulating subjects reproduced this pattern exactly. Since Bem's subjects were merely observing the behavior of others, rather than writing the essays themselves, they could not be experiencing cognitive dissonance. So when their predictions about the attitudes expressed by Cohen's subjects coincided with the actual responses of the latter groups, it suggested that Cohen's subjects, themselves, might not be experiencing any dissonance. They might only have been observing their own behavior.

Dissonance Theorists' Reactions to Criticism

It was now the dissonance theorists' turn to cry, "Artifact!" In the first of these studies Carlsmith, Collins, and Helmreich (1966) pointed out that the essay-writing task employed by Janis and Gilmore (1965) and Elms and Janis (1965) was not really comparable to the face-to-face deception required of subjects in the original Festinger and Carlsmith experiment. There is simply not the degree of commitment inherent in writing an anonymous essay that there is in taking a public stance that conflicts with your private beliefs. In effect, this argument held that the "counterattitudinal" actions required in the two incentive studies were neither committing enough nor discrepant enough to arouse any cognitive dissonance.

To test this idea Carlsmith, Collins, and Helmreich had subjects either write essays or engage in face-to-face deception for one of three levels of payment—$.50, $1.50, or $5—in a factorial design (as discussed in Chapter Two). The results showed the predicted interaction between nature of task and level of payment: when the task was writing an essay which described a boring procedure as fun and interesting, the more subjects were paid for their essays the more favorable their own attitudes became; but when the task was face-to-face deception of another subject by describing the same boring procedure as interesting and fun, the more subjects were paid the *less* their private attitudes changed. In short, incentive findings were obtained for essay writing but dissonance findings were obtained for face-to-face deception.

In the second major dissonance response to the incentive theory work, Linder, Cooper, and Jones (1967) argued that Rosenberg's (1965) "two-experiment" design obscured the role of commitment in the production of dissonance. These investigators pointed out that for dissonance effects to occur, the amount of money involved in the counterattitudinal behavior must be known by the subject *at the time he or she decides whether or not to participate.* If you have already agreed to an unpleasant task and I offer to pay you for accomplishing it, you will evaluate it more highly the more I pay you (an incentive effect). But if the amount of reward is made part of your decision, then the principle of insufficient justification should take over. Linder, Cooper, and Jones argued that subjects in Rosenberg's experiment committed themselves to participate in the "other little experiment" by announcing that they would wait for Rosenberg to finish his work, and further by walking to another part of the building where the "other experiment" was being conducted. These actions constituted a decision to participate regardless of the rewards involved, so naturally those rewards produced incentive effects.

In a procedure that has become a model for later attempts at arti-fact discovery, Linder, Cooper, and Jones included one complete set of conditions that exactly paralleled Rosenberg's conditions. They then included another set of conditions designed to remove the arti-fact: subjects in these conditions were specifically told *not* to decide whether to participate in the "other experiment" until *after* they had heard all that the experimenter had to say (obviously including the amount of money to be involved). This design is known as a balanced replication, a design which includes both conditions that reproduce the artifact and conditions that show how it can be eliminated. And the results supported the predictions. In the No-choice conditions in which subjects were simply sent to the "other experiment," incentive effects were obtained, but in the Free Decision conditions in which subjects waited until after they had been told of the amounts before deciding to participate, dissonance effects were obtained.

Not only did the dissonance theorists point out artifacts in the incentive research, they also identified artifacts in the interpersonal simulations (Jones, Linder, Kiesler, Zanna, and Brehm, 1968; Piliavin, Piliavin, Loewenton, McCauley, and Hammond, 1969). Specifically, these investigators noted that one aspect of the information available to a "real" subject that is unavailable to a simulating subject is the "real" subject's initial attitude on the topic in question. Both these sets of investigators conducted balanced replications of Bem's simula-tions in which similar results were obtained when no information was provided the simulating subjects about the "real" subjects' initial attitudes. But when information *was* provided about the subjects' initial attitudes, the simulators made predictions that differed from the results obtained with "real" subjects. It appeared, as Piliavin et al. (1969) noted, that Bem's simulators had made the right answers for the wrong reasons.

Extensions and Reinterpretations

At this stage in the development of the controversy, most of the re-searchers involved reached the conclusion that I hope you have also reached: dissonance theory can account for some of the counteratti-tudinal advocacy results, incentive theory can account for some of the results, and self-perception theory can account for some of the results. Furthermore, it became clear that the theorists of different persuasions were much more effective in convincing themselves than in convinc-ing each other. Reviews of the literature by incentive theorists were published which concluded that the findings on the whole supported incentive theory (Elms, 1967; Janis, 1968; Rosenberg, 1968); exten-sions of the dissonance work (Cooper, 1971; Collins and Hoyt, 1972) found consistent evidence for dissonance theory, provided there was a strong personal responsibility for the decision felt by the subjects; and replies by the self-perception theorists (Bem, 1968; Bem and McConnell, 1970; Bem, 1972) took issue with the criticisms that had been leveled at interpersonal simulations. All these extensions and reinterpretations helped to clarify the conditions under which one theory as opposed to another might provide the best account of the experimental findings, and in so doing, they all helped to reveal just how complex were the phenomena that seemed so simple right after the Festinger and Carlsmith study.

Recent Attempts at Resolution

The trend toward clarification and integration of various theoretical viewpoints has continued in recent research. With regard to the long-standing dissonance-incentive controversy, Gerard, Connolley, and Wilhelmy (1974) have argued that depending upon the degree of justification for engaging in a counterattitudinal behavior, both dissonance and incentive effects are possible. When there is insufficient justification dissonance effects will be obtained; when the justification is sufficient and appropriate there will be no attitude change at all; and when the justification is too great there will be incentive effects. In short, if I pay you either too little (dissonance) or too much (incentive) to perform a behavior with negative consequences, your attitude toward that behavior will become more favorable. It remains to be seen whether this attempted integration will withstand the test of future experimental research and criticism.

With regard to the self-perception–dissonance controversy, research by Taylor (1975) suggests that the self-perception explanation may be limited to cases in which the person is either unsure of, or not strongly committed to, his or her initial attitudes. On the other hand, research in an area that has become known as oversufficient justification (Nisbett and Valins, 1971) shows support for the self-perception approach. Oversufficient justification deals with extrinsic payment for something that the person would do otherwise (a proattitudinal, rather than counterattitudinal, action). In cases of oversufficient justification, there should be no dissonance: it is certainly not dissonant to be rewarded for having fun. But the self-perception analysis is the same as for the case of insufficient justification. A person who is receiving a large external payment for engaging in a proattitudinal action should evaluate his or her behavior and conclude that it has been produced not by intrinsic interest, but rather by the external reward. If for some reason the external reward is then taken away, the person should become *less* interested in the activity than he or she was before there was an extrinsic reward. This damaging effect of external reward has been obtained in several studies with young children (Lepper and Greene, 1975; Lepper, Greene, and Nisbett, 1973), and if it also holds for adults it could have important consequences for a wide variety of social behaviors.

It should be emphasized that the stages just outlined in the controversy between dissonance theory and two alternative explanations trace a typical, rather than an exceptional, course in the development of theory in social psychology. What begins as a simple statement (e.g., dissonance will be produced whenever one cognitive element implies the opposite of another) becomes, through continuous refinement, a more complex but more accurate statement (dissonance will be created whenever a person feels personally responsible for actions that lead to negative consequences). Along the way new methods are developed (evaluation-apprehension reduction techniques, interpersonal simulations, balanced replications), new pitfalls are discovered, and new areas of research grow out of attempts to resolve theoretical controversy. Perhaps the greatest compliment that can be paid to the theory of cognitive dissonance is the recognition of its extensive role in this continuing process.

Summary of Dissonance Theory

Cognitive dissonance theory is a strictly intrapersonal consistency theory, and the fact that its elements are *propositions* reflecting a person's view of the social world and his or her own behavior attests to this intrapersonal focus. These propositions (p. 245) can be *consonant* (if one implies another), *dissonant* (if one implies the opposite of another), or *irrelevant* (if the two carry no mutual implications). The *magnitude* of dissonance (p. 247) will increase as the number of dissonant cognitions increases and as the importance of those dissonant cognitions increases, but it will decrease as the number and importance of consonant cognitions increases. Once dissonance has been aroused, it can be *reduced* (p. 248) by changing one or the other element, by altering the importance of the elements involved, or by adding elements consonant with the discrepant behavior. The magnitude of dissonance cannot be estimated accurately in advance of the induction of dissonance, and it can be difficult to measure all the possible modes of dissonance reduction. Dissonance theory has been involved in a continuing controversy with incentive theory and self-perception theory (p. 250), which provide alternative explanations for many of the results obtained in dissonance research. This controversy has contributed to theoretical refinements in all three areas, and has produced important methodological contributions as well.

Suggested Additional Readings

ABELSON, R. P., ARONSON, E., McGUIRE, W. J., NEWCOMB, T. M., ROSENBERG, M. J., and TANNENBAUM, P. H. (Eds.) *Theories of cognitive consistency: A sourcebook.* Chicago: Rand McNally, 1968. At the time it was published, this book was the last word on all cognitive consistency theories. It contains contributions by nearly all the major theorists and researchers, and includes integrative summaries at the ends of sections. Very heavy reading for beginners.

ARONSON, E. The theory of cognitive dissonance: A current perspective. In L. Berkowitz (Ed.) *Advances in experimental social psychology.* Vol. 4. New York: Academic Press, 1969. Pp. 2–35. The most recent readily available statement of dissonance theory. This paper deals with some of the criticisms that have been raised against the theory as they are seen by one of the early supporters of the theory.

BEM, D. J. *Beliefs, attitudes, and human affairs.* Belmont, Calif.: Brooks/Cole, 1970. A short and highly readable book on the social consequences of attitudes. This book places its emphasis on the syllogistic structure of attitudes, but also contains elements of the dissonance–self-perception controversy.

BEM, D. J. Self-perception theory. In L. Berkowitz (Ed.) *Advances in experimental social psychology.* Vol. 6. New York: Academic Press, 1972. Pp. 2–62. A very thorough, but still readable, presentation of self-perception theory. This paper gives an analysis of the dissonance–self-perception controversy from the viewpoint of the latter theory's originator.

ELMS, A. C. (Ed.) *Role-playing, reward, and attitude change.* New York: Van Nostrand, 1969. An excellent collection of the major research papers in the early stages of the controversy between dissonance theory and the alternative explanations of incentive and self-perception.

FELDMAN, S. *Cognitive consistency: Motivational antecedents and behavioral consequents.* New York: Academic Press, 1966. An important collection of papers by major consistency theorists, with selections that concentrate on the degree to which inconsistency may possess motivating properties. Longer, more integrative chapters than in the Abelson et al. book, and probably much easier reading for students unfamiliar with the area.

GREENWALD, A. G., BROCK, T. C., and OSTROM, T. M. (Eds.) *Psychological foundations of attitudes.* New York: Academic Press, 1968. A collection of chapters on various aspects of attitude theory. Explicitly prepared to focus on aspects of attitude organization *other than* consistency theory, this volume gives the reader an idea of the breadth of the field. Some of the approaches included are learning theory, personality theory, and various functional theories.

ZIMBARDO, P. G., and EBBESEN, E. B. *Influencing attitudes and changing behavior.* Reading, Mass.: Addison-Wesley, 1969. An excellent introduction to attitude change research and techniques of attitude measurement, with an overview of cognitive dissonance research.

An individual's judgment of a message will depend on his or her own position on the issue.

Photo by Paul Seder

Principles of Attitude Change
Chapter Seven

We have previously discussed the cognitive, affective, and behavioral components of a single attitude (Chapter Five), and the organizational principles that might apply to sets of attitudes: horizontal and vertical structure, and cognitive consistency (Chapter Six). From these discussions, we have already learned a good deal about attitude change. But much of that knowledge has dealt with resistance rather than change. The component analysis suggests that cognitively based attitudes will be more responsive to new information, but that emotionally based attitudes will not. From the syllogistic model of attitude organization we learn that the more horizontal and vertical interconnections an attitude has, the more difficult it will be to change. In a similar manner, an attitude that is balanced, congruous, or consonant with a number of others (or with behavior) will be more resistant to change than is an attitude that is less consistent with the person's other beliefs and opinions. These principles of attitude organization set the limits within which direct attempts at influence have some chance of success. As we see in this chapter, however, the instigation of attitude change is more complicated than it would appear to be. First we distinguish between real and apparent attitude change, then we go on to examine some of the functions of attitudes, and finally we turn to sources of resistance to and facilitation of change.

REAL OR APPARENT CHANGE?

The first problem we encounter in considering attitude change is the difficulty of distinguishing between true change in an internal attitude (called *private acceptance*) and mere conformity in overt behavior (called *public compliance*). To the extent that attitudes can lead to behavior, private acceptance should produce the most enduring changes. Suppose that I am in the business of making candy bars, and that these candy bars are always sold in opaque wrappers. Even though I must print the weight of the enclosed bar on the wrapper, I have discovered that I can make every fifth bar smaller, thereby cheating some of the customers and saving myself a lot of money. Now suppose that you represent a consumer group, and by weighing my candy bars you have found me out. What will you do about it? One possibility would be to threaten to bring legal action if you catch me shortchanging bars again. That would produce compliance—I would stop shortchanging as long as you were watching me—but not necessarily private acceptance (I might go right back to my old ways the minute that you stopped watching). From your viewpoint, and also from society's viewpoint, private acceptance would be preferable. How can such private acceptance be attained?

One answer is suggested by Kelman's (1961) analysis of the processes of attitude change. Considering attitude change attempts in the broader perspective of social influence, Kelman argued that at least three different processes could be distinguished: compliance, identification, and internalization. In Kelman's terms, compliance is the observable change in behavior in the direction advocated by the influencing agent and is, therefore, equivalent to the public compliance referred to previously. Compliance takes place as a result of threatened punishment or promised reward, and behavior so affected may revert back to its original character once the rewarding or punishing agent leaves the scene. Your threats have not changed my attitude toward my customers; all they have accomplished is to make me want to keep from getting caught.

In contrast to compliance, identification and internalization are both aspects of private acceptance. They differ in the motivation presumed to account for that private acceptance. Identification is private acceptance based on a "satisfying self-defining relationship" (p. 63) between the target person (me) and the change agent (you). To the extent that my self-image depends on having you think of me as a respected businessman, you may be able to influence me to identify with your requests. Note that I privately accept your view not because I have considered it and think it to be morally correct, but rather because I consider providing full portions to be "good business." I have identified with your notion of what a "respected businessman" should be, and if I do not privately accept your request that I not cheat my customers, I will lose an important part of my identity. Kelman (1961) uses the process of identification to account for the formation of attitudes in children who are socialized by their parents (classic "identification" in a Freudian sense), and for the attitude change that occurs in more extreme socialization experiences as well. For example, a new recruit in the armed forces will adopt a great many attitudes held by the military through identification, because his or her self-image (identity) is so dependent upon the relation to the group.

The other sort of private acceptance, internalization, is based on the target person's belief that the position advocated is "congruent with his value system"(p. 65). Here private acceptance comes about not because of the instrumental value of the attitude, but because holding that attitude is a valuable end in itself. If I believe that it is morally and ethically correct for business people to deal with their customers in a forthright and honest way, then I will deal with my own customers according to those principles. The basis for judgment will by *my own value system,* not the views of the consuming public. Although the process of internalization has quite a rational sound to it, it may not be entirely a rational process. Suppose that my own values held, for some reason, that one should cheat one's customers as much as possible. We would like to think of this as an irrational view of business practices, but any attitude consistent with this orientation would be adopted through a process of internalization. It does not matter what consumers think about the issue—I will shortchange or not depending only on my own value system.

In summary, *compliance* is superficial behavioral change "because I have to," *identification* is private acceptance that occurs "because it is expected of me," and *internalization* is private acceptance that takes place "because it is right." To induce compliance in a target person, the change agent must identify the threats and rewards, limit the behavioral choices, and constantly engage in surveillance to ensure that there will be no backsliding. To induce identification, the change agent needs to make salient to the target person the role expectations for his or her behavior, and to make it attractive for the target person to live up to those role expectations. Since this is an internal change, no surveillance is necessary as long as the role expectations remain clear and attractive. To induce internalization, the change agent must convince the target person that the behavior is value relevant, and this task will be simplest when the change agent is credible (i.e, shares the target person's value system). Again, since the change is an internal one, no surveillance is necessary (unless, of course, there is a basic change in the target person's value structure). Thus real attitude change can be distinguished from apparent change by whether or not surveillance is necessary and by whether external threats and/or rewards are involved. Within the domain of private acceptance, identification and internalization can be distinguished from each other by whether the change agent's influence attempts are stated in terms of role expectations or basic values, respectively.

THE FUNCTIONS OF ATTITUDES

Four Functions

The discussion of identification and internalization leads naturally to consideration of the several functions that attitudes may serve for the person who holds them. Perhaps the most comprehensive theory, developed by Katz and his associates (Katz, 1960; Katz and Kahn, 1966; Katz and Stotland, 1959), identifies four different functions of attitudes:

1. The instrumental function: *People will develop positive attitudes toward people and objects that facilitate their achievement of desired goals, and will develop negative attitudes toward people and objects that frustrate the achievement of those goals.* This functional category corresponds roughly to Kelman's (1961) idea of identification. Each evaluation depends on the fact that holding a particular attitude has some end beside itself. If the candy-making businessman has a positive attitude toward his customers, that attitude will help increase his sales (i.e., will have some instrumental value) quite apart from the ethical, moral, or value justification for being pleasant. It should be noted that the instrumental function is for a privately accepted attitude what superficial compliance is for overt behavior: each helps the individual achieve desired goals, and neither is an end in itself.

2. The value-expressive function: *People will develop attitudes that are consistent with, and expressive of, their broader value system.* A person who places a high value on human life will develop attitudes against capital punishment, in favor of medical aid to people in underdeveloped countries, and in favor of various social programs designed to make life easier for underprivileged people. This functional category is roughly equivalent to private acceptance through Kelman's (1961) process of internalization, since its defining characteristic is congruence with the person's value system.

3. The knowledge function: *People will develop attitudes that help bring structure to their social worlds.* These attitudes simplify a person's experience, provide organizing principles, and guide information gathering on topics of importance to the person. Another way to describe these attitudes is to compare them to the *attributions* (see Chapter Four) that an individual makes for the causes of the actions of other people. We try to explain and predict the actions that others take, and some of these attributional explanations (e.g., "he is an extremely evil person") sound much like attitudes. There is a cognitive categorization of the person's behavior, an implicit evaluation of that behavior ("evil" is probably "bad"), and an implicit behavioral predisposition ("stay away from him").

4. The ego-defensive function: *People will develop at least some attitudes which have the effect of shielding them from conscious recognition of their own inadequacies and failings.* An excellent example is the attitude of racism (Chapter Five) which can have any number of ego-defensive expressions. These could include "I wouldn't have so much trouble getting a job if they weren't given preferential treatment," or "I don't have anything to do with them, because you can't trust any of them to be fair with you." Ego-defensive attitudes

deny or distort reality in order to protect the person holding them from having to admit some of his or her own negative characteristics.

Implications for Change

The major contribution to our understanding of attitude change that is provided by the functional approach is the specification of some of the conditions under which attitudes might change. For example, providing a person with correct information will change a knowledge attitude that had been based on faulty information, but it might have little effect on a value-expressive attitude. In addition, the suggestion that attitudes can serve the process of ego defense carries substantial implications for attitude change. An instrumental attitude can be altered simply by changing the reinforcements (rewards or punishments) associated with that attitude, and a knowledge attitude can be altered by correcting misinformation about the world. A value-expressive attitude that is inconsistent with the person's value system could be changed by pointing out the inconsistency, and a consistent value-expressive attitude might be changed by a rational discussion of the entire value system. But the arguments against a strongly held ego-defensive attitude are, themselves, likely to be misinterpreted, distorted, or denied. It is unlikely that we can reduce individuals' prejudice by convincing them that the problem is really their own inadequacy. So instead of dealing only with the attitude, we must try to deal with the circumstances that produce the inadequacy itself. For example, racial tension could be reduced if there were plenty of jobs to go around for everyone.

In short, the functional theory of attitudes suggests that before we can accurately predict the difficulty of changing a particular attitude, we must know the function which that attitude serves for the individual. This is, as we have seen, an intuitively pleasing formulation. But well-articulated measures of the various functions do not exist, and the research based on this approach (e.g., Katz, Sarnoff, and McClintock, 1956; McClintock, 1958; Stotland, Katz, and Patchen, 1959) has not produced clear-cut findings. And indeed, it would be very difficult to identify people whose attitudes served ego-defensive functions, since the more successfully those attitudes worked, the less defensive the individual would appear on the surface. Despite these difficulties, the functional theory of attitudes can suggest some of the reasons for resistance to attitude change. We now turn to consideration of specific sources of resistance to attempts at attitude change.

SOURCES OF RESISTANCE TO ATTITUDE CHANGE

A person will be reluctant to change an attitude (1) if it has numerous horizontal and vertical connections to other parts of his or her attitude structure; (2) if it is supported by a great many consistent cognitions; or (3) if it serves ego-defensive purposes. In each of these cases the resistance to change arises from the existing psychological support for the attitude, and in principle that resistance should be constant, no matter what form the influence attempt takes. Taking an ego-defensive attitude as an example, if you maintain a racially biased attitude in order to shore up your lagging self-esteem, then the message I use to try to change that attitude will make little difference. I can present rational arguments, I can insult you for holding such a biased opinion, I can use **prestige suggestion** and tell you that your favorite movie star doesn't feel the way you do, or I can even try to force you into counter-attitudinal behavior such as signing a petition supporting school integration and busing. But unless I accompany these techniques with a strong boost to your self-esteem (from a direction irrelevant to the attitude), I will not succeed in producing any significant or lasting change. In other cases in which the background of psychological support for the attitude is not quite so strong, the manner in which I conduct my influence attempt *can* make a difference in the outcome, and we shall now consider two such instances.

Resistance Arising from Discrepancy

Suppose that you are a social science major and are asked to participate in a debate with two other students, one a humanities major and one a natural science major. Each of you is to persuade the audience that his or her approach should be adopted by everyone and that the other two areas of inquiry should be discarded altogether. It is reasonable to expect that the members of the audience will be relatively committed to their own positions, but it is possible that the way you state your case might have some bearing on the outcome of the debate. In order to win, you need to hold all your social science majors in line while changing the opinions of a number of other people, so that when the issue comes to a vote there will be a plurality of the audience on your side. You are in the fortunate position of having more in common with each of the other areas than they have in common with each other. Should you try to convert a few from each other area, or should you aim your message at one group alone?

The answer depends upon the *discrepancy* between the position you advocate and the original position of the hearers. For example, if you assert that "Chemistry is nonsense" you may win some friends among the humanities majors, but you will make some confirmed enemies among the natural science students and you may even lose the support of the biologically oriented psychologists. The ways in which people react to attitude statements like this one can be described in terms of a theory of social judgment first elaborated by Sherif and Hovland (1961). The essential principle of social judgment theory is that *an individual's own position on an issue will influence his or her perception of attitude statements about that issue.* This fundamental assumption can be seen in a wide variety of social judgment theories (e.g., Eiser and Stroebe, 1973; Fishbein and Ajzen, 1975; Helson, 1964; Sherif, Sherif, and Nebergall, 1965; Upshaw, 1969), but we shall concentrate primarily on the version proposed by Sherif and Hovland.

Latitudes of Acceptance, Rejection, and Noncommitment

For example, imagine a scale of attitudes toward a specific natural science (chemistry) that runs from one extreme (Highly Favorable) to the other (Highly Unfavorable). Both the "own positions" of members of your audience and the scale values of various possible messages could be located on this scale. For example, a senior chemistry major planning graduate work in the discipline should have a very favorable "own position," a student planning graduate work in biology might be expected to have a moderate "own position" on chemistry; and a student who almost didn't get into graduate school in English because he had flunked chemistry would have a highly unfavorable attitude toward the subject. Just as the members of the audience can be located on the scale of attitudes toward chemistry, so can possible messages you might use in the debate (e.g., "Chemistry is nonsense" is Highly Unfavorable).

Social judgment theory proposes that an individual's evaluation of a message will depend on the discrepancy between the recipient's own position and the scale position of the message. This idea is represented in three zones or *latitudes* thought to surround an individual's own position. These are (1) a latitude of acceptance which encloses all the messages that might be accepted by the recipient, even though they do not coincide exactly with his or her own position; (2) a latitude of rejection which encloses all the messages that will be rejected out of hand; and (3) a latitude of noncommitment which encloses all the remaining possible messages. Examples of these latitudes are shown in Figure 7-1 for an ardent chemistry major (whose own position is F) and for a biology major (whose own position is taken to be D). The

FIGURE 7-1
Assimilation and contrast in acceptance of persuasive communications.

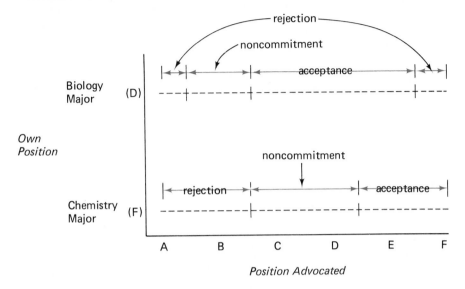

Statement of Positions Advocated

A = Chemistry is worthless.
B = Chemistry may have some value.
C = Chemistry is helpful to any science major.
D = Chemistry provides an excellent example of
      the practical applications of science.
E = Chemistry is a terrific major.
F = Chemistry is the only path to knowledge and truth.

latitudes shown have all been set arbitrarily, to illustrate that they may differ for different people. In practice, however, the latitudes can be defined empirically by having an individual accept or reject a series of statements which cover the entire range of the scale.

Consider first the judgments of the ardent chemistry major. He really believes that chemistry is the only path to knowledge and truth (F), but he can also accept the idea that chemistry may be [just] a terrific major field (E). He is not terribly concerned about whether chemical research produces practical benefits (D), and he hasn't thought too much about the field's potential for other science majors (C), so these messages fall into his region of noncommitment. He must, of course, reject the notion that chemistry has "some value" (B), because that statement would be perceived as suggesting that there were cases in which it had no value, and must also reject the idea that chemistry is worthless (A). The biology major takes the position that chemistry has significant practical applications (D) and can also accept either the idea that chemistry can be a terrific major (E) or the argument that it is useful for any science major (C). She has no particular commitment about the assertion that chemistry may have some value (she thinks that it does, and she is not sensitive to the other possible meaning of the statement). But she cannot accept either the idea that chemistry is worthless (A) or the view that it is the only path to knowledge and truth (F). Thus each student's opinion of the statements in this series will be based in part on his or her own position on the issue.

Assimilation, Contrast, and the Perception of Discrepancy

Social judgment theory was originally derived from classic psychophysical methods, in which subjects are to give psychologically based descriptions of various physical stimuli. For example, suppose that you are asked to estimate the "heaviness" of a series of lifted weights by comparing each weight in the series to a *standard,* or anchor, weight. Your judgments of the heaviness of all the weights in the series will be affected by the weight of the standard. If this standard is heavier than most of the weights in the series, you will underestimate most of the weights. If the standard is lighter than most of the weights in the series, you will overestimate their heaviness. Weights that are close to the standard will be *assimilated* to its value (judged closer than they really are), while weights distant from the standard will be *contrasted* with its value (judged even further away than they really are).

In attitude issues, as opposed to psychophysical judgments, the standard is considered to be your own original position on the issue. Messages that are close to your own position (that is, messages that fall into your latitude of acceptance) will be assimilated to your own position. Consequently, the assimilated messages will produce only slight attitude change (since you mistakenly believe that they are just alternative ways to state your own position). Messages that are far away from your own position (that is, ones that fall into your latitude of rejection) will be contrasted with your initial position and will be seen as further away than they really are. Contrasted messages will exert no pressure toward attitude change. Messages that fall into your latitude of noncommitment are the only ones that have any chance of producing significant *movement* in your initial position on the issue. If these messages are persuasively delivered, making you pay attention to them in a way that changes your noncommitment into acceptance, then they will have produced some attitude change. So, to return to the debate example, social judgment theory would have you direct your comments toward the humanities majors and natural science

majors who have some interest in social science in an attempt to
change a few minds in each category (without losing any of your own
following).

Implications of Assimilation/Contrast for Scaling

The assimilation/contrast hypothesis of social judgment theory is
in conflict with another attitude-related viewpoint. You will remember
from the discussion of attitude scaling in Chapter Five that the first
step in the construction of a Thurstone scale is to establish scale
values for the attitude statements to be used in the scale. To obtain
estimates of these scale values all the statements were to be sorted
into eleven categories of favorability toward the attitude object, and
the judges who were to perform this sorting were to do so *without
reference to their own feelings about the attitude object*. But social
judgment theory suggests that this will be an impossible task. Early
research on the topic (Beyle, 1932; Ferguson, 1935; Hinckley, 1932;
Pintner and Forlano, 1937) seemed to bear out Thurstone and Chave's
(1929) assumption that judges could disregard their own attitudes, but
the balance of later studies support the position of social judgment
theory (e.g., Ager and Dawes, 1965; Dawes, Singer, and Lemons, 1972;
Hovland and Sherif, 1952; Koslin and Parmagent, 1969; Zavalloni and
Cook, 1965). As social judgment theory suggests, individuals with
extreme positions on attitude issues make estimates of the scale value
of statements which differ from the estimates made by judges with
more moderate positions.

Discrepancy and Attitude Change

To return to the issue of attitude *change*, there is one experiment
most often referred to as an illustration of the effects of assimilation
and contrast on attitude change. This study, by Hovland, Harvey, and
Sherif (1957), investigated the effects of various persuasive communications on attitudes toward the use of alcohol. In the course of an
Oklahoma referendum on abolishing the prohibition against the sale of
alcoholic beverages (the referendum had failed by a narrow margin),
a number of groups had become vocally identified with extreme positions on the issue. These ranged from the Women's Christian Temper-
ance Union to an association of liquor dealers (and a group of the
experimenters' friends). For social judgment theory, the crucial question was, "Will a person's attitude change in response to a persuasive
message depend in part on his or her original position on the issue?"
Three groups of subjects were selected to represent various positions:
the "wets" consisted of people "personally known to the experimenters
or their assistants," the "moderates" were a group of college students,

and the "drys" were members of the WCTU, Salvation Army members, and students from divinity schools or church-affiliated colleges.

All the subjects were first asked to identify their "most preferred" position on a scale of nine position statements. These position statements ranged from one that described alcohol as "the curse of mankind" to one that asserted that people simply cannot get along without alcohol. From one to three weeks after their initial positions had been assessed, subjects were exposed to a persuasive communication that was slightly on the "wet" side: it advocated carefully regulated and limited sale of alcohol for special occasions only. After hearing this communication, subjects again indicated their own "most preferred" position on the issue.

What predictions should social judgment theory have made? First, the theory would predict that the slightly wet communication would be perceived differentially, depending upon the original position of the hearer. The extreme drys should contrast the communication and see it as wetter than it really is; the extreme wets should see it as dryer than it really is, and only the moderates should judge its scale position with any accuracy, although they should assimilate the communication toward their own positions. This prediction received some support: the drys did contrast the communication, seeing it as substantially wetter than it really was. Some contrast was also shown by the extreme wets, and there was a small degree of apparent assimilation by the moderates, but neither of these latter findings was particularly striking. A second prediction made by the theory was that the greatest degree of attitude change would be produced in those subjects for whom the communication was *moderately* discrepant. The results were consistent with this prediction, as there was very little attitude change among people at either extreme of the scale. Most of the attitude change occurred among people whose original positions were moderately discrepant from the communication.

Although these results were generally favorable to the social judgment theory, a number of important criticisms, both of this experiment and of the overall approach, have recently been raised. Consider the results of the experiment. The strongest evidence in favor of the social judgment theory was the fact that there was virtually no attitude change among people holding extreme positions. But as Zimbardo and Ebbesen (1969) have pointed out, this finding can be explained without need for the social judgment theory. Remember that the extreme drys were members of the WCTU, while the extreme wets included liquor dealers. It is difficult to imagine how one persuasive communication in an experimental setting could change the attitudes of either of these groups. It might be the high *involvement* of these groups in their respective positions on the issue, rather than the extremity of the position alone, which precluded attitude change. This is the sort of risk that an experimenter runs in an attempt to use naturally existing groups of research subjects instead of randomly assigning subjects to experimental treatments. As we noted in Chapter Two, the gains in external validity achieved through naturalistic experiments may be attained at the cost of internal validity.

The criticism of the subject selection applies only to this particular experiment, but the issue of involvement raises a more general problem in explaining social judgment phenomena (Upshaw, 1969). To recall material from Chapter Three, our social world can be thought of as being represented by a set of cognitive categories. When we approach an unfamiliar person or are faced with an unfamiliar attitude issue, our categorization of the person or issue is a simple one. As we become more familiar with the person, or as we learn the nuances of the issue, our cognitive category becomes more differentiated—we see finer shades of personality or meaning. Thus increased involvement with an attitude issue may change the nature of the *scale* used to make the judgments.

Suppose, for example, that you were interested in having two people rate five candidates for public office: a "conservative Republican," a "moderate Republican," a "conservative Democrat," a "moderate Democrat," and a "liberal Democrat." Further assume that one of your subjects was very heavily involved in politics, while the other was only an occasional (and straight-ticket) voter. For the involved politician, able to distinguish among candidates by their stands on a variety of issues, you might not have provided enough categories. Is the moderate Democrat in favor of increasing defense spending, or does he think it should be cut? How about public assistance, job programs, and health insurance? But for the straight-ticket voter, five categories would be too many. What difference does the shading make? A Republican is a Republican and a Democrat is a Democrat. It is important to note that not only do the individualized judgment scales (called **personal reference scales** by Upshaw, 1969) of the two subjects differ from each other, they both differ from the response categories that you have provided. So the judgments of candidates that you obtain may reflect a true assimilation/contrast effect, or they may represent a difference in personal reference scale, or they may simply be an artifact of the response categories you have provided.

Given these differences in scales of judgment, it is not too surprising that there have been often inconsistent results across experiments designed to test predictions from social judgment theory. In one attempt to increase the precision of the theory, Sherif, Sherif, and Nebergall (1965) explicitly measured the involvement of subjects in an attitude issue apart from their positions on the issue. These investigators discovered that higher involvement, regardless of position on the issue, increases the size of the latitude of rejection while decreasing both the latitude of acceptance and the latitude of noncommitment. In another approach to the problem of increasing precision, Upshaw (1969) reports a series of experiments to demonstrate how an individual's personal reference scale can be measured using an unlimited response language. For example, Upshaw asked subjects to indicate their moral outrage at a number of criminal offenses by placing an amount of sand equivalent to their censure of the offense into a small bucket. The sand was then weighed to determine the degree of censure for each offense.

The inclusion of involvement as a separate factor in social judgment and the use of unlimited response languages have permitted better tests of the social judgment theory's explanation of attitude change in terms of assimilation and contrast. Particularly when involvement is also considered, the greatest attitude change does seem to follow communications of moderate discrepancy (Sherif and Sherif, 1969). Although there have been some failures to confirm individual predictions, one recent review of the social judgment literature (Eiser and Stroebe, 1973) concludes that there is, on balance, strong support for the basic idea that an individual's judgment of a social attitude will depend on his or her own position on the issue.

Resistance Arising from Restrictions of Freedom

Resistance to persuasive communications that arises from assimilation/contrast depends on the discrepancy between one's own position and the position advocated in the communication. As the discrepancy increases, the probability of acceptance of the advocated position will decrease (Fishbein and Ajzen, 1975). Surprisingly enough, there may also be resistance to persuasion even when the position advocated is *identical* to the recipient's initial position, and this resistance will be engendered by the forcefulness of the persuasive attempt. Suppose that you are planning to spend your spring break from classes at one of the popular Florida resorts. That is your initial position on the issue and the choice that you would make if I said nothing to you about it, or even if I said, "Do you want to go to Florida over spring break?" But what if I said, "This year you have absolutely no choice. You *must* go to Florida for spring break." You might reply, "Nuts to you—I am going skiing in Utah instead!"

What is happening here? In one sense, I am just strongly advocating a position you already hold, so we might expect that you would simply agree with me. But in another sense, I am suggesting that the

decision is not really yours to make, but that you are required to do
what I want you to do. This threatened reduction in your decision
freedom is the essential element in the arousal of what Brehm (1966,
1972) has called psychological reactance. Reactance is a negative
motivational state (it is presumed to be unpleasant) specifically directed
toward restoring a lost decision freedom. In our example, I have not
attacked your attitude position (indeed, I have agreed with it), but I
have severely restricted your freedom to make whatever choice of
vacation spot you might want to make. The only way you can restore
your threatened freedom is to change *away* from the position I have
advocated, even though that is "cutting off your nose to spite your
face." Reactance theory argues that you cannot afford to let me continue to think that I can make all your choices for you.

The amount of psychological reactance that is produced by a
threat to your behavioral freedom will depend on the number of
freedoms threatened (greater reactance with threat to more freedoms),
on the future implications of the threat (greater reactance when the
threat carries with it the promise of future threats to come), and on the
source of the threat to freedom (greater reactance against a personal,
rather than impersonal, threat to freedom). Thus the greatest reactance
should be produced by a personal restriction of many freedoms
that implies similar restrictions will be forthcoming in the future. But
even with impersonal and immediate restrictions some reactance is
likely. Suppose that you approach a vending machine on a hot day and
stand there for a moment trying to decide whether to choose a sugar-
free soft drink (your normal favorite) or a soft drink with sugar added
to it. You finally decide to try something different, insert your money,
and press the button. Then a little light comes on that tells you to
"make another selection please," forcing you to choose your normally
preferred drink. Do you hit the machine for restricting your freedom
to choose as you wish? Whether you do or not, you surely will feel
frustration.

Not only does this example illustrate some basic reactance principles, it also suggests one of the problems connected with testing for
reactance in the experimental laboratory. One description of the
vending machine's "behavior" is that it restricted your freedom of
choice. Unfortunately, there is another plausible description of the
machine's behavior: it has frustrated your goal-directed actions. And,
as theorists from Dollard, Doob, Miller, Mowrer, and Sears (1939)
onward have suggested, frustration leads to aggression. So one of the
problems in reactance research has been to design experimental settings that would induce reactance without also producing frustration
in the subjects.

One of the early experiments testing reactance theory predictions for attitude change was conducted by Sensenig and Brehm (1968). In this study reactance was produced by implied (rather than explicit) threats to freedom, and a number of additional measures were collected to rule out the alternative explanation in terms of frustration. Subjects were asked to indicate their attitudes on a number of issues, and then were told that they would be asked to write essays supporting one side or the other for five of these attitude issues. The subjects were run in pairs, and each member of the pair was led to believe (1) that the other girl would make the choices for both of them as to which side of the issue to support, and (2) that her own preferences would be taken into account before the decision was made. In a Low Implied Threat condition, the subjects were informed that the other person would make the choice only on the first of the five issues; in a High Implied Threat condition, the other person was to make the choices on all five attitude issues. In both of these conditions the actual induction of reactance was accomplished by means of a note delivered to the subject (ostensibly coming from the other subject) which said, "I've decided that we will both agree [disagree] with [the attitude issue in question]." This note was prepared by the experimenter, and it agreed with the subject's initial position on the issue. Yet it appeared to come from the other woman (who could not be expected to know the subject's position), so it seemed to make the decision without taking into account the subject's preferences. As a result, the note should have aroused reactance.

Before writing her first essay, each subject was asked to indicate her "actual feelings" on the issue (the first issue was always the question of federal aid to private colleges), and this indication of "actual feeling" could then be compared to the subject's previously measured position on the issue.

Superficially, the reactance-induction note does not seem like a very important restriction of freedom—particularly when the restriction is limited to the first essay. The results confirm this impression, showing no difference between the Low Implied Threat condition and a Control condition in which the subject's preferences had been taken into account. There was, however, a significant difference between the High Implied Threat condition and these other two conditions, with subjects in the High Threat condition changing their opinions about federal aid *away from* their original positions. In short, the High Threat subjects reacted against the high implied threat to their freedom to express preferences by changing their attitudes.

In the case of this experiment, as opposed to the case of our vending machine example, it is difficult to argue that the same outcome could have come about as a result of frustration. For one thing, frustration theory does not make a *directional* prediction: there is no reason to believe that a frustrated subject should change away from her initial position rather than reasserting that position even more strongly than before. Another argument against frustration is based on the subject's evaluations of the other subject (who had presumably performed the restriction of freedom). In this situation a subject frustrated enough to change her attitude should also have been frustrated enough to derogate the person considered responsible. But there were no significant differences across conditions in either the rated likability or competence of the other subject, so it seems unlikely that any frustration was produced by the induction of reactance.

Reactance theory predictions have been successfully confirmed in a number of different experimental settings, and many of these studies are reviewed in books by Brehm (1966) and Wicklund (1974) and in an article by Wortman and Brehm (1975). On the basis of the reactance findings, particularly in the area of attitude change, it can be concluded that not only moderate discrepancy from the initial position of the recipient, but also *moderation* in the influence attempt is necessary to avoid resistance to the persuasive message.

Resistance Arising from Advance Warning

Inoculation Against Counterpropaganda

Social judgment theory leads us to expect that the most persuasive messages will be those which are moderately discrepant from the recipient's initial position. Reactance theory leads us to expect that the most persuasive messages will be those which are expressed in terms of moderate forcefulness. Suppose that you have carefully constructed and presented a convincing case in favor of your position on a specific issue, and your success in this endeavor is indicated by noticeable change in the recipient's attitude. How do you make this change a relatively permanent one, so that the recipient will not change to a different position as soon as another persuasive communicator comes along?

One answer is suggested by a theory of inoculation proposed by McGuire (1964). Based on an analogy to medicine, and on research that has found a two-sided presentation of an issue to be more effective than a one-sided presentation (e.g., Hovland, Lumsdaine, and Sheffield, 1949; Jones and Brehm, 1970; Lumsdaine and Janis, 1953; McGinnies, 1966), inoculation theory argues that a weak dose of possible counterarguments can immunize the hearer against much of the effect that those counterarguments might later have. If at the time you initially change the person's attitudes you also try to deal with some of the arguments against your own position, the change you produce in the recipient's attitudes is more likely to withstand later attack.

Suppose that you belong to a national organization for owners of firearms, and that I am trying to convince you to support a complete ban against possession of any handguns—target pistols, antiques, pistols for "protection," and the well known Saturday-night specials. To give me even a remote chance of success, we must first assume that you are not a very active member of the gun organization and that you have some doubts about its position on this issue. My proposal is still moderately discrepant from your initial position (at the very least it is dissonant with the position of an organization you value). Further, we will assume that I make my case in a way that does not threaten your freedom to believe what you want to believe. My message will probably include several elements necessary to support my position, such as statistics on the number of murders with guns committed not by "criminals," but by husbands and wives whose arguments get out of control; public statements by conservative big-city mayors and by chiefs of police in favor of outlawing the possession of handguns; and a number of arguments in support of the statement that handguns have no value for recreation. If my message is a convincing one, and if I have a firm belief in the power of dissonance reduction, then I might be tempted to stop there, trusting the dissonance aroused by my message to change your attitude.

But inoculation theory suggests that I should include some additional elements in the message—specificially, some points from the other side. I know perfectly well that you will be bombarded with information from your organization and that this information will be totally opposed to any sort of regulation of control of guns whatsoever. If my message is to have any lasting effect on your attitudes, I must include something that will try to deal with this later "counterpropaganda" to which I know you will be exposed. Fortunately for me, your organization's positions are so well known that it is not difficult for me to construct weak versions of their positions, which I can then *refute*. For example, I can say, "Now they will tell you that with guns outlawed, only outlaws will have guns. Why do you suppose that the police chiefs (who, after all, are supposed to deal with those outlaws) are not worried about that? And since you are much more likely to be accidentally (or intentionally) shot *by a member of your own family* than by an 'outlaw,' a complete ban on handguns will actually *reduce* your chances of getting shot even if the outlaws still continue to carry guns. Besides, you are proficient enough with your rifle so that you could easily use it against an intruder without the risk of shooting yourself that a handgun carries." There are, of course, other aspects to the position of your organization, and I should try to deal with those in a similar manner.

An Example of Inoculation

How well does inoculation work? As of this writing, no researcher has actually attempted the difficult sort of persuasive communication and inoculation illustrated in the example, but the theory has received support in a variety of other contexts. The first experiment demonstrating the effectiveness of inoculation was conducted by McGuire and Papageorgis (1961). These investigators first identified a set of what they called *cultural truisms*, beliefs that are so widely shared that a person would not ever have heard them attacked and might even think that they could not be attacked. The examples used included "It is a good idea to brush your teeth after every meal," "The effects of penicillin have been, almost without exception, of great benefit to mankind," and "Everyone should get a yearly chest x-ray to detect signs of TB at an early stage."

The actual experiment (diagrammed in Table 7-1 for a hypothetical cultural truism) involved two separate sessions, a "defense" session followed by an "attack" session. The subject's final attitudes toward the truisms were measured at the conclusion of the attack session. In the defense (first) session each truism was stated and was accompanied by a defense of the position expressed in the truism.

There were two different sorts of defenses. The *supportive* de-

TABLE 7-1
A hypothetical inoculation experiment

TRUISM TO BE ATTACKED: "APPLE PIE IS THE ALL-AMERICAN FAVORITE DESSERT."

	First Experimental Session (Defense)	Second Experimental Session (Attack)
Supportive Defense:	An apple a day keeps the doctor away.	Too much apple pie causes stomach cancer.
Refutational Defenses:		
Refutational —same:	Even though some of the ingredients in apple pie can cause cancer, you would have to eat a whole pie a day for a year before you would get into any trouble.	Too much apple pie causes stomach cancer.
Refutational —different:	Even though some of the ingredients in apple pie can cause cancer, you would have to eat a whole pie a day for a year before you would get into any trouble.	The flour and shortening wasted in making apple pie could be better used to feed hungry people.

fenses consisted of additional arguments in favor of the position taken by the truism, while the *refutational* defense briefly mentioned (and then refuted) some of the arguments that could be raised against the truisms. In the attack (second) session, each truism was restated, and then each was attacked in detail. There were two different kinds of attacks used for different truisms: half the attacks were simply detailed statements of the same counterarguments previously employed in the refutational defense (called the *refutational-same* attacks), but half the counterarguments were totally new ones that had not been previously used (called the *refutational-different* attacks). After the attack session concluded, the subjects' attitudes toward the several truisms were assessed. The results showed that the refutational defenses had been more successful in *inoculating* the subjects against attack than had the supportive defenses. In addition, the refutational defenses proved to be almost as successful against different counterarguments as they were against the counterarguments that had been previously refuted.

Apparently, a refutational defense against an anticipated counterargument can inoculate the hearer against the potential force of that counterargument. To return to the terms of our example, if I can somehow inoculate you against the idea that "only outlaws have guns," that inoculation may also help me prevail against "taking away our guns is the first step on the path to dictatorship." The effectiveness of inoculation against future counterarguments has been demonstrated in a number of experiments (summarized in McGuire, 1964, 1969), and the success of the technique indicates that resistance to persuasion can be induced in the course of establishing the initial attitude. Whether this presents advantages or difficulties to the potential changer of attitudes depends upon whether you are the change-agent doing the inoculating, or whether you are having to change attitudes where a previous inoculation has taken place.

SOURCES OF FACILITATION

We have seen that in order to have persuasive impact, a communication should be moderately discrepant from the recipient's existing opinion—just enough to arouse some inconsistency, but not so much as to be dismissed out of hand. In addition, the communication must not threaten or undermine the recipient's self-esteem, or appear to reduce his or her freedom to make an informed decision individually. But within these limits, are there other factors that can enhance the effectiveness of a persuasive communication? We correctly assume that the answer to this question is an affirmative one. Two categories of such other factors are the characteristics of the communication, and the participation of the recipient in the process of persuasion.

Facilitation Arising from the Communication and its Presentation

Are highly credible people more influential than communicators with lower credibility? Is a message that presents both sides of a controversial issue more effective or less effective than a message that presents only one side of the issue? Does frightening a recipient by pointing out the disastrous consequences of his or her present attitude make the person more or less susceptible to the new position advocated? If there are two sides to the story, does it matter which is presented first? What happens to the effectiveness of a persuasive communication over time? Research designed to provide answers to these and other similar questions began in earnest near the end of World War II in what was to become the Yale Communication and Attitude Change Program, under the direction of Carl Hovland.

The Yale Program

The Yale Program produced four volumes of research reports (Hovland, Janis, and Kelley, 1953; Hovland, 1957; Hovland and Rosenberg, 1960; and Sherif and Hovland, 1961) which addressed communicator credibility, the order of presentation of material, cognitive consistency, and social judgment (assimilation and contrast) respectively. In part because of the sheer volume of research, and in part because of the high stature of many of the social psychologists associated at various times with the program, it was thought that the program's findings had adequately answered many of the important questions. For example, Hovland and Weiss (1951) found that high-credibility communicators would be more effective in producing attitude change than would low-credibility communicators. Hovland, Lumsdaine, and Sheffield (1949) showed that with an intelligent audience and a controversial subject matter, presenting both sides of the issue would be more effective than presenting just one side. Janis and Feschbach (1953) found that moderately threatening fear appeals produced greater attitude change in the direction advocated by the communication than did highly threatening fear appeals. And several investigators associated with the program (Hovland, Lumsdaine, and Sheffield, 1949; Hovland and Weiss, 1951; Kelman and Hovland, 1953) all found evidence of a "sleeper effect": the tendency of some communications to produce more attitude change after a time delay of up to a month than they produced immediately after their delivery.

In recent years, however, attempts to replicate some of these early "reliable" findings have failed, leading a number of different reviewers (e.g., Fishbein and Ajzen, 1975, for communicator credibility; Gillig and Greenwald, 1974, for the sleeper effect; Kiesler, Collins, and Miller, 1969, for the entire program; and Leventhal, 1970, for the issue of fear appeals) to argue that at best the Yale Program just suggested some good leads. It is instructive to reconsider some of that early research in light of today's more sophisticated methods and standards. Let us take the example of the study by Hovland and Weiss (1951). This experiment is a good example because it illustrates the approach of the program, because it deals with two of the issues (credibility and the sleeper effect) that many people had until recently considered resolved by the program's research, and because it had achieved the status of a "classic" experiment—being widely reported, reprinted, and discussed in textbooks. But its conclusions are suspect, as both Fishbein and Ajzen (1975) and Gillig and Greenwald (1974) have pointed out.

A Reexamination of Communicator Credibility

The Hovland and Weiss (1951) experiment was designed to determine the effects on persuasion of having either an affirmative or a negative position on an issue of contemporary interest taken either by a high-credibility source or a low-credibility source. There were four different issues: should antihistamine drugs continue to be sold without a doctor's prescription; can a practicable atomic-powered submarine be built at the present time; is the steel industry to blame for the current shortage of steel; and as a result of television will there be a decrease in the number of movie theaters in operation by 1955. Each subject read a statement about each of the four issues. The two variables of interest (credibility and position on the issue) were arranged in a factorial design (see Chapter Two) so that each subject received a different treatment combination on each issue. In other words, across the four issues, a subject would receive two affirmative arguments (one from a high-credibility source, one from a low-credibility source) and two negative arguments (one high credibility, one low credibility).

A few days before the experiment was conducted, all the subjects were asked to indicate their positions on the four issues and their rating of the "trustworthiness" of the eight sources later to be used as high- and low-credibility communicators. (In both cases, the relevant issues or sources were embedded in a larger list of possibilities.) Then the subjects were exposed to a booklet containing the persuasive communications on the four topics, and after they had read these communications their attitudes were again measured. Finally, there was a third assessment of the subjects' attitudes on the issues four weeks after the experiment to test for the presence of a sleeper effect.

The results of the experiment were presented in terms of the percentage of net opinion change in the direction of the position advocated by the communication. That is, for each issue, a certain percentage of the subjects changed from their own original position *toward* the position advocated in the communication, a certain percentage of the subjects changed from their own original position *away from* the position advocated in the communication (almost a reactance effect), and a certain percentage of the subjects maintained their original position regardless of the nature of the communication. The *net opinion change* was the percentage changing toward the communication minus the percentage changing away from the position of the communication. Over the four different issues, this net percentage opinion change was 23.0 percent for high-credibility sources, but only 6.6 percent for low-credibility sources. These results were interpreted as evidence in favor of the prediction that high-credibility sources would be more effective than would low-credibility sources.

Unfortunately, as Fishbein and Ajzen (1975) have noted, there was significant net opinion change on only two of the four issues (atomic submarines and the steel shortage), and the differences obtained on these two measures were so great as to boost the overall average to such a point that it, too, became significant. Some of the difficulties in the experiment can be illustrated by considering the issue that produced the greatest difference between high-credibility sources and low-credibility sources (atomic submarines). Most attitude change researchers have suggested that *credibility* involves at least two different dimensions, expertise and trustworthiness (e.g., see reviews by McGuire, 1969; Triandis, 1971). People will think that you are credible if you know what you are talking about, either through experience or training, and if they think that you have nothing to gain personally by advocating the position you take. For the atomic submarine issue, the "high-credibility" source was Dr. Robert Oppenheimer, a well-known physicist, while the "low-credibility" source was *Pravda*, the official newspaper of the Communist Party. We would probably agree that both trustworthiness differences and expertise differences would contribute to the subjects' varying impressions of the two sources used here, but only "trustworthiness" was used as the standard for establishing that the "credibility" manipulation had been successful. Worse still, the low-credibility source carried strong political overtones (remember that those were the days of the cold war between the Soviet Union and the United States). These confounding factors make it very difficult to determine whether the final results of net opinion change were actually due to change in the subjects' attitudes, differential perception of the messages (what Fishbein and Ajzen call "reception"), or to a differential willingness to *admit* having been influenced by one source or the other.

If these confounding factors in the credibility manipulation were not enough of a problem, there is also room for legitimate disagreement about the extent to which the issues were really what we would consider *attitude* issues. Of the four topics, only movie theaters and antihistamine drugs are likely to be part of the subjects' personal experience before the experiment. It would be surprising if the subjects had possessed any more than the vaguest beliefs about the steel shortage and atomic submarines, and it would be still more difficult to argue that they had any strong emotional reactions to these two topics. But as we learned in Chapter Five, an attitude is supposed to consist of three components: belief, emotion, and behavioral predisposition. A good case can be made that the two issues showing change actually involved only one of these three (belief). So even without the problems of the credibility manipulation, it might be inappropriate to interpret the results in terms of attitude change (rather than *belief* change). And if the effects of credibility are limited to changes in beliefs about which the individual is initially uncertain, the psychological importance of expertise and trustworthiness is diminished.

One final aspect of the research that should be noted is the fact that the Hovland and Weiss study found further evidence for the sleeper effect. After four weeks, the net opinion change in the high-credibility groups dropped from 23.0 percent to 12.3 percent, while the net opinion change in the low-credibility groups increased from 6.6 percent to 14.0 percent. In short, after a period of four weeks, net opinion change was approximately the same in both of the credibility groups. The sleeper effect has always been defined as the *increase* in persuasive power of a message (usually from an untrustworthy source) over a long period of time. But as Gillig and Greenwald (1974) noted, the evidence used by Hovland and Weiss (and by other investigators who have obtained favorable results) is a statistical interaction between credibility and time. The concept of an interaction was more fully discussed in Chapter Two, but here it involves both a slight increase in the low-credibility groups *and an equal decrease in the high-credibility groups*. In short, while the definition of the effect involves only the rise in *one group*, the evidence taken as supporting the existence of that effect mistakenly includes the decrease in the

other group as well. And in an extensive series of studies designed
to remedy this problem, Gillig and Greenwald (1974) found no support
whatsoever for the increase taken by itself.

Recent criticism of the research growing out of the Yale Program
has not been confined to the Hovland and Weiss (1951) study and has
served to reopen most of the questions that had previously been
thought answered. What began as simple questions about the characteristics
of persuasive communications have become complex questions
about the circumstances in which those communications produce
one effect rather than another. Thus, "are highly credible communicators
more effective than communicators of lower credibility?"
has been prefaced by "When" and by "Why." In a similar way, researchers
now ask, "Under what circumstances will highly threatening
fear communications be more effective than moderately threatening
ones, and when will these effects be reversed?" When will presenting
one side first benefit that side, and when will it be harmful to that
position? And even more importantly, how do many of these message
and source characteristics interact to produce (or inhibit) attitude
change? As of this writing, the major contribution of the "characteristics
of the communication" research is not the answers obtained,
but the complexity revealed in the original questions. It remains the
task of future research to establish what aspects of the communication
reliably lead to greater probability of attitude change.

Facilitation Arising from the Participation of the Recipient

In contrast to questions about the nature and presentation of the
communication, questions about the effects on attitude change of
participation by the recipient of a message have frequently led to
replicable findings. For example, the idea that public advocacy of an
attitude will lead to change in the direction advocated is a fairly consistent
finding in social psychological research on attitude change. As
we saw in Chapter Six, there is still a great deal of theoretical controversy
about the reason for this experimental result (in terms of
dissonance, incentive, or self-perception theory). But regardless of
the theoretical explanation, there is widespread agreement on the
empirical generalization that advocacy leads to attitude change.

In the case of public advocacy, the person engaging in the advocacy
is also the "recipient" of his or her own persuasive message. The
subjects in a forced compliance experiment are persuaded by their
own messages and by the fact of their compliance, but their behavior
has typically been elicited by a request from the experimenter.
Effective as public advocacy is, it is not the only sort of participation

by the communication recipient. For our purposes it will be useful to distinguish among three different levels of recipient participation: *no* participation, *induced* participation, and *informed* participation. The category of no participation includes such techniques as classical conditioning and mere exposure; induced participation includes the now-familiar forced compliance and the foot-in-the-door technique; and the category of informed participation includes methods such as group discussion.

No Participation

CLASSICAL CONDITIONING. To begin with an approach familiar to every introductory psychology student, there is evidence that attitudes, like other social behaviors, can be formed through processes of *classical conditioning* (Lott and Lott, 1968; Staats, 1968; Zanna, Kiesler, and Pilkonis, 1970). The basic idea of classical (or Pavlovian) conditioning is that an initially neutral stimulus will become endowed with positive or negative properties through its repeated association with other stimuli which are inherently positive or negative. (The evening news could be a neutral stimulus to the viewer unless associated with eating dinner, at which point it would become positive.)

In one of the early studies of the classical conditioning of attitudes, Lott and Lott (1960) had groups of third- and fifth-grade children play a noncompetitive board game. Each play group was composed of three children from the same classroom who had *not* previously chosen each other as friends on a questionnaire collected in class. Therefore, at the beginning of the experiment it was assumed that the children had approximately neutral attitudes toward each other. During the course of the play, some of the children in each group were rewarded for their successes at the game, while other children in the same group were not rewarded for success. Different numbers of children (zero, one, two, or three) were rewarded in different groups so that the play of the game would not appear to have been rigged. At the conclusion of the day, all the children were given another questionnaire, which asked them to select from the members of the class *two* children with whom they would like to take an imaginary vacation. Children who had been in the rewarded play groups were more likely to select the other members of that group than were children who had been in groups not rewarded for success. Thus the presence or absence of reward produced differences in the friendship choice— we prefer associates who are a part of a positive experience we shared with them.

MERE EXPOSURE. Not only is it possible for attitudes to be classically conditioned, it is also possible for favorableness toward an attitude object to increase simply with repeated presentation of the object (with no reward at all). In a series of experiments Zajonc (1968) found that the rated "favorability" of various stimuli (nonsense words, photographs of faces, and even Chinese-like pictograms) increased with repeated presentation. No matter what the stimulus was, the more frequently it was presented (up to a maximum of twenty-five times) the more favorably it was evaluated. Zajonc referred to this phenomenon as the effect of *mere exposure*, and suggested that it might serve as a confounding factor in studies that attempt to show attitude change through various conditioning procedures. After all, in any conditioning procedure the attitude object is *repeatedly* paired with the positive or negative stimulus that serves as reward or punishment. How much of the conditioning effect is due to the presence of the reward or punishment, and how much is based simply upon repeated presentation? This question has not yet been satisfactorily answered, but a number of studies have been performed to explore the characteristics of the mere exposure effect (Berlyne, 1970; Brickman, Redfield, Harrison, and Crandall, 1972; Burgess and Sales, 1971; Matlin, 1971; Stang, 1973, 1975).

One of the conclusions of much of the research dealing with mere exposure is that there are limits to its effectiveness. For example, imagine eating your favorite food. Pleasant experience? Now imagine eating absolutely nothing else for a month. Still pleasant? In a modification of the mere exposure position Berlyne (1970) and Stang (1973) have suggested that a two-factor theory provides a better explanation of the results. The two factors thought to be involved are a "learning" factor and a "satiation" factor, and the two together determine the attitude toward the object.

In the early stages of exposure to a novel stimulus, repeated presentations facilitate the learning of the stimulus. This learning of a novel stimulus is considered to be pleasurable (and is likened to the exploratory behavior observed in children), so during the learning phase the rated favorableness of the attitude object increases with repeated presentation. But as the presentation wears on—after the stimulus has been successfully learned—further presentation just produces boredom. Thus the two-factor theories argue that Zajonc's findings represent only the first phase of mere exposure. His stimuli were complex and novel, so they most probably required even more than twenty-five trials to be learned. Consequently, all his ratings of increased favorableness with increased presentation frequency occurred during the learning phase, before satiation had set in. The first assumption of the two-factor theory (that learning can be fun) has received support in a recent study by Stang (1975) in which the rated pleasantness of Turkish words followed the pattern of the learning curves for various exposure durations. During the learning of these words, pleasantness increased with learning. It would appear that the mere exposure effects thus parallel the politician's intuitive notions about how to conduct a reelection campaign: see that you get enough publicity so that people are learning your name, but don't get "overexposed" and don't "peak too early." Just when increasing familiarity turns from pleasure to contempt still remains to be established.

Induced Participation

In an important sense, of course, *any* participation in an activity designed to change attitudes may be an induced participation. There are only occasional cases in which we actively seek change in our attitudes, such as voluntary participation in psychotherapy. For our purposes, however, the category of induced participation will be restricted to those instances in which there is deliberate concealment of the goal of attitude change.

FORCED COMPLIANCE. The most familiar experimental example of induced attitude change is the forced compliance technique employed in studies of cognitive dissonance (these studies, and some alternative explanations, are discussed more fully in Chapter Six). The success of changing attitudes through forced compliance depends not only on concealing the goal of attitude change, but also on establishing in the subject's mind the illusion of being personally responsible for the decisions that are made. When these decisions lead to negative consequences, dissonance is presumably aroused, and this dissonance leads to attitude change. There are other explanations for the effects of forced compliance in terms of incentive theory and self-perception theory but, as we noted earlier, the important point for our purposes is that public advocacy produces attitude change.

THE FOOT-IN-THE-DOOR TECHNIQUE. One of the ways that the forced compliance procedure differs from processes of attitude change in the real social world is that there is only a single experimental trial for any given attitude. The request from the experimenter is an all-or-nothing affair. In contrast, most attempts to produce attitude change in the real world involve gradual and repeated requests that ultimately lead to performance of what would previously have been a "counter-attitudinal" action. Suppose I own an automobile dealership and the only models I can get from the factory have automatic transmission and factory-installed air conditioning. Let's also suppose that you are interested in a new car, but that you have always considered automatic transmission and factory air conditioning frivolous and wasteful. Do I tell you the whole story of my offerings in a newspaper advertisement, so that the only people who will respond are ones who want exactly what I have to sell? Certainly not. I talk of "stupendous savings," of my dealership's "care for its customers," and of our "excellent service record." Since those are things that every car buyer would like, you may decide to visit me. You don't know it yet, but you have just taken the first small step toward counterattitudinal action. My first task is not to convince you to buy a particular car, but simply to "get my foot in the door" (or, more appropriately for this example, to get your foot into my door).

Do I hit you with the full package when you arrive at my showroom? Again, certainly not. I try to ascertain your likes and dislikes, show you features of the car, and try to discover how you feel about various accessories. When I discover that you don't want the only thing I have, I don't talk about the equipment you dislike. I try to get you to take a test drive. If you agree to do so, then I suggest that we have enough in common so that we really ought to "talk a little business." (You are getting more and more committed with every action.) You may now agree to talk with me, just to find out how much your old car is worth, and that gives me my last needed optunity. If I can make you an offer that is sufficiently better than you might have expected, then I will have sold you something that you initially did not want. The process has been a gradual one, with your commitment increasing slightly at each successive level of the interchange. I will be more successful in getting you to accede to my final large request to sign on the dotted line if I have previously been able to get you to agree to smaller requests along the way.

That agreement to small initial requests can produce greater compliance with later requests of a more important nature has been demonstrated in two studies by Freedman and Fraser (1966). In one study, these investigators asked housewives to agree to a large request of placing a big sign in their front yards for a week. In the other study the large request was permitting a team of five or six researchers to spend two hours in their homes categorizing their household products. Some of these housewives had previously been asked to comply with a smaller request (such as placing a three-inch sign in one of their windows, or answering a series of eight consumer-oriented questions), while other subjects had not been previously approached. When there had been no prior contact, only 25 percent of the subjects agreed to comply with the large request. In contrast, when there had been an earlier smaller request, over 55 percent of the subjects agreed to comply with the large request. It should be noted in passing that in no cases did subjects actually have to comply with the large request to which they had agreed. The experimenter simply thanked the agreeable subject and stated that he was just collecting names of people who would be willing to help, and that he would notify them if it was necessary to use them. These experiments thus support the salesperson's intuitive belief that it always helps to "get your foot in the door."

Informed Participation: Group Discussion

The final category of the recipient's participation includes all those attitude change procedures in which there is full and informed involvement by the person whose attitudes are to be changed. One of the earliest examples of this approach, the *group discussion method* developed by Lewin (1958) and his students, was discussed previously in Chapter One. The basic idea is that many of an individual's attitudes are reinforced and maintained by the social groups to which he or she belongs. Fraternities and sororities often differ in their ideas about the relative importance of various aspects of campus life, occupational organizations typically share certain attitudes, and political parties have formally stated platforms which justify their positions on issues of importance. If it is possible to change the entire group's position through group discussion, then individual members' attitudes may also undergo dramatic and lasting change.

The first step in achieving attitude change through discussion is the unfreezing of the group's initial position on the issue. This is followed by moving the group to a new attitude, and then by refreezing the attitude at its new value. The unfreezing of the group's initial attitude may be accomplished by the presentation of new information, or by pointing out how a change would be in the group's best interest. For example, the purpose of a political party is to field candidates who can win elections. Suppose that time after time the party's candidates lose, and the public opinion polls indicate that there are aspects of the party's platform that the electorate simply cannot support. This information alone would be sufficient to unfreeze the party's position, and discussion at party conventions might reveal a new position to which the party could move. Formal adoption of this change in position would serve to freeze the platform at the new value, and members who placed the party high in their priorities would change their own attitudes to agree with the new position. (Members who could not support the new elements of the platform would probably leave the party.)

The specific effects that groups can have on the attitudes of their members will be discussed more fully in Chapter Twelve, but for our purposes here it is enough to note that these effects can be substantial. In one of the first studies of group participation in decision making, Coch and French (1948) compared the attitudes toward new working conditions of employees who had been permitted to have either full participation, representative participation, or no participation in the design of the changes to be implemented. Not surprisingly, the resulting attitudes were the most positive when there had been full participation in designing the new conditions, but even the representative participation group showed positive change. In another example, described in Chapter One (Lewin, 1947), more housewives actually served previously unattractive meats (beef hearts, sweetbreads, kidneys) after discussion to consensus than after hearing persuasive communications advocating use of these meats, but with no discussion. Similar shifts in group-maintained attitudes have been found in other contexts by Newcomb (1943), who studied the political attitudes of students in a women's college; by Siegel and Siegel (1957), who investigated the relationship between housing choice among college undergraduates and authoritarianism; and by Cook (1970), who investigated the reduction of prejudice through intergroup contact and exchange. It is apparent that full and informed participation, like induced participation, can lead to change in important social attitudes. And given the results of classical conditioning and mere exposure studies, we may conclude that virtually any participation by the recipient of a message can serve to facilitate attitude change.

ETHICAL ISSUES IN ATTITUDE CHANGE

In many of the experiments discussed in this and the preceding chapter, experimenters have deliberately concealed the fact that the goal of the research was the production of attitude change. This concealment, like other forms of experimental deception (treated more fully in Chapter Two), raises ethical questions. Just how serious are the risks to the subjects, and do the potential benefits of the research outweigh these risks? Unfortunately, as we noted earlier, it is sometimes difficult to attain both these goals within the framework of a single experiment. Using materials and issues of very little importance to subjects would certainly help to protect the self-esteem of a subject who happened to be persuaded to change his or her opinion, but would such research have sufficient internal and external validity to warrant taking the subject's time?

Obtaining the subject's informed consent prior to the research, by describing the experiment in detail before the subject makes the decision to participate, will reduce the risk, but it may also enhance demand characteristics. And if the informed consent is not based on *complete* information, the act of obtaining consent may in actuality be a sort of forced compliance procedure: the subject might then be more dramatically affected by any adverse effects of the experiment, believing that he or she had been warned and had freely chosen to suffer them anyway. In the vast majority of attitude change (and other) research, experimenters are conscientious about meeting their responsibilities to their subjects. These standards for experimenters are high, and should remain so, but some additional observations may help us to keep our perspective.

Unlike other forms of experimental deception, the deliberate attempt to produce attitude change has innumerable counterparts in the everyday world. The merchant who lures you into a store with the promise of free gifts or great bargains is really trying to get you to purchase something more expensive. The advertiser who claims that his or her products will make you more attractive and self-assured is concerned with your attitude change toward buying, not your self-image. The politician who accuses opponents of association with undesirable people or unpopular causes is not merely informing the public, but is trying to get your vote. The list could go on and on. We are continually bombarded by persuasive messages that play upon our desires, our uncertainties, and our fears. So to be subjected to attitude change attempts in a laboratory is not exactly a novel experience for us. Indeed, some of the comparisons between the laboratory and the real social world suggest that we might have greater cause for ethical concern in the latter.

The first such comparison deals with the importance of the attitudes and behaviors in question. It is difficult to imagine that many subjects suffered psychological damage from writing an essay favoring police intervention in campus disturbances (Cohen, 1962), supporting a governing board's decision to forbid a postseason football game (Rosenberg, 1965), or favoring the continuation of a ban against campus appearances by radical speakers (Linder, Cooper, and Jones, 1967). Even when the behavior was performed outside a laboratory setting (e.g., Freedman and Fraser, 1966), placing a three-inch sign in one's window does not seem terribly important. In contrast, attitude changes in everyday life lead to consequences of much greater importance. The unwary buyer who gets "sold" something he or she cannot really afford, the cosmetic purchaser who buys something that may be harmful either personally or to the environment, and the voter who helps contribute to a candidate's landslide election victory may all live to regret their changed attitudes.

A second difference between laboratory studies of attitude change and attempts at persuasion in the real world is the presence of a debriefing. When laboratory experiments carry risk to the subjects, there is careful debriefing designed to minimize those risks. For example, in any of the forced compliance research in which the behavior called for is face-to-face deception of another person (e.g., Carlsmith, Collins, and Helmreich, 1966; Festinger and Carlsmith, 1959) the subject's self-esteem may be threatened by the realization that he or she can be induced to lie for (in some cases) very little justification. But the debriefing is designed to let the subject "off the hook" by emphasizing that his or her behavior should be attributed to the overwhelming power of the situation, rather than to a character failing.

A disturbing contrast to the experimenter's care in a forced compliance study is provided by the interrogation procedures often employed by police officials to obtain confessions from criminal suspects. These procedures have been discussed in detail by Inbau and Reid (1962), with critical comments by Zimbardo (1970). According to Zimbardo, the entire relationship between detectives and suspect is distorted in a number of ways designed to produce a confession. The detectives may exaggerate the amount or quality of the physical evidence in their possession, they may suggest that they are only trying to "help" the suspect (conveniently ignoring that interrogation is fundamentally an adversary procedure), or they may play on a subject's guilt about other issues to elicit a confession about the issue at hand. One other popular strategy involves a distortion of sociopsychological characteristics of the participants: the so-called good cop–bad cop routine, in which one interrogator appears to be pleasant and kind while the other appears to be on the verge of a physical attack against the suspect. Once a confession is signed, there is no retraction by the police on the grounds of their overwhelming control of the situation, and there is no revelation of the interrogator's true purposes. If it is possible to generalize from interrogation (and to a lesser extent, from advertising) it would appear that in the real world of attitude change the higher the stakes to the subject, the *less* likely there is to be a debriefing.

It is not our purpose here to minimize the ethical questions raised by attitude change research by comparing them favorably to the ethical problems found in real-world attempts to change attitudes. But the prevalance of everyday persuasion, and the importance of many of the attitudes involved, suggests that we should maintain a certain degree of perspective. Perhaps more ethical concern should be directed toward the pressures toward change that are so common in our society.

Summary

When we speak of modifying a person's attitudes, we should distinguish between mere public compliance with our requests (which will vanish when our surveillance is lifted) and private acceptance of the position we advocate. This private acceptance can come about either through identification (p. 267) or through internalization (p. 267). We must also recognize that an individual's attitudes serve several psychological functions, including expressing values (p. 269), serving as descriptions of people who facilitate or hinder goals (p. 269), bringing order to social knowledge (p. 269), and helping to maintain ego defenses (p. 269).

A person will be reluctant to change attitudes that serve ego defensive purposes, or that have numerous horizontal and vertical interconnections, or that are consistent with most of the person's other cognitions. In addition to these general sources of resistance to change, several other kinds of resistance may be developed by particular aspects of the persuasive communications used. An attitude change attempt that advocates a position highly discrepant from the recipient's original position will have less chance of success than a communication of more moderate discrepancy (p. 272). A communication that restricts the recipient's freedom to believe as he or she chooses will create reactance (p. 279) that will lead to rejection of the influence attempt. And the success of an attack on an existing attitude may depend on whether the recipient has been inoculated (p. 281) against such attacks by previous refutations of mild versions of possible attacks.

Sources of facilitation of attitude change include the characteristics of the communication and the participation of the recipient. Much of the early work on the characteristics of effective communications grew out of the Yale Communication and Attitude Change Program, but an unfortunate number of findings from that program have not replicated in recent years. With regard to facilitation from participation by the recipient, there is reason to believe that attitude change can come about through *mere exposure* (p. 291) and *classical conditioning* (p. 290) with no active participation by the recipient; through the induced participation found in cases of *forced compliance*

(p. 292) or *foot-in-the-door* (p. 292) techniques; and through the full and informed participation common to *group discussion* (p. 294) of attitude issues. Receptivity to attitude change typically increases with increasing participation by the recipient.

Both experimental methods designed to produce attitude change in the laboratory and the powerful attitude change techniques so frequently employed for personal gain in the everyday world raise ethical questions that we must face, as researchers and as citizens.

Suggested Additional Readings

EISER, J. R., and STROEBE, W. *Categorization and social judgement.* New York: Academic Press, 1972. Although it is a bit technical in presentation, this book provides an excellent recent discussion of developments in the social judgment approach to attitude change.

GREENWALD, A. G., BROCK, T. C., and OSTROM, T. M. *Psychological foundations of attitudes.* New York: Academic Press, 1968. This book contains broad, integrative chapters by major investigators in attitude change. It does not include sections on cognitive consistency theory, but has two chapters on classical conditioning of attitudes and a good chapter on reactance theory.

ROSNOW, R. L., and ROBINSON, E. J. *Experiments in persuasion.* New York: Academic Press, 1967. This collection of readings includes many of the important Yale Program studies, as well as other experiments dealing with various aspects of attitude change. Some of the topics included are fear-arousing communications, inoculation theory, and the foot-in-the-door technique.

ZIMBARDO, P. G., and EBBESEN, E. B. *Influencing attitudes and changing behavior.* Reading, Mass.: Addison-Wesley, 1969. This highly readable book contains a critique of social judgment theory, discussions of forced compliance and classical conditioning of attitudes, and a long section on the practical aspects of attitude change.

The self is often considered to be the totality of answers to the question "Who am I?"

The Self
Chapter Eight

Engaging in meditation, playing handball, and asking your neighbor for an opinion of your new automobile all have something in common. Each of these activities can serve to reveal to you a different aspect of your self. But there is more to the self than inner experience, observable abilities, and material possessions. It also includes such elements as social perceptions, attitudes, personality characteristics, motives, and emotions. In short, the self is often considered to be the totality of the answers to the question "Who am I?" Perhaps because of its breadth as a concept, the self has assumed a prominent role in a wide variety of social and psychological theories. Psychologists interested in personality dynamics have concentrated on the *conscious* determinants of the self (e.g., Erikson, 1968; Jourard, 1964; Maslow, 1961; Rogers, 1959), while traditional clinical theories have emphasized *unconscious* or *irrational* forces involved in the development of the self (e.g., Freud, 1933; Jung, 1953; Sullivan, 1953). For their part, social psychologists have been preoccupied with the idea of *self-evaluation* (e.g., Bem, 1972; Duval and Wicklund, 1972; Festinger, 1954; Jones and Nisbett, 1971; Schachter, 1964) and the resulting *self-concept* or *self-esteem* (e.g., Coopersmith, 1967; Janis and Field, 1959; Rosenberg, 1965; Ziller, 1973). Finally, sociologists have explored the *social context* of the individual self (e.g., Cooley, 1902; Goffman, 1959; Mead, 1934; Parsons, 1968; Thomas and Znaniecki, 1958).

Unfortunately, this extensive interest in the self has not been reflected in the development of a unified body of theory. As Gordon and Gergen (1968) point out, researchers in each discipline tend to lose sight of progress in related areas, and in few cases has this been more true than in the area of the self. There is, however, one recurrent theme that is most important for our purposes: *the conflict between pressures toward accuracy and pressures toward distortion* both in the acquisition of knowledge about the self and in the public behavior that reveals the self. Social psychology's particular concern is the joint influence of personal and situational factors on individual behavior, and both of these sorts of factors play a part in the conflict between accuracy and distortion.

Let's consider an example. Suppose that you are attempting to evaluate your social self to determine whether you have a real chance of developing a close relationship with an attractive person of the opposite sex. Put very simply, you want to find out if you are "good enough" to be considered a worthy partner. So you ask your friends for their opinions. What sort of information do you *really* want, and what sort are they likely to give you? You would like to be told if they think you have no chance at all, so you won't make a fool of yourself by attempting the impossible. But at the same time you would relish at least a few compliments. What your friends tell you may depend in part on the attractiveness of the intended partner, in part on your actual social stimulus value, and in part on their desire to maintain your friendship. They will probably tell you if they think you have no chance with the person, but even under these circumstances they may refrain from being "brutally frank" about your shortcomings. Thus there are situational and personal factors involved in your search for information, and in the provision of that information by your friends. And in each case, there is some conflict between pressures toward accuracy and pressures toward distortion.

Our discussion in this chapter concentrates on this conflict and is limited to the *social self*. We emphasize the uniquely social features of (1) the process of self-evaluation and (2) the public behavior of the self. Those aspects of the self that are more closely associated with personality development (e.g., self-actualization) and with clinical applications of self theory (e.g., irrational determinants of the self, the apparent changes in the self-concept that accompany emotional disorder) will be omitted. Such omissions would be lamentable in a volume devoted entirely to the self, but they do seem justified for an introductory text in social psychology.

The earliest contributions of interest to a social view of the self are the suggestion by James (1892) that there are multiple social selves, and the idea that self-knowledge can be obtained from the impressions of other people (Cooley, 1902; Mead, 1934). Most later work in social psychology builds on these two foundations, taking from James the various components of the self, and taking from Cooley and Mead the principle that self-evaluation can best be thought of as a *social* process involving the external social world. After examining these two "traditional" conceptions of the social self, we turn to the *process of self-evaluation*, including the two functions of reference groups (Hyman, 1942; Kelley, 1952); the process of social comparison (Festinger, 1954); the assessment of emotional states (Schachter, 1964); the self-perception of attitudes (Bem, 1967, 1972); and the development of self-esteem (Coopersmith, 1967). Finally we discuss the *public behavior of the self* under normal circumstances (Goffman, 1959; Jourard, 1964) and under extreme circumstances in which self-awareness is either experimentally heightened (Duval and Wicklund, 1972) or dramatically decreased (Zimbardo, 1970).

THE SOCIAL SELF: ORGANIZATION AND INTERACTION

Multiple Social Selves

The *Me*

One of the earliest descriptions of the self that is of interest to social psychologists is the characterization suggested by William James (1892). James first distinguished between the self as an active, conscious agent (called the *I*) and the self as an object of reflection (called the *Me*). The **Me** consists of the *sum total of all that a person can call his or her own* and is divided into three categories: the constituents of the *Me*, the emotions to which those constituents may give rise, and the actions that result from the emotions. The category of *constituents*, in turn, includes the material self, the spiritual self, and the several social selves. These aspects of the self are shown in Figure 8-1. You have only a single material self, and it includes your body, your home, and your other material possessions (such as that car you so proudly display to your neighbor). In the same way, you have only a single spiritual self. It consists of all your psychological faculties and dispositions, such as personality traits, verbal skills, attitudes, social perceptions, and that inner experience you seek through meditation. Both the material self and the spiritual self are presumed to remain constant and complete, no matter what the social situation.

In contrast, you are presumed to have *multiple* social selves, one for each person who carries an image of you in his or her mind. This suggests that you might have hundreds of social selves, but James (1892) points out that for all practical purposes the number can be reduced to one social self for each class or group of people who recognize you as an individual. Thus you have one social self that is revealed to your close friends, another that is presented to your parents, and a different one seen by your instructors. This is not to say that you are a "different person" around each of these groups of people, but rather to suggest that the *elements* of your self that are disclosed in each situation may well be different.

The material self, the spiritual self, and the social selves complete the constituents of the *Me*. The second aspect of the *Me* is the *emotions* to which these constituents give rise. James considers these emotions to fall into two broad classes, *self-complacency* (such as pride and arrogance) and *self-dissatisfaction* (such as humility or despair). These emotions are produced when the *Me* is evaluated,

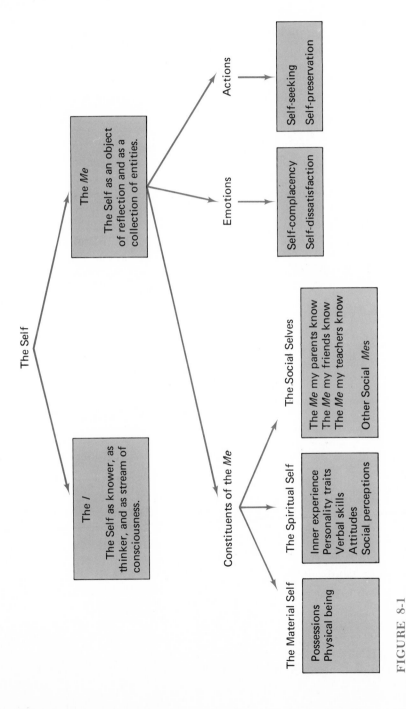

FIGURE 8-1
The components of the self, as outlined by William James (1892).

either by your *I* or by other people who are important to you. In many cases the nature of the emotion (positive or negative) will depend as much on the circumstances of the evaluation as on the characteristic being judged. For example, if you have much of your self invested in material possessions, you will be happy when they are becoming more valuable, but you will be sad if they are lost. If you are concentrating on your spiritual self, you might be pleased with your keen sense of smell when you walk into a florist's shop, but you would be unhappy if your home was downwind from a paper manufacturing plant. Finally, if all the people around you are singing your praises (positively evaluating your social selves), you can't hear enough; but if no one has a good word to say, it is easy to hear too much.

The third component of the *Me* consists of the *actions* that can be produced by the constituents of the *Me* either directly, or indirectly through the emotions. There are two general classes of actions: *self-preservation* and *self-seeking*. The first set is directed toward maintenance of the self as it exists in the present, and these actions of self-preservation include physical responses (startle reactions, bodily self-defense) and social behaviors designed to protect the integrity of the spiritual or social selves. If, for example, you suffer a heavy blow to your self-esteem through an unpleasant interchange with another person, you may need to spend some recuperative time alone (to "pull yourself together") before returning to social activities. The second set of actions, self-seeking, consists of behaviors designed to provide for the future and to enhance the self, rather than merely to maintain the status quo. And, as the name suggests, self-seeking may not always be a purely rational process. We shall return to this point later.

The *I*

If the *Me* is the sum total of the content of the self, then the I is the ongoing process of consciousness. It is the pure ego, the knower, the thinker, or as James describes it the *organized stream of consciousness*. Since the *I* is a process, rather than a collection of empirical entities, it is more difficult to describe in concrete terms than is the *Me*. While the *I* can reflect upon the contents of consciousness, it is not simply the aggregate of those contents. While it can be thought of as participating in the direction of purposeful behavior, it is not the same thing as the actions that are taken. Nor is it considered "an unchanging metaphysical entity like the Soul, or a principle like the transcendental Ego" that exists apart from time and space (James, 1892, p. 215). The *I* participates in causation of behavior and in the evaluation of the *Me*, but it is not thought to be a causal force apart from consciousness. Rather it *is* the dynamic process of consciousness; the awareness of self and of individuality.

Accuracy and Self-Enhancement

There are two aspects of James's analysis of the self that are most important from our perspective: the idea of multiple social selves, and the actions taken for the benefit of the self. To begin with there will be times when your multiple social selves get in each other's way. For example, your friends may ask you to spend the weekend sailing with them, but you have an assignment due on Monday, and you have just received a letter from your parents wondering when you will have enough free time to come home for a weekend. Part of your self-concept is based on a positive evaluation by your friends of the social self you reveal to them, but your self-concept is also boosted by the positive opinions of your instructors and your parents. Yet in this situation it is impossible for you to live up to everyone's expectations, and so you suffer from what Gross, Mason, and McEachern (1957) call role conflict. Such role conflict arises whenever you perceive that there are incompatible expectations for your behavior that are the result of the different roles you occupy. To resolve role conflict you must choose one set of expectations to follow, and because of this choice there may be distortion in other roles and expectations. For example, you might rationalize your choice of sailing with your friends on the grounds that "I am in college to make life-long friendships as well as to do homework. Besides, my parents can't really want to see me again so soon—I went home just a couple of months ago." The existence of role conflict demonstrates that our multiple social selves are not always in harmony with each other.

In addition, the actions of the self present an even greater potential for conflict between accuracy and distortion. Consider what is involved in self-preservation. To protect your self you should have accurate information about impending threats and about ways to minimize those dangers. How much preparation is really necessary to pass a difficult required course? What balance between academic work and extracurricular activities is appropriate for your occupational and personal goals? Are you likely to find a particular social relationship rewarding, or will it be too stressful? In each of these instances the goal of self-protection would best be served by accurate information. But in each case self-seeking or self-enhancement would be better served by a distortion of reality. Given the best possible circumstances, you would *like* to think it easy to pass the course, to believe that you can handle an extensive extracurricular life while maintaining a high academic average, and to have a degree of self-assurance that would permit you to gain from almost any relationship. When your goal is self-seeking you may emphasize your strengths, minimize your weaknesses, strive to achieve beyond your capacity, and overestimate the extent to which fortune will smile upon you. In the opposition between self-preservation and self-seeking we can see the beginning of the conflict between accuracy and distortion in self-knowledge and self-expression.

The Looking-Glass Self

If it is true, as James (1892) suggests, that we have multiple social selves, how do these relationships with other people affect our own self-concept? Early interest in this question can be traced to the origin (Cooley, 1902) of the sociological tradition that has become known as symbolic interactionism (Mead, 1934; Rose, 1962). This approach describes social encounters in terms of their *meaning* and their *value*. People exist in a symbolic, as well as a physical, environment where even physical objects assume importance because of their social meaning. A building is not important because of its physical characteristics —walls, floor, roof, doors, windows—but because of its social significance as a gathering place for people. Similarly, the importance of a social interaction is derived not from the physical fact of the encounter, but from the meaning it holds for the participants. Is the meeting a business transaction, or an exchange of pleasantries between casual acquaintances, or an angry debate between partisans for different political causes? In addition to its social meaning, an encounter or an interaction has a particular *value* to the participants (and to observers). This value is usually phrased in positive or negative terms. For example, a conservationist may agree with a campground developer that construction of buildings in a wilderness area has a social meaning of "increased public use of the area." For the developer this would be a good thing; for the conservationist it might be a bad thing.

So far we have been speaking as if meanings and values were developed in individuals without any communication among people. But the "interaction" in symbolic interactionism refers specifically to the fact that people *do* communicate with each other, thereby providing the opportunity for meanings to be learned and values to be exchanged. Because we share a common language and have the ability for symbolic thought, we can (at least in principle) put aside our own concerns to look at the world from the view of other perceivers.

Certainly we do not do this all of the time, or even often enough, but as Mead (1934) put it, we are able to *take the role of the other*. We can empathize with the feelings and attitudes of others by symbolically stepping into each other's shoes.

The ability to take the role of another person has an important implication for the development of self-concept. When I take another's view of the social world, one of the things that I will see is, obviously, my self. Not surprisingly, Cooley (1902) described the resulting picture as a looking-glass self with three major components. The first component is our social meaning: our imagination of our appearance to the other person, that person's estimate of our behavior and our motives. The second component is our social value: our imagination of the evaluative judgment that the other person would make about the behavior he or she sees. The third component is some form of self-feeling (such as pride or shame) that arises from what we believe the other person's evaluation of us to be. Here our emotions arise not from our own evaluation of our social selves, but rather from the evaluation that we believe is being made by the other person. In keeping with James's (1892) idea of multiple social selves, Cooley points out that the looking glass is not a "mere mechanical reflection" (p. 152) since it will differ depending upon whose view we take. The great surgeon who takes pride in a professional reputation for technical brilliance might feel shame should his or her patients discover that some of this expertise had been attained at their risk. The looking glass can be tarnished by self-preservation and self-seeking; and the interesting question "What does he *really* think of me?" is made even more intriguing by the relative infrequency with which it is asked.

THE PROCESS OF SELF-EVALUATION

The assertion that we possess multiple social selves and the idea that we can learn of these selves through the opinions of others together serve as the foundation for most social psychological study of the self. But these two ideas still leave some important questions unanswered. Whose opinions of us are the most valuable, and for what purposes? When do we desire accurate information, and when do we want to be misled? How do we assess our attitudes and emotions? What consequences does all of this self-assessment have for our self-esteem? In this section of the chapter we examine some recent formulations that suggest answers to these questions.

Perhaps nothing is more basic to self-evaluation than comparison of the self with other people. We obtain estimates of our abilities, confirmation for our opinions, and judgments of our self-worth from other people. This principle of comparison was inherent in the ideas of James (1892) and the symbolic interactionists (Cooley, 1902; Mead, 1934), and it can be seen in a wide variety of other social evaluation theories (summarized by Pettigrew, 1967). For our purposes the most important of these theories are the *reference group theory* of Hyman (1942), the *social comparison theory* of Festinger (1954), and the *cognitive labeling theory* of Schachter (1964). The first deals with the choice of comparison groups, the second concentrates on the selection of individual comparison persons within a group, and the third shows how social factors can influence even private experiences such as emotions.

Reference Groups

According to reference group theory (Hyman, 1942; later extended by Kelley, 1952; and by Merton, 1957), a reference group is any group that is used as a standard for self-evaluation or attitude formation, regardless of whether it is also a membership group for the person doing the comparing. For example, you may compare your attitudes toward getting high grades with the attitudes held by members of a fraternity or sorority, even though you do not belong to such a group yourself. If you use the group as an example of what your attitudes ought to be, then it is serving as a *positive* reference group; if you use it as an example of what your attitudes should not be, then it is a *negative* reference group. In either case, the group is serving what Kelley (1952) called the comparison function. It does not attempt to set or enforce particular rules for your behavior, but merely serves as a standard of comparison.

But a reference group may perform another function as well—what Kelley (1952) calls the normative function—especially if you have or desire membership in the group. In this case the group establishes rules for your behavior—group *norms*—and enforces your adherence to these norms by providing appropriate rewards and punishments. If you actually belong to a fraternity or sorority, the evaluations that other members make of you as a person may well depend upon your expressed agreement with the group's attitudes toward study habits, social life, and participation in school activities. And the fewer outside sources of self-evaluation you have, the more you will need to conform to the group's requirements.

As Pettigrew (1967) notes, most of the research on aspects of reference group theory has concentrated on the normative function of reference groups. The best known of these studies is the large-scale investigation of attitudes toward public affairs conducted at Bennington College by Newcomb (1943). The research began with the first class of graduating seniors in 1935 and continued until 1939. During this time over six-hundred students participated in a variety of measures, some dealing with presidential preferences, some with political attitudes (such as those toward unemployment, rights of organized labor, and welfare payments) made salient by the New Deal policies of the federal government, and some with mutual friendship choices and ratings of personal prestige. Most of the students had come from urban, high socioeconomic standing, politically conservative families, and Newcomb was interested in determining what changes in attitudes might develop as a consequence of the students' exposure to a liberal and politically active faculty.

In terms of the theory, the membership group consisted of the entire student body, but there were at least three major possibilities for reference groups: family and friends at home, the faculty, or other students at the college. Within this last category were the campus leaders (who were, for the most part, quite liberal), the majority of other students (who typically became more liberal from their freshman year to their senior year), and a small minority of students who maintained their conservatism throughout their four years of college. Support for the reference group analysis is provided by the fact that the most liberal students identified most strongly with the liberal elements of the community, while students who remained conservative identified with their families and underestimated the degree of liberalism present in the college environment. In addition, the normative aspects of the situation were apparent in the interview responses of conservatives, many of whom noted their isolation from the larger social system of the campus community.

In the normative and comparison functions of a reference group we can see the conflicting pressures toward accuracy and distortion. When a reference group serves only a comparison function for you, you can be relatively honest with yourself about your position and that of the group (except for some constraints of social desirability). But when the reference group also has normative power over you, differences between its opinion and your own may have detrimental effects on your self-interest. As a result you may misjudge the group's position (the case of the conservative Bennington students who dramatically underestimated the liberalism of the college environment), or you may find it necessary to shift your opinion so that it more closely matches the opinion of the group. In terms of Kelman's (1961) three processes of opinion change (discussed in Chapter Seven), change that follows a comparison with a reference group would most probably be identification, while change that occurs through normative pressure would be compliance.

Social Comparison Among Individuals

Reference group theory is useful for describing comparisons with identifiable groups of people, but it does not attempt to deal with the numerous comparisons that we make with other individuals. This is the province of Festinger's (1954) social comparison theory (not to be confused with his dissonance theory, discussed in Chapter Six). Although the complete statement of social comparison theory is quite detailed, for our purposes it can be summarized in three fundamental propositions: (1) People have a drive to evaluate their opinions and abilities. (2) In the absence of "objective" bases for comparison, this need can be satisfied by "social" comparison with other people. (3) Such social comparisons will, when possible, be made with similar others. Let us take a closer look at these propositions.

Two Kinds of Evaluation

What does it mean to say that people have a drive to evaluate their opinions and abilities? The two key words in this proposition are "drive" and "evaluate." Although motivational theorists disagree about the precise meaning of the term *drive*, there is concurrence that drivelike states can be inferred from the behavior that follows a *deprivation* (Cofer and Appley, 1964). If we make you go without food for a few days, you will behave as if you had a hunger *drive*—you will seek food, perform various tasks to try to obtain it, and devour any food you happen to get. In a similar, though less extreme, manner, if we deprive you of information about your opinions and abilities, you will behave as if you had a drive to acquire that knowledge. The minute you acquire a new skill, you will want to find out how your ability compares with that of others who possess the skill. As soon as a new means of travel is invented—be it swamp buggy, airboat, or snowmobile—someone will decide to hold races to see who can drive it the fastest. The same thing is true, although not quite so obviously, for opinions. We want to determine where our opinions fit with those of other people, and we want to see what others might think of us for holding one opinion or another. Thus it is appropriate to postulate the existence of a drive for evaluation of opinions and abilities.

But what about the evaluation? You may have noticed that our examples involve two different sorts of evaluations. Although Festinger (1954) used the term to mean "find the location of," a number of

other writers have pointed out that it could also be used to mean
"place a value upon." For example, you may discover that your tennis
ability is located at the high-ability end of the scale (there are few
people whom you cannot beat), but how much this discovery adds to
your self-esteem will depend on the value you place on being good
at tennis. These two different goals for evaluation have been described
in various ways. Latané (1966), for example, makes the distinction
between self-evaluation and self-enhancement. Singer (1966) distinguishes evaluation of the opinion or ability from evaluation of the
self for *holding* the opinion or *possessing* the ability. The distinction
is the same in each case. Necessity for such a distinction arises because we value some opinions more than others, and because we
prize great ability. For example, if we use some test of mechanical
aptitude to determine that 95 percent of people have more mechanical
aptitude than you do, we have not merely provided you with information about your location. None of us wants to think that he or she is
among the worst 5 percent at anything, so the test outcome may be
damaging to your self-esteem. As we shall see in a moment, it is important to distinguish between the "location" and "valuation" senses
of *evaluate.*

Objective versus Social Comparison

The second basic proposition of social comparison theory states
that when information about opinions and abilities cannot be obtained
from objective sources, it will be gathered through comparison with
other people. To set the stage for the two sorts of comparison, Festinger first draws a distinction between *physical reality* and *social
reality.* Physical reality is an objective world of time and space containing objects whose characteristics can be specified with certainty.
This physical reality is equivalent to the physical environment in symbolic interactionist theory. In contrast to this objective world, social
reality (analogous to the symbolic environment) consists of an interpersonal world of subjective judgments. Physical reality is thought to
be preferred as a source of information, but there are times when the
social reality assumes predominance. For example, it was once
thought that tomatoes were poisonous to human beings. Given this
social reality, who would perform the first physical test by tasting a
tomato? As another example, suppose you were about to learn some
possibly negative things about yourself. Would you rather get the information from an unimpeachable objective source, or from a social
source which could be discounted as unreliable? Probably the latter.
The theory's assumption that physical reality is the preferred source

of information has not been adequately tested, and these examples suggest that it should receive more attention in the future.

The critical difference between an objective comparison and a social comparison is that the former *can* be tested against physical reality, not that such a test will necessarily be made. To illustrate the difference, suppose that I am approached by a shady character who offers to sell me a "diamond" for zircon prices. I may have reason to believe that the stone is, in fact, a diamond, and this would agree with the social reality that is expressed by the fellow. But I do not have to rely upon his word alone. I can rub the stone across a piece of glass, safe in the knowledge that only a real diamond will produce a scratch in the glass. My belief that the stone is a diamond can be checked against objective physical reality to determine whether it is correct. In contrast, many of our beliefs rest entirely upon the judgments of others. Suppose, for example, that I believe that people's privacy should be respected by the police and the government, no matter who the people in question might be. There is no physical test that I can perform to decide whether this belief is "correct," either in the sense of agreeing with universal ethical principles, or in the sense of being so positively valued that holding the belief will increase my self-esteem. These latter judgments must be made by social comparison with other people.

The Importance of Similarity

The third fundamental assumption of social comparison theory is that *similar* others will be most often chosen for purposes of evaluation. Why should I choose a similar other? Intuitively we might think that such a choice could serve both evaluative goals. Suppose that I want to find the location of one of my political beliefs—that the government and police should respect an individual's privacy—and I compare myself with extremists at both ends of the political spectrum. If I discover that anarchists also want privacy (so their bomb factories won't be discovered) and law-and-order conservatives want privacy (so the meetings of their vigilante groups won't be disturbed), does that really tell me anything more about the location of my belief, or about its correctness? Probably not. And if my purpose was self-aggrandizement for holding a correct belief, it certainly wouldn't improve my self-image to be associated with either comparison group. Similar others provide me with a more precise estimate of where in the spectrum my opinion falls. In addition, because they share my values, they are more likely to commend me for the beliefs I hold. Thus it would appear that comparing with people whose values are more like mine would not only provide me with a more precise location for my opinion, it would also provide me with a better chance of increasing my self-esteem.

Social Comparison of Abilities

THE UNIDIRECTIONAL DRIVE UPWARD. An interesting complication arises in the choice of a comparison other when the question is one of *ability* rather than opinion. Festinger states that "there is a unidirectional drive upward in the case of abilities which is largely absent in opinions." In short, we like to see ourselves as continually performing "better." Because of this high value placed on good performance, it might not always be best to choose a similar other for comparison: if the choice is *too* similar, and if there is competition, you might lose. Do you really want to know where your ability lies enough to risk being defeated at an activity you value?

In part because the predictions for comparison choices are more complicated for ability comparison, and in part because the experimental operations necessary to conduct the research are simpler, social comparison of abilities has received more experimental attention than any other aspect of social comparison theory. Consider an experimental example (Wheeler, Shaver, Jones, Goethals, Cooper, Robinson, Gruder, and Butzine, 1969). Suppose that I give you, together with eight other people, a test which purportedly measures one of your cognitive abilities. Before the test begins I say that I will assign each of the nine of you an identifying code letter (from A through I), but in fact I give each of you the same Letter (H). Next I describe the test of cognitive functioning, pointing out that it measures an ability not ordinarily included in standard intelligence tests (so that you won't be able to use your past performance in such tests as a standard for comparison). The description of the test differs across groups of nine subjects. For half the groups, the test is described in positive terms, as a test of "intellectual flexibility." For the other half of the groups of nine, the test is described as measuring "intellectual rigidity," a very undesirable trait.

After a brief description of the meaning of flexibility or rigidity, you take the test. Then I score the nine tests and tell each of you your score in private. Next I suggest that all of you might be interested in the performance of the group, so I write a rank order of the identifying letters on the blackboard. This rank order is shown in Table 8-1 and, as you can see, numerical values are given only for the highest rank (person G), the lowest rank (person B), and the median rank (person H). The numerical values for the two ends of the scale are only approximate in the information I write on the blackboard, and each of the nine subjects believes that the 310 for H is

TABLE 8-1
Information presented to subjects prior to comparison choice selection

Rank Order	Numerical Score
G	550-600
I	
D	
A	
H (subject's score)	310
F	
C	
E	
B	25-75

Adapted from Wheeler et al. (1969).

his or her own score. Finally, I offer to let you all see one other exact score, and ask you to indicate which one that will be. This is your choice of a comparison other. Which score will you choose to see?

COMPARISON CHOICES. If comparison of abilities in this experiment followed the pattern suggested earlier for opinions, the choices should be about evenly distributed between the two most similar people (A and F), regardless of whether the dimension has been described in positive or negative terms. But remember that in the case of abilities there is thought to be a *unidirectional drive upward*—we all like to see our abilities as slightly better than they really are. By comparing ourselves to people who are slightly better off, we may be able to change our own self-image in much the same way that we try to change the attitudes of others by presenting them with information that is slightly discrepant from their original position (this social judgment theory of attitude change is discussed more fully in Chapter Seven). But just as there are limits to assimilation, so there ought to be limits to self-enhancing social comparison. For example, we should not choose to see the "best" possible score (numerically the highest in the positive condition, numerically the lowest in the negative condition), because that comparison would only serve to remind us of how far we have to go. Extending the analogy to social judgment a bit more, these "best" scores should be contrasted with our own. Taking all these considerations into account, we might expect that the predominant comparison choice would be person A in the positive condition, person F in the negative condition. In each of these cases the comparison choice would be *slightly better off* than the subject.

When this experiment was actually performed (Wheeler et al., 1969), the data did seem to support the prediction. In the positive conditions, 47 percent of the subjects chose person A (slightly better off than themselves), and in the negative conditions 43.8 percent of the subjects chose person F (again, slightly better off than themselves). From these data alone it would be tempting to conclude that the subjects were trying to enhance their self-esteem by assimilating their own scores to the score of a person who was slightly better off. But the next most frequent first choice for comparison was the *most desirable* score (the highest numerical score in the positive condition, the lowest numerical score in the negative condition). It is difficult to see how this choice could have served the purpose of self-enhancement. Indeed, on motivational grounds alone, the most desirable score should have been contrasted with the subject's own score, so that the subject would not "suffer by comparison." Consequently, it appears as though choice of the most desirable score can only serve the informational purpose of defining the scale.

INFORMATION AND MOTIVATION. What does all of this tell us about the factors that might influence choice of a comparison other? Perhaps the most general conclusion is that both informational and motivational goals are involved in the choice. There has been some experimental support for the informational goal of defining the scale (Arrowood and Friend, 1969; Radloff, 1966; Thornton and Arrowood, 1966); some support for the motivational goals of self-enhancement and self-protection (Friend and Gilbert, 1973; Hakmiller, 1966; Wheeler, 1966; Wheeler et al., 1969); and some evidence that both informational and motivational objectives may be involved in comparison choice (Gruder, 1971; Jones and Regan, 1974; Zanna, Goethals, and Hill, 1975). On balance, the research in social comparison justifies Festinger's (1954) original assumption that people have a drive to evaluate their opinions and abilities. It also justifies the distinction between the two senses of *evaluate*, and it provides evidence that similar others are involved in a preponderance of comparison choices. This choice of similar others is especially likely, as two of the recent studies (Jones and Regan, 1974; Zanna, Goethals, and Hill, 1975) indicate, when the question to be answered is "What can I *do* with the ability," rather than "How much of the ability do I possess?" Apparently we do evaluate constituents of our social selves through comparison with other people, and in many cases these comparisons are made with others who are similar to us on attributes related to the comparison. In the next section we shall see that social comparison may apply in the assessment of emotional states, as well as in the evaluation of opinions and abilities.

Assessment of Emotional States

Early Theories of Emotion

Of all the aspects of your social self, intense emotional experiences would seem to be the most subjective and private. The joy of giving birth, the profound grief at the loss of a loved one, the contentment with a life well spent—these emotions are very difficult to convey to other people who have not shared the same circumstances. Yet many emotional states can be verbally described, and shared, through literature, drama, and conversation. And an extension of social comparison theory suggests that labels provided by others can be combined with internal physiological arousal to *produce*, not merely communicate, the subjective experience of emotion (Schachter, 1964). We shall take a closer look at this theory after briefly considering some alternative positions on the origin of emotion.

Let us take fear as an example of an emotion to be understood. In terms of self-assessment, how do you know when you are afraid? The first answer to this question to have substantial impact upon psychological interest in emotion was proposed by James and Lange (1922). They suggested that the subjective experience of emotion was the consequence of visceral changes and feedback from skeletal muscles. You have the emotional experience of fear because you are running from a large brown bear that just stood up in the middle of your hiking trail. The threat from the bear not only produces running behavior, it also produces visceral changes—a surge of adrenaline, increases in heart rate and respiration—that are interpreted as the emotional experience of fear. Thus emotion is the result of feedback to the brain from *peripheral* organs in the body. This bodily reaction theory of emotion is usually called a *peripheral* theory, to indicate that the source of emotional experience is outside the brain. Peripheral theories require two fundamental assumptions. First, there must be a different pattern of physiological arousal for each different emotion. Second, any visceral arousal must be accompanied by some emotional experience. Both of these assumptions are necessary for the one-to-one correspondence between visceral arousal and emotion postulated by the theory, but an early critique by Cannon (1927) undercut both assumptions.

On the basis of experimental and surgical evidence, Cannon (1927) raised five different objections to the peripheral theory, but only two of these objections are still considered serious criticisms (Leventhal, 1974). These two criticisms are (1) that artificial arousal of the visceral changes associated with strong emotion (for example, through the administration of drugs) does not produce those strong emotions, and (2) that visceral changes occur so slowly that it is difficult to see how they can produce emotions that are often felt instantaneously. It doesn't take you three or four minutes to be frightened by the bear; you are scared the second it rears up and growls.

If emotions are not the result of visceral changes, what does produce them? Cannon's (1927) answer was that both the visceral changes and the subjective experience are produced by activation of a part of the *central nervous system*, specifically the thalamus. According to this theory, the external stimulus (the bear) activates particular structures in the brain, and this activation leads to both the overt behavior (running) and the internal changes (visceral arousal and the experience of fear). Because it attributed emotional experience to changes in the brain, Cannon's theory is known as a *central* theory. But as Leventhal (1974) points out, the activation theory describes only the neurophysiology of emotion, not the psychology of emotion, and certainly not the *social* psychology of emotion. Emotional experiences are still ultimately attributable to particular arousing stimuli, except that now the intervening internal process is thought to be in the brain rather than in the viscera.

The Social Psychology of Emotion

WAITING ALONE OR TOGETHER. The beginning of social psychology's concern with emotional experience is usually traced to the influential work of Schachter and his associates (e.g., Schachter, 1959, 1964; Schachter and Singer, 1962; Schachter and Wheeler, 1962). And the first studies in this series (Schachter, 1959) can be regarded as extensions of social comparison theory. The same factors that give rise to the drive for social comparison of an opinion or ability—uncertainty about the opinion or ability, coupled with a reason to try to reduce the uncertainty—might produce attempts to compare emotional experiences. To test this idea, Schachter (1959) performed an experiment in which groups of five to eight female undergraduates were brought into a laboratory containing an impressive array of electrical hardware. The subjects were met by an experimenter who introduced himself as "Dr. Gregor Zilstein, of the Medical School's Department of Neurology and Psychiatry." As if this introduction were not frightening enough, "Zilstein," who was wearing a white lab coat with a stethoscope drooping out of one pocket, then described the experiment as a study of the physiological effects of electric shock. The subjects were to be given an "intense" series of electric shocks which were "quite painful," although they would "do no permanent damage." This introduction concluded, "Zilstein" went on to say that the subjects would have to wait for a few moments while he finished setting up and calibrating the equipment. Each subject was given the option of waiting alone or waiting together with other female undergraduate students, but there were two different descriptions of these other students. In the Same State condition the other students were described as waiting for the same experiment, while in the Different State condition the students were described as waiting to talk with their professors.

The prediction from social comparison theory is that there would be a stronger preference toward waiting with others when those others *were similar to the subject,* in short, when they were also waiting to take part in the experiment. It is doubtful that you will learn just how frightened you should be of Dr. Zilstein and his shock machine if you are sitting in a room with people who are there for an entirely different purpose. The data supported the prediction, with stronger preferences indicated in the Same State condition. The dependent variable of interest was the subject's choice of where to wait, so the experiment was terminated as soon as the choices had been made (no subjects were actually shocked). Since the experiment did not include observation of the subjects while they were waiting, it cannot conclusively establish that the desire for social comparison of emotional states led to the choices of waiting, but later research (Darley and Aronson, 1966; Gerard, 1963; Gerard and Rabbie, 1961; Wrightsman, 1960) has ruled out most of the other possible explanations.

COGNITIVE LABELING OF EMOTION. In Schachter's (1959) first series of experiments the emotion (fear) was induced by the threatening situation. All that social comparison with other subjects could provide was some estimate of the degree of fear that was justified. The next step in the research demonstrated that the *quality* of the emotion, not just its degree, could be determined by comparison with other people. The classic experiment by Schachter and Singer (1962) illustrates this approach. In this study subjects were injected with epinephrine (adrenaline), which produces some heart palpitations, hand tremor, rapid breathing, and a warm feeling of flushing. All the subjects had been led to believe that the injection was an experimental vitamin supplement ("suproxin"), but some (the Informed group) had been told to expect these side effects as a result of the injection. When the symptoms did occur this Informed group of subjects would have an appropriate *label* for their subjective feelings. A second group of subjects (the Ignorant group) was given the injection with no prior warning about the symptoms to follow, and a third (Misinformed) group was told that "suproxin" should produce side effects of numbness, itching, and slight headache (all obviously inappropriate to explain the symptoms actually induced). This Misinformed group was included as a control against later emotional differences based solely on physiological introspection, and a second control group was given an injection of saline solution (and no prior instructions).

There is usually a three- to five-minute delay before the onset of symptoms after an injection of epinephrine (this, of course, was the basis of one of Cannon's objections to the body reaction theory of emotion), and during this time the subject was joined by an experimental confederate. The confederate had been trained to act in either an angry manner or an euphoric manner. Thus, for subjects *without* an adequate explanation for their impending symptoms, the actions of the confederate could provide an appropriate cognitive label. The results of the experiment confirmed the predictions: subjects in the groups without a prior explanation for their physiological arousal (Ignorant and Misinformed groups) adopted the label provided by the confederate's behavior, while Informed subjects did not.

These results, as well as findings from a similar experiment by Schachter and Wheeler (1962), led Schachter (1964) to propose a cognitive labeling theory of emotion in which both physiological and cognitive elements are required for the subjective experience of emotional states. The physiological component provides the basis for the experience, and the cognitive component provides a label for that experience. Just how external stimuli create physiological arousal is not clearly spelled out in the theory (all of the emotion theories are relatively vague on this point), but the importance of the cognitive label is convincingly demonstrated. In normal circumstances, adults have difficulty separating the cognitive label from the physiological arousal, but labeling theory simply suggests that the labels are learned during childhood experience. To buttress the case for learning, Schachter cites the physiological effects of smoking marijuana—vertigo; a sensation of floating; increased appetite; increased sensitivity to pressure, touch, and pain; and decreased muscular coordination—and wonders "Given such symptoms, should the smoker describe himself as 'high' or as 'sick'?" (1964, p. 77). His answer to the question is that the smoker must *learn* to call these symptoms pleasurable. It is plausible to argue that similar learning could occur in the labeling of other sorts of arousal as well.

Misattribution of Emotion

The cognitive labeling theory thus describes emotional experience as consisting of two largely independent components, arousal and cognition. The very independence of these two components raises some intriguing questions. Can people make mistaken estimates of the *degree* of their arousal? The success of such techniques as acupuncture and hypnosis in producing anesthesia might depend on this sort of misattribution. Can people be induced to misattribute the *source* of their arousal, in much the same way that Schachter and Singer's (1962) subjects were induced to err in the naming of their emotional experience? Might such induced misattribution serve therapeutic purposes? Research growing out of the cognitive labeling approach indicates that the proper answer to all these questions is a qualified yes.

THE DEGREE OF AROUSAL. First consider judgments of the degree of physiological arousal. In a technique that has since come to be known as the "false heart rate feedback" method, Valins (1966) showed slides of female nudes to male undergraduate students who had been wired with dummy electrodes. These electrodes ostensibly measured the subject's heart rate, and the resulting rate was played back to the subject over a loudspeaker. On a randomly selected few of the slides, the programmed heart rate either increased or decreased appreciably, although it remained constant over the remainder of the slides. Attractiveness ratings of the slides were obtained as each slide was shown, and at the conclusion of the experiment the subjects were told that they could take a few of the slides with them, as a reward for participating in the experiment. On both the attractiveness ratings made during the study and the slide choices made at its conclusion, subjects showed a definite preference for slides on which there had been a presumed heart rate change, regardless of whether that presumed change had been an increase or a decrease.

Apparently subjects can be misled into believing that they have been emotionally aroused by a stimulus. Interestingly enough, the reverse also appears to be true. For example, in a similar false heart rate study, Valins and Ray (1967) showed slides of snakes and of the word *shock* to people who had admitted being afraid of snakes. Presentation of the word *shock* was accompanied by a mild shock to the fingers, and by a change in the programmed heart rate. Presentation of the snake slides was *not* accompanied by any change in programmed heart rate. After several trials of this procedure, experimental subjects (who had been told that the heartbeat was their own) were able to approach a small boa constrictor more closely than were control subjects who had been told that the heartbeat was not their own. The experimental subjects may well have observed their own (presumed) arousal, noted that there was no arousal accompanying presentation of the "feared" object, and concluded that they must not be as fearful of snakes as they had originally thought. If this sort of explanation sounds familiar, that is because of its similarity to the self-perception theory of attitude organization (Bem, 1972) discussed in detail in Chapter Six.

The ease with which people can be misled about the presence or absence of arousal (in the form of false heart rate feedback) led Valins (1970) to propose that with low levels of arousal the *cognition* of arousal may be more important in the production of an emotional experience than is the actual arousal. This is a substantial modification of Schachter's (1964) formulation, because it suggests that not even the physiological arousal is necessary for many emotional experiences. It is a purely cognitive interpretation of emotion. Certainly it does not apply to cases of extreme emotion—fear, rage, disgust—in which the internal cues are quite powerful. But neither does Bem's self-perception theory of attitudes apply when the internal cues are clear. Support for Valins's (1970) position has come from several recent experiments (Barefoot and Straub, 1971; Goldstein, Fink, and Mettee, 1972; Misovich and Charis, 1974), and it would appear that quite a variety of everyday "emotional" experiences might be produced more by the cognition of arousal than by the actual existence of arousal.

THE SOURCE OF AROUSAL: THERAPEUTIC MISATTRIBUTION. Next let us turn to the misattribution of the source of arousal. In an early study of this sort, Nisbett and Schachter (1966) gave subjects a placebo pill and then administered an increasingly intense series of electric shocks. Half the subjects had been led to expect some autonomic arousal as a "side effect" of the pill, and these subjects showed a much greater shock tolerance before reporting pain. The major contribution of this research was to apply the misattribution paradigm to a natural emotion of general concern. Few of us will ever be in a position to listen to an amplified version of our heartbeat while viewing either attractive or frightening stimuli. Even if we are conscious of our heart rate, it is not programmed to *change* our emotional experiences. But all of us suffer pain now and then, and for many of us that experience may be as much "in our heads" as in our bodies. The results of Nisbett and Schachter's experiment make us wonder to what extent aspirin and other pain relievers can act as placebos that rely for their effectiveness on the belief that they will relieve pain.

The potential therapeutic benefit from induced cognitive misattribution of the source of arousal is perhaps best illustrated by the work of Storms and Nisbett (1970). These investigators attacked a common problem—insomnia—that appears tailor-made for solution with a misattribution therapy. What happens when you are tense and think you will have difficulty getting to sleep? You know that you need the rest, but you are afraid that you will not be able to sleep. You lie down and try to take your mind off your problems, but the harder you try the more wide awake you become. Confirming your worst fears, you are not able to get to sleep. But what if you could attribute your sleeplessness to some emotionally irrelevant external stimulus? Storms and Nisbett tried to answer this question by giving insomniac subjects a placebo pill which was described as producing alertness, high temperature, and heart rate increases. Since all these physiological symptoms typically accompany insomnia, subjects receiving the pill could readily attribute their arousal to the drug, rather than to the fears and worries that had previously been keeping them awake. As anticipated, the subjects reported being able to get to sleep earlier on nights when they took the pills than on nights when they did not. Thus the misattribution of arousal to an emotionally irrelevant external stimulus helped alleviate a disturbing emotional problem. This was also the case in Valins and Ray's (1967) work with snake phobics; other therapeutic applications for misattributions are suggested by Ross, Rodin, and Zimbardo (1969), and by Nisbett and Valins (1971).

In this section we have seen that an important aspect of the social self—emotional experience—may be produced or changed by various combinations of internal cues (physiological arousal) and external labels. Experimental manipulation of the latter can alter the subjective experience of emotion, change the individual's ability to cope with stress (Lazarus, 1966), or aid in the solution of emotional problems. Outside the usual laboratory settings, the relative balance between internal and external cues had been linked to cigarette smoking be- havior (Herman, 1974), choice of a dangerous occupation (Shaver, Turnbull, and Sterling, 1973), and the development of obesity (Schachter, 1964, 1971). For example, Schachter (1971) found that, compared to normal people, the obese are more sensitive to the ex- ternal cues for eating (appearance, taste, and texture of food) and less sensitive to the internal cues of hunger and satiety. Obese people eat when food seems attractive, regardless of whether or not they are hungry, and this leads to an intake of calories that is substantially in excess of the amount normally needed. At this point we should note that a good deal of behavior, as well as much of emotional experience, may be determined by people and stimuli out- side the self.

Self-Perception of Attitudes

We may base some of our attitudes on those held by reference groups that are important to us, and we may evaluate the location and social value of other attitudes through processes of social com- parison. But what of the formation of attitudes when there is no clear position available for comparison? Is it possible that some self- evaluation is present in these cases as well? The self-perception theory of Bem (1967, 1972) suggests that there is. You will recall that the basic premise of Bem's approach is that people do observe both their own behavior and the situational context in which it occurs in much the same way that they observe the behavior of other people. The self infers its "attitude" toward a particular attitude object on the basis of internal feelings and external rewards or punishments. Because Bem's theory was discussed in detail in Chapter Six, all we shall try to do here is place it in the larger framework of the self-evaluation principles we have just considered (looking-glass self, social comparison, cognitive labeling).

In many ways Bem's self-perception approach is quite similar to other views of self-evaluation, but there is one critical difference: the focus is on one's *own* behavior, rather than on the behavior of others or the cues they provide. First, the looking-glass self has us taking the role of significant other people, and evaluating ourselves as we guess they might evaluate us. This is not direct self-observation, but observation through the eyes of another. Next, social comparison describes ways in which we learn about, and judge, our opinions and abilities by means of explicit references to the opinions and abilities of others. Certainly some evaluation of self follows social comparison, but the principal source of information is the behavior of others. Finally, cognitive labeling theory concentrates on the emotional labels provided by the external environment and by the actions of other people. There is much more emphasis on internal states (e.g., physiological arousal) in cognitive labeling theory than in either symbolic interactionism or social comparison, but the major role is still given to the externally based label. Thus, while all the self-evaluation theories discuss some form of interchange between the self and the social environment, self-perception theory can be distinguished from the others by its more exclusive concern with direct observation of one's own behavior.

THE DEVELOPMENT OF SELF-ESTEEM

Successes and Pretensions

Because of its concern with direct observation of the self, the self-perception theory of attitudes brings us a bit closer to that all-important personal estimate of worthiness, *self-esteem*. Indeed, a major study of self-esteem (Coopersmith, 1967) defined the term as a set of self-evaluative *attitudes*. Whether the evaluative behavior involves modeling an attitude after one held by a desirable reference group, comparing ability with a similar (but slightly better off) other, avoiding excessive fear by obtaining appropriate emotional labels for threatening situations, or weighing the relative contributions of internal and external sources of an attitude, the ultimate goal is the same: protection or enhancement of self-esteem.

Just as the topic of evaluation of the social self must begin with the ideas of James (1892), so a discussion of self-esteem must begin with his definition:

$$\text{Self-esteem} = \frac{\text{Successes}}{\text{Pretentions}}$$

According to this definition, what you think of yourself will depend upon the degree to which your actual successes coincide with the goals and aspirations you have set for yourself. The first thing to notice about this definition is that your "pretensions" can be considered *internal* standards over which you have substantial control, both in the selection of which aspects of self you consider important and in the level of performance you expect to attain on each of those aspects. Suppose that I ask you to tell me something you are proud of, and you reply, "I can almost always break 90 when I play golf." What is involved in this assertion of self-esteem? To begin with, you have chosen to tell me about your athletic ability (rather than your musical talent or your interpersonal skills), and this choice reflects the importance to you of the general arena of athletics. Within this arena, you have further confined your pretensions to a specific game, rather than attempting to assert that you have an equal competence in other sports as well. And finally, you have set a numerical score of 90 as your **level of aspiration** (Gardner, 1939; Lewin, Dembo, Festinger, and Sears, 1944), that standard of performance which will determine whether your self-evaluation is positive or negative. If you obtain a score lower than 90 you will be pleased with yourself; if you do not break 90 you will be unhappy with your game. The choice of "athletics," the choice of "golf," and the score of 90 are all standards for evaluation that you set for yourself.

Once the standards have been set, you evaluate your performance against that standard, and it is in this judgment of your "success" that many of the self-evaluation theories we have discussed come into play. If your chosen athletic ability is tennis instead of golf, there is no objective standard (the score of 90) against which to judge your success. Your achievements in tennis must be gauged against the play of various opponents, through a process of social comparison. In the same way, if what you value is your ability to keep cool when others around you are "losing their heads," you will need to do some social comparison of emotional state. And finally, if you derive much of your self-esteem from thinking that you are an intellectually independent person, you will need to evaluate the extent to which your attitudes are determined by internal, as opposed to external, forces. Among the social evaluation theories previously considered, only reference group theory might be more appropriate for setting pretensions than for evaluating successes.

One final feature of the definition deserves comment. Since self-esteem is the ratio of success to pretensions, you can raise your overall level of self-esteem either by increasing your successes or by *decreasing your pretensions*. If you and I play golf together, and your goal is to break 90 while my goal is to lose fewer than a dozen balls in the ponds and in the rough, I can play much, much worse than you do and still feel more success at the end of the round. My pretensions are so much lower that it takes very little success to keep me happy. Unfortunately, one of the most difficult tasks in the maintenance of self-esteem is the setting of *realistic* aspirations. Particularly in the case of abilities, there is that "unidirectional drive upwards" with which to contend.

The explicit comparison between actual ability, performance, or personality and the internal standards of aspiration can be seen in most of the recent descriptions of self-esteem (e.g., Bills, Vance, and McLean, 1951; Coopersmith, 1967; Diggory, 1966; LaForge and Suczek, 1955; Wylie, 1961; Ziller, 1973). Some of these measures are verbal, some are nonverbal; some ask the subject to make a direct comparison of success to pretensions, others simply assume that individual pretensions can be equated with more general societal expectations for "good" characteristics. The wide range of measurement possibilities can be illustrated by two of the scales. The scale developed by Bills, Vance, and McLean (1951) is perhaps the most literal translation of James's (1892) ideas. It asks the subject to give three answers to each of forty-nine self-descriptive traits: how often the trait is characteristic of him, how often he would like for it to be so, and how he feels about possessing the characteristic. The first of these is the measure of successes (called the real self), the second is the measure of pretensions (called the ideal self), and the third is a measure of the importance of the trait in question. The person's self-esteem is defined as the *discrepancy* between real self and ideal self, a rather direct analog to James's conception of self-esteem.

In contrast to this sort of measure is the scale developed by Ziller (1973). In one form of this scale subjects are presented with a horizontal row of six circles and are asked to indicate which circle corresponds to the self and which circles correspond to significant other people (such as "someone who is flunking," or "the strongest person you know"). The crucial measure of self-esteem is how far to the *left* in the row the person places himself or herself, on the grounds that in our culture there is a "norm of hierarchical ordering of social objects in a horizontal line from left to right" (p. 11). In the case of this measure, successes are represented by the placement of the self and pretensions are considered to be implicit in the ordering from left to right.

External Factors Influencing Self-Esteem

Socialization Experiences

Although we have concentrated on the relationship between success and pretensions as a major determinant of self-esteem, there are other influences on self-esteem that are largely outside the control of the person. These begin in childhood with the actions of the parents and continue into adulthood with the responses of peers and significant reference persons. In an extensive study of preadolescent children (ages ten to twelve), Coopersmith (1967) found three separate factors leading to the development of high self-esteem: parental *acceptance* of the children, clearly defined and enforced *limits* on behavior, but *respect* for individual action within those prescribed limits. The parents of high-self-esteem children were themselves "active, poised, and relatively self-assured individuals who recognize the significance of childbearing and believe they can cope with the increased duties and responsibilities it entails" (p. 237). The sort of parents we have and the way they dealt with us when we were children are profound influences on our later self-esteem over which we obviously have no personal control.

Race and Sex

Another set of influences on self-esteem over which we have no control includes all our physical characteristics—race, sex, attractiveness. Yet others may judge us in terms of these characteristics, and we may incorporate those judgments (faulty though they may be) into our impressions of ourselves. One of the earliest demonstrations of how these "biosocial" attributes can affect self-esteem was the classic study of Clark and Clark (1947), which showed that black children chose a white doll and rejected a black doll when asked to select the one that was nice, or with which they would like to play. Since the children were aware of both the color of the doll and their own skin color, the investigators made a convincing case that this culturally approved choice nevertheless constituted a denial of self-worth. We might hope that recent emphasis on racial pride among black people (e.g., Carmichael and Hamilton, 1967) would have changed these preferences, but with few exceptions (Hraba and Grant, 1970) studies conducted in the past few years (e.g., Asher and Allen, 1969; Greenwald and Oppenheim, 1968; Morland, 1970; Porter, 1971) have obtained essentially similar results.

Another so-called biosocial attribute than can have lasting effects on self-esteem is sex, with conditions favoring higher self-esteem for males and lower self-esteem for females. At first you might think, "Of course, the traditional sex roles for women have always been of lower prestige than the roles prescribed for men, and women develop lower self-esteem as a consequence of this difference in role expectation." But some of the influences on a woman's self-esteem are much more subtle than that. Remember that self-esteem is defined as the ratio of successes to pretensions, so that successes are supposed to have a positive effect on self-worth. But there are two different judgments involved in the determination of a "success." First, there is the question of whether the behavioral outcome was truly a success, in the sense that objective observers (not just you) would consider it to be one. Second, there is a determination of the causes for that success, and there is some recent evidence that this attribution of causes is made differently depending upon whether the person involved is a man or a woman.

For example, Deaux and Emswiller (1974) asked subjects to explain the success of a stimulus person on a perceptual task of identifying familiar objects shown as part of a confusing background. This stimulus person was described as being either male or female, and the objects were either traditionally male-oriented (such as a wrench or a tire jack) or traditionally female-oriented (such as a mop or a double-boiler). It was implied that male stimulus persons should do better on the male-oriented materials and female stimulus persons should do better on the female-oriented materials. The results showed that when the female succeeded at the male-oriented task, her performance was attributed to luck, while male success at the female-oriented task was attributed to ability. What is most interesting for our purposes is that these evaluations were the *same* whether they were made by male or female subjects. Other studies of the attribution of causality for success (e.g., Feather and Simon, 1975; Feldman-Summers and Kiesler, 1974) have also found a consistent denial of the ability of successful female stimulus persons. In all these studies the female subjects view their successes as caused by factors other than their ability, and this denial of ability can be interpreted as inconsistent with the development of high self-esteem. Admittedly the implications are not quite as direct as the black child's preference for a white doll, but the consequences for self-esteem may be just as real.

Physical Attractiveness

Finally, it will come as no surprise to you that your physical attractiveness will have a substantial effect on your self-esteem, particularly to the degree that your self-impression is based upon the opinions of others (the looking-glass self). The effect of physical attractiveness begins early in socialization and continues into adulthood, as pointed out in an extensive review by Berscheid and Walster (1974a). Differences in physical attractiveness among preschool children affect the way that the children judge each other (Dion and Berscheid, 1972), with unattractive children considered by their peers to be more aggressive and antisocial (defined as "fighting a lot," "hitting and yelling at the teacher," and "saying angry things"). This tendency to equate physical unattractiveness with antisocial behavior can also be seen in the evaluations of children made by adults (Dion, 1972). In this study college females evaluated the reported misbehavior of a seven-year-old child. The reports were ostensibly based on daily reports of elementary school teachers and related an incident that was either mild or serious. Attached to each report was a picture of the child, and four different sorts of pictures were used—attractive boy, attractive girl, unattractive boy, and unattractive girl. The results showed that when the transgression was mild (such as stepping on the tail of a sleeping dog) there were no differences in evaluation based on the attractiveness of the child. But when the transgression was serious (e.g., throwing sharp stones at a dog which cut one of its legs), it was excused as a result of a temporary mood for attractive children but condemned as a product of an antisocial character for the unattractive children.

In both of these studies it seems that "what is beautiful is good, and what is ugly is bad." Unfortunately for less attractive children (and adults), support for this general proposition has been obtained in a wide variety of settings: the evaluation of intellectual potential by teachers (Clifford and Walster, 1973), dating choice (e.g., Berscheid, Dion, Walster, and Walster, 1971; Huston, 1973; Murstein, 1972), and even judgments of criminal guilt (Efran, 1974; Landy and Aronson, 1969). There are some limits to the application of this stereotype (Dermer and Thiel, 1975; Sigall and Ostrove, 1975), but its broad area of application cannot help but limit the self-esteem of people who, through no fault of their own, are low in physical attractiveness. Attractiveness, like race and sex, may thus affect self-esteem in ways that cannot easily be countered by internal manipulation of successes and pretensions.

THE PUBLIC SELF: MASK OR REALITY?

In the broadest sense, of course, any of your behavior that is observed by another person is a public expression of your self. The clothes you wear, your posture and body language, your words and how you say them, the actions you perform and the actions you refuse to take—

these are some of the cues that other people will use to try to determine what you are "really" like. Their impressions of you are formed
according to the same principles of social perception (described in
Chapters Three and Four) that apply to your understanding of others.
In this section, however, the emphasis is on the *control* you choose
to exert over the information your actions convey. Are the multiple social selves described by James (1892) merely masks you wear on
different occasions? Or do they all reveal something of the "real you"?
What factors affect your honest disclosure to other people? What are
the consequences of making you "self-conscious," or of making you
anonymous? In trying to answer some of these questions, it will be
useful to distinguish between the normal circumstances of everyday
interaction and the extreme pressures on the social self that are inherent in some less frequent situations.

Concealment and Disclosure in Daily Interaction

Whether it is in the evaluation of an ability, the assessment of an
emotion, or the development of self-esteem, the social context plays
an important role in the characteristics of the self. As we have noted
throughout this chapter, this search for the social self is influenced
at times by a desire for accurate self-appraisal and at times by a
desire for self-enhancement. This conflict can also be seen in the
public behavior of the self and is represented by the distinction between self-presentation (Goffman, 1959, 1967) and self-disclosure
(Jourard, 1964, 1971).

Self-Presentation

Self-presentation, defined as the creation and maintenance of a
public self, occurs in what Goffman (1959, 1967) suggests is a highly
structured and ritualized interaction. As we noted in Chapter Three,
each participant in the interaction brings to it a *line* (view of the
situation and the people involved), a central element of which is the
face (the positive social value the person claims for himself or herself).
This face is essentially a public expression of self-worth, and it is enhanced both by what is revealed and by what is withheld. Making an
analogy to the theater, Goffman suggests that each participant in an
interaction is engaged in a *performance* designed as much for its
effects on the *audience* as it is for honest and open expression of the
self. This is not to say that the person is hypocritical about his or
her performance and face—in fact, the person may really come to
believe in the front being presented (like the politician who is too

busy being a legislator to notice a few campaign irregularities here and there).

Since an individual's face is a public expression of self, he or she has a vested interest in maintaining and enhancing this face. The same is true of all the participants in the interaction, and there is an implicit rule of reciprocity: you help protect and maintain my face, and I will do the same for you, so that neither of us will suffer a loss of face in the interaction. Continuation of the encounter depends upon mutual acceptance of this social contract, as indicated by the nature of the corrective process (the *interchange*) that follows a blunder. Suppose that you and I are discussing a mutual acquaintance, and I suggest that the person is so obnoxious that only equally unpleasant people can stand him. As it happens, you have some of the same reservations about the individual that I do, but despite those reservations you have agreed to take an apartment with the person for the summer. The first step in the interchange is the *challenge*, in which the blunder is brought to the offender's attention (you inform me somewhat icily of your plans). The second step is the *offering*, in which the offender has the opportunity to correct the error (I try to recover by saying that of course I didn't mean *you*, that you will probably be very good for the person). Next (if the interaction is to continue) there is your *acceptance* of my offering, followed by my *thanks* for your graciously letting me recover my face. Unless my original statement was made maliciously (e.g., I had prior knowledge of your plans and was just trying to tar you with the same brush I used on the other person), there is a distinct "We're all in this together; let's try to make the best of a bad situation" character to the interchange.

Self-Disclosure

One of the most striking aspects of Goffman's description of interaction is the degree to which it is a description of social roles rather than of people. The contractual nature of the relationship, the processes of self-presentation or face work, and the interchange that follows a threat to face all remain constant, regardless of who the participants in the interaction might be. No doubt this description is accurate for a wide variety of social settings, and, indeed, it might even be considered "normal" by virtue of its prevalence. But a growing number of psychologists would agree with Jourard (1964) that what is normal may not always be psychologically *healthy*. To support his position, Jourard (1964) draws on his experience as a clinical practitioner, pointing out that much of psychotherapy consists of listening sympathetically to intimate revelations that the client may not have disclosed to anyone else. To share yourself honestly with another human being is to admit your fears and desires, and consequently to know yourself. In contrast, to "play a role" or to hide your real self from others is to provide for yourself an internal stress. According to Jourard (1964), this stress is "subtle and unrecognized, but none the less effective in producing not only the assorted patterns of unhealthy personality which psychiatry talks about, but also the wide array of physical ills that have come to be recognized as the province of psychosomatic medicine" (p. 33).

It should be noted, however, that even Jourard does not encourage us to disclose all our intimate secrets to everyone we meet. Healthy personality only requires complete self-disclosure to at least one other *significant* person—a close friend, a marriage partner, a parent, or, if it comes to that, a therapist. But there can be too much of a good thing. We are embarrassed by someone who describes his or her psychological or medical problems in excessive detail, and we find ourselves wondering whether the person is obtaining some unhealthy gratification from these troubles. Some recent experimental work in self-disclosure (Chaikin and Derlega, 1974; Chaikin, Derlega, Bayma, and Shaw, 1975; Cozby, 1973) lends support to this idea, indicating that too much disclosure, as well as too little disclosure, might be related to faulty psychological adjustment.

What governs the degree of self-disclosure? First consider some of the consistent findings. Jourard (1971) reported in a series of studies that females disclose more to each other than do males, women tend to receive more disclosure than do men, and the amount of information revealed is highly correlated with the amount received. This last phenomenon, designated the dyadic effect by Jourard (1964), is the most consistent result obtained in self-disclosure research (e.g., Altman, 1973; Cozby, 1973; Davis and Skinner, 1974; Derlega, Harris, and Chaikin, 1973; Jourard and Friedman, 1970; Marlatt, 1971; Rubin, 1975; Worthy, Gary, and Kahn, 1969). What do these effects have in common? They all illustrate that the process of self-disclosure, like the process of self-presentation, depends upon the existence of a social *relationship* between the two parties involved. Whether the conversation is between an experimenter and a person waiting for a plane at an airport (Rubin, 1975) or between an interviewer and an interviewee (Davis and Skinner, 1974; Jourard and Jaffe, 1970), self-disclosure implies the same sort of mutual commitment found in the maintenance of face.

At this juncture it is difficult to say with any assurance just how much of everyday social interaction is myth and how much is reality. What is most intriguing is that both seem to require mutual commitment and reciprocity. If you commit a social blunder that threatens your face, only my commitment to continuation of the interaction leads me to help you try to restore your position in the ritual. But if we are to get to know each other better, our commitment to that goal requires some honest self-disclosure. A great deal of our interpersonal behavior is specified by the roles that we play, and, as we shall see in the next section, those roles can have powerful effects on our behavior that simply would not be possible if we were "pretending." But just as a great deal of our behavior can be characterized in role terms, *changes* in the depth of a relationship probably will not occur in the absence of self-disclosure. Strangers become acquaintances and acquaintances become friends through mutual sharing of aspirations and anxieties, through the revelation of an increasing amount of previously concealed material. Friendship develops by adding reality without completely destroying myth.

Unusual Situations for the Self

The everyday interaction of the self is, as we have seen, a mixture of role and real self. Even in the most superficial self-presentation, the individual must focus enough attention on his or her true characteristics to ensure that undesirable material does not inadvertently slip out. Similarly, even in the most real and honest self-disclosure there must be some minimal awareness of role requirements helping to direct that disclosure toward good friends (or complete strangers) rather than toward casual acquaintances. Thus in most circumstances there is some degree of balance between self-awareness and role awareness. But there are other cases in which self-consciousness can be increased to an uncomfortable level (giving a report to a large class, meeting your steady date's parents for the first time, participating in some forms of encounter groups), and cases in which individuality can be all but destroyed (being in a mass demonstration, working in an office which has rows of identical desks almost as far as the eye can see, going to prison). What happens to public behavior of the self under these circumstances?

Objective Self-Awareness

First let us consider the case of increased attention to the self. Suppose one of your professors asks you to make a report to the class on a topic of importance. You read the material in advance, take voluminous notes, outline what you are going to say, maybe even practice your talk on some good friends, but when the time comes you cannot help but be nervous. You are afraid you will say something stupid, or boring, or worse, and you don't know how you will ever make it through the whole class period. According to a recent theory by

Duval and Wicklund (1972), your discomfort is the result of objective self-awareness—heightened recognition of your self as a social object. In a sense you join the audience and evaluate your own performance even as you are giving it. This idea of objective self-awareness is obviously an extension of the symbolic interactionists' conception of the looking-glass self, except that there is one added ingredient. In the case of the looking-glass self your emotional reaction of pride or shame is based on your imagination of the evaluations of *other* people; in the case of objective self-awareness what is important is your *own* evaluation of yourself. Other people are not even necessary. In fact, many of the studies of objective self-awareness simply use the presence or absence of a mirror as the experimental manipulation (e.g., Carver, 1974; Duval and Wicklund, 1973; Ickes, Wicklund, and Ferris, 1973; Scheier, Fenigstein, and Buss, 1974).

Why should your own response to your self be a critical one? After all, you are thought to have control over the level of your pretensions, and other people have at least some favorable things to say about you. There might be several reasons. First, you know your shortcomings much better than do the outside observers of your behavior (there are some aspects of your self that you do not disclose even to your close friends). Second, although you have control over your pretensions, your private aspirations for your self may follow Festinger's (1954) principle of a unidirectional drive upwards. The pretensions you announce to the public are modest enough so that you have an excellent chance of achieving them, but you might privately have hoped to do even better. Third, nobody is perfect. If you are realistic about your self, you will always be able to find some aspect of your behavior that could be improved. Normally you put these flaws in proper perspective to maintain your self-esteem, but when your attention is forced on your self as a social object this balancing is more difficult to accomplish. As a consequence of objective self-awareness, then, you are likely to be excessively self-critical, taking more of the blame for negative occurrences (Duval and Wicklund, 1973) and expressing a lower self-esteem (Ickes, Wicklund, and Ferris, 1973).

Anonymity and Deindividuation

If objective self-awareness can make you excessively self-critical, anonymity might keep you from being self-critical enough. This possibility has guided social theory about group behavior ever since LeBon (1895) argued that in a crowd a person might entirely lose "conscious personality," causing the person to act "in utter contradiction with his character and habits" (p. 34). We shall return to some of these group dynamics in more detail in Chapter Thirteen. In contrast, the effects of anonymity on the behavior of *individuals* have received much less attention, with Zimbardo (1970) able to conclude that only three earlier accounts (Festinger, Pepitone, and Newcomb, 1952; Singer, Brush, and Lublin, 1965; Ziller, 1964) dealt with the phenomenon that has come to be known as **deindividuation**. As described by Zimbardo (1970), the process of deindividuation consists of a decreased concern for social evaluation (either self-evaluation or the evaluation of the self by other people). This decreased concern for social evaluation can be characterized as a loss of identity, individuality, or distinctiveness, and it is reflected in *lowered restraints* against inappropriate behavior (particularly of a negative or hostile form). Some of the possible antecedents of deindividuation might include anonymity, the diffusion of responsibility for action among a large number of members of a group, and altered states of consciousness produced by drugs, stress, or lack of sleep (Zimbardo, 1970).

The behaviors that follow deindividuation are not only irrational, impulsive, and atypical for the person involved, they must also be *self-reinforcing* in the sense that they are not under the control of discriminative stimuli in the environment. The behavior, once begun, carries through to a conclusion on the basis of its own momentum. An excellent example of a self-reinforcing behavior, cited by Zimbardo (1970) and based on an account by the undersea explorer Jacques Cousteau, is the "dance of death" of killer sharks that have surrounded a passive victim. The sharks circle for hours until one of them takes the first bite. Then all the sharks attack in a fury until there is virtually nothing left of the victim, and if one of the attackers is injured in the melee it, too, becomes a victim. Perhaps some of the popularity of Benchley's (1974) book and the film *Jaws* is based on our fascination with (as well as our horror of) behavior that seems totally out of control.

Deindividuation in human beings does not often produce behavior that even approaches this extreme, although some inner-city riots in the late 1960s, many of the lynchings of blacks in the old South, and some of the actions of political terrorist organizations have had a similar mindless quality to them. More frequently, deindividuation leads to the performance of behaviors that would otherwise be inhibited; to a lack of restraint rather than a complete loss of control. This difference can be seen in many of the studies reported by Zimbardo (1970). For example, in one study groups of undergraduate females were asked to administer electric shock to another woman, ostensibly for the purpose of observing her emotional reactions to stress. Half of the subjects were made anonymous by placing hoods over their heads, while the other half of the subjects were individuated by introducing them to each other and having them wear nametags throughout the course of the experiment. The hooded subjects gave the victim shocks that were, on the average, twice as long as those administered by the other subjects, but, even in the deindividuated (hooded) group the shocks were neither as long, nor as frequent, as was theoretically possible.

In another study a ten-year-old automobile was left without license plates and with its hood up on a New York City street (a "control" automobile in the same condition was left at the same time on a street in Palo Alto, California) and observed continuously for sixty-four hours. The car left in Palo Alto was not disturbed during the observation period. But in New York, different groups of vandals began systematically stripping the abandoned automobile within ten minutes of the researchers' departure. Within thirty-six hours the New York car had become the target of random destruction, but even here the destruction did not begin until *after* all the usable parts had been removed (Zimbardo, 1970). Vandalism, yes, but not an irrational all-consuming destruction beginning with the first act of looting.

DEINDIVIDUATION IN A SIMULATED PRISON. One final example (Haney, Banks, and Zimbardo, 1973) deserves more detailed comment for a number of reasons. Like the preceding studies, it illustrates the extent to which deindividuation can produce undesirable behavior without complete loss of control. More important, it shows that deindividuation can be the consequence not only of anonymity, but also of *the normal performance of a social role*. Finally, since it deals with the effects of imprisonment, it has strong implications for social policy. The subjects were undergraduate males who had volunteered for a two-week psychological study, for which they were to be paid $15 per day. The subjects were informed at the outset that the research was a simulation of a prison environment, and they were prescreened on a variety of psychological tests in order to exclude any individuals who might have had problems that would have been exacerbated by their participation in the study. Half of the remaining twenty-four subjects were randomly assigned to be "prisoners" and half were assigned to be "guards." Only nine prisoners and nine guards took part at any one time; the remainder were on "standby" in case they were needed.

The nine subjects who were to be the first prisoners were arrested at their homes by the local police and were transported without explanation to the city jail, where they were fingerprinted, blindfolded, and placed in holding cells. They were then taken by the experimenters from the jail to a simulated prison, constructed in the basement of one of the academic buildings. Upon their arrival at the "prison" the prisoners were searched, stripped naked, deloused, and issued uniforms which were designed to humiliate them even further. These uniforms consisted of a hospital gown worn without underwear (to make the prisoners feel emasculated), a cap make from a nylon stocking (to remove any individuality of hair style), a heavy chain locked around one ankle (to serve as a constant reminder of the oppressiveness of the environment), and a pair of flip-flop sandals.

The individuality of the guards was also reduced, by providing them with khaki uniforms, nightsticks borrowed from the local police, and reflecting sunglasses which prevented anyone from seeing their eyes. The guards worked three at a time in rotating eight-hour shifts, and they were given no special training for their roles. They were just told to do what was "necessary to maintain law and order" in the prison environment. There was no prearranged schedule of operation, so the three guards on duty at any time had complete authority to establish rules of conduct, kinds of activities that would be permitted, times at which these activities could take place, and punishments for infractions of rules or for displays of "improper attitude."

The first full day passed uneventfully, with the guards beginning to exercise their authority, but on the second day there was a rebellion. The prisoners barricaded themselves in their cells, removed their caps, and taunted the guards. The guards responded by calling in everyone who was off duty and putting down the rebellion by force. Realizing that they could not all continue to serve twenty-four-hour shifts, the guards resorted to psychological tactics to break the prisoners' solidarity. They arbitrarily dispensed special privileges to some prisoners, and as the days passed became increasingly capricious in their administration of the prison, often refusing requests by the prisoners even to go to the bathroom. During the same time, the prisoners were becoming more and more accepting of their total helplessness.

By the sixth day of the study, it had become apparent that not only were the guards and prisoners virtually *living* their randomly assigned roles, but so were the prison superintendent (Zimbardo), the prisoners' relatives (who had been permitted the opportunity to visit), a former prison chaplain who had been invited to evaluate the validity of the simulation, and even an attorney requested by some of the prisoners through the chaplain. The simulation was terminated at this point, and a series of encounter groups was conducted, first among the guards, then among the prisoners, and finally included all the participants in the study. The purpose of these sessions was to try to deal with the changes in themselves that all the participants observed during the course of the simulation. The relationship of master to slave tends to dehumanize both, although in different ways: the guards became part of an oppressive social system, and the prisoners became that system's unprotesting victims.

SIMULATION, ETHICS, AND SOCIAL POLICY. This prison simulation raises some profound ethical and social questions, precisely because of its apparent success at producing deindividuation. Ever since the early stages of research in social psychology there has been disagreement over the ethical justification for various experimental and observational procedures. Many of these problems are discussed in Chapter Two, but a recurring concern (Aronson and Carlsmith, 1968) has been the use of deception to create "experimental realism" for the subjects in research. It has been argued that role playing is an ineffective tool for producing experimental realism (Aronson and Carlsmith, 1968; Freedman, 1969), and the preponderance of opinion at the time Zimbardo and his colleagues conducted their simulation would not have predicted the extremes in behavior that were actually observed. There was no deception in the prison simulation—all participants knew in advance what was planned—but nobody was prepared for the powerful effects on all participants that the roles would have. In retrospect we might be tempted to label the simulation unethical, but we might not have done so in advance. It is the very success of the procedure that gives us pause as researchers.

It is also the success of the simulation that raises serious questions of social policy. There is ample anecdotal evidence to support the assertion that particular roles and particular situations can deindividuate and dehumanize the people involved in them. But because the evidence is primarily anecdotal, it can be dismissed as peculiar either to the individuals or to the times. The results of this simulation, however, like the results of Milgram's destructive obedience research (discussed more fully in Chapter One), refuse to go away. Remember that the participants were *randomly assigned* to their roles of prisoner and guard, precluding any self-selection of a role congruent with personal characteristics. Moreover, none of the personality tests administered in the preliminary screening predicted the extent of the effects observed or the individual differences in behavior that emerged (particularly among the guards). And finally, the whole enterprise had been billed in advance as *research*, a situation (unlike real prison) which any participant could leave at any point. All these factors work against the effectiveness of the simulation. Its results suggest how truly awesome might be the deindividuating effects of a real prison, or for that matter, of any total institution in which a person *becomes* his or her role.

Summary

The self consists of social perceptions, attitudes, personality characteristics, motives, material possessions, and conscious experience, but the aspect of self most important to social psychologists is the way

in which that self interacts with the social environment. We have
multiple social selves (p. 304), each slightly different and each relating
to a different group of other people. We learn to evaluate our social
selves in part by considering the impression we make on others (the
looking-glass self [p. 309]), and our public behavior may depend on
the balance between the roles that we play and the elements of
self that remain constant across situations. In public behavior, as well
as in the course of acquisition of knowledge about the self, there is a
recurrent conflict between pressures toward accuracy and pressures
toward distortion through self-aggrandizement.

The process of self evaluation includes the choice of reference
groups (p. 310) which may set standards for our behavior. These
groups may simply provide us with models of appropriate behavior
(the comparison function [p. 310]), or they may administer rewards
and punishments designed to enforce their standards (the normative
function [p. 310]). On an individual, rather than group, level we
attempt to evaluate our opinions and abilities by engaging in social
comparison (p. 312) with similar others. These comparisons permit us
to find the location of our beliefs and abilities, and provide self-
validation which can enhance self-esteem. In much the same way that
we evaluate our opinions and abilities through social comparison, we
may also assess our emotional states by means of the cognitive labels
(p. 321) provided by the social context. Particularly in novel situations,
our judgments about the degree to which we are physiologically
aroused, or about the source of that arousal, may be susceptible to
influence by the social cues available to us. In some cases experimentally induced *misattribution* (p. 321) of emotional arousal may
have therapeutic value.

The impressions that we have of our self-worth, designated by the
term *self-esteem* (p. 325), will depend on circumstances both within
and beyond our control. One critical aspect of self-esteem is the degree to which our successes in life correspond to the pretensions
(p. 326) we set for ourselves, and this component of self-esteem can
be measured by a comparison between real self (p. 327) and ideal
self (p. 327). We have control over our pretensions, and we can raise
our self-esteem either by increasing our successes or by decreasing
the goals we set for ourselves. There are, however, significant contributors to self-esteem (or lack thereof) that are beyond our direct
control, including the child-rearing practices of our parents and
various of our biosocial attributes such as race, sex, and physical
attractiveness.

The conflict between accuracy and distortion is represented in
the public behavior of the self by the opposing processes of *self-
presentation* (p. 331) and *self-disclosure* (p. 332). Self-presentation

occurs in ritualized interaction in which the major element of interest is the role (p. 332) taken by each individual and maintained by mutual commitment of the group. On the contrary, honest self-disclosure involves the admission of basic desires and fears, and the ability to disclose these to at least one other significant person may be a sign of a healthy (p. 332) (as opposed to normal) personality. In extreme circumstances objective self-awareness (p. 334) can lead to exaggerated self-criticism, while deindividuation (p. 336) can produce a variety of socially undesirable or inappropriate responses.

Suggested Additional Readings

DERLEGA, V. J., and CHAIKIN, A. L. *Sharing intimacy: What we reveal to others and why.* Englewood Cliffs, N.J.: Prentice-Hall, 1975. A short, readable introduction to the area of self-disclosure. Includes sections on disclosure reciprocity, making friends, disclosure in marriage, disclosure in psychotherapy, and the ethics of research in self-disclosure. Less technical than the book by Jourard (1971).

GERGEN, K. J. *The concept of self.* New York: Holt, Rinehart and Winston, 1971. An introduction to some of the theory and research in self-concept. Identifies several critical issues in self theory, traces the development of the self-concept, and outlines some of the relationships between the self and various facets of interpersonal behavior. A good overview of the area.

GORDON, C., and GERGEN, K. J. *The self in social interaction.* Vol. 1. New York: Wiley, 1968. An extensive collection of theory and research on the self, consisting of short chapters. Includes contributions by nearly all the major authorities, and introductory sections by the authors. At times this is quite technical material, but the volume is an excellent resource for interested students.

SCHACHTER, S. *Emotion, obesity, and crime.* New York: Academic Press, 1971. The most recent volume dealing with the cognitive labeling theory of emotion, showing its application to the problems of obesity and the psychological description of repeated offenders. Pretty technical.

ZIMBARDO, P. G. The human choice: Individuation, reason, and order versus deindividuation, impulse, and chaos. In W. J. Arnold and D. Levine (Eds.) *Nebraska symposium on motivation, 1969.* Lincoln: University of Nebraska Press, 1970. Pp. 237–307. A comprehensive report of a program of research on deindividuation, including a theoretical model of the process. Technical in places, but interesting reading. (This report does not include the prison experiment.)

A great deal of interpersonal behavior is learned through imitation of models, rather than through direct trial and error.

Reinforcement and Exchange in Social Behavior
Chapter Nine

As we have noted at several points throughout the book, social psychology is the scientific study of the social behavior of the individual person. Nearly all the material presented up to this point has dealt with psychological processes *within* the individual which influence that social behavior. We have examined social perception (Chapters Three and Four), describing the cues that might be used in the formation of impressions and the perceiver's own contributions to the impressions obtained of other people and their reasons for acting. Next we considered another aspect of the individual—social attitudes—outlining the components of attitudes and suggesting how they are organized and changed (Chapters Five, Six, and Seven). Finally, we turned to the person's evaluation and presentation of the social self (Chapter Eight).

At each stage of this focus on the individual person, we have discussed the theories developed by scientific social psychology to account for the phenomena of interest. And, not surprisingly, the great majority of these theories have been primarily intrapersonal in nature. The integration of perceptual information and the making of dispositional attributions; the formation of attitudes and the maintenance of cognitive consistency; the social comparison of abilities and the cognitive labeling of emotion all involve processes within a single individual. There is very little of a truly *interpersonal* nature in any of these theories, and the social benefits (gains or losses) that may accompany the various processes are of less importance than the manner in which each process is presumed to function. For example, the theory of cognitive dissonance presumes that dissonance is unpleasant and consonance is pleasant, but the major task of the theory is to describe *how* dissonance, once aroused, can successfully be reduced.

But now our focus shifts from the individual to the interpersonal, so the social benefits and costs of action become paramount. The topics to be discussed in the remainder of the book all involve a social exchange among participants: helping and attraction (Chapter Ten), competition and aggression (Chapter Eleven), interpersonal influence (Chapter Twelve), and group processes (Chapter Thirteen). These social exchanges are best described in terms of the rewards achieved and the costs incurred by participants in the exchange. To provide a conceptual framework for most of the remaining material, the present chapter discusses a number of theories based on the general idea of reward and cost. Because it is intended to be a general introduction to principles of social exchange, this chapter concentrates on a single body of theory more exclusively than have any preceding chapters.

THE PRINCIPLE OF REINFORCEMENT

The Hedonistic Calculus and the Law of Effect

Many of the origins of social psychology can be traced to the philosophy of earlier times, and nowhere is this more true than in the case of social exchange. One of the first explanations of human behavior held that people were motivated to seek pleasure and avoid pain. In Western philosophy this principle was represented in the views of Bentham (1789), who devised what he called a hedonistic calculus for analyzing pleasure and pain. Bentham recognized that there could be different sources of pleasure and pain, but he argued that all of these could be characterized with respect to a number of *dimensions* such as duration, intensity, certainty, and extent (will other people be involved in the experience?). There could also be individual differences among people in what they found pleasurable or painful, but the behavioral prediction remained the same: people should act in ways that will maximize their pleasure and minimize their pain.

This doctrine of hedonism was first formally expressed in psychology in the Law of Effect proposed by Thorndike (1898). According to Thorndike, any behavior that led to pleasure would be "stamped in," and any behavior that led to pain would be "stamped out." Behaviors that consistently produced pleasurable consequences would thus be more likely to occur in the future actions of the individual. Thus the *effect* of an action might actually serve as the *cause* of future behavior. And because the effect was observable, it could be used to account for the occurrence of future action without having to assume the existence of any intervening cognitive processes such as "motives" or "expectations." Let's consider a concrete example. Suppose that you are a student in my class, and that early in the term you ask a very perceptive question. If my immediate response is to commend you for your insight (and then to give a satisfactory answer to the question) the frequency with which you ask questions in class would presumably increase. It is assumed that the commendation is pleasurable to you, and that achieving that pleasurable effect will increase the chances of your asking questions in the future. Thorndike would not assume that you "expected" commendations in the future, only that this one commendation had "stamped in" your question-asking behavior.

Modern Behaviorism

Concentration on observable actions and effects is, of course, the hallmark of Skinner's (1953, 1971) behaviorism, but Skinner has taken the argument one step further. He refers to the Law of Effect as the principle of reinforcement, and defines a *positive reinforcer* as any stimulus that increases the probability of an action that it follows. Likewise, a *negative reinforcer* is any stimulus that decreases the probability of the behavior that it follows. Notice that this is a dramatic shift in emphasis from the early doctrine of hedonism. Where Bentham proposed ways to distinguish one subjective experience of pleasure or pain from another such experience, Skinner defined "pleasure" (positive reinforcement) or "pain" (negative reinforcement) solely in terms of its effects on behavior. My commendation for your asking perceptive questions is considered to be positively reinforcing *only* if the frequency of your questions increases.

A number of writers (e.g., Berger and Lambert, 1968; Gergen, 1969; Sahakian, 1974) have noted some major conceptual difficulties with this approach. Foremost among the difficulties is the *circular* character of such a strict definition of reinforcement. What is a positive reinforcer? It is any stimulus that leads to an increase in the probability of the behavior it follows. And why does the probability of an action increase? Because that action has been positively reinforced. There is no means for determining whether a stimulus will be a positive reinforcer apart from observing its effects. This circularity is of only minor importance when one is dealing with animal subjects over which one has virtually complete control, but it presents substantial difficulties when dealing with people. You can give your experimental pigeon almost any single stimulus, observe its behavior, and be relatively certain that any change in the pigeon's actions is a direct result of the stimulus change that you have made. So the question "What is positively reinforcing?" is easy to answer by well-controlled experiments. But if your subject is a human being, you simply do not have sufficient control over that person's environment (and we would hope that you could never exert that degree of control) to be able to say for sure whether the subject's changes in behavior are the result of your manipulation, of some uncontrolled environmental event, or of a change in the subject's willingness to cooperate. Under these circumstances it would seem necessary to include the person's human qualities and capacities in the reinforcement equation. This task has fallen to the social learning theories, to which we now turn.

SOCIAL LEARNING THEORY

Expectancy, Value, and Imitation

Beginning with your earliest experiences as an infant, and continuing through your development into adulthood (and beyond), other people try to influence your social behavior. Your parents try to socialize you by teaching you which interpersonal behaviors are appropriate, which are forbidden, and which depend upon the circumstances. In order to get along with your peers you may have to learn an entirely different set of social rules, and even after you have achieved adulthood you may need to alter your actions in response to increased responsibilities and a changing social climate. In short, through most of your life you will literally be *learning* how to behave. How can we account for this social learning?

If the behavior is one that you have performed before and the only change is one involving the rate at which you emit the action, a modified reinforcement position is sufficient. But even here, social learning theories shy away from the extreme form of behaviorism exemplified by Skinner's views. For example, the social learning theory of Rotter (1954) includes a nonobservable *expectancy* about the likelihood of reinforcement, and a nonobservable *value* of each possible incentive. For example, a business executive's willingness to take a risk for his or her company will depend on both the likelihood of success and the size of the profit that might be achieved. Behavior is determined jointly by expectancy and value. The higher the value of the incentive, and the more certain the expectancy that the reinforcement will be forthcoming, the greater the probability of the action. Here the observable characteristics of the reward are less important than the individual's subjective estimates of value and expectancy. This view takes into account some of the complexity of human social behavior, but it shares with more behavioristic analyses one major deficiency: it cannot adequately account for the emergence of *novel* social behaviors (Bandura and Walters, 1963).

Some of your social behavior can be learned while doing it (the principle behind on-the-job training), and some can be learned through what Skinner would call successive *approximations* (e.g., the transition from a skateboard to water skis to single skiing to surfing). But a great deal of your interpersonal behavior is learned through *imitation* of various models, rather than through direct trial and error. The social learning theory of Bandura and Walters (1963), later extended by Bandura (1971), gives imitation the predominant role. Novel social behaviors are first learned through the observation of models, and these newly learned behaviors are then either strengthened through positive reinforcement or weakened through the absence of reinforcement (or occasionally through negative reinforcement). This sequence of events can be used to explain the acquisition of deviant (socially undesirable) actions, as well as the learning of conforming (socially acceptable) ones.

An Example: Imitation of Aggression

When successive reinforcement leads to gradual change in behavior, Bandura and Walters argue that an observer who imitates the actions of a model will give a more or less complete performance of the action on the very first try. The extent of this mimicry is illustrated in an experiment by Bandura, Ross, and Ross (1963a) which, because of its procedure and subject matter, had social policy implications quite apart from its theoretical significance. The investigators were interested in the modeling of aggression by preschool children as a function of the nature of the model and the way in which aggression was observed. There were three experimental conditions: a Live condition in which the model was an adult and the subject was seated in the same room with the model; a Film condition in which the subjects observed a film of the human model; and a Cartoon condition, also filmed, in which the adult was dressed as a cartoon character. There were two control conditions, one in which there was no model at all and one in which the adult model engaged in nonaggressive activity.

In all the model conditions the model was given a number of toys to play with, including a set of Tinkertoys, a small wooden mallet, and a five-foot inflated plastic "Bobo" doll. This doll has the figure of a clown painted on one side and has a curved and weighted base, so that no matter what is done to it the doll will return to a standing position. There was a ten-minute observation period in each model condition. In the Nonaggressive model condition the live model simply spent all of this time quietly assembling the Tinkertoys. In the three Aggressive conditions (Live, Film, and Cartoon), however, the model spent nine of the ten minutes attacking the Bobo doll. Some of these aggressive actions toward the doll were merely punching and the accompanying verbal aggression ("Pow," "Hit him down"). But because punching was something that the children were likely to do even without any demonstration, a series of distinctive acts of aggression was also included in the model's repertoire. These actions were (1) pushing the Bobo doll onto its back, sitting on top of it, and repeatedly hitting it on the nose; (2) tossing the doll into the air; (3) hitting the doll over the head with the wooden mallet; and (4) kicking the doll around the room.

After observing the model or the film each child in an experimental group was given a frustrating experience in order to instigate the child to aggression. (For the control subjects who did not observe any model, this was the beginning of the experiment.) The child was taken into a room with several very attractive toys and told that he or she could play with them. After a brief period just long enough to let the child get involved with one of these toys, the experimenter changed her mind and said that since these were her very best toys she didn't let just anyone play with them. She then announced that she was going to save them for the other children, and led the child to another room. This room contained a three-foot Bobo doll, a number of other aggressive toys (dart guns, a mallet and peg board), and some nonaggressive toys (crayons and coloring paper, dolls, cars and trucks, and farm animals).

The child remained in this room for a period of twenty minutes (during which time the experimenter sat inconspicuously in a corner) and was observed through a one-way mirror. Behavior was scored according to a number of predetermined categories, but of primary interest to us are the direct imitations of the distinctive aggressive actions previously exhibited by the models. The results strongly supported the social learning predictions, with children in the Aggressive model conditions displaying a large number of responses which exactly duplicated the distinctive actions of the aggressive models. Virtually no such distinctive actions occurred in either the Nonaggressive model condition or the No-model control condition. In addition, the children shown the Nonaggressive model exhibited significantly more behavior characteristic of their subdued model than did children in the No-model control condition. Children in this experiment adopted the behavior of the models they had observed, even though they, themselves, had received no prior reinforcement for these distinctive behaviors. Thus novel responses can be learned simply through observation.

From the standpoint of social policy, it is important to note that there were no differences in the aggressive behavior of the children viewing different sorts of aggressive models. Children who saw the filmed cartoon character and children who saw the filmed human models imitated just as many of the distinctive acts of aggression as did children who had witnessed the live performance of the adult model. This suggests, among other things, that televised acts of aggression (even of the stylized sort found in cartoons) may be imitated by children who have been frustrated in their goal-directed behavior. There is a great deal of controversy over the precise effects of televised violence, however, and we shall postpone further discussion of the policy issues until that controversy has been examined more fully in Chapter Eleven.

The Informational Value of Reinforcement

Although Bandura and Walters (1963) emphasize the role of imitation in the production of novel responses, their social learning theory also rests heavily upon the principle of reinforcement. Once a new response occurs in a person's repertoire, its future prevalence will be determined largely by the reinforcement that it receives. Any behavior, be it prosocial or antisocial, that receives positive reinforcement will be more likely to recur in the future. Consistent with the findings from animal studies of reinforcement schedules, social behaviors that receive only partial, or intermittent reinforcement will show greater increases in strength, and greater resistance to extinction, than will social behaviors that receive continuous positive reinforcement. For example, Cowan and Walters (1963) found that seven-year-old boys who were rewarded every time they hit an automated doll (a continuous schedule of reinforcement) were *less* aggressive in a later free play session than were boys who were rewarded only every sixth time they hit the doll (an intermittent schedule). Bandura and Walters illustrate the importance of intermittent reinforcement with the example of a whining, demanding child: the parent first ignores the unpleasantness but finally attends to the child's request. This intermittent positive reinforcement only serves to strengthen the child's undesirable behavior.

Not only does social learning theory rely upon the principle of reinforcement for the maintenance of social behavior, Bandura and Walters (1963) also extend the concept of reinforcement by demonstrating that it can have *informational* as well as motivational properties. When I commend you for asking perceptive questions in class, I am not only boosting your ego (the motivational function of reinforcement), I am also showing you and the other members of the class that such behavior is socially acceptable (the informational function). Indeed, as far as the other students are concerned, information about what I expect in the classroom is the thing of value in my commendation of you. They learn whether to try to imitate your performance from the reinforcement you receive: if you are rewarded, it is safe for them; if you are punished, they had better refrain from making the same mistakes. This imitation of successful models and tendency not to imitate unsuccessful models has been obtained in a number of studies dealing with the imitation of aggressive responses by children (Bandura, 1965; Bandura, Ross, and Ross, 1963b; Kuhn, Madsen, and Becker, 1967; Walters and Willows, 1968). Thus vicarious reinforcement as well as direct reinforcement can play a part in social learning.

Most of the research accomplished within the framework of social learning theory concentrates on the behavior of children (e.g., Bandura and Perloff, 1967; Bates, 1975; Mischel and Grusec, 1966; Weiner and Dubanowski, 1975) because it is during childhood that the vast majority of social learning occurs. But it would be a mistake to conclude that imitation ceases after a person reaches adulthood. (Consider for example the amount advertisers spend obtaining product endorsements from famous people whose choices we are expected to imitate.) And it would also be a mistake to conclude that the effects of social reinforcements become substantially less pronounced as we get older. We are all susceptible to a little flattery here and there, and we become increasingly aware of the social costs incurred (and the rewards derived) from our relationships with other people. If there is any apparent change from childhood, it is that as adults our imitation of others, and our search for social rewards, becomes more deliberate. This more or less conscious weighing of the social alternatives is at the heart of several theories of interaction.

EXCHANGE THEORY

The fundamental assumption of various theories of social exchange (e.g., Blau, 1968; Homans, 1961; Thibaut and Kelley, 1959) is that in their interpersonal relations, as well as in their own lives, people will seek to maximize their pleasure and minimize their pain. We form friendships on the basis of mutual trust and support, we avoid social entanglements that we believe might be too costly, we join groups that will provide us with personal rewards. The principles of social exchange are most easily described when there are only two people (a *dyad*) involved, so our discussion of social exchange will concentrate on the theory of dyadic interaction developed by Thibaut and Kelley (1959). This theory draws upon the principle of reinforcement and upon aspects of economics and sociology, and it suggests that each participant in an interaction brings along a *repertoire* of possible behaviors that could be performed. The pleasure or pain experienced by each participant will thus depend jointly upon his or her own actions and on the actions of the other person. The theory diagrams the interaction possibilities in the form of a matrix, which can be used to illustrate some of the relationships that are possible. In addition, the theory suggests how each participant might evaluate his or her rewards from the interaction.

The Interaction Matrix

Suppose that I am your employer, and that you have been working for me long enough so that you think it might be time for a raise in your salary, particularly since you have just completed a major piece of work that is important to me and to the company. We meet in the hallway one day, and there are a number of different behavioral possibilities for each of us. For my part, I can choose to say something about your work or I can ignore it; I can give you a pleasant greeting, ask you about your family, say a brusque hello, or even just grunt as I walk by. Your possible behaviors are a bit more limited. If you are really interested in a raise, you can't afford to be openly hostile to me, nor can you appear to be obsequious. You might just say hello, you could ask my advice on a problem, or you could come right out and ask me for a raise. Some of these possibilities are diagramed in the interaction matrix shown in Figure 9-1.

In the diagram I am person A (the Superior) and you are person B (the Employee). My behaviors are referred to as a_1 (Cheery Greeting), a_2 (Compliment on Work), and a_3 through a_n (the complete set of remaining actions that I could take). Your alternatives are b_1 (Request Advice), b_2 (Request Raise), and b_3 through b_k (the complete set of remaining actions that you could take). The final subscripts are different (a_n as opposed to b_k) to indicate that the number of alternatives open to one participant may not be the same as the number of alternatives open to the other person. Each cell of the resulting matrix represents a specific interaction outcome. For example, in cell a_1b_1 I could give you a Cheery Greeting and you could Request Advice; in Cell a_1b_2 you could think that my good humor made me approachable for a raise.

Costs, Rewards, and Goodness of Outcomes

Let us take a closer look at just the first two possible actions for each of us (the four interaction cells a_1b_1, a_1b_2, a_2b_1, and a_2b_2). Exchange theory assumes that each action, whether it be one of yours or one of mine, has associated with it a certain cost, and some reward.

FIGURE 9-1
The matrix of interaction possibilities. (Adapted from Thibaut and Kelley, 1959, p. 14)

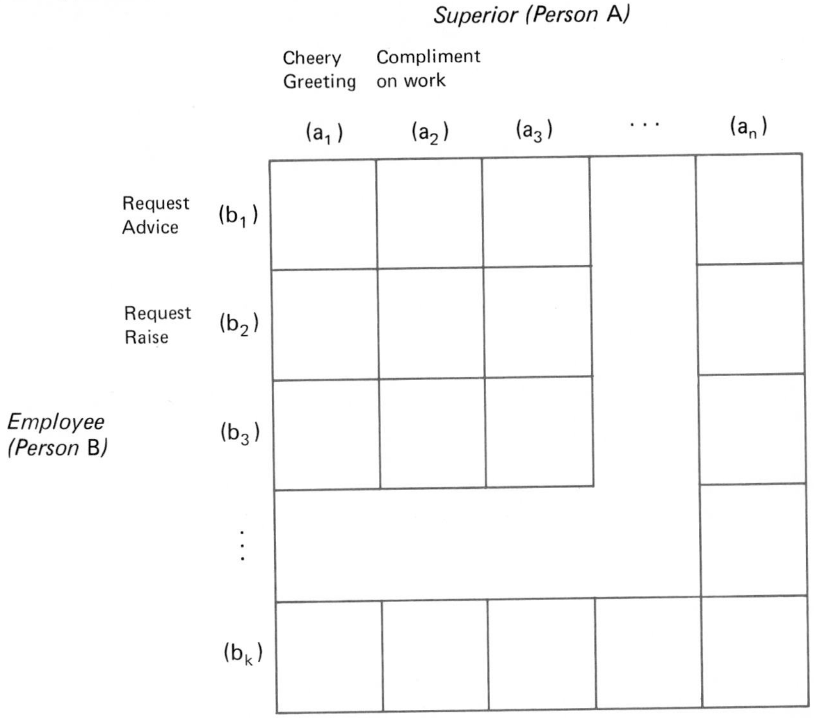

The *cost* of an action will include the pure physical effort involved in performing the action, the time it takes to perform the action, and the social cost that might accrue as a result of the action. The *physical* cost of an action to one person will remain virtually the same regardless of the behavior of the other person, but the *social* cost may change as a consequence of the other's behavior. For example, I expend the same amount of physical effort, and take the same amount of time, to compliment you on your work whether you respond by asking for advice or by asking for a raise. But the social cost to me is much greater in the latter case. I have committed myself to a high evaluation of your worth to the company, and I am thus in a bad position to argue that you do not deserve the raise you request. Costs of a behavior may change over time, as a result of physical fatigue or as a consequence of a social analog of fatigue: your request for advice may be a pleasant consultation the first time or two, but if you keep it up I will think you incapable of accomplishing anything without being led by the hand.

Just as every behavior has some cost, each also leads to some *reward*. But unlike the costs, the rewards are almost entirely determined by the behavior of the other person. There is some intrinsic reward—no matter whether I give a cheery greeting or a compliment, I can enhance my self-esteem by thinking of myself as a forthright and pleasant executive—but the effects of this self-administered pat on the back can be dramatically outweighed by your behavior. I will be rewarded by your asking for advice, while a request for a raise will give me no reward whatsoever. Rewards can change over time, usually decreasing with the repetition of an action. For me to compliment you once indicates that I have been paying close attention to your work, while for me to repeat my congratulations every time we meet suggests to you that I am routinely doling out praise that may have very little to do with your actual performance.

Exchange theory assumes that both costs and rewards can be quantified in terms of whatever units of measurement are appropriate for the relationship. To illustrate the computations, let us assume for the moment that my complimenting you might cost me 5 such units if all you did was ask for advice, but it might cost me 25 units if you then asked for a raise. In the same way, if you were asking advice you might obtain a reward of 6 units from my cheery greeting, but you might get a reward of 10 units from my compliment. In each behavioral instance the cost of producing the action is subtracted from the reward obtained in order to arrive at the goodness of the outcome, or the profit for the action. A complete set of hypothetical rewards, costs, and resulting profits is shown in Figure 9–2 for the four interaction possibilities. In each cell the numbers *above* the diagonal line refer to the outcomes of Person A (in this example the Superior), while the numbers *below* the diagonal line in each cell refer to the outcomes of Person B (the Employee). It should be noted that the costs (C), rewards (R), and profits (P) shown in the diagram have been arbitrarily set for purposes of illustration. In actual fact the specific numbers might be quite difficult to determine.

Win-Stay, Lose-Change

What sort of implications does this diagram have for the course of our interaction together? Suppose that the first time we meet in the hall I compliment your work and you immediately ask for a raise (cell a_2b_2). Your profit from that interchange is +5, but my "profit" is in fact a *loss* of −30. You will probably never receive another compliment from me for any reason. I have lost, so I will change my behavior. On the other hand, you receive a positive outcome (+5), so you

FIGURE 9-2
*Rewards (R), Costs (C), and Profits (P) in a hypothetical inter-
action between an Employee and a Superior.*

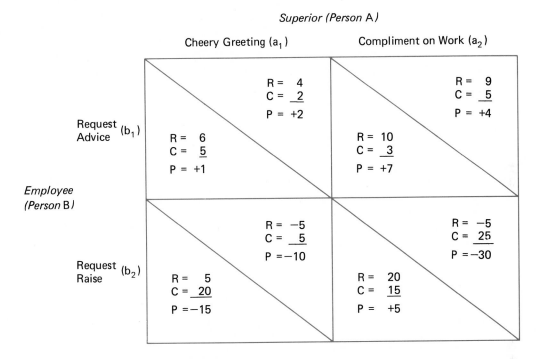

are likely to repeat your request the next time we meet, even though
I only give you a cheery greeting (cell a_1b_2). This time we both lose.
You decide that I am not going to give you a raise, no matter what
the circumstances, so you drop that behavioral option. I decide that
you have some compulsion to request raises, regardless of what I do,
so I might as well give you deserved compliments (since I have no
intention of granting your request for a raise). The consequence of
these choices by the two of us is to move the interaction into cell
a_2b_1, where it will remain because of the positive profits we both
receive from that relationship. This general principle of behavioral
movement is called the win-stay, lose-change rule. Any action that
leads to a positive outcome will be repeated, while any action that
leads to a negative outcome will be changed. The relationship will
stabilize in a cell which consistently offers positive profits to both
participants. Notice that this win-stay, lose-change rule is to an interaction between two people what the principle of reinforcement is to
the behavior of a single individual. Mutually rewarding actions will

be "stamped in," while cells that punish either participant will be "stamped out."

In the interaction matrix shown in Figure 9-2 there are obviously four possible places where the relationship could begin (the four cells). Three of these (a_1b_2, a_2b_1, and a_2b_2) all lead to the final outcome described above, a settlement on a_2b_1. There is, however, one other possibility. If we begin our interaction with a Cheery Greeting and a Request for Advice (a_1b_1) we both obtain positive outcomes, and we might become "stuck" in that cell, never realizing that other more mutually profitable alternatives exist. Although in real life this is certainly a possibility (as when you and a friend both incorrectly assume that the other would not enjoy an activity—"I didn't know you liked _____"), it is minimized by the fact that there is usually considerable *sampling* of various interaction alternatives at the beginning of a relationship.

Evaluation of Outcomes

Two Different Standards

We have examined the computation of rewards, costs, and profits in a relationship, and we have seen the effects that these profits have on the selection of mutually agreeable patterns of interaction. A traditionally "behavioristic" analysis would simply end here, satisfied that a description of the behavior would be a sufficient explanation of the interaction. But the exchange theory goes one step further to suggest how you might *feel* about your outcomes in a relationship. According to Thibaut and Kelley (1959), there are two different standards against which a person can evaluate the *outcomes* (profits or losses) from a relationship. The first of these standards is the comparison level (CL), defined as the average value of all the outcomes known to the person, each weighted by its momentary salience. In the course of your experience you have participated in a wide variety of relationships, with parents, friends, co-workers, teachers, and numerous other people. The exchange theory asserts that you ought to be able to quantify the outcomes obtained from these relationships and use that average value as a standard against which to compare your present outcomes. The addition of the phrase "each weighted by its momentary salience" indicates that when you are judging a particular relationship, the comparison level will be based only on the experiences you consider relevant. For example, your interactions with your professors would properly be compared to experiences with teachers (and perhaps other authority figures), but might not properly be compared to interactions with good friends. The comparison level can change over time—as your general level of outcomes improves (or declines) so does your comparison level— and it can be specific to the sort of situation as well as to the people involved. Singing songs around a campfire on a beautiful evening in the mountains may or may not be comparable to singing in other places and at other times.

The second standard against which outcomes can be evaluated is called the **comparison level for alternatives** (abbreviated CL_{alt}) and is defined as the level of outcomes prevailing in the best currently available alternative to the present relationship. Here the standard for comparison is not a weighted average of other salient possibilities, but rather is simply the level that could be attained in *any* alternative to the present relationship, regardless of whether that alternative was the same sort of experience. These alternatives include the alternative of solitude, as well as relationships that include other people. When you are sitting in a lecture hall on a sunny spring day, the CL may well be based on other lectures, but the CL_{alt} may be going to the beach. Thus you might choose to cut a lecture that would, by a different standard, ordinarily have been considered quite good.

The Nature of the Relationship: Attraction and Dependence

The nature of the relationship will depend on the relative positions of the two comparison levels and your outcomes, as shown in Table 9-1. When your outcomes are better than both your comparison level (CL) and your comparison level for alternatives (CL_{alt}) we might describe your attitude toward the relationship as one of Contentment. This will be a stable relationship not only because it will be seen as positive (better than CL), but also because it is better than anything else that is available. The next possibility shown has your outcomes higher than your CL, but *lower* than your CL_{alt}, and we have chosen to characterize your attitude toward this relationship as one of Pleasure. You will enjoy the interaction, but it might be unstable because of the other attractive possibilities also available. Whenever your outcomes exceed your CL, as they do in both Contentment and Pleasure, Thibaut and Kelley say that *attraction* to the relationship will be the result.

The next possibility is not so pleasant. When your outcomes are below your CL but still above your CL_{alt}, Thibaut and Kelley assert that you will feel *dependence* upon the relationship. It does not live up to your expectations, but it is much better than whatever else is available to you. For example, this is the sort of situation confronting a person who does not like his or her job. The person can't be

TABLE 9-1

Nature of the bond to a relationship as a function of the Comparison Level (CL), the Comparison Level for Alternatives (CL_{alt}), and the goodness of outcomes

	NATURE OF THE BOND TO THE RELATIONSHIP			
	ATTRACTION		DEPENDENCE	
	CONTENTMENT (STABLE)	PLEASURE (UNSTABLE)	(STABLE)	DISSATISFACTION (UNSTABLE)
Goodness of Outcomes →	Outcomes	CL_{alt}	CL	CL, CL_{alt}
		Outcomes	Outcomes	
	CL, CL_{alt}	CL	CL_{alt}	Outcomes

Adapted from Thibaut and Kelley, 1959, pp. 24–25, and Swensen, 1973, pp. 228–229.

happy with it, but even as bad as it is, it is better than no job at all (or than other worse jobs that might be available). It should be noted that this condition of dependence is quite stable and could not be explained by a simple reinforcement theory which considered only the outcomes presently being experienced. These outcomes are negative, and by themselves ought to destroy the relationship. They do not do so only because the other alternatives are even worse. But to take into account those other alternatives requires some *cognitive* mechanism not found in the extreme behaviorism of some reinforcement theories (such as Skinner's). Thus the idea of the comparison level for alternatives—like the idea of the informational value of vicarious reinforcement found in social learning theory—is a significant addition to the basic principle that people will try to maximize their gain. They will, but they will also try to minimize their losses.

The last possibility shown in Table 9-1 is what we have chosen to characterize as an attitude of Dissatisfaction. In this case the interaction is highly unstable (indeed, it is about to be ended), because the person finds that the outcomes from the relationship are far below *both* his or her comparison level and the comparison level for alternatives. There is no attraction to the relationship, and no dependence upon it, so it will quickly be terminated.

To conclude our discussion of the evaluation of outcomes, let us return to the encounter between the Superior and the Employee. Of the four possibilities for interaction depicted in Figure 9-2, the most likely outcome will be the cell a_2b_1, since it is the natural outcome of three of the four beginnings. In this Compliment-Advice cell the Superior achieves an outcome (profit) of +4, while the Employee achieves an outcome (profit) of +7. How should these outcomes be judged? For purposes of evaluating any given interaction, Thibaut and Kelley suggest that the CL can be assumed to be *near zero*. Remember that the CL is the average value of all of the outcomes known to the person (which are salient at the time). Some of these outcomes will have been good (a positive sign) and some will have been bad (a negative sign), with the overall average approximating zero. Since there are changes in the CL which reflect both the salience of past relationships and the passage of time (overall improvement or decline in typical outcomes), the absolute value of the CL will not be exactly zero. But for the purpose of evaluating any specific interaction the question is still "How much better [more positive] or worse [more negative] is *this* interaction than the relationships to which I am accustomed?" The most faithful numerical representation of this question requires setting the CL to approximately zero. Thus, in the example both the Employee and the Superior are receiving outcomes that are above CL in cell a_2b_1. So long as they continue that joint interaction pattern (within the limits of fatigue), we would expect them both to continue to be attracted to the relationship.

Correspondence of Outcomes

The Compliment-Advice cell of Figure 9-2 represents a profit for both the Employee and the Superior, while the Greeting-Raise cell (a_1b_2) represents a substantial loss for each participant. In each of these cases the outcomes achieved by the Employee correspond to the outcomes achieved by the Superior, and although the actual values are much less, the same correspondence can be seen in the Greeting-Advice cell (a_1b_1). Imagine, for a moment, that the interaction matrix were extended to include a large number of behaviors by each of the participants. We could then examine all the cells of the matrix to determine how the profits of one person are related to the profits of the other. If over a broad range of behaviors the two participants either gain together or lose together, their relationship would be described as one of high correspondence of outcomes. High correspondence of outcomes can be seen in helping relationships that call for reciprocation of favors, and in friendship development and mutual attraction when each participant's gains are accompanied by the gains of the other participant. We shall return to these situations in Chapter Ten.

But what about the one exceptional cell in Figure 9-2? In this Compliment-Raise cell (a_2b_2) the Employee gains, but the Superior loses. If the matrix were extended and the large majority of cells followed this pattern, we would say that the relationship was characterized by a very *low* correspondence of outcomes. In the language of game theory (Luce and Raiffa, 1957), low correspondence of outcomes is at best a mixed-motive game: a game in which the most favorable outcome carries the greatest risk. In such a game each participant must choose between maximizing immediate gain and minimizing long-term losses. When there is perfect *non-correspondence* of outcomes, the situation is described as a zero-sum game: whatever gains the one participant achieves are obtained at the expense of the other participant. To illustrate these differences, consider the case of a star NBA basketball player. No matter how well that individual can play, he cannot beat the other team singlehandedly. Therefore he depends upon the cooperation of his four teammates, and to receive their cooperation he must at least some of the time be a "team player." So within his own team, his situation is a mixed-motive game. He can make those fantastic plays that have earned him his reputation as a star only if his teammates will pass the ball to him at the critical moment. In order to compete (be the best player on his team) he must also cooperate. Although the star player has mixed motives toward his teammates, his motives toward the opposition are purely competitive. Because, as any number of famous coaches will tell you, there can be only one winning team. Athletic contests, like poker games and many social relationships, are zero-sum games. There is a winner whose victory is achieved at the expense of those who lose. These competitive social relationships will be discussed more fully in Chapter Eleven.

By assuming that costs, rewards, and the resulting outcomes can be quantified, exchange theory adds to the principle of reinforcement and permits us to (a) predict the course of a relationship (through the win-stay, lose-change rule), (b) assess each participant's attraction to, and dependence upon, the relationship, and (c) describe interactions as primarily cooperative or primarily competitive. Various features of the Thibaut and Kelley (1959) model of social exchange have received experimental support, including the win-stay, lose-change rule (Kelley, Thibaut, Radloff, and Mundy, 1962), some of the attitudinal effects of the magnitude of the CL (Friedland, Arnold, and Thibaut, 1974), and the prediction of cooperation and competition (Rabinowitz, Kelley, and Rosenblatt, 1966). The theoretical model has been used to account for features of social power (Schopler, 1965) and group problem solving (Kelley and Thibaut, 1969), and its implications for cooperation and competition will also be seen in later chapters.

For our purposes, however, there is one gap in the exchange model. All the standards that a person uses in order to assess his or her satisfaction with, or dependence upon, a relationship are drawn from personal experience. Both the CL and the CL_{alt} are internal standards of comparison against which the interpersonal outcomes from interaction are measured. This does not make the exchange theory any less interpersonal, since the outcomes being evaluated are produced by interaction, and since the consequences of satisfaction and dependence are, themselves, interpersonal consequences. But it can in some cases reduce the predictive value of the theory. For example, if your outcomes exceed your CL and your CL_{alt}, you ought to be Content (see Table 9-1). But what if the *other* person involved in the interaction is getting even greater rewards from it than you are? Will surpassing your own standards be sufficient for happiness? Probably not. You may well be dissatisfied because you think that, pleasant as the interaction is, you are not benefitting from it nearly as much as is the other participant. In short, one of the elements in your judgment of satisfaction is a social comparison of your outcomes with the outcomes of the other person, and there is no provision in exchange theory for this comparison. Such comparisons are the subject matter for the theories to which we now turn.

FAIRNESS IN SOCIAL EXCHANGE

A common observation among professors is that there are only two categories of students who complain about their grades on examinations—those who flunk and those who just missed getting an A. In fact the latter group is usually more vocal. It is easy to understand the position of the students who have failed, since failing grades are usually below both CL and CL_{alt} and have serious implications for continuation in school as well. But most exchange theories have difficulty explaining the strong reactions of the other dissatisfied students. Even though grade averages continue to rise in most colleges and universities, a grade of B is not yet a "bad" grade, so what is the basis for complaint? First let us consider the idea of distributive justice.

The Principle of Distributive Justice

Relative Deprivation

If you question one of the students who is complaining about receiving a B, the first explanation you get for dissatisfaction is the difficulty of gaining admission to graduate schools. There is also a bit of the "undirectional drive upward" entering into the student's social comparison of his or her abilities (see Chapter Eight). But if you probe a little further, you discover that part of the student's objection is based on the fact that his or her outcome (the B) is the same as the outcome received by other people in the class, many of whom put far less into the course. The "high B" is psychologically different from the "low B," but this difference is not reflected in the final grade on the transcript. The student believes that the rewards have not been dispensed in a manner that is proportional to the effort involved.

This social comparison of rewards and effort first came to the attention of social psychologists through the large-scale study by Stouffer and his associates of American troops during World War II (Stouffer, Suchman, DeVinney, Starr, and Williams, 1949). These investigators reported that men in the Army Air Corps were much less satisfied with opportunities for promotion than were men in the Military Police. What is surprising is that the promotions in the Air Corps were extremely fast, while promotions in the Military Police were very slow. Why should the Air Corps troops have been unhappy with objectively better outcomes? Stouffer and his colleagues attributed this inconsistency to what they called *relative deprivation*. In the Air Corps, the rapid rate of promotion led to a high expectation of promotion, so any man who was not promoted felt deprived relative to other members of the unit. It was not a man's objective standing, but rather his standing in relation to his peers that was important.

Profits and Investments

At another level, the issue can be drawn in terms of the fairness with which the available rewards were dispensed. But what is meant by "fairness"? According to Homans (1961), the principal criterion for determining the fairness of a distribution of rewards ought to be the *investments* made by each party in an interaction. In his elaboration of the idea of relative deprivation, Homans argued that **distributive justice** would obtain in a relationship between two people (A and B) when

$$\frac{A's\ profits}{A's\ investments} = \frac{B's\ profits}{B's\ investments}$$

A person's investments include age, experience, education, interpersonal skills, and active contributions to the interaction. Profits are determined by subtracting costs (time, money, effort, and so forth) from rewards, as was the case in Thibaut and Kelley's (1959) exchange theory. Notice that the person's costs are not necessarily the same as his or her investments. If you and I spend an hour talking about social psychology, I may feel that distributive justice requires that my profits be greater than yours. The cost to each of us (say, in time) is the same, but my investments in social psychology are greater than yours, and those investments need to be compensated by higher rewards in order to achieve distributive justice.

The principle of distributive justice has been extended to include relationships between more than two parties (Homans, 1961), such as the triad consisting of two employees and an employer. The two workers compare their investments in the company against the salaries they are paid to see whether they are being treated fairly. In this case, the difference between costs and investments becomes even clearer. For example, each worker may spend exactly the same time, and exactly the same effort, to produce the same amount of the company's product. But the worker with seniority will be dissatisfied if his or her investment of previous years is not reflected in salary. In all these cases of distributive *injustice*, it is clear that the party who feels unfairly treated will be dissatisfied with the relationship, but as Adams (1965) points out, the principle of distributive justice makes few predictions about the behavior that might be undertaken in order to remedy the injustice. To make such predictions, Adams combined the principle of distributive justice with some features of cognitive dissonance theory (Festinger, 1957, discussed in Chapter Six) to develop what he called an *equity* theory of social exchange.

Equity Theory

Recognition and Relevance of Inputs

Whereas the principle of distributive justice concentrates on a condition of equality between two participants in a social exchange,

Adams (1965) and later writers as well (e.g., Walster, Berscheid, and Walster, 1973) have focused on the antecedents and consequences of *inequity*. In his discussion of equity theory, Adams (1965) adopted the general formula presented by Homans (1961) suggesting that a condition of equity between participants in an interaction obtains when each person's outcomes are proportional to his or her inputs:

$$\frac{\text{A's Outcomes}}{\text{A's Inputs}} = \frac{\text{B's Outcomes}}{\text{B's Inputs}}$$

In this expression, Outcomes are equivalent to Profits in the distributive justice principle, and Inputs are equivalent to Investments. There is, however, a more psychologically based description of the Inputs. Whereas Homans (1961) treated all investments in the same terms, whether or not they were *recognized* by the participants and whether or not they were considered *relevant* to the exchange, Adams (1965) distinguished among Inputs on these two grounds. Any attribute—experience, race, attractiveness, sex, possession of certain tools, interpersonal skills, age, seniority—that is recognized by either party in an interaction has the potential to become an Input. But some of these Inputs will be relevant to the exchange at hand, while some will not. And the presence or absence of perceived inequity may depend as much upon the degree of agreement about the relevance of an Input as it does on the actual value of an Outcome.

For example, many industries used to discriminate against blacks and other minorities in terms of hiring, salary, and promotion. Passage of the civil rights laws and issuance of later governmental regulations on affirmative action then changed the balance, by suggesting preferential treatment for minorities in order to redress past injustices. This policy works reasonably well when there is full employment, but what happens in a recession? If an employer follows the usual rule of "last hired—first fired," minority workers will believe that they are being inequitably treated, but if the employer tries to maintain the level of minority employees, the workers with seniority will feel inequitably treated. The issue is not whether layoffs are necessary in hard economic times, but rather whether "being a victim of past discrimination" is a *relevant* input. Workers with seniority claim, of course, that seniority alone is the relevant input, while minority workers argue that past discrimination is also relevant.

Consequences of Inequity

In addition to distinguishing between relevant and irrelevant inputs, Adams (1965) outlines the behavioral consequences of perceived inequity. When you receive outcomes that are proportionally too small for your inputs, you will experience a psychological tension (usually labeled as "anger"), and this tension will lead you to try to remove the inequity. Similar tension ("guilt") will be aroused if the rewards you receive are proportionally too great for your inputs, although in this case the tension will be mitigated somewhat by the pleasure of maximizing your own outcomes. If this use of an internal state of tension to account for a person's reactions to a situation in the environment (inequity) sounds familiar to you, it should. Adams patterned his model after cognitive dissonance (Festinger, 1957), and as we saw in Chapter Six, dissonance is an internal state that is presumed to have motivating properties.

How can the internal tension arising from inequity be resolved? Adams suggests several different possibilities: (1) changing your own inputs or outcomes, (2) acting on the other person to change his or her inputs or outcomes, (3) choosing a different person for comparison, (4) cognitively distorting your inputs or outcomes, or those of the comparison person, and (5) leaving the field entirely.

The Case of Underpayment

Let us consider how each of these mechanisms might work in the case of *under*payment. Suppose that you are working for me. You compare your salary with that of some of my other employees, and this comparison suggests to you that you are being discriminated against. The first possibility is for you to reduce your inputs, by producing less work on the job, by increasing your absenteeism, or even by sabotaging some of the products you have access to. Next you might try to increase your outcomes, by padding your expense account or by pilfering from my supplies. (It is interesting to note in this connection that the large majority of shoplifting is done by the *employees* of the businesses affected.) If you cannot alter your own inputs or outcomes, you might try to get the comparison person(s) to restore equity by working harder themselves. If none of the behavioral alternatives succeeds in redressing the balance, you might distort either your own inputs or outcomes, or the inputs or outcomes of others. For example, you might be able to convince yourself that although your salary may not be high enough, you could not easily find another job that provided you with such pleasant working conditions. If these tactics fail, you might search for a different comparison group, but Adams suggests that this alternative is a very difficult one to take. Finally, your last resort is to remove yourself from the inequitable situation by finding a job in which you feel fairly compensated.

A number of field studies in businesses (Homans, 1953; Jacques, 1961) and laboratory experiments (Austin and Walster, 1974; Leventhal, Weiss, and Long, 1969; Thibaut, 1950) indicate that people will take direct action to increase their rewards if they believe they are being underpaid. As an example, in 1975 the firefighters of Kansas City, Missouri, went out on strike demanding to have their salary scale equated with the salaries paid to police officers in the same city. All these examples are consistent with Adams's (1965) model, but do we really need the concept of equity in order to explain them? Why not simply say that underpayment creates dissonance (or even "anger"), and it is *this* state, rather than a tension presumed to arise from inequity, which accounts for the reactions? What we have here is another case in which two different theories make exactly the same prediction. Is the second theory really necessary?

The Case of Overpayment

You may remember from Chapter Six that this is the same sort of question which arose in the initial stages of the controversy between cognitive dissonance theory and self-perception theory for the case of insufficient justification. People who performed counterattitudinal actions for small rewards could have changed their attitudes in order to reduce dissonance, or they could have taken their behavior (as well as their internal reactions to the task) into account and perceived their attitudes to be more positive than we would have expected them to be. There the explanatory value of self-perception became clearest in the case of *over*sufficient justification, which presumably should have produced no cognitive dissonance. The same is true for equity theory. In the case of underpayment, both dissonance and inequity might lead to attempts to redress the imbalance. But overpayment should create only inequity, not dissonance. And since we would need a concept similar to inequity in order to account for the reduction of imbalance generated by overpayment, it is more parsimonious to let the same concept apply to the situation of underpayment as well.

In part because the concept of inequity applies more convincingly to cases in which the person is *better off* than those with whom he or she compares, most of the research conducted within the framework of equity theory has dealt with overpayment (Adams, 1965; Walster, Berscheid, and Walster, 1973). To use a typical illustration, suppose that you were asked to work with a partner on a task for which the two of you were to receive a monetary reward. The amount of the reward would depend upon the total amount of work completed by the two of you together, although you were to work independently on the task. After you have completed your part of the task, and without reuniting you with your "partner" (who is really an experimental confederate), the experimenter informs you of how much you have contributed to the team effort. Specifically, you are told either that you have provided 65 percent of the team's total, or that you have provided 35 percent, with the remainder in each case being the contribution of your partner. Then the experimenter tells you that you have randomly been chosen to divide the team's earnings ($2.05) between you and your partner. The crucial question is, how much do you take for yourself?

When Leventhal and Michaels (1969) actually performed such an experiment, they discovered that subjects would allocate earnings in proportion to their own perceived inputs (their contribution to the outcome). Subjects who thought that they had contributed only 35 percent of the outcome took less reward for themselves than did subjects who believed they had contributed 65 percent of the outcome. Thus the subjects tried to make their rewards consistent with their inputs, as equity theory would predict. There is some controversy (Shapiro, 1975) over whether the results of such *reward allocation* studies reflect a drive toward equity or a desire for equality, but predictions from equity theory have been supported in a number of different contexts as well. For example, when subjects are overpaid for a task, they try to work harder than if they have been fairly paid, or underpaid (Adams, 1963; Adams and Jacobsen, 1964). This is an adjustment of inputs, rather than outcomes, but the purpose is still the maintenance of equity.

Equity and Exploitation

In all the examples we have considered so far, both the person who is evaluating the equity of the relationship (referred to as Person), and the person or group used for comparison purposes (referred to as Other) have had their outcomes determined by some third party. This is obviously the case in most business organizations, where only a few people have the power to set their own salaries. The remainder of the workers and managers compare the salaries they are given with the salaries and wages received by their fellows. It is also the case in most experimental settings. If the dependent variable is reward allocation, the experimenter arbitrarily establishes each subject's inputs, and if the dependent variable is alteration of input, the experimenter establishes the rewards provided (in order to produce conditions of perceived underpayment or overpayment). And finally, the equity model originally proposed by Adams (1965) also emphasizes the case in which one recipient of benefits compares those rewards with the outcomes of another recipient.

Recently, however, the equity model has been extended to include cases in which Person has *produced* the outcomes of Other (Walster, Berscheid, and Walster, 1973). Included in this category are instances in which the Person is an exploiter and the Other is exploited (the harm-doer and the victim), and instances in which the Person is a helper and the Other is a recipient of that help. Consider, for example, the harm-doer and the victim. The theory holds that a harm-doer will feel tension from producing the harm, and this will lead to an attempt to restore equity. This attempt at equity restoration can take the form of compensation (returning the victim to his or her former state, or providing restitution for his or her losses), or it can take the psychological tack of reducing the victim's inputs by asserting that for some reason the victim deserved to suffer. We shall return to a more detailed consideration of these attempts at equity restoration in the discussion of altruism and helping behavior (Chapter Ten). For now it is sufficient to note that equity theory makes the same predictions about the removal of inequity regardless of whether it was originally brought about by the Person or by some third party.

Equity theory represents a further step in the application of reinforcement principles to social interaction. It assumes, as do social learning theory and exchange theory, that people will try to maximize their interpersonal outcomes. But whereas social learning theory asserts that people will imitate success, and exchange theory proposes that people will evaluate their own outcomes against internal standards (CL and CL_{alt}), equity theory suggests that the successes of other people will enter into the calculation of one's own outcomes. There is some disagreement about whether equity theory might involve internal standards as well as external ones (Austin and Susmilch, 1974; Lane and Messé, 1972; Messé and Lane, 1974), but the principal focus of the theory does require comparison of one's own outcomes with the outcomes of others. Whereas Thibaut and Kelley's (1959) model shows how a relationship might develop in order to maximize the rewards of both participants, equity theory concentrates on the possible consequences of a failure to achieve parity. Like the notion of relative deprivation and the principle of distributive justice, equity theory argues that people will be dissatisfied if they believe they are being treated unfairly. But unlike these other two principles, equity theory identifies specific actions that might be taken in order to bring the situation into (at least) psychological balance, whether the original source of the injustice was the Person or a third party.

The theories discussed in this chapter all deal with the development, maintenance, and evaluation of interpersonal interaction, whether that interaction is a helping relationship, a friendship, an adversary relationship, or the search for individual goals through group membership. These principles of social exchange, occasionally combined with elements of the cognitive theories we have studied in earlier chapters, provide the framework necessary for much of the material in chapters to follow.

Summary

Interpersonal behavior can be characterized as a social *exchange* (p. 344) between people, and these social exchanges typically involve both costs and rewards to the participants. A fundamental assumption of all theories of interpersonal behavior is that, on balance, a person will perform those actions which produce the greatest rewards (at the least cost). Social behavior which leads to positive reinforcement should be strengthened, while social behavior which leads to negative reinforcement should be weakened. The three theories described in this chapter deal with the development, maintenance, and evaluation of such social behavior.

Social learning theory (p. 347) suggests that novel social behavior is first learned through *imitation* (p. 347) of adult models, particularly when these models are rewarded for their actions. In this case the reinforcement received by the model serves as information to the person about which behaviors are acceptable and appropriate for the circumstances. Once a novel action has been learned through imitation, its strength will depend on the reinforcement it receives, and on whether that reinforcement is administered according to a *continuous* or an *intermittent* schedule (p. 350).

The theory of social exchange (p. 351) assumes that each participant in dyadic interaction brings a repertoire of possible actions, and that the goodness of each person's outcomes will be jointly determined by the behaviors of both parties. During the development of a relationship there will be sampling of the various cells of the interaction matrix (p. 352), with each person's course of action being subjected to a win-stay, lose-change rule (p. 355). Each participant in the interaction will evaluate his or her outcomes in terms of two standards of comparison, the comparison level —CL—(p. 356) and the comparison level for alternatives—CL_{alt}—(p. 357). The relative value of the person's outcomes, the CL, and the CL_{alt} will determine both the person's *attraction* (p. 357) to the relationship and his or her *dependence*

(p. 357) upon it. Across all cells of the interaction matrix it is possible to assess the correlation between the losses and gains of one person and the losses and gains of the other, or their **correspondence of outcomes** (p. 359). Low correspondence of outcomes produces competition, while high correspondence of outcomes produces cooperation.

The principles of **relative deprivation** (p. 362) and **distributive justice** (p. 363) and the theory of **equity** (p. 363) all suggest that a person's satisfaction with the outcomes received will in part depend upon the outcomes that other comparison persons are receiving. When the person believes that his or her outcomes are not proportional to inputs, the perceived overpayment or underpayment, or **inequity** (p. 364), will lead to corrective action. To restore equity to a relationship the person may take direct action to change his or her inputs or outcomes (or those of the comparison person), may engage in a psychological distortion of the various inputs and outcomes, or may leave the field. Although equity theory is most clearly relevant to business relationships, it also applies to cases of exploitation and helping behavior.

Suggested Additional Readings

ADAMS, J. S. Inequity in social exchange. In L. Berkowitz (Ed.) *Advances in experimental social psychology.* Vol. 2. New York: Academic Press, 1965. Pp. 267-299. This fairly technical paper provides a thorough coverage of laboratory and field research relevant to the original formulation of equity theory.

BANDURA, A., and WALTERS, R. J. *Social learning and personality development.* New York: Holt, Rinehart and Winston, 1963. This short book contains a complete statement of the authors' version of social learning theory.

BERKOWITZ, L., and WALSTER, E. *Advances in experimental social psychology.* Vol. 9: *Equity theory.* New York: Academic Press, 1976. In a departure from its usual format, this volume of the *Advances* series is devoted entirely to one theoretical issue. It contains an annotated bibliography of equity research and chapters on such topics as reward distribution, equity and the law, and an extended model of social exchange. At times difficult, but a thorough and interesting review of equity research and theory.

GERGEN, K. J. *The psychology of behavior exchange.* Reading, Mass.: Addison-Wesley, 1969. This highly readable book includes sections on social learning, social exchange, and features of interpersonal bargaining and negotiations.

THIBAUT, J. W., and KELLEY, H. H. *The social psychology of groups.* New York: Wiley, 1959. Although it is a bit technical in places, this book presents a complete statement of exchange theory that should be of value to interested students. Particularly important is the generalization of the theory to apply to triads (three-person) and larger groups.

Surprisingly, only recently have social psychologists turned their attention to positive social behavior.

Photo courtesy Martin W. Sandler

Positive Forms of Social Behavior
Chapter Ten

Perhaps no personal quality is considered more "human" than the ability to care for others, and the self-sacrifice which that caring often entails. A passing stranger rushes into a burning building to save a person trapped inside. People who have little money of their own contribute to innumerable charitable organizations. Entire communities pull together to rebuild after a disaster. But positive social behavior is not limited to helping. Good friends share adventures, joys, and sorrows. Lovers become passionately devoted to each other. Our history and literature are filled with such examples, but surprisingly only recently have social psychologists turned their attention to these actions (e.g., Berscheid and Walster, 1969; Huston, 1974; Latané and Darley, 1970; Macaulay and Berkowitz, 1970). This is most probably because most social psychological research has been problem oriented, concentrating on topics such as prejudice, competition, and conformity rather than more positive social behaviors.

In this chapter we consider two principal forms of positive behavior, helping and interpersonal attraction. You will notice common themes in our discussion of both topics. First, there is a common thread of theory—reward, cost, reinforcement—running through both areas. In the case of altruistic action, reinforcement is a theoretical problem to be dealt with, since altruism ought to be action not motivated by personal gain. The solution typically adopted is to define "objective altruism" in terms of observable criteria that rule out external gain but do not attempt to deny the increases in self-esteem that follow performance of a helping action. In general terms, the absence of reward is the rule, and occasional reinforcement is the exception. For interpersonal attraction, this relation is reversed. Some form of reinforcement is the preferred explanation for most of interpersonal attraction, although there are occasional instances in which costs, not rewards, produce increased liking.

The second common theme in the discussion of the two topics is the emphasis on the interchange between the people involved. As noted in Chapter Nine, our emphasis has shifted from a focus on the individual person to consideration of that person's dealings with other people. Until now we have been attempting to explain social behavior in terms of two different sets of factors: the personal characteristics of the individual, and the characteristics of the situation in which the individual's actions occur. To these we must now add a third source of influence, the *relationship* between the person whose actions we seek to understand and the person who is the beneficiary or target of those actions. In the case of helping behavior, the influence of the relationship between the two can best be seen in work on the social responsibility norm, a norm which requires that we help those who are dependent upon us. In the case of attraction, the strong effects of attitude similarity upon the development of liking provide the best example of the influence of the relationship between subject and target person.

One final note about the material in this chapter and succeeding ones. As the behavior we study becomes more complex and more interpersonal, the task of explanation changes. In some ways our explanations will be more complex, such as those involving the effects of the relationship between two or more people as well as the situational factors and personal characteristics of the people involved. But in other ways our explanations will become simpler, as will your task of understanding them. The interpersonal theories discussed in Chapter Nine, which apply to helping, attraction, and many of the topics yet to come, are themselves less complex than many of the theories we have considered earlier, such as attribution theory (Chapter Four) and the cognitive consistency theories (Chapter Six). In large measure this difference reflects the domain of behavior covered by the theory. A theory with a restricted range of application can be more specific in accounting for the behavior of interest without exceeding our ability to follow its explanations. But a theory which attempts to deal with a wide range of action must keep its explanatory principles simple or risk losing its audience through boredom, disbelief, or mis-understanding.

As a result of the decrease in theoretical complexity, you will notice a change in the nature of theoretical disagreements. For example, you may recall from Chapter Six that the controversy among dissonance theory, incentive theory, and self-perception theory over the proper explanation for insufficient justification effects was often quite narrowly drawn. Slight changes in experimental methods were all that was necessary to produce results more favorable to one theory than to the others. This sort of disagreement will not be seen in the area of interpersonal processes. Critics of one theoretical approach will point to a whole area of behavior, rather than a specific set of experimental operations, where the theory appears inadequate. Resolution of these major arguments will refine the theories involved, and these refinements will, in time, narrow the issue. At this writing, however, breadth of explanatory power is necessarily more important than theoretical precision in the interpersonal theories, and you should keep this distinction in mind as you read. As social psychologists learn more about interpersonal phenomena, theories will become more precise.

Altruism and Helping Behavior

THE PROBLEM OF DEFINITION

Motives and Self-Sacrifice

In common usage the term *altruism* usually refers to intentional, self-sacrificing behavior that benefits other people. We can all think of actions we would describe as altruistic—the missionary who is devoted to improvement of living conditions in a primitive society, the country doctor who maintains a practice for the good of the community though barely able to cover expenses, the passerby who intervenes in an emergency at considerable personal risk—and most of these examples are consistent with the popular definition. But illustrations of a concept do not constitute the sort of operational definition (see Chapter Two) required for scientific research.

For example, consider the requirement that altruistic behavior be self-sacrificing in the light of the principles of reinforcement and exchange discussed in Chapter Nine. As Rosenhan (1972) has noted, altruistic action presents a paradox for reinforcement theory, since by definition such behavior would appear to have costs which exceed its rewards. Perhaps people might occasionally engage in actions of this kind, but how could we account for an entire lifetime of "altruism"? There are three possible explanations, but each would have an important limitation. First, we could argue that altruism is simply the exception that proves the rule of reinforcement. Our continued self-seeking can be justified on the grounds that occasionally we do give something for nothing. This explanation sounds plausible, but it fails to tell us anything about why altruism occurs. A second possibility is to assume that the life-long altruists are simply not in touch with the rewards and costs of their behavior. But this lack of contact with reality would make altruists so abnormal that their behavior would be of little interest to social psychologists who presume to deal with the social actions of a majority of people. Finally, we could suggest that life-long altruists are really pursuing goals that they find rewarding. In this instance their rewards would outweigh their costs; it is just that their system of costs and rewards differs from that of most people. This final explanation leaves the principle of reinforcement intact, but it does so at the expense of part of the definition of "altruism." The self-sacrifice is gone.

If the problem of self-sacrifice were not troublesome enough, there is also difficulty in establishing objective criteria for distinguishing between altruistic and nonaltruistic action. Suppose we adopt a criterion based on the *motives* behind the action. Then we would say that a philanthropist who donated a million dollars to charity in order to achieve a tax reduction was not altruistic, while a poor person who gave ten dollars to the same charity was altruistic, because the motives were pure. This sounds fine at first, but what about the effects of the action? There is no doubt that the philanthropist's donation will accomplish more good than will the poor person's donation. And what about the case of a person who intervenes in an accident (with pure motives of helpfulness) but inadvertently prevents the victim from receiving professionally trained help? Will we judge such a person as altruistic even though the actions had negative consequences? Probably not. At this point we are ready to admit that we would like to consider some actions altruistic (or not) because of their motives and regardless of their consequences, while considering others altruistic because of their consequences and regardless of their motives. In our everyday lives, this solution is probably widely adopted. But it is unsatisfactory for research. The difficulty is that the choice of whether to consider motives or effects is an individual value judgment not based on any objectively specifiable criteria.

Objective Altruism

For all these reasons, it is not surprising that social psychologists interested in positive social behavior have either defined the object of study as *helping behavior* rather than "altruism" (e.g., Latané and Darley, 1970), or have side-stepped some of the conceptual problems by concentrating exclusively on observable criteria (e.g., Krebs, 1970; Leeds, 1963; Macaulay and Berkowitz, 1970; Wispé, 1972). We shall adopt the latter approach, and will distinguish objective altruism both from helping behavior and from the subjective altruism based on individual value judgments of motives and effects. There is general agreement that what we are calling objective altruism must meet three different tests. First, the action must be *voluntary*, rather than coerced by social pressure. Second, it may produce *no external rewards* for the actor. Self-administered pats on the back are permitted, and there is no requirement for self-sacrifice. Third, it must actually *benefit* the recipient. Good intentions are, unfortunately, not enough. When defined according to these three criteria, objective altruism can be regarded as a special case of helping behavior. Only the third criterion, actual benefit, is necessary for an act to be helpful, but the other two are required before that helpful action can be considered a case of objective altruism.

How does this objective altruism square with the principle of reinforcement and the social exchange theories discussed in Chapter Nine? To begin with, it does not contradict the principle of reinforcement, because it does permit internal, self-administered rewards which could outweigh the costs of action. Such internal motives as sincere concern for others, empathy with a suffering victim, or even a desire to avoid the guilt that would follow a failure to help can all lead to behavior that would be objectively altruistic. Although it does not contradict the principle of reinforcement, objective altruism does exclude the receipt of the rewards that might be gained through social exchange. Thus aiding a good friend (who might be expected to return the favor) would be helping, but not objective altruism. Performing the same actions for strangers (with whom no future relationship is contemplated) would qualify as objective altruism.

When we compare the definition of objective altruism to the common usage of the term, we discover that scientific precision has been gained at the expense of some of the richness of the term. *Objective altruism,* like its common language counterpart, assumes that altruistic actions are intentional (rather than accidental) and reflect the actor's character. External rewards are precluded by both definitions, although objective altruism does not require self-sacrifice. The greatest difference between the two conceptions is in the way they deal with internal motives. Objective altruism concentrates on results, assuming that the absence of social pressure and external reward will be sufficient to ensure that the actor's motives were pure. But this definition in terms of outcomes makes it impossible for us to consider objectively altruistic any actions—even those of heroic proportions—which fail in the attempt. Although this restriction is necessary to avoid the subjective value judgments about the purity of a person's motives, it does diminish the intuitive appeal of the idea. Perhaps after greater experience in the study of positive social behavior social psychologists will be able to extend their operational definitions to encompass some of the additional judgments implicit in the intuitive idea of altruism.

Having outlined the criteria for objective altruism, we now turn to some of the personal and situational factors that influence its occurrence. For ease of presentation we shall distinguish between "normal" circumstances in which help might be rendered and the special case of bystander intervention in emergency situations. In the absence of an emergency, objective altruism will be affected by a variety of factors, including social norms, situational variables, and internal states of the actor. As examples of these factors we shall consider, respectively, the norms of reciprocity and social responsibility, the situational factor of modeling, and the internal motives to restore equity and avoid guilt. There are other factors which may affect objective altruism, but a complete review is beyond the scope of this chapter. As a result our discussion will be restricted to factors that have received a substantial proportion of the attention of researchers. For a more extended treatment of helping in nonemergency situations, you might read review papers by Berkowitz (1972) and Krebs (1970), a special journal issue edited by Wispé (1972), or a book by Macaulay and Berkowitz (1970). A thorough discussion of helping in emergencies can be found in a book by Latané and Darley (1970).

OBJECTIVE ALTRUISM IN NONEMERGENCY SITUATIONS

The Effects of Norms

Reciprocity

Even the theories of social interaction that assume that people will try to maximize their outcomes do not suggest that interaction can be sustained through reward seeking alone. If you recall the example in Chapter Nine of the Employee and the Superior that was used to illustrate some of the concepts in Thibaut and Kelley's (1959) exchange theory, you will remember that positive outcomes were obtained by both participants only if the Employee did not ask for a raise when meeting the boss in the hallway. Continuation of their *informal* interaction depended upon the Employee's tacit acceptance of a particular social rule: do not ask for a raise during an informal conversation. This rule, which specified the expected or appropriate behavior for a particular interaction setting, is simply one example of a *social* norm. In its most general sense the norm serves as a guideline for action, no matter who the participants in the interchange might be. For example, whether you are a mail clerk or an executive vice-president, a casual encounter in the hallway with the boss is neither the time nor the place to request an increase in salary.

Thus, one element of social exchange is the norm, which facilitates interaction by specifying which actions are appropriate in which settings. And as several writers (e.g., Gouldner, 1960; Homans, 1961) have noted, the most basic of these norms is the norm of reciprocity. Interaction, after all, is the mutual exchange of rewards. I will not continue an interaction with you (provided, of course, that I have some realistic alternative) if you never reciprocate the pleasant outcomes I give to you. In his analysis of the reciprocity norm, Gouldner (1960) argued that it establishes at least two "minimal demands: (1) people should help those who have helped them, and (2) people should not injure those who have helped them" (p. 171). The reciprocity norm creates an obligation for repayment that must be satisfied if the interaction is to continue. In addition to these positive demands, the norm of reciprocity also suggests that it is fair to retaliate for evils or injustices done.

Evidence for the existence of a reciprocity norm comes from our own social experience (as represented in the admonition to "do unto others as·you would have them do unto you," or in the justification "an eye for an eye. . .") and from a number of research studies. For example, Staub and Sherk (1970) gave pairs of children an opportunity to interact with each other while listening to a tape-recorded story. One child in each pair had previously received several pieces of candy which could be shared with the other as they heard the story. Later in the experiment the two children were asked to make drawings, but they were provided with only one crayon—and this was given to the second child (who had not previously been given the candy by the experimenter). The results showed a strong reciprocity effect. The more candy the second child had received from his or her peer, the more time he or she shared the crayon; if the first child had been obviously selfish with the candy, the second reciprocated by being selfish with the crayon. So reciprocity was involved both in the positive action of sharing and in the retaliatory action of denial. In a similar matching of reciprocation, Pruitt (1968) found that college undergraduates gave more to a partner in an experimental game when they had previously received a great deal from the partner, and when the partner's previous gift amounted to a greater percentage of his or her resources. The norm of reciprocity demands not only repayment in kind, but also repayment in degree.

The obligation created by reciprocity can lead to negative consequences if there is suspicion about the donor's motives (Brehm and Cole, 1966; Jones, 1964; Schopler and Thompson, 1968) or if repayment in kind and/or degree is impossible. Consider how you feel when your friend gives you a birthday present that is far beyond your expectations. You may try to justify the gift on the grounds that you really deserved it, but deep down you may think that your friend must "want something" in return. This principle appears to apply whenever the recipient is unable to repay in kind, as in the case of massive foreign aid to underdeveloped countries. Gergen and Gergen (1971) provided evidence of this problem when they interviewed recipients of United States foreign aid. They discovered that a country that offers aid with no strings attached is seen either as "manipulative" or as "naive."

This analysis was extended in some experimental research conducted in Sweden, Japan, and the United States (Gergen, Ellsworth, Maslach, and Seipel, 1975). Participants in an experimental game received help, in the form of additional chips to invest in the game, from another player who ostensibly had either Large Resources or Small Resources. Within each of the Resource conditions there were three degrees of obligation attached to the gift: No Repayment, Repayment With Interest, and Repayment Without Interest. The Large Resources–No Repayment condition, of course, corresponds to the usual situation that obtains in the provision of foreign aid. At the conclusion of the game the subjects were asked to say how highly they thought of their benefactor, and the results indicated what can happen when reciprocity is neither demanded nor possible. Subjects were more positive in their evaluations of the Small Resources donor than the Large Resources donor, and they were more positively disposed toward a benefactor who wanted exact repayment (Repayment Without Interest) than toward a benefactor who demanded either greater repayment or no repayment at all.

Social Responsibility

Since reciprocity is defined as an aspect of an ongoing exchange, its obligations lead only to helping behavior, not to objective altruism. You help your friend either because you owed him or her a favor, or because you expect reciprocation in the future. But why do you help a stranger? Could social norms also account for some of the occurrence of objective altruism? An affirmative answer to this question was suggested by Berkowitz and Daniels (1963), who extended the concept of reciprocity to encompass any dependent other, not just dependent others who happen to be in exchange relationships with the benefactor. This extension of reciprocity is called the social responsibility norm, and it holds that people should help anyone in a dependent position. Berkowitz and Daniels (1963) obtained evidence for the existence of a social responsibility norm in two experiments that became models for this sort of research. Subjects were asked to serve as "workers" whose task was to construct paper boxes for a peer who was described as a "supervisor." The studies purported to be tests of supervisory skill, so there was the possibility that the supervisor might earn a prize, although there were no external rewards for the subjects serving as workers. The supervisor's dependency on the subject was manipulated by convincing the subjects that the supervisor's chances of winning the prize depended either to a great deal (High Dependency) or very little (Low Dependency) on the productivity of the worker.

The most convincing evidence in favor of the social responsibility norm was provided by the second experiment, in which the dependency manipulation was combined in a factorial design with *when* the supervisor was supposed to find out about the worker's performance (either Immediately or over a month Later). Notice that the High Dependency–Later condition meets all the criteria for objective altruism. There are no external rewards for the subject, there is no possibility of a social exchange, the worker is in a position to benefit the supervisor, and there is no social pressure (apart from the pressure implicit in the fact that the experimenter will know about the worker's performance, a point to which we shall return in a moment). What happened? The results showed a main effect for dependency, with the High Dependent supervisor receiving more help than the Low Dependent supervisor, and this was true even when the supervisor would not find out until much later just how much the worker had done.

These results would appear to rule out nearly all the explanations for altruism except adherence to a norm of social responsibility. There is, however, the problem of the experimenter's knowledge of the worker's performance. From the subject's point of view this might have exerted social pressure to help, or it might have led to an expectation of approval from the experimenter. To rule out this potential source of confounding, Berkowitz, Klanderman, and Harris (1964) conducted another worker-supervisor experiment in which subjects were led to believe that even the experimenter would not discover what the subject's performance had been until over a month after the study had been completed (by putting the worker's output in a cardboard box that would remain sealed until all the data had been collected). The results confirmed those found earlier, with more help given to the dependent other, even though *nobody* but the subject would know about his or her performance until much later.

Other studies have also found results consistent with the existence of a social responsibility norm (many of these are summarized by Berkowitz [1972] and by Staub [1972]), and the general normative approach to objective altruism has also been taken by Schwartz (1968, 1970), who considers the benefactor's acceptance of personal responsibility for the dependent other a crucial link in the chain leading toward help. But a normative approach to objective altruism cannot by itself be a sufficient explanation for the behavior. In the experiments by Berkowitz and his associates, the social responsibility norm was made salient by experimental design. Subjects were put into a position which gave them the responsibility for the fate of another person, and in the high dependency conditions, at least, this fact was made rather obvious. But in the much more complex world outside the laboratory, "social responsibility" may not always be uppermost in our minds. There must be some aspect of the situation which brings the social responsibility norm to our conscious attention before that norm can be a guideline for helping behavior.

The Effects of the Situation: Modeling

In our discussion of social learning theory (Chapter Nine), we noted the powerful effects on a child's behavior that the aggressive actions of an adult model can have. This influence of the model is not limited to cases of antisocial action; modeling can also serve as the basis for the performance of positive social behavior. In addition, models can affect the behavior of adults in much the same way that they affect the behavior of children. The salesperson who plants an accomplice to express appreciation for the product, the politician who brings along an entourage of enthusiastic supporters, and the evangelist who concludes a presentation with a dramatic conversion of several members of the audience are all relying on models to influence the reactions of the remaining observers. Thus it is not surprising to learn that a number of experimental studies of helping have found that the presence of a model can increase the prevalence of objective altruism. What is more interesting is the wide variety of modeling effects. Let us take a closer look at some of this research.

In an early series of studies conducted outside the laboratory, Bryan and Test (1967) found increased helping in two different situations in which there was a helpful model. The first study measured the willingness of motorists to stop and help a woman whose automobile appeared to be disabled. There were two experimental conditions: In the Model condition the motorists had just driven past another disabled vehicle whose driver was receiving help. Both this incident and the test car situation were staged by confederates of the experimenter. In the No Model condition there was no good example provided. As expected, more help was rendered in the Model condition. Similar effects for the influence of a helpful model were obtained in the second experiment, which involved donations to a Salvation Army kettle in a shopping center.

Apparently observation of a helpful model will increase the likelihood of helping. But what accounts for this effect? Is it that the model's actions make the social responsibility norm salient, or that they merely suggest alternative courses of behavior that the observer might otherwise not have considered? The available experimental evidence indicates that both explanations may be partially correct. For example, in a study by Macaulay (1970) college students were given the opportunity to make donations as they passed a table set up in the student union building. The donations were tabulated immediately after a model had loudly announced to the person sitting at the table that she either would, or would not, make a donation. No matter what the model said, there were more donations immediately following her speech than there were in control periods when no model was present. The fact that donations increased even when the model stated that she would *not* donate suggests that her refusal made other passersby conscious of their own social responsibility to help. But these results are clouded by the fact that the legitimacy of the charity—either a starvation relief agency or a political committee—did not affect the rate of donation. Yet the social responsibility norm would predict differences based on the legitimacy of the appeal.

In another experiment which varied the behavior of a model and the legitimacy of the cause, Wagner and Wheeler (1969) arranged for Navy enlisted men and recruits to overhear a model being asked to donate to a fund. The worthiness of the cause was also varied by describing the fund as necessary either to fly in the immediate family of a serviceman who was dying, or to augment the funds of a local servicemen's club. The subjects in the Positive model condition overheard the model agreeing to donate, while subjects in a Negative model condition overheard the model refuse to give anything. The subjects were then asked to make a donation of their own. The results showed that compared to a control condition (in which the subjects were asked to make their own contributions before they had overheard the model's response) more money was donated in the Positive condition, but *less* money was donated in the Negative condition.

Whereas Macaulay had obtained increased donation after a negative model, this experiment found decreased donation after a negative model. But like the earlier study, the presumed worthiness of the cause had no effect whatsoever on the amount given. These results suggest that there must be more to helping than a norm of social responsibility (or there would have been greater help given the worthy causes), and that there must be more than the specific actions of a model (otherwise negative models should produce consistent failures to help). In short, we might do well also to consider the potential effects of individual differences within the observers. How do they interpret the situation, and do their own characteristics enter into the decision of whether to help?

The Effect of Internal States: Guilt

The popular literature is filled with examples of how guilt can influence human behavior. We read of parents who try to use their children's guilt about the normal transgressions of childhood to control the children's future behavior, and we suspect that psychotherapists spend a great deal of time with adults who have had this experience as children. We learn of obvious mistakes made by a criminal we had considered clever, and we think that the person might have wanted to be caught and punished. Even when positive social behavior is concerned, guilt may play a causal role: we expect harm-doers to want to provide restitution to their victims, and we wonder whether at least part of the reason for a philanthropist's large donations to charity might be guilt over wealth in the midst of poverty. As it happens, there is a substantial amount of research evidence indicating that guilt can motivate helping behavior.

Restoration of Equity

Much of this research has been conducted within the conceptual framework of equity theory (Walster, Berscheid, and Walster, 1973), with the clearest application of the theory being the case in which the helper is a former harm-doer trying to square accounts with a recipient who has been his or her victim. As Walster, Berscheid, and Walster (1973) note, you may have either of two reactions to a person you have harmed, and these two reactions are likely to be mutually exclusive. First, you might justify your behavior and the victim's suffering—thereby restoring psychological equity—by convincing yourself that the victim was a bad person who deserved to suffer. This *derogation of the victim* has been obtained in a number of studies in which subjects have observed the apparent suffering of a victim who, through no fault of behavior, was experiencing a purportedly painful series of electric shocks as part of a learning experiment (Lerner, 1970; Lerner and Matthews, 1967; Lerner and Simmons, 1966). Although this research has usually been conceptualized as demonstrating the need people have to believe in a "just world" in which people get what they deserve (and deserve what they get), it can also be thought of as an example of the restoration of equity. The second possible reaction that you might have to a person you have harmed is one of *compensation*, providing the victim with rewards or help that will restore equity. The two techniques of compensation and derogation do appear to be mutually exclusive (Walster and Prestholdt, 1966), and the likelihood of compensation actually being provided will be greatest when the available compensation is neither too much nor too little (Berscheid and Walster, 1967; Berscheid, Walster, and Barclay, 1969). As equity theory predicts, you want to provide the victim with appropriate and adequate compensation, but not excessive compensation.

Suppose that you choose to compensate your victim. How does equity theory account for this choice? The theory assumes that you feel two different sorts of distress upon harming another person (Walster, Berscheid, and Walster, 1973). The first of these is called retaliation distress—the simple fear that the victim, or some outside person, or the Fates will restore equity to the relationship not by helping the victim but by punishing you. The second sort of distress is called self-concept distress, arising from an inconsistency between your behavior and your internalized values that prescribe fairness and equity. It is fair to say that self-concept distress is roughly equivalent to the state we have been calling "guilt." In the absence of any potential for the victim (or others) to retaliate, a choice of compensation will be attributed to guilt; in the presence of retaliatory potential your choice will probably be attributed to retaliation distress, on the assumption that the latter is more threatening than guilt. You have no control over the actions that others might take against you in order to restore equity, but you do have at least nominal control over the recriminations you direct at yourself.

The Problem of Generality

Restoration of equity in order to reduce guilt is a clear possibility when the harm-doer compensates the victim, but does guilt enter into helping when the helper is not the same person who caused the harm? And can guilt drive a harm-doer to be helpful, even though the beneficiaries are not the people he or she has injured? Several experiments suggest that the answer to both of these questions is yes.

With regard to the guilt of a person who witnesses but does not cause harm to another, consider an experiment by Rawlings (1970). In this study subjects participated in an ostensible auditory discrimination learning task. They were to report the number of tones heard against a background of white noise (a sound like the buzz that occurs between stations on a radio), and their partner was to record this information.

In one experimental condition (the Reactive Guilt condition), the partner received a mild electric shock every time the subject made an error—the subject thus caused the partner's discomfort. In another experimental condition (Noncontingent Guilt) the partner was shocked on a random schedule which had nothing to do with the subject's performance. The situation was arranged so that the partners of subjects in both conditions received the same number of shocks. Next the subjects were given *new* partners for a second phase of the experiment in which they could choose to share the shocks administered for errors. Both the Reactive Guilt and Noncontingent Guilt subjects shared these shocks with their new partners to a greater extent than did control subjects, and there were no differences between the two guilt conditions. These results indicate that both causing harm to another and merely witnessing that harm can lead to helping behavior—even when the recipient is a different person from the one who was harmed initially. Other experiments in which subjects are induced to cause harm and are then given the opportunity to be helpful to unharmed third parties have obtained quite similar results (Carlsmith and Gross, 1969; Freedman, Wallington, and Bless, 1967).

Before we generalize these results to the case of the robber-baron who must contribute to charity in order to salve his conscience, three notes of caution are in order. First, since "guilt" is an internal state that cannot be measured directly, there is always the possibility that these experiments have produced results for some other reason. For example, since most of the studies have involved public behavior of the subject (public at least to the extent that the experimenter knows about it), the internal state leading to helping might plausibly be described as *shame*, rather than as guilt. Or there might be no internal state at all. This is the same problem of measurement that arises in connection with any intervening variable (dissonance is a prime example). The only solution to the problem is to conduct a wide variety of studies that will rule out other plausible alternatives, a solution which may already have been achieved (Freedman, 1970).

The second note of caution is based on an important difference between experimental procedures for inducing guilt and the presumed causes of guilt under circumstances outside the laboratory. In all the experimental studies it has been necessary to *force* subjects into behaving in a manner contrary to their moral codes. Under these circumstances it is not surprising that the subjects have an internal reaction that can be called guilt. But people who voluntarily cause others to suffer may not have the sort of moral code that will lead them to feel guilty about their actions, or they would not have engaged in those actions to begin with. There is some evidence from interviews with confidence men (Goffman, 1952) and juvenile delinquents (Sykes and Matza, 1957) indicating that such people do feel guilty about their behavior, but these anecdotal reports cannot be taken as conclusive evidence on the point. After all, it is socially desirable to tell the interviewer that you feel guilty for actions of which you know he or she disapproves.

Finally, it is interesting to note that altruistic behavior can be the consequence not only of negative internal states (such as guilt), but also the result of a positive internal state such as happiness (Aderman, 1972; Rosenhan, Underwood, and Moore, 1974), empathy with the person in need of help (Aderman and Berkowitz, 1970; Aderman, Brehm, and Katz, 1974), or similarity to that person (Hornstein, Masor, Sole, and Heilman, 1971; Sole, Marton, and Hornstein, 1975). These results are not surprising, but they do illustrate some of the complexity of nonemergency helping. We have seen that social norms of reciprocity and social responsibility do not always appear to produce helping, that similar performances by models may have very different effects, and that a variety of internal emotional states may lead to helping. Exchange and equity theories can account for much of this nonemergency helping, but a complete theoretical description will have to deal more thoroughly with all aspects of the phenomenon.

OBJECTIVE ALTRUISM IN EMERGENCIES

The Failure to Act

Intervention into an emergency situation should be slightly simpler to explain than is nonemergency helping, if only because the need for quick action ought to preclude consideration of some of the long-term consequences of the action. But even in emergencies the reasons for acting, or for failing to act, are not always as obvious as they might seem. For example, let us look at one widely reported failure to intervene (e.g., Latané and Darley, 1970; Rosenthal, 1964). In the early hours of a March morning a young woman returned from her job, parked her car in a lot near her apartment building, and started walking the short distance to the front door. A man who had been standing in the parking lot suddenly attacked her, stabbing her with a knife. The woman screamed for help, some lights went on in the building, a man called out, and the attacker got in his car and drove away. Then the lights in the building went out and the attacker returned to stab her again. Lights went on again, windows were opened, and the attacker drove off. By now the woman had managed to crawl to the doorway of the building, but the attacker returned a third time, fatally stabbed her, and drove away. The entire sequence of events took more than half an hour and was observed by *thirty-eight* witnesses (Rosenthal, 1964), but not a single person intervened.

What makes this tragic incident important is, unfortunately, not that it occurred at all—similar murders happen with frightening regularity; nor is it particularly noteworthy that the murder took place in New York City, since incidents like this one can be found in most major cities and smaller towns as well. What is important is that this case marked the beginning of serious inquiry into the reasons why virtually none of the bystanders took even the minimal action of notifying the police. In interviews with psychologists, sociologists, and psychiatrists, Rosenthal (1964) obtained a variety of explanations for the witnesses' failure to intervene, but a consistent theme was "apathy"—the result of depersonalization and dehumanization in a large city. This explanation has the ring of intuitive plausibility, but as Latané and Darley (1970) point out, it may not be a correct interpretation: "The 38 witnesses . . . did not merely look at the scene once and then ignore it. Instead they continued to stare out of their windows at what was going on. Caught, fascinated, distressed, unwilling to act but unable to turn away, their behavior was neither helpful nor heroic; but it was not indifferent or apathetic either" (p. 4).

Diffusion of Responsibility

Rather than attempting to answer the general question "What leads people to help others?" Latané and Darley (1970) and other social psychologists who have studied bystander intervention have tried to identify particular characteristics of emergency situations that either promote or inhibit intervention. The first of these experiments (Darley and Latané, 1968) was designed to determine the effects on helping of the number of bystanders who witnessed an incident. Remember that one of the internal states thought to influence helping in a nonemergency situation is an acceptance of personal responsibility for the victim (Schwartz, 1970). When there are numerous witnesses to an event, this personal responsibility becomes *diffused* among the witnesses, with the possible result that none of them will take any action. If you are alone with a person who suddenly collapses, you know that if help is to be rendered you will have to be the one to do it. You have complete responsibility for the person's fate. But if you and a number of your friends are all present, the responsibility is diffused among you all, and this may make each of you less likely to help.

To test this idea Darley and Latané (1968) had male and female undergraduates at New York University overhear what they thought was an epileptic seizure suffered by one participant in a discussion of personal problems. The subjects had been told that the purpose of the research was to discuss the sorts of problems faced by students who were adjusting to college and to life in the city. Ostensibly to preserve the anonymity of the subjects, but really to remove the obviously responsible experimenter from the situation, the subjects were told that they would have the opportunity to talk about their experiences with other students, but that the experimenter would not listen in on this initial discussion. Each subject was placed in a room alone and was given a pair of earphones through which the instructions were delivered and the subject could hear the statements of other participants. The subjects were to talk in turn, with a mechanical switch allowing each person's microphone to be on for a period of two minutes, during which time all other microphones would be off. This was done so that when the "seizure" occurred the subjects would be unable simply to discuss it with the other participants.

The future victim spoke first and said that he found it difficult to adjust to New York City and to his studies. Then with obvious embarrassment he admitted that he was prone to seizures, especially when he was under pressure. Other participants then took their turns presenting their problems (including the real subject), and finally the switching apparatus returned to the victim. This time, after making a few relatively calm comments, the victim became increasingly incoherent, spluttering that he was having a seizure and asking for help. After about seventy seconds the victim appeared to have had a complete breakdown.

Although the incident in this experiment was mild by comparison, the witnessing subject was placed in much the same position as the witnesses of the murder described earlier. The subject was confronted with a clear behavioral choice—to intervene or not to intervene—and was isolated from other witnesses so that there could be no discussion of the matter. There were three experimental conditions. In all these there was only one naive subject run at a time (speeches of the other participants, including the victim, had been tape recorded), but from the subject's point of view there were either Two people (the subject and the victim), Three people (subject, victim, one other), or Six people (subject, victim, four others) taking part in the experiment.

If the idea of diffusion of responsibility is correct, then the proportion of witnesses helping the victim should have decreased as the size of the group increased from Two to Six, and the results of the experiment confirmed this prediction. When only the subject and victim were present, 85 percent of the subjects reported the emergency to the experimenter before the end of the apparent seizure. When the apparent group size was Three, this proportion decreased to 62 percent, and when the subjects thought that there were four other observers (Six condition) the percent responding by the end of the seizure decreased dramatically to 31 percent. Not only did a greater proportion of the subjects respond in the Two condition, those who responded did so more quickly (an average of 52 seconds) than did subjects in the Three condition (93 seconds) and the Six condition (166 seconds). Thus increased group size, and presumably more greatly diffused responsibility, led to a decrease in an individual's tendency to intervene and help.

As Latané and Darley (1970) have noted, these percentages only represent the likelihood that a *particular* bystander will intervene, not the likelihood that the victim will receive help. An appropriate mathematical transformation can be used to change the individual probability to an estimate of the likelihood that at least one bystander will help. When this calculation is made, it shows that the victim is equally likely to receive help in all conditions, but that help will be rendered more quickly in the Two and Three conditions than in the Six condition. These findings and others reported by Latané and Darley (1970) indicate that one important situational influence of helping may be the number of bystanders involved.

A Model of Intervention Decisions

To account for some of the bystander intervention effects, Latané and Darley (1970) have proposed a model of the intervention process which incorporates elements of exchange theory (Chapter Nine) and social comparison theory (Chapter Eight). The model is outlined in Figure 10-1 and shows that there are five basic steps leading to intervention in an emergency situation. The first of these is to *notice* that something is wrong, and this is not as trivial a step as it might seem.

FIGURE 10-1
A model of the bystander intervention process. (Adapted from Latané and Darley, 1970, pp. 31–36)

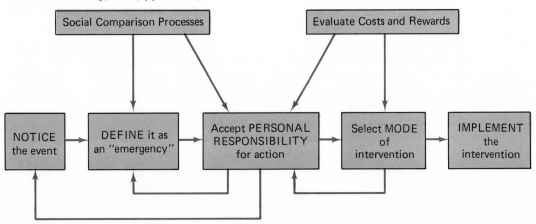

For example, remember how you felt the first time you drove into a large city during rush hour. You were probably so intent on staying in the proper lane of traffic and avoiding accidents that you noticed very little except for the other cars near you. Had there been some sort of emergency on a sidewalk or in the entrance to a building, you would have missed it completely. The more familiar the surroundings and the less you need to "tune them out" because they are noisy or unpleasant, the more likely you will be to notice an emergency should one occur.

After noticing something amiss, the observer must *define* the event as an "emergency." At this point in the decision chain, social comparison processes can affect the outcome. Remember that we evaluate our opinions and abilities against social standards whenever objective standards are not available. There are, of course, emergencies in which the need for immediate intervention is obvious, and we shall return to these in a moment. But in many cases of potential emergency, there may be few objective standards for appropriate behavior. Are the screams you hear from inside a house the sounds of an attack or just the accompaniment to a family quarrel? Does the smoke coming from the rear of a building indicate that the building is on fire or just that someone is burning trash? To borrow an idea from Froman (1971), is that man collapsed on the sidewalk having a heart attack or is he lying in wait for you? In either case, what should you do about it? If you are alone when you are confronted by such possible emergencies, you will have to decide for yourself, but if there are other people around you will probably study their reactions to determine what your own should be. In short, you will engage in social comparison to reach a definition of the situation.

If you decide that what you are viewing is a real emergency, the next step in the decision process is the acceptance of *personal responsibility* for whatever action might be necessary. Both social comparison and the evaluation of costs and rewards will enter into this commitment. If you know you have the technical competence to deal with the problem you will be more likely to intervene than if you do not know what to do (Schwartz and Clausen, 1970), and you will be more likely to take responsibility if you know that others are unable to help (Bickman, 1971). But how can you judge your ability against that of a group of strangers? Only through social comparison. Even if you determine that you can help, the social costs of intervention—which may range from making a fool of yourself, to making the situation worse, to getting sued, injured, or killed for your trouble—may keep you from taking personal responsibility for action. Indeed, as Figure 10-1 shows, Latané and Darley (1970) suggest that your desire to avoid personal responsibility may cycle the decision process backward, getting you to change your definition of the event as an emergency or to pretend that you didn't even notice that the event was happening.

After you have accepted personal responsibility for action, you must still decide which course of action to take. You have committed yourself to "getting involved"; the only question is to what degree. Should you intervene *directly* in the emergency, doing what you can for the victim yourself? Or should you take the *indirect* course of notifying the proper authorities? Although direct intervention is the more obvious choice, it also has the greater social cost, and this may lead you to cycle one step back, avoiding personal responsibility by "leaving the situation to the experts." Once you have decided that you will intervene, either directly or indirectly, the last step in the process, *implementing* the decision, follows rather naturally.

Ambiguity, Social Comparison, and Costs/Rewards

The decision process model of bystander intervention is primarily useful in explaining instances of potential emergencies, in which the situation is ambiguous. In such circumstances the need for extensive social comparison may serve to inhibit intervention. When you are looking at the reactions of others (and they are observing your reactions), you want to be certain of the situation before committing yourself to an action that may be inappropriate. We are taught to respond unemotionally—to "look before we leap"—and we hesitate to do something that others will think foolish. The more bystanders there are in an ambiguous situation, the more hesitation there will be. The importance of ambiguity in mediating the inhibitory effect of a larger number of bystanders is illustrated in two experiments by Clark and Word (1974). In these two studies it was found that more help was given a technician who had appeared to suffer a severe electrical shock when that incident occurred in the full view of the subject (no ambiguity) than when it had occurred out of the subject's view (some ambiguity). More importantly, the subjects were run either alone or in pairs, and this difference in group size affected helping (less help from the pairs) only when the situation was ambiguous. The social constraints against intervention in an ambiguous situation should be even more powerful in larger groups.

In contrast, when the need for intervention is clear, the first two steps of the decision process model (and, consequently, much of the social comparison) will be omitted. There is no need for social comparison to determine whether or not an emergency exists, and the fear of behaving inappropriately will be greatly reduced. In a clear emergency in which it is apparent that no specialized skills are required, the major influence on the decision process will be the costs of intervention to the potential helper. For example, you may recall the field experiment conducted in the New York subways by Piliavin, Rodin, and Piliavin (1969) discussed in Chapter Two. In that study, people riding in a subway car were exposed to a victim who was either black or white and who collapsed in the center of the car shortly after the train left the platform. On approximately half of the trials within each victim race the victim appeared to be ill, but on the other half he appeared to be drunk. No one riding in the car could fail to notice the incident, and few would have considered it anything but an emergency. What happened in this clear case? On sixty-two of the sixty-five trials the victim received help even before the model (who had been planted to increase the likelihood of helping) could perform his act of intervention. The only three trials on which no help was rendered prior to intervention by the model all involved a drunk victim, and this suggested that the social costs to the helper might play an important role.

This influence of social costs can be seen in a variety of different circumstances. It is not surprising to learn that people will be more likely to help when they have time to spare than when they do not (Darley and Batson, 1973); that they will generally help people of the same race more quickly than people of a different race (West, Whitney, and Schmedler, 1975) although this same-race helping can be affected by situational factors (Piliavin, Rodin, and Piliavin, 1969; West, Whitney, and Schmedler, 1975; Wispé and Freshley, 1971); or that females will be helped more often and more quickly than will males (Clark, 1974; Darley and Latané, 1970; West, Whitney, and Schmedler, 1975).

In a less obvious example of the cost of helping, Piliavin and Piliavin (1972) found that a bloody victim will receive less help than a nonbloody one. We would expect just the opposite result, on the grounds that a bloody victim would probably need help more. But this greater need creates higher costs for the potential helper: more opportunity to inadvertently make the situation worse, more commitment of time and resources to get the victim to the hospital, the fear that whoever caused the victim to bleed may return and attack the helper as well. These results indicate that in some cases the people who need help the most may, because of the costs to the potential helpers, be least likely to receive aid.

The fact that costs incurred by the potential helper may influence the decision to intervene or the course of action (direct or indirect) taken does not eliminate bystander intervention from the class of

objectively altruistic actions. Such intervention is still voluntary action
that helps the victim and earns no external reward, so it still satisfies
all the criteria for objective altruism. But it is also the result of a
decision, and this decision can be influenced by the costs to the
potential helper, by the ambiguity of the situation, and by the number
of other bystanders and their reactions to the incident.

Let us return again to the thirty-eight witnesses of a murder. It is
easy to imagine that many of the witnesses at first considered the
incident to be a lover's quarrel, failing to define the situation as an
emergency. Then just as the observers might have been ready to accept
the personal responsibility for calling the police, the assailant drove
off and the emergency was over. When the attacker returned, it is possible that the passage of time justified the assumption that somebody
had surely called the police. Then the emergency apparently ended
again, and when it began for the third time people might have been
so committed to inaction that they could not at that late time notify
the police. Their decision process had cycled from one step to another
without ever leading to an acceptance of personal responsibility for
intervention, with tragic consequences for the victim. Perhaps understanding the nature of the process will keep us all from becoming
trapped in a cycle of indecision should we ever be faced with similar
circumstances.

SUMMARY

The scientific study of positive social action requires an operational
definition of terms that deals with observable antecedents and consequences, rather than with the motives leading to action. By this sort
of definition, *helping behavior* (p. 377) is any action which benefits
another person, and **objective altruism** (p. 377) is a special case of
helping behavior. Not only must objective altruism benefit the recipient, it must also be a voluntary action that earns no external rewards
for the actor.

In situations in which no emergency exists, helping behavior can
be produced in response to social norms, the presence of models in
the situation, and internal feeling states such as guilt or happiness.
The norm of **reciprocity** (p. 379) is fundamental to social exchange
and leads to helping behavior, while the norm of **social responsibility**
(p. 381), which does not depend on exchange, can lead to objectively
altruistic action. Helpful *models* (p. 383) may contribute to objective

altruism by making the social responsibility norm more salient, but models who refuse to help may also increase the likelihood that people who observe their refusals will help. One explanation for the differences in response to models may be that the observation creates different internal states (p. 385) in different observers. Individual differences can produce a variety of responses to a victim which range from *derogation* (p. 385) of the victim on the grounds that suffering was deserved to *compensation* (p. 385) of a victim in order to restore equity. Compensation is particularly likely when the helper is the same person who caused the original harm and when an appropriate level of compensation is possible.

The failure to intervene in emergency situations has sometimes been attributed to the apathy of the bystanders, but it may be more appropriate to view the act of intervention as the final step in a decision process (p. 391) which is influenced by *social comparison* and evaluation of the *costs* associated with various forms of intervention. This decision process has five steps: *noticing* (p. 391) the situation, *defining* (p. 392) it as an emergency, *accepting* personal responsibility (p. 392) for the action, *selecting* a mode (p. 393) of intervention and *implementing* (p. 393) the decision. The potential actor can *cycle* (p. 392) from one step in the decision process to a previous step if the situation is ambiguous or if the costs of intervention are too great, never reaching the final step of implementing the intervention.

Interpersonal Attraction

As we have seen, a substantial amount of helping behavior, and all objective altruism, is independent of the *external* rewards so prevalent in other forms of social exchange. This contrasts with the case of interpersonal attraction, a positive form of social behavior that is heavily dependent upon mutual reward (Aronson, 1970; Berscheid and Walster, 1969; Homans, 1961). Indeed, as you will recall from Chapter Nine, one definition of attraction to a relationship, and presumably to the other people in that relationship, requires that rewards received surpass both the comparison level and the comparison level for alternatives (Thibaut and Kelley, 1959). Thus, while reward is excluded from objective altruism, it is practically essential for interpersonal attraction.

AN ATTITUDE OF FAVORABILITY

What does it mean to say that you are attracted to a person? Think of some of the words that could be used to describe a relationship between two people—respect, admiration, friendship, liking, love. Can these be used interchangeably? Does the use of one necessitate the use of others? Occasionally so, but much of the time probably not. For example, you can respect a professor whom you do not like; you can develop a friendship with a person whose faults you cannot admire; you can like a person for a long time without having that liking become love. Each descriptive word has a slightly different meaning, and often these differences are important. But each word also represents a favorable, or positive, evaluation of the target person. In order to recognize some of the complexity of interpersonal attraction, and simultaneously provide a conceptual definition that is clear enough to serve as the foundation for research, many social psychologists would agree with Berscheid and Walster (1969) that attraction can be defined as an attitude of favorability toward the target person.

Let us consider this attitude of favorability in terms we have used earlier (Chapters Five and Six). Compared to other attitudes, interpersonal attraction is probably less cognitive and more emotional, with more clearly identifiable behavioral consequences. The cognitive component of your attraction toward another person might include your perception of the other's competence, your estimate that many of the person's beliefs are similar to yours, and your judgment of the person's ability to provide you with social rewards. The affective component might include the value you place on the qualities the person possesses, the pleasure you receive from rewards actually provided, and some indefinable "chemistry" of immediate liking. The behavioral component could include your willingness to help the other person, the words you use to describe him or her to a third person, and the amount of time you choose to spend together. The fact that there are numerous different aspects of attraction would be accounted for by saying that the attitude of favorability had an extensive horizontal structure, with a great many syllogistic chains contributing to the final conclusion.

Since interpersonal attraction is a positive social behavior, its existence is more easily documented (indeed, its prevalence may tend to be overestimated) than is the existence of socially undesirable attitudes such as racism. A person will try to show positive actions while attempting to conceal negative feelings. Moreover, researchers have developed a wide array of measures of attraction, including such social dependent variables as friendship choice (Deutsch and Collins, 1951; Festinger, Schachter, and Back, 1950; Sherif, Harvey, White, Hood, and Sherif, 1961); behavioral indicants such as doing favors (Brehm and Cole, 1966) and use of personal space (Little, 1965; Rosenfeld, 1965); and physiological measures such as GSR (Porier and Lott, 1967, discussed more fully in Chapter Five); as well as more typical verbal reports made on attitude scales.

If there are significant limitations to the study of interpersonal attraction, they center on one basic issue—duration. First, most of the measures are administered in a single experimental session, rather than being repeated over a long period of time. Second, most of the relationships that have been investigated are themselves of short duration: first impressions, casual friendships, or short-term dating relationships. Indeed, Huston (1974) estimates that perhaps 80 percent of the social psychological research on attraction consists of single-session studies of short-term relationships. There are exceptions, such as Newcomb's (1961) study of the development of acquaintance and friendship in a college dormitory and Altman and Taylor's (1973) research on the changes that occur in self-disclosure over a time period of more than a year, but even these studies might more properly be considered to cover the formative stages of a relationship than to cover its maintenance extended through time. As a result, many social psychologists would agree with Levinger and Snoek (1972) that present research tells us more about the early stages of an encounter than it does about the later stages of a strong relationship. You should keep this limitation in mind as we consider some of the antecedents of attraction.

THE MEASUREMENT OF ATTRACTION

Friendship Choice

Because it has served as a model for a number of measurement procedures, the topic of friendship choice deserves further comment. One of the earliest attempts to assess interpersonal attraction by means of friendship choice was the sociometric method developed by Moreno (1934). To illustrate the method, imagine that you are in a small class with a number of people (say, eight others) whom you know, but not well. I ask each of you to write down the names of no more than *two* other people (the number listed can change, and two is used here only to simplify the example) with whom you would like to become "good friends." Then I collect the papers, assign a number to each of you, and construct a diagram known as a sociogram based on your responses. Such a sociogram is shown in Figure 10-2, with each arrow indicating a friendship choice. The sociogram indicates that Person #1 wrote down the names of Person #2 and Person #3; that Person #2 reciprocated Person #1's choice and in addition chose Person #5; Person #3 also reciprocated the choice of Person #1 while making the additional selection of Person #5; the remaining choices can be described in similar terms. As the diagram indicates, Person #5 is the most popular (the "star") with a total of five choices (since he was limited to listing two people himself, we do not know how many of those five he would actually reciprocate). Person #9 is somewhat of an outcast (the "isolate"), being chosen for friendship by nobody else in the group.

The choices used to construct a sociogram can be spontaneous and virtually unlimited, they can be inferences made by the investigator from interviews conducted with the subjects (rather than explicit choices by the subjects themselves), or they can be direct answers to a restricted set of questions, as in our example. When the choices are responses to direct questions, it will make quite a difference which specific questions are asked. Suppose that instead of asking you to pick the two people you would like to have for good friends I ask you to pick the two people you would most like to have on your team if I were to split the nine of you into three groups competing for a single prize. You might choose for teammates the two most uncom-

FIGURE 10-2
A sociogram of friendship choice. (Adapted from Moreno, 1934, p. 32)

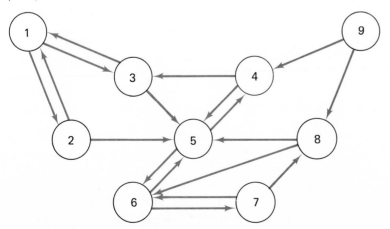

promising and fiercely competitive people in the class, but most probably you would not select these same people to be your good friends.
Indeed, a consistent finding in the study of leadership in small groups
is that the people selected for task leadership are not often chosen
to maintain the emotional needs of the group (Bales, 1958; Gibb,
1969; Halpin, 1966; Stogdill, 1969). We shall return to this issue in
Chapter Thirteen; for now it is sufficient to point out that a carefully
constructed set of sociograms can be used to distinguish among the
various senses of interpersonal attraction.

Attitude Scaling Approaches

This attempt to differentiate one sort of attraction from another is
also present to some degree in attitude scaling approaches to interpersonal attraction, although most of these studies tend to be more
concerned with the antecedents and consequences of attraction than
with the diversity of ways in which that attraction might be expressed.
Two examples illustrate this approach. The first of these is the work of
Byrne (1961, 1971) and his associates, which concentrates on the
relationship between attitude similarity and liking; the second is the
research on love recently conducted by Rubin (1970, 1973).

The major finding of the program of research by Byrne—that
attraction will increase as a direct function of attitude similarity—will
be discussed more fully at a later point. The scales used to measure
liking in this research, however, are drawn directly from sociometric
studies. One of these scales asks the subject to judge how much he or
she would like to have the stimulus person as a work partner (the
task-oriented choice), while another scale asks the person to indicate
how much he or she likes the stimulus person (the friendship choice).
These two ratings are embedded in a short series of other scales which
include estimates of the stimulus person's morality, intelligence, personal adjustment, and knowledge of current events. The entire in-
ventory is known as the Interpersonal Judgment Scale (Byrne, 1971).
In most cases interpersonal attraction is simply considered to be the
sum of the scores on the work partner and liking scales (Byrne, 1971),
although all the ratings have occasionally been used to indicate attraction (Byrne, London, and Reeves, 1968).

It is easy to conceive of attitude measurement techniques to
assess liking, but it is much more difficult to imagine how "love"
could be translated into the unemotional and objective terms of an
attitude scale. After all, we usually think of love as a rather special
human emotion, the proper subject for poets and songwriters, but
not for social scientists. Even research on dating and marriage deals

with the formal characteristics of the relationship—number of dates
per week, presence of a marriage certificate, length of the relationship
—rather than with the nature of the affective bond between the two
people. Yet the study of this romantic bond is just what Rubin (1970,
1973) attempted. In analyzing the treatment of romantic love (as
opposed to, for example, the love of a parent for a child) in philosophy
and literature Rubin identified two common themes, *needing* and
giving. Romantic love is usually thought to involve physical or emotional need, represented in a strong attachment to the object person,
and to involve an altruistic caring for that person's own needs.

In an attitude scaling procedure much like those discussed in
Chapter Five, Rubin constructed a large number of attitude statements relating to liking and loving and administered these items to a
group of judges who tried to sort them into liking, caring, and needing
categories based on their content. Items that were consistently sorted
in the appropriate categories were further refined by having 182
dating couples at the University of Michigan complete both the liking
and loving items as they would apply (a) to their dating partner, and
(b) to a same-sex close friend. Rubin found that for the liking items
there was not much difference between the total scores for liking of
friend and liking of partner, but that for the loving items there were
large differences between the totals for partners and the totals for
friends. These differences showed partners loved much more than
friends, as expected. These results, and further analyses of the correlations among the various items, suggested that the two scales did, in
fact, measure different aspects of attraction.

In later work Rubin (1974) has reported further refinements of the
liking and loving scales, such that each scale now consists of nine
items. The liking scale consists of items related to liking, admiration,
maturity, personal adjustment, responsibility, and respect, while the
love scale consists of items relating to caring and need. Examples of
these love scale items are "I would do almost anything for _____,"
"I would forgive _____ for practically anything," and "It would be
hard for me to get along without _____." For each item on either
the love scale or the liking scale, the subject is asked to say how much
the statement is true for the stimulus person in question (i.e., partner
or friend). If the statement is "not at all true" a score of 1 is given for
that item, if the statement is "definitely true—agree completely," a
score of 9 is given for that item, and the levels of agreement between
these two extremes receive appropriate scores between 1 and 9. Thus,
for the total of nine items in each scale, the possible scores range
from a low of 9 to a high of 81. The data presented by Rubin (1974)
suggest that on such nine-item scales the average liking scores for
friends and partners would be approximately 60. Love scores for

partners would be about 65, while love scores for friends would be closer to 40. These differences indicate how attitudinal research can take into account the different dimensions of attraction while maintaining the overall view of attraction as an attitude of favorability.

SOME ANTECEDENTS OF ATTRACTION

If we think of interpersonal attraction as an attitude that can be affected by rewards, we can use principles of exchange theory (Chapter Nine) and cognitive consistency theory (Chapter Six) to make predictions about what factors might influence the development of attraction. As an alternative to theory-based predictions, we might try to make guesses based on the popular wisdom about attraction, but its inconsistency would make this a difficult task. For example, consider the potentially important environmental variable of *propinquity* or physical closeness. Does attraction increase with physical separation ("absence makes the heart grow fonder"), or does separation cause a decrease in attraction ("out of sight, out of mind")? The popular wisdom permits both predictions, but on the grounds that physical proximity is usually necessary for the provision of rewards, exchange theory would suggest that propinquity would be a necessary condition for the development and maintenance of attraction.

In much the same way, we might guess that the interpersonal variable of *similarity* should influence attraction. But again the popular wisdom makes opposite predictions. Does attraction increase with similarity ("birds of a feather flock together"), or are attraction and similarity negatively correlated in general ("opposites attract")? Here several of the theories we have considered would lead to the expectation that similarity should increase attraction. Balance theory argues that you should have positive feelings for those with whom you agree, social comparison theory (Chapter Eight) suggests that similar others will reward you with comparisons that are likely to be both more meaningful and more ego enhancing, and exchange theory implies that similar others may be able to provide you with a wider range of rewarding interactions.

Finally, the ideas of exchange theory suggest that certain *personal qualities* of the target person ought to be related to the development of attraction. Specifically, you should prefer people who want to reward you and who are capable of doing so. One of the best predictors of a person's desire to give you social rewards should be the person's attitude toward you, so exchange theories would predict that you should be more attracted to people who express liking for you than to people who do not think highly of you. As far as capability to bestow rewards is concerned, in any culture that places a high value upon good looks, physically attractive people should have more to give; in any culture that values success, competent people should be better able to deliver. So in contemporary American society, competent and physically attractive people would be liked more than incompetent and unattractive people. Exchange and reinforcement theorists do not argue that this preference is necessarily morally correct, only that it is highly likely.

All these factors assume, to one degree or another, that interpersonal attraction is strongly influenced by rewards received. Indeed, the relationship between each factor and interpersonal attraction can be regarded as an aspect of the general rule that rewards increase attraction. A considerable amount of experimental evidence supports this general rule (e.g., see reviews by Aronson, 1970; Berscheid and Walster, 1969; Byrne, 1971), and compared to the inconsistency of common sense statements about attraction the general rule is a significant improvement. We now consider propinquity, similarity, and personal qualities in more detail, showing some of the ways in which these variables influence attraction, but also pointing out some of the exceptional cases. It should be noted that these variables do not exhaust the list of contributors to attraction, although they are the ones that have received the most attention from social psychologists. For a more complete picture of interpersonal attraction you might want to read the short book by Berscheid and Walster (1969) or the collection of more technical papers edited by Huston (1974).

Propinquity

Advertisements for long-distance telephone calls notwithstanding, the best way to give, and receive, rewards through social interaction is in person. So physical proximity, and the opportunity for interaction that it provides, will have substantial impact on the development of liking. This has been illustrated in a classic study of housing patterns and friendship conducted at the Massachusetts Institute of Technology by Festinger, Schachter, and Back (1950). The university maintained a housing project for married students which was called Westgate West and consisted of a total of seventeen two-story buildings, with each building divided into ten apartments as diagramed in Figure 10-3. For the most part students who were assigned to live in the project did not know each other in advance, and more importantly,

FIGURE 10-3
A Westgate West residential unit. (Adapted from Festinger, Schachter, and Back, 1950, p. 36)

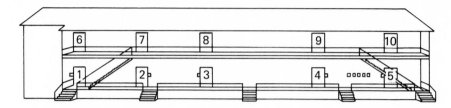

they were assigned as apartments became available so they had no choice in which apartment they occupied. To determine the effect of living in the project on friendship choices, participation in the governing body of the project, and a variety of other attitudes, the researchers conducted extensive interviews with the residents of the project. These interviews were conducted after the tenants had lived in the project for some time, and one of the first questions asked each couple was which three other couples they saw socially most frequently.

Proximity was measured in functional units rather than in terms of actual physical distance, with the units based on doors passed and stairways climbed in order to reach the other apartments. Thus next-door neighbors on the same floor were counted as a single unit apart, even though the distance between apartment #3 and apartment #4 was almost twice the distance between #3 and #2. The results showed that next-door neighbors on the same floor were named as good friends 41 percent of the time, while people two units away on the same floor were named only 22 percent of the time and people the farthest away on the same floor were named only 10 percent of the time. Overall, the residents living on the same floor were more likely to be friends than residents living on different floors, and very seldom were close friends found in different buildings.

As noted by Freedman, Carlsmith, and Sears (1974), there are a number of reasons why proximity might lead to attraction, including anticipatory dissonance avoidance, familiarity, predictability, and the maintenance of balance. At first you might give a close neighbor every possible benefit of the doubt, overlooking faults so that the interaction necessitated by your proximity will not be unpleasant. This sort of anticipatory dissonance avoidance has been demonstrated by Darley and Berscheid (1967), who found that subjects evaluated a stimulus person with whom they expected to interact more favorably than a comparable stimulus person with whom no interaction was anticipated. Close proximity also leads to familiarity with each other's habits and preferences, and familiarity alone (the "mere exposure" discussed in Chapter Seven) can lead to greater liking within limits of novelty and interest (Freedman, Carlsmith, and Suomi, 1969; Saegert, Swap, and Zajonc, 1973). Not only are we familiar with people who live nearby, we cannot help but be aware of their habits and preferences: when they go to work, what sort of friends they already have, the kinds of parties they give, and (in many apartment buildings and dormitories) even what they say to each other in ostensible privacy. As a result their behavior is more predictable, and we are less likely to offend them inadvertently and more likely to learn in what ways their attitudes are similar to our own. Finally, once a relationship is established, the interaction forced by proximity may lead us to ignore minor difficulties that might otherwise lessen liking.

As powerful as proximity is in the development of attraction, it has significant limitations. If your new neighbors have a barking dog which keeps you awake at night, no amount of pleasant interaction during the day will produce unqualified liking. These are situational limitations on the effects of proximity, but there may be personal limitations as well. For example, Wrightsman and Cook (1965) examined the personality characteristics of initially prejudiced white subjects who were given prolonged positive contact with blacks in a work setting. These investigators found that subjects whose attitudes did not change in a more positive direction were lower in self-esteem and had more negative views of people in general than subjects whose attitudes did become less prejudiced. People need to like themselves and to maintain open minds toward others in order to come to like a broad sampling of other people.

Finally, the frustrations often found in close relationships may become so great that even an initially favorable evaluation is not sufficient to guarantee harmony and mutual reward. Considering the exceptions to the rule that proximity leads to liking, it may be more appropriate to argue that proximity serves to enhance whatever emotion predominates—attraction or repulsion. Given our initial tendency to give others the benefit of the doubt, proximity may encourage the development of a relationship. And given our needs to maintain cognitive consistency, proximity may keep us from noticing minor faults. But when those faults can no longer be overlooked, proximity may magnify unpleasantness into hatred. Eloquent testimony to this aspect of proximity is provided by the high proportion of homicides committed by members of the victim's immediate family.

Similarity

If propinquity is often regarded as an essential condition for the development of attraction (on the grounds that rewards are most easily exchanged in person), similarity is often cited as a reason that such rewards are forthcoming. Attitude similarity contributes to balance, and thus to a relation of liking. Similar others provide us with the best social comparison—both the most accurate and the most likely to be self-enhancing. The interaction matrix of similar people will have more possibility for mutual reward, and hence a higher correspondence of outcomes. Similar people will be more likely to believe the same inputs are relevant in the determination of equity, and they may also judge the outcomes by the same standards. For these reasons and others, it has long been assumed that similarity will lead to attraction, and the extensive program of research by Byrne (1961, 1971) and his associates provides a great deal of evidence to support this assumption.

An Experimental Example

Suppose that you were a subject in one of these experiments. Early in the school term you would have been given a standardized attitude scale (Byrne, 1971) to obtain your opinions on twenty-six different issues, including school activities, political parties, religious beliefs, and sexual customs. Some weeks later you would be asked to serve as a subject in a study of interpersonal judgment, and your task would be to make a number of judgments about a person based on limited information, specifically consisting of the person's answers to the same twenty-six-item attitude scale. You might learn about the person's attitudes by reading what was purported to be his or her answer sheet, by listening to a tape recording in which the person described his or her answers, by watching a sound film of the person's responses, or by being present when the person was interviewed by the experimenter. No matter what the stimulus mode, you would learn just how much this person's attitudes agreed with your own. Then you would be asked to use the Interpersonal Judgment Scale mentioned earlier to estimate the person's knowledge of current events, intelligence, morality, and personal adjustment and to indicate how much you liked the person as an individual and as a work partner. The ratings on these last two scales would be added together to determine your attraction toward the person. What sort of ratings would you make?

If you were responding the way most subjects in these experiments did, you would indicate more attraction toward people who were similar to you. Indeed, most of the research shows that attraction increases as a direct function of the proportion of agreement: the higher percentage of statements on which the stimulus person agrees with you, the more attraction you express toward that person. This relationship has been found to hold across modes of stimulus presen-

tation, and across a wide variety of subject populations, including
hospitalized surgical and psychiatric patients, primary and secondary
school children, clerical workers, and participants in federal job-
training programs.

The Law of Attraction?

In an attempt to account for this rather consistent finding, Byrne
(1969, 1971; Byrne and Nelson, 1965) has proposed a law of attraction
which states that "attraction toward X [some object or person] is a
positive linear function of the proportion of positive reinforcements
received from X [the object or person]" (1969, p. 67). This explanation
of similarity attraction in terms of reinforcement assumes that similarity is positively reinforcing, an assumption which has been successfully tested by using attitude statements that agreed with the subject's
position to teach a small-large discrimination in a learning study
(Golightly and Byrne, 1964), and by measuring the physiological
consequences of agreement and disagreement (Gormly, 1974). In addition, though most of the research has dealt with attitude similarity,
the same positive linear function has been obtained with other sorts
of similarity as well, such as economic level, psychological defense
mechanisms, and self-concept (Byrne, 1969).

Has the attitude similarity–attraction research really produced a
"law" of attraction based on reinforcement, or are there still significant
exceptions to this relationship between reinforcement and attraction?
Critics of Byrne's approach (e.g., Aronson, 1970; Murstein, 1971)
would point out that (a) the experimental paradigm might not generalize well to situations outside the laboratory, (b) there are cases in
which similarity appears to be unpleasant and difference seems pleasant, and (c) on the more general question, there is a sizable body of
research that conflicts with the hypothesized relationship between
reinforcement and attraction. Let us consider these objections in
turn.

Certainly Byrne's work demonstrates that if we know nothing
about a person but attitudes, we will evaluate the person more positively if those attitudes resemble our own. But as Murstein (1971) has
noted, this restricted experimental paradigm may not generalize well.
When you meet a person for the first time you don't administer an attitude scale before you make any attempts to be friendly. The person's
attitudes on crucial issues may not be obvious until the relationship
has progressed quite far. Indeed, as the study by Newcomb (1961) of
acquaintance processes in a college dormitory showed, the first element of friendship is proximity. Only after a semester of getting to
know each other better did the students' attitudes before the school

year started become the best predictor of their friendship choices. We approach a new relationship cautiously, revealing a little of ourselves at a time and expecting reciprocal self-disclosure. Gradually this reciprocal disclosure enables us to penetrate each other's masks and defenses (Altman and Taylor, 1973), but the process can be short-circuited at any time. And the depth of agreement may be more important than the simple proportion of agreement. If you disagree with another person about the moral justification for war or the value of human life, extensive agreement about superficial issues may not be sufficient to maintain the relationship.

Complementarity in Attraction

Quite apart from the question of how well the similarity-attraction paradigm may generalize, there is some doubt as to whether similarity is always rewarding. For example, consider similarity of personality rather than of attitude. In long-term relationships, this sort of similarity might turn out to be uninteresting. As Winch (1958) suggested in his detailed study of the personality characteristics and personal needs of twenty-five married couples, strong relationships may be built on complementarity. On such important dimensions as dominance-submission and nurturance-receptivity, Winch found that the needs of one spouse often complemented the needs of the other. Dominant husbands tended to have submissive wives; dominant wives tended to have submissive husbands. Although support for the idea of need complementarity has not always been obtained in other studies, a recent review (Swensen, 1973) concludes that complementarity does influence friendship and marriage choices. In other research involving personality similarity, Novak and Lerner (1968) have shown that subjects find it threatening to learn that they are personally similar to a person who is mentally unstable, and research by Shaver (1970) and by Schroeder and Linder (1976) shows that personal similarity to a stimulus person who accidentally causes harm can also be threatening. You don't want to think that you could make the same mistakes, so similarity that could lead to negative outcomes is unpleasant.

It should be noted that these latter studies present difficulties of interpretation only for the specific issue of similarity-attraction, not for the larger principle which explains attraction in terms of positive reinforcement. The reinforcement theorist could easily argue that whenever similarity leads to rewards (as mediated, for example, by shared attitudes) it will lead to attraction, and that whenever similarity leads to punishment (such as boredom or threat) it will reduce attraction. Thus the larger principle of reinforcement can accommodate both cases of similarity-attraction and cases in which attraction is increased by personal differences. This resolves some of the specific problems, but the general issue still remains: Does attraction only follow positive reinforcement, or are there instances in which pain and suffering lead to greater attraction?

Suffering

Many of the studies conducted to test cognitive dissonance theory (summarized in Chapter Six) suggest that there will, indeed, be times when interpersonal attraction will be enhanced by suffering. Particularly relevant are the experiments that have dealt with the relationship between the *severity of an "initiation"* and subsequent attraction toward that group (Aronson and Mills, 1959; Gerard and Matthewson, 1966). In the first of these studies, Aronson and Mills asked female undergraduates to volunteer to participate in a group discussion of the psychology of sex. Each subject was tested individually, and there were three conditions: a Severe initiation condition, a Mild initiation condition, and a No-initiation control condition.

In all three conditions the subjects listened to a dull discussion on the reproductive habits of animals and then rated the topic and the participants in the discussion. In the No-initiation condition the subjects simply listened to the discussion (which was actually a tape recording) without any prior test. But in the two initiation conditions subjects were told that they would have to pass a "screening test" before listening to the discussion. The ostensible purpose of this screening test was to ensure that subjects would not be too shy to participate in the discussion. In the Severe initiation condition the screening test required the female subject to read aloud (to the male experimenter) a rather explicit passage from a contemporary novel and a list of twelve obscene words. In the Mild initiation condition the subject had to read aloud a number of words related to sex which were not obscene.

The results of the experiment showed that subjects in the Severe initiation condition expressed the most positive feelings toward the dull group discussion and the participants in that discussion. These results support the prediction from dissonance theory but conflict with the principle of reinforcement. There were, however, a number of alternative explanations for the findings. For example, perhaps the Severe initiation subjects were simply more "relieved" at passing the difficult test, and this relief was reflected in their ratings.

Many of these alternatives were later ruled out by Gerard and Matthewson's (1966) conceptual replication of the earlier study. Instead of using sexual material for the initiation, these investigators employed a short series of either mild or painful electric shocks (the mild and severe initiations). The topic of the discussion group was changed from sexual behavior to cheating in college, and some of the subjects evaluated the discussion without thinking that it was a group they would later join. The results of the experiment replicated those of Aronson and Mills (1959), with higher ratings of the discussion group obtained when there had been a severe initiation, and the variations in procedure effectively ruled out a number of alternative explanations.

These experiments show that punishment suffered in order to join a group can enhance liking for the group. Such results pose a problem for reinforcement theories of attraction, which assume that attraction will increase with the rewards obtained from a relationship. To be fair to the reinforcement position, it should be noted that there may be differences between the attraction expressed toward a group and the liking shown for an individual person. In addition, the punishment in these experiments was administered not by the object of attraction, but by a third party—the experimenter. For both of these reasons the severity-of-initiation studies do not provide a perfect comparison to the similarity-attraction work of Byrne (1971) and his associates. A better comparison would be obtained if the object of liking delivered the punishments, and if that object were a person rather than a group. As we shall see in a later section on gain and loss, research by Aronson and Linder (1965) meets these criteria and still contrasts with what would be expected on the basis of reinforcement alone.

Personal Qualities of the Stimulus Person

Physical Attractiveness

From the viewpoint of reinforcement theory, propinquity makes reward possible, similarity makes reward likely, and the personal characteristics of the stimulus person set limits on how much reward is available. For example, consider physical attractiveness as a basis for heterosexual attraction. A number of experiments reviewed by Berscheid and Walster (1974a) indicate that people do equate attractiveness with positive aspects of character and behavior—what is beautiful is good. In one such study, Dion, Berscheid, and Walster (1972) found that physically attractive people were expected to be more sensitive, kind, strong, poised, modest, sociable, outgoing, and sexually responsive than were physically less attractive people. This physical attractiveness stereotype held for both male and female stimulus persons, and it did not differ between male and female subjects. Later research has suggested that there may also be some negative characteristics such as vanity and egotism associated with physical attractiveness, but even this study replicated many of the positive qualities of the stereotype (Dermer and Thiel, 1975).

The relationship between physical attractiveness and ability to bestow interpersonal rewards can be illustrated in a number of ways. In a study of the ways in which a woman's appearance might be related to her marriage choice, Elder (1969) found that women who married above their working-class origins were, on the average, prettier as adolescents than were those who did not marry above their original level. Studies of satisfaction with partners who had been provided by computer blind date services have indicated that physical attractiveness is the most important determinant of desire to date the partner again (Brislin and Lewis, 1968; Tesser and Brodie, 1971), and research by Berscheid, Dion, Walster, and Walster (1971) extended this analysis to the active choice of a dating partner. These investigators found some evidence for preference of attractive people, but they also found strong support for a matching principle: people tended to select dates whose attractiveness was similar to their own. Apparently physical attractiveness not only signifies how much social reward might be available, but also indicates how likely it is that such rewards will be forthcoming. We prefer attractive people to unattractive ones, but we also expect attractive people to be more discriminating themselves. Thus the preference for more attractive people is moderated by a fear of being rejected. Exactly these results have been found for the dating preferences of male students by Huston (1973).

Competence

In the same way that we prefer physically attractive people to people who are unattractive, we prefer people who are competent to those who are incompetent (Spence and Helmreich, 1972; Stotland and Hillmer, 1962). But here again there is some moderation of preference. We like those who are competent enough to reward us, but people who are perfect might have nothing to do with us. You can probably think of a classmate who seems to breeze through school with high grades while spending more time on extracurricular activities than on studies. And you might even be able to bring yourself to like such a person if he or she would only make a mistake every now and then!

The humanizing influence of making a mistake has been demonstrated in an experiment by Aronson, Willerman, and Floyd (1966). These investigators had subjects listen to a tape recording of what was purported to be a preliminary session for choosing a person to represent the university in a nationally televised quiz program for college students. In fact, there were two different tapes, one in which the person appeared to be extremely competent (answering 92 percent of the very difficult questions correctly) and one in which he appeared to be incompetent (answering only 30 percent correctly). For half of the subjects within each of these competence conditions, the end of the questions ended the tape, and those subjects then completed a number of rating scales to describe the stimulus person. For the other half of the subjects in each competence condition the tape continued. The interviewer offered the candidate a cup of coffee, there was the sound of confusion, and the candidate was heard lamenting that he had spilled the coffee all over his new suit. At the conclusion of this incident the tape ended and the subjects made their ratings of the stimulus person. The results showed that overall the competent stimulus person was seen as more attractive than the incompetent, but more importantly, he was judged even *more* attractive when he spilled coffee on himself than when he did not. In contrast, the incompetent stimulus person was seen as even less attractive when the accident came after his poor performance.

The research on competence, like the research on physical attractiveness, can easily be interpreted in terms of reinforcement. All that is necessary is to assume that the actual reward value of a stimulus person is a combination of what rewards that person has to give and how likely it is that you will be the recipient. The highly competent, but human, person won't hold your own failings against you. This view of actual reward as the product of the *magnitude of the incentive* and the *probability* that the incentive will be forthcoming is implicit in most reinforcement theories relating to human behavior, and is explicit in the social learning theory of Rotter (1954) and other approaches based on his formulation (as noted in Chapter Nine). Thus reinforcement principles can be used to account for attraction to physically attractive people, as well as dating choice of partners who match and for the attraction to competent people, especially the highly competent but humanized ones. As the reward value of a person (the magnitude of the incentives he or she has to offer times the likelihood that they will be offered) increases, so does your attraction toward that person.

Gain and Loss of Esteem

As we noted earlier, the evaluations that a person makes about you ought to be a fairly good indication of whether he or she will bestow social rewards upon you. And to the extent that the likelihood of such rewards increases your attraction toward the person, your attraction should increase with the frequency of the person's positive evaluations of you. This is simply another way to state Byrne's "tentative law of attraction." We have seen, however, that there are exceptions to this view of interpersonal attraction. Many of the findings that do not quite fit—propinquity can lead to hatred, similarity can be threatening, competence that approaches perfection can be too much of a good thing—can be interpreted in a reinforcement framework by adding the concept of likelihood of reward to the idea of amount of reward available. But other conflicting findings, such as the severity of initiation research, cannot be integrated easily into the reinforcement approach.

An important exception to the reinforcement position depends on the *sequence* of the rewards that are delivered. Suppose that you came to a conference in my office on several different occasions, and that on each of these occasions I made a summary evaluation of your performance. If my comments were always positive, you would be happy about it, but you might wonder whether I was paying enough attention to tell when you did something wrong. On the other hand, if my comments began quite negatively and then became more positive, you might think that I was a discerning fellow, and that you had succeeded in earning my respect. What should happen to your attraction for me in each case? The "law of attraction" states that attraction is determined only by the proportion of positive reinforcements, and since this proportion is higher (actually 100 percent) in the first case, that law would predict greater attraction when my comments were all positive. But a more cognitive approach might argue that since the negative comments establish my discernment beyond a doubt, my later positive comments would mean much more to you than would an unchanging string of positive evaluations. This line of reasoning predicts greater attraction in the changing condition, even though fewer positive reinforcements are delivered.

To compare these two predictions Aronson and Linder (1965) designed an experiment which required subjects to engage in a series of seven conversations with another person (actually an experimental confederate). As a result of these conversations the confederate provided evaluations of the subjects, and there were four different patterns of evaluation. In the All Positive condition the confederate described the subject in glowing terms after each of the seven conversations, while in the All Negative condition she described the subject as dull, unintelligent, and ordinary in a variety of ways after each of the seven conversations. In addition to these two constant conditions, there were two changing conditions: a Negative-Positive one in which the first three evaluations were negative, the fourth was neutral, and the last three were positive; and a Positive-Negative condition which was the mirror image of the Negative-Positive.

On the grounds that changes in evaluation would imply discernment, Aronson and Linder predicted that the two changing conditions would produce ratings of attractiveness that were more extreme than the ratings in the two constant conditions. That is, not only would the Negative-Positive produce *more* attraction than the All Positive, the Positive-Negative would produce *less* attraction than the All Negative. The results showed that, as expected, the Negative-Positive confederate was liked better than the All Positive confederate. The comparison between Positive-Negative and All Negative was in the expected direction, with the Positive-Negative liked less, but the difference was not statistically significant. Thus there was strong evidence for what Aronson and Linder called a *gain* effect (change from negative to positive produced more attraction than all positive), and marginal support for a *loss* effect (change from positive to negative produced less attraction than all negative). Similar results have been obtained in other studies (Gerard and Greenbaum, 1962; Mettee, 1971; Mettee, Taylor, and Friedman, 1973), and a recent study using nonverbal cues to coolness or warmth rather than verbal evaluations (Clore, Wiggins, and Itkin, 1975) has obtained strong gain and loss results.

The gain-loss results, like the severity of initiation findings, contradict the predictions about attraction that would be made on the basis of any theory of reinforcement (such as Byrne's "law of attraction") that does not itself contain a strong cognitive component. Just counting the reinforcements delivered is not enough. But these results do not contradict all theories of social behavior based on the principle of reinforcement: given a liberal interpretation of what constitutes an "interaction," the exchange theory of Thibaut and Kelley (1959) can handle these apparent exceptions to reinforcement with little difficulty. The gain-loss phenomenon can be accounted for by suggesting that the early trials set a comparison level for that particular relationship against which the later outcomes are evaluated. This is what leads to the feeling of "gain" in the Negative-Positive and to the feeling of "loss" in the Positive-Negative. To account for the severity of initiation findings, it is possible to argue that the unpleasant interaction with the experimenter (either reading obscene words, or receiving electric shocks) is a comparison level against which even a dull discussion group has certain advantages.

Arousal and Attraction

Throughout the chapter we have been describing attraction as an attitude of favorability toward the stimulus person. In closing let us consider the affective component of that attitude. You may recall from

Chapter Eight that Schachter (1964) has proposed a two-factor theory of emotion. This theory holds that an emotional experience requires both physiological arousal and an appropriate cognitive label for that arousal. When there is some ambiguity about the source of the arousal, the necessary cognitive label may be provided by cues in the situation, and in some cases this can lead to misattribution of the emotion. Recently some investigators (e.g., Berscheid and Walster, 1974b) have suggested that, especially in the case of romantic liking, Schachter's theory should lead us to wonder just how much of passion depends on the target person and how much depends on other aspects of the situation.

Imagine that you are on a first date with an attractive person, on your way to a concert to be followed by a small party. You have been looking forward to the date with anticipation, but also with some apprehension about making a good impression. The concert involves several of your favorite performers, and many of your good friends will be at the party. During the evening you will be trying to guess whether your date is having a good time, and you will be evaluating your own feelings as well. Let's examine the things that might be contributing to your own state of physiological arousal. There will be the apprehension about the impression you are making, there will be the pleasure of the concert, there will be the company of your friends, and of course the attraction you feel toward your date. But will each of these be separately identified and properly labeled? Or will all the sources of arousal be combined and mistakenly attributed to the most salient feature of the situation—your date?

In their explanation of romantic love Walster and Berscheid (1971; Berscheid and Walster, 1974b) argue that *misattribution* is the more likely outcome, and there is some experimental evidence that supports this interpretation. For example, Brehm, Gatz, Goethals, McCrimmon, and Ward (1970) found that even a wholly irrelevant source of emotional arousal might be erroneously attributed to the attractiveness of a potential date. In this study male undergraduates were led to believe that they would later receive a series of electric shocks and then were interviewed by an attractive female student. Compared to a control group which had received no threat, the threatened subjects rated the woman as more attractive and expressed a greater interest in dating her. Apparently even the arousal generated by fear can be misinterpreted as a product of attraction, and in Chapter Eleven we shall see that similar misattribution can enhance aggressive tendencies as well. Whenever the true source of arousal is ambiguous or not attended to, a highly salient situational cue can direct the course of the emotional experience.

At this point it may be appropriate to ask again, "What leads to interpersonal attraction?" We have seen that the best answer is "sometimes propinquity, sometimes similarity, and sometimes personal characteristics; usually reinforcement, but occasionally not." Do not be discouraged by the close resemblance between this answer and the popular wisdom "birds of a feather flock together, but sometimes opposites attract." Social psychologists studying interpersonal attraction may not have produced a wide variety of counterintuitive findings, but they have discovered many of the conditions under which different features of common sense analysis seem to apply. More importantly, the experimental research on interpersonal attraction can be placed in the context of existing theory (especially exchange theory), leading to predictions that cannot be made on the basis of common sense alone and contributing to our understanding of attraction as one more aspect of positive social behavior.

SUMMARY

Interpersonal attraction is most frequently considered to be an *attitude of favorability* (p. 397) toward another person or toward a group. But it is a complex attitude, reflected in such particular dimensions as respect, liking, friendship, and the needing and giving that are characteristic of love. Because attraction between people is socially approved, liking is less difficult to measure than are socially undesirable attitudes, although most experimental research in the area deals only with single measurements of attraction between relative strangers.

Liking can be assessed through sociograms of friendship choices (p. 399) and a variety of social, behavioral, and physiological measures as well as through traditional forms of attitude measurement. These attitude questionnaires can be as narrowly focused as the two attraction items on the Interpersonal Judgment Scale, or as broadly conceived as the liking and love scales used to distinguish liking from romantic love.

Among the antecedents of interpersonal attraction are *propinquity* (p. 403), *similarity* (p. 405), and some of the *personal characteristics* (p. 410) of the stimulus person. Other things being equal, people will become attracted to others with whom they come in frequent contact, to people whose attitudes are similar to their own, and to those whose personal characteristics suggest both an ability and a willingness to provide them with rewards. All these factors assume that liking will increase with the exchange of rewards, and a law of attraction (p. 407) has been proposed which states that attraction will increase as a positive linear function of the proportion of rewards provided.

There are, however, important exceptions to this general rule that reinforcement increases liking. The entire body of cognitive dissonance research, especially studies dealing with severity of initiation (p. 409), would suggest that punishment, as well as reward, can enhance liking. In long-term relationships, complementarity (p. 408) of personality may be more important than similarity, and there are times when similarity can be threatening rather than rewarding. Research on the gain and loss(p. 412) of esteem indicates that a particular combination of negative and positive evaluations (negative followed by positive) can lead to greater liking for the evaluator than a series of entirely positive evaluations. Finally, an extension of the cognitive labeling theory of emotion suggests that romantic attraction may be enhanced through *misattribution* (p. 415) of arousal from other sources. By charting the course of the general rule of reinforcement, and by noting its exceptions, scientific study of interpersonal attraction can lead to better understanding of the affective tie between people.

Suggested Additional Readings

BERSCHEID, E., and WALSTER, E. H. *Interpersonal attraction.* Reading, Mass.: Addison-Wesley, 1969. This short book is a very good introduction to a variety of topics in interpersonal attraction and concentrates particularly on the reward value of the target persons. Readable and recommended.

HUSTON, T. L. (Ed.) *Foundations of interpersonal attraction.* New York: Academic Press, 1974. A collection of chapters written by leading researchers. The book is intended for an audience of social psychologists, so it will be a bit technical for many students.

LATANÉ, B., and DARLEY, J. M. *The unresponsive bystander: Why won't he help?* Appleton-Century-Crofts, 1970. This book summarizes the authors' program of research on bystander intervention in emergency situations, taking the position that situational factors are of paramount importance. Although it is basically a research report, it is written in a manner designed for nontechnical readers.

MACAULAY, J. R., and BERKOWITZ, L. *Altruism and helping behavior.* New York: Academic Press, 1970. A collection of chapters, like those in the Huston book written by leading researchers and largely for a professional audience. But it will not be too formidable for interested students.

In the real social world, we face a confusion of inconsistent attitudes toward competition and aggression.

Photo by Paul Seder

Competition and Aggression

Chapter Eleven

Not all social behavior is as positive as the altruism and attraction we have just considered. Indeed the lessons of history and the contemporary records of crime indicate that there has always been and currently is a vast amount of aggressive and antisocial behavior present in human society. Among the industrialized countries, America's criminal records paint a particularly gloomy picture. The Federal Bureau of Investigation's Uniform Crime Reports for 1974 recorded more than 450 thousand aggravated assaults, more than 400 thousand robberies, over 55 thousand forcible rapes, and more than 20 thousand murders. On the average this is equivalent to one violent crime every *thirty-three seconds* of each day in the year (Kelley, 1975). It is important to note that these figures represent only crimes of violence against persons; property crimes (such as arson, burglary, and vandalism) only add to the total. Even worse, an accepted (but probably conservative) estimate places the number of crimes actually committed at *double* the number reported to the police (Mulvihill and Tumin, 1969). And finally, there is a great deal of everyday aggression that occurs apart from criminal offenses.

But aggression and violent crime are not the only examples of antisocial action: corporations make huge domestic political contributions, or payments to agents of foreign governments, in order to ensure their competitive position; economic or "white collar" crime costs the country millions of dollars a year; the effects of economic and social competition can be seen in everything from the actions of a politician who uses position for personal financial gain to the behavior of a student who cheats on an examination in order to improve a grade. It would seem that competition, like aggression, might have predominantly negative effects on society. But is this necessarily true? Aren't there times when competition benefits society and when aggression is encouraged? What exactly do we mean by competition and aggression? What social and personal factors lead to the occurrence of competition? of aggression? Can any of the theories of social psychology we have discussed earlier (especially in Chapter Nine) shed light on these phenomena? The purpose of this chapter is to suggest answers to some of these questions. We begin with a definition of competition, then consider situational factors in competition (reward structure, presence of threat) and individual differences in competitive desires (such as achievement motivation). Next we turn to a definition of aggression, then examine the predisposition toward aggression and the responses to frustration. We conclude with a description of the effects of witnessing aggression (the problem of filmed and televised violence).

Competition

THE DEFINITION OF COMPETITION

When we speak of competition, or of aggression, we are confronted by definitional problems quite different from those encountered in the description of positive social behavior. You will remember that the common usage of the term *altruism* included an element of self-sacrifice that could not be represented in any operational manner satisfactory for the needs of social science. In a sense, the common language term was a bit too specific. In contrast, the normal usage of *competition* and *aggression* encompasses too many different meanings: the terms are not precise enough. For example, to say that two parties are in competition for scarce resources usually means each is actively trying to get more than an equal share, at the other's expense. But to say that there is stiff competition for admission to graduate schools only means that many of the applicants are well qualified and that there are more applicants than openings. No direct confrontation among applicants is implied, and the final outcome is under the control of third parties (the admissions committees) rather than under the control of either competitor. Stretching the definition even further, some businesses claim that their prices are "competitive," meaning only that they are no higher than usual, not that they are substantially lower.

Most social psychologists would restrict the meaning of the word competition to a variation of its first usage, requiring that one person's gains be achieved at the other's expense, and requiring the outcome to be determined primarily by the actions of the competing parties. Such a definition can be stated most precisely in terms of Thibaut and Kelley's (1959) exchange theory. You will recall from Chapter Nine that an interaction between two or more people can be described by the degree of correspondence of outcomes for the participants. In a dyad, if one person's most profitable choices also provide good outcomes for the other, there is high correspondence of outcomes. Alternatively, if one's most profitable choices provide bad outcomes for the other, then there is low correspondence of outcomes. **Competition** thus occurs whenever all participants strive to achieve their individual goals in an interaction characterized by low correspondence of outcomes. This is a definition of competition that takes into account both the nature of the situation (low correspondence of outcomes) and ·

the actions taken by the participants (the striving to achieve one's own goals).

The definition of competition in terms of correspondence of outcomes encompasses both those cases in which there is only one winner and one loser and those cases in which there are numerous winners with varying degrees of success. In a winner-take-all contest there is a perfect negative correspondence of outcomes: every gain by one person is matched by an equal loss to the other. When you match wits with a confidence man, every dollar he gains is a dollar you have lost, and the interaction as a whole has a *zero sum* (his gains minus your losses equals zero). In the other sort of competitive interaction the correspondence of outcomes is low, but not perfectly negative. For example, in automobile races, professional tennis and golf tournaments, and college classes, rewards await the several people who finish at the top of the group. But since these rewards (be they prize money or high grades) do not come directly from the "losers," the interaction as a whole has a non-zero sum. Strong competition obviously can occur in both situations.

FACTORS CONTRIBUTING TO COMPETITION

Why do some people seem to have a relentless drive for competition, even if their achievements must be obtained at the expense of other people? When does the legitimate and beneficial competition inherent in so many relationships become destructive exploitation? How does the size of the rewards to be gained affect competition? How do differences in power and resources among competing parties influence the course of competition? Perhaps most important, how should social psychology attempt to answer these questions? Given the prevalence of competition in our society, it might seem appropriate to assess the personalities of successful individuals, to observe the frequent negotiating sessions between management and labor, or to assess the social reforms achieved by special interest and minority groups. But because of the complexity of the social world, and the problems inherent in attempting to infer causality from events not under direct control of the observers, the great majority of social psychological research on competition involves experimental analogs of the instances of competition found in the world outside the laboratory. In this section we shall present some of the common research techniques, discuss the conclusions drawn from this research, and elaborate on one individual difference variable considered important in competition—the need for achievement.

Experimental Methods for the Study of Competition

The Prisoner's Dilemma

One of the first requirements needed to conduct research on competition is an appropriate dependent variable, one that represents the essential elements of competition and can be easily measured, yet is responsive to variations in experimental procedure. If you were brought into a laboratory and asked to take part in something resembling a television game show in which there were monetary prizes, and it was made clear that the questions to be asked would be a good indication of your basic intelligence, virtually no experimental variations would lessen either your desire to win or your anxiety over losing. The experimental task must moderate these incentives and reactions by becoming a more distant abstraction from normal competitive situations. Social psychologists found such an abstraction in a situation originally described as part of game theory (a branch of decision-making theory)—the Prisoner's Dilemma (Luce and Raiffa, 1957).

Suppose that you and a co-conspirator are taken into custody by the police on suspicion of having committed a crime—for example, an armed robbery. The prosecuting attorney is certain that you have committed the crime, but because of a legal technicality knows that conviction will be impossible without a confession from at least one of you. The two of you are led to separate interrogation rooms, where the prosecutor points out to each of you (alone) that you have two alternatives: either you can confess to the armed robbery, or you can refuse to confess. Then the prosecutor outlines the possible consequences. If both of you confess, you will both be convicted and the prosecution will recommend moderately harsh sentences for you both. If neither of you confesses to the armed robbery, you both will still be convicted of illegal possession of a firearm, which carries a shorter sentence than the minimum for robbery. If, however, one of you confesses while the other does not, the one who confesses will be permitted to plea-bargain to an even lesser charge, while the one who does not confess will "get the book thrown at him." These consequences, represented as months of possible sentence, are shown in Figures 11-1 and 11-2. Figure 11-1 shows a verbal description of the sentences that might be imposed for the various outcomes, and

FIGURE 11-1
Verbal description of the Prisoner's Dilemma. (After Luce and Raiffa, 1957)

Prisoner A *(You)*

		Not Confess	Confess
Prisoner B *(Your Friend)*	Not Confess	One year for both	One month for A Ten years for B
	Confess	Ten years for A One month for B	Five years for both

Figure 11-2 is a numerical representation of those sentences, showing the number of months that will be taken away from your life of freedom.

A Mixed-Motive Game

The Prisoner's Dilemma is one sort of **mixed-motive** game. It exhibits neither the consistent high correspondence of outcomes found in pure cooperation, nor the consistent low correspondence of outcomes found in pure competition. In the two cells where you and your co-conspirator make the same decision (either to confess or not confess), your outcomes are identical (perfect high correspondence of outcomes). In the two cells where the two of you reach different decisions, there is a low correspondence of outcomes—one of

FIGURE 11-2
Numerical representation of the Prisoner's Dilemma, scaled in months of imprisonment. (After Luce and Raiffa, 1957)

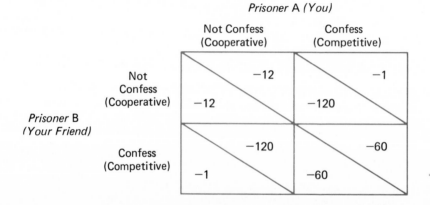

Prisoner A *(You)*

Not Confess (Cooperative) / Confess (Competitive)

Prisoner B *(Your Friend)*

Not Confess (Cooperative): −12 / −12 ; −1 / −120

Confess (Competitive): −120 / −1 ; −60 / −60

you will get away with a light sentence while the other receives a harsh penalty. What action should you take? The answer to this question will depend on a variety of factors such as how much you trust your co-conspirator, how cooperative a person you are, the particular characteristics of the payoffs involved (just how long all the sentences are), and whether there is only a single opportunity to make the choice or whether (as is the case in experimental research) there are repeated plays of the game.

As indicated in Figure 11-2, *the cooperative choice in the Prisoner's Dilemma game is to remain firm and not confess.* This may sound confusing at first, because in most cases we describe a prisoner who is helping the prosecutor as cooperative. But that is society's view, not the view of the other person in the interaction (the co-conspirator). From the standpoint of the co-conspirator, the Not Confess choice is the truly cooperative one. Not only does that choice open up the opportunity for both of you to prove that there is honor among thieves (and get away with moderately light sentences), it demonstrates that you trust your co-conspirator not to take advantage of the situation by turning state's evidence and putting you away for a long time. In contrast, *the choice to confess is actually the competitive choice,* since from the co-conspirator's point of view a five-year sentence for both of you would be preferable to a ten-year sentence served alone.

All the outcomes in the original example of the Prisoner's Dilemma are negative, but the essential structure of the game does not require that this be true. The essential structure is shown in Figure 11-3, in which letters have been substituted for the numerical payoffs. If both participants make the cooperative choice (C or C'), they will both receive a payoff of S; if both make the competitive choice (D or D'), they will both receive a payoff of T; if their choices differ, the one

FIGURE 11-3
Schematic representation of the general payoff matrix for the Prisoner's Dilemma.

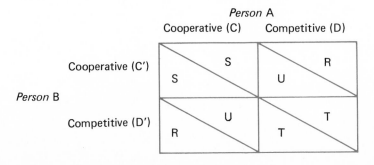

making the competitive choice will receive R, while the other will receive U. The essential character of the dilemma will be preserved in any payoff matrix where the inequality

$$R > S > T > U$$

holds true. This permits researchers to use a form of the Prisoner's Dilemma game that contains only positive payoffs, such as the one shown in Figure 11-4. In research these payoffs can represent either points gained or money earned on every trial of the game. Especially in the all-positive form, the game represents a wide variety of competitive situations—businesses exchanging market information, athletes playing "for themselves" versus for their teams—in which there is a conflict between achievement of individual objectives and achievement of the highest *mutual* profit.

Cooperation or Competition?

Suppose that you were serving as a subject in a study of competition using the Prisoner's Dilemma game. You would be shown the payoff matrix and would be asked to make a choice (C or D) on a number of trials that could range from a single play (Terhune, 1970) to as many as several hundred trials (Rapoport, Chammah, Dwyer, and Gyr, 1962), although the usual number is between twenty-five and fifty. In most studies you would never see your opponent, who would be described to you by the experimenter. In fact you would typically be playing against a standard or *programmed* opponent, because the experimenter would be interested in your reactions to a standard performance by your ostensible rival. Your choice and the opponent's choice are made simultaneously, and on any trial your dilemma is to decide whether you should make the cooperative (C) response in the hope that the opponent will do the same (thus maximiz-

FIGURE 11-4
Positive payoffs in a Prisoner's Dilemma game.

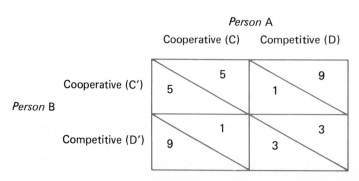

ing the joint profit achieved by the two of you), or whether instead you should make the competitive (D) choice in the hope that you can exploit your opponent and maximize your own outcomes. Extensive research with the Prisoner's Dilemma (e.g., see reviews by Apfelbaum, 1974; Gergen, 1969; Nemeth, 1972; Oskamp, 1972; Vinacke, 1969) has suggested several factors that will affect whether you choose to cooperate or compete. These can be grouped into four general categories—the structural characteristics of the game, your personality and motives, the personal characteristics of the opponent, and the opponent's apparent strategy—and we shall consider one example of each category.

GAME STRUCTURE. Not too surprisingly, changing the relative values of the various payoffs can affect the degree of cooperation. The reason that you occasionally try to exploit your opponent instead of cooperating all the time is that by engaging in exploitation you stand to gain relatively more than you would through constant cooperation. Suppose you were playing the game shown in Figure 11-4 against an opponent who seemed to be making just random choices, 50 percent of the time selecting C′ and the other 50 percent of the time selecting D′. Let us consider your *expected gains* from either cooperation or competition. If you chose C all the time and the opponent continued random choices, half of the time you would gain 5, half of the time you would gain 1. Your expected gain would be an average of the two or $(5 + 1)/2 = 3$. In contrast, if you chose the competitive response (D) every time, your expected gain would be $(9 + 3)/2 = 6$. Obviously, if your opponent were making random choices it would pay you to select the competitive move all the time. Your average expected gain is twice as much from competing as from cooperating, and that ought to be enough to overcome any qualms you have about appearing exploitative to the experimenter.

Now assume that you are still playing against the same randomly choosing opponent, but imagine that the R value of 9 has been changed to 6, and the T value of 3 has been changed to 2. The matrix still meets the definition of a Prisoner's Dilemma ($R > S > T > U$), but your expected gain from competing has been reduced dramatically to $(6 + 2)/2 = 4$. This may not be enough better than the 3 expected from cooperating for you to be willing to present yourself to the experimenter as an exploitative person. The fact that the particular values used in the payoff matrix influence the level of cooperation has been demonstrated primarily through comparisons between the Prisoner's Dilemma and other experimental games (e.g., Enzle, Hansen, and Lowe, 1975; Gallo and McClintock, 1965; Oskamp, 1972; Sermat, 1964), but it is reasonable to believe that the relative size of payoffs should also affect games which meet the definition of a Prisoner's Dilemma.

Since the relative size of the payoffs appears to influence competition, we might also expect that the absolute value of the payoffs would affect the outcome. Subjects competing for points might engage in a good deal of mutual exploitation, but subjects playing for substantial sums of money ought to be more concerned with maximizing joint profits. Surprisingly, the research evidence does not bear out this expectation. There have been studies which found greater cooperation among subjects playing for real money as opposed to imaginary money (Radlow, Weidner, and Hurst, 1968), but other studies have shown the reverse (Gumpert, Deutsch, and Epstein, 1969) and still others have found no differences at all between small and large monetary payoffs (Oskamp and Kleinke, 1970).

PLAYER'S CHARACTERISTICS. With the exception of sex (females tend to be more cooperative than males), few enduring individual difference variables have been found to exert strong influence on long-term competition in experimental games. In one-trial play of the Prisoner's Dilemma Terhune (1970) reports cooperation from *achievement*-oriented subjects, a defensive competition (making the D choice with the expectation that the opponent will also do so) from *affiliation*-oriented subjects, and exploitative competition (making the D choice with the expectation that the opponent will *not* do so) from *power*-oriented subjects. But as the experimental games lengthened, and as the characteristics of the payoff matrices changed in the direction of fostering greater competition, these personality differences exerted much less influence on the outcome.

What does seem to make a difference are the more transient motives that players either bring to the contest or have instilled in them when they arrive. For example, Kelley and Stahelski (1970) found that self-expressed competitors expected all their opponents to be competitive, while self-expressed cooperators expected wide variations in the inclinations of their opponents. Even more importantly, Deutsch (1960) demonstrated that the motivating instructions given to subjects about to play a Prisoner's Dilemma game could greatly affect the level of cooperation. In this experiment all subjects used the same payoff matrix, but there were three different descriptions of the subject's task in the game. In the *competitive* instruction condition the subjects were told that they should try not only to win as much as they could for themselves but also to do as much better than their opponents as they could. In the *individualistic* instruction condition the subjects were told only to win as much as possible for themselves, with no mention made of the opponent's winnings.

Finally, in a *cooperative* instruction condition the subjects were asked to take an interest in the other person's welfare, and were told that the other would be taking an interest in their welfare. There was only one play of the game, for imaginary winnings as high as $10. Cooperative choices were made by nearly 90 percent of the subjects given cooperative instructions, by only 35 percent of the subjects given individualistic instructions, and by fewer than 15 percent of the people given competitive instructions. When subjects were permitted to communicate with each other about the game before making their choices, the cooperation increased in all conditions, although it still remained the lowest in the competitive instruction group. Apparently your own motives or goals for the interaction will influence your choice of whether to cooperate or compete.

OPPONENT'S CHARACTERISTICS. Not only your own motives, but also the characteristics of the opponent will affect cooperation and competition. Imagine that you are about to play some kind of game —chess, tennis, horseshoes—against a single opponent. If you both view the contest as just a game, you will play to win but you will not try to exploit the other just to achieve this end. If, however, your opponent has an inflated self-opinion, you may try a little harder to bring the person into touch with reality, and if he or she appears to be weak you may try to take advantage of this weakness. On a broader scale, how many times have you heard national leaders suggest that safety lies in strength ("force is all they understand," "cuts in the defense budget might be interpreted as a sign of weakness")? Will people actually put up strong defenses against potentially threatening opponents, and will they also take advantage of the weak?

Experimental evidence from Prisoner's Dilemma research suggests that the answer to both of these questions is yes. In one such study Marlowe, Gergen, and Doob (1966) had subjects play thirty trials of a Prisoner's Dilemma game against a (programmed) partner who made 70 percent cooperative responses. The game was described as a decision task, and the subjects were told that in order for them to have some impression of their opponents the two would exchange self-ratings before beginning play. Each subject was then asked to fill out a number of self-rating scales, and these answers were collected by the experimenter for transmission to the subject's opponent. Then the experimenter returned with what were purported to be the opponent's rating scales. There were two different conditions: the "opponent" described himself either as ineffective and lacking in self-confidence (Self-effacing) or as extremely capable and self-confident (Egotistical). To complete the factorial design, half of the subjects within each of these confidence conditions were told that they would have the opportunity after the experiment to meet with their opponent to discuss the decisions that they had reached (Anticipation of Interaction), while the other half of the subjects within each condition were told that they would not be able to see their opponents after the session (No Anticipation). Following delivery of these instructions subjects played the Prisoner's Dilemma game for the thirty trials.

As predicted, the subjects made more competitive choices against the Egotist when they anticipated having to meet with him after the experiment than when they did not ever expect to see him again. In a relationship that has the potential for becoming a long-term interaction, it is important to indicate at the very beginning that you are no pushover, and the best way to do that in this context is to be exploitative yourself (force is the only thing they understand). But what if the opponent appears so powerless that he could not possibly be a threat? It is disappointing to learn that in the Self-effacing Opponent condition the greater exploitation occurred when no future interaction was anticipated. Indeed, the highest overall level of competitive choices (an average of twenty-three out of the thirty trials) was obtained in the Self-effacing Opponent–No Anticipation condition. Those who argue that it is a mistake to appear weak seem to be correct. This apparently applies to the perceptions engendered by strategy (to which we now turn) as well as to the perceptions engendered by apparent personality characteristics.

OPPONENT'S STRATEGY. In the Prisoner's Dilemma game there are three basic possible strategies for the (programmed) opponent to take. The first is *unconditional cooperation*, in which the opponent repeatedly makes the cooperative choice regardless of the real subject's choice. The second general strategy is *unconditional competition*, in which the opponent continually makes the competitive choice regardless of the subject's choice. There can, of course, be different levels of these two strategies, with 50 percent of each being the middle ground, but in both cases the proportion of cooperative to competitive responses is set beforehand and bears no relation to the subject's own strategy. The third general class is called the contingent or "tit-for-tat" strategy, and in this case the choice of the programmed opponent on any trial is determined by the choice of the subject on the *preceding* trial. There can be mixtures of these three general classes of strategy in any particular Prisoner's Dilemma game, but here it is sufficient simply to discuss the basic classes.

When one considers strategy, as well as when one considers the opponent's personal characteristics, it appears that people will take advantage of others if they believe that such exploitation will not be

punished. In a study by Shure, Meeker, and Hansford (1965), subjects played a Prisoner's Dilemma game against an opponent who was
an avowed pacifist (by virtue of his Quaker background). The pacifist's strategy was unconditionally cooperative, and he even refused
to employ an outside punishment (electric shock) as retaliation for
exploitation. The more the subjects learned about this pacifist's behavior and intentions, the more they exploited him. As Nemeth (1972)
has pointed out, the subjects were urged by their constituents (who
were actually experimental confederates) to assume the aggressive
role in the game, so it was impossible to tell for certain whether the
subjects were responding to this peer pressure or were just using
that pressure as a justification for the hostile actions they would have
taken even in the absence of constituent pressure. It should be noted,
however, that although the pressure from constituents may cloud the
results of this experiment, the presence of pressure more closely
approximates the situation as it might occur in the world outside the
laboratory.

Among the three basic strategies, the contingent one produces by
far the highest levels of cooperation across a variety of settings
(Nemeth, 1972). This might be because the contingent strategy allows
a form of implicit communication between the participants that would
otherwise not be possible (Jones and Gerard, 1967; Nemeth, 1972). In
the usual Prisoner's Dilemma game no communication is permitted
during play of the game, and contingency in strategy might be seen
as one way to restore this usual element of bargaining and negotiation.
Of course contingency might also be required to "back up" any
threats that might be made through ordinary channels of communication. Perhaps early in the series of trials a contingent strategy means,
"Look, I will cooperate if you will," an implicit communication of a
proposed joint strategy for the game. In the later stages of the series
the same contingency might mean, "You had better stop trying to take
advantage of me," an implicit communication of threat. Either the
suggestion of a strategy or the vow to retaliate ought to enhance
cooperation.

Communication and Power in Bargaining

As we have seen, the only communication permitted in the context of a Prisoner's Dilemma game is the implicit communication
inherent in the contingent stragegy. As Nemeth (1972) has noted, this
is a serious limitation in the external validity of the Prisoner's Dilemma. Whether the particular issue is competition for scarce resources, labor negotiations, an athletic contest, or business decisions,
competition in the real social world typically involves some formal

communication between the competing parties. This communication may not always be honest (bluffing and deceit may be widespread), but it nevertheless is present in the situation. Another limitation in the original Prisoner's Dilemma format is that the two competing parties are of equal power: there is a match between the best outcomes available to each and the worst outcomes available to each. Neither party can force the other to risk any more than he or she personally stands to lose. This situation, like the lack of formal communication, reduces the generalizability of research conducted using the Prisoner's Dilemma. To fill these gaps in knowledge researchers have developed a variety of other experimental games. Foremost among these is the Trucking Game developed by Deutsch and Krauss (1960), which can include both formal communication and the potential for establishing differential power between the two parties.

THE TRUCKING GAME. The Trucking Game is a mixed-motive game for two players, each of whom assumes the role of a trucking company (either Acme or Bolt) that wants to move a cargo from a point of origin to a destination. For every completed trip by a player, that player will receive a payment of 60 cents minus the "operating expenses" for the trip (determined by the time taken to complete the journey). The game is electrically operated, so that the timing is accomplished automatically, and the road map provided to the subjects is shown in Figure 11-5. As you can see from the diagram, there are two possible routes that each player might take. The main route (represented by the solid line) is constructed so that its middle third is one lane. If both trucks are to use this main road one must wait at the entrance while the other passes through the one-lane section. The time involved in the use of the main road is such that the trucker who passes through immediately will earn a profit of 15 cents (60 cents payment minus 45 cents operating expenses) while the trucker who waits will earn nothing (60 cents minus 60 cents in operating expenses) for that trial. In addition to the main route each company has unrestricted access to an alternate route (the dotted lines), but this alternate is so much longer that its use results in a *loss* of 10 cents for the trial.

EFFECTS OF THREAT. The optimal strategy in this game is, of course, a cooperative alternation, with one party earning the profit on one trial and the other party earning the profit on the next trial. Such a cooperative strategy would produce an average winning (over the twenty trials of the game) of $1.50 per person (15 cents profit on each of ten trials, no profit and no loss on the rest). In the first experiment using the Trucking Game Deutsch and Krauss (1960) were interested in the effects that *threat* would have on the level of cooperation. The

FIGURE 11-5
The road map for the Trucking Game. (Adapted from Deutsch and Krauss, 1960, p. 183)

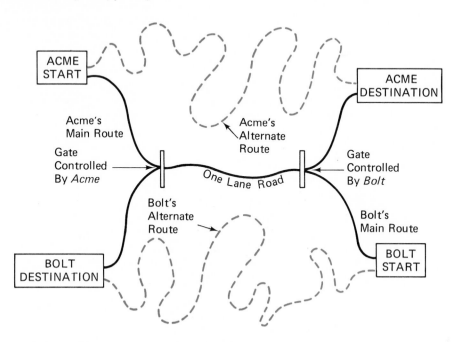

presence of threat was made possible by the use of the gates shown at each end of the one-lane stretch of the main road. If a gate was operable (this was up to the experimenter) the player who controlled the gate could choose to close it, permitting his or her truck to pass through but preventing the other's truck from passing. There were three experimental conditions: In the No Threat condition neither gate was operable; in the Unilateral Threat condition only Acme's gate was operable; in the Bilateral Threat condition both gates were operable. Now consider the power of each participant to punish the other. In the No Threat condition neither player has any potential to punish the other without also losing, and this correspondence of outcomes is even more direct than in the Prisoner's Dilemma game. In the Unilateral Threat condition Acme is endowed with an additional source of power quite apart from the ability to block the opponent's truck with his or her own. Finally, in the Bilateral Threat condition both participants are endowed with this possibility for overkill. How might these variations in threat affect the process of competition?

The subjects in this first experiment were female employees of the Bell Telephone Company (remember that females are typically more cooperative in mixed-motive games than are males) who played twenty trials against each other (not against a programmed opponent). Neither member of the pair knew who the other was, and no communication was permitted in this study. The effects of threat were striking. In the No Threat condition mutual accommodation emerged without formal communication such that the average winnings were slightly over $1 for each subject (out of a possible $1.50). In the Unilateral Threat condition both players *lost* money, with the more powerful Acme averaging losses of $1.19 and the weaker Bolt averaging losses of $2.87. In the Bilateral Threat condition the losses to both sides were even greater, with the average for both approximately $4.38. (None of the "losses" incurred by the subjects was actually collected by the experimenter.) It is important to note that most of these losses are *worse* than the −$2.00 which would have been lost by consistent taking of the alternate route.

THREAT AND COMMUNICATION. Apparently the issue became maximizing the suffering of the opponents, rather than maximizing one's own gains or minimizing one's own losses. There is, however, another possibility. Perhaps the use of the external threat, like the contingent strategy in the Prisoner's Dilemma game, is an attempt at implicit communication, the "you had better believe me" part of developing a strategy for the game. To evaluate the use of threat as communication Deutsch and Krauss (1962) replicated the original study, only this time permitted formal communication between the two competitors. Interestingly enough, the greatest amount of formal communication occurred in the No Threat condition, less occurred in the Unilateral Threat condition, and in the Bilateral Threat condition the two participants hardly spoke to each other. The large losses incurred in the Bilateral Threat condition thus appear to be the result of injury inflicted for punishment's sake, not for the sake of communication.

A slightly different outcome was obtained in a recent study (Smith and Anderson, 1975) which included both a manipulation of threat availability and a manipulation of possibility for communication. These investigators used a version of the Trucking Game, but changed the payoffs to higher monetary incentives whose value was randomly varied across trials to preclude discovery of the "obvious" strategy of alternation. They found that when no formal communication was permitted the presence of threat did improve the level of cooperation. But when full communication was allowed, the presence of threat *decreased* the likelihood of cooperation. Thus threat may serve as part of the implicit communication between competing parties, but if there is already full communication, threat will just get in the way of settlement of the dispute. Imagine for a moment that these results could be generalized to interpersonal or even international conflict, as many researchers in the area might argue. Such findings would suggest, for example, that the huge nuclear stockpiles maintained by the United States and the Soviet Union once served as implicit communication leading to an increased probability of cooperation. As direct communication—hotlines, diplomatic contacts, formal negotiations—increases, the maintenance of large stockpiles will only inhibit cooperation and may lead to aggression.

But can the findings from laboratory studies of cooperation and competition be generalized to this degree? There are arguments on both sides of the question. For example, Nemeth (1972) has suggested that the limited communication inherent in the Prisoner's Dilemma game makes it difficult to generalize beyond the walls of the laboratory, but this objection cannot apply to versions of the Trucking Game in which communication is permitted and sometimes even encouraged. Another limitation is that experimental studies typically involve pairs of subjects engaged in a temporary dyadic relationship, rather then groups of societies involved in numerous simultaneous (and long-lasting) relationships. Finally, there are the usual qualms about the artificial nature of the experimental situation and the personal characteristics of the college undergraduate subjects, but at the same time it is apparent that the subjects find partipating in these bargaining studies quite ego-involving. More importantly, the experimental techniques do seem to capture some of the essential elements of conflicts in the outside world. On balance it is fair to say that many social psychologists would share Deutsch's (1969) view that although laboratory study of cooperation and competition must be generalized with care, it is still socially relevant science.

Achievement Motivation and Competition

Throughout this chapter we have argued that competition can best be thought of as an interaction in which there is low correspondence between the outcomes of the two participants. Various structural features of the interaction—such as the nature of the payoffs to both parties, the temporary motives of each participant, the ease of communication, and the distribution of power—will affect the degree of competition, but these alone cannot account for the diversity in responses in competitive situations. For example, consider the realm of academic accomplishment. The external situation composed of your professors' expectations, the scarcity of places in graduate and professional schools, the competition for jobs at the completion of undergraduate education, and the institution's own requirements for maintenance of good academic standing is the same for nearly all students. Yet the reactions to these external pressures differ greatly. Some of you elect to pursue membership in Phi Beta Kappa, some of you are more concerned with the breadth and depth of your educations than with the grades you happen to obtain, and some of you may decide to drop out of college altogether. Only a relatively enduring personality or motivational variable can account for these differences, and the *need for achievement* is such a variable. Our treatment of competition will conclude with a discussion of achievement motivation.

Measurement of Achievement Needs

In his comprehensive theory of personality, Murray (1938) argued that behavior could be explained by describing both the individual's relatively enduring predispositions to action (called *needs*) and the situational factors (called by the general name environmental *press*) which might contribute to or inhibit the expression or one or more of those needs. In many ways this is a very social description of personality, and the measuring instrument that Murray (1938) developed to assess personal needs involved judgment of social stimuli. This instrument, the *Thematic Apperception Test* (TAT), consists of a series of twenty pictures of ambiguous situations, such as a picture of a college-age youth sitting at a desk with a book open before him. Rather than concentrating on the book, the youth is resting his head on his hand as he gazes out at the viewer (you). The TAT is based on the presumption that a person's fantasy life will reveal important characteristics about personality, so the person who is being tested is asked to make up a story about each of the twenty pictures. The person is usually given from three to five minutes to write down the short story, and each story is to describe such things as what has led up to the situation in the picture, what is wanted and by whom, and what will happen in the future. The stories are later content-analyzed to determine which needs predominate.

When the goal is the measurement of achievement motivation alone, only four of the twenty pictures are typically used (McClelland, Atkinson, Clark, and Lowell, 1953) and each story is scored for a number of different aspects of achievement motivation. For example, a story receives one point if the entire theme is achievement oriented, an additional point for an apparent state of need, another point for the anticipation of success in obtaining a desired goal, additional points for mentioning obstacles that might be in the way of achievement or for describing contributory forces in the social environment.

Using the content coding categories outlined by McClelland et al. (1953), a total of as much as 15 points might be given to a story high in all aspects of achievement motivation. This scoring system is described in detail in a manual by Atkinson (1958) based on the procedures suggested by McClelland et al. (1953), and an excellent summary of the method can be found in Brown (1965). Anyone interested in measuring achievement motivation using the TAT must first establish reliability as a scorer by comparing his or her scoring of a standard set of stories against the scores for those stories presented in the manuals. Raters following the prescribed methods can usually attain quite high levels of reliability, and there is evidence that the validity of the scoring system (the degree to which the actual behavior of high-scorers differs from the behavior of low-scorers) also seems to be good (see Weiner, 1972, for a review).

It should be noted that the content analysis of stories written about the four TAT pictures will reveal only the subject's interest in successful achievement, what Atkinson (1958; Atkinson and Feather, 1966) has called the *motive to approach success* (abbreviated M_S). According to this later version of achievement theory a person's tendency to approach an achievement-oriented task will be determined by the motive to approach success (M_S), the probability of obtaining success [$P(S)$], and the positive incentive value that such success would have (I_S). The theory states that this incentive value will decrease as the probability of achieving success increases, much the same way that cognitive dissonance theory (Chapter Six) argues that we like best things we must work hardest to obtain.

But there is more to the attempting of tasks than the certainty of success: there is also the possibility of failure and the negative consequences that this failure would carry with it. When you are about to make an oral report to a very important class, you hope to do a good job (the desire to achieve success) but you are also anxious about making a fool of yourself (what Atkinson calls the *motive to avoid failure*, abbreviated M_{AF}). This motive to avoid failure cannot be measured from the achievement imagery found in the TAT responses so it must be estimated in some other way. Traditionally, achievement researchers have used the Mandler-Sarason (1952) Test Anxiety Questionnaire (TAQ) to estimate the motive to avoid failure, since it deals with anxiety in what most people would consider to be an achievement-related situation. More recently, however, Mehrabian (1969) has developed an objective scale of achievement motivation which measures both the motive to achieve success and the motive to avoid failure, and it may be used instead of the TAT and TAQ.

The tendency to avoid achievement-related situations is considered to be a function of the motive to avoid failure (M_{AF}), the probability of failure (which, of course, is unity minus the probability of success), and the incentive value of failure. Just as the incentive value for success varies inversely with the probability of success, the incentive value of failure varies inversely with the probability of failure (or *positively* with the probability of success). In short, the more likely you are to succeed at a task [the higher $P(S)$], the less reward you will achieve for succeeding and the more pain you will suffer for failing. You can't gain much credit for succeeding at an easy task, but should you fail at an easy task you will be roundly denounced as incompetent.

Achievement theory thus argues that your tendency to approach a task will depend upon the probability of success at the task, and upon what Atkinson calls **resultant achievement motivation**: the strength of your motive to achieve success minus the strength of your motive to avoid failure ($M_S - M_{AF}$). If you are very high on the motive to achieve success and very low on the motive to avoid failure, your resultant achievement motivation will be quite high (a positive number). If you are high on both motives, or low on both, your resultant achievement motivation will be at an intermediate level (a numerical value around zero). Finally, if your motive to achieve success is low and your motive to avoid failure is high, your resultant achievement motivation will be low (a negative number).

How do these various tendencies become expressed in action? The theory states that the tendency to undertake any task related to achievement (T_A) will be the product of resultant achievement motivation ($M_S - M_{AF}$) times the relevant probability estimates (since the incentive values are related to these probability estimates they cancel out):

$$T_A = (M_S - M_{AF}) \times [P(S)] \times [1 - P(S)]$$

Thus both the personal factor of resultant achievement motivation and the environmental factor of task difficulty jointly determine the tendency to undertake an achievement-related task. M_S and M_{AF} are usually computed in *standard scores* (or z scores) which seldom differ from zero by more than 3 points (+3 to −3). As a result, the value of resultant achievement motivation will generally vary between an extreme high of 6 [+3 − (−3) = 6] to an extreme low of −6 [−3 − (+3) = −6].

Let us consider an example of just how this formula might predict the choice of an achievement-related task. Suppose that you are about to select your college major, and you have narrowed the choice to two alternatives. Both subjects are equally interesting to you, but your family expects you to do graduate work and you realize that you will have to keep your grades up in order to gain entrance to graduate school. Assume that getting good grades would be relatively easy in one subject [say the probability of success would be high, $P(S) = .9$], but more difficult in the other [$P(S) = .5$]. Further assume that your resultant achievement motivation is high [$+2 - (-2) = 4$]. Substituting these numbers in the formula we obtain a value for the easy major of

$$T_A = [+2 - (-2)] \times (.9) \times (.1) = +.36$$

but for the moderately difficult major a value of

$$T_A = [+2 - (-2)] \times (.5) \times (.5) = +1.00$$

What this means is that people who are high in resultant achievement motivation will tend to choose tasks of intermediate difficulty over tasks that are either very easy or very difficult. This tendency of people in whom $M_S > M_{AF}$ to select intermediate difficulty tasks has been demonstrated in a number of different experiments. For example, Atkinson and Litwin (1960) permitted subjects to select the distance from which they would try to toss rings over a peg, and found that subjects who were high in resultant achievement motivation showed a clear preference for moderate distance (8 to 9 feet).

But what about the people who are low in resultant achievement motivation? If your M_S were -1 and your M_{AF} were $+3$, your tendency to approach the easy major would be

$$T_A = [-1 - (+3)] \times (.9) \times (.1) = -.18$$

while for the moderately difficult major your tendency to approach would be

$$T_A = [-1 - (+3)] \times (.5) \times (.5) = -.50$$

As these formulas indicate, people who are low in achievement motivation will generally try to avoid achievement situations (the "approach" tendency is negative). Within these general fear-of-achievement situations, however, the ones of intermediate difficulty are the most threatening. Easy tasks will permit success, and extremely difficult tasks will provide a ready excuse for the anticipated failure. So if you are high in resultant achievement motivation (that is, if $M_S > M_{AF}$) you will choose the moderately difficult major, but if you are low in resultant achievement motivation ($M_S < M_{AF}$) you will choose the easy major. Further, if the choice were between the moderately difficult one and an extremely difficult major, those for whom $M_S > M_{AF}$ would again choose the task of intermediate difficulty, while those for whom $M_S < M_{AF}$ would now choose the extremely difficult major. This general prediction has been confirmed in two studies of occupational choice (Mahone, 1960; Morris, 1966) which found that students for whom $M_S > M_{AF}$ had occupational preferences which generally corresponded to their level of competence while students for whom

$M_S<M_{AF}$ often held occupational preferences that were more likely to be either too easy or too difficult when compared with the actual level of competence.

Persistence, the Protestant Ethic, and the Causes of Success

There is substantial support for the achievement theory prediction that people high in resultant achievement motivation prefer tasks of intermediate or moderate difficulty, but apart from the two studies of occupational choice the evidence is less clear that people who are low in achievement motivation will choose either too difficult or too easy tasks (Atkinson, 1964; Feather, 1967; Karabenick, 1972; Trope, 1975). While this aspect of the theory remains to be confirmed in a convincing manner, there is general agreement (Atkinson, 1964; Weiner, 1974) that there are important behavioral differences between people who are high in resultant achievement motivation and people who are low. Highs initiate achievement-related activities, lows have to be forced into them; highs work at such tasks more diligently than do lows; and highs will persist even when confronted by failure while lows are only too willing to stop at the first lack of success.

Let us illustrate how these differences might be related to competition by examining the idea of persistence in the face of failure. We hold in high admiration those who succeed against all odds, and in the popular wisdom a "true competitor" is a person who keeps on trying as hard as possible even though he or she is not always successful. No matter whether competition is limited to the play of an experimental game, broadened to include other interactions in which there is a low correspondence of outcomes between the participants, or generalized to social and economic competition on a grand scale, there will always be some losses mixed in with the wins. Thus the critical question for sustained competition is not "What leads people to attempt competitive tasks?" but "How do the people who can maintain their competitive interest after occasional failures differ from people who resign after the slightest setback?" We shall consider two quite different answers to this question, both derived from the basic datum that persistence is greater among people higher in resultant achievement motivation.

The first approach deals with the socialization of achievement motivation. Are there any differences between the parents of high-motive children and low-motive children, particularly in terms of their child-rearing practices? In order to examine this issue Winterbottom (1953) obtained estimates of the motive to approach success from a sample of twenty-nine boys between the ages of eight and ten, and conducted extensive interviews with the mothers of these boys. Each

mother was asked to indicate by what age she had expected her child
to attempt or accomplish a number of things, including doing well
in competition, knowing his way around the city, making his own
friends, and trying new things for himself. Winterbottom found that on
these four items in particular the mothers of high-achievement boys
expected much earlier self-reliance than did the mothers of low-
achievement boys. She suggested that these activities, as opposed to
the normal caretaking activities which the parent would be forced to
do if the child did not do them for himself (getting dressed, getting
ready for bed), constituted *independence training.* In addition to
their greater stress on early self-reliance and independence, the
mothers of high-achievement sons rewarded success with physical
affection rather than with verbal praise. You may recall from Chapter
Eight that one of the determinants of self-esteem identified by
Coopersmith (1967) was parental respect for individual initiative within well-defined but broad limits. The production of high achievement
motivation would seem to occur when this respect for initiative turns
to the active *encouragement* of initiative and the substantial reward
for success.

Even though many of Winterbottom's results have been confirmed
in later research (see an extensive review by Brown, 1965), it would
be a mistake to conclude that independence training is the only
difference between those who turn out to be highly achievement-
oriented and those who do not. Her correlational study could not
establish the direction of a causal relationship (see Chapter Two
and Chapter Four), the sample was a restricted one, and surely there
is more to the socialization experience than independence training.
What is more important about these results is that they provided the
link which enabled McClelland (1961) to suggest that the development of achievement motivation in sons was a social-psychological
mechanism intervening between the religious movement of Protestantism and the rise of modern capitalism, in short *a psychological account of the Protestant Ethic* (Weber, 1930). The Protestant emphasis
upon achievement, devotion to duty, and self-reliance should be just
the constellation of parental attitudes that would produce high achievement motivation in children. This achievement motivation should be
reflected in the occupational choices of the children (an emphasis
upon the entrepreneurial role) and later in the economic growth of
the countries involved.

In an imaginative test of this proposition McClelland and his
associates (McClelland, 1961) compared the level of achievement
imagery (of the motive-to-approach-success sort) present in the children's stories of twenty-three countries during the years 1920–1929
to the economic growth (represented by per capita income and per

capita kilowatt hours of electricity generated!) in those countries in 1950. This roughly 25-year time span would have been sufficient for those who were children in 1920–1929 to have reached the point of making their contributions to the economic output of their country. Corrections were made for the damaging effects of wars that might have occurred, for the absolute level of economic development of the countries involved, for the disparities in natural resources, and for a number of other potential confounding factors. After all the corrections had been made, the data demonstrated a significantly positive correlation: the higher the level of achievement imagery in the children's stories, the higher the level of economic development 25 years later. Thus it appeared that the religious training of Protestantism produced a particular sort of independence training, this independence training produced high achievement motivation, and this achievement motivation was, in turn, reflected in economic growth. Later research suggested that Protestantism might not be a necessary part of the chain. Any religion stressing direct communication with God (rather than communication through an intermediate priesthood) would produce independence training, and then the rest of the chain would follow (Brown, 1965).

Apparently, early independence training will affect achievement motivation and later persistence and competition. In the second approach to our question Weiner (1974; Weiner, Frieze, Kukla, Reed, Rest, and Rosenbaum, 1972; Weiner and Kukla, 1970) has shown that there are reliable differences in the ways that high-achievement-motive people, as opposed to lows, perceive the causes of their successes and failures. Selecting from among the components of action first identified by Heider (1958; as described earlier in Chapter Four), Weiner (1974) points out that there are four basic contributors to success or failure: ability, task difficulty, effort, and luck.

These four components can be classified as shown in Table 11-1 by virtue of whether they are *stable* or *variable* properties and by virtue of whether they are considered to be *internal* to the person or aspects of the *external* environment. Thus ability is a stable internal property which enters into task success, and luck is a variable external property. In a number of research studies Weiner (1974) demonstrated that people who are high in resultant achievement motivation attribute success to ability but attribute failure to lack of effort. In direct contrast, people low in resultant achievement motivation attribute failure to a lack of ability and are more likely to attribute success to good luck, or at least not to an internal disposition. In short, high-achievement-motive people see themselves as the cause of their

Table 11–1
Classification of the perceived contributors to achievement behavior

STABILITY OF THE PROPERTY	LOCATION OF THE PROPERTY	
	INTERNAL TO THE PERSON	IN THE EXTERNAL ENVIRONMENT
Stable	Ability	Task Difficulty
Variable	Effort	Luck

Adapted from Weiner (1974)

successes and look upon their failures as the result of a lack of effort—leading them to try even harder in the face of occasional setbacks. Low-achievement-motive people see their failures as the result of a stable disposition (lack of ability) which cannot be changed, so they avoid achievement tasks in order to preserve what little self-esteem they can still maintain. Since most achievement tasks contain elements of both ability and effort, these errors in causal attribution tend to become self-fulfilling.

Achievement Motivation in Women: Fear of Success?

The vast majority of research on achievement motivation has employed male subjects, primarily because the TAT-TAQ technique for measuring achievement motivation has proved unreliable with female subjects. In an attempt to account for this difficulty Horner (1972) has argued that while achievement, ambition, and competitiveness may be desirable for males (i.e., may have a positive incentive value), the same characteristics may be widely perceived as being undesirable or unfeminine for females. Consequently, while the congruence between achievement and role expectations leads to a desire for success among males, the inconsistency between achievement and the traditional role expectations for females leads them to *fear success*. It is important to note that this is not the same as a desire for failure which precludes attempts at success; rather, it is a fear which increases as the probability of success increases: potentially highly successful women should suffer more from fear of success than should women who never attempt to achieve.

To test for the existence of the fear of success Horner (1972) described a number of ambiguous situations to male and female subjects and asked them to describe what was happening and what would happen in the future. The crucial situation described a stimulus person who places at the top of a medical school class after final examinations for the first term. The stimulus person was identified by name (Anne or John) and the pronouns used in the story further reinforced the sexual identification of the stimulus person. Male subjects received a version containing only John, while female subjects received a version containing only Anne. The stories written in response to the situation were coded for fear of success if they contained any of several themes. These themes (and examples of them) were negative consequences of success (e.g., loss of a valued male friend), future activities away from success (e.g., become a housewife after completion of medical school), direct expression of conflict about success, denial of responsibility for achieving success (e.g., this semester was just good luck), or bizarre or inappropriate responses (such as one suggesting that Anne was really a code name for a nonexistent person).

The results of this part of Horner's research showed that 65.5 percent of the female subjects wrote stories showing fear of success in response to the cue name Anne, while only 9.1 percent of the male subjects wrote fear of success stories in response to the cue name John. Horner interpreted these findings, and the results from a second experimental session involving the completion of a number of tasks, as confirming the existence of a *motive to avoid success.*

Not surprisingly, these results generated a great deal of interest. They served the conceptual function of explaining why traditional measures of achievement motivation might not apply to females at the same time that they suggested that the prevailing role expectations for women might be having quite detrimental effects on them. Unfortunately, the balance of research conducted since Horner's original study indicates that while the conceptual idea may have merit, it has not yet been satisfactorily confirmed. Critics soon pointed out a number of difficulties in Horner's work, not the least of which was that Anne's success was in one of the most male-dominated professions. Indeed, when other researchers gave the Anne cue to *male* subjects, well over half of the male subjects also wrote stories showing fear of success (Feather and Raphelson, 1974; Monahan, Kuhn, and Shaver, 1974; Robbins and Robbins, 1973). In a comprehensive review of the fear of success literature, Zuckerman and Wheeler (1975) illustrate other methodological problems with Horner's study, discuss the consistencies and inconsistencies in subsequent work, and present alternative measures of the fear of success. Their overall conclusion is that while the idea of fear of success has intuitive appeal because of its promise to resolve a problem inherent in the traditional measurement of achievement motivation, its existence and characteristics remain to be confirmed by future research.

The fact that traditional achievement measurement techniques have such low reliability for females is a serious limitation for the theory of achievement motivation. But despite this problem, there is consistent support for the role of independence training and for the analysis of causal attribution for success. Taken together these two ideas suggest one important way in which high achievement motivation—reflected in persistence in the face of failure—might affect willingness to engage in sustained competition. We now turn from this pursuit of one's own goals to the intentional injury of other people—the topic of aggression.

Aggression

THE DEFINITION OF AGGRESSION

If anything, our everyday uses of the word *aggression* are even more confusing than such uses of the word *competition.* We describe the physical attack by one person against another as aggression unless the attacker is in a role (soldier, police officer) in which physical attacks against selected other people are sanctioned. We describe a particularly hard-hitting professional football player as aggressive, but we use the same label for a salesperson who is assertively promoting a product. We often refuse to take some actions by asserting that to do so would "do violence" to our moral principles, and nations sometimes describe the self-interested economic policies of their adversaries as "acts of aggression." It would be tempting to suggest that the concept of aggression is really quite clear, that it is only our everyday language which is imprecise. But there are important contradictions in the scientific definitions offered for the concept of aggression (see discussions of the concept by Bandura, 1973; Johnson, 1972; and Kaufmann, 1970).

More often than not these contradictions reflect differences in theoretical approach, rather than disagreements about which particular behaviors should be labeled aggressive. For example, there is a continuing debate as to whether aggression is primarily instinctual or primarily a response to external instigation. On one side of the issue are Freud (1933, 1950) and the ethologists (scientists who study animal social behavior in its natural setting), such as Lorenz (1966); on the other side are most social psychologists. Freud traced aggressive impulses to a death instinct (called Thanatos) whose aim is to destroy life. This death instinct is presumably manifest in self-destructive behavior (of which suicide would be the final step) and in aggression directed outward toward other people. From a slightly different perspective, Lorenz argues that aggression between members of the same species (*intraspecific* aggression) serves evolutionary purposes. Intraspecific aggression, properly regulated by rituals and inhibitions developed over time, disperses the population to take maximum advantage of the available food and encourages selective breeding among the most hardy. Thus while Freud and Lorenz might disagree on the precise functions of aggression, both argue that it is an instinctual drive that is virtually impossible to modify.

In rather direct contrast to this view is the position taken by most social psychologists who have studied the problem of aggression. The environmentalist position was first proposed by Dollard, Doob, Miller, Mowrer, and Sears (1939). This now-classic work argued that aggression was *always* the consequence of *frustration*, which was defined as interference with a goal-directed response. As Kaufmann (1970) has noted, it was not specifically stated whether this relationship between frustration and aggression was supposed to be innate or learned, but the occurrence of aggression was quite clearly attributed to conditions in the external environment, not to aggressive instincts within the person. Later discussions by social psychologists have suggested that frustration may not always lead to aggression (Berkowitz, 1962); that aggression can be either an intentional action (Berkowitz, 1975) or not necessarily intentional (Buss, 1961); and that which actions are designated as aggressive may depend as much upon the value judgments of the observers as upon the nature of the action (Bandura, 1973). But despite these differences of opinion (which we shall consider in more detail later), all these theorists place little stock in the notion of an aggressive instinct.

Perhaps the only common element in all the various definitions of aggression is the idea of *injury to the target*. The injury may be physical or psychological, the attempt at injury may be successful or unsuccessful, the target may be a person or an inanimate object, the source of the attempt at injury may be an aggressive instinct or an environmental frustration, the attempt at injury may be guided by intention or it may not, and the aggressor may or may not be in close proximity to this target. Obviously a definition this general will be of little use to us, so some additional conditions must be imposed. First, since our interest is human social behavior, let us restrict the class of targets to persons. Second, to rule out the possibility of aggression-by-accident let us side with those (e.g., Bandura, 1973; Berkowitz, 1975; Kaufmann, 1970) who argue that the actor's intentions must be considered. Finally, let us distinguish between injury to the self and injury to others by restricting aggression to the latter circumstances.

These three restrictions are probably sufficient for our purposes, and they leave us with a definition of **aggression** as intentional action directed toward the injury of another person. This definition is not much different from the original one proposed by Dollard et al. (1939) —"a response having for its goal the injury of a living organism" (p. 11)—even though we have considered some of the arguments raised in the intervening years. Such a definition permits us to describe as "aggressive" those actions that produce psychological injury as well as those that produce physical injury, and those actions that fail in the attempt as well as those that succeed. In this latter respect the definition of aggression differs from the one proposed in Chapter Ten for objective altruism. There, actions with positive intentions were not sufficient, because of the difficulty of determining the intentions apart from the effects of action. To recall Heider's distinction between ambiguous mediation and synonymous mediation (Chapter Three), an aggressive action is likely to be synonymous with an aggressive intention. In contrast, the specific intention giving rise to a helpful action is ambiguous—it may be altruism, but it may also be self-interest or ingratiation. Thus only those actions that produced benefit for the recipient and no external rewards for the benefactor could qualify as objectively altruistic. In the present case the actor's aggressive intentions are clear from the actions, even though those actions may not be successful in inflicting harm because of the superior power of the target person.

Finally, although the definition of aggression is stated in terms of injury to the target, aggressive actions are not without consequences to the actor. Whether the action is presumed to be instinctive or learned it can be argued that aggression involves rewards to the actor. If aggression is really the discharge of an accumulated instinctual drive, according to Freudian theory such a release of tension would be pleasurable. On the other hand, if aggression is regarded as having some causes that are external to the person (such as frustrations), the social learning that would have to be involved would include the rewards or punishments that accompany performance of aggressive behaviors. In either case it is reasonable to suggest that aggression, like competition, can be seen as one example of social exchange. The aggressor and the target are in an interaction in which each one's outcomes are determined by the joint behavior of the two. For example, whether the aggressive action succeeds in producing injury to the target person will depend on the particular form of aggression chosen by the attacker and on the defenses against that attack mounted by the target. The situation involves a low correspondence of outcomes, but because the target's costs may far exceed the aggressor's rewards the interaction as a whole has a non-zero (usually negative) sum. In this way at least, and perhaps in others as well, aggression and competition can be seen in the same light.

INSTIGATION AND MAINTENANCE OF AGGRESSION

Although the problem of aggression is as old as recorded history, the scientific study of aggression is a relatively recent development. This scientific interest may be attributable as much to the emergence of competing theories of aggression as to the social consequences of the problem. Is aggression innate, or is it learned? How can aggression be controlled and reduced? What role, if any, does society play in fostering aggression, and can society itself survive if aggression is permitted to grow unchecked? These questions all deal with the source of *instigation to aggression*. Our definition of aggression as intentional action directed toward the injury of another person identifies the immediate or proximate cause of an aggressive action as the actor's intention to produce harm. Thus the social and scientific question becomes, "What was the source of the intention, what *instigated* the aggressive intention?" Beginning with Freud's (1933) suggestion that aggression is only an interpersonal manifestation of individual death instinct, and continuing through some recent theories that argue that aggression is a joint product of cognitive and motivational factors (e.g., Kaufmann, 1970; Tannenbaum and Zillman, 1975), there have been widely differing answers to this question. These theories can be grouped into three categories defined by the presumed source(s) of instigation. Some theories hold that aggression is instigated by *internal* pressures much the same way that a balloon will burst if inflated too much. Others hold that the instigation to aggression is wholly *external*, the natural reaction to conditions in the environment. Finally, there are theories that suggest that a particular act of aggression may be the result of both internal and external factors. We shall briefly consider these categories of theory and then examine a single social problem—televised violence—to suggest which sort of theory best accommodates the available experimental evidence.

Theories of Internal Instigation

Freud's Instinctive Theory

Freud was the first to suggest psychological factors in aggressive behavior, and in his early work (1920) he considered aggression to be a response to the thwarting of the person's pursuit of pleasure or avoidance of pain. Confronted with the problem of explaining sadism and self-destructive behavior, Freud later (1933, 1950) postulated the existence of a death instinct (Thanatos) which opposed the life instinct (Eros) and tried to reduce the organism to its inanimate state. Both actions of self-destruction (as minor as nail-biting and as serious as suicide) and acts of aggression directed at others are thought to be manifestations of this death instinct.

In this view the death instinct is a constant source of aggressive impulses. Many of these can be displaced onto nonhuman targets (such as the hunting of animals for sport), and others can be sublimated, or channeled into socially acceptable activities (everything from contact sports to merciless political satire). But substitutes cannot be satisfactory indefinitely; eventually the death instincts will be discharged in an act of overt aggression. This model of aggressive instinct has often been described by an analogy to the hydraulic system of a reservoir. Thanatos is an underground spring feeding a small stream of aggressive impulses, but this stream is dammed up by societal prohibitions against the expression of aggression. Some socially acceptable spillways in the dam permit a portion of the pressure to be relieved, but eventually the stream will overflow its banks in periodic discharges of aggression.

Lorenz's Instinctive Theory

A similar "hydraulic" theory of human aggressiveness has been advanced by Lorenz (1966), based on his extensive study of aggression among infrahuman animals in their natural settings. Lorenz shares with Freud the position that human aggression is innate rather than learned, but he attributes such aggressiveness to an aberration in the evolutionary process of natural selection. According to Lorenz's theory, human beings, like their infrahuman counterparts, are endowed with an instinct for fighting which serves to disperse the population (thus providing for better utilization of resources) and to ensure mating among only the most hardy. But unlike other animals, human beings are not naturally endowed with lethal weapons (fangs, claws, crushing strength). As a result humans have never developed the instinctual inhibitions against killing that are thought to be practically universal among the lower animals. Throughout most of human history this lack of inhibitions against killing presented no problems, but when humans developed a technology capable of producing a tremendous variety of lethal weapons the inevitable result was a dramatic increase in aggression, violence, and war.

Although Lorenz's position and similar generalizations from animal behavior by other writers such as Ardrey (1966) and Morris (1967) have gained wide popular appeal, they have been met with skepticism in the scientific community. A collection of papers edited by Montagu (1968) is particularly critical of Lorenz's observations of animal behavior and of his generalizations to humans, and the vast majority of research by social scientists is contradictory to the instinctual position (Bandura, 1973; Berkowitz, 1975).

For example, let us consider the idea of territoriality. One of the evolutionary purposes usually thought to be served by intraspecies aggression is the distribution of the population across the available resources—the establishment and maintenance of territoriality (Altman, 1975; Johnson, 1972; Klopfer, 1969). People build fences and personalize their homes and offices, they react with discomfort to invasion of their personal space (Chapter Three), and they defend their neighborhoods against what they perceive to be intrusions from outsiders. And in many of these instances the reactions to intruders are quite aggressive and violent. But is the simple presence of the intruders the cause of the reaction (as it would be among animals), or is it the *symbolic value* of the intrusion that leads to the reaction? The small town that is openly hostile to anyone who tries to settle there may be friendly to outsiders who just come to visit; discomfort from invasions of personal space arises not because the resources (such as oxygen) have become restricted, but because the social meaning of the intrusion causes embarrassment or fright. Extensive experimental research on crowding (Freedman, 1975) has indicated that whether density is pleasant or unpleasant will depend on the social situation. Under some circumstances it appears that increased density can even enhance pleasure (for example, compare a crowded party or dance floor with one that is underpopulated). The general conclusion to be drawn from these examples and from experimental research is that direct generalization from animal to human behavior is tenuous even when an issue as basic as territoriality is concerned. This suggests that other potential sources of instigation to aggression found among animals should be generalized to humans with even greater caution.

Although the present weight of scientific evidence argues against the instinctive theories, the idea that aggression can be instigated by internal factors cannot be dismissed entirely. And to the degree that internal sources of instigation are unmodifiable by events in the external world, the validity of these theories paints a pessimistic picture of our ability to reduce and control aggression. We may dam and attempt to drain the reservoir, but eventually the aggressive drive will lead to some form of destructive behavior. We shall return to this point after discussing other theories about the instigation to aggression.

Theories of External Instigation

The Frustration-Aggression Hypothesis

As noted earlier in this chapter, the frustration-aggression hypothesis first proposed by Dollard, Doob, Miller, Mowrer, and Sears (1939) is the foremost example of a purely environmentalist or external theory of the instigation of aggression. These theorists avoided taking a position on the question of whether the *relationship* between frustration and aggression was instinctive or learned, but they did argue that (a) frustration always leads to aggression, and (b) aggression is always the consequence of frustration. In other words, frustration will produce only aggression—not coping behavior, not withdrawal, not tearful helplessness. And aggression can be brought about only by frustration, not by pain, not by deprivation, not by reward. This is an extremely restrictive interpretation of the relationship between external frustration and acts of aggression, and in a later paper Miller (1941) modified the position considerably. Miller still maintained that frustration was the only antecedent of aggression, but he suggested that such frustration would lead to the *instigation* of aggression, not necessarily to an overt aggressive act. This modification of the original hypothesis makes it possible for features of the situation to prevent the occurrence of aggression even though the instigation to aggression may be present, and in so doing it increases the scope of the formulation.

Aversive Events and Cues to Aggression

Recently the frustration-aggression hypothesis has been extended even further in a reformulation by Berkowitz (1969). Since the publication of the original hypothesis a large amount of experimental research had been performed to explore various aspects of the relationship between frustration and aggression, and in reviewing this literature Berkowitz (1969) concluded that two additional modifications of the hypothesis were justified. First, the antecedents of aggression should be expanded to a general class of *aversive events*, of which frustration is only one specific sort. Research with animals had indicated that aggressive responses could be brought about by pain (Lagerspetz and Nurmi, 1964; Ulrich, Wolff, and Azrin, 1964) even when external cues were largely absent (Scott, 1966), and by other aversive events such as hunger (predatory aggression) and a need for territorial defense (Moyer, 1967). Second, Miller's (1941) modification was extended slightly to incorporate all of the *aggressive cues* present in the situation. Some of these relevant cues might enhance aggression, and cues that aggression is somehow inappropriate in the situation might inhibit its expression. The function of aggressive cues can be seen in the research of Bandura, Ross, and Ross (1963a) on the imitation of aggression (described more fully in Chapter Nine); in the finding by Berkowitz and Geen (1967) that there was more aggression against a target person who resembled the victim in an aggressive film than against a target person who did not resemble the victim even when the only source of resemblance was the first name of the two people; and in the finding by Berkowitz and LePage (1967) that the mere presence of weapons in the situation would enhance aggressive responding.

This reformulation of the frustration-aggression hypothesis thus holds that a variety of aversive events can create an instigation to aggression, conceived of as a state of emotional arousal or a readiness to engage in aggressive behavior. It is important to note that even though this readiness is an internal state, it is nearly always the direct product of some aversive stimulus in the external environment. Thus, in contrast to the instinctive theories of aggression, the reformulation still places most of the sources of instigation *outside* the person. Given the readiness to engage in aggressive behavior, the occurrence (or inhibition) of an overt aggressive action will be influenced heavily by another external factor, the stimulus characteristics of the situation.

Although this reformulation of the frustration-aggression hypothesis can account for a high proportion of the data on aggression, there is reason to believe that at least some internal factors must also be considered. For example, Burnstein and Worchel (1962) found less aggression against a person who kept interrupting a group discussion if that person appeared to be hard of hearing (wore a hearing aid) than if he did not. In the latter case his interruptions seemed arbitrary and were followed by aggression, while in the former case the interruptions were justified. What differed between these two conditions was the subject's *internal* interpretation of the reasons for the blocking of the group's goal. In addition to the possibility of cognitive factors influencing aggression, there are wide individual differences in reactions to situational frustration, and these also suggest that internal differences may play a part in the response to instigation. We now turn to theories that explicitly encompass both external and internal sources of instigation to aggression.

Combinatorial Theories

Excitation-Transfer Theory

In Berkowitz's reformulation of the frustration-aggression hypothesis, aversive events in the environment are thought to produce a state of emotional arousal or readiness to aggress (the instigation), and if the situational cues suggest that aggression is appropriate an aggressive overt response will occur. The internal state of arousal is thus relatively specific to both the aversive events and to the aggressive response. But you may recall from the discussion of Schachter's (1964) theory of emotion in Chapter Eight, and from some of the research on attraction in Chapter Ten, that there is reason to believe that the subjective emotional experience is not specific to an identifiable state of physiological arousal. Indeed, there is strong evidence that both the internal arousal and a cognitive label for that arousal (usually provided by the environment) are required for the experience of an emotion. Does this mean that other sources of arousal (besides aversive events) might also contribute to the instigation to aggression? In their excitation-transfer theory of the facilitation of aggression Tannenbaum and Zillman (1975) argue for an affirmative answer to this question.

Specifically the theory holds that once there has been an initial instigation to aggression by an aversive event, adding to the person's arousal by other means will increase the strength of the aggressive response. In a typical experiment a subject first will be angered by an experimental confederate who insults the subject's intelligence. This aversive event presumably produces the initial instigation to aggression. Then in a second phase of the experiment the subject is exposed to a film or videotape which has either Aggressive or Nonaggressive (e.g., erotic or humorous) Content. Finally, the aggressive response is measured by permitting the subject to deliver electric shocks to the confederate as negative reinforcement for mistakes in what is purported to be a "learning" task (this latter portion of the research is typical of most studies of aggression in the laboratory). Results from a number of different experiments have indicated that the greatest aggressive reactions are produced in the Aggressive Content conditions, but that overt aggression is greater in the Nonaggressive Content conditions than in nonarousal control conditions (Tannenbaum and Zillman, 1975). Apparently even nonaggressive content can energize an aggressive response once there has been an appropriate instigation.

Social Learning Theory

There is a common thread among all the external instigation and combinatorial instigation theories we have considered so far. All assume that aggressive actions are specific responses to the instigation provided by aversive events of one sort or another. Certainly the excitation-transfer theory suggests that other sources of arousal can *enhance* the aggressive response, but even this theory presupposes the existence of an appropriate prior instigation. But is instigation always necessary for aggression? In a laboratory setting it probably is, since no subject would want to appear aggressive without good reason, but what about aggression and violence in the real social world? Is it reasonable to argue that the purse snatcher who pushes the victim to the ground was instigated to aggression? What about the juvenile gang that sets drunks on fire "just for kicks"? Or the professional killer who murders for hire? Or for that matter, what about armies engaged in battle? It strains credibility to argue that in all these cases there has been a specific instigation to aggression or even to argue that, in the absence of an aversive instigation, aggression is the result of innate aggressive instincts (Freud and Lorenz) or of characterological defects (Fromm, 1975). It is much more plausible to suggest that while aggression may often be the response to the push of aversive instigation, it may also be the response to the pull of rewards anticipated for successful aggression. Aggression may thus be an *instrumental activity* as well as a *hostile response* to thwarting.

Because it includes both the possibility of instigation from aversive events and the possibility of aggression in order to achieve anticipated rewards, the social learning analysis of aggression outlined by Bandura (1973) is the most comprehensive of the aggression theories. You will recall from Chapter Nine that social learning theory asserts that imitation and vicarious reinforcement as well as the more direct attainment of desired goals will influence social behavior. In contrast to the strict environmentalist view of reinforcement effects maintained by Skinner (1971) and other behaviorists, social learning theory includes emotional states and cognitive functions such as anticipation and expectancy within its broad framework of explanatory principles. Particularly important are the cognitive representations of the reinforcement contingencies that will accompany anticipated actions: "If I behave aggressively in this situation, will I get away with it?" The assumption that such cognitive representations of the contingencies exist is inherent in many of society's attempts to control aggressive behavior, ranging all the way from the parent's threats against an errant child to the legal threats of punishment for criminal behavior.

By including anticipated consequences to be gained by aggression social learning theory broadens our view of the possible antecedents of aggression. In a similar manner the theory proposed by Bandura (1973) employs the principles of social learning to expand the possible responses to instigation. As noted previously, Berkowitz (1969) pointed out the importance of the cues in the situation for determining the scope of the aggressive response. But his reformulation of frustration-aggression dealt with two basic response options: aggression and nonaggression. There was no attempt to distinguish among various possibilities in the nonaggression category. Bandura's (1973)

social learning model, however, suggests that, depending upon the
individual's social learning history and upon the stimulus features of
the situation, an instigation can lead to behavior as diverse as dependency, withdrawal, constructive problem solving to overcome
an obstacle, or outright aggression. Finally, Bandura reviews a great
deal of research that indicates that changes in stimulus and reinforcement conditions can transform aggression into other (more
socially desirable) responses. The social learning approach to the
study and control of aggression is particularly relevant for the social
policy question we now consider: the effects of televised violence.

Theory and Practice: The Issue of Televised Violence

Television has practically become a way of life in America. Most
adults get their news from television; a home is more likely to have a
television set than to have any other electrical appliance; when
summer vacation and weekends are counted, children spend more
time in front of television sets than they spend in school (Liebert,
Neale, and Davidson, 1973). Both the advertisers who pay for commercial programs and the creators of children's programs on noncom-
mercial television obviously believe that television can have
significant effects on behavior, and the research evidence supports
this belief.

What concerns us here is the effect that televised violence may
have on the actions of people who view such violence. Is the immediate and in-depth coverage of terrorist activities and attempts at
assassination of political leaders likely to contribute to increases in
these antisocial actions? Do crime-oriented commercial shows encourage criminal behavior and teach people how to be more successful criminals? Does the violence exhibited even by the heroes of these
shows and by the "good guys" in children's cartoons teach the lesson
that violence is not only an accepted means of resolving conflict, but
the preferred solution? In recent years questions such as these have
become of increasing concern to the television industry, to regulatory
agencies, and to the public.

In conceptual terms all these questions can be reduced to a
central issue: whether the observation of televised aggression increases or decreases the level of aggression subsequently displayed by
the viewer. The research by Berkowitz (1965, 1969) and by Tannenbaum and Zillman (1975) indicates that people who are already
instigated to aggression will behave more aggressively after viewing
violent episodes than after viewing control (nonaggressive) material.
But what about viewers who are not already instigated to aggression

at the time of their exposure to the aggressive content? This question has implications for theory as well as for social policy, because the various theories of aggression can be shown to make one of two opposing predictions. On the one hand there is the prediction that the observation of aggression will serve as a vicarious outlet for aggressive impulses that would otherwise be manifest in overt behavior. On the other hand, there is the view that the observation of aggression will teach aggression as a way of resolving conflict, thus increasing the probability of future aggression by the viewers. Let us take a closer look at these two differing predictions.

The Catharsis Hypothesis

The suggestion that observed aggression will decrease overt aggression is known as the catharsis hypothesis, and it assumes a reservoir model of aggression. The catharsis hypothesis was first formally advanced in the original frustration-aggression doctrine (Dollard, Doob, Miller, Mowrer, and Sears, 1939), but it was derived from earlier Freudian theory. Although the frustration-aggression theory assumes that all instigation to aggression is external to the person, while the instinctive theories of Freud and Lorenz assume that instigation is internal, the source of the instigation is not a critical element of catharsis. The point is that *whatever* the source of the instigation, that instigation will create a reservoir of aggressive impulses which will have to be reduced. This reduction can occur through displacement, through sublimation, or through the vicarious experience of observing aggression and violence (catharsis).

The best evidence for the catharsis hypothesis comes from an extensive field study by Feshbach and Singer (1971). These investigators used as subjects over four hundred preadolescent and adolescent boys who were living either in college-preparatory boarding schools or in public institutions for homeless boys. Within each sort of institution half of the boys were randomly assigned to watch programs high in aggressive content while the other half of the boys were assigned to watch programs of low aggressive content. Both groups of boys were required to watch at least six hours of television per week for six weeks, and during this time they were rated on aggressiveness by the house staff using a behavior rating scale devised by the investigators. The results showed that in the public institutions the level of aggressiveness declined among the boys watching the aggressive material but increased among the boys watching the nonaggressive material. In the private boarding schools the reverse pattern of results appeared, but here the differences were not statistically significant.

On balance these results support the catharsis hypothesis, with a television diet of aggressive content leading to a decrease in expressed aggression, at least among the boys in the public homes. Although Feshbach and Singer had taken what methodological precautions they could, there are often problems in a field experiment. For example, the boys in the nonaggressive conditions demanded to be permitted to see "Batman" even though its content was aggressive. The ratings of aggressiveness were made by the house staff, who could not help but know each boy's experimental condition, and this might have made some differences in the ratings. Most importantly, there was some evidence that the aggressive programs were liked more by all the boys (Chaffee and McLeod, 1971). If this is true, then it is reasonable to argue that the boys in the nonaggressive condition were suffering frustration as a result of the prohibition against watching programs they would otherwise have watched. This frustration, rather than the lack of catharsis, might have produced the increase in their level of aggressive behavior. Finally, Liebert, Neale, and Davidson (1973) describe two other field studies that failed to replicate Feshbach and Singer's (1971) findings.

Social Learning and Increased Aggression

These difficulties cast doubt on the catharsis hypothesis, and most subsequent social psychological research on the problem indicates that the doubts are justified. Indeed, instead of decreasing the level of aggression, exposure to *televised violence appears to increase* overt aggression (Liebert, Neale, and Davidson, 1973; Tannenbaum and Zillman, 1975). If we recall the other theories of aggression—the reformulation of frustration-aggression, the excitation-transfer theory, and social learning theory—we can see why this might be the case. First, suppose that the viewing child is instigated to aggression before watching the program. (Ask a parent, or an adolescent child, how smoothly the parent-child relationship is going and you will have no trouble imagining that there is some instigation to aggression.) In the terms of Berkowitz's (1969) reformulation of the frustration-aggression doctrine, the televised violence would serve as an aggressive cue establishing the appropriateness of releasing the aggressive impulses. In addition, the excitation-transfer theory of Tannenbaum and Zillman (1975) suggests that the excitement of the program itself may be misattributed to a desire to behave aggressively. We normally do not think of television programs as being highly arousing events, but they do produce changes in physiological arousal (Cline, Croft, and Courier, 1973; Geen and Rakosky, 1973; Tannenbaum and Zillman, 1975). Because we do not regard the program as the source of this arousal, we have no external label for the subjective feeling and may mistakenly think it part of our anger at having been instigated to aggression. Thus given a prior instigation the televised violence may indicate that aggression is appropriate and may also increase the level of aggression that is later expressed.

But what if there is no prior instigation to aggression? The social learning viewpoint taken by Bandura (1973) predicts that observation of televised violence will still increase subsequent aggression. Recall that this model postulates two quite different reasons for aggressive action: the aversive events described by many other theories, and the use of aggression as a means of obtaining rewards in the absence of any aversive instigation. Let us concentrate upon the latter reason for aggression. A detailed analysis of the content of television programs conducted by Larsen (1968) found that violent methods were the single most widely employed means of reaching desired goals. It is probable that the content of television programming has moderated somewhat in the intervening years, but it is also highly likely that this instrumental use of aggression still occupies a central role in program content.

How well do children learn this lesson? A large number of experimental studies shows that the lesson is learned vey well indeed. Children produce "carbon copy" imitations of aggressive actions they have witnessed (Bandura, Ross, and Ross, 1963a), and they retain this imitative behavior as long as eight months after witnessing a single ten-minute episode (Hicks, 1968). A majority of children will report that they would like to emulate a character who accomplishes ends through violence as long as that violence is not punished, and the imitation of aggression increases with the justification given for that aggression even among college students (Meyer, 1972). Instigation to aggression reliably increases the level of subsequent aggressive behavior, but these studies support the social learning view that aggression can be taught in the absence of any instigation at all.

The social learning theory analysis thus argues that with or without prior instigation televised violence is likely to increase subsequent aggression, and the great preponderance of the research evidence confirms this prediction (Goranson, 1970; Liebert, Neale, and Davidson, 1973; Tannenbaum and Zillman, 1975). Included in this supporting evidence is a massive study undertaken by the United States Surgeon General (described by Cater and Strickland, 1975) which includes seven volumes of reports by researchers using a variety of experimental and nonexperimental procedures and an extensive array of dependent variables. There is evidence that the instigational effects of observed violence are not confined to the medium of television (Leyens, Camino, Parke, and Berkowitz, 1975); there are occasional studies which fail to find instigational effects (e.g., Manning and Taylor, 1975); and there are still those who doubt the relationship between observed violence and aggression (Howitt and Cumberbatch, 1975). But there is general agreement among researchers in the area that televised violence in particular serves as an instigation to later aggressive behavior (Tannenbaum and Zillman, 1975).

A CONCLUDING COMMENT

In this chapter we have seen that competition and aggression, like the positive social behaviors of altruism and attraction, can be influenced by both situational factors and personal characteristics. Competition can be increased by changing the payoffs for success, by suggesting individualistic goals, or by altering the apparent characteristics of the opponent. But over the long term an individual person's participation in competition may also be affected by his or her level of resultant achievement motivation. Aggression can reliably be instigated by aversive events, but it can also be the learned solution to the problem of obtaining one's own ends.

If competition and aggression are like the positive social behaviors in their dependence upon both personal and situational factors, they are unlike altruism and attraction in their characterization by society. We foster competition among children by training them to be self-sufficient, we further encourage competition by rewarding good performance in school, and competition is presumed to be an essential element of our economic system (although there may be some doubt about this). In these and other ways we label competition as positive and healthy, and we profess to be surprised when our children seem uncaring for the welfare of others, when students cheat on examinations in order to maintain high grade averages, and when businesses make illegal payments and campaign contributions. We discourage individual aggression through socialization and a legal system that punishes violence, asserting all the while that there must be better ways of resolving interpersonal conflicts. Yet at the same time we do little to restrict the contradictory lessons taught by television, we reinstitute capital punishment for certain crimes, and we insist that our armed forces be the most powerful in the world.

We began this chapter by pointing out the confusion in common-language definitions of competition and aggression. After some refinements of the terms we were in a position to see what situational and personal factors might affect these two behaviors, at least in the context of scientific research. When we wonder how many of these research findings might be applied in the real social world, we face a different confusion—one of inconsistent social attitudes toward competition and aggression. Easy generalization from research to interpersonal behaviors of competition and aggression may well require the resolution of some of these attitudinal inconsistencies.

Summary

People are said to be in competition (p. 421) if their interaction is characterized by a low correspondence of outcomes and if each party to the interaction is striving to achieve individual goals. The process of competition may be studied in the laboratory in a variety of mixed-motive (p. 424) games such as the Prisoner's Dilemma game or the Trucking Game. Research with these and other experimental games has demonstrated that competition can be increased by changes in the structure of the game, by inducing *individualistic motives* (p. 428) in the participants, by the unilateral or bilateral possession of *threat* (p. 432), by an opponent's unconditional *strategy* (p. 430), or even by some of the opponent's personal characteristics. Cooperation will be enhanced if the parties are allowed to communicate with each other, provided that this communication is used for coordination rather than for transmission of threats. Although these laboratory studies of competition have the usual problems of external validity, many of the principles derived from such research can be applied to problems of competition in the real social world.

Among the personal factors that may affect an individual's willingness to engage in sustained competition is his or her level of resultant achievement motivation (p. 438). Both a *motive to achieve success* (p. 437), traditionally measured by pictures selected from the Thematic Apperception Test (TAT), and a *motive to avoid failure* (p. 437), usually measured by the Test Anxiety Questionnaire (TAQ), enter into this resultant achievement motivation. People in whom the resultant level is high will tend to choose tasks of intermediate difficulty and will attribute their success to internal causes. In contrast, people who are low in resultant achievement motivation will be more likely to choose tasks that are either much too difficult or much too simple, and they will make internal attributions for failure. Early independence training (p. 441) is likely to produce high achievement motivation, and the effects of such motivation can be seen in indexes of economic growth. A persistent problem is that the measurement of achievement motivation is often unreliable for women. It has been suggested that this is because a woman's achievement motivation may be complicated by a *fear of success* (p. 443), but the research evidence on this point is presently inconclusive.

Human aggression (p. 447) can be defined as intentional action directed toward the injury of another person, and theories of the origin of aggression can be distinguished from each other on the basis of whether they view the source of instigation (p. 448) as inherent in the person, as coming from the external environment, or as the result of some combination of the two. Foremost among the internal theories are the instinctive theories of Freud and Lorenz, but most of the research in social psychology supports either the frustration-aggression hypothesis (p. 451) and its modifications or the more inclusive *social learning theory* (p. 453). In recent years there has been an increasing controversy over the possible role of televised violence in the instigation of aggression in society. In keeping with the instinctive theories and with early frustration-aggression theory, it was first thought that televised violence might provide catharsis (p. 456) for aggressive impulses that would otherwise be expressed in socially destructive ways. Subsequent research in a wide variety of settings, however, indicates that, in keeping with social learning theory, televised violence may actually increase the level of aggression that is later expressed.

Suggested Additional Readings

APFELBAUM, E. On conflicts and bargaining. In L. Berkowitz (Ed.) *Advances in experimental social psychology.* Vol. 7. New York: Academic Press, 1974. Pp. 103–156. A review of research using mixed-motive games which takes into account the social nature of such interactions. A bit technical at times.

BANDURA, A. *Aggression: A social learning analysis.* Englewood Cliffs, N.J.: Prentice-Hall, 1973. This is an extensive review of theory and research on aggression, concentrating on the social learning position, but with coverage of the major alternatives as well. More difficult reading than the book by Johnson (following).

BERKOWITZ, L. (Ed.) *Roots of aggression: A re-examination of the frustration-aggression hypothesis.* New York: Atherton Press, 1969. This is a collection of many of the classic experiments done to test aspects of the frustration-aggression hypothesis.

JOHNSON, R. N. *Aggression in man and animals.* Philadelphia: Saunders, 1972. This moderately sized book begins with discussion of the evolutionary purposes served by aggression in animal societies, then turns to theories of human aggression and concludes with the problem of violence in human society. A thorough yet readable treatment of the variety of behaviors that can be subsumed under the heading of aggression.

WEINER, B. *Theories of motivation: From mechanism to cognition.* Chicago: Markham, 1972. This rather technical book contains an extensive discussion of achievement motivation theory and research.

We are usually aware of attempts by others to influence our actions, and of our own attempts to change the behavior of other people.

Social Influence
Chapter Twelve

Of all the topics of interest to scientific social psychology, social influence perhaps best matches intuitive conceptions of what the subject matter of the discipline ought to be. We may not be attuned to the accuracy or error of our social perceptions, we may not be conscious of all the factors shaping our social attitudes and self-concept, we may not reflect upon the degree to which our own actions might help or harm other people. Yet we are usually aware of the attempts by others to influence our actions, and of our own attempts to change the behavior of other people. From the intuitive point of view this process of mutual influence is the real stuff of social behavior: we plead, we bargain, and we threaten in order to have our views prevail, we resist attempts to change our own behavior, and the society passes laws to keep this mutual influence within acceptable bounds.

Social influence, like competition and aggression, may be a positive phenomenon or a negative one, depending upon the circumstances of influence and upon the value system of the person making the judgment. Suppose, for example, that a new industrial plant is planned for some vacant land near a park. The workers and merchants who would benefit by the presence of the plant will try to get the approval of the local governing body, while the people who fear that the park will be destroyed will argue against such approval. Each side will see its own efforts as legitimate attempts to exert influence for the betterment of the community and will think the other group's efforts unjustified and improper. From the standpoint of scientific social psychology, both groups are engaged in a process of social influence. Their ultimate goals differ, but the means they employ to achieve those goals may be identical.

In this chapter we take a closer look at the process of social influence. We begin with some broad questions about the process, distinguishing between power and influence, illustrating some of the bases of social power, and recalling a distinction drawn in Chapter Seven between public compliance and private acceptance. In the next section we discuss the ways in which one individual may exert influence over another, noting the role played by personal factors such as Machiavellianism and by situational variables such as direct orders. Then we turn to the issue of individual conformity with group opinion, showing how this conformity may arise from either informational or normative pressures. Finally we consider social influence as an interaction, discussing the possible role of an active minority in bringing about social change.

AN OVERVIEW OF POWER AND INFLUENCE

Let us suppose that your professor has announced that there will be an important examination early next week. You know that you need time to study, and as late as Friday afternoon you intend to spend most of the weekend in the library, preparing for the test and catching up on your other work. If you actually did spend a great deal of time studying, we might say either that the professor had power over you or that the professor had influenced your behavior. But now imagine that late Friday evening some of your close friends decide to take a really special weekend trip, leaving early Saturday morning and returning late Sunday night. They urge you to come along, and against your better judgment you decide to do so. In this case it is clear that the professor has exerted very little influence on your action, but what can we say about the professor's power? Is the power less because there was no influence, or will the power just be implemented in a different way (by punishing you with a bad grade for your poor performance on the test)?

Although some theorists who are concerned with organizational decision making (Dahl, 1957; March, 1957) equate power with influence, social psychologists more typically distinguish between the two (Cartwright, 1959; Schopler, 1965; Thibaut and Kelley, 1959). In terms of our example, the decision theories would say that in the second case the professor had no power (you went on the weekend trip anyway), while the social psychological theories would argue that what had changed was the professor's influence, not power. We shall adopt this latter position and define social power as the capacity of a person or group to affect the behavior of another person or group. Implicit in this idea of capacity to affect behavior is the qualification "other things being equal." Under normal circumstances you probably would have spent the weekend studying, and you might even have been able to disregard distractions of an ordinary sort. Only the prospect of an uncommonly attractive distraction kept the professor's power from affecting your action over the weekend (and you realize that this power may result in later unpleasantness).

In contrast to power, social influence can be defined as attitudinal or behavioral change brought about by the application of social power. Although such change is often correlated with the power of the influencing agent, the relationship between power and influence is *nonsymmetrical:* power is a prerequisite for the occurrence of influence, but a lack of influence does not necessarily imply a lack of power. If the professor had no social power, he or she could not influence you to spend the weekend studying, even under the best of conditions. But the fact that you choose not to comply with the professor's wishes does not diminish his or her social power, it only indicates that there are more powerful agents influencing you to do otherwise.

Field Theory and Forces

The distinction between power and influence can best be illustrated in terms of Lewin's (1942, 1951) field theory of social behavior. This theory holds that the social person exists in a field of forces that affect his or her actions. This total field of environmental factors and personal desires is called the life space, and a simple diagram of a life space is shown in part A of Figure 12-1. The large ellipse represents the life space, while the small circle represents the person (P). The area outside the circle but within the ellipse represents the subjective or phenomenological environment; that is, the environment *as it is perceived by the person.* (In part A of the figure this area is shaded.) At any moment in time the person's behavior is a joint function of his or her own desires, goals, and abilities and the pressures and constraints the person perceives in the environment. In terms of the theory, behavior (b) is a function of the person (P) and the environment (E), or

$$b = f(P,E)$$

This functional relationship should be quite familiar to you by now, since throughout the book we have emphasized that both situational factors and personal dispositions determine social behavior. Indeed, we have suggested that among the behavioral sciences social psychology is unique for its concentration upon the combination of these two classes of factors.

The example of the student who chooses not to study is shown in parts (B) and (C) of Figure 12-1. Part (B) is a diagram of the situation as it existed until late Friday afternoon, with the student fully intending to approach the negatively valued goal of spending the weekend in the library, because of the force (F) exerted by the professor. This force is a *vector,* which has both a direction and a certain strength. In the absence of other outside influences the force would have been sufficient to overcome the negative value of the goal. But as part (C) shows, the situation is complicated by the invitation from friends to take a weekend trip. The trip is a positive goal that the student would approach on his or her own, and there is the added force (F_2) provided by the urging of friends. Since the second force is greater than the

FIGURE 12-1
*Diagrams of the life space. (A) shows the person (P) surrounded
by the social environment (E). (B) shows the force (F) exerted by
the professor to induce the student (P) to approach the negatively
valued goal (G −) of studying for the examination. (C) shows the
force (F₁) exerted by the professor on the student (P) and the
opposing force (F₂) exerted by the student's friends to approach
the positively valued goal (G +) of taking the weekend trip with
them. (Adapted from Lewin, 1946)*

A

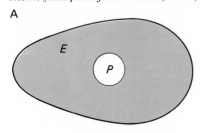

B

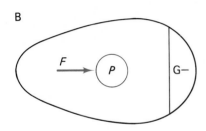

C

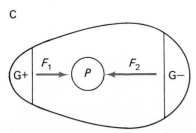

first, and in the opposite direction, the student will end up taking the
trip (and perhaps paying the consequences on the day of the test).

In terms of field theory, an individual's *power* can be thought of
as his or her force vector (F_1 is the power of the professor, F_2 is the
power of the friends). The social *influence* is the *resultant* of all of
the forces acting upon the person. In this situation, since F_2 is much
greater than F_1, and in the opposite direction, the resultant is a vector
directed toward the positively valued goal, with a value equal to $F_2 -
F_1$. The professor's power (represented by F_1) is not diminished by the

actions of the student, it is only overcome by the more powerful force exerted by the student's friends. This conception of power and influence in terms of forces and their resultant, respectively, will be useful to us in our later discussion of the factors which contribute to the power of individuals over each other and the power of groups over their members.

Sources of Social Power

If we continue with the example of the student taking the weekend trip for a moment, we can identify some of the important sources of social power. In an analysis based on field theory, French and Raven (1959) distinguished among five different types of power: *reward, coercive, legitimate, referent, and expert power.* For purposes of illustration these are usually described separately, but any single powerful agent is likely to derive power from more than one source at a time.

Reward power and coercive power are based on aspects of social exchange that we have considered before (e.g., in Chapter Nine). I have reward power over you if I can govern either the likelihood that you will receive rewards or the amount of the rewards that you obtain. Reward power is nothing more or less than my ability to provide you with positive reinforcements, or with outcomes that in terms of Thibaut and Kelley's (1959) exchange theory would be *above* both your comparison level (CL) and your comparison level for alternatives (CL_{alt}). In contrast, coercive power is based on the fact that I can provide you with negative reinforcements, or with outcomes that would be *below* your CL (in the next section we shall discss what might happen if these punishments are also below your CL_{alt}.

Legitimate power is derived from the previous socialization of the person upon whom such power is to be used. If you have been taught that your "elders," your professors, your supervisors have the right to ask you to perform certain tasks for them, then they have legitimate claims to power over you. Legitimacy often combines with reward and coercive power. We respect the rights of police officers to enforce the laws (even though we may disagree with a particular application of those laws), but we would not respect the attempts by vigilante groups to enforce exactly the same laws. The limitations on legitimate power include the nature and extent of your socialization, as well as the degree to which the powerful agent represents the class of people whom you endow with legitimate power. Just as we would think it improper for vigilante groups to enforce traffic laws, we might think it improper for police officers to enforce laws that regulate private morality. There will be more disagreement about the sorts of behavior that can be regulated than about the kinds of agents who might be justified in exercising legitimate power.

Referent power is derived from a desire for identification with the powerful agent. Here identification is defined as it was in the discussion of Kelman's (1961) three processes of attitude change (Chapter Seven): acceptance of influence in order to ensure a satisfying self-defining relationship. Those whom you desire to emulate will have referent power over you. Doing their bidding will make a positive contribution to your self-concept.

Finally, **expert power** rests on the fact that the powerful person has skills or knowledge that you lack or need. If you believe that such a person is acting in good faith and being truthful, you will follow his or her recommendations for your activities.

In our example, the professor can be seen to possess reward power (the ability to give you a good grade on the test), coercive power (the ability to flunk you), and legitimate power (his or her giving of tests and your taking them is part of the educational enterprise). To the extent that the test is seen as the professor's way of measuring your knowledge of the material, he or she may have expert power. And to the extent that being thought of as a "conscientious student" is important to you, the professor may also have some degree of referent power. In contrast, your friends can only exert reward power (the pleasure of the journey and of their company), and some referent power (you want to be thought of as a reliable friend).

With all the different sources of power available to the professor, why did you decide to take the trip with your friends? The answer is, of course, that what finally determines your decision is the total amount of force that each party is able to bring to bear upon you, not the variety of sources contributing to that power. There will be cases in which the source of the influencing agent's power will affect the amount of power he or she can wield (rewards obviously generate less resistance than punishments, so fewer rewards are needed to create the same amount of power), but even here the crucial variable is the total amount of power possessed by the influencing agent.

Counterforces Against Social Influence

The analysis of power in terms of forces brought to bear upon the target person can be extended to include the target person's tendency to resist or avoid the intended influence. We now briefly consider four different counterforces available to the target person: inertia, resistance, avoidance, and opposition. All four of these counterforces will have the effect of reducing the level of influence (the actual change in attitude or behavior), and the last two may also limit the amount of power that the influencing agent is willing to exercise (as opposed to the power that the influencing agent possesses). The power that the influencing agent is willing to exercise is called usable power, and in a moment we shall see why this is typically a smaller amount than the total power available to the influencing agent.

Inertia and Resistance

Only rarely does someone pressure you to do something you were about to do anyway, and in such a case the restriction of your behavioral freedom might generate psychological reactance (discussed more fully in Chapter Seven). In most instances of social influence, the influencing agent's goal is to change your attitude or behavior from what it would have been without intervention. The first source of force against influence will simply be the *inertia* inherent in your normal behavior. You get accustomed to a particular way of perceiving the social environment, to a set of social attitudes, or to a pattern of interpersonal behavior, and it requires a special effort to change from that routine. You may not even claim that your way is the best way, just that it is comfortable for you. This behavioral inertia is a nonspecific sort of resistance to social influence: it will act as a counterforce against any influence attempt, no matter what the direction of the applied force.

In contrast to the nonspecific character of inertia, *resistance* is a counterforce specifically induced by the character of the influence attempt. Resistance, like reactance, is a response to a threatened freedom. But it is produced by an attempt to *change* your behavior, rather than an attempt to require you to do what you were already about to do. What would it mean to change in the direction advocated by the powerful person? By accepting influence you not only change your behavior, you also imply that future influence attempts by the powerful agent will be successful. You sacrifice a certain amount of personal freedom. And the greater the threatened freedom, the greater the resistance. Suppose that two people ask you to change one of your behaviors, and one of the influencing agents is a person you will never see again while the other is a person with whom you interact on a regular basis. Both requests will produce the same counterforce from inertia, but the second will produce the greater resistance. Thus resistance is the social influence counterpart of reactance.

Avoidance and Opposition

A third response to the influence attempt is to leave the situation entirely. This *avoidance* response is not so much a true counterforce against the influence attempt as it is a demonstration that the powerful person cannot even force you to subject yourself to continued pressure. The avoidance response in social influence corresponds to the response in a conflict situation of "leaving the field" (Lewin, 1933; Miller, 1944).

Finally, the most direct counterforce against an influence attempt is direct *opposition:* the exercise of power by the target person against the would-be influencing agent. In terms of our earlier example, avoidance of the professor's power might be accomplished by a psychologically induced trip to the college infirmary on the day of the examination, while opposition might be shown by negativistic and argumentative behavior in class—you may still flunk, but you will succeed in ruining the class for everyone else. (Please do not take this particular illustration too literally!)

Usable Power

The avoidance and opposition sesponses, and their effect on the usable power of the powerful person, can be shown more clearly in terms of Thibaut and Kelley's (1959) exchange theory (discussed more fully in Chapter Nine). According to this theory, *social power* is defined as the range of outcomes through which one participant in the interaction can move the other. This definition simply makes more specific our earlier definition of social power as the capacity to affect the social behavior of another person or group. If I can give you both highly positive outcomes and highly negative outcomes, my power over you is greater than it would be if the range of outcomes were smaller. But there is a limit to my willingness to exercise this power to control your outcomes, and two different factors contribute to the limit. If I consistently provide you with outcomes that are below your comparison level for alternatives, you will avoid my power by leaving the situation. Thus my *usable power* is first restricted to the range of outcomes through which I can move you and still stay above your CL_{alt}.

There is a second restriction on my power, and this corresponds to the counterforce of opposition. In most of the discussion so far we have assumed that the powerful person is basically indifferent to the behavior of the target person. Certainly the powerful agent would find compliance by the target person more satisfying than defiance, but other than this difference in satisfaction we have assumed that there was little opportunity for the target person to affect the outcomes of the powerful agent. In most social relationships, however, this is not the case. The agent and the target person are in a relationship that either has proven valuable to both in the past or promises to do so in the future, and each has a range of outcomes through which he or she can move the other. *The higher the correspondence of those joint outcomes the less usable power the influencing agent possesses.* If by giving you punishments for noncompliance I dramatically lower my own outcomes, I will be careful about issuing threats. Only in the case of low correspondence of outcomes (e.g., competition or aggression) will the influencing agent's own outcomes allow the use of a broad range of threats, and in this case the influencing agent's usable power is still limited to the amount of punishment you will accept before leaving the relationship entirely. So both the CL_{alt} (avoidance) and the correspondence of outcomes (opposition) restrict the absolute power of an influencing agent to a smaller range of usable power.

Compliance or Acceptance?

The final distinction that should be drawn before we move on to deal with the factors that affect power and influence is the distinction made earlier (Chapter Seven) between *public compliance* and *private acceptance.* As the poet Ferlinghetti has asserted, "Just because you have silenced a man does not mean you have changed his mind." The target of social influence may publicly comply with the influence attempt, all the time intending privately to find a way to sabotage the influencing agent's wishes. Although the definition of social influence is broad enough to include attitude change, most research has concentrated on public conformity rather than on private acceptance because the dependent variables have been behavioral changes rather than changes in private attitudes or opinions. In the destructive obedience research of Milgram (1963), for example, the principal research question was "How many subjects will administer the highest shock possible?" (a question of behavioral conformity), rather than "What will the subjects think about the legitimacy of this experiment?" (a question of private acceptance).

This is not to say that private acceptance is unimportant to social influence. In Thibaut and Kelley's (1959) view, continuance of the interaction depends upon the internal satisfaction of the less powerful person (unless, of course, there is dependence upon a relationship that consistently provides outcomes below CL but above CL_{alt}). Variations in the bases of social power also ought to affect private acceptance in different ways. Legitimate power should produce more private acceptance than power deemed illegitimate; rewards ought to produce a greater probability of private acceptance while coercion ought to engender compliance alone. The effectiveness of both referent power and expert power depends entirely upon private acceptance.

Informational versus Normative Social Influence

Deutsch and Gerard (1955) used the designation informational social influence to refer to social power that produces private acceptance, in order to reflect the fact that such power achieves its ends by providing the target person with the information needed to make a wise decision individually. In contrast to this benign persuasion is the group or individual pressure brought to bear on the target person in an attempt to induce a change in behavior, not because the change would make the person's actions somehow "correct," but because the change would permit the person either to obtain rewards or to avoid punishments. Deutsch and Gerard (1955) have called this sort of pressure normative social influence to denote that it achieves success through the imposition of norms on the target person, with the implication that sanctions could follow a failure to adhere to these norms.

Both forms of social influence are related to concepts that we have considered in earlier chapters. Specifically, you may recall that in Chapter Eight we outlined Kelley's (1952) distinction between the two sorts of self-evaluation functions that can be served by a group—the comparison function and the normative function. If a group (or an individual person) merely serves as an example for behavior and you are free to follow the example or not, that reference group serves the comparison function. If in addition the reference group establishes rules for your behavior and enforces those rules with sanctions, then it is also serving a normative function. (This function is most frequently seen in membership groups.)

The effects of social influence can also be described in terms of Kelman's three processes of attitude change (discussed more fully in Chapter Seven). Kelman (1961) distinguished between compliance (behavioral acquiescence without any internal attitude change) and two kinds of internal change: identification and internalization. We have already seen that referent power is based on the target person's identification with the influencing agent, and that expert power achieves its success through the internalization of the expert's recommendations. Normative social influence is the most likely to produce compliance without private acceptance, while informational social influence is most likely to produce some form of private acceptance. Whether this private acceptance is identification or internalization may well depend upon the basis of the influencing agent's power.

A Summary of Social Influence Processes

So far we have had a characterization of the process of social influence, a description of the bases of social power, and an outline of the possible responses to influence. In addition we have recalled from earlier chapters material on the role that different sorts of groups can play in social influence, and a distinction among three kinds of attitude change. The way in which all these aspects of social influence might be interrelated is summarized in Table 12-1. Thus, for the case of "persuasion" we see that informational social influence is exerted by groups or individuals serving the comparison function. These are reference groups or individuals who derive their power from expertise, the legitimacy of their position, or their ability to serve as examples (referents) for the target person. The solid arrows indicate that in this process of informational social influence, expert power and legitimate power will most often produce private acceptance through internalization, while referent power will most often produce private acceptance through identification.

In contrast, the "pressure" of normative social influence will be exerted by groups or individuals who serve the normative function. If the influencing agent is a reference group it will most typically also be a membership group, or if the agent is an individual, it will probably be someone in a stable relationship with the target person. These influencing agents derive their power primarily from the rewards they dispense and the punishments they threaten to administer. The solid arrows indicate that such tactics are most likely to produce overt compliance without private acceptance. Over the long term (indicated by the dotted arrows) there is the possibility that rewards will lead to identification and that compliance with threats might (through dissonance reduction) eventually have the same end.

The relationships outlined in Table 12-1 are not intended to exhaust the possible combinations of nature of influence, source of power, and character of response to the influence attempt. Indeed, we have already noted that the bases of power themselves seldom appear in pure form. The table does identify the conceptual similarities between aspects of social influence and related material considered in earlier chapters, and it does show that social influence is composed of a number of dimensions: the nature of the influencing agent, the source of the agent's power, and the nature of the response. In this respect our view of social influence draws on a number of other formulations (Allen, 1965; Gamson, 1968; Jahoda, 1959; Stricker, Messick, and Jackson, 1970; Willis, 1965) that argue that social influence is a multidimensional concept. The final resultant pressure on the target person can still be represented by the familiar single force vector, just so we keep in mind that there are a variety of different components contributing to that force and that there are several possible responses to the force that may be taken by the target person. Unfortunately, much of the research on conformity and social influence—with its stress on the dependent variable of behavioral compliance—necessarily oversimplifies the process.

TABLE 12-1
Classification of social influence processes showing the conceptual differences between "persuasion" (informational social influence) and "pressure" (normative social influence)

CHARACTERISTIC	CONCEPTUAL TERMS USED TO DESCRIBE THE CHARACTERISTIC				
Influence process (Deutsch & Gerard, 1955)	Informational social influence			Normative social influence	
Function of the reference individual or group (Kelley, 1952)	Comparison function			Normative function	
Base of power (French & Raven, 1959)	Expert	Legitimate	Referent	Reward	Coercive
	↓	↓	↓	↓	↓
Process of change (Kelman, 1961)	Internalization	Internalization	Identification	Compliance	Compliance

THE INFLUENCE OF ONE INDIVIDUAL OVER ANOTHER

Machiavellianism: Influence as an Interpersonal Style

We have discussed some of the complexities of the social influence process, and now we turn to the process in action. Our first concern is the people who wield social power—not those who come by their power through legitimate position or expertise, but those who seem able to achieve their ends in an interaction even without the trappings of office. Can these extremely successful manipulators be distinguished from other people, and what tactics do they employ? In order to answer these questions, Christie and his associates (reported in Christie and Geis, 1970) began by studying historical treatments of social power and influence, including two works by Niccolò Machiavelli: *The Prince* and the *Discourses*. In *The Prince* (originally published in 1532) Machiavelli not only gave advice about tactics of social influence, he also made a number of specific statements about the nature of humanity. On the assumption that people who would follow Machiavelli's advice about social influence might also share his views of human nature, Christie and his colleagues collected a wide variety of statements from *The Prince*, and added some others of their own, in a first attempt to measure individual differences in manipulativeness.

Construction of a Machiavellianism Scale

The complete set of statements was edited and some of the wordings were reversed (e.g., Machiavelli's views on the cowardice of most people became "Most men are brave") to guard against the *acquiescence* response set: in answering questionnaires, people (some more than others) tend to agree with the items as worded no matter what the content of the items might be. Under these circumstances, if all the items contributing to the final score are worded in the positive direction, a subject's score will be artificially inflated by this tendency to agree. The edited statements were then presented in a Likert format (degrees of agreement or disagreement, as discussed more fully in Chapter Five) to undergraduate students at three universities. Correlations were computed on the results to determine how well each of the seventy-one items corresponded to the total score. Fifty of the seventy-one items correlated significantly with the total score, and these were subjected to an item analysis to eliminate overlapping items, to choose those which were most discriminating, and to include a variety of content. The result was a Likert-format scale of twenty items, half worded in the positive direction and half worded in the negative direction.

This version of the scale (called the Mach IV) contained three subscales: one dealing with interpersonal tactics, one concerned with general views of human nature, and one dealing with abstract or generalized morality. Sample items from each scale are presented in Table 12-2. Strong agreement with a positively worded item (denoted M+) or strong disagreement with a negatively worded item (denoted M−) contributes to a high score on Machiavellianism. As you might imagine from the nature of the items shown in Table 12-2, some of the early research with the Mach IV showed that the scale was much too highly correlated with measures of social desirability. This correlation was high negative, with people who were high in social desirability scoring low in Machiavellianism. To counter this problem, a forced choice version of the scale was constructed (the Mach V).

In this final version of the scale every Machiavellian-keyed item (M+ or M−) was placed in a triad with two other items. One of the additional items was matched in social desirability (SD) with the Machiavellian-keyed item, while the third item was a *buffer* which differed in social desirability. Thus, when the Machiavellian-keyed

TABLE 12-2
Selected items from a test of Machiavellianism

Interpersonal Tactics
> Positive Wording: The best way to handle people is to tell them what they want to hear. (M+)
> Reversed Wording: Honesty is the best policy in all cases. (M−)

Views of Human Nature
> Positive Wording: It is hard to get ahead without cutting corners here and there. (M+)
> Reversed Wording: Most people are basically good and kind. (M−)

Abstract Morality
> Positive Wording: People suffering from incurable diseases should have the choice of being put painlessly to death. (M+)
> Reversed Wording: All in all, it is better to be humble and honest than important and dishonest. (M−)

Adapted from Christie & Geis (1970).

item was worded in the positive direction, it would have a low social desirability value, and so would the matched item. The buffer in such a triad would have a much higher social desirability value. For example, consider one of the items from Table 12-2. In the Mach V its triad became:

A. The best way to handle people is to tell them what they want to hear. (M+, SD = 2.80)
B. People are getting so lazy and self-indulgent that it is bad for our country. (Matched, SD = 2.80)
C. It would be a good thing if people were kinder to others less fortunate than themselves. (Buffer, SD = 4.35)

For each triad respondents were supposed to say which of the three items was *most like* their own opinions, and which of the three was *least like* their own opinions. Given this particular triad, a person whose first concern was making the socially desirable response would obviously say that Item C was most like his or her opinion (since it has a high social desirability value of 4.35). But what about the choice between the other two? Ideally the socially desirable response is to deny both, but the instructions prohibit this. So which one the respondent chooses to identify as least like him will depend not on the social desirability of the item, but on its *content*. If he is a high Machiavellian, he will say that the matched item (B) is least like his opinion, while if he is low in Machiavellianism he will say that the Machiavellian-keyed item (A) is least like his opinion. Of course, a high Machiavellian who was *not* concerned with positive self-presentation would simply endorse the Machiavellian item (A). But by combining the Machiavellian items with matched and buffer items, Christie and Geis have provided a method for measuring what many people consider a socially undesirable trait in a manner uncontaminated by social desirability constraints.

What Are Machiavellians Like?

What sort of person scores high on these tests? First let us see what personal characteristics do *not* seem related to Machiavellianism. A wide variety of studies reported by Christie and Geis (1970) indicates that Machiavellianism is not significantly correlated with IQ; data from Wrightsman and Cook (1965) show no important correlations between Machiavellianism and racial attitudes; a national survey conducted in 1963 by the National Opinion Research Corporation (1970) found no correlation between Machiavellianism and political party or candidate preference; Christie and Geis (1970) report few significant relationships between Machiavellianism and personality measures such as the need for achievement, the overall level of anxiety, and authoritarianism.

These results suggest that Machiavellianism is more of an *interpersonal style* than a personality trait, and other research confirms this interpretation. For example, Exline, Thibaut, Hickey, and Gumpert (1970) had subjects participate in a set of decision tasks with an experimental confederate. In the middle of this series of tasks the experimenter was called out of the room for "a long-distance telephone call." In his absence the confederate looked at the answers for the remaining tasks with such a flourish that it implicated the subject in his cheating. The experimenter then returned, the series of tasks was completed, and the experimenter expressed amazement at the success of the pair, first implicitly and then explicitly accusing them of cheating. The dependent variable of interest to us is the amount of eye contact maintained by the subject with the experimenter, both during this period of accusation and in a subsequent two-minute period. Compared to low Machiavellians, the high Machiavellians actually *increased* their amount of eye contact after the formal accusation. After an accusation of unethical behavior, it is the high Mach, rather than the honest person, who will look you in the eye.

What Social Conditions Favor Machiavellians?

This experiment, and a large number of others reported by Christie and Geis (1970), establish the high Mach as a manipulator of other people, suggesting both aspects of disposition and characteristics of the situation that permit the person to make the most of available opportunities. The principal dispositional difference between the high and the low scorer is that high Machs show much *greater emotional detachment* in the interpersonal situation. They are oriented toward cognitions—rules of the game, rational solutions to problems— rather than toward the persons who may be taking part in the interaction. They initiate and control the structure of the interaction, setting limits, defining goals, recommending procedures, while low Machs accept and follow the structure set up by others. Finally, high Machs are highly resistant to sheer social pressure. They can be persuaded by rational arguments (informational social influence) just as easily as can low Machs, but they are much less susceptible to normative social influence attempted by other parties in the interaction.

High Machs are best able to take advantage of their substantial emotional detachment in interactions that provide advantages for them at the expense of the low Mach. The "best" situation, from the standpoint of the high Mach, is one that involves *face-to-face interaction*, that has some *latitude for improvisation*, and that offers the possibility for the high Mach to *arouse irrelevant affect* in the other participants. Machiavellianism is, as we have seen, less of a personality trait than in an interpersonal style, and it is a style that cannot be effective except in person. There cannot be a fixed structure for the interaction, and there cannot be sufficient time for the other participants to reflect upon the situation before taking action. The interaction must be face-to-face so that the high Mach can concentrate on strategy while the low Mach gets personally involved with the other participants; there must be enough flexibility in the rules of the interaction so that the high Mach can tailor new rules to his or her own needs; and there must be the potential for playing on the emotions of the people who are likely to take their own positions seriously. High Machs cannot be wedded to ideological commitments of their own, for then they would be unable to make the necessary compromises (it is not surprising that Machiavellianism is unrelated to political preferences), and they must be well enough adjusted so that personal problems do not complicate their goals in the interaction. Given these limits on disposition and situation, the high Mach can be an extremely successful agent of social influence even in the absence of any obvious source of social power.

Direct Influence: Obedience to Authority

A vast amount of social influence among individuals takes place in the context of giving and following orders. Obviously the armed forces depend upon the "chain of command" for everything from the completion of routine clerical tasks to successful performance in battle, but the relationship between supervisor and subordinate can also be found in any stable organization. In most of these cases the orders are not stated directly, but they still rest upon a tacit agreement between supervisor and subordinate that the former's status provides the legitimate authority to exercise social influence. The boss may say to an assistant, "Will you please prepare this report for me," the department chairman may ask a new assistant professor, "Do you think you could teach introductory psychology next term," or your apartment manager may ask politely if it is possible for you to keep your parties just a bit more quiet. But no matter how pleasantly the request is phrased, it contains an implicit threat. An employee who hopes to continue to receive salary increases will not often disregard the requests of the employer. A professor who hopes to maintain the esteem of colleagues will not refuse to carry his or her share of the teaching responsibilities. A tenant who wishes to stay in the apartment complex will not take the manager's advice too lightly.

The Danger of Uncritical Acceptance of Influence

This sort of individualized normative social influence depends both on the provision of appropriate rewards for compliance and on the threat of punishment for failure to comply. It also depends on the target person's belief that the influence attempt is justified and that the influencing agent is acting within the bounds of legitimate authority. The smooth operation of any structured organization depends upon the acceptance by subordinates of the legitimate directives issued by their supervisors. But the process of individual normative social influence is so prevalent that its uncritical acceptance may have disastrous consequences. In 1971 a platoon of American soldiers under the command of Lt. William Calley murdered twenty-two Vietnamese men, women, and children in the village of My Lai. The participating soldiers asserted that they had been ordered to shoot, and in his subsequent trial Lt. Calley argued that he, too, had been following orders. In 1973, it was disclosed that the acting director of the Federal Bureau of Investigation, L. Patrick Gray, had destroyed papers and documents that might have proved politically embarrassing to the Nixon administration. In 1975, a Senate committee revealed that the Central Intelligence Agency had attempted several times in the preceding years to assassinate Cuba's leader Fidel Castro. These are not isolated instances, only well-known ones, and they can tell us something about the process of individual normative social influence.

There are three common threads in these examples that are relevant for our purposes. First, people who did not originate the idea for each action were nevertheless involved in the action—in an important sense they were following orders. Second, it has been virtually impossible to pinpoint the responsibility for initiating each action. Lt. Calley is the only one to have been convicted of a crime or otherwise held personally responsible in a formal proceeding, and there is some reason to think that at least the climate leading to his order to shoot was the responsibility of his superiors. Third, the disclosure of each event was accompanied by a public outcry sufficient to indicate a general lack of approval for the action that had been taken. Thus, after the fact there was doubt about the legitimacy of the actions, but at the time of compliance the various subordinates did not consider the requests made of them to be illegitimate. It would be tempting to condemn the participants in these incidents, attributing the occurrence to some flaws in their characters, but to do so would be to deny the power of the situation and the degree to which all of us are likely to do what is asked of us.

Destructive Obedience

The experiments on destructive obedience conducted by Milgram (1963, 1965) are perhaps the most convincing demonstration of this tendency to follow orders. A massacre of people considered to be "the enemy" can be attributed to the conditions under which a guerrilla war must be fought, the mistakes of an appointed official can be thought of as misguided loyalty, and the excesses of an agency might be attributable to overzealous performance of its mandate. Whether any of these reasons serves as a sufficient excuse for the action taken is a personal value judgment. For our purposes here, the critical point is that these attributions to the specific circumstances suggest that only in rare cases will people succumb to destructive individualized social influence. The major contribution of Milgram's research is to demonstrate just how widespread such influence can be.

You will recall from Chapter One that the subjects in Milgram's first experiment (1963) participated individually with an experimental confederate in what was described as a learning study. The subject was always chosen to "teach" the confederate a series of paired associates by administering an increasing level of electric shock for every successive failure during testing. The situation was purposely contrived so that the subject would be placed in the position of following orders from the experimenter to continue giving these electric shocks long after they had obviously become intolerably painful to the "learner." The dependent variable was the point on the shock scale (ranging from an ostensible 15 volts to an ostensible 450 volts) at which the subject adamantly refused to proceed, even after prodding by the experimenter. Contrary to all advance predictions, fully 60 percent of the subjects continued with the procedure until they were administering the maximum shock to an unresponsive learner. For these subjects the experimenter's attempted influence was highly successful.

How are these findings to be explained? First let us consider the obvious sources of power over the subject that were available to the experimenter. Coercive power must be ruled out because no subject was ever threatened with punishment for failure to comply. Reward power is also an unlikely explanation, because it was repeatedly stated that the subject's payment for participation was for simply showing up at the laboratory, not for any actions he or she might take during the experiment. It is doubtful that the experimenter was a positive referent for many of the subjects, in view of what he was asking them do so. What is left? Assume for the moment that from the subject's perspective, the experimenter is both the legitimate authority and the resident expert. In the research setting the experimenter is supposed to "know what he is doing," and subjects are not surprised to be asked to perform tasks "for science" that they might otherwise consider trivial, unusual, or even dangerous. Given this perception of the situation, it is not surprising that the subjects complied with the experimenter's demands.

In later versions of the experiment, however, Milgram (1965) moved from the psychology laboratory at Yale to a run-down brownstone building in Bridgeport, Connecticut. Compliance was somewhat lower in that setting than in the Yale laboratory, although a majority of subjects still complied. This argues against an explanation in terms of legitimate and expert power, leaving us with the impression that none of the bases of power alone provides a convincing explanation of the effect. In other changes, Milgram substituted a variety of different victim behaviors and altered the proximity of the experimenter to the subject and the subject to the victim. All these variations affected the dependent variable (percent compliance) to some degree. Compliance decreased when the experimenter gave his instructions over the telephone instead of in person, and decreased still further when the instructions were delivered by a tape recorder with no experimenter present. Subject compliance also decreased when the victim was brought into the same room with the subject, and still further when the subject was required to hold the victim's hand on a shock plate in order to administer punishment. Even in this last condition, however, over 30 percent of the subjects followed instructions to the bitter end.

As Milgram (1965) has noted, the destructive obedience paradigm is an excellent example of the analysis of social influence in terms of the forces brought to bear upon the subject's actions. There is an internal restraining force against injuring another person, and this is enhanced by the immediacy of the victim. Opposing this force toward morality is the force exerted by the experimenter. Contributing to this force might be at least some legitimacy inherent in the research process (no matter what the setting), the experimenter's willingness to accept the responsibility for the outcome, and the experimenter's immediacy to the subject.

One might perceive all these factors as specific to the experimental setting, but before we become complacent let us see how well they generalize to the real social world. There we do not often deal with experimenters, but we *do* interact with people in positions of legitimate authority, we recognize that the responsibility for an action lies with the person who orders that action performed, and we are all too willing to leave the decision making to "the experts," who presumably have more information than is available to us. From the child who says to a parent "All right, if you say so" in a tone of voice that clearly indicates who will be at fault if there is trouble, to the congressman who argues that the president should be allowed to make important decisions "because he has all the information," people serve as the instruments of legitimate authority, only too pleased to shift to others the responsibility even for their own actions. It is certainly true that questioning every attempt at legitimate social influence would be detrimental to society. But a failure to recognize the power of the situation and a wholly uncritical acceptance of all individualized normative social influence may be equally dangerous. A reasonable compromise can be reached only if we attend to the situation in which individual influence occurs and consider the forces affecting our actions. Similar precautions are relevant for group influence on individual behavior, the topic to which we now turn.

GROUP INFLUENCE OVER THE INDIVIDUAL

Conformity

Much of our social behavior is influenced not only by the other individuals in our lives, but also by the social groups that are important to us. A social group is more than a statistical aggregate (such as people over forty, college graduates, or two-car families); it is a collectivity that has psychological implications for the individual. As Kiesler and Kiesler (1969) have noted, a group will carry psychological implications for the individual only if that person (1) is *aware* of the other members of the group, (2) either *defines himself* as a member of the group or would like to do so, and (3) feels that the group is emotionally or cognitively personally *significant.* Since the reference group serves as a standard for self-evaluation (see Chapter Eight), its effects are achieved principally through informational social influence. When the reference group is also a membership group, its effects may then be accomplished primarily through normative social influence. It should be emphasized that in many real social groups these distinctions will be blurred: reference groups often double as membership groups, serving both the comparison function and the normative function (Kelley, 1952; Newcomb, 1943; Siegel and Siegel, 1957).

According to one accepted definition, conformity is a change in behavior or belief toward a group as a result of real or imagined group pressure (Kiesler and Kiesler, 1969). Let us see how this definition compares with the terms we have been using to describe other forms of social influence. To begin with, conformity is a form of influence (change). When this conformity is in belief it corresponds to private acceptance; when the change is in behavior it is equivalent to public compliance. The private acceptance is probably based on identification, rather than internalization, because the influence is the result of pressure. Finally, distinction between real pressure and imagined pressure reflects the difference between normative social influence and informational social influence. Thus, conformity is a more inclusive term than most we have used in this chapter, since it applies to any sort of influence by a group on an individual, as long as the change by the individual is in the direction of the group's position.

But conformity is not the only possible response to group pressure. At least two other possible responses have received attention: independence and anticonformity. In terms of the counterforces to social influence we outlined earlier in the chapter, independence could encompass the counterforces of inertia and resistance (the target person could steadfastly maintain his or her own position despite the group pressure), or it could be reflected in avoidance (the target person could leave the sphere of influence of the group). The other response to group pressure, anticonformity (action in direct opposition to group norms), corresponds to the counterforce of opposition and would be reflected in an active attempt to sabotage the group's objectives. Just as in the case of individual social influence, the target person's response to group pressure will depend upon the balance of forces present in the situation. If the group is highly attractive to the target person, if it has the capability of helping the target person achieve personal goals, or if the person has few alternative relationships available, the pressure to conform will be increased. If the group has little attractiveness compared to the alternatives, the pressure it can exert (usable power) will decrease. We now examine more closely both informational and normative social influence as they might be exerted by a group on an individual.

Group Informational Social Influence

Sherif's Study of Autokinetic Effects

In Chapter One we described Sherif's (1936) pioneering research on the formation of social norms for perceptual judgments. Despite its expressed concern with "norms," this research actually typifies the process of informational social influence rather than normative social influence: the group simply defined the perceptual situation for the individual, and there were not even implied sanctions for failure to adhere to the group standards. You will recall that Sherif employed the autokinetic effect—the perceptual illusion that occurs when a person views a point of light in a darkened room—to study the formation of norms for judgment. In the first series of trials the subjects privately estimated how much the light appeared to move; in a second series of trials these judgments were announced out loud and the several subjects converged on a common norm for perceived movement. In the final stage of the experiment the subjects once again made their judgments privately, and these private judgments remained quite close to the norm established in the second stage of research.

Imagine that you had been a subject in this experiment, and suppose that you believe the point of light to be moving around through an arc of more than a foot (this sort of estimate would be much higher than the average). You have never been in a situation precisely like the experimental setting, and you are quite uncertain about most of your answers. There are no objective standards against which you can evaluate your perceptual experience. In the second set of trials, the responses of the other subjects permit you to judge your own perceptual experience through social comparison (discussed in Chapter Eight). You have no reason to doubt the reports of other subjects, but you learn that they are quite different from your own. These other reports constitute the **social reality** (Festinger, 1950) of the situation, and it makes you uncomfortable to express an opinion that differs so greatly from this social reality. According to social comparison theory (Festinger, 1957), this dependency on the prevailing social reality will exert pressure upon you to change at least your public report of your perceptual experience, if not the experience itself. The fact that in the third session of the experiment your privately reported judgments still follow the previously established norm indicates that the informational social influence has produced private acceptance, as well as public compliance. You have changed your view of the phenomenon not because the group was explicitly threatening you with sanctions for your "errors," but because you have used the group opinion to define the situation for you.

Norm Transmission Through Information

The informational social influence present in Sherif's research differs from much of that found in the real social world in one respect. The group standard did not exist prior to the public judgments made by all the subjects. Strictly speaking, only the subjects whose initial public judgments differed from the later norm actually *conformed* to that norm. Those whose initial judgments were near the later norm did not actually *change* their beliefs, and no group pressure to change was ever exerted upon them. In most cases of comparison with a group outside the laboratory, however, the group has an existing position on the issue in question in advance of the comparison by the target individual. The particular target person may be ignorant of the group's stand, but at least the position is not in the process of development at the time of comparison. This characteristic of the procedure limits the external validity of Sherif's research to cases of norm formation, but a later study with the autokinetic effect extends the findings to a preexisting norm.

In this study of norm transmission (Jacobs and Campbell, 1961), subjects were placed in the autokinetic situation in groups of four. Each group member made public judgments of the degree of movement for thirty trials. At the conclusion of the first block of thirty trials, one subject in the group was replaced by a new subject, and then the group made another thirty judgments. Then a second "experienced" group member was replaced by a naive subject, and this process of judgment and replacement of the most experienced member continued for a total of eleven blocks of thirty trials in each block. Thus, by the end of the fourth block of trials, all the subjects who had been present during the first block had been replaced.

For each new replacement, the first series of thirty trials consisted of a comparison between his or her own perceptions and the previously established norm for the group—just the sort of situation that might prevail in the real social world. There were two conditions in Jacobs and Campbell's experiment. In the Control condition the very first group consisted of four naive subjects, but in the Arbitrary Norm condition the very first group consisted of three experimental confederates and one naive subject. The confederates had been instructed to make extreme judgments of movement, averaging 16 inches of movement per trial. Not surprisingly, the first naive subject placed in with the three confederates also made estimates of movement that were extreme (more than 14 inches per trial on the average). In short, this subject conformed to the group's preestablished norm, although the judgments were not quite as extreme as those of the confederates.

What is more interesting than the naive subject's conformity to the arbitrary norm is that this norm was *transmitted* to later replacement subjects, even after all the confederates had been replaced. Each new replacement in the Arbitrary Norm group made judgments that were less extreme than those made by the previous replacement, but until the *seventh* trial block (long after all confederates had departed) the judgments in the Arbitrary Norm condition were more extreme than the judgments in the Control condition. The arbitrary norm had been successfully transmitted to several "generations" of naive subjects.

This experiment serves as more than an illustration of informational social influence. It also serves as a model for too many organizations, bureaucracies, and informal social groups. Laws are left on the books long after the function they originally served is no longer needed; informal groups cling to traditions that have become outmoded; bureaucrats insist that certain procedures must be followed because in their memory "it has always been done that way." In most of these instances the original procedures and judgments were not arbitrary (unlike the situation in Jacobs and Campbell's experiment) but they nevertheless impede social change which might be highly constructive. People begin to feel comfortable with the rules they have privately accepted, and their cognitive consistency needs preclude any dramatic shifts in belief just to accommodate the views of "newcomers." Informational social influence may not be as effective as normative social influence in producing immediate public compliance, but because of the inertia present in private acceptance, its long-term effects may be much stronger.

A Step Toward Normative Social Influence

The Asch Experiment

The research by Sherif (1936) and by Jacobs and Campbell (1961) shows how informational social influence can produce both compliance and acceptance when the stimulus situation is ambiguous. No normative pressure is needed, because the information provided by the group serves to define the situation for the target person. But what happens when the group judgment quite clearly differs from objective reality as perceived by the target person? In order to answer this question, Asch (1951) conducted what has become a classic study of social influence. Imagine for a moment that you were a subject in such an experiment. You would arrive at the laboratory to find eight other subjects (all of whom were actually confederates) already seated in chairs that had been arranged in a semicircle in front of a blackboard. You would take the only vacant seat, the second one from the end of the semicircle. After appropriate introductions the experimenter would describe the task as one of visual discrimination and would show you a sample of the stimulus materials. These would be vertical lines drawn on large pieces of cardboard. Two pieces of carboard would be placed on the chalk rail of the blackboard at a time, one containing the *standard* line (from 2 inches long in some cases to 10 inches long in others) and the other containing a set of three *comparison* lines—one the same length as the standard, one longer, and one shorter. Your task in the experiment would simply be to say which of the comparison lines was equal in length to the standard line. Unlike estimation of movement in the autokinetic situation, this judgment task is unambiguous, and if you were to make the judgments all by yourself you would make virtually no errors.

Ostensibly so that the experimenter could keep track of the judgments, all of you would be asked to make your decisions out loud, beginning with the person on the other end of the semicircle from you. Thus by the time you announce your decision, you would have heard the judgments made by seven of the other eight people. In the typical experiment there would be eighteen judgment trials, and on six of these (the "neutral" trials) all the other people would report judgments that agreed with your perceptual experience. On the other twelve trials (the "critical" trials), however, every other "subject" would report what seemed to you to be the *wrong* choice. The question is, how will you respond when confronted by a unanimous majority whose opinion differs so widely from your own perceptual experience? Will you report what you see, or will you conform to their erroneous judgment?

Factors Contributing to Conformity

Research through the years with the Asch situation has demonstrated that the answer to this question depends upon a number of factors. Even with a judgment as unambiguous as the one in Asch's (1951) experiment, errors were made on approximately one-third of the critical trials and, not surprisingly, greater *ambiguity* of the task enhances conformity (Allen, 1965; Crutchfield, 1955). Asch found extensive individual differences, with some subjects remaining independent on almost all critical trials and other subjects yielding on virtually all. The *independent* subjects (those who conformed less than half the time) were either quite confident of their responses or were withdrawn and nervous. The *yielding* subjects (those who conformed on half or more of the trials) most frequently distorted their judgment (actively considered the possibility that the majority was wrong, but adopted its position as a way to resolve their own uncertainty), sometimes distorted their action (knowing quite well that the majority was wrong, but conforming only to go along with the group), and infrequently distorted their perception (thinking that the majority had been factually correct).

These specific differences between independents and yielders seem to be related to personality variables (Crutchfield, 1955), but the other conformity effects seem attributable to situational variables. In a review of conformity research, Allen (1965) shows that there is greater conformity when the responses by the subject are made *publicly* rather than privately, when the *attractiveness* of the group is high rather than low, when the members of the group are *similar* to each other rather than different (in sex, ability), and when the issue in question is relatively *unimportant* to the individual who is under pressure. All these factors can be seen as contributing to the forces impinging upon the target person. The force of the group is increased by its attractiveness, cohesiveness, similarity among members, and demand for public responses. The resistance available to the target person will depend on his or her certainty (determined by the ambiguity of the task) and willingness to take a stand on the issue (importance).

One aspect of the situation that has received a great deal of attention is the nature of the majority, and the available research evidence suggests that *unanimity* is much more important than the sheer *size* of the majority. In his initial series of studies Asch (1951) found that a unanimous majority of sixteen was no more effective in producing conformity than was a unanimous majority of three. With very few exceptions (e.g., Gerard, Conolley, and Wilhelmy, 1968) subsequent research confirms the finding that conformity does not increase with size of the majority as long as the majority is at least three (Allen, 1965; Graham, 1962; Rosenberg, 1961). In contrast to the marginal effects of changes in group size (beyond three), changes in the unanimity of the majority have a profound effect on the degree of conformity. Again in the initial series of studies Asch (1951) found that the percentage of errors dropped from 32 percent to 5 percent with the addition of a *single* confederate who consistently agreed with the naive subject against the majority. It is possible that this drop in conformity to the erroneous judgment by the target person was caused by the fact that the dissenting confederate was *agreeing with the subject*, not just dissenting from the majority view. But an experiment by Allen and Levine (1968) rules out this possibility: their dissenting confederate consistently made judgments that were even more erroneous than those made by the majority. Although this dissenter thus also disagreed with the subject, conformity was substantially reduced.

There are problems inherent in the Asch experiments (and others like them), but on balance they represent the process of group normative social influence perhaps as well as laboratory research can. Conformity in the laboratory is not pure normative social influence, since the group gives no direct orders and there are no sanctions applied for failures to conform. The consequences of independence are far less serious than in pure cases such as a child's failure to obey her parents, a soldier's refusal to follow the orders of his superior, or a citizen's public civil disobedience. But the independent subjects in group conformity experiments do suffer unpleasant consequences, if only self-doubt and fear of being rejected by the majority of the group, and it is very difficult to justify the use of stronger sanctions on either methodological or ethical grounds. Milgram's obedience research raises serious ethical questions, and such influence might be even more dangerous if exerted by a group. In addition, a number of researchers have pointed out that the typical conformity experiment already suffers from possible experimenter expectancy effects and demand characteristics (Adair, 1972; Godwin and Restle, 1974; Nosanchuck and Lightstone, 1974). And finally, as noted earlier in the chapter, concentration on the behavioral response of public compliance does not quite do justice to the complexity of the social influence process. Despite these difficulties, experiments of group pressure on individuals do demonstrate the power of a unanimous majority to change beliefs and behavior.

SOCIAL INFLUENCE AND SOCIAL CHANGE

The Readiness to Accept Influence

We have seen that an individual's social power, or that of a group, can be derived from a variety of sources, that the application of this power may induce a number of counterforces, and that the response to attempted social influence may range from resistance and anticonformity through public compliance to private acceptance. Across all the examples and all the research there are two basic factors that appear to contribute to the target person's final willingness to accept social influence. These are *uncertainty* about the correct, or appropriate, response and the *personal advantage* that might be gained by compliance. Any single instance of social influence need not involve both factors; indeed, the former is more typical of informational social influence while the latter is more characteristic of normative social influence. But together the two factors have a good deal of explanatory value.

Let us consider first the influence of one individual over another. In an interaction between a high Mach and a low Mach, the high's wishes will typically prevail, and this can be described in terms of uncertainty. For the high Mach the latitude for improvisation represents an opportunity to structure the situation to his or her own advantage, but for the low this flexibility increases uncertainty about what responses might be appropriate. The high's concentration on cognitions leads the person to discard personal feelings as irrelevant to the task at hand, but such personal feelings and emotional involvements complicate the low Mach's social decisions.

When the interaction is between a legitimate authority and a target person (rather than between people of differing Machiavellianism), uncertainty and personal advantage would both contribute to the willingness to accept influence. Milgram's subjects, and their counterparts in the real social world, do as they are told unless they become convinced that it would be morally wrong to do so. In their uncertainty about their responsibilities in the situation, they rely on the judgment of the expert and the legitimacy of his or her authority. Most of their previous social learning has taught them that it is more costly to disobey the requests of legitimate authority than to comply with those requests, and if there is any doubt at all they will be more likely to comply.

Uncertainty and personal advantage can also be seen in the individual's response to group pressure. In the autokinetic situation, we see an excellent example of the effects of uncertainty. Here the group serves to define the situation for the individual, and to reduce perceptual ambiguity the subject engages in social comparison (which in past experience outside the laboratory has proved quite helpful) and shifts his or her judgments to agree with the discovered consensus. In the Asch situation there is no question about the perceptual judgment, but there is a high degree of confusion regarding the "correct" response in the situation. Of course there are individual differences in perceptual acuity in everyday situations, but to find yourself a minority of one cannot help but shake your self-confidence. And in this case there is comfort in being wrong with others instead of being correct but alone.

In part because of the research conducted on the topic, the term *conformity* has acquired pejorative connotations. When we hear of people who conform we often get a mental picture of the mindless subjugation of individual wills to the arbitrary whims of a powerful authority. We would do well to remember that while some conformity may in fact be mindless, much of the acceptance of social influence may be the result of active processes—social comparison to reduce uncertainty, and the desire to maximize outcomes—that in other circumstances would lead to effective individuality.

Contingency in Interaction

As we have noted several times during this chapter, one way to conceive of the process of social influence is to ask what the target person would have done without influence from others, and then to compare this to his or her actions following intervention by the influencing agent. But it is unlikely that this intervention will produce a completely changed target person—some actions will still be the result of the person's own wishes. In addition, because of the target person's ability to resist, to avoid, or to oppose influence, the powerful agent's actions may also be affected by the target person's behavior. The two parties must be regarded as participating in an interaction in which each one's actions are partly determined by his or her own goals and partly determined by the actions of the other. The relative social influence exerted by one party upon the other can be described in terms of a model of interaction proposed by Jones and Gerard (1967).

If we imagine two parties to an interaction, in this case the influencing agent and the target person, and consider that each party may (or may not) have a *plan* for the interaction and may (or may not) alter this grand design in response to the actions of the other, then there are four kinds of interaction possible. These four sorts of interaction are shown in Figure 12-2 as they might progress through time. Both the responses of the influencing agent and the responses of the target person are shown, with the arrows indicating whether those responses have been produced by one's own plan, the responses of the other person, or some combination of the two. The first sort of interaction, which Jones and Gerard (1967) called **pseudocontingency**, is the limiting case of social interaction. Pseudocontingency is illustrated by actors following a script, or by a target person who

FIGURE 12-2
Contingency of interaction between an influencing agent and a
target person. (Adapted from Jones and Gerard, 1967)

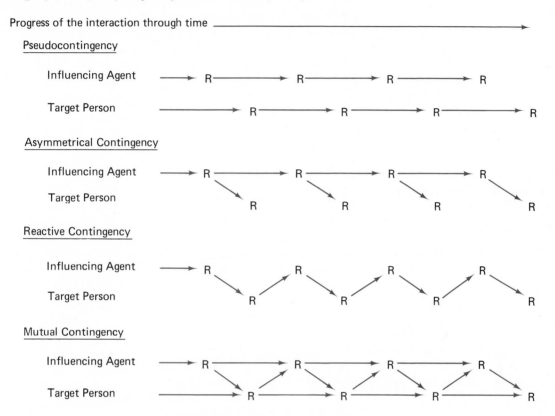

happens to change his or her actions just after being asked to, even
though intending to make the change all along. Each participant's
response (R) is determined by his or her own plan, with no consideration for the other's behavior. In terms of social influence, of
course, this case represents no influence at all.

The second case, called **asymmetric contingency**, is typical of the
interaction between an extremely powerful influencing agent and a
weak target person. The agent's actions are determined by this plan
alone, with no concern for the target person's responses. In contrast, the target person has no plan; his or her actions are determined
entirely by the influencing agent. This is an extreme form of social
influence found in concentration camps, some prisons, and occasional
mental hospitals. The influencing agents in these instances have
virtually complete control over the behavior of the target persons,
and there are few limits on their power.

The third case, **reactive contingency,** can best be illustrated by such things as panics, anarchy, or political terrorism. The influencing agent may have started the interaction with a plan, but after the target person's first response all either of them can do is quite literally react to the other's earlier behavior. For example, a government might issue stiff curfew regulations in order to prevent demonstrations, but then people would demonstrate against the curfew, the demonstrators would be jailed, there would be riots against the incarceration of peaceful demonstrators, troops would be called out to disperse the riots, and pretty soon the situation is completely out of the control of either party to the interaction. This is the logical extreme of interpersonal social influence, because neither party is able to follow any sort of internal plan for the interaction.

Finally, there is **mutual contingency** in which each party's actions are partly the result of his or her plan and partly the result of the other's actions. This last category is thought to typify true interaction and may be the most prevalent form of social influence. The influencing agent has a plan for the interaction, and in some important ways this agent's influence attempts affect the behavior of the target person. Yet the target person, too, has a plan for the interaction, and his or her compliance, acceptance, or resistance will affect the subsequent behavior of the influencing agent. This is the mutual influence found in nearly all relationships from friendship to formal negotiations between nations.

Active Minorities and Social Change

The fact that most social influence takes the form of mutual contingency makes explicit what has been an implicit assumption throughout this chapter: the process of social influence is an interactive, *reciprocal* process. Only in extreme circumstances is there a total lack of correspondence between the outcomes of the influencing agent and the target person, so those with social power can seldom actually use all they possess. Not only is their freedom of action thus restricted to a smaller range of usable power, but influencing agents must also change some of their subsequent actions to accommodate the target person's desires. Failure to do so risks alienating the person to such a degree that he or she will have no alternatives available except dramatic opposition. The result can be seen in such things as inner-city riots, prison uprisings, and political terrorism which, from the view of their perpetrators, may be the only rational solution left (Gamson, 1968; Nieburg, 1969).

Violence for the sake of a cause may be the final step in a target person's attempt to mitigate the power of an overbearing influencing agent, but precisely because social influence is a reciprocal process this last step is usually unnecessary. Most of the research discussed in this chapter, and indeed most of the social influence literature in social psychology, takes the perspective of the influencing agent (Apfelbaum, 1974; Moscovici and Faucheux, 1972), examining conformity by the minority. But there are some exceptions. Recall for a moment the Jacobs and Campbell (1961) study of the transmission of an arbitrary norm in the autokinetic situation. That study showed that when the first "generation" of subjects was three-fourths confederates who made extreme judgments, it took six additional generations to bring the movement estimations down to the level maintained throughout by control subjects. Every replacement subject in the Arbitrary Norm condition was influenced by the prevailing norm. But another way to look at the results of that experiment is to say that each new replacement moved the Arbitrary Norm condition a little farther in the direction of reality, exerting a *minority influence* on the perceptual judgments of the majority. Several recent studies have confirmed this finding, showing that a determined and consistent minority can cause the majority to question its own position (Moscovici and Faucheux, 1972).

This interchange between majority and minority, or between influencing agent and target person, is not characteristic only of social influence. It is also at the core of social change. In the exchange among people, or between people and social institutions, no party to the interaction can adhere completely to his or her own plan, oblivious to the behavior of the other participants. The mutual contingency of social influence will eventually produce changes in the powerful agent, as well as changes in the target of influence.

Summary

In an interaction between an influencing agent and the person who is the target of that influence, social power (p. 465) is the influencing agent's capacity to produce change, while social influence (p. 465) is the actual attitudinal or behavioral change produced by the influence attempt. The force that the agent can exert may not be the only force acting upon the target person, and that person's actions can be considered to be the *resultant* (p. 467) of all of the forces in the target person's life space.

An influencing agent may derive power from any of five different sources: ability to reward the target person, ability to punish the target person, legitimate and accepted authority, the target person's desire to emulate him or her, or his or her expertise. No matter what its source, the influencing agent's theoretical capacity to produce change will usually be restricted by the correspondence of outcomes with the target person, and by that person's alternative relationships, to a smaller range of **usable power** (p. 471). The process of persuasion, or **informational social influence** (p. 473), is most likely to lead to private acceptance, in the form of either identification or internalization. In contrast, the social pressure inherent in **normative social influence** (p. 473) will probably lead to public compliance without private acceptance.

Some influencing agents who are high in **Machiavellianism** (p. 475) can produce behavioral change even without obvious sources of power, as long as the interaction is face-to-face, with latitude for im- provisation and the opportunity to inject irrelevant affect into the situation. Even in the absence of differences in interpersonal style, the role relationship between a supervisor and a subordinate can dic- tate compliance by the subordinate. Research on destructive obedience illustrates just how far this tendency to "follow orders" may extend.

A **social group** (p. 483) is a collectivity which has psychological implications for the person and, like the individual influencing agent, groups can exert either informational or normative social influence over the target person. Research with the autokinetic effect shows how the **social reality** (p. 485) established by a group can affect an individual's judgments, even when this social reality is an arbitrary and erroneous one. Although it does not contain the explicit rewards and punishments usual in normative social influence, the Asch situa- tion demonstrates the group's power to produce public compliance, at least as long as the majority opinion is *unanimous* (p. 489).

A target person who is uncertain about the correct behavior for the situation or who finds it to his or her personal advantage to comply will more readily accept social influence regardless of the objective facts. But as the characterization of social influence in terms of **mutual contingency** (p. 494) makes clear, the interchange between agent and target is a *reciprocal* (p. 494) one. Not only can the target restrict the group's usable power, he or she may also exert a *minority influence* (p. 495) on the group's judgment through consistency and deter- mination.

Suggested Additional Readings

ALLEN, V. L. Situational factors in conformity. In L. Berkowitz (Ed.) *Advances in experimental social psychology.* Vol. 2. New York: Academic Press, 1965. Pp. 133–175. This is a thorough review of early research on the factors affecting individual conformity to group pressure.

CHRISTIE, R., and GEIS, F. L. *Studies in Machiavellianism.* New York: Academic Press, 1970. Although it reports the details of scale construction, scoring methods, and numerous experimental studies on the characteristics of the high Mach, this remains an entertaining and readable book.

KIESLER, C. A., and KIESLER, S. B. *Conformity.* Reading, Mass.: Addison-Wesley, 1969. This is a good introduction to research and theory on individual conformity to group pressure.

MOSCOVICI, S., and NEMETH, C. Social influence II: Minority influence. In C. Nemeth (Ed.) *Social psychology: Classic and contemporary integrations.* Chicago: Rand McNally, 1974. This is an extensive review of the success that a group minority may have in changing the opinions of the majority.

WHEELER, L. *Interpersonal influence.* Boston: Allyn & Bacon, 1970. This highly readable book takes a historical approach to the study of social influence, including the research of Sherif, Asch, the group discussion work of Lewin, and more recent material on social comparison and behavioral contagion.

Group membership may simply be an end in itself.

Photo by Melissa Hayes

The Individual and the Group
Chapter Thirteen

At the beginning of this book we constructed a definition of scientific social psychology as the study of the personal and situational factors that influence the social behavior of the individual. In keeping with this definition we chose the individual person as the unit of analysis, examining social perceptions, attitudes, self-concept, and social motives before turning to interactions with other people. Even our definition of a social group as a collectivity with psychological implications for the individual (Chapter Twelve) is consistent with this level of analysis. We have, of course, referred to social groups throughout the book, whenever their influence on the individual was clear. Thus we have seen that reference groups can serve as sources of self-evaluation, that deindividuation can accompany the anonymity of being just one among many, and that groups can exert conformity pressures upon their members. But until now we have not chosen to describe social behavior from the perspective of the group. We do so in this final chapter in order to show the person's place in the group, and to suggest the individual's role in the larger social context.

The numerical range of the social group logically extends from the dyad through the organization and nation to the human group as a whole, and there is a new set of problems for study at every level. There are, however, some common elements. Whatever the size of the group, its members must be able to communicate with each other, and often this communication takes place according to some formalized *communication structure*. Again, almost regardless of the size of the group, it will have a recognized *leader*. The leader may have been elected or appointed to a position in the formal structure of the group or may have simply emerged from among the remainder of the group members during the formative stages of the group, but in either case he or she will be more than just another member of the group. Finally, whether the group's purposes include the completion of specific goals, the maintenance of a group or national identity, or merely the pursuit of mutual enjoyment and satisfaction, the group will need to *make decisions* that will affect its future. Our introduction to the social psychology of groups therefore includes discussion of these three common elements: communication, leadership, and group decision-making processes. The limited scope of the chapter requires that we omit some material of interest, such as the formation of coalitions among members of a group (Caplow, 1968), the problems of cooperation and competition between groups (Sherif, 1966), the collective behavior characteristic of large groups (Smelser, 1963), and the development of social movements (Toch, 1965), but this material would take us too far from our concentration on the individual's actions and role in the social group.

COMMUNICATION WITHIN THE GROUP

The Structure of Communication

What factors may contribute to a disgruntled citizen's complaint that "big government just doesn't listen to ordinary people any more"? Or to an unhappy industrial worker's assertion that an impending strike is the result of a "failure of communication between the employees and the management of the company"? Or even to a student's belief that his university treats him "like a number, not like a person"? In part these complaints may be traced to the sheer size of the institution involved, and in part they may serve as rationalizations for intended actions against the organization or institution. But these complaints may also reflect the actual *structure of communication* within the organization. Direct, face-to-face contact with decision makers, if possible at all, will require penetration of several layers of administrative bureaucracy. And at any point along the way a complaint may be misunderstood, unsatisfactorily answered by someone without the necessary authority to provide relief, or arbitrarily discarded.

Communication Networks

Small groups in which most of the participants are of equal status initially are quite different from formal organizations, but even in small groups the structure of communication can have important social consequences. For example, suppose that you and four other people are brought together in a laboratory setting and asked to solve a number of simple problems. Each of you would be given part of the information necessary to solve the problem, but no one individual would control the manner in which communication was permitted among the five of you, and this would constitute the experimental variable. Some of the possible communication patterns are shown in Figure 13-1. Each solid line represents a two-way communication linkage between two people. Each pattern, or **communication network** has been given a descriptive name, as indicated in the figure.

Let us take a closer look at the flow of communication within each network. Suppose that you took the position of person s in each network. In the chain and the circle you could communicate directly with two other people (r and t), but in the Y or the wheel you could communicate directly only with person r. In any network your *dis-*

FIGURE 13-1
Some possible communication networks among five people. (A)
The "chain." (B) The "circle." (C) The "Y." (D) Two equivalent
representations of the "wheel." (Adapted from Bavelas, 1950,
and Leavitt, 1951)

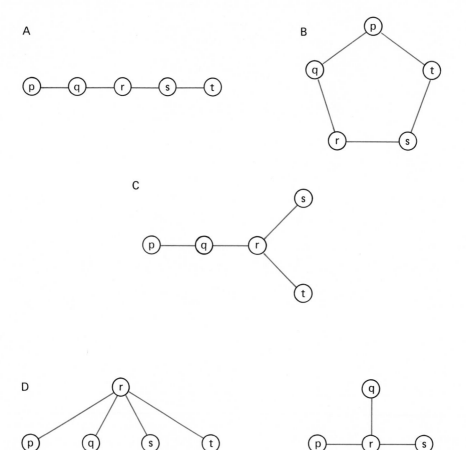

tance from other participants will be defined as the number of steps
required for communication. *Direct* communication requires only one
step, *indirect* communication requires an additional step for each
intervening person. So while your distance from *t* in the chain is a
value of 1, your distance from *p* in the same chain is a value of 3 (*s* to
r, r to *q,* and *q* to *p*) steps. The circle network immediately appears to

be "leaderless," with no one position having an advantage, while the wheel obviously gives a great advantage to the person occupying position r. This intuitive impression is borne out when the importance of each position is computed according to a method suggested by Bavelas (1950), based on the distances involved for each position.

Relative Centrality

In the chain network, the distance from s (your position) to p is 3, from s to q is 2, from s to r is 1, and from s to t is 1, for a summed distance of 7. Computations of this sort for all positions in a chain network are shown in part A of Figure 13-2. The grand total of all of the distances involved in a chain network is 40. To determine the importance of each position in the chain, simply divide the total number of distances (40) by the sum of the distances for each position. The result is the relative centrality of the position, and these values for the chain are directly below the positions in part A of Figure 13-2. The relative centrality values for the chain will confirm your intuitive impressions from sitting on the side of a long table during a formal dinner. Position r is the most central, positions q and s are less central, and positions p and t are the most peripheral. In part B of Figure 13-2, computations of relative centrality are shown for the wheel network, and here position r's advantage is even greater (a relative centrality of 8.0 as opposed to 6.7 in the chain). If the same computations are made for the other networks, position r obtains a value of 7.2 for the Y and 5.0 for the circle.

Within any particular network, the relative centrality of any position can be compared to that of other positions. In much the same manner, one sort of network can be compared for centrality of organization to another network using the *difference* between the most advantaged position and the least advantaged position. Thus in the circle (the least centralized) network, each position has a relative centrality of 5.0, and so the difference between any two positions is 0. In the chain, the difference between position r and the "worst" position (either p or t) is $6.7 - 4.0 = 2.7$. The next most centralized network is the Y, and there the difference between r and p is $7.2 - 4.0 = 3.2$. And finally, the most centralized network is the wheel, with a difference between r and any other position being $8.0 - 4.6 = 3.4$.

Social Consequences of Structure

What are the social consequences of the structure of communication within a small group? To answer this question Leavitt (1951) conducted an experiment in which five-person groups, arranged as wheels, chains, or circles, tried to solve a problem. Each person was

FIGURE 13-2
Computation of the relative centrality of each position in a
chain network (A) and a wheel network (B). (Adapted from
Bavelas, 1950)

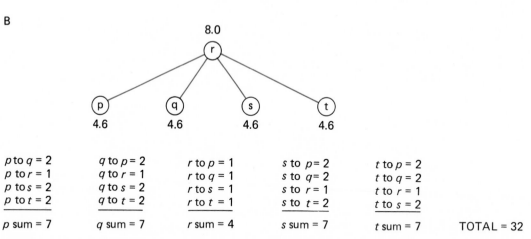

A

p to q = 1	q to p = 1	r to p = 2	s to p = 3	t to p = 4
p to r = 2	q to r = 1	r to q = 1	s to q = 2	t to q = 3
p to s = 3	q to s = 2	r to s = 1	s to r = 1	t to r = 2
p to t = 4	q to t = 3	r to t = 2	s to t = 1	t to s = 1
p sum = 10	q sum = 7	r sum = 6	s sum = 7	t sum = 10

TOTAL = 40

$$\text{The relative centrality for a position} = \frac{\text{Total for all positions}}{\text{Sum for the position in question}}$$

B

p to q = 2	q to p = 2	r to p = 1	s to p = 2	t to p = 2
p to r = 1	q to r = 1	r to q = 1	s to q = 2	t to q = 2
p to s = 2	q to s = 2	r to s = 1	s to r = 1	t to r = 1
p to t = 2	q to t = 2	r to t = 1	s to t = 2	t to s = 2
p sum = 7	q sum = 7	r sum = 4	s sum = 7	t sum = 7

TOTAL = 32

given a card upon which had been printed five symbols. Only one of
the five symbols appeared on all five cards, and the group's task was
to determine which symbol was common to all participants. The subjects were forced to communicate with each other through written
messages which were relayed by the experimenter (so that the experimenter could control the structure of the network). The participants
indicated their choices of the correct symbol by closing switches
which illuminated lights on a panel monitored by the experimenter.
Incorrect choices could thus be counted, and the task was completed

when all five participants made the correct choice. At the conclusion of the experimental task, the subjects were asked whether their group had a leader (and, if so, what position he or she occupied in the network) and how their morale had been during the performance of the task.

These and other dependent variables were nearly always ordered according to the centrality either of the networks, or of the positions within the networks. For example, the group's efficiency in completing the task increased from the circle to the chain, to the Y, to the wheel. Although the more centralized networks were more efficient, the subjects found them less pleasant, reporting the highest morale in the circle, less in the chain, less in the Y, and the least in the wheel. Within networks, subjects who occupied central positions enjoyed the task the most and were consistently nominated as the leader of the group. Subjects who occupied the most peripheral positions were the least happy with their performance and were almost never nominated as the leader of the group.

Since this original study by Leavitt (1951), a great deal of research has been conducted on the characteristics of various communication networks. Much of this literature has been reviewed by Collins and Raven (1969), who conclude that many of Leavitt's findings remain valid. There are inconsistencies from one experiment to another, but in general the efficiency of a group increases with the centralization of its communication network. In contrast, the morale of the group as a whole *decreases* with increasing centralization of the network. Considering each position within any network rather than the network as a whole, the occupants of relatively central positions like the task more and are nominated more frequently for leadership roles than are the occupants of more peripheral positions.

The Nature of Communication

As we have seen, the structure of communication permitted within a group and an individual's place in that structure will affect both efficiency and satisfaction. These two aspects of group performance can also be seen in the nature of the communications exchanged between members of a small group. It is generally agreed (e.g., Bales, 1950, 1970; Borgatta, 1962) that a member's participation in a group can be characterized along the relatively independent dimensions of group locomotion (Festinger, 1950), or progress toward the group goal, and group maintenance (Thibaut and Kelley, 1959), the facilitation of pleasant interaction among group members. Any group that is not organized for purely social purposes will have some sort of task to perform—a committee reaching a decision, a work group completing a product, or even a group of friends organizing a party. Although group success requires concerted task effort by members of the group, that task-directed behavior can proceed smoothly only if the members of the group remain amicable. People whose feelings are consistently ignored will not remain productive members of the group.

Interaction Process Analysis

How can we tell whether a particular action by a group member is a contribution primarily to the task achievement or to the social maintenance of the group? In the first attempt to deal with this problem Bales (1950) developed an objective interaction scoring system known as *Interaction Process Analysis* (IPA). He began with the basic distinction between task achievement and social maintenance and suggested that each of these dimensions might find expression in two different ways in the group. First, in order to achieve the group's goal, the members will need to share relevant information: some people will ask questions, others will give answers. And second, although group success will require mutual cooperation and good feeling, a scoring system should provide for disruption as well: the social process may sometimes be positive and sometimes negative. These divisions produce four different classes of behavior, and Bales then outlined three more specific elements of each class, for a total of twelve interaction categories (shown in Table 13-1).

TABLE 13-1
The scoring categories of Interaction Process Analysis

Social-emotional area

Positive Reactions	1. *Shows solidarity:* gives reward, help
	2. *Shows tension release:* jokes, laughs
	3. *Agrees:* accepts, complies, concurs

Task area

Answers	4. *Gives suggestion:* direction, not command
	5. *Gives opinion:* expresses feeling, evaluates
	6. *Gives information:* repeats, clarifies
Questions	7. *Asks for information*
	8. *Asks for opinion*
	9. *Asks for suggestion*

Social-emotional area

Negative Reactions	10. *Disagrees:* rejects, resists compliance
	11. *Shows tension:* withdraws from field
	12. *Shows antagonism:* asserts self, deflates others

Adapted from Bales (1950).

To illustrate how these categories can be employed to assess the nature of an interaction, let us consider an example drawn from research on small-group communication. Suppose you bring a group of subjects together in a room equipped with one-way mirrors so that you can observe the discussion without actually being present in the same room. So that all your groups will be discussing the same issues, you might provide them with a standard case to discuss, such as the one used by Schachter (1951) and others. This case describes the life history of a fictitious juvenile delinquent named Johnny Rocco, and the case ends with Johnny about to be sentenced for a minor crime. The group's task is to take the role of the juvenile authorities and decide which of several possible punishments should be imposed. After making the appropriate introductions, you leave the group alone to discuss the case and come to a decision about the punishment. While the group is engaged in its task you and your assistants try to code everything that is communicated (verbally or nonverbally) into the appropriate Bales category.

As it happens, one person starts off by saying, "I think the guy should get the book thrown at him" (category 5), and another person nods her agreement (category 3). A third person then says that he thinks such a punishment would be too harsh (category 10), while a fourth asserts that any punishment at all is a "dumb idea" (category 12). A fifth person then says that she thinks both arguments have some merit (category 1), and suggests that before any more discussion takes place it might be a good idea to see just which punishment each person would select (category 4). This is done, and the discussion then continues as you and your assistants code everything that is communicated. When you are through you will have a profile for the group showing what proportion of the discussion occurred in each of the twelve categories, and (if you have been keeping your records separate for each participant) you will also have such a profile for each individual member of the group.

Group Maintenance and Emergent Leadership

In one of the early applications of Interaction Process Analysis, Bales (1955) found that category 5 (Gives Opinion) was the most prevalent in groups discussing human-relations problems, with a total of over 30 percent of the communicative acts falling in this category. Category 6 (Giving Information) was the next most frequent at nearly 18 percent, closely followed by Category 3 (Shows Agreement) at 16 percent. None of the remaining categories received more than 8 percent. If we consider the four major divisions rather than the twelve categories, the results show that 56 percent of the time was spent in problem-solving action—the Answers class including categories 4, 5, and 6—while almost 26 percent was devoted to group maintenance activity (the Positive Reactions class including categories 1, 2, and 3). The remaining 18 percent of the time was split between Questions (7 percent) and Negative Reactions (11 percent), with most of the latter representing Disagreement (category 10). Even in a highly task-oriented group whose members do not anticipate future interaction, a fair proportion of the time is devoted to keeping things running smoothly. And though there is naturally some disagreement, there is little tension and virtually no open antagonism.

The Interaction Process Analysis scores for members of a group can also be used to examine the phenomenon of **emergent leadership**. At the beginning of the experimental session the group is leaderless. No one is appointed to be in charge, and since there is full communication among all participants there is no built-in structural bias in favor of any one member. Nevertheless, at the conclusion of the experimental session two different sorts of leaders seem to emerge. In most groups there seemed to be one person who took charge of the task, contributed a great deal to the discussion, and was perceived as having the "best ideas." Bales (1955) refers to this emergent leader as the *task specialist*. In addition, there typically was a different person who showed the greatest amount of agreement, tension release, and solidarity. This *social emotional specialist* was usually the best liked, even though his other contributions to the task were not great. Just as there are two dimensions to the group process—efficiency and morale—there seem to be *different* people in each group whose specialty is one dimension or the other. As we shall see in the next section, this finding has also been obtained in groups with formal leadership structures.

In the years since the introduction of Interaction Process Analysis there have been refinements in the technique designed to make the scoring more precise (Borgatta, 1962), and other coding systems have been developed to measure different aspects of group process (Mann, 1967). Despite these developments, Interaction Process Analysis remains a popular method for assessing group dynamics. More recently Bales (1970) has reported an extensive series of studies (founded on IPA) leading to a theoretical model of the relationship between an individual's personality characteristics and mode of participation. The IPA scoring technique, together with its methodological and theoretical extensions, illustrates both the contributions that an individual might make to the group and some of the effects on the individual that might follow group participation. Thus the nature of communication within a group, as well as the structural characteristics of that communication process, can help to determine the group's efficiency and the morale of its members.

GROUP LEADERSHIP

Leader Characteristics

Personality Traits

What makes a good leader of a group? Is it charisma, interpersonal skill, or just being in the right place at the right time? Does the nature of the group make any difference? Will someone who is an excellent leader of a small group also be an outstanding head of a large formal organization? These questions have concerned social psychologists as well as personnel managers and voters for years, and the first studies of leadership perhaps naively began collecting evidence on the personality traits of successful leaders. In a review of this evidence, Gibb (1969) reports early research showing that leaders, as compared to relevant followers, tended to be taller, more interpersonally attractive, more intelligent, more self-confident, better adjusted, and more dominant. Yet, as Gibb points out, the most striking thing about all these presumed correlates of leadership is how *little* importance they seem to have from one situation to another. Of all the traits, only intelligence is consistently associated with leadership, and even here the relationship must be qualified. The overall correlations are usually low, and while task leaders tend to be more intelligent than their followers, the same differential does not hold for social-emotional leaders (Cattell and Stice, 1954). It also appears that leaders cannot exceed their followers in intelligence by too wide a margin or they lose their effectiveness (Gibb, 1969). Thus, despite some popular historical examples to the contrary (Alexander the Great, Napoleon, Hitler, de Gaulle), most of the research evidence does not support the "Great Man theory" that a particular constellation of physical and psychological traits will produce a renowned leader regardless of the circumstances or opportunities.

Behavior in the Group

If potential leaders cannot be reliably identified on the basis of physical and personality traits, can they be selected on the basis of their behavior in the group situation? The work of Bales (1959, 1970) would certainly suggest that they might. Especially when compared with the inconsistency of the trait research, the consistent differentiation between task specialists and social-emotional specialists in Bale's experimental groups indicates that these two domains of behavior might discriminate between leaders and followers. In an attempt to measure the varieties of leadership behavior Hemphill (1950) and his associates (Halpin and Winer, 1952) constructed questionnaires designed to assess several a priori dimensions of leadership activity. These questionnaires were then administered to a large group of subjects, and the responses were factor analyzed to describe the results. This factor analysis revealed four different aspects of leadership behavior, two of which accounted for nearly 85 percent of the variance in the ratings. These two were *consideration*—the extent to which the leader is considerate of the feelings of followers— and *initiating structure*—the extent to which the leader organizes the group, its activities, and his or her relationship to the group.

Items that contributed to these two factors have been grouped into the Leadership Behavior Description Questionnaire, or LBDQ (Halpin, 1966), consisting of thirty descriptive statements (fifteen for each factor). The consideration items deal with the leader's openness, warmth for the followers, and willingness to consult with the followers before taking action. The initiating structure items deal with the maintenance of standards of performance, the clarity of rules and expectations, and the guidance of individual responsibilities in the achievement of the group goal. If these two factors sound familiar to you, they should. They are for a formal group (with a designated leader) virtually the same behaviors we have seen before in the social-emotional specialist and task specialist found in the leaderless groups. The dimensions of consideration and initiating structure do seem to be independent (Greenwood and McNamara, 1969), although the leaders of highly successful groups often show ability in both areas (Halpin, 1953; Hemphill, 1955). Apparently the leaders of formal groups, like the leaders of informal groups, can be identified by their actions.

A Model of Leadership Effectiveness

The early search for personality characteristics that would be associated with effective leadership did not prove to be productive because of the wide variety of situations in which leadership must be exercised and because of the differences in leader behavior that are often called for. The shift to investigation of leader behavior provided a more accurate picture of formal leadership styles—consideration or initiation of structure—but that research was only suggestive for the issue of leadership effectiveness. It is easy to think of situations in which a leader who was high on consideration but low on structure might be ineffective (such as an Army infantry captain in combat). In the same way there are situations in which a high-structure but low-consideration leader might be ineffective (such as in group psychotherapy). So when the question is effectiveness rather than leader behavior, it would make better sense to consider both the leader's style and the nature of the situation. This is just what Fiedler's (1964, 1971) contingency model of leadership effectiveness does, by assuming that the success of any personal style will be contingent upon certain specifiable characteristics of the situation.

The Leader's Attitudes Toward Co-Workers

The contingency model of leadership effectiveness takes a slightly different approach to the measurement of leader characteristics from that employed by Hemphill (1950) and his associates. Their Leader Behavior Description Questionnaire to measure consideration and initiating structure was an instrument that was completed not by the leader but by his or her subordinates. But Fiedler was interested in the leader's own attitudes. Since so many of the LBDQ items are socially desirable, it would hardly make sense to ask the leaders to use the scale to describe themselves. In fact, any *direct* attempt to measure the leader's behavior toward most of the subordinates would be similarly affected by social desirability. Because of these problems Fiedler decided on an indirect measure of the leader's attitudes toward subordinates, on the assumption that those attitudes would be reflected in the leader's behavior.

Even this attitude scale was designed to make negative statements socially acceptable. The leader is asked to think of all of the people with whom he or she has ever worked, and to select the one who was the most difficult to get along with. This person is the leader's *"least-preferred co-worker"* (to put it mildly), and the leader is asked to describe the person on a series of bipolar adjective scales arranged in a format similar to the semantic differential (discussed more fully in Chapter Five). The Least-Preferred Co-worker (LPC) scale includes items such as pleasant-unpleasant, distant-close, and productive-unproductive, with each item scored as an eight-point scale with high scores indicating positive qualities. Some leaders will find positive qualities even in the people they dislike, and these leaders will have high LPC scores. Other leaders will be less charitable toward their least-preferred co-workers, and they will have low LPC scores. In the terms we have used earlier, the High LPC leader is a social-emotional specialist, high on consideration, while the Low LPC leader is the task specialist, high on initiating structure. Thus the LPC scale—administered to the leaders themselves—can be used to classify leaders into the same two general categories produced by the LBDQ, which is administered to the subordinates.

The Favorability of the Situation

But the categorization of leaders is only half the task of measuring leadership effectiveness. The other half is categorization of the situations, and Fiedler (1964) suggests that three different aspects of the situation should be considered. These are (1) the *affective relations* between the leader and the members, (2) the degree of *structure* inherent in the task to be accomplished by the group, and (3) the *power position* of the leader. The affective relations factor is presumed to be the "most important, single determinant of group processes which affect team performance" (Fiedler, 1964, p. 159). A leader who is liked and accepted by subordinates (whether this acceptance is for the leader's good ideas or social-emotional maintenance ability) can get the maximum performance from those subordinates under a wide variety of conditions. The second factor, task structure, refers to the clarity or ambiguity of the task. When the group's task is a highly specific one, such as assembling part of an automobile or executing a standard play in a football game, the leader's job is easier than when the task is ambiguous (discussing the social implications of a novel or developing a policy to increase company profits). Finally, the third factor refers to what French and Raven (1959) would call legitimate power (see Chapter Eleven)—the leader's traditionally recognized authority.

To keep the theory to a manageable size, each situational component is considered as a dichotomy. Leader-member relations are divided into those that are good and those that are moderately poor, assuming that if the leader-member relations are very poor the group will disintegrate (we shall return to this point a bit later). The task is considered to be either structured or unstructured, and the leader's position power is classified as either strong or weak. These dichotomous factors can be combined in what amounts to a factorial design $(2 \times 2 \times 2)$ to produce eight different characterizations of the situation, as shown in Figure 13-3. Each characterization, or *octant*, is thus a combination of the three situational factors. You will notice that Figure 13-3 shows nine octants, instead of the eight produced by the combinations. This ninth octant (called V-A) had to be added to the conceptual model after it became clear that with a high degree of task clarity a leader with a great deal of legitimate power could get subordinates to perform even if his or her affective relations with them were terrible (instead of just moderately poor).

The octants are ordered (I through V-A) according to their overall *favorability toward the leader*. The best situation for a leader is one in which affective relations are good, the task is clear, and the

FIGURE 13-3
Curve indicating the optimal leadership style (permissive and considerate versus managing and controlling) required by each of several situations, as predicted by the contingency model of leadership effectiveness. (Adapted from Fiedler, 1964)

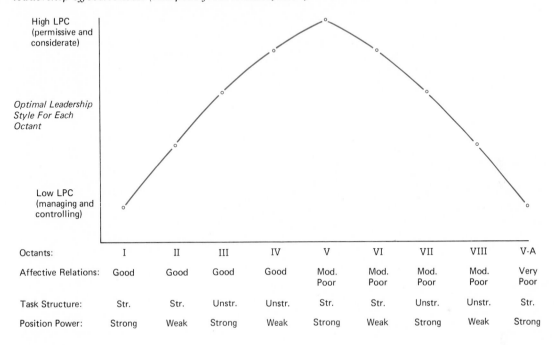

Octants:	I	II	III	IV	V	VI	VII	VIII	V-A
Affective Relations:	Good	Good	Good	Good	Mod. Poor	Mod. Poor	Mod. Poor	Mod. Poor	Very Poor
Task Structure:	Str.	Str.	Unstr.	Unstr.	Str.	Str.	Unstr.	Unstr.	Str.
Position Power:	Strong	Weak	Strong	Weak	Strong	Weak	Strong	Weak	Strong

leader's legitimate power is strong (Octant I). The three factors affecting the situation are listed in the order of their importance, with the least important (position power) alternating from octant to octant. The differences in importance can readily be seen if we examine changes away from the best possible circumstances (Octant I) in a single factor at a time. If the affective relations remain good and the task remains clear, a change in position power from strong to weak only changes the octant by one (I to II). If affective relations remain good and power remains strong, a change in the task structure from structured to unstructured changes the octant number by two (I to III). But if the affective relations change from good to moderately poor while the other two factors remain the same, the octant number changes by *four* (I to V). Thus, affective relations is the most important factor, followed by task structure, followed by position power, and successive changes in these factors produce the ordering of favorability shown in Figure 13-3.

Tests of the Contingency Model

The fundamental hypothesis of the contingency model is that *"the type of leader attitude* [permissive and considerate as opposed to managing and controlling] *required for effective group performance depends upon the degree to which the group situation is favorable or unfavorable to the leader"* (Fiedler, 1964, p. 164; emphasis in original). As the curve in Figure 13-3 indicates, the low LPC leaders (who are managing, controlling, and highly directive) perform best in situations that are either very favorable or very unfavorable. In the favorable situations (Octants I, II, III) the group is ready to be told what to do, and this suits the leader's inclinations. In the unfavorable situations (Octants VII, VIII, V-A) the group will disintegrate unless the highly controlling Low LPC leader can keep everyone in line. In a sense, when the conditions are favorable, the Low LPC's personal characteristics and attitudes cannot spoil the situation for the group, and in the unfavorable situations these abrasive qualities serve to hold the group together. (The image of the oppressive drill instructor in an armed forces boot camp comes to mind for Octant V-A.)

In rather direct contrast to the Low LPC leaders, the High LPC leaders perform best in the moderately unfavorable condition (Octants IV, V, and VI). There the situation is marred either by an unstructured task, weak position power, or moderately poor relations, but a diplomatic, tactful, and sensitive leader (High LPC) can help the group overcome the adverse situational conditions. The leader's permissiveness and consideration will keep the members from feeling threatened, and his or her nondirective stance may produce voluntary cooperation within the group—"Let's all try to make the best of a bad situation."

To test the contingency model, Fiedler has conducted a great many studies correlating the LPC scores of leaders with the performance, productivity, or effectiveness of the groups involved. For example, Octant I and V differ only in the affective relations between the leader and the group members. In both cases the task is clear and the leader's position power is strong, as would be the case in military organizations. Fiedler (1955) was able to study B-29 bomber crews and Army tank crews in which the leader-member relations were either good or moderately poor. He found, as predicted by the contingency model, that the task-oriented Low LPC leaders were more effective when relations were good, but that the social-emotional-oriented High LPC leaders were more effective when

leader-member relations were moderately poor. Over a period of
more than a decade a wide variety of studies has been conducted
comparing performance across octants, and Fiedler (1964, 1971) reports evidence that closely follows the theoretical curve shown in
Figure 13-3.

As impressive as some of the evidence appears, the contingency
model is not without problems. To begin with, most of the comparisons that support the model are correlations between LPC scores
and group performance. In the moderately unfavorable octants (IV
through VII) these correlations are positive (indicating that High
LPC scores are associated with success by the group). In the very
favorable octants (I through III) and the very unfavorable octants
(VIII and V-A) these correlations are negative, indicating that Low
LPC scores are associated with group success. In most of the research, however, the individual correlations are *not* statistically
significantly different, even though they are in the directions predicted by the model. And, as some critics have pointed out (e.g.,
Graen, Alvares, Orris, and Martelle, 1970), the use of a weak criterion
like directionality rather than a strong criterion like statistical significance does not help our confidence in the validity of the theory.
In addition, there has also been some question about the LPC scale
itself, with Fishbein, Landy, and Hatch (1969) suggesting that it might
tell us more about specific Least-Preferred Co-workers than about
the leader. Leaders who have had unfortunate experiences with really
troublesome subordinates will obviously have lower LPC scores than
will leaders who have been fortunate enough not to have supervised
any obnoxious people. Despite these problems with the evidence
for the theory, the contingency model remains the best available
account of leadership effectiveness. Because it attempts to include
both the presumed characteristics of the leader and the presumed
nature of the situation, the contingency model exemplifies social
psychology's concern with the joint effects of personal dispositions
and situational factors on social behavior.

GROUP DECISION PROCESSES

We have seen that the communication structure within a group can
affect member satisfaction and group efficiency, and that leadership
effectiveness can best be evaluated by considering the relevant
aspects of the situation as well as the interpersonal style of the leader.
But a social group is more than a collection of individuals, it is a

unit that must coordinate its activity in order to achieve its objectives. Not all a group's decisions can be—or should be—made by the leader alone. Much of the time the decisions about the group's priorities, plans, and actions will be *group decisions* arrived at only after some discussion among the membership. What can social psychology tell us about these decisions?

Successful group activity depends upon coordinated action taken by all the members of the group, even by those who might have initially opposed the course of action to be taken. Since so few group functions will have unanimous support, the group will frequently be in the position of asking at least some of its members to set aside their own individual goals in favor of the group's goal. To understand why these members will usually comply, it is important to know why individuals join groups in the first place.

Attraction to the Group

Social and Emotional Needs

Many of the sources of attraction to groups are the same as sources of attraction to individuals, discussed earlier in Chapter Ten. Remember that Aronson and Mills (1959) and Gerard and Matthewson (1966) found that the more severe the initiation, the greater the liking expressed for a rather dull group. Certainly these were experimentally created groups, but it is reasonable to suggest that even with real social groups the more you invest in your decision to join, the more attractive you are likely to find the group and the more committed to it you are likely to be. Another important illustration is the desire to join positive reference groups. Just as you are attracted to individuals who hold attitudes similar to yours, you will be attracted to groups with attitudes and values that are compatible with yours. In Chapter Two we described the "Seekers" Group (Festinger, Riecken, and Schachter, 1956), which believed that the world was doomed but that a small number of the faithful would be saved by a spaceship which would carry them to a better place. Admittedly, this group had a limited appeal, but there are many groups today which attract members through their strong belief systems. Finally, you may seek social comparison with a group of people in much the same way that you might seek it with an individual. In Chapter Eight we discussed Schachter's (1959) research on the social reduction of fear. In those experiments subjects who were anxious over the impending experimental treatment chose to wait with others who were in the same state.

These examples illustrate one major category of reasons for

attraction to social groups: those groups can serve *social and emotional needs*. Attraction can follow dissonance reduction, discovery of similar beliefs, or successful social comparison. In addition, participation in a group can provide prestige, a sense of self-definition, or the feelings of belonging that are necessary to overcome loneliness. Group membership may simply be an end in itself. To the extent that this is true, attraction toward the group may parallel the reasons for attraction to individuals.

The Instrumental Functions of Groups

But participation in a group may serve more than social-emotional needs; it may also serve the *instrumental* function of enabling the individual to achieve goals as a member of the group that would not be attainable alone. Farmers organize cooperatives in order to get higher prices for their produce and purchase their supplies at reduced rates; workers join unions in order to improve their bargaining position with employers; individuals join political and charitable organizations to accomplish ends that would be difficult for individuals to bring about. Groups that are high in meeting the social-emotional needs of their members will be primarily concerned with group maintenance activities, while groups that are formed to achieve instrumental goals will be high in task-oriented activities. Which sort of leadership is more appropriate for the group will, of course, depend upon the nature of the group itself.

Just as the two sorts of leadership are found to varying degrees in most groups, the two different sources of attraction are also typically found together in the same setting, often by intent of the group. For example, most enlightened business organizations will strive to have their employees satisfy some of their emotional needs through identification with the company. They will provide security, status, and individual recognition, as well as a salary. The employees will then come to develop a "company loyalty" that extends beyond the remunerative relationship that exists between an organization and the people whose wages it pays. Businesses that take the position that all they need to provide for their employees is a paycheck place their workers in a relationship that exchange theory (Chapter Nine) would describe as dependence, rather than in a relationship of attraction. In doing so, they risk high absenteeism, frequent turnover of personnel, and a high proportion of mistakes in production.

Not only employers but also voluntary organizations (social clubs, interest groups, political parties) should provide a variety of ways for members to satisfy their emotional needs as well as to achieve their task objectives. In terms of field theory (discussed in Chapter Twelve), each inducement provided by a group is a different *force* acting upon individuals to keep them in the group. When the group asks its members to forego some of their individual objectives in order to achieve the group goal, the forces acting on individuals to keep them in the group will become of paramount importance. A politician who is more interested in running for office than in the principles his or her party stands for will switch parties if he or she loses the nomination. An executive whose company has not attended to his or her psychological needs may leave the company rather than move to an undesirable location, even though that move would be a promotion. In general, the smaller the total of forces acting to keep the individual in the group, relative to the demands that the group makes on its members, the more likely it is that dissatisfied individuals will leave the group.

Group Cohesiveness

The attraction of individuals to the group, and their tendency either to stay or to leave, are ideas that make intuitive sense. But how can these be more precisely characterized and measured? The examples we have used suggest that we might describe attraction in terms of exchange theory. An individual would be attracted to any group that provided outcomes above his or her comparison level (CL) and would be dependent upon any group which provided outcomes below CL but still above the comparison level for alternatives (CL$_{alt}$). Thus, in terms of exchange theory, attraction to a relationship with a group would have exactly the same determinants as attraction to a relationship with another individual. At first this seems a satisfactory solution to the problem, but it has a significant drawback: it does not adequately describe the relationship among *all* the members of the group.

What we really need to know is how closely knit the entire group might be, not how attractive it might seem to a single person. For this reason, most social psychologists (e.g., Cartwright and Zander, 1968) use the term cohesiveness to describe the members' commitment and attraction to their social group. Cohesiveness is not an element of the relationship between one member and the group, it is a property of the entire group. And it is more than the attractiveness of the group to an outsider; it also takes into account the extent to which participation in the group satisfies the member's own needs. Thus, for example, militant groups of either the far left or the far right might be highly cohesive, even though to most of us they would not be attractive.

Although cohesiveness is a property of the group, it can be measured by variations of the sociometric technique (Moreno, 1934) described in Chapter Ten for the assessment of interpersonal attraction among individuals. You may recall from Chapter Ten that in order to construct a sociogram of a group, you would ask each member of the group to select a limited number of other people toward whom he or she has positive feelings. These positive feelings might be the "liking" accorded social-emotional specialists, and in that case the questions asked would deal with friendship choice. Or the positive feelings might be the "respect" accorded task specialists, and in that case the questions asked would deal with competence in task performance. It should be clear by now that the sort of answers you would get would depend upon the goal of the group (social or task), as well as on the nature of the questions that you asked.

When sociometric methods are used for friendship choice, the dependent variable of interest might be the number of times that a particular individual was chosen (popularity). In the same way, Bales (1955) used frequency of choice to establish emergent social-emotional leaders (with the question phrased in terms of "best-liked" person) and emergent task leaders (person with the "best ideas"). By contrast, when sociometric methods are used to establish the cohesiveness of the group as a whole, the dependent variable of interest is not any single member's frequency of choice, but rather a comparison between choices made within the group and choices made outside the group. For example, in their study of friendship patterns in a housing development (described in Chapter Ten) Festinger, Schachter, and Back (1950) used the ratio of friendship choices made *within* an apartment unit to friendship choices made *outside* of the unit as an index of the cohesiveness of the unit. Another way to use sociometric methods to compare the cohesiveness of different groups is to determine the number or proportion of reciprocated choices within the groups, assuming that the highly cohesive groups should have a high proportion of reciprocated choices. However cohesiveness is measured, the greater the cohesiveness the more demands the group can place upon its members before they drop out of the group. In the next sections we consider some of these demands and the implications they carry, both for the individual group members and for the group as a whole.

Pressures Toward Uniformity of Opinion

Social Reality and Group Locomotion

In an early analysis of social communication within small groups, Festinger (1950) distinguished between two different sources of pressure toward uniformity of opinion within social groups: social reality and group locomotion. It is consistent with Festinger's analysis for us to describe these two sources in terms we have been using throughout the chapter. Groups that exist primarily to serve social-emotional needs will be most successful if they can create an atmosphere, a social reality (as contrasted with objective reality), that validates the opinions of the members. Through the process of social comparison with the opinions of other members of this positive reference group, members can learn that they are, indeed, attractive, important, and useful human beings. Satisfaction among the members of a social-emotional group can be maintained only as long as the social reality has some basis in fact, or as long as there are no dissenting voices. But if the group is infiltrated by a subversive who insists that the emperor really is wearing no clothes, the social reality will collapse. To preserve its view of reality the group must insist on uniformity of opinion (at least on relevant issues). The pressure toward uniformity is no less strong in a task-oriented group, but here its source is the need for *group locomotion*—movement toward the group goal. Achievement of task objectives requires coordinated and concerted effort on the part of all members of the group, and once a decision has been reached about a course of action, those who continue to maintain conflicting positions will simply get in the way.

Effects of Cohesiveness: An Experimental Demonstration

In both the social-emotional group and the task group it is presumed that the greater the cohesiveness of the group, the greater the pressure toward uniformity of opinion. This direct relationship between cohesiveness and pressure toward uniformity has been demonstrated in a now-classic study by Schachter (1951). Suppose that you had been a subject in this experiment. You would have volunteered to participate in a "club" and would have arrived for the first meeting of the group. After some appropriate preliminaries (more about these later), you and the four or five other people in the group would be asked to discuss the Johnny Rocco case described earlier and to arrive at a consensus about the punishment that should be imposed for Johnny's violations of the law. To begin the discussion, the experimenter would ask each of you to state a position on the question of punishment, in much the same way that subjects in an Asch-type conformity experiment are asked to make their choice of the proper comparison line. So you each state a position, and the last person to state an initial position takes a stand that is as far as possible *away* from the opinion of the rest of the group. By now, you would have guessed (although the real subjects did not) that this *deviate* was in fact a confederate of the experimenter.

MANIPULATION OF COHESIVENESS AND RELEVANCE. How do the real subjects react to the programmed deviate? The answer depends on the *cohesiveness* of the group and on the degree to which the entire issue of Johnny Rocco is *relevant* to the ostensible purposes of the club you have all joined. There were two levels of cohesiveness in the experiment, determined by whether the subjects had been assigned to a club of their choice or to one they were not particularly interested in. Thus cohesiveness was manipulated by varying the extent to which the group met the needs and desires of its members. The experiment was a factorial design, so within each level of cohesiveness, discussion of the Johnny Rocco case seemed consistent with the purposes of half of the clubs but inconsistent with the purposes of the other half.

The High Cohesiveness–Relevant discussion groups were all *case study* clubs organized for the purpose of providing advice to judges and lawyers about the treatment of juvenile delinquents (so the issue was relevant), and all the members of these groups had chosen case study as their first choice of a club (so the groups were highly cohesive). The High Cohesiveness–Irrelevant discussion groups were all *movie* clubs that had presumably been organized to preview films for a local theatre to estimate how successful those films would be with a college audience (so the Rocco case was completely out of line with the purpose of the club). All the members of these clubs had chosen the movie club as their first choice.

The Low Cohesiveness–Relevant discussion groups were all *editorial* clubs that had been organized ostensibly to provide advice on the format, editorial policy, and feature articles for a new national magazine. Discussion of the Rocco case was thus quite consistent with the feature article portion of the group's purposes. But all the members of these editorial clubs had expressed little or no interest in the editorial club, saying that they would have preferred the case study club. Thus, although the issue was equally relevant in both cases, the members of editorial clubs would have preferred to have been in a different club. (To make certain that the subjects assigned to the Low Cohesiveness groups would actually show up for the experiment, all subjects were told that they would not learn of their club assignment until they arrived for the first meeting.) And, finally, the Low Cohesiveness–Irrelevant discussion groups were all *radio* clubs whose ostensible purpose was market research similar to that of the movie clubs (so that discussion of the Rocco case was irrelevant to the task at hand), and the members of these radio clubs had all originally stated a preference for the movie clubs.

REJECTION OF THE DEVIATE. Now let us return to treatment of the deviate. As the discussion progressed in each experimental group, observers recorded the frequency and nature of communications addressed to the deviate. At the end of the experiment sociometric rankings were gathered from all the participants. First let us consider communication. In the High Cohesiveness–Relevant groups, communication to the deviate increased sharply at the beginning of the meeting, but then fell off when it became clear that he was not going to change his position. In all other experimental conditions there was gradual increase in communication to the deviate throughout the meeting. A group will try to change the position of a deviate in order to achieve uniformity of opinion, but if uniformity is extremely important these attempts will cease early if they do not succeed and will be followed by rejection. To illustrate this rejection, consider the sociometric rankings. These showed that with relevance held constant, the more cohesive the groups were, the more they rejected the deviate. In addition, with cohesiveness held constant, the more important the issue was, the more the deviate was rejected. And, finally, the greatest rejection of the deviate was (not surprisingly) in the High Cohesiveness–Relevant condition. The more cohesive the group and the more important the issue, the less tolerance there will be for disagreement.

The Development of Groupthink

The results of Schachter's (1951) experiment are consistent with a number of things we have learned about attitude change, social comparison, and social influence. For example, you may recall from Chapter Seven that a persuasive communication on an issue of importance will be effective in changing attitudes only if it falls within the recipient's latitude of noncommitment. A position that is too far away will be contrasted and seen as even more extreme. But when the issue is very important, this latitude of noncommitment *shrinks* so that in the High Cohesiveness–Relevant condition the deviate's position is rejected, while in the other conditions the latitude of noncommitment remains large enough to include his position. Thus in the High Cohesiveness–Relevant condition the deviate is seen not only as stubborn, but also as *different,* and just as attitude similarity can contribute to attraction (Chapter Ten), attitude dissimilarity can contribute to rejection. This line of reasoning obviously places a significant restriction—in terms of the importance of the issue—on the potential for minority influence in a group setting (Chapter Twelve). The committed and consistent minority may be successful in altering the judgments of the remainder of the members of a group only on issues that are not critical to the group's objectives.

False Consensus

Rejection of the deviate in Schachter's experiment has implications not only for psychological theory, but also for social policy decision-making processes. To avoid rejection by the others in the group, a member may conform or remain silent, hiding reservations about an important group decision precisely when he or she should be voicing those reservations. The consensus achieved under these circumstances will be a *false* consensus, with the apparently uniform social reality dangerously out of touch with the objective reality outside the group. The group then becomes the victim of what Janis (1972) has called groupthink, a group preoccupation with unanimity that renders ineffective any critical evaluation of the situation.

As an example of groupthink in social policy decision making, Janis (1972) describes in detail the abortive Bay of Pigs invasion of Cuba planned and conducted in 1961 by then-President John Kennedy and his advisors. In the invasion attempt some fourteen hundred poorly equipped Cuban exiles landed at the Bay of Pigs in Cuba, expecting (as did Kennedy and his advisors) that a minimal show of force would be all that was necessary to begin a popular rebellion against Cuba's dictator Fidel Castro. Some twelve hundred of the invading exiles were captured and later ransomed by the United States government for $53 million in food and drugs. From the standpoint of the United States, everything about the operation went as badly as it possibly could have. For the policy maker and the social scientist alike, the crucial question is how such gross miscalculations could have been made. Illustrating his argument with material from transcripts of the development of the invasion plan, Janis (1972) argues that groupthink is the most plausible explanation. Groupthink is highly probable whenever (1) the decision-making group is a highly cohesive one, (2) the group is insulated from outside opinion, and (3) the policy under consideration has been strongly endorsed by the leader of the group. Under these conditions, what group member would be willing to risk status (or even membership) in the group by pointing out flaws in the leader's reasoning?

Reducing the Illusions

Once groupthink has arisen on an issue, the reluctance of members to voice their objections leads to an *illusion of unanimity*, a false consensus that does not veridically reflect even social reality. This false consensus, in turn, leads to an *illusion of invulnerability:* after all, if none of the bright and capable people in this group, familiar with the issues as they are, can see any flaws in the plan, then that plan must be correct. Once critical thinking has been suspended, the group tends to ignore whatever contradictory information may become available from outside the group. For example, Janis notes that even after newspapers began printing rumors of the impending invasion, President Kennedy and his advisors remained convinced that the invasion could be kept secret from the Cuban government and armed forces. The group simply hardens its position, perhaps to resolve dissonance created by the conflicting information, just as the Seekers began to proselytize after the anticipated doomsday passed uneventfully. It thinks in simplistic and stereotyped terms about the problem, and develops a *rationale* to justify its actions.

Although the Bay of Pigs invasion may be the best-known example of groupthink in action, it is by no means the only one. A number of historical case studies described by Janis (1972), the ill-fated attempt by the Nixon administration to cover up the Watergate break-in, and some of the activities of the Central Intelligence Agency might also qualify as examples of groupthink. Nor is the problem limited to governmental decision. Decisions made by businesses, universities, and informal social groups as well often show the characteristics of groupthink. How can this distortion of the decision-making process be avoided? Janis (1972) makes a number of specific suggestions, including bringing in outside experts who are encouraged to challenge the views of the group, having one member of the group play "devil's advocate" on any questions of importance, and teaching the leader of the group to accept criticism and refrain from stating his or her own position on the issue. Explicit procedures for the expression of disagreement and reservations must be institutionalized in the group in order to overcome the all-too-natural pressures toward uniformity of opinion.

Choice Shifts in Group Discussion

As we have just seen, the pressures toward uniformity of opinion within a group may lead to groupthink if a highly cohesive group with a strong, opinionated leader is insulated from outside opinion. But even if the group is essentially leaderless, even if there is full discussion of the issues, and even if the group is not isolated from outside opinion, it may make a group decision that would differ from the individual decisions made privately by its members. This is one conclusion from an extensive series of experimental studies of a phenomenon originally called the *shift to risk*, or "risky shift," but later described in broader terms as a **choice shift** in group discussion (Pruitt, 1971).

The Choice Dilemmas

The phenomenon can best be illustrated by asking you to imagine that you are a member of a small, leaderless experimental group that has been formed to discuss a number of decision problems. Each of these decision problems, or *choice dilemmas* (Wallach and Kogan, 1959), describes a choice that must be made by a stimulus person. For example, one stimulus person must decide whether to leave a steady job with a modest salary for a potentially more rewarding position with a newly formed company whose future is uncertain. Another must choose between attending a high-prestige graduate program whose standards he might not be able to meet and attending a school of much lower prestige from which he would certainly receive a degree. Still another must decide whether to marry a particular person after advice to the couple from a marriage counselor suggests that their marriage might be a good one, but that happiness is not assured. There are twelve choice dilemmas such as these, and your task is to serve as an advisor to the central person in each story. In each case you are asked to indicate the *lowest* probability of success that you would require before you would encourage the stimulus person to choose the risky but more desirable alternative (in these examples the more risky alternatives are, respectively, taking the new job, attending the high-prestige university, and getting married). The amount of risk that you are willing to take on each choice dilemma is simply the probability estimate you give. If you are willing to take one chance in ten of success before advising the stimulus person to forge ahead, you are obviously more risky than if you would insist on a probability level of five chances in ten.

It is clear that the probability level you require is a measure of your willingness to take risks (or at least to encourage others to do so), but what exactly is the risky shift? That shift is a group-produced effect, in some ways similar to the convergence around a common norm found in the perceptual judgments made in Sherif's (1936) studies with the autokinetic phenomenon. The risky shift was first observed by Stoner (1961), who was interested in group decisions on the choice dilemma problems. Small groups of subjects were brought together and presented with the choice dilemmas. Each member of the group first recorded a private opinion about the probability of success required, then the group discussed the issue, and finally each member recorded a private opinion again. Interestingly enough, the results showed that for most of the twelve choice dilemmas the group's required probability of success was lower (more risky) than the average of the original private opinions, and this *shift to risk* during the group discussion was in many cases retained in the subsequent private judgments. Just as in the autokinetic situation, group discussion produces convergence of opinion around a common norm, and that norm is to some degree maintained in later private judgments.

Diffusion of Responsibility and Personal Values

But there are two crucial differences between convergence on the choice dilemmas and convergence in the autokinetic situation. First, the choice dilemmas describe situations that have *value connotations* —taking business risks, competing in contests of various sorts, or making decisions that can affect future life—while the autokinetic situation is a relatively value-free perceptual judgment. Second, and more important, convergence on the choice dilemmas was preponderantly in a *particular direction*, with more risky decisions apparently made by groups than by individuals. Prior to the publication of these findings, it had been assumed that if a decision had to be made on a controversial or uncertain issue, a decision-making "committee" would typically arrive at a more conservative solution than would a single person acting alone. The risky shift found by Stoner (1961) and subsequently replicated by others suggested that just the opposite might be true. This possibility seemed to carry such important implications for group decision making in a variety of contexts that a great deal of effort was devoted to attempts to explain the risky shift.

An obvious possibility is that the subjects in the experiment are perfectly willing to make risky decisions for some *other* person but would not do so if they were to suffer the consequences of failure themselves. This artifact of the procedure was quickly ruled out by having subjects decide on their own chances of experiencing noxious physical effects such as nausea from smelling a chemical (Bem, Wallach, and Kogan, 1965). The first theoretical explanation to receive attention was the idea that in the group setting each member is less personally responsible for the outcome (and consequently less to blame for a potential failure). With this *diffusion of responsibility* (Wallach, Kogan, and Burt, 1967) among members of the group, the group can afford to make a more risky decision. You may remember from Chapter Ten that Latané and Darley (1970) suggested that diffusion of responsibility for aiding a victim might contribute to bystander unresponsiveness in an emergency. There it was argued that diffusion of responsibility produced a *failure* to take the risk of intervening, while here it is argued that the same diffusion of responsibility should produce a *greater* likelihood of risky action. The two are obviously contradictory, but fortunately for conceptual clarity, the diffusion of responsibility explanation of the risky shift has not been supported by most of the evidence (Pruitt, 1971).

A second explanation, suggested by Brown (1965), was that in our culture a positive *value* is placed on taking (reasonable) risks, especially if those are entrepreneurial or competitive risks. As it happens, nine of the twelve items in the set of choice dilemmas deal with just this sort of risk. This value explanation suggests that in the course of normal self-presentation the members of the group desire to make public statements that indicate that they subscribe to this positive view of reasonable risk. During the group discussion the "conservatives" realize that they have not gone far enough, and they shift in the risky direction in order to regain their stature with the group.

Perhaps the most important contribution of the value theory was its implication that the shift ought to be greatest on those items that are most entrepreneurial or competitive in tone. This implication caused investigators to look more closely at the specific items, discovering to their surprise that a few of the items produced consistent *conservative* shifts, such as the marriage item mentioned above. Whether the group's opinion is more risky or less risky than the opinion of the individuals in the group thus depends on the *content* of the issue being discussed. Consequently, it is more appropriate to refer to the group-induced changes as a *choice shift*, rather than as a shift in a particular direction (Pruitt, 1971). The discovery that some choice dilemma items produce conservative shifts, and the finding that shifts occur on attitude dimensions (Moscovici and Zavalloni, 1969) as well as on the risk dimension, makes the idea of the choice shift less of a novelty and brings the question of its causes back into the realm of the mutual social influence that occurs in the group setting (Cartwright, 1971).

Communication, Leadership, and Group Decision

The social group may, indeed, make decisions that will differ from the decisions that would be made by an individual person. In part those differences will depend on the structure of communication processes within the group, in part they will be determined by the emergent and formal leadership of the group, and in part they will be the result of the group's cohesiveness and its resulting pressure toward uniformity of opinion. Participation in a group is an excellent example of the mutual contingency of social interaction and influence. Each member of the group brings individual social perceptions, attitudes, and social motives. These individual characteristics influence the "plan" of the group, both in setting its objectives and in accomplishing the group locomotion necessary to achieve those objectives. But by the same token the group's objectives and the process of achieving the group's goal will affect the individual's "plan," occasionally requiring the alteration of some of these personal attitudes and the relinquishing of some of these personal goals.

As we have so often noted before, the task of scientific social psychology is to develop theories and conduct research that will increase our understanding of human social behavior. Much of that social behavior can be properly regarded as individual action, but some of it can also be regarded as the result of a social exchange between the individual and various social groups.

How do we account for these social exchanges? One approach is to adopt the viewpoint of the group and ask how groups produce various sorts of self-presentations, how they affect the self-concepts and attitudes of their members, and how their norms influence the individual's behavior in subtle ways as well as through explicit demands for conformity. Such an approach focuses on the group and its characteristics, placing the individual group members in the background. This concentration upon group processes was characteristic of early work in social psychology, and it continued to be a dominant theme through the 1950s (Steiner, 1974). A different approach concentrates on the individual, relegating group influences to a secondary role. Here the focus is on the internal causes of social behavior— ways of integrating perceptual information, processes of social attribution, needs for cognitive consistency and self-esteem, rewards and costs of social exchange as viewed by the participants in a relationship. This latter approach has been the dominant theme of recent social psychology, and it is obviously inherent in our definition of the discipline as the study of the personal and situational factors that affect *individual* social behavior.

Throughout the book we have adhered to this individualistic position, turning to a person's interactions with others only after considering that person's social perceptions, attitudes, self-concept, and social motivation. Given an individualistic definition of social psychology, the present chapter is the logical conclusion to our progression from simpler internal processes to more complex interpersonal ones. In this chapter we have examined communication within a small group, the emergence and influence of group leaders, and various aspects of group decision making. The study of interaction among members of a social group is perhaps as far as we can venture without losing sight of the individual. But it would be a mistake to think that this conclusion to an individualistically defined social psychology also marks the end of significant influences on social behavior. From here the trail simply leads to other disciplines: to sociology, which concentrates on human groups and institutions, and to anthropology, which places those institutions in proper cultural context. It may be more appropriate to regard the material outlined in this chapter as a continuation rather than as an end; as an introduction to other fields rather than as a conclusion to this one.

Summary

A **social group** is a collectivity that has psychological implications for the individual. Such groups can be characterized by the degree to which they provide social-emotional rewards for their members, and also by the degree to which they attempt to achieve well-defined group goals. The functioning of a group, and the place of the individual in that group, will be affected by the communication structure of the group, the nature of the group's leadership, and the processes involved in group decisions.

The flow of communication in a group can be described in terms of various **communication networks** (p. 501), including such models as the chain, the circle, the Y, and the wheel. The communication *distance* (p. 501) between members of the group will differ depending on the pattern of the communication network, as will the **relative centrality** (p. 501) of each position in the network. Measures of group efficiency and measures of member satisfaction with the group performance are usually rank-ordered according to the degree of centralization in the communication network: the more centralized the network is, the more efficient the group tends to be in performing a well-defined task, but the less pleased the members are with their participation in the group. In addition, the peripheral members of any network express less satisfaction with their group membership than do the more central members.

Regardless of the structure of communication within a social group, the content of that communication can be examined through use of *Interaction Process Analysis* (p. 506). In groups without formal structure or established leadership most of the communication among members is related to the task objectives of the group, with the next most frequent type of communication consisting of group maintenance activities. Two different roles—the *task specialist* (p. 508) and the *social-emotional specialist* (p. 508)—typically emerge in the group, and these roles are usually occupied by different people.

When the group does have a formal leadership position, the group leader will tend to be taller, more interpersonally attractive, more intelligent, more self-confident, and more dominant than the other members of the group. Yet the most striking thing about these characteristics of group leaders is how little importance they seem to have from one situation to another. More important than the leader's personal characteristics is his or her behavior toward members of the group, with highly successful leaders showing *consideration* (p. 510) for group members and *initiating structure* (p. 510) in the group's activities. Perhaps the best description of leadership effectiveness is provided by the **contingency model** (p. 511), which takes into account both the leader's characteristics and the nature of the situation. In this model, leaders are classified according to their opinions of their least-preferred co-workers and situations are categorized along the dimensions of affective relations between the leader and the members, the degree of structure in the task of the group, and the position power held by the leader. Tests of the contingency model indicate that highly managing and controlling leaders will be most effective when the situation is either quite favorable or quite unfavorable, while permissive and considerate leaders will be most effective in moderately unfavorable circumstances.

Successful group activity requires that at least some decisions be made by the group as a whole, rather than exclusively by the leader, and a variety of factors will affect these group decision processes. Groups can serve social-emotional functions and/or instrumental functions for their members, and the degree to which the group meets all of its members' needs will determine the **cohesiveness** (p. 518) of the group. The more cohesive the group is, the more *pressure toward uniformity of opinion* (p. 519) there will be, and the more likely the group will be to reject any member who consistently takes a deviant position. An extreme example of this effect can be seen in the phenomenon of **groupthink** (p. 523): members of a highly cohesive group that is insulated from outside opinion may tend to accept without question a policy that is strongly endorsed by the group leader. The resulting *illusion of unanimity* (p. 523) leads to an *illusion of invulnerability* (p. 523) regarding the group's position on the issue. Since the social reality in such a group may be completely out of touch with objective reality, disastrous miscalculations can occur. Even in a leaderless group with full discussion of the issues, the group setting may induce a **choice shift** (p. 524) in member attitudes away from the attitudes or judgments that the members would have made privately.

Suggested Additional Readings

CARTWRIGHT, D., AND ZANDER, A. (Eds.) *Group dynamics: Research and theory.* (3rd ed.) New York: Harper & Row, 1968. This is an excellent collection of classic studies in group dynamics, including material on cohesiveness, group standards, communication, and leadership. Each section begins with an introduction by the editors.

COLLINS, B. E., AND RAVEN, B. H. Group structure: Attraction, coalitions, communication, and power. In G. Lindzey and E. Aronson (Eds.) *Handbook of Social Psychology.* (2nd ed.) Vol. 4. A comprehensive though quite technical review of communication networks, theories of group structure, and coalition formation in small groups.

FIEDLER, F. E. A contingency model of leadership effectiveness. In L. Berkowitz (Ed.) *Advances in experimental social psychology.* Vol. 1. New York: Academic Press, 1964. Pp. 149–190. This is a brief presentation of the contingency model of leadership effectiveness, including a review of some of the relevant research. Readable, even though a bit technical.

PRUITT, D. G. Choice shifts in group discussion: An introductory review. *Journal of Personality and Social Psychology,* 1971, 20, 339–360. A thorough summary of the explanations that have been suggested for the presence of the risky shift and other group-induced shifts in member attitudes and judgments.

From here the trail leads to other disciplines. . . .

Photo by Paul Seder

One View of Social Psychology
An Epilogue

Throughout this book the major emphasis has been placed upon the theory and research of scientific social psychology rather than upon the practical problems to which those concepts and findings might be applied. We have discussed theories of social perception and attribution rather than dealing at length with suggestions for reducing ethnic or racial stereotyping. We have presented theories of attitude organization and change rather than giving specific instructions to would-be persuaders. We have described models of social exchange and interpersonal influence instead of discussing particular techniques for increasing social attractiveness or effectiveness or enjoyment of interaction. This emphasis is not meant to suggest that practical applications are unimportant. Indeed, most of the examples used in this book were intentionally designed to show how theoretical ideas could be applied to familiar situations in everyday life. What the emphasis upon theory does reflect is the belief that concepts need to be taught, whereas practical applications are likely to suggest themselves to people who know the concepts.

THEORY AND APPLICATION

Once the approach, the research, and the theories of contemporary social psychology have been communicated, it becomes appropriate to conclude by showing how the whole discipline—not just a selected theory or two—might have practical applications. Perhaps the best case for the social relevance of social psychology was made in the work of Kurt Lewin (1890–1947), and it is principally for this reason that Lewin is generally regarded as the intellectual father of the discipline. Lewin wrote extensively on the applications of social psychological theory to practical social problems, and was one of the founders of the Society for the Psychological Study of Social Issues. His methodological contributions were substantial, and his guiding principle that there "is nothing so practical as a good theory" (1951, p. 169) has served as the inspiration to later generations of social psychologists. After considering two examples of Lewin's approach, we shall use his balance between theory and application as a standard against which to evaluate the current status of social psychology and to estimate its prospects for the future.

In the early chapters of this book we distinguished between the implicit social psychology of the untutored observer and the systematic methods of scientific social psychology. We pointed out that reliance on personal experience can lead to the derogation as "trivial" of results that agree with expectations, and to the rejections as "counterintuitive" of findings that do not square with experience. For this reason personal experience cannot be permitted to substitute for systematic methods. Experience can and does serve, however, as a rich source of *hypotheses* to be tested by scientific methods, and one incident attributed to Lewin illustrates this quite well.

There is a story, confirmed by at least one observer (Marrow, 1969), concerning Lewin and his students at the Psychological Institute of the University of Berlin and their frequent gatherings to talk at the Schwedische Café near the Institute. The several participants in these informal gatherings typically ordered a variety of foods and drinks, and one certain waiter was always able to remember each person's order without the benefit of any written notes. When someone asked for the check, the waiter would simply recall exactly what each person had ordered. On one of these occasions, several minutes after the bill had been paid, Lewin asked the waiter to provide another accounting of the orders. The waiter declared indignantly that the matter had been settled, that he could not remember.

Why would something be so precisely remembered, then so quickly forgotten? For Lewin, the question seemed to suggest the presence of a psychological *tension* created with the taking of the order and discharged with the payment of the bill. As long as the tension was present, there would be no difficulty in remembering the orders, but as soon as the tension has been discharged, the orders would be forgotten. To test this idea one of Lewin's students, Bluma Zeigarnik, conducted a series of experiments, and the results are the well-known *Zeigarnik effect*: interrupted tasks will be recalled much better than completed tasks (indicating that some tension still remains in the case of the incompleted tasks). The concept of psychological tension assumed a fundamental role in Lewin's field theory, serving as the basis for the valences, forces, and barriers described in Chapter Twelve. Thus the sensitive observation of a simple social behavior contributed to the development of a complex psychological theory.

But Lewin was much more than a sophisticated observer of human behavior, building theory by taking ideas from his personal experience. He was also an advocate of what had become known as **action research:** the application of social psychological theory and methods in the attempt to solve social problems. An excellent example of action research is discussed in Chapter One. You may recall that this experiment used group discussion to change the eating habits of families, increasing their use of beef hearts, sweetbreads, and kidneys in order to conserve other cuts of meat needed for the troops during the Second World War. The conclusions of the study do require some qualifications, but the research still stands as an excellent example of the attempt to apply theory and research to the solution of practical problems.

THE PRESENT STATE OF SOCIAL PSYCHOLOGY

Why does a waiter forget the orders as soon as the bill is paid? How can social attitudes be changed? Even in answering such practical questions, personal experience cannot be an adequate substitute for systematic research. Scientific theories will have a decided advantage over the popular wisdom of "common sense," but in their development of theory social psychologists should not lose sight of social reality. They should draw upon everyday social behavior for testable hypotheses, and they should apply their theories to matters of everyday concern. The relationship between theory and practice is a reciprocal one: applied questions can contribute to the development of theory, and conceptual ideas can contribute to the solution of social problems. This is Lewin's legacy to social psychology. How well do the data and theory of contemporary social psychology measure up to this standard?

Are the data of contemporary social psychology in touch with everyday social reality? This is an extremely important question because of the special relationship between theory, research, and everyday behavior. For the most part the theories considered in this book claim to explain aspects of everyday behavior. Yet most were formulated in the context of known research findings and were tested by subsequent research rather than by attempts at practical application. If for some reason the relevant research does not adequately represent social reality, then the theory's explanatory value cannot be determined. For example, do the conceptual ideas invoked to account for the risky shift in group discussion (Chapter Thirteen) generalize to risk taking outside the laboratory? This depends on whether the laboratory task—choice dilemmas—represents the essence of risk taking in the real social world, and there is good reason to believe that it does not (Dion, Baron, and Miller, 1970; Smith, 1972).

Even if the research task or setting captures the essential features of the comparable everyday situation, there is no guarantee that the *findings* of research will automatically generalize beyond the observational or experimental setting. You will remember from Chapter Two that research findings may be distorted by a variety of biases. Subjects may respond in a socially desirable way. Experimenters may inadvertently convey their own expectations for the outcome. The demand characteristics of the setting may affect the subjects' responses. The presence of an observer may change the behavior of the people being observed. The subjects chosen for study may not be representative of the larger population. These sources of difficulty must be minimized and the research should be conceptually replicated before the findings can be generalized to the real social world with any degree of confidence.

As a discipline, social psychology has been more successful at eliminating threats to internal validity than at increasing external validity. It has been more effective in designing procedures that capture the essential features of everyday behavior than in testing those procedures on representative groups of subjects (unfortunately concentrating almost exclusively on college undergraduates). And it has been less concerned with replication of findings than with further extensions of knowledge. Notwithstanding the limitations, it is fair to suggest that the data of contemporary social psychology do generally reflect social reality. Certainly there are some exceptions, but entire areas of present interest—such as attribution, helping behavior, attraction, and aggression—continue Lewin's tradition of drawing testable hypotheses from the observation of everyday behavior.

So the data of social psychology are in reasonable touch with social reality, drawing upon interesting questions in everyday experience as a source of researchable hypotheses. Thus the data approximate Lewin's standards. Can the same be said for contemporary theories? Once developed, can the theories be applied to practical problems, or do they become so esoteric that they are only of interest to what Smith (1972) calls the "priestcraft"? Probably the best answer to this question is "a little of each." Social psychologists have typically been more interested in the basic research that leads to conceptual development than in the applied research that contributes to the solution of social problems. As a result, theories typically undergo a great deal of refinement before their practical applications are ever determined, and in occasional instances conceptual issues are carried well beyond the point of diminishing returns. But to say that a theory has never been applied to a practical problem is *not* to say that practical application is impossible.

Why, then, has there been so little emphasis upon the practical applications of social psychological knowledge? There are several answers to this question, some related to the professional interests and aspirations of social psychologists, and some related to the theories themselves. It just happens to be true that more social psychologists, are interested in basic research and theoretical refinement than in applied research. This natural preference is exaggerated by a system of academic and professional incentives that also favors research publication over the solution of practical problems. Further, the labeling of a particular societal condition as a "social problem" is a value judgment rather than a scientific judgment. We noted early in the book that although social psychology is not itself value-free, it does not assume the role of making your value judgments for you. And individual social psychologists are understandably reluctant to put themselves in a position they would consider inappropriate for their discipline.

Even if there is general agreement on the existence of a specific social problem, a social psychologist may be reluctant to suggest a solution based on theory (and an intelligent audience may harbor doubts about the solution) because of the nature of contemporary theories. Some theories may seem too *artificial* to have general applicability, others may appear to be too *complex* to offer the straightforward alternatives desired by policy makers, and still others may be so *controversial* that no single policy recommendation seems advisable. Work in experimental games (Chapter Eleven) is often accused of artificiality, but it does have concrete applications in bargaining situations ranging from labor negotiations to dealing with political terrorists. Attribution theory (Chapter Four) might seem an overly complex description of a simple process of social perception, but it nevertheless provides insight into the practical problems of determining criminal guilt or the presence of mental disorder. Theoretical explanations of the effects of role playing on attitude change (Chapter

Six) are highly controversial, yet all suggest that the technique might be valuable in reducing tensions between groups of people who would otherwise be natural adversaries.

There are problems with contemporary theories, but important social questions will not often wait until sufficient data have been gathered. In the absence of recommendations based on tentative theories, policy decisions will be made out of convenience or tradition, disregarding possible social consequences. Under these circumstances a recommendation based on inconclusive research or an artificial, complex, or controversial theory might have been preferable. Contemporary social psychology might surprise Lewin, not because its theories have no practical utility but because its practitioners typically do not actively seek to apply them.

PROSPECTS FOR THE FUTURE

In the past few years social psychology has been undergoing a searching reexamination of its methods, theory, and accomplishments as a discipline. Surveys of major journals have found a heavy reliance on manipulative laboratory experiments (Fried, Gumpper, and Allen, 1973; Helmreich, 1975; Higbee and Wells, 1972), although there is still some applied research being conducted (Nelson and Kannenberg, 1976). Critics within the field have variously argued that there has been too much research with too little theoretical guidance (Kruglanski, 1975), that some of this research is conducted more to demonstrate the investigator's ingenuity than to produce scientifically valuable data (Ring, 1967), and that whatever the investigator's motivation, the use of methods such as deception is ethically unacceptable (Kelman, 1968). Whether they subscribe to these particular criticisms or not, most commentators (Helmreich, 1975; McGuire, 1973; Smith, 1972) agree that social psychology would profit from a return to Lewin's values for the discipline, specifically from a greater emphasis on applied problems.

Throughout this book we have seen the difficulty of predicting the future behavior of a single individual; predicting the course of a discipline can only be more hazardous. Yet there are presently some trends that suggest increasing attention to practical applications of theory and research. A survey of graduate students and faculty in psychology (Lipsey, 1974) showed a majority favoring involvement in the problems of society, so the calls for application should be falling on receptive ears. Researchers trained in the traditional experimental mold have turned their attention to such practical concerns as environmental crowding (Freedman, 1975; Stokols, 1972), education (Gerard and Miller, 1975; Weiner, 1974), and the law (Miller, 1975; Shaver, Gilbert, and Williams, 1975). Recent issues of the *Journal of Social Issues* have addressed such problems as population control (Back, 1974), pornography (Wilson and Goldstein, 1973), and civil liberties (Zalkind, 1975), to mention just a few. These trends suggest that it is possible to agree with Smith (1972) that social psychology has traded "more on promise than on performance," while at the same time accepting Helmreich's (1975) conclusion that the promise is great.

For a few of you the choice of a course in social psychology may have been the first step on the road to a professional career in the area. For others it may have been a convenient way to satisfy a requirement. For many it may have been a reflection of natural curiosity about social behavior. Whatever your reasons for choosing the course and whatever your expectations for its content, this text had several responsibilities to you. Certainly it should have tried to enhance your understanding of social behavior. But it should not have tried to offer simple answers to complex social questions. It should have taught you about contemporary theories, because these theories serve to organize some of the complexity that actually exists. It should have shown you how research is conducted, because guessing how people *might* behave is no substitute for observing what they actually *do*. Finally, it should have discharged these responsibilities without losing your interest. Only you can judge the extent to which these goals have been met.

Glossary

Words in *italics* indicate other glossary entries.

acquiescence   The *response set* representing a tendency to agree with attitude statements regardless of their content.

action research   Application of social psychological research methods and theory to the solution of social problems.

aggression   Intentional action directed toward the injury of another person. (See *catharsis hypothesis*, *excitation-transfer theory*, and *frustration-aggression hypothesis*)

altruism   Intentional, self-sacrificing behavior that benefits other people. (See *objective altruism*)

ambiguous mediation   In social perception, the case in which an individual's action might reflect any one of several underlying *personal dispositions*. (See *synonymous mediation*)

anticonformity   The counterforce to *conformity* representing an active attempt to sabotage the group's objectives. (See *independence*)

archival methods   Research procedures in which records established and maintained for some other purpose are analyzed to test hypotheses in social psychology.

artifact   In research, a spurious finding resulting not from real psychological differences, but from procedural errors.

associative bond   In *congruity theory*, an assertion of a connection between a source and an object. (See *dissociative bond*)

asymmetric contingency   A social interaction in which one person's responses are determined by his or her internal plan, while the other person's responses are entirely contingent on the actions of the first person. (See *mutual contingency*, *pseudocontingency*, and *reactive contingency*)

attitude   An organized predisposition to respond in a favorable or unfavorable manner toward a specified class of social objects.

attraction   An *attitude* of favorability toward a person. (See *complementarity*, *gain-loss theory*, and *law of attraction*)

attribution processes   The cognitive processes through which perceivers interpret the actions of other people (and in some cases their own actions as well).

attributional criteria   The attributional criteria are distinctiveness, consistency, and consensus. An attribution will be made to a distinctive entity when the response to the entity is consistent over time and modality, and when there is consensus among observers about the response.

authoritarian personality   A *personality syndrome* presumed to consist of rigid adherence to conventional moral values, an emphasis on power and toughness, and a deference to higher authority.

balance theory   A *cognitive consistency* theory of attitude organization which posits two primary relationships—liking and *unit formation*—between cognitive elements. Imbalance in the system is presumed to be unpleasant, and to motivate the person to make whatever attitudinal changes are necessary to restore balance.

balanced replication   An experimental design that includes both conditions necessary to reproduce earlier findings thought to be *artifacts*, and conditions designed to rule out the effects of those artifacts.

behavioral intention   In the *information-processing model* of attitude organization, a specific response tendency reflecting the more general predisposition toward the attitude object.

behaviorism   The approach to psychology that explains behavior entirely in terms of observable stimuli and observable responses rather than, e.g., in terms of intervening cognitive processes inferred from overt behavior.

belief congruence   The degree to which the beliefs of one person agree with the beliefs of another.

belief premise   In the *syllogistic model* of attitude organization, the premise that states the person's beliefs about the non*criterial attributes* of the attitude object. (See *evaluative premise*)

belief strength   In the *information-processing model* of attitude organization, the respondent's subjective probability that an attitude object actually possesses the characteristic in question.

catharsis hypothesis   The hypothesis that suggests that the observation of aggression would decrease later aggressive behavior. (See *frustration-aggression hypothesis*, *social learning theory*, and *vicarious reinforcement*)

central traits   In impression formation, the important characteristics or traits (such as warm-cold) that seem to exert an organizing influence on other traits involved in the impression.

choice shift   Originally described in the more limited terms of a "risky shift," this is the tendency of a group to make a decision after discussion that differs from the decision that would be made by pooling the individual, private decisions of group members.

coercive power   The *social power* derived from an ability to provide a target person with negative *reinforcements*. (See *expert power*, *legitimate power*, *referent power*, and *reward power*)

cognitive complexity   The presumed sophistication of the cognitive categories a person employs to describe events and people in the social world.

cognitive consistency model   Any of several models of attitude organization—e.g., *balance, congruity*, or *dissonance*—based on the premise that people seek to maintain consistency among their attitudes, or between their attitudes and behavior.

cognitive dissonance theory   A *cognitive consistency* theory of attitude organization that posits three possible relations between pairs of cognitive elements—consonance, irrelevance, and dissonance. Dissonance arises when one element implies the obverse of the other element, and this dissonance serves as a motivation for attitude change.

cognitive labeling theory   An outgrowth of *social comparison theory* that holds that the experience of an emotion requires both internal physiological arousal and an external cognitive label for that arousal.

cohesiveness   The mutual commitment and attraction of members to their *social group*; the sum of forces that hold the group together.

communication network   A pattern of the two-way flow of communication among members in a *social group*.

comparison function   The function served by a *reference group* when that group is used either as an example of what attitudes and behavior should be (a positive reference group) or what they should not be (a negative reference group). (See *normative function*)

comparison level (CL)   In *exchange theory*, one standard for evaluating the *goodness of outcomes*: the average value of all outcomes known to the person, each weighted by its momentary salience. (See *comparison level for alternatives*)

comparison level for alternatives (CL$_{alt}$)   In *exchange theory*, one standard for evaluating the *goodness of outcomes*: the level of outcomes prevailing in the best currently available alternative to the present relationship. (See *comparison level*)

competition   The sort of interaction that occurs when all participants strive to achieve their individual goals in a situation characterized by low *correspondence of outcomes*.

complementarity   The principle which states that long-term (e.g., marital) relationships may be based as much on complementary personality characteristics as on *attitude* similarity. (See *law of attraction*)

compliance   Observable change in behavior in the direction advocated by an influencing agent. This overt change need not be accompanied by any internal attitude change. (See *identification, internalization*)

conceptual replication   A test of a single conceptual idea using procedures which differ from those employed in preceding tests of the conceptual idea.

conformity   A change in belief or behavior toward a group as a result of real or imagined group pressure. (See *anticonformity, independence*)

congruity theory   A *cognitive consistency* theory of attitude organization which describes both sources of statements and objects of those statements on a seven-point scale. Unless the source and object have the same scale positions on this evaluative scale, the incongruity will serve as a motivation for attitude change.

constructive process   In the perceptual arc, the perceiver's interpretation of a *proximal stimulus*.

contingency model   A model of leadership effectiveness that holds that the efficacy of various leadership styles will depend on the characteristics of the situation. Situations are described in terms of the affective relations among group members, the structure of the task, and the power position of the leader. Leader characteristics are described on a dimension from managing and controlling to permissive and considerate.

contingent strategy   A strategy for repeated plays of the *Prisoner's Dilemma Game*, or for other *mixed-motive games*, in which one player's move on any trial depends on the other player's move on the preceding trial.

correlation coefficient   A statistical measure of the association between two variables. Represented by the symbol r, the correlation coefficient can range from a numerical value of $+1.00$ (a perfect positive relationship between the two variables) through a value of 0 (no relationship between the two variables) to a value of -1.00 (a perfect inverse relationship between the two variables).

correlation matrix   An array of all the possible correlations between scores on several different tests or measures.

correspondence of inference   The degree to which a stimulus person's actions, and the *personal disposition* presumed to account for the action, can be described in the same terms. The greater the correspondence, the greater the perceiver's certainty about the attribution.

correspondence of outcomes   In an interaction described by *exchange theory*, the degree to which one person will increase the other's rewards simply by pursuing his or her own goals.

counterattitudinal advocacy   Advocacy by a subject of a position inconsistent with his or her own attitudes as a result of a *forced compliance* technique. Counterattitudinal advocacy is presumed to create *cognitive dissonance*, which, in turn, produces attitude change consistent with the position publicly advocated.

covariation (principle of)   The attribution theory principle that holds that an effect will be attributed to a presumed cause that is present when the effect is present and absent when the effect is absent.

credibility (of communicator)   The believability of a person who attempts persuasive communication, usually thought to be based on the communicator's expertise and trustworthiness.

criterial attribute   An essential attribute of an object or person that helps to define the category to which that object or person belongs. For example, the sexual organs are criterial attributes for the determination of gender.

debriefing   The postexperimental interview designed to ascertain the subject's suspicions, reveal and explain the experimental deceptions, and remove residual effects of the manipulations.

defensive attribution   A self-protective denial of a stimulus person's responsibility for negative outcomes. This denial is based on threat from the stimulus person's circumstances and from the perceiver's personal similarity to the stimulus person.

deindividuation   The decreased concern for social evaluation (either self-evaluation or evaluation of the self by others) brought about by anonymity, altered states of consciousness, or diffusion of responsibility for action among members of a group. This loss of identity is reflected in lowered restraints against inappropriate, negative, or hostile behavior.

demand characteristics   The sum total of all the cues that convey an experimental hypothesis (not necessarily the correct hypothesis) to the subject.

dependent variable   The measured response in an experiment; the behavior expected to change as a result of changes in the *independent variable*.

differential accuracy   A perceiver's ability to distinguish the degree to which different people possess varying amounts of various personality traits.

displacement   The Freudian defense mechanism that holds that some id impulses that cannot be directed at a primary target person can be shifted to a similar, but less inhibiting, second person.

dissociative bond   In *congruity theory*, the denial of a connection (or the rejection of a connection) between a source and an object. (See *associative bond*)

distal stimulus   In perception, a physical object or social entity external to the perceiver.

distributive justice   A principle for evaluating the fairness of a comparison of rewards. If the ratio of one person's profits to investments is equal to the ratio of the other person's profits to investments, then distributive justice is said to occur.

dyadic effect   The fact that in an interaction the amount of personal information disclosed by one participant will be positively correlated with the amount disclosed by the other participant.

effect dependence   In socialization, the fact that nearly all a young child's rewards and punishments are mediated by its parents. (See *information dependence*)

ego-defensive function   People will develop *attitudes* that have the effect of shielding them from conscious recognition of their own inadequacies and failings. (See *instrumental function, knowledge function*, and *value-expressive function*)

electromyography   The procedure for measuring the neural impulses generated by implicit (or minute) muscle movements using extremely sensitive physiological recording equipment.

emergent leadership   In an informal *social group*, the gradual assumption by one or more members of the social *role* of group leader.

empathy   The state of experiencing an emotion felt by another person.

empirical replication   A research study in which all procedures are kept as nearly identical as possible to procedures employed in a preceding study. Sometimes called "exact" replication.

equal-appearing intervals   The initial sorting of items in a *Thurstone scale* creates an approximation of a true *inverval scale* in which the eleven sorting categories appear to represent psychologically equal intervals.

equity theory   A theory that expands on the principle of *distributive justice*, and states that equity occurs between participants in an interaction when each person's outcomes are proportional to his or her inputs. Inputs must be relevant and recognized, and inequity can be reduced by alterations in outcomes or inputs, by cognitive distortion of the situation, or by leaving the field.

evaluation apprehension   An experimental subject's concern about attaining a positive evaluation of his or her behavior from the experimenter.

evaluative premise   In the *syllogistic model* of attitude organization, the premise that states the person's affective, emotional, or evaluative reaction to the characteristics associated with the attitude object in the *belief premise*.

exchange theory   A theory of interpersonal behavior that holds that (1) people seek to maximize their pleasure and minimize their pain in interaction, and (2) social encounters can best be described as exchanges of rewards among participants.

excitation-transfer theory   A *cognitive labeling* theory of the facilitation of aggressive behavior. The theory holds that once there has been instigation to *aggression*, adding to the person's arousal by other (nonaggressive) means will enhance the aggressive response.

experimental realism   The degree of psychological impact that the experimental setting and manipulations have on the subject.

experimenter expectancy   An *artifact* in experimental research based on the experimenter's unintentional communication to the subject of results anticipated for the research.

expert power   The *social power* derived from skills or knowledge lacked by the target person. (See *coercive power*, *legitimate power*, *referent power*, and *reward power*)

external validity   The extent to which the findings of research will generalize beyond the confines of the particular setting or procedures. (See *internal validity*)

face   In the analysis of *self-presentation* in social interaction, the positive social value that each participant claims for himself or herself.

factor analysis   A statistical procedure for determining the number of fundamental dimensions underlying a set of ratings or personality traits. The procedure is designed to explain the greatest amount of variation in the ratings in as few underlying dimensions as possible.

factorial experiment   An experiment in which there are systematic variations in more than one *independent variable*. Each independent variable then becomes one factor in the experiment.

falsifiability   A prerequisite for calling a set of propositions a theory; the extent to which, in principle, cases can be found to which the theory does not apply. If a proposition cannot be tested, or if it applies to all conceivable situations, then it is not falsifiable, and not properly regarded as a theory.

field experiment   An experiment performed outside a laboratory but containing a manipulation controlled by the experimenter.

field theory   The general theory of human motivation that holds that a person's behavior will be determined by a total field of personal desires and environmental factors. (See *life space*)

forced-choice format   A format for an attitude or personality scale consisting of item pairs (or occasionally item triads). The respondent produces a self-description through a forced choice between the elements of each pair. These elements are matched in social desirability, but only one of each pair is keyed for the attitude or personality characteristic in question.

forced compliance   The experimental procedure used to induce *cognitive dissonance* by making a subject perform a counterattitudinal behavior while leaving the subject with the illusion that he or she has freely chosen to perform that behavior.

frustration-aggression hypothesis   The hypothesis that suggests that all aggressive behavior is the product of frustration, and that frustration inevitably leads to aggression.

gain-loss theory   A theory of interpersonal *attraction* that holds that a person's attraction toward an evaluator will depend not on the proportion of positive evaluations rendered, but rather on the sequence of those evaluations. (See *law of attraction*)

Gestalt   An organized perceptual whole, or unit.

goodness of outcome   In *exchange theory*, the psychological representation of a person's profit (reward-cost) for any particular behavior. (See *comparison level, comparison level for alternatives*)

group locomotion   Movement of a *social group* toward its collective goal. A source of pressure toward uniformity of opinion within the group.

group maintenance   Actions by group members which are directed toward facilitation of pleasant interaction among the group.

groupthink   A group preoccupation with unanimity of opinion (usually in order to facilitate achievement of a group goal) that renders ineffective any critical evaluation of the situation.

hedonistic calculus   Bentham's early analysis of human motivation in terms of a fundamental desire to seek pleasure and avoid pain. Included in the analysis was an attempt to specify the dimensions— e.g., duration, intensity, certainty—that could characterize sources of pleasure and pain.

horizontal structure   In the *syllogistic model* of *attitude* organization, the number of different syllogistic chains leading to exactly the same attitudinal conclusion. (See *vertical structure*)

the *I*   That part of *self* which is pure ego—thinker, knower, organized stream of conscious awareness. (See *the* Me)

ideal self   In some measures of self-esteem, the list of personal characteristics that the respondent considers desirable. This contrasts with the *real self*, the characteristics the respondent claims to possess.

identification   Private acceptance of influence based on a satisfying self-defining relationship between the influenced person and the influencing agent. (See *compliance, internalization*)

incentive theory   An attitude change theory, based on the principle of *reinforcement*, that holds that attitude change should increase with increases in the external rewards for change. This view contrasts with the position of *cognitive dissonance theory.*

independence   A counterforce to *conformity* representing a refusal to comply with the group's objectives (either by maintaining one's own position or by leaving the group). (See *anticonformity*)

independent variable   The variable selected or manipulated by an experimenter in order to determine its effects on behavior. The independent variable may be under the experimenter's control (i.e., the experimental conditions) or it may be a characteristic of the subjects (e.g., sex) expected to affect behavior in the experimental setting. (See *dependent variable*)

index numbers   Numbers which have been corrected for the base rate of occurrence of the phenomena they represent. Although there would be more blue-eyed people in a large group than in a small group, the percentage (an index number) might be the same in both groups.

information dependence   In socialization, the fact that most of a child's knowledge about the social world is derived from information provided by parents. (See *effect dependence*)

information integration theory   A mathematical model of impression formation that holds that both the scale value (positivity) of an adjective and its normalized weight combine to produce the final impression.

information-processing model   A model of attitude organization that describes a social attitude as the product of *belief strength* times the evaluation (positive or negative) of the characteristic.

informational social influence   The *social power* of persuasion that produces private acceptance by providing the target person with the information needed to make a wise decision. (See *normative social influence*)

informed consent   An ethical guideline for psychological research that holds that a potential subject should agree to participate only after receiving a detailed description of the research project.

inoculation   An attitude consolidation technique based on an analogy to medicine. If a person can be exposed to a weakened version of possible counterpropaganda, the person will become more resistant to any effects from that later counterpropaganda.

instrumental function   Favorable *attitudes* will be developed toward people and objects which facilitate achievement of goals; unfavorable attitudes will be developed toward people and objects that frustrate goal attainment. (See *ego-defensive function, knowledge function*, and *value-expressive function*)

insufficient justification   A conceptual explanation for the attitude change that occurs following *counterattitudinal advocacy*. The minimal external rewards for such behavior are insufficient to justify having performed the actions, *cognitive dissonance* results, and this leads to attitude change.

interaction effect   In a factorial experiment, the statistical effect due to a combination of factors, over and above the effects that the factors might have individually.

interaction matrix   In *exchange theory*, the set of interaction possibilities formed by the conjunction of one person's possible behaviors with the other person's possible behaviors.

intermittent reinforcement   The provision of reward not for every occurrence of an action, but only occasionally (often according to a prearranged schedule of *reinforcement*).

internal validity   The extent to which the findings of research reflect the actual psychological differences thought to be measured; freedom from artifacts or confounding. (See *external validity*)

internalization   Private acceptance of influence based on the influenced person's belief that the position advocated is congruent with his or her own value system. (See *compliance, identification*)

interpersonal simulation   A technique devised to test the *self-perception theory* of attitude change. In this technique the simulating subjects are given information about the situation confronting a person in a *forced compliance* experiment and are asked to predict that person's attitudes.

interval scale   A numerical scale of measurement for ordering observations in which there is an arbitrary zero point. Identical numerical differences along the scale are presumed to represent identical degrees of difference between the observations being scaled. (See *nominal scale, ordinal scale,* and *ratio scale*)

item analysis   Any of several procedures for determining the suitability of an individual item for inclusion in an attitude scale. One such procedure measures the degree to which each item in an attitude scale correlates with the total score (less that item) on the scale.

item pool   The complete set of attitude or opinion statements (often ranging up to 100 such statements) from which items to be included in a *Thurstone scale* or a *Likert scale* are to be selected.

just world (need to believe in a)   A self-protective distortion in *attribution* based on a belief that people who suffer deserve to suffer, either through a behavioral mistake or through a character flaw.

kinesic cues   Cues in social perception arising from the body movements—e.g., posture, gestures, facial expressions—of a stimulus person.

knowledge function   People will develop *attitudes* that help bring structure and organization to their social worlds, and help to explain social events. (See *ego-defensive function, instrumental function,* and *value-expressive function*)

latitude of acceptance In the *social judgment theory* of attitude change, the area moderately discrepant from a target person's own accepted by the recipient, even though they are not identical to the recipient's position. (See *latitude of noncommitment, latitude of rejection*)

latitude of noncommitment In the *social judgment theory* of attitude change, the area moderately discrepant from a target person's own position. This area encloses all messages that will be neither immediately accepted nor immediately rejected. (See *latitude of acceptance, latitude of rejection*)

latitude of rejection In the *social judgment theory* of attitude change, the area that encloses all messages so far from the recipient's own position that they will be rejected out of hand. (See *latitude of acceptance, latitude of noncommitment*)

law of attraction The proposition that states that *attraction* toward an object or person is a positive linear function of the positive *reinforcements* received from the object or person. A typical experimental procedure equates positive reinforcements received with degree of similarity in *attitudes.* (See *complementarity* and *gain-loss theory*)

Law of Effect The first psychological representation of hedonism (See *hedonistic calculus*), which held that behavior leading to pleasure would be "stamped in," but behavior leading to pain would be "stamped out."

legitimate power The *social power* derived from acceptance by the target person of the authority inherent in the influencing agent's social *role.* (See *coercive power, expert power, referent power,* and *reward power*)

level of aspiration A self-imposed expectation for task performance that will determine whether the self-evaluation is positive or negative following actual task performance.

life space In *field theory,* the total field of environmental factors and personal desires perceived by the person at any given moment in time.

Likert scale An attitude scale that requires respondents to indicate the degree of their agreement or disagreement with a set of statements about the attitude object. The respondent's score is the sum of his or her responses to the individual statements.

linear transformation The transformation of a numerical scale accomplished by adding or subtracting a constant, or by multiplying or dividing by a constant.

locus of control   A person's generalized expectancy about whether his or her rewards will be contingent on his or her own actions (internal control) or on factors in the environment (external control).

looking-glass self   The proposition from *symbolic interactionism* that holds that one's self-concept will be determined in large part by imagining one's social value to other people.

Machiavellianism   The interpersonal style characterized by the manipulation of other people in order to gain one's own ends.

main effect   In a factorial design, the statistical effect due to variations in a single factor, disregarding the influence of other factors.

matching principle   A statement of the fact that people tend to select dates whose physical attractiveness is close to their own.

the *Me*   The *self* as an object of reflection, consisting of material possessions, psychological faculties, social behaviors, and the emotions to which these elements give rise. (See *the* I)

mean score   The arithmetic average of a group of scores.

median   The mid-point of a set of scores; that point above which (or below which) exactly half of the scores lie.

mixed-motive game   An interaction in which there is a low *correspondence of outcomes*, such that if both participants pursue their own immediate goals, both will lose. The very best outcome for each participant also carries the highest risk.

multiple operationism   Use of different operations to measure a concept within the context of a single research study.

mundane realism   The degree of correspondence between the experimental task and the actions a subject might perform in everyday life outside the laboratory.

mutual contingency   A social interaction in which each participant's actions are partly determined by his or her own plan and partly determined by the other's actions. (See *asymmetric contingency*, *pseudocontingency*, and *reactive contingency*)

naive psychology   The systematic attribution theory that attempts to account for the way in which an untrained (naive) observer might explain the causes of behavior.

natural experiment   An experiment in which the manipulation is accomplished by an environmental or situational change not under the experimenter's control.

nominal scale   A scale of measurement by which observations can be classified, but not ordered. (See *interval scale*, *ordinal scale*, and *ratio scale*)

noncommon effects   In correspondent inference theory, the effects produced by one behavioral choice but not by an alternative choice.

nonverbal leakage   The information from a stimulus person's nonverbal behavior that conflicts with the person's verbal message.

non-zero sum game   A game in which one person's gain is not necessarily the other person's loss. Includes cooperation as well as *mixed-motive games*.

norm   A set of expectations for behavior in a particular situation, regardless of the *roles* held by the participants.

normative function   The function served by a *reference group* when that group establishes rules (*norms*) for behavior and provides rewards and punishments to enforce those rules. The normative function is typically limited to cases in which the target person holds (or desires) membership in the reference group. (See *comparison function*)

normative social influence   The *social power* of reward and punishment that produces behavioral *compliance*, but may not produce any private acceptance of the position advocated. (See *informational social influence*)

objective altruism   Voluntary action by an actor that benefits another person with no external rewards for the actor. (See *altruism, reciprocity norm, social responsibility norm*)

objective self-awareness   Heightened recognition of the self as a social object, brought about by focusing one's attention on oneself.

operational definition   A definition of a conceptual variable stated in terms of the procedures or operations performed to measure the concept. "Twelve hours since the last meal" is an operational definition of hunger.

ordinal scale   A numerical scale of measurement by which observations can be rank-ordered. (See *interval scale, nominal scale,* and *ratio scale*)

oversufficient justification   External reward for something that the person would normally have done without that reward. Used as a test of the *self-perception theory* of attitude change. Contrasts with *insufficient justification*.

paralinguistic cues   In social perception, cues to a stimulus person's characteristics that are contained in the person's manner of speaking. These cues include, for example, dialect, loudness, and rate of speech.

participant observation   The recording of behavior by an observer who also takes part in the group's activities. Participant observation may be partially concealed (the subjects know the observer is recording their actions, but do not know precisely what is being recorded) or fully concealed (the subjects are unaware that any record of their actions is being taken).

peer nomination method   A method for studying a perceiver's implicit personality theory. A number of rating dimensions (e.g., weak-strong) are presented to the perceiver, who nominates a specific person to represent each end of every dimension.

percept The phenomenal experience of an object, person, or situation; the way that object, person, or situation appears to the perceiver.

perceptual defense A presumably subconscious attempt by a perceiver to screen out a stimulus that would be threatening if it were consciously perceived.

personal constructs The unique set of dimensions a person uses to describe and explain social behavior, role relationships, and personal characteristics.

personal disposition An enduring personality characteristic, behavioral style, or other reason for acting. (See *attribution processes*)

personal reference scale An individualized scale of social judgment that takes into account both the psychological distance from one end of the scale to the other and the number of categories or divisions in that distance. The later distinctions are accomplished through the use of an *unlimited response language.*

personal space The spatial area immediately surrounding a person that the person considers to be his or her own.

personality syndrome A unified collection of personality traits.

phi phenomenon The perceptual experience of apparent movement which can occur while viewing lights flashing on and off in sequence.

plausible rival hypotheses Potential explanations for research findings that are derived either from alternative theoretical viewpoints or from the presence of *artifacts* in the research procedures.

p-o-x triad In *balance theory*, a triad consisting of the person (p) whose viewpoint is taken, another person (o), and an object (x) associated in some positive or negative way with both people. Such a triad would be balanced if, for example, p and o both like each other and also like x.

prestige suggestion A method of persuasive communication that employs positive statements about an attitude object made by well-known and highly valued individuals.

primacy effect In impression formation or persuasive communication, the tendency for material presented at the beginning of a sequence to have a greater effect than material presented at the end of the sequence.

prior entry effect In social categorization, the error that results from the fact that early information contributes to the formation of a category more than later information will contribute to change in the category.

Prisoner's Dilemma Game A *mixed-motive game* in which the payoffs for joint *competition* and joint cooperation fall between the payoffs for the combination of cooperation and competition (the competing person wins the most, the cooperating person loses the most).

proxemics   The study of the social meanings of various interpersonal differences.

proximal stimulus   In perception, the local and immediate representation of a *distal stimulus* at the sense organs.

pseudocontingency   The limiting case of social interaction in which participants who are really following their own internal plans appear to be responding to each other. An example is a group of actors following the cues in a script, but appearing to be responding to each other. (See *asymmetric contingency, mutual contingency,* and *reactive contingency*)

ratio scale   A numerical scale of measurement having an absolute zero point. Not only must equal numerical intervals represent equal differences in the observations being scaled, but a ratio of two numbers on the scale must represent an equivalent ratio in the observations being scaled. (See *interval scale, nominal scale,* and *ordinal scale*)

reactance   The specific negative motivational state directed toward restoring lost decision freedom.

reactive contingency   A social interaction in which each participant's behavior is entirely contingent on the immediately preceding action of the other. (See *asymmetric contingency, mutual contingency,* and *pseudocontingency*)

reactivity   The extent to which research findings are distorted by the subjects' knowledge that they are participating in research.

real self   In some measures of self-esteem, the personal characteristics the respondent claims to possess. This contrasts with the *ideal self*, the list of such characteristics the respondent considers desirable.

reciprocity norm   The social *norm* that requires that (1) people should help those who have helped them, and (2) people should not injure those who have helped them. (See *social responsibility norm*)

reference group   Any social group used as a standard for self-evaluation or attitude formation. The group may be used either as an example to follow (a positive reference group) or as an example to avoid (a negative reference group). (See *comparison function* and *normative function*)

referent power   The *social power* derived from the target person's desire for *identification* with the powerful agent. (See *coercive power, expert power, legitimate power,* and *reward power*)

reinforcement (principle of)   The representation in modern *behaviorism* of the early *Law of Effect*: Behavior followed by positive consequences (positive reinforcement) will become more likely to recur; behavior followed by negative consequences (negative reinforcement) will be less likely to recur.

relative centrality   In a *communication network*, the importance of a particular position as measured by dividing the distances from that position to all others into the sum total of the distances for the entire network.

representativeness   Similarity in psychological characteristics or experience between subjects in research and the population from which those subjects were drawn (or to which the researcher hopes to generalize).

response set   A systematic tendency to answer questions in a way determined not by the content of the question, but by its form or by the characteristics of the possible answers. (See *acquiescence* and *social desirability*)

resultant achievement motivation   The strength of the motive to approach success (usually measured by a version of the Thematic Apperception Test) minus the motive to avoid failure (usually measured by the Test Anxiety Questionnaire).

retaliation distress   According to *equity theory*, one of the two sorts of distress felt by a harm-doer: fear that the victim, or some outside agency, will restore equity by punishing the harm-doer. (See *self-concept distress*)

reward power   The *social power* derived from an ability to provide a target person with positive *reinforcements*. (See *coercive power*, *expert power*, *legitimate power*, and *referent power*)

role   The set of behavioral expectations for a person who performs a particular social function. Examples would be "parent," "student," and "supervisor." (See *norm*)

role conflict   Perceived incompatibility of the expectations inherent in several simultaneously occupied social *roles*.

selective deposit   In *archival methods*, the possibility that some records will have been kept more fully than others, either because of deliberate action by the record keepers or simply because of contemporary social custom.

selective survival   In *archival methods*, the possibility that some records will not last as long as others, either because of natural decay or because of deliberate destruction.

self   The totality of answers to the question "Who am I?" including, for example, inner experience, awareness, observable abilities, and material possessions.

self-concept distress   According to *equity theory*, one of the two sorts of distress felt by a harm-doer: the loss of self-esteem that accompanies behavior inconsistent with equity and fairness. (See *retaliation distress*)

self-perception theory   A theory that holds that people learn of their own attitudes and reasons for behaving by observing their behavior in much the same way that another person might observe them. In the area of attitude change, this view contrasts with that of *cognitive dissonance theory*.

semantic differential   A scaling technique that employs a series of adjective pairs to measure the connotative meaning of words and concepts, or to assess social attitudes.

simple observation   The recording of the public behavior of subjects, without their awareness and without any interference in the situation by the observer.

social comparison theory   A theory of self-evaluation that holds that (1) people have a drive to evaluate their opinions and abilities, (2) in the absence of objective standards this evaluation will occur through social comparison with others, and (3) such social comparisons will usually be made with similar others.

social desirability   The *response set* representing a tendency to respond in a socially approved manner regardless of the content of the behavior requested or the questions asked.

social group   A collectivity that has psychological implications for the individual, based on the person's awareness of the other group members, his or her membership (or desired membership) in the group, and the emotional significance of the group.

social influence   Attitudinal or behavioral change brought about by the application of *social power*. Social influence is a result, whereas social power is a capacity.

social judgment theory   A theory of attitude change that considers the position advocated in relation to the target person's initial position on the issue. Persuasive communications falling in the *latitude of acceptance* may produce slight change, those falling in the *latitude of noncommitment* will produce greater change, and those falling in the *latitude of rejection* will produce no change.

social learning theory   A theory of interpersonal behavior that emphasizes the role of *reinforcement* in the development and maintenance of social interaction patterns. Some social learning theories concentrate on imitation and *vicarious reinforcement*, others deal with expectancy and value, but all share the view of social development as a learning process.

social power   The capacity of a person or group to affect the behavior of another person or group. In terms of *exchange theory*, the range of outcomes through which one person can move another. Implicit in each of these definitions is the qualification "other things being equal." Social power contrasts with *social influence*.

social reality   The group consensus about a situation or attitude issue derived from *social comparison* among group members.

social responsibility norm   A social *norm* that holds that people should help anyone in a dependent position. (See *reciprocity norm*)

sociogram   A diagram showing the interpersonal relationships among members of a group. Often such diagrams illustrate friendship choices or co-worker preferences, showing both reciprocated and nonreciprocated choices.

speaker state signal   The nonverbal and *paralinguistic cues* that together indicate that a listener wants to take a turn at speaking.

standard deviation   A statistical measure of the dispersion of a set of scores, derived from the squared deviation of each score in the set from the overall *mean score* of the set.

statistically significant   An experimental result is considered to reflect real psychological differences (rather than chance fluctuations) if the results of appropriate tests are statistically significant. Findings are usually considered statistically significant if they would have occurred fewer than 5 times in 100 by chance.

sublimation   The Freudian defense mechanism that holds that some unacceptable id impulses can be channeled into socially acceptable behaviors.

syllogistic model   A model of attitude organization that describes a social attitude as the syllogistic conclusion of two premises: a *belief premise* representing opinions about the object's characteristics, and an *evaluative premise* reflecting the person's affective reaction to the object.

symbolic interactionism   A theory of social behavior that describes social encounters in terms of their symbolic meaning and the value of that meaning to participants in the encounter.

synonymous mediation   In social perception, the case in which an individual's action unequivocally reflects a single underlying *personal disposition*. (See *ambiguous mediation*)

Thurstone scale   An attitude scale made up of statements with known scale values. These scale values have previously been determined in a sorting procedure designed to produce *equal appearing intervals*. A respondent's attitude score is taken to be the mid-point of the scale values of all items agreed with.

trait implication method   A method for studying a perceiver's implicit personality theory that assesses the extent of the perceiver's belief that the presence of one trait (e.g., "warm") implies the presence of another (e.g., "sociable").

unfreezing/moving/refreezing   The process of attitude change presumed to occur as a result of group discussion of an issue anchored in the social group. A communicator using this process would first unfreeze the group's attitude, then move the group to a new position, and finally refreeze the attitude in the new position.

unit formation   In *balance theory*, the relationship of association—through kinship, proximity, similarity, formal organizations, owning, or other factors—between cognitive elements.

unlimited response language   In the measurement of social *attitudes* according to the respondent's *personal reference scale*, a response continuum with no fixed or apparent categories. An example would be the size or weight of small piles of sand used to assess favorability toward a number of attitude objects.

unobtrusive measures   Physical or psychological measures obtained without the subject's awareness. Such measures avoid *reactivity*.

usable power   The *social power* that an influencing agent is willing to exercise. Because the target of influence can typically provide the powerful person with some negative reinforcements, or simply leave the relationship altogether, usable power is usually some proportion of actual social power.

value-expressive function   People will develop *attitudes* that are consistent with, and expressive of, their broader value systems. (See *ego-defensive function*, *instrumental function*, and *knowledge function*)

veridicality   The extent to which a *percept* corresponds to objective reality.

vertical structure   In the *syllogistic model* of *attitude* organization, the length of the syllogistic chain leading to a particular attitudinal conclusion.

vicarious reinforcement   In *social learning theory*, the process of increasing the likelihood of recurrence of an action by permitting the actor to observe a model being rewarded for the same action.

win-stay, lose-change rule   In an interaction described by *exchange theory*, the informal rule dictating that a participant should continue to perform an action leading to reward, but should cease performing an action leading to punishment.

z **score**   A statistically derived measure of the degree to which an observation or response differs from the *mean score* of a relevant group of observations. The z score is computed by finding the difference between a score and the mean, and then dividing this difference by the *standard deviation* of the group of observations. As a result the z score seldom has a value larger than $+3$ or smaller than -3.

zero-order belief   In the *syllogistic model* of *attitude* organization, a primitive and fundamental belief (such as a belief in the validity of sensory experience) that rests on faith rather than on any prior reasoning.

zero-sum game   An interaction in which there is a perfect negative *correspondence of outcomes*: one person's gains are identical in magnitude to the losses of the other.

References

CHAPTER 1

AJZEN, I. Effects of information on interpersonal attraction: Similarity versus affective value. *Journal of Personality and Social Psychology*, 1974, 29, 374–380.

ALLPORT, G. W. The historical background of modern social psychology. In G. Lindzey (Ed.) *Handbook of social psychology* (1st ed.). Vol. 1. Reading, Mass.: Addison-Wesley, 1954. Pp. 3–56.

BEIER, E. G., ROSSI, A. M., and GARFIELD, R. L. Similarity plus disssimilarity of personality: Basis for friendship? *Psychological Reports*, 1961, 8, 3–8.

BENNETT, E. B. Discussion, decision, commitment, and consensus in "group decision." *Human Relations*, 1955, 8, 251–274.

BENTHAM, J. *An introduction to the principles of morals and legislation.* (First published 1789.) Oxford: Clarendon Press, 1879.

BERSCHEID, E., and WALSTER, E. H. *Interpersonal attraction.* Reading, Mass.: Addison-Wesley, 1969.

BYRNE, D. *The attraction paradigm.* New York: Academic Press, 1971.

CARTWRIGHT, D. Risk-taking by individuals and groups: An assessment of research employing choice dilemmas. *Journal of Personality and Social Psychology*, 1971, 20, 361–378.

CATTELL, R. B., and NESSELROADE, J. R. Likeness and completeness theories examined by 16 personality factors measures on stably and unstably married couples. *Journal of Personality and Social Psychology*, 1967, 7, 351–361.

COMTE, A. *The positive philosophy.* Vol. 1. (Original French ed. 1830). Transl. London: Trubner, 1853.

COMTE, A. *The positive polity.* Vol. 2. (Original French ed. 1852). Transl. London: Longmans, Green, 1975.

FESTINGER, L. A theory of social comparison processes. *Human Relations*, 1954, 7, 117–140.

FESTINGER, L. *A theory of cognitive dissonance.* Stanford, Cal.: Stanford University Press, 1957.

FESTINGER, L., and CARLSMITH, J. M. Cognitive consequences of forced compliance. *Journal of Abnormal and Social Psychology*, 1959, 58, 203–210.

FITZGERALD, F. SCOTT. *This Side of Paradise*. New York: Charles Scribner's Sons, 1920.

HOBBES, T. *Leviathan*. 1651. As noted in B. Russell, *A history of western philosophy*. New York: Simon and Schuster, 1945. Pp. 546–557.

HUME, D. *Treatise of human nature*. 1739. As noted in B. Russell, *A history of western philosophy*. New York: Simon and Schuster, 1945. Pp. 659–674.

KANT, I. *The critique of pure reason*. (1st ed.) 1781. As noted in B. Russell, *A history of western philosophy*. New York: Simon and Schuster, 1945. Pp. 701–718.

KAPLAN, M. F., and ANDERSON, N. H. Information integration theory and reinforcement theory as approaches to interpersonal attraction. *Journal of Personality and Social Psychology*, 1973, 28, 301–312.

KELLEY, H. H., and THIBAUT, J. W. Group problem solving. In G. Lindzey and E. Aronson (Eds.) *Handbook of social psychology*. (2nd ed.) Vol. 4. Reading, Mass.: Addison-Wesley, 1969. Pp. 1–101.

KERCKHOFF, A. C., and DAVIS, K. E. Value consensus and need complimentarity in mate selection. *American Sociological Review*, 1962, 27, 295–303.

KOGAN, N., and WALLACH, M. A. *Risk-taking: A study in cognition and personality*. New York: Holt, 1965.

LEVINGER, G. Note on need complementarity in marriage. *Psychological Bulletin*, 1964, 61, 153–157.

LEWIN, K. Group decision and social change. In T. Newcomb and E. Hartley (Eds.) *Readings in social psychology*. New York: Henry Holt, 1947. Pp. 330–344.

LEWIN, K. Problems of research in social psychology. In D. Cartwright (Ed.) *Field theory in social science: Selected theoretical papers by Kurt Lewin*. New York: Harper & Row, 1951. Pp. 155–169.

LINDZEY, G. (Ed.) *Handbook of social psychology*. Reading, Mass.: Addison-Wesley, 1954.

LINDZEY, G., and ARONSON, E. (Eds.) *Handbook of social psychology*. (2nd ed.) Reading, Mass.: Addison-Wesley, 1969.

LOCKE, J. *An essay concerning human understanding*. 1690. As noted in B. Russell, *A history of western philosophy*. New York: Simon and Schuster, 1945. Pp. 604–647.

MCDOUGALL, W. *An introduction to social psychology*. London: Methuen, 1908.

MILGRAM, S. Behavioral study of obedience. *Journal of Abnormal and Social Psychology*, 1963, 67, 371–378.

MURCHISON, C. (Ed.) *A handbook of social psychology*. Worcester, Mass.: Clark University Press, 1935.

NEWCOMB, T. M. *The acquaintance process*. New York: Holt, Rinehart, and Winston, 1961.

ORNE, M. T. On the social psychology of the psychological experiment: With particular reference to demand characteristics and their implications. *American Psychologist*, 1962, 17, 776–783.

ROETHLISBERGER, F. J., and DICKSON, W. J. *Management and the worker: An account of a research program conducted by the Western Electric Company, Hawthorne Works, Chicago.* Cambridge, Mass.: Harvard University Press, 1939.

ROSENBERG, M. J. When dissonance fails: On eliminating evaluation apprehension from attitude measurement. *Journal of Personality and Social Psychology*, 1965, 1, 28–42.

ROSENTHAL, R. *Experimenter effects in behavioral research.* New York: Appleton-Century-Crofts, 1966.

ROSS, E. *Social psychology: An outline and source book.* New York: Macmillan, 1908.

SAHAKIAN, W. *Systematic social psychology.* New York: Chandler, 1974.

SHERIF, M. *The psychology of social norms.* New York: Harper & Row, 1936.

TRIPLETT, N. The dynamogenic factors in pacemaking and competition. *American Journal of Psychology*, 1897, 9, 507–533.

WINCH, R. F. *Mate-selection: A study of complementary needs.* New York: Harper & Row, 1958.

ZAJONC, R. Social facilitation. *Science*, 1965, 149, 269–274.

CHAPTER 2

ARONSON, E., and CARLSMITH, J. M. Experimentation in social psychology. In G. Lindzey and E. Aronson (Eds.) *Handbook of social psychology.* (2nd ed.) Vol. 2. Reading, Mass.: Addison-Wesley, 1968. Pp. 1–79.

BARBER, T. X., and SILVER, M. J. Fact, fiction, and the experimenter bias effect. *Psychological Review*, 1968, 70, No. 6, Part 2.

CAMPBELL, D. T. Factors relevant to the validity of experiments in social settings. *Psychological Bulletin*, 1957, 54, 297–312.

CAMPBELL, D. T., and FISKE, D. W. Convergent and discriminant validation by the multitrait-multimethod matrix. *Psychological Bulletin*, 1959, 56, 81–105.

CAMPBELL, D. T., SIEGMAN, C., and REES, M. B. Direction-of-wording effects in the relationships between scales. *Psychological Bulletin*, 1967, 68, 293–303.

CHESLER, M., and SCHMUCK, R. Participant observation in a super-patriot discussion group. *Journal of Social Issues*, 1963, 19, 18–30.

CONN, L. K., EDWARDS, C. N., ROSENTHAL, R., and CROWNE, D. Perception of emotion and response to teachers' expectancy by elementary school children. *Psychological Reports*, 1968, 22, 27–34.

CRANO, W. D., and BREWER, M. B. *Principles of research in social psychology.* New York: McGraw-Hill, 1973.

CROWNE, D. P., and MARLOWE, D. *The approval motive.* New York: Wiley, 1964.

DURAND, J. Mortality estimates from Roman tombstone inscriptions. *American Journal of Sociology*, 1960, 65, 365–373.

EDWARDS, A. L. *The social desirability variable in personality assessment and research.* New York: Holt, 1957.

Esquire. The great celebrity ball. November, 1974, 108–109.

FESTINGER, L., REICKEN, H. W., and SCHACHTER, S. *When prophecy fails.* Minneapolis, Minn.: University of Minnesota Press, 1956.

FREEDMAN, J. L. Role-playing: Psychology by consensus. *Journal of Personality and Social Psychology,* 1969, 13, 107–114.

KELMAN, H. C. *A time to speak: On human values and social research.* San Francisco: Jossey-Bass, 1968.

LUCE, R. D., and RAIFFA, H. *Games and decisions.* New York: Wiley, 1957.

McGUIRE, W. J. Suspiciousness of experimenter's intent. In R. Rosenthal and R. L. Rosnow (Eds.) *Artifact in behavioral research.* New York: Academic Press, 1969. Pp. 13–58.

McNEMAR, Q. Opinion-attitude methodology. *Psychological Bulletin,* 1946, 43, 289–374.

MERTON, R. *Social theory and social structure.* Glencoe, Ill.: Free Press, 1957.

MILGRAM, S. Behavioral study of obedience. *Journal of Abnormal and Social Psychology,* 1963, 67, 371–378.

OKSNER, P. W., and SHAVER, K. G. Level of experimental sophistication, self-esteem, and attitudes toward psychological research following deception. Paper presented at the meeting of the Southern Society for Philosophy and Psychology, Knoxville, Tenn., 1973.

ORA, J. P. Personality characteristics of college freshman volunteers for psychological experiments. Unpublished master's thesis, Vanderbilt University, 1966.

ORNE, M. T. The demand characteristics of an experimental design and their implications. Paper presented at the American Psychological Association meeting, Cincinnati, Ohio, September, 1959.

ORNE, M. T. On the social psychology of the psychological experiment: With particular reference to demand characteristics and their implications. *American Psychologist,* 1962, 17, 776–783.

ORNE, M. T. Demand characteristics and the new concept of quasi-controls. In R. Rosenthal and R. L. Rosnow (Eds.) *Artifact in behavioral research.* New York: Academic Press, 1969. Pp. 143–179.

PILIAVIN, I. M., RODIN, J., and PILIAVIN, J. A. Good samaritanism: An underground phenomenon? *Journal of Personality and Social Psychology,* 1969, 13, 289–299.

PILIAVIN, J. A., and PILIAVIN, I. M. Effects of blood on reactions to a victim. *Journal of Personality and Social Psychology,* 1972, 23, 353–361.

POPPER, K. R. *The logic of scientific discovery.* New York: Basic Books, 1959.

RORER, L. G. The great response-style myth. *Psychological Bulletin,* 1965, 63, 129–156.

ROSENBERG, M. J. When dissonance fails: On eliminating evaluation apprehension from attitude measurement. *Journal of Personality and Social Psychology,* 1965, 1, 28–42.

ROSENBERG, M. J. The conditions and consequences of evaluation apprehension. In R. Rosenthal and R. L. Rosnow (Eds.) *Artifact in behavioral research.* New York: Academic Press, 1969. Pp. 279–349.

ROSENTHAL, R. *Experimenter effects in behavioral research.* New York: Appleton-Century-Crofts, 1966.

ROSENTHAL, R., and FODE, K. L. The effect of experimenter bias on the performance of the albino rat. *Behavioral Science*, 1963, 8, 183–189. (a)

ROSENTHAL, R., and FODE, K. L. Three experiments in experimenter bias. *Psychological Reports*, 1963, 12, 491–511. (b)

ROSENTHAL, R., and JACOBSEN, L. *Pygmalion in the classroom: Teacher expectation and pupils' intellectual development*. New York: Holt, Rinehart, and Winston, 1968.

ROSENTHAL, R., and ROSNOW, R. L. The volunteer subject. In R. Rosenthal and R. L. Rosnow (Eds.) *Artifact in behavioral research*. New York: Academic Press, 1969. Pp. 59–118.

ROSS, H. L., and CAMPBELL, D. T. The Connecticut speed crackdown: A study of the effects of legal change. In H. L. Ross (Ed.) *Perspectives on the social order*. New York: McGraw-Hill, 1968. Pp. 30–35.

SCHACHTER, S., and SINGER, J. E. Cognitive, social, and physiological determinants of emotional state. *Psychological Review*, 1962, 69, 379–399.

SEEMAN, J. Deception in psychological research. *American Psychologist*, 1969, 24, 1025–1028.

SILVERMAN, I., SCHULMAN, A. D., and WIESENTHAL, D. L. Effects of deceiving and debriefing psychological subjects on performance in later experiments. *Journal of Personality and Social Psychology*, 1970, 14, 203–212.

SLETTO, R. F. *A construction of personality scales by the criterion of internal consistency*. Hanover, N.H.: Sociological Press, 1937.

STRICKER, L. J. The true deceiver. *Psychological Bulletin*, 1967, 68, 13–20.

THIBAUT, J. W., and RIECKEN, H. W. Some determinants and consequences of the perception of social causality. *Journal of Personality*, 1955, 24, 113–133.

WEBB, E. J., CAMPBELL, D. T., SCHWARTZ, R. D., and SECHREST, L. *Unobtrusive measures: Nonreactive research in the social sciences*. Chicago: Rand McNally, 1966.

WEICK, K. E. Systematic observational methods. In G. Lindzey and E. Aronson (Eds.) *Handbook of social psychology*. (2nd ed.) Vol. 2. Reading, Mass.: Addison-Wesley, 1969. Pp. 357–451.

CHAPTER 3

ALLPORT, F. H. *Theories of perception and the concept of structure*. New York: Wiley, 1955.

ANDERSON, N. H., and HUBERT, S. Effects of concomitant verbal recall on order effects in personality impression formation. *Journal of Verbal Learning and Verbal Behavior*, 1963, 2, 379–391.

ASCH, S. E. Forming impressions of personality. *Journal of Abnormal and Social Psychology*, 1946, 41, 258–290.

BATESON, G., JACKSON, D. D., HALEY, J., and WEAKLAND, J. H. Toward a theory of schizophrenia. *Behavioral Science*, 1956, 1, 251–264.

BRUNER, J. S. Going beyond the information given. In J. S. Bruner, E. Brunswik, L. Festinger, F. Heider, K. F. Muenzinger, C. E. Osgood, and

D. Rapaport (Eds.) *Contemporary approaches to cognition.* Cambridge, Mass.: Harvard University Press, 1957.

BRUNSWIK, E. *Wahrnemung und Gegenstandwelt.* Leipzig and Vienna: Deuticke, 1934.

DUNCAN, S., JR., and NIEDEREHE, G. On signalling that it's your turn to speak. *Journal of Experimental Social Psychology,* 1974, 10, 234–247.

EKMAN, P. Communication through nonverbal behavior. In S. S. Tomkins and C. E. Izard (Eds.) *Affect, cognition, and personality.* New York: Springer, 1965. Pp. 390–442.

EKMAN, P. The recognition and display of facial behavior in literate and non-literate cultures. *Proceedings, American Psychological Association Convention,* 1968, 3, 727.

EKMAN, P. Universals and cultural differences in facial expression of emotion. In J. K. Cole (Ed.) *Nebraska Symposium on Motivation, 1971.* Lincoln, Neb.: University of Nebraska Press, 1972. Pp. 207–283.

EKMAN, P., and FRIESEN, W. V. Nonverbal leakage and clues to deception. *Psychiatry,* 1969, 32, 88–105.

EKMAN, P., and FRIESEN, W. V. Constants across culture in the face and emotion. *Journal of Personality and Social Psychology,* 1971, 17, 124–129.

EKMAN, P., and FRIESEN, W. V. Detecting deception from the body or face. *Journal of Personality and Social Psychology,* 1974, 29, 288–298.

EKMAN, P., FRIESEN, W. V., and ELLSWORTH, P. *Emotion in the human face: Guidelines for research and an integration of findings.* New York: Pergamon Press, 1972.

EKMAN, P., FRIESEN, W. V., and TOMKINS, S. S. Facial affect scoring technique (FAST): A first validity study. *Semiotica,* 1971, 3, 37–58.

ELLSWORTH, P., CARLSMITH, J. M., and HENSON, A. The stare as a stimulus to flight in human subjects: A series of field experiments. *Journal of Personality and Social Psychology,* 1972, 21, 302–311.

EXLINE, R. Visual interaction: The glances of power and preference. In J. Cole (Ed.) *Nebraska Symposium on Motivation 1971.* Lincoln, Neb.: University of Nebraska Press, 1972. Pp. 163–206.

FELEKY, A. M. *Feelings and emotions.* New York: Pioneer Press, 1924.

FRIJDA, N. H. Recognition of emotion. In L. Berkowitz (Ed.) *Advances in experimental social psychology.* Vol. 4. New York: Academic Press, 1969. Pp. 167–223.

GOFFMAN, E. *The presentation of self in everyday life.* Garden City, N.Y.: Doubleday, 1959.

GIBSON, J. J. *The perception of the visual world.* Boston: Houghton Mifflin, 1950.

GORDON, C. Self conceptions: Configurations of content. In C. Gordon and K. J. Gergen (Eds.) *The self in social interaction.* Vol. 1. New York: Wiley, 1968.

HALL, E. T. *The silent language.* New York: Fawcett, 1959.

HALL, E. T. *The hidden dimension.* New York: Doubleday, 1966.

HALL, E. T. Proxemics. *Current Anthropology,* 1968, 9, 83–95.

HARGREAVES, W. A., and STARKWEATHER, J. A. Recognition of speaker identity. *Language and Speech,* 1963, 6, 63–67.

HEIDER, F. *The psychology of interpersonal relations.* New York: Wiley, 1958.

IZARD, C. E. Cross-cultural research findings on development in recognition of facial behavior. *Proceedings, American Psychological Association Convention*, 1968, 3, 727.

IZARD, C. E. The emotions and emotion constructs in personality and culture research. In R. B. Cattell (Ed.) *Handbook of modern personality theory.* Chicago: Aldine, 1970.

JONES, E. E., and GERARD, H. B. *Foundations of social psychology.* New York: Wiley, 1967.

KANFER, F. H. Verbal rate, content, and adjustment ratings in experimentally structured interviews. *Journal of Abnormal and Social Psychology*, 1959, 58, 305–311.

KANFER, F. H. Verbal rate, eyeblink, and content in structured psychiatric interviews. *Journal of Abnormal and Social Psychology*, 1960, 61, 341–347.

KELLEY, H. H. The warm-cold variable in first impressions of persons. *Journal of Personality*, 1950, 18, 431–439.

KINZEL, A. Body buffer zone in violent prisoners. *American Journal of Psychiatry*, 1970, 127, 59–64.

KOFFKA, K. *Principles of gestalt psychology.* New York: Harcourt, Brace, 1935.

KÖHLER, W. *Gestalt psychology.* New York: Liveright, 1929.

KUHN, M. H., and McPARTLAND, T. S. An empirical investigation of self-attitudes. *American Sociological Review*, 1954, 19, 68–76.

LABOV, W. The logic of nonstandard English. In F. Williams (Ed.) *Language and poverty: Perspectives on a theme.* Chicago: Markham, 1970. Pp. 153–189.

LIPPMANN, W. *Public opinion.* New York: Harcourt, Brace, 1922.

LUCHINS, A. S. Primacy-recency in impression formation. In C. I. Hovland (Ed.) *The order of presentation in persuasion.* New Haven, Conn.: Yale University Press, 1957. Pp. 33–61.

MAHL, G. F. Speech disturbances and emotional verbal content in initial interviews. Paper presented at Eastern Psychological Association meetings, 1957.

MEHRABIAN, A. Inference of attitude from the posture, orientation, and distance of a communicator. *Journal of Consulting and Clinical Psychology*, 1968, 32, 296–308.

SCHLOSBERG, H. The description of facial expressions in terms of two dimensions. *Journal of Experimental Psychology*, 1952, 44, 229–237.

SOMMER, R. *Personal space: The behavioral basis of design.* Englewood Cliffs, N.J.: Prentice-Hall, 1969.

SOSKIN, W. F., and KAUFFMAN, P. E. Judgment of emotion in word-free voice samples. *Journal of Communication*, 1961, 11, 73–80.

TOMKINS, S. S. *Affect, imagery, consciousness.* Vol. 1: *The positive affects.* New York: Springer, 1962.

TOMKINS, S. S. *Affect, imagery, consciousness.* Vol. 2: *The negative affects.* New York: Springer, 1963.

THURSTONE, L. L. *Multiple factor analysis.* Chicago: University of Chicago Press, 1947.

WEITZ, S. (Ed.) *Nonverbal communication: Readings with commentary.* New York: Oxford University Press, 1974.

WERTHEIMER, M. Experimentelle Studien über das Sehen von Bewegung. *Zeitschrift für Psychologie*, 1912, 61, 161–265.

WISHNER, J. Reanalysis of "impressions of personality." *Psychological Review*, 1960, 67, 96–112.

WOODWORTH, R. S. *Experimental psychology*. New York: Holt, 1938.

YNGVE, V. H. On getting a word in edgewise. *Papers from the sixth regional meeting, Chicago Linguistic Society*, 1970, 567–577.

CHAPTER 4

ADORNO, T. W., FRENKEL-BRUNSWIK, E., LEVINSON, D. J., and SANFORD, R. N. *The authoritarian personality*. New York: Harper, 1950.

AJZEN, I. Attribution of dispositions to an actor: Effects of perceived decision freedom and behavioral utilities. *Journal of Personality and Social Psychology*, 1971, 18, 144–156.

ALLPORT, F. H. *Theories of perception and the concept of structure*. New York: Wiley, 1955.

ALLPORT, G. W. *Pattern and growth in personality*. New York: Holt, Rinehart, and Winston, 1961.

ANDERSON, N. H. Primacy effects in personality impression formation using a generalized order effect paradigm. *Journal of Personality and Social Psychology*. 1965, 2, 1–9.

ANDERSON, N. H. A simple model for information integration. In R. P. Abelson, E. Aronson, W. J. McGuire, T. M. Newcomb, M. J. Rosenberg, and P. H. Tannenbaum (Eds.) *Theories of cognitive consistency: A sourcebook*. Chicago: Rand McNally, 1968. Pp. 731–743.

ANDERSON, N. H. Cognitive algebra: Integration theory applied to social attribution. In L. Berkowitz (Ed.) *Advances in experimental social psychology*. Vol. 7. New York: Academic Press, 1974. Pp. 1–102.

ANDERSON, N. H., and BARRIOS, A. A. Primacy effects in personality impression formation. *Journal of Abnormal and Social Psychology*, 1961, 63, 346–350.

ANDERSON, N. H., and HUBERT, S. Effect of concomitant verbal recall on order effects in personality impression formation. *Journal of Verbal Learning and Verbal Behavior*, 1963, 2, 379–391.

ANDERSON, N. H., and JACOBSON, A. Effect of stimulus inconsistency and discounting instructions in personality impression formation. *Journal of Personality and Social Psychology*, 1965, 2, 531–539.

ASCH, S. E. Forming impressions of personality. *Journal of Abnormal and Social Psychology*, 1946, 41, 258–290.

ASHLEY, W. R., HARPER, R. S., and RUNYON, D. L. The perceived size of coins in normal and hypnotically induced economic states. *American Journal of Psychology*, 1951, 64, 564–572.

BIERI, J. Complexity-simplicity as a personality variable in cognitive and preferential behavior. In D. W. Fiske and S. R. Maddi (Eds.) *Functions of varied experience*. Homewood, Ill.: Dorsey Press, 1961.

BRUNER, J. S. Going beyond the information given. In J. S. Bruner, E. Brunswik, L. Festinger, F. Heider, K. F. Muenzinger, C. E. Osgood, and D. Rapaport (Eds.) *Contemporary approaches to cognition*. Cambridge, Mass.: Harvard University Press, 1957.

BRUNER, J. S., and GOODMAN, C. D. Value and need as organizing factors in perception. *Journal of Abnormal and Social Psychology*, 1947, 42, 33–44.

BRUNER, J. S., and POSTMAN, L. Symbolic value as an organizing factor in perception. *Journal of Social Psychology*, 1948, 27, 203–208.

BRUNER, J. S., SHAPIRO, D., and TAGUIRI, R. The meaning of traits in isolation and in combination. In R. Taguiri and L. Petrullo (Eds.) *Person perception and interpersonal behavior*. Stanford, Cal.: Stanford University Press, 1958. Pp. 277–288.

BRUNER, J. S., and TAGUIRI, R. The perception of people. In G. Lindzey (Ed.) *Handbook of social psychology*. Vol. 2. Reading, Mass.: Addison-Wesley, 1954. Pp. 634–654.

BRUNSWIK, E. *Wahrnemung und Gegenstandwelt*. Leipzig and Vienna: Deuticke, 1934.

BUCKHOUT, R. Eyewitness testimony. *Scientific American*, 1974, 231, 23–31.

BYRNE, D., CLORE, G. L., GRIFFITT, W., LAMBERTH, J., and MITCHELL, H. E. Information integration theory and reinforcement theory as approaches to interpersonal attraction. *Journal of Personality and Social Psychology*, 1973, 28, 313–320.

CATTELL, R. B., and WENIG, P. W. Dynamic and cognitive factors controlling misperception. *Journal of Abnormal and Social Psychology*, 1952, 47, 797–809.

CHAIKIN, A. L., and DARLEY, J. M., JR. Victim or perpetrator: Defensive attribution of responsibility and the need for order and justice. *Journal of Personality and Social Psychology*, 1973, 25, 268–275.

CHRISTENSON, L. Person perception accuracy as a function of ethnic group and familiarity. *Perceptual and Motor Skills*, 1970, 31, 510.

CHRISTENSON, L. The influence of trait, sex, and information on accuracy of personality assessment. *Journal of Personality Assessment*, 1974, 38, 130–135.

CHRISTIE, R., and COOK, R. A guide to published literature relating to the authoritarian personality through 1956. *Journal of Psychology*, 1958, 45, 171–199.

CHRISTIE, R., and GEIS, F. L. (Eds.) *Studies in Machiavellianism*. New York: Academic Press, 1970.

CHRISTIE, R., and JAHODA, M. (Eds.) *Studies in the scope and method of "The authoritarian personality."* New York: Macmillan (Free Press), 1954.

CLINE, V. B. Interpersonal perception. In B. A. Maher (Ed.) *Progress in experimental personality research*. Vol. 1. New York: Academic Press, 1964. Pp. 221–284.

CRONBACH, L. J. Processes affecting scores on "understanding of others" and "assumed similarity." *Psychological Bulletin*, 1955, 52, 177–193.

DEUTSCH, M., and KRAUSS, R. M. *Theories in social psychology.* New York: Basic Books, 1965.

EDWARDS, B. C., and MCWILLIAMS, J. M. Expressor sex, perceiver personality, and cognitive perception. *Journal of Psychology,* 1974, 87, 137–141.

ERIKSEN, B. A., and ERIKSEN, C. W. *Perception and personality.* Morristown, N.J.: General Learning Press, 1971.

FISHBEIN, M., and HUNTER, R. Summation versus balance in attitude organization and change. *Journal of Abnormal and Social Psychology,* 1964, 69, 505–510.

HARVEY, O. J., HUNT, D. E., and SCHRODER, H. M. *Conceptual systems and personality organization.* New York: Wiley, 1961.

HASTORF, A. H., RICHARDSON, S. A., and DORNBUSCH, S. M. The problem of relevance in the study of person perception. In R. Taguiri and L. Petrullo (Eds.) *Person perception and interpersonal behavior.* Stanford, Cal.: Stanford University Press, 1958. Pp. 54–62.

HASTORF, A. H., SCHNEIDER, D. J., and POLEFKA, J. *Person perception.* Reading, Mass.: Addison-Wesley, 1970.

HATCH, R. S. *An evaluation of a forced choice differential accuracy approach to the measurement of supervisory empathy.* Englewood Cliffs, N.J.: Prentice-Hall, 1962.

HEIDER, F. *The psychology of interpersonal relations.* New York: Wiley, 1958.

HENDRICK, C. Averaging *vs.* summation in impression formation. *Perceptual and Motor Skills,* 1968, 27, 1295–1302.

HJELLE, L. Personality characteristics associated with interpersonal accuracy. *Journal of Counseling Psychology,* 1969, 16, 579–581.

HOCHBERG, J. E., and GLEITMAN, H. Toward a reformulation of the perception-motivation dichotomy. In J. S. Bruner and D. Krech (Eds.) *Perception and personality: A symposium.* Durham, N.C.: Duke University Press, 1950.

HODGES, B. Adding and averaging models for information integration. *Psychological Review,* 1973, 80, 80–85.

HOWES, D. H., and SOLOMON, R. L. Visual duration threshold as a function of word probability. *Journal of Experimental Psychology,* 1950, 41, 401–410.

HYMAN, H. H., and SHEATSLEY, P. B. "The authoritarian personality"—a methodological critique. In R. Christie and M. Jahoda (Eds.) *Studies in the scope and method of "The authoritarian personality."* New York: Macmillan (Free Press), 1954. Pp. 50–122.

JONES, E. E., and DAVIS, K. E. From acts to dispositions: The attribution process in person perception. In L. Berkowitz (Ed.) *Advances in experimental social psychology,* Vol. 2. New York: Academic Press, 1965. Pp. 219–266.

JONES, E. E., DAVIS, K. E., and GERGEN, K. J. Role playing variations and their informational value for person perception. *Journal of Abnormal and Social Psychology,* 1961, 63, 302–310.

JONES, E. E., and HARRIS, V. A. The attribution of attitudes. *Journal of Experimental Social Psychology,* 1967, 3, 1–24.

JONES, E. E., KANOUSE, D. E., KELLEY, H. H., NISBETT, R. E., VALINS, S., and WEINER, B. (Eds.) *Attribution: Perceiving the causes of behavior.* Morristown, N.J.: General Learning Press, 1972.

JONES, E. E., ROCK, L., SHAVER, K. G., GOETHALS, G. R., and WARD, L. M. Pattern of performance and ability attribution: An unexpected primacy effect. *Journal of Personality and Social Psychology*, 1968, 10, 317–340.

JONES, E. E., WORCHEL, S., GOETHALS, G. R., and GRUMET, J. F. Prior expectancy and behavioral extremity as determinants of attitude attribution. *Journal of Experimental Social Psychology*, 1971, 7, 59–80.

KAPLAN, M., and ANDERSON, N. H. Information integration theory and reinforcement theory as approaches to interpersonal attraction. *Journal of Personality and Social Psychology*, 1973, 28, 301–312.

KELLEY, H. H. The warm-cold variable in first impressions of persons. *Journal of Personality*, 1950, 18, 431–439.

KELLEY, H. H. Attribution theory in social psychology. In D. Levine (Ed.) *Nebraska symposium on motivation 1967*. Lincoln, Neb.: University of Nebraska Press, 1967. Pp. 192–238.

KELLEY, H. H. *Attribution in social interaction*. Morristown, N.J.: General Learning Press, 1971.

KELLEY, H. H. The process of causal attribution. *American Psychologist*, 1973, 28, 107–128.

KELLEY, H. H., and STAHELSKI, A. The inference of intention from moves in the prisoner's dilemma game. *Journal of Experimental Social Psychology*, 1970, 6, 409–419.

KELLY, G. A. *The psychology of personal constructs*. (1st ed.) Vols. 1 and 2. New York: Norton, 1955.

KELLY, G. A. *A theory of personality: The psychology of personal constructs*. New York: Norton, 1963.

KIRSCHT, J. P., and DILLEHAY, R. C. *Dimensions of authoritarianism: A review of research and theory*. Lexington, Ky.: University of Kentucky Press, 1967.

LAMBERT, W. W., SOLOMON, R. L., and WATSON, P. D. Reinforcement and extinction as factors in size estimation. *Journal of Experimental Psychology*, 1949, 39, 637–641.

LEON, M., ODEN, G. C., and ANDERSON, N. H. Functional measurement of social values. *Journal of Personality and Social Psychology*, 1973, 27, 301–310.

LERNER, M. J. The unjust consequences of a need to believe in a just world. Paper presented at the meeting of the American Psychological Association, New York, September, 1966.

LERNER, M. J., and MATTHEWS, G. Reactions to the suffering of others under conditions of indirect responsibility. *Journal of Personality and Social Psychology*, 1967, 5, 319–325.

LEVINE, R., CHEIN, I., and MURPHY, G. The relation of the intensity of a need to the amount of perceptual distortion. *Journal of Psychology*, 1942, 13, 283–293.

MARTIN, J. G., and WESTIE, F. R. The tolerant personality. *American Sociological Review*, 1959, 24, 521–528.

MCARTHUR, L. A. The how and the what of why: Some determinants and consequences of causal attribution. *Journal of Personality and Social Psychology*, 1972, 22, 171–193.

MCGINNIES, E. Emotionality and perceptual defense. *Psychological Review*, 1949, 56, 244–251.

MEAD, G. H. *Mind, self, and society*. Chicago: University of Chicago Press, 1934.

MESSICK, D. W., and REEDER, G. D. Roles, occupations, behaviors, and attributions. *Journal of Experimental Social Psychology*, 1974, 10, 126–132.

NEWCOMB, T. M. *The acquaintance process*. New York: Holt, Rinehart, and Winston, 1961.

NEWTSON, D. Dispositional inference from effects of actions: Effects chosen and effects forgone. *Journal of Experimental Psychology*, 1974, 10, 489–496.

NISBETT, R. E., and VALINS, S. Perceiving the causes of one's own behavior. In E. E. Jones, D. E. Kanouse, H. H. Kelley, R. E. Nisbett, S. Valins, and B. Weiner (Eds.) *Attribution: Perceiving the causes of behavior*. Morristown, N.J.: General Learning Press, 1972. Pp. 63–78.

NORMAN, W. T. Toward an adequate taxonomy of personality attributes: Replicated factor structure in peer nomination personality ratings. *Journal of Abnormal and Social Psychology*, 1963, 66, 574–585.

OSGOOD, C. E., SUCI, G. J., and TANNENBAUM, P. H. *The measurement of meaning*. Urbana, Ill.: University of Illinois Press, 1957.

PASSINI, F. T., and NORMAN, W. T. A universal conception of personality structure? *Journal of Personality and Social Psychology*, 1966, 4, 44–49.

POSTMAN, L., BRUNER, J. S., and McGINNIES, E. Personal values as selective factors in perception. *Journal of Abnormal and Social Psychology*, 1948, 43, 142–154.

PROSHANSKY, H. M., and MURPHY, G. The effects of reward and punishment on perception. *Journal of Psychology*, 1942, 13, 295–305.

RODIN, M. J. The informativeness of trait descriptions. *Journal of Personality and Social Psychology*, 1972, 21, 341–344.

ROKEACH, M. *The open and closed mind*. New York: Basic Books, 1960.

ROSENBERG, M. J. The conditions and consequences of evaluation apprehension. In R. Rosenthal and R. L. Rosnow (Eds.) *Artifact in behavioral research*. New York: Academic Press, 1969. Pp. 279–349.

ROSENBERG, S. Mathematical models of social behavior. In G. Lindzey and E. Aronson (Eds.) *Handbook of social psychology*. (2nd ed.) Vol. 1. Reading, Mass.: Addison-Wesley, 1968. Pp. 179–244.

ROSENBERG, S., and SEDLAK, A. Structural representations of implicit personality theory. In L. Berkowitz (Ed.) *Advances in experimental social psychology*. Vol. 6. New York: Academic Press, 1972. Pp. 235–297.

ROTTER, J. B. Generalized expectancies for internal versus external locus of control of reinforcement. *Psychological Monographs*, 1966, 80, 1–28.

SCHAFER, R., and MURPHY, G. The role of autism in a visual figure-ground relationship. *Journal of Experimental Psychology*, 1943, 32, 335–343.

SHAVER, K. G. Defensive attribution: Effects of severity and relevance on the responsibility assigned for an accident. *Journal of Personality and Social Psychology*, 1970, 14, 101–113.

SHAVER, K. G. *An introduction to attribution processes*. Cambridge, Mass.: Winthrop, 1975.

SHAW, M. E., and SULZER, J. L. An empirical test of Heider's levels in attribution of responsibility. *Journal of Abnormal and Social Psychology*, 1964, 69, 39–46.

SNYDER, M., and JONES, E. E. Attitude attribution when behavior is constrained. *Journal of Experimental Social Psychology*, 1974, 585–600.

SORRENTINO, R. M., and BOUTILIER, R. G. Evaluation of a victim as a function of fate similarity/dissimilarity. *Journal of Experimental Social Psychology,* 1974, 10, 83–92.

SOSIS, R. H. Internal-external control and the perception of responsibility of another for an accident. *Journal of Personality and Social Psychology,* 1974, 30, 393–399.

STEINER, I., and JOHNSON, H. Authoritarianism and "tolerance of trait inconsistency." *Journal of Abnormal and Social Psychology,* 1963, 67, 388–391.

STOTLAND, E., SHERMAN, S., and SHAVER, K. G. *Empathy and birth order: Some experimental explorations.* Lincoln, Neb.: University of Nebraska Press, 1971.

TAFT, R. The ability to judge people. *Psychological Bulletin,* 1955, 52, 1–23.

TAFT, R. Accuracy of empathic judgments of acquaintances and strangers. *Journal of Personality and Social Psychology,* 1966, 3, 600–603.

TAGUIRI, R. Person perception. In G. Lindzey and E. Aronson (Eds.) *Handbook of social psychology.* (2nd ed.) Vol. 3. Reading, Mass.: Addison-Wesley, 1969. Pp. 395–449.

THOMPSON, D. D. Attributions of ability from patterns of performance under competitive and cooperative conditions. *Journal of Personality and Social Psychology,* 1972, 23, 302–308.

THURSTONE, L. L. *A factorial study of perception.* Chicago: University of Chicago Press, 1944.

TUPES, E. C., and CHRISTAL, R. E. Stability of personality trait rating factors obtained under diverse conditions. *USAF WADC Technical Note,* 1958, No. 58–61.

VERNON, P. E. Some characteristics of the good judge of personality. *Journal of Social Psychology,* 1933, 4, 42–58.

WALSTER, E. Assignment of responsibility for an accident. *Journal of Personality and Social Psychology,* 1966, 3, 73–79.

WARR, P. B., and KNAPPER, C. *The perception of people and events.* London: Wiley, 1968.

WEINER, B. *Achievement motivation and attribution theory.* Morristown, N.J.: General Learning Press, 1974.

WISHNER, J. Reanalysis of "Impressions of personality." *Psychological Review,* 1960, 67, 96–112.

WRIGHTSMAN, L. S. Attitudinal and personality correlates of presidential voting preferences. Paper presented at the meeting of the American Psychological Association, Chicago, September, 1965.

CHAPTER 5

ALLPORT, G. W. Attitudes. In C. Murchison (Ed.) *Handbook of social psychology.* Worcester, Mass.: Clark University Press, 1935. Pp. 798–884.

ALLPORT, G. W. *The nature of prejudice.* Reading, Mass.: Addison-Wesley, 1954.

ALLPORT, G. W. *The nature of prejudice.* (Abr. ed.) New York: Doubleday, Anchor Books, 1958.

ALLPORT, G. W., and KRAMER, B. M. Some roots of prejudice. *Journal of Psychology*, 1946, 22, 9–39.

ARONSON, E., and CARLSMITH, J. M. Effect of severity of threat on the devaluation of forbidden behavior. *Journal of Abnormal and Social Psychology*, 1963, 66, 584–588.

BANDURA, A., and WALTERS, R. *Social learning and personality development.* New York: Holt, Rinehart, and Winston, 1963.

BOGARDUS, E. S. Measuring social distances. *Journal of Applied Sociology*, 1925, 9, 299–308.

BRIGHAM, J. C. Ethnic stereotypes. *Psychological Bulletin*, 1971, 76, 15–38.

BRIGHAM, J. C. Ethnic stereotypes and attitudes: A different mode of analysis. *Journal of Personality*, 1973, 41, 206–233.

BROWN, R. *Social psychology.* Glencoe, Ill.: Free Press, 1965.

BYRNE, D., and WONG, T. J. Racial prejudice, interpersonal attraction, and assumed similarity of attitudes. *Journal of Abnormal and Social Psychology*, 1962, 65, 246–253.

CAMPBELL, A. *White attitudes toward black people.* Ann Arbor, Mich.: Institute for Social Research, 1971.

CARMICHAEL, F. F., and HAMILTON, C. V. *Black power: The politics of liberation in America.* New York: Random House, 1967.

COOK, S. W. Motives in a conceptual analysis of attitude-related behavior. In W. J. Arnold and D. Levine (Eds.) *Nebraska Symposium on Motivation, 1969.* Lincoln, Neb.: University of Nebraska Press, 1970. Pp. 179–231.

DAWES, R. M. *Fundamentals of attitude measurement.* New York: Wiley, 1972.

DEFLEUR, M. L., and WESTIE, F. R. Verbal attitudes and overt acts: An experiment on the salience of attitudes. *American Sociological Review*, 1958, 23, 667–673.

DILLEHAY, R. C. On the irrelevance of the classical negative evidence concerning the effect of attitudes on behavior. *American Psychologist*, 1973, 10, 887–891.

DOLLARD, J., DOOB, L. W., MILLER, N. E., MOWRER, O. H., and SEARS, R. R. *Frustration and aggression.* New Haven, Conn.: Yale University Press, 1939.

EHRLICH, H. J., and RINEHART, J. W. A brief report on the methodology of stereotype research. *Social Forces*, 1965, 43, 564–575.

FENDRICH, J. M. A study of the association among verbal attitudes, commitment, and overt behavior in different experimental situations. *Social Forces*, 1967, 45, 347–355.

FISHBEIN, M. The prediction of behavior from attitudinal variables. In K. K. Sereno and C. C. Mortensen (Eds.) *Advances in communication research.* New York: Harper and Row, 1972.

FISHBEIN, M., and AJZEN, I. Attitudes and opinions. *Annual Review of Psychology*, 1972, 23, 487–543.

FISHBEIN, M., and AJZEN, I. *Belief, attitude, intention, and behavior: An introduction to theory and research.* Reading, Mass.: Addison-Wesley, 1975.

FREUD, S. *New introductory lectures on psychoanalysis*. New York: Norton, 1933.

GILBERT, G. M. Stereotype persistence and change among college students. *Journal of Abnormal and Social Psychology*, 1951, 46, 245–254.

GLUECK, S., and GLUECK, E. *Unraveling juvenile delinquency*. New York: Commonwealth Fund, 1950.

GREEN, B. F. Attitude measurement. In G. Lindzey (Ed.) *Handbook of social psychology*. Vol. 1. Cambridge, Mass.: Addison-Wesley, 1954.

GREEN, J. A. Attitudinal and situational determinants of intended behavior to Negroes. Paper presented at the meeting of the Western Psychological Association, Vancouver, June, 1969.

HARDING, J., KUTNER, B., PROSHANSKY, H., and CHEIN, I. Prejudice and ethnic relations. In G. Lindzey and E. Aronson (Eds.) *Handbook of social psychology*. (2nd ed.) Vol. 5. Reading, Mass.: Addison-Wesley, 1969. Pp. 1–76.

HAYS, W. L. *Statistics for psychologists*. New York: Holt, Rinehart and Winston, 1963.

HOROWITZ, E. L., and HOROWITZ, R. E. Development of social attitudes in children. *Sociometry*, 1938, 1, 301–338.

HUGHES, E. C., and HUGHES, H. M. *Where peoples meet: Racial and ethnic frontiers*. Glencoe, Ill.: Free Press, 1952.

JONES, E. E., and GERARD, H. B. *Foundations of social psychology*. New York: Wiley, 1967.

JONES, E. E., and SIGALL, H. The bogus pipeline: A new paradigm for measuring affect and attitude. *Psychological Bulletin*, 1971, 76, 349–364.

JONES, J. M. *Prejudice and racism*. Reading, Mass.: Addison-Wesley, 1972.

JONES, R. A., and ASHMORE, R. D. The structure of intergroup perception: Categories and dimensions in views of ethnic groups and adjectives used in stereotype research. *Journal of Personality and Social Psychology*, 1973, 25, 428–438.

JONES, R. L. (Ed.) *Black psychology*. New York: Harper & Row, 1972.

KARLINS, M., COFFMAN, T. L., and WALTERS, G. On the fading of social stereotypes: Studies in three generations of college students. *Journal of Personality and Social Psychology*, 1969, 13, 1–16.

KATZ, D., and BRALY, K. W. Racial stereotypes of one-hundred college students. *Journal of Abnormal and Social Psychology*, 1933, 28, 282–290.

KELLY, G. A. *A theory of personality: The psychology of personal constructs*. New York: Norton, 1963.

KIESLER, C. A., COLLINS, B. E., and MILLER, N. *Attitude change: A critical analysis of theoretical approaches*. New York: Wiley, 1969.

KUTNER, B., WILKINS, C., and YARROW, P. R. Verbal attitudes and overt behavior. *Journal of Abnormal and Social Psychology*, 1952, 47, 649–652.

LaPIERE, S. T. Attitudes vs. actions. *Social Forces*, 1934, 13, 230–237.

LERNER, M. J., and MATTHEWS, G. Reactions to suffering of others under conditions of indirect responsibility. *Journal of Personality and Social Psychology*, 1967, 5, 319–325.

LIKERT, R. A technique for the measurement of attitudes. *Archives of Psychology*, 1932, No. 140, 5–53.

LORENZ, K. *On aggression.* New York: Harcourt, Brace, and World, 1966.

LOYE, D. *The healing of a nation.* New York: Norton, 1971.

McGUIRE, W. J. The nature of attitudes and attitude change. In G. Lindzey and E. Aronson (Eds.) *Handbook of social psychology.* (2nd ed.) Vol. 3. Reading, Mass.: Addison-Wesley, 1969. Pp. 136–314.

OSGOOD, C. E., SUCI, G. J., and TANNENBAUM, P. H. *The measurement of meaning.* Urbana, Ill.: University of Illinois Press, 1957.

OSTROM, T. M. The bogus pipeline: A new *ignis fatuus? Psychological Bulletin,* 1973, 79, 252–259.

PETTIGREW, T. F. *Racially separate or together?* New York: McGraw-Hill, 1971.

PORIER, G. W., and LOTT, A. J. Galvanic skin responses and prejudice. *Journal of Personality and Social Psychology,* 1967, 5, 253–259.

RANKIN, R. E., and CAMPBELL, D. T. Galvanic skin response to Negro and white experimenters. *Journal of Abnormal and Social Psychology,* 1955, 51, 30–33.

ROKEACH, M. *The open and closed mind.* New York: Basic Books, 1960.

ROKEACH, M., SMITH, P. W., and EVANS, R. I. Two kinds of prejudice or one? In M. Rokeach (Ed.) *The open and closed mind.* New York: Basic Books, 1960. Pp. 132–168.

ROSS, E. *Social psychology: An outline and source book.* New York: Macmillan, 1908.

SCHACHTER, S. The interaction of cognitive and physiological determinants of emotional state. In L. Berkowitz (Ed.) *Advances in experimental social psychology.* Vol. 1. New York: Academic Press, 1964. Pp. 49–80.

SHAW, M. E., and WRIGHT, J. M. *Scales for the measurement of attitudes.* New York: McGraw-Hill, 1967.

SHERIF, M., and SHERIF, C. *Social psychology.* New York: Harper & Row, 1969.

SIGALL, H., and PAGE, R. Current stereotypes: A little fading, a little faking. *Journal of Personality and Social Psychology,* 1971, 18, 247–255.

SOUTHALL, S. E. *Industry's unfinished business.* New York: Harper, 1950.

STEIN, D. D., HARDYCK, J. E., and SMITH, M. B. Race *and* belief: An open and shut case. *Journal of Personality and Social Psychology,* 1965, 1, 281–289.

THURSTONE, L. L. Attitudes can be measured. *American Journal of Sociology,* 1928, 33, 529–554.

THURSTONE, L. L. *The measurement of social attitudes.* Chicago: University of Chicago Press, 1932.

THURSTONE, L. L., and CHAVE, E. J. *The measurement of attitude.* Chicago: University of Chicago Press, 1929.

TRIANDIS, H. A note on Rokeach's theory of prejudice. *Journal of Abnormal and Social Psychology,* 1961, 62, 184–186.

VIDULICH, R. N., and KREVANICK, F. W. Racial attitudes and emotional response to visual representations of the Negro. *Journal of Social Psychology,* 1966, 68, 85–93.

WESTIE, F. R., and DEFLEUR, M. L. Autonomic responses and their relationship to race attitudes. *Journal of Abnormal and Social Psychology,* 1959, 58, 340–347.

WHITING, J. W. M., and CHILD, I. L. *Child-training and personality: A cross-cultural study.* New Haven, Conn: Yale University Press, 1953.

WICKER, A. W. Attitudes versus actions: The relationship of verbal and overt behavioral responses to attitude objects. *Journal of Social Issues,* 1969, 25, 41–78.

WILLIAMS, R. M., JR. *Strangers next door.* Englewood Cliffs, N.J.: Prentice-Hall, 1964.

WILNER, D. M., WALKLEY, R. P., and COOK, S. W. Residential proximity and intergroup relations in public housing projects. *Journal of Social Issues,* 1952, 8, 45–69.

WRIGHTSMAN, L. S. *Social psychology for the seventies.* Belmont, Calif.: Wadsworth, 1972.

CHAPTER 6

ABELSON, R. P. Psychological implication. In R. P. Abelson *et al.* (Eds.) *Theories of cognitive consistency: A sourcebook.* Chicago: Rand McNally, 1968. Pp. 112–139.

ABELSON, R. P., ARONSON, E., MCGUIRE, W. J., NEWCOMB, T. M., ROSENBERG, M. J., and TANNENBAUM, P. H. (Eds.) *Theories of cognitive consistency: A sourcebook.* Chicago: Rand McNally, 1968.

ABELSON, R. P., and ROSENBERG, M. J. Symbolic psycho-logic: A model of attitudinal cognition. *Behavioral Science,* 1958, 3, 1–13.

ARONSON, E. The psychology of insufficient justification: An analysis of some conflicting data. In S. Feldman (Ed.) *Cognitive consistency: Motivational antecedents and behavioral consequents.* New York: Academic Press, 1966. Pp. 115–136.

ARONSON, E. Dissonance theory: Progress and problems. In R. P. Abelson *et al.* (Eds.) *Theories of cognitive consistency: A sourcebook.* Chicago: Rand McNally, 1968. Pp. 5–27.

ARONSON, E. The theory of cognitive dissonance: A current perspective. In L. Berkowitz (Ed.) *Advances in experimental social psychology.* Vol. 4. New York: Academic Press, 1969. Pp. 2–35.

ARONSON, E., and CARLSMITH, J. M. Effect of the severity of threat on the devaluation of forbidden behavior. *Journal of Abnormal and Social Psychology,* 1963, 66, 584–588.

ARONSON, E., and MILLS, J. The effect of severity of initiation on liking for a group. *Journal of Abnormal and Social Psychology*, 1959, 59, 177–181.

BEM, D. J. An experimental analysis of self-persuasion. *Journal of Experimental Social Psychology*, 1965, 1, 199–218.

BEM, D. J. Self-perception: An alternative interpretation of cognitive dissonance phenomena. *Psychological Review*, 1967, 74, 183–200.

BEM, D. J. The epistemological status of interpersonal simulations: A reply to Jones, Linder, Kiesler, Zanna, and Brehm. *Journal of Experimental Social Psychology*, 1968, 4, 270–274.

BEM, D. J. *Beliefs, attitudes, and human affairs.* Belmont, Cal.: Brooks/Cole, 1970.

BEM, D. J. Self-perception theory. In L. Berkowitz (Ed.) *Advances in experimental social psychology.* Vol. 6. New York: Academic Press, 1972. Pp. 2–62.

BEM, D. J., and McCONNELL, H. K. Testing the self-perception explanation of dissonance phenomena: On the salience of premanipulation attitudes. *Journal of Personality and Social Psychology*, 1970, 14, 23–31.

BREHM, J. W. Postdecision changes in the desirability of alternatives. *Journal of Abnormal and Social Psychology*, 1956, 52, 384–389.

BREHM, J. W., and COHEN, A. R. (Eds.) *Explorations in cognitive dissonance.* New York: Wiley, 1962.

BREHM, M. L., BACK, K. W., and BOGDANOFF, M. D. A physiological effect of cognitive dissonance under stress and deprivation. *Journal of Abnormal and Social Psychology*, 1964, 69, 303–310.

BROWN, R. *Social psychology.* New York: Free Press, 1965.

CARLSMITH, J. M., COLLINS, B. E., and HELMREICH, R. L. Studies in forced compliance: I. The effect of pressure for compliance on attitude change produced by face-to-face role playing and anonymous essay writing. *Journal of Personality and Social Psychology*, 1966, 4, 1–13.

CARTWRIGHT, D., and HARARY, F. Structural balance: A generalization of Heider's theory. *Psychological Review*, 1956, 63, 277–293.

CHAPANIS, N. P., and CHAPANIS, A. Cognitive dissonance: Five years later. *Psychological Bulletin*, 1964, 61, 1–22.

COHEN, A. R. An experiment on small rewards for discrepant compliance and attitude change. In J. W. Brehm and A. R. Cohen (Eds.), *Explorations in cognitive dissonance.* New York: Wiley, 1962. Pp. 73–78.

COLLINS, B. E., and HOYT, M. F. Personal responsibility-for-consequences: An integration and extension for the "forced compliance" literature. *Journal of Experimental Social Psychology*, 1972, 8, 558–593.

COOPER, J. Personal responsibility and dissonance: The role of foreseen consequences. *Journal of Personality and Social Psychology*, 1971, 18, 354–363.

CROCKETT, W. H. Balance, agreement, and subjective evaluations of the P-O-X triads. *Journal of Personality and Social Psychology*, 1974, 29, 102–110.

DARLEY, J. M., JR., and BERSCHEID, E. Increased liking caused by the anticipation of personal contact. *Human Relations*, 1967, 20, 29–40.

DEMBROWSKI, T. M., and PENNEBAKER, J. W. Reactions to severity and nature of threat among children of dissimilar socioeconomic levels. *Journal of Personality and Social Psychology*, 1975, 31, 338–342.

DEUTSCH, M., and COLLINS, M. E. *Interracial housing: A psychological evaluation of a social experiment.* Minneapolis, Minn.: University of Minnesota Press, 1951.

EBBESEN, E. B., BOWERS, R. J., PHILLIPS, S., and SNYDER, M. Self-control processes in the forbidden toy paradigm. *Journal of Personality and Social Psychology*, 1975, 31, 442–452.

ELMS, A. C. Role playing, incentive, and dissonance. *Psychological Bulletin*, 1967, 68, 132–148.

ELMS, A. C. (Ed.) *Role playing, reward, and attitude change.* New York: Van Nostrand, 1969.

ELMS, A. C., and JANIS, I. L. Counter-norm attitudes induced by consonant versus dissonant conditions of role-playing. *Journal of Experimental Research in Personality*, 1965, 1, 50–60.

FEATHER, N. T. The prediction of interpersonal attraction. *Human Relations*, 1966, 19, 213–237.

FELDMAN, S. (Ed.) *Cognitive consistency: Motivational antecedents and behavioral consequents.* New York: Academic Press, 1966.

FESTINGER, L. *A theory of cognitive dissonance.* Stanford, Cal.: Stanford University Press, 1957.

FESTINGER, L. (Ed.) *Conflict, decision, and dissonance.* Stanford, Cal.: Stanford University Press, 1964.

FESTINGER, L., and CARLSMITH, J. M. Cognitive consequences of forced compliance. *Journal of Abnormal and Social Psychology*, 1959, 58, 203–210.

FESTINGER, L., SCHACHTER, S., and BACK K. *Social pressures in informal groups: A study of human factors in housing.* New York: Harper, 1950.

FISHBEIN, M., and COOMBS, F. S. Basis for decision: An attitudinal analysis of voting behavior. *Journal of Applied Social Psychology*, 1974, 4, 95–124.

FREEDMAN, J. L. Long-term behavior effects of cognitive dissonance. *Journal of Experimental Social Psychology*, 1965, 1, 145–155.

FULLER, C. H. Comparison of two experimental paradigms as tests of Heider's balance theory. *Journal of Personality and Social Psychology*, 1974, 30, 802–806.

GERARD, H. B., CONNOLLEY, E. S., and WILHELMY, R. A. Compliance, justification and cognitive change. In L. Berkowitz (Ed.) *Advances in experimental social psychology.* Vol. 7. New York: Academic Press, 1974. Pp. 217–248.

GERARD, H. B., and FLEISCHER, L. Recall and pleasantness of balanced and unbalanced cognitive structures. *Journal of Personality and Social Psychology*, 1967, 7, 332–337.

GERARD, H. B., and MATTHEWSON, G. C. The effects of severity of initiation on liking for a group: A replication. *Journal of Experimental and Social Psychology*, 1966, 2, 278–287.

GREENWALD, A. G., BROCK, T. C., and OSTROM, T. M. (Eds.) *Psychological foundations of attitudes.* New York: Academic Press, 1968.

HEIDER, F. Social perception and phenomenal causality. *Psychological Review*, 1944, 51, 358–374.

HEIDER, F. Attitudes and cognitive organization. *Journal of Psychology*, 1946, 21, 107–112.

HEIDER, F. *The psychology of interpersonal relations*. New York: Wiley, 1958.

JANIS, I. L. Attitude change via role-playing. In R. P. Abelson *et al.* (Eds.) *Theories of cognitive consistency: A sourcebook*. Chicago: Rand McNally, 1968. Pp. 810–818.

JANIS, I. L., and GILMORE, J. B. The influence of incentive conditions on the success of role playing in modifying attitudes. *Journal of Personality and Social Psychology*, 1965, 1, 17–27.

JONES, E. E. *Ingratiation: A social psychological analysis*. New York: Appleton-Century-Crofts, 1964.

JONES, E. E., and GERARD, H. B. *Foundations of social psychology*. New York: Wiley, 1967.

JONES, R. A., LINDER, D. E., KIESLER, C. A., ZANNA, M., and BREHM, J. W. Internal states or external stimuli: Observers' attitude judgments and the dissonance theory/self-perception controversy. *Journal of Experimental Social Psychology*, 1968, 4, 247–269.

JORDAN, N. Behavioral forces that are a function of attitudes and of cognitive organization. *Human Relations*, 1953, 6, 273–287.

KERLINGER, F. N. The social attitudes scale. In M. E. Shaw and J. M. Wright (Eds.) *Scales for the measurement of attitudes*. New York: McGraw-Hill, 1967. Pp. 322–324.

LEPPER, M. R., and GREENE, D. Turning play into work: Effects of adult surveillance and extrinsic rewards on children's intrinsic motivation. *Journal of Personality and Social Psychology*, 1975, 31, 479–486.

LEPPER, M. R., GREENE, D., and NISBETT, R. E. Undermining children's intrinsic interest with extrinsic rewards: A test of the overjustification hypothesis. *Journal of Personality and Social Psychology*, 1973, 28, 129–137.

LEPPER, M. R., ZANNA, M. P., and ABELSON, R. P. Cognitive irreversibility in a dissonance reduction situation. *Journal of Personality and Social Psychology*, 1970, 16, 191–198.

LINDER, D. E., COOPER, J., and JONES, E. E. Decision freedom as a determinant of the role of incentive magnitude in attitude change. *Journal of Personality and Social Psychology*, 1967, 6, 245–254.

McGUIRE, W. J. The current status of cognitive consistency theories. In S. Feldman (Ed.) *Cognitive consistency: Motivational antecedents and behavioral consequents*. New York: Academic Press, 1966. Pp. 1–46.

McGUIRE, W. J. The structure of human thought. In R. P. Abelson *et al.* (Eds.) *Theories of cognitive consistency: A sourcebook*. Chicago: Rand McNally, 1968. Pp. 140–164.

MILLER, H., and GELLER, D. Structural balance in dyads. *Journal of Personality and Social Psychology*, 1972, 21, 135–138.

NEWCOMB, T. M. Interpersonal balance. In R. P. Abelson *et. al.* (Eds.) *Theories of cognitive consistency: A sourcebook*. Chicago: Rand McNally, 1968. Pp. 28–51.

NISBETT, R. E., and VALINS, S. *Perceiving the causes of one's own behavior*. Morristown, N. J.: General Learning Press, 1971.

NUTTIN, J. M., JR. Attitude change after rewarded dissonant and consonant "forced compliance": A critical replication of the Festinger and Carlsmith experiment. *International Journal of Psychology*, 1966, 1, 39–57.

OSGOOD, C. E., SUCI, G. J., and TANNENBAUM, P. H. *The measurement of meaning*. Urbana, Ill.: University of Illinois Press, 1957.

OSGOOD, E. C., and TANNENBAUM, P. H. The principle of congruity in the prediction of attitude change. *Psychological Review*, 1955, 62, 42–55.

PILIAVIN, J. A., PILIAVIN, I. M., LOEWENTON, E. P., McCAULEY, C., and HAMMOND, P. On observers' reproductions of dissonance effects: The right answers for the wrong reasons? *Journal of Personality and Social Psychology*, 1969, 13, 98–106.

PRICE, K. O., HARBURG, E., and NEWCOMB, T. M. Psychological balance in situations of negative interpersonal attitudes. *Journal of Personality and Social Psychology*, 1966, 3, 255–270.

RODRIGUES, A. Effects of balance, positivity, and agreement in triadic social relations. *Journal of Personality and Social Psychology*, 1967, 5, 472–475.

ROSENBERG, M. J. When dissonance fails: On eliminating evaluation apprehension from attitude measurement. *Journal of Personality and Social Psychology*, 1965, 1, 28–42.

ROSENBERG, M. J. Hedonism, inauthenticity, and other goads toward expansion of a consistency theory. In R. P. Abelson *et al.* (Eds.) *Theories of cognitive consistency: A sourcebook*. Chicago: Rand McNally, 1968. Pp. 73–111.

TANNENBAUM, P. H. The congruity principle: Retrospective reflections and recent research. In R. P. Abelson *et al.* (Eds.) *Theories of cognitive consistency: A sourcebook*. Chicago: Rand McNally, 1968. Pp. 52–72.

TAYLOR, S. E. On inferring one's attitudes from one's behavior: Some delimiting conditions. *Journal of Personality and Social Psychology*, 1975, 31, 126–131.

THIBAUT, J. W., and KELLEY, H. H. *The social psychology of groups*. New York: Wiley, 1959.

WATERMAN, C. K., and KATKIN, E. S. The energizing (dynamogenic) effect of cognitive dissonance on task performance. *Journal of Personality and Social Psychology*, 1967, 6, 126–131.

WELLENS, A. R., and THISTLETHWAITE, D. I. Comparison of three theories of cognitive balance. *Journal of Personality and Social Psychology*, 1971, 20, 82–92.

WHITNEY, R. E. Agreement and positivity in pleasantness ratings of balanced and unbalanced social situations: A cross-cultural study. *Journal of Personality and Social Psychology*, 1971, 17, 11–14.

WIEST, W. M. A quantitative extension of Heider's theory of cognitive balance applied to interpersonal perception and self-esteem. *Psychological Monographs*, 1965, 79, Whole No. 607.

WILLIS, R. H., and BURGESS, T. D. G. Cognitive and affective balance in sociometric dyads. *Journal of Personality and Social Psychology*, 1974, 29, 145–152.

WYER, R. S., JR. *Cognitive organization and change: An information-processing approach*. Potomac, Md.: Erlbaum, 1974.

ZANNA, M. P., and COOPER, J. Dissonance and the pill: An attribution approach to studying the arousal properties of dissonance. *Journal of Personality and Social Psychology*, 1974, 29, 703–709.

ZIMBARDO, P. G., and EBBESEN, E. B. *Influencing attitudes and changing behavior*. Reading, Mass.: Addison-Wesley, 1969.

CHAPTER 7

ADORNO, T. W., FRENKEL-BRUNSWIK, E., LEVINSON, D. J., and SANFORD, R. N. *The authoritarian personality*. New York: Harper, 1950.

AGER, J. W., and DAWES, R. M. The effect of judges' attitudes on judgment. *Journal of Personality and Social Psychology*, 1965, 1, 533–538.

BERLYNE, D. E. Novelty, complexity, and hedonic value. *Perception and psychophysics*, 1970, 8, 279–286.

BEYLE, H. C. A scale of measurement of attitude toward candidates for elective governmental office. *American Political Science Review*, 1932, 26, 527–544.

BREHM, J. W. *A theory of psychological reactance*. New York: Academic Press, 1966.

BREHM, J. W. *Responses to loss of freedom: A theory of psychological reactance*. Morristown, N. J.: General Learning Press, 1972.

BRICKMAN, P., REDFIELD, J., HARRISON, A. A., and CRANDALL, R. Drive and predisposition as factors in the attitudinal effects of mere exposure. *Journal of Experimental Social Psychology*, 1972, 8, 31–44.

BURGESS, T. D. G., II, and SALES, S. M. Attitudinal effects of "mere exposure": A re-evaluation. *Journal of Experimental Social Psychology*, 1971, 7, 461–472.

CARLSMITH, J. M., COLLINS, B. E., and HELMREICH, R. L. Studies in forced compliance: I. The effect of pressure for compliance on attitude change produced by face-to-face role playing and anonymous essay writing. *Journal of Personality and Social Psychology*, 1966, 4, 1–13.

COCH, L., and FRENCH, J. R. P. Overcoming resistance to change. *Human Relations*, 1948, 1, 512–532.

COHEN, A. R. An experiment on small rewards for discrepent compliance and attitude change. In J. W. Brehm and A. R. Cohen, *Explorations in cognitive dissonance*. New York: Wiley, 1962. Pp. 73–78.

COOK, S. W. Motives in a conceptual analysis of attitude-related behavior. In W. J. Arnold and D. Levine (Eds.) *Nebraska symposium on motivation, 1969*. Lincoln, Neb.: University of Nebraska Press, 1970. Pp. 179–231.

DAWES, R. M., SINGER, D., and LEMONS, F. An experimental analysis of the contrast effect and its implications for intergroup communication and the indirect assessment of attitude. *Journal of Personality and Social Psychology*, 1972, 21, 281–295.

DOLLARD, J., DOOB, L. W., MILLER, N. E., MOWRER, O. H., and SEARS, R. R. *Frustration and aggression.* New Haven, Conn.: Yale University Press, 1939.

EISER, J. R., and STROEBE, W. *Categorization and social judgement.* New York: Academic Press, 1973.

FERGUSON, L. S. The influence of individual attitudes on construction of an attitude scale. *Journal of Social Psychology*, 1935, 6, 115–117.

FESTINGER, L., and CARLSMITH, J. M. Cognitive consequences of forced compliance. *Journal of Abnormal and Social Psychology*, 1959, 58, 203–210.

FISHBEIN, M., and AJZEN, I. *Belief, attitude, intention, and behavior: An introduction to theory and research.* Reading, Mass.: Addison-Wesley, 1975.

FREEDMAN, J. L., and FRASER, S. C. Compliance without pressure: The foot-in-the-door technique. *Journal of Personality and Social Psychology*, 1966, 4, 195–202.

GILLIG, P. M., and GREENWALD, A. G. Is it time to lay the sleeper effect to rest? *Journal of Personality and Social Psychology*, 1974, 29, 132–139.

GREENWALD, A. G., BROCK, T. C., and OSTROM, T. M. (Eds.) *Psychological foundations of attitudes.* New York: Academic Press, 1968.

HELSON, H. *Adaptation-level theory.* New York: Harper & Row, 1964.

HINCKLEY, E. D. The influence of individual opinion on construction of an attitude scale. *Journal of Social Psychology*, 1932, 3, 283–296.

HOVLAND, C. I. (Ed.) *The order of presentation in persuasion.* New Haven, Conn.: Yale University Press, 1957.

HOVLAND, C. I., HARVEY, O. J., and SHERIF, M. Assimilation and contrast effects in reactions to communication and attitude change. *Journal of Abnormal and Social Psychology*, 1957, 55, 244–252.

HOVLAND, C. I., JANIS, I. L., and KELLEY, H. H. *Communication and persuasion.* New Haven, Conn.: Yale University Press, 1953.

HOVLAND, C. I., LUMSDAINE, A. A., and SHEFFIELD, F. D. The effects of presenting "one side" versus "both sides" in changing opinions on a controversial subject. In C. I. Hovland, A. A. Lumsdaine, and F. D. Sheffield, (Eds.) *Experiments on mass communication.* Princeton, N. J.: Princeton University Press, 1949. Pp. 201–227.

HOVLAND, C. I., and ROSENBERG, M. J. (Eds.) *Attitude organization and change.* New Haven, Conn.: Yale University Press, 1960.

HOVLAND, C. I., and SHERIF, M. Judgmental phenomena and scales of attitude measurement: Item displacement in Thurstone scales. *Journal of Abnormal and Social Psychology*, 1952, 47, 822–832.

HOVLAND, C. I., and WEISS, W. The influence of source credibility on communication effectiveness. *Public Opinion Quarterly*, 1951, 15, 635–650.

INBAU, F., and REID, J. *Criminal interrogation and confessions.* Baltimore, Md.: Williams & Wilkins, 1962.

JANIS, I. L., and FESCHBACH, S. Effects of fear-arousing communications. *Journal of Abnormal and Social Psychology*, 1953, 48, 78–92.

JONES, R. A., and BREHM, J. W. Persuasiveness of one- and two-sided communications as a function of awareness there are two sides. *Journal of Experimental Social Psychology*, 1970, 6, 47–56.

KATZ, D. The functional approach to the study of attitudes. *Public Opinion Quarterly*, 1960, 24, 163–204.

KATZ, D., and KAHN, R. L. *The social psychology of organizations*. New York: Wiley, 1966.

KATZ, D., SARNOFF, I., and McCLINTOCK, C. Ego-defense and attitude change. *Human Relations*, 1956, 9, 27–45.

KATZ, D., and STOTLAND, E. A preliminary statement to a theory of attitude structure and change. In S. Koch (Ed.) *Psychology: Study of a science*. Vol. 3: Formulations of the person and the social context. New York: McGraw-Hill, 1959. Pp. 423–475.

KELMAN, H. C. Processes of opinion change. *Public Opinion Quarterly*, 1961, 25, 57–78.

KELMAN, H. C., and HOVLAND, C. I. "Reinstatement" of the communicator in delayed measurement of opinion change. *Journal of Abnormal and Social Psychology*, 1953, 48, 327–335.

KIESLER, C. A., COLLINS, B. E., and MILLER, N. *Attitude change: A critical analysis of theoretical approaches*. New York: Wiley, 1969.

KOSLIN, B. L., and PARMAGENT, R. Effects of attitude on the discrimination of opinion statements. *Journal of Experimental Social Psychology*, 1969, 5, 245–264.

LEVENTHAL, H. Findings in the study of fear communications. In L. Berkowitz (Ed.) *Advances in experimental social psychology*. Vol. 5. New York: Academic Press, 1970. Pp. 119–186.

LEWIN, K. Frontiers in group dynamics: Concept, method, and reality in social science; social equilibria and social change. *Human Relations*, 1947, 1, 5–42.

LEWIN, K. Group decision and social change. In E. E. Maccoby, T. M. Newcomb, and E. L. Hartley (Eds.) *Readings in social psychology*. (3rd ed.) New York: Holt, Rinehart, and Winston, 1958. Pp. 197–212.

LINDER, D. E., COOPER, J., and JONES, E. E. Decision freedom as a determinant of the role of incentive magnitude in attitude change. *Journal of Personality and Social Psychology*, 1967, 6, 245–254.

LOTT, A. J., and LOTT, B. E. The formation of positive attitudes toward group members. *Journal of Abnormal and Social Psychology*, 1960, 61, 297–300.

LOTT, A. J., and LOTT, B. E. A learning theory approach to interpersonal attitudes. In A. G. Greenwald, T. C. Brock, and T. M. Ostrom (Eds.) *Psychological foundations of attitudes*. New York: Academic Press, 1968. Pp. 67–88.

LUMSDAINE, A. A., and JANIS, I. L. Resistance to "counterpropaganda" produced by one-sided and two-sided "propaganda" presentations. *Public Opinion Quarterly*, 1953, 17, 311–318.

MATLIN, M. W. Response competition, recognition, and affect. *Journal of Personality and Social Psychology*, 1971, 19, 295–300.

MCCLINTOCK, C. Personality factors in attitude change. *Dissertation Abstracts*, 1958, 18, 1865.

MCGINNIES, E. Studies in persuasion: III. Reactions of Japanese students to one-sided and two-sided communications. *Journal of Social Psychology*, 1966, 70, 87–93.

MCGUIRE, W. J. Inducing resistance to persuasion: Some contemporary approaches. In L. Berkowitz (Ed.) *Advances in experimental social psychology*. Vol. 1. New York: Academic Press, 1964. Pp. 191–229.

MCGUIRE, W. J. The nature of attitudes and attitude change. In G. Lindzey and E. Aronson (Eds.) *Handbook of social psychology*. (2nd ed.) Vol. 3. Reading, Mass.: Addison-Wesley, 1969. Pp. 136–314.

MCGUIRE, W. J., and PAPAGEORGIS, D. The relative efficacy of various types of prior belief-defense in producing immunity against persuasion. *Journal of Abnormal and Social Psychology*, 1961, 62, 327–337.

NEWCOMB, T. M. *Personality and social change*. New York: Dryden, 1943.

OSGOOD, C. E., and TANNENBAUM, P. H. The principle of congruity in the prediction of attitude change. *Psychological Review*, 1955, 62, 42–55.

PINTNER, R., and FORLANO, G. The influence of attitude upon scaling of attitude items. *Journal of Social Psychology*, 1937, 8, 39–45.

ROSENBERG, M. J. When dissonance fails: On eliminating evaluation apprehension from attitude measurement. *Journal of Personality and Social Psychology*, 1965, 1, 28–42.

ROSNOW, R. L., and ROBINSON, E. J. *Experiments in persuasion*. New York: Academic Press, 1967.

SENSENIG, J., and BREHM, J. W. Attitude change from an implied threat to attitudinal freedom. *Journal of Personality and Social Psychology*, 1968, 8, 324–330.

SHERIF, M., and SHERIF, C. W. *Social psychology*. New York: Harper & Row, 1969.

SHERIF, M., and HOVLAND, C. I. *Social judgment: Assimilation and contrast effects in communication and attitude change*. New Haven, Conn.: Yale University Press, 1961.

SHERIF, C. W., SHERIF, M., and NEBERGALL, R. E. *Attitude and attitude change: The social judgment-involvement approach*. Philadelphia: W. B. Saunders, 1965.

SIEGEL, A. E., and SIEGEL, S. Reference groups, membership groups, and attitude change. *Journal of Abnormal and Social Psychology*, 1957, 55, 360–364.

STAATS, A. W. Social behaviorism and human motivation: Principles of the attitude-reinforcer-discriminative system. In A. G. Greenwald, T. C. Brock, and T. M. Ostrom (Eds.) *Psychological foundations of attitudes*. New York: Academic Press, 1968. Pp. 33–66.

STANG, D. J. Six theories of repeated exposure and affect. *JSAS Catalog of selected documents in psychology*, 1973, 3, 126.

STANG, D. J. Effects of "mere exposure" on learning and affect. *Journal of Personality and Social Psychology*, 1975, 31, 7–12.

STOTLAND, E., KATZ, D., and PATCHEN, M. The reduction of prejudice through the arousal of self-insight. *Journal of Personality*, 1959, 27, 507–531.

THURSTONE, L. L., and CHAVE, E. J. *The measurement of attitude.* Chicago: University of Chicago Press, 1929.

TRIANDIS, H. C. *Attitude and attitude change.* New York: Wiley, 1971.

UPSHAW, H. S. The personal reference scale: An approach to social judgment. In L. Berkowitz (Ed.) *Advances in experimental social psychology.* Vol. 4. New York: Academic Press, 1969. Pp. 315–372.

WICKLUND, R. A. *Freedom and reactance.* New York: Academic Press, 1974.

WORTMAN, C. B., and BREHM, J. W. Responses to uncontrollable outcomes: An integration of reactance theory and the learned helplessness model. In L. Berkowitz (Ed.) *Advances in experimental social psychology.* Vol. 8. New York: Academic Press, 1975. Pp. 277–336.

ZAJONC, R. B. The attitudinal effects of mere exposure. *Journal of Personality and Social Psychology Monograph Supplement*, 1968, 9, Part 2, 1–27.

ZANNA, M. P., KIESLER, C. A., and PILKONIS, P. A. Positive and negative attitudinal affect established by classical conditioning. *Journal of Personality and Social Psychology*, 1970, 14, 321–328.

ZAVALLONI, M., and COOK, S. W. Influence of judges' attitudes on ratings of favorableness of statements about a social group. *Journal of Personality and Social Psychology*, 1965, 1, 43–54.

ZIMBARDO, P. G. The psychology of police confessions. In *Readings in Psychology Today.* Del Mar, Calif.: CRM, 1970. Pp. 101–107.

ZIMBARDO, P. G., and EBBESEN, E. B. *Influencing attitudes and changing behavior.* Reading, Mass.: Addison-Wesley, 1969.

CHAPTER 8

ALTMAN, I. Reciprocity of interpersonal exchange. *Journal for the Theory of Social Behavior*, 1973, 3, 249–261.

ALTMAN, I., and TAYLOR, D. A. *Social penetration processes: The development of interpersonal relationships.* New York: Holt, Rinehart and Winston, 1973.

ARONSON, E., and CARLSMITH, J. M. Experimentation in social psychology. In G. Lindzey and E. Aronson (Eds.) *Handbook of social psychology.* (2nd ed.) Vol. 2. Reading, Mass.: Addison-Wesley, 1968. Pp. 1–79.

ARROWOOD, A. J., and FRIEND, R. M. Other factors determining the choice of a comparison other. *Journal of Experimental Social Psychology*, 1969, 5, 233–239.

ASHER, S. R., and ALLEN, V. L. Racial preference and social comparison processes. *Journal of Social Issues*, 1969, 25, 157–166.

BAREFOOT, J. C., and STRAUB, R. B. Opportunity for information search and the effect of false heart-rate feedback. *Journal of Personality and Social Psychology*, 1971, 17, 154–157.

BENCHLEY, P. *Jaws.* Garden City, N. Y.: Doubleday, 1974.

BEM, D. J. Self-perception: An alternative explanation of cognitive dissonance phenomena. *Psychological Review*, 1967, 74, 183–200.

BEM, D. J. Self-perception theory. In L. Berkowitz (Ed.) *Advances in experimental social psychology*. Vol. 6. New York: Academic Press, 1972. Pp. 2–62.

BERSCHEID, E., DION, K. K., WALSTER, E., and WALSTER, G. W. Physical attractiveness and dating choice: A test of the matching hypothesis. *Journal of Experimental Social Psychology*, 1971, 7, 173–189.

BERSCHEID, E., and WALSTER, E. Physical attractiveness. In L. Berkowitz (Ed.) *Advances in experimental social psychology*. Vol. 7. New York: Academic Press, 1974. Pp. 157–215.

BILLS, R. E., VANCE, E. L., and MCLEAN, O. S. An Index of Adjustment and Values. *Journal of Consulting Psychology*, 1951, 15, 257–261.

CANNON, W. B. The James-Lange theory of emotions: A critical examination and an alternative theory. *The American Journal of Psychology*, 1927, 34, 106–124.

CARMICHAEL, F. F., and HAMILTON, C. V. *Black power: Politics of liberation in America*. New York: Random House, 1967.

CARVER, C. S. Facilitation of physical aggression through objective self-awareness. *Journal of Experimental Social Psychology*, 1974, 10, 365–370.

CHAIKIN, A. L., and DERLEGA, V. J. Variables affecting the appropriateness of self-disclosure. *Journal of Consulting and Clinical Psychology*, 1974, 42, 588–593.

CHAIKIN, A. L., DERLEGA, V. J., BAYMA, B., and SHAW, J. Neuroticism and disclosure reciprocity. *Journal of Consulting and Clinical Psychology*, 1975, 43, 13–19.

CLARK, K. B., and CLARK, M. P. Racial identification and racial preference in Negro children. In T. M. Newcomb and E. L. Hartley (Eds.) *Readings in social psychology*. New York: Holt, 1947. Pp. 169–178.

CLIFFORD, M. M., and WALSTER, E. The effect of physical attractiveness on teacher expectation. *Sociology of Education*, 1973, 46, 248–258.

COFER, C. N., and APPLEY, M. H. *Motivation: Theory and research*. New York: Wiley, 1964.

COOLEY, C. H. *Human nature and the social order*. New York: Scribner's, 1902.

COOPERSMITH, S. *The antecedents of self-esteem*. San Francisco: Freeman, 1967.

COZBY, P. C. Self-disclosure: A literature review. *Psychological Bulletin*, 1973, 79, 73–91.

DARLEY, J. M., JR., and ARONSON, E. Self-evaluation vs. direct anxiety reduction as determinants of the fear-affiliation relationship. *Journal of Experimental Social Psychology*, 1966, 2 (Supplement 1), 66–79.

DAVIS, J. D., and SKINNER, A. E. G. Reciprocity of self-disclosure in interviews: Modeling or social exchange? *Journal of Personality and Social Psychology*, 1974, 29, 779–784.

DEAUX, K., and EMSWILLER, T. Explanations of successful performance on sex-linked tasks: What is skill for the male is luck for the female. *Journal of Personality and Social Psychology*, 1974, 29, 80–85.

DERLEGA, V. J., HARRIS, M. S., and CHAIKIN, A. L. Self-disclosure reciprocity, liking, and the deviant. *Journal of Experimental Social Psychology*, 1973, 9. 277–284.

DERMER, M., and THIEL, D. L. When beauty may fail. *Journal of Personality and Social Psychology*, 1975, 31, 1168–1176.

DIGGORY, J. S. *Self-evaluation*. New York: Wiley, 1966.

DION, K. K. Physical attractiveness and evaluations of children's transgressions. *Journal of Personality and Social Psychology*, 1972, 24, 207–213.

DION, K. K., and BERSCHEID, E. Physical attractiveness and social perception of peers in preschool children. Minneapolis, Minn.: Unpublished manuscript, University of Minnesota, 1972.

DUVAL, S., and WICKLUND, R. A. *A theory of objective self-awareness*. New York: Academic Press, 1972.

DUVAL, S., and WICKLUND, R. A. Effects of objective self-awareness on attribution of causality. *Journal of Experimental Social Psychology*, 1973, 9, 17–31.

EFRAN, M. G. The effect of physical appearance on the judgment of guilt, interpersonal attraction, and severity of recommended punishment in a simulated jury task. *Journal of Research in Personality*, 1974, 8, 45–54.

ERIKSON, E. *Identity: Youth and crisis*. New York: Norton, 1968.

FEATHER, N. T., and SIMON, J. G. Reactions to male and female success and failure in sex-linked occupations: Impressions of personality, causal attributions, and perceived likelihood of different consequences. *Journal of Personality and Social Psychology*, 1975, 31, 20–31.

FELDMAN-SUMMERS, S., and KIESLER, S. B. Those who are number two try harder: The effect of sex on attributions of causality. *Journal of Personality and Social Psychology*, 1974, 30, 846–855.

FESTINGER, L. A theory of social comparison processes. *Human Relations*, 1954, 7, 117–140.

FESTINGER, L., PEPITONE, A., and NEWCOMB, T. M. Some consequences of deindividuation in a group. *Journal of Abnormal and Social Psychology*, 1952, 47, 382–389.

FREEDMAN, J. L. Role-playing: Psychology by consensus. *Journal of Personality and Social Psychology*, 1969, 13, 107–114.

FREUD, S. *New introductory lectures on psychoanalysis*. New York: Norton, 1933.

FRIEND, R. M., and GILBERT, J. Threat and fear of negative evaluation as determinants of locus of social comparison. *Journal of Personality*, 1973, 41, 328–340.

GARDNER, J. W. Level of aspiration in response to a prearranged sequence of scores. *Journal of Experimental Psychology*, 1939, 25, 601–621.

GERARD, H. B. Emotional uncertainty and social comparison. *Journal of Abnormal and Social Psychology*, 1963, 66, 568–573.

GERARD, H. B., and RABBIE, J. M. Fear and social comparison. *Journal of Abnormal and Social Psychology*, 1961, 62, 586–592.

GOFFMAN, E. *The presentation of self in everyday life*. Garden City, N.Y.: Doubleday, 1959.

GOFFMAN, E. *Interaction ritual*. Garden City, N.Y.: Doubleday, Anchor Books, 1967.

GOLDSTEIN, D., FINK, D., and METTEE, D. Cognition of arousal and actual arousal as determinants of emotion. *Journal of Personality and Social Psychology*, 1972, 21, 41–51.

GORDON, C., and GERGEN, K. J. (Eds.) *The self in social interaction*. Vol. 1: Classic and contemporary approaches. New York: Wiley, 1968.

GREENWALD, H. J., and OPPENHEIM, D. B. Reported magnitude of self-misidentification among Negro children—artifact? *Journal of Personality and Social Psychology*, 1968, 8, 49–52.

GROSS, N., MASON, W. S., and MCEACHERN, A. *Explorations in role analysis: Studies of the school superintendency role*. New York: Wiley, 1957.

GRUDER, C. L. Determinants of social comparison choices. *Journal of Experimental Social Psychology*, 1971, 7, 473–489.

HAKMILLER, K. L. Threat as a determinant of downward comparison. *Journal of Experimental Social Psychology*, 1966, 2 (Supplement 1), 32–39.

HANEY, C., BANKS, C., and ZIMBARDO, P. C. Interpersonal dynamics in a simulated prison. *International Journal of Criminology and Penology*, 1973, 1, 69–97.

HERMAN, C. P. External and internal cues as determinants of the smoking behavior of light and heavy smokers. *Journal of Personality and Social Psychology*, 1974, 30, 664–672.

HRABA, J., and GRANT, G. Black is beautiful: a re-examination of racial preference and identification. *Journal of Personality and Social Psychology*, 1970, 16, 398–402.

HUSTON, T. L. Ambiguity of acceptance, social desirability, and dating choice. *Journal of Experimental Social Psychology*, 1973, 9, 32–42.

HYMAN, H. The psychology of status. *Archives of Psychology*, 1942, No. 269.

ICKES, W. J., WICKLUND, R. A., and FERRIS, C. B. Objective self-awareness and self-esteem. *Journal of Experimental Social Psychology*, 1973, 9, 202–219.

JAMES, W. *Psychology: The briefer course*. New York: Holt, 1892.

JAMES, W., and LANGE, G. C. *The emotions*. Baltimore, Md.: Williams & Wilkins, 1922.

JANIS, I. L., and FIELD, P. Sex differences and personality factors related to persuasibility. In C. I. Hovland and I. L. Janis (Eds.) *Personality and persuasibility*. New Haven, Conn.: Yale University Press, 1959. Pp. 55–68.

JONES, E. E., and GERARD, H. B. *Foundations of social psychology*. New York: Wiley, 1967.

JONES, E. E., and NISBETT, R. E. *The actor and the observer: Divergent perceptions of the causes of behavior*. Morristown, N.J.: General Learning Press, 1971.

JONES, S. C., and REGAN, D. T. Ability evaluation through social comparison. *Journal of Experimental Social Psychology*, 1974, 10, 133–146.

JOURARD, S. *The transparent self: Self-disclosure and well-being*. Princeton, N.J.: Van Nostrand, 1964.

JOURARD, S. *Self-disclosure: An experimental analysis of the transparent self*. New York: Wiley, 1971.

JOURARD, S., and FRIEDMAN, R. Experimenter-subject "distance" and self-disclosure. *Journal of Personality and Social Psychology*, 1970, 15, 278–282.

JOURARD, S., and JAFFE, P. E. Influence of an interviewer's disclosure on the self-disclosing behavior of interviewees. *Journal of Counseling Psychology,* 1970, 17, 252–257.

JUNG, C. G. *The collected works of C. G. Jung.* Vol. 12: Psychology and alchemy. New York: Pantheon, 1953.

KELMAN, H. C. Processes of opinion change. *Public Opinion Quarterly,* 1961, 25, 57–78.

KELLEY, H. H. Two functions of reference groups. In G. E. Swanson, T. M. Newcomb, and E. L. Hartley (Eds.) *Readings in social psychology.* (2nd ed.) New York: Holt, Rinehart, and Winston, 1952. Pp. 410–414.

LaFORGE, R., and SUCZEK, R. The interpersonal dimension of personality: III. An interpersonal check list. *Journal of Personality,* 1955, 24, 94–112.

LANDY, D., and ARONSON, E. The influence of the character of the criminal and victim on the decisions of simulated jurors. *Journal of Experimental Social Psychology,* 1969, 5, 141–152.

LATANÉ, B. Studies in social comparison—introduction and overview. *Journal of Experimental Social Psychology,* 1966, 2 (Supplement 1), 1–5.

LAZARUS, R. S. *Psychological stress and the coping process.* New York: McGraw-Hill, 1966.

LeBON, G. *Psychologie des foules.* Paris: F. Olean, 1895. (Transl. *The crowd.* London: T. Fisher Unwin, 1896.)

LEVENTHAL, H. Emotions: A basic problem for social psychology. In C. Nemeth (Ed.) *Social psychology: Classic and contemporary integrations.* Chicago: Rand McNally, 1974. Pp. 1–51.

LEWIN, K., DEMBO, T., FESTINGER, L., and SEARS, P. S. Level of aspiration. In J. McV. Hunt (Ed.) *Personality and the behavior disorders.* Vol. 1. New York: Ronald Press, 1944. Pp. 333–378.

MARLATT, G. A. Exposure to a model and task ambiguity as determinants of verbal behavior in an interview. *Journal of Consulting and Clinical Psychology,* 1971, 36, 268–276.

MASLOW, A. Peak experiences as acute identity-experiences. *American Journal of Psychoanalysis,* 1961, 21, 254–260.

MEAD, G. H. *Mind, self, and society.* Chicago: University of Chicago Press, 1934.

MERTON, R. K. *Social theory and social structure.* (Rev. ed.) Glencoe, Ill.: Free Press, 1957.

MISOVICH, S., and CHARIS, P. C. Information need, affect, and cognition of autonomic activity. *Journal of Experimental Social Psychology,* 1974, 10, 274–283.

MORLAND, J. A comparison of race awareness in northern and southern children. In M. Goldschmid (Ed.) *Black Americans and white racism: Theory and research.* New York: Holt, Rinehart, and Winston, 1970. Pp. 25–32.

MURSTEIN, B. I. Physical attractiveness and marital choice. *Journal of Personality and Social Psychology,* 1972, 22, 8–12.

NEWCOMB, T. M. *Personality and social change.* New York: Dryden, 1943.

NISBETT, R. E., and SCHACHTER, S. Cognitive manipulation of pain. *Journal of Experimental Social Psychology,* 1966, 2, 227–236.

NISBETT, R. E., and VALINS, S. *Perceiving the causes of one's own behavior.* Morristown, N.J.: General Learning Press, 1971.

PARSONS, T. The position of identity in the general theory of action. In C. Gordon and K. G. Gergen (Eds.) *The self in social interaction*. Vol. 1: Classic and contemporary approaches. New York: Wiley, 1968. Pp. 11–24.

PETTIGREW, T. F. Social evaluation theory: Convergences and applications. In D. Levine (Ed.) *Nebraska symposium on motivation, 1967*. Vol. 15. Lincoln, Neb.: University of Nebraska Press, 1967. Pp. 241–311.

PORTER, J. D. *Black child, white child; the development of racial attitudes*. Cambridge, Mass.: Harvard University Press, 1971.

RADLOFF, R. Social comparison and ability evaluation. *Journal of Experimental Social Psychology*, 1966, 2 (Supplement 1), 6–26.

ROGERS, C. R. A theory of therapy, personality, and interpersonal relationships, as developed in the client-centered framework. In S. Koch (Ed.) *Psychology: Study of a science*. Vol. 3. New York: McGraw-Hill, 1959. Pp. 184–256.

ROSE, A. M. (Ed.) *Human behavior and social processes: An interactionist approach*. Boston: Houghton Mifflin, 1962.

ROSENBERG, M. *Society and the adolescent self-image*. Princeton, N.J.: Princeton University Press, 1965.

ROSS, L. D., RODIN, J., and ZIMBARDO, P. G. Toward an attribution therapy: The reduction of fear through induced cognitive-emotional misattribution. *Journal of Personality and Social Psychology*, 1969, 12, 279–288.

RUBIN, Z. Disclosing oneself to a stranger: Reciprocity and its limits. *Journal of Experimental Social Psychology*, 1975, 11, 233–260.

SCHACHTER, S. *The psychology of affiliation*. Stanford, Cal.: Stanford University Press, 1959.

SCHACHTER, S. The interaction of cognitive and physiological determinants of emotional state. In L. Berkowitz (Ed.) *Advances in experimental social psychology*. Vol. 1. New York: Academic Press, 1964. Pp. 49–80.

SCHACHTER, S. *Emotion, obesity, and crime*. New York: Academic Press, 1971.

SCHACHTER, S., and SINGER, J. E. Cognitive, social, and physiological determinants of emotional state. *Psychological Review*, 1962, 69, 379–399.

SCHACHTER, S., and WHEELER, L. Epinephrine, chlorpromazine, and amusement. *Journal of Abnormal and Social Psychology*, 1962, 65, 121–128.

SCHEIER, M. F., FENIGSTEIN, A., and BUSS, A. Self-awareness and physical aggression. *Journal of Experimental Social Psychology*, 1974, 10, 264–273.

SHAVER, K. G., TURNBULL, A. A., and STERLING, M. P. Defensive attribution: The effects of occupational danger and locus of control; perceiver sex and self-esteem. *JSAS Catalog of Selected Documents in Psychology*, 1973, 3, 48.

SIGALL, H., and OSTROVE, N. Beautiful but dangerous: Effects of offender attractiveness and nature of the crime on juridic judgment. *Journal of Personality and Social Psychology*, 1975, 31, 410–414.

SINGER, J. E. Social comparison—progress and issues. *Journal of Experimental Social Psychology*, 1966, 2 (Supplement 1), 103–110.

SINGER, J. E., BRUSH, C. A., and LUBLIN, S. C. Some aspects of deindividuation: identification and conformity. *Journal of Experimental and Social Psychology*, 1965, 1, 356–378.

STORMS, M. D., and NISBETT, R. E. Insomnia and the attribution process. *Journal of Personality and Social Psychology*, 1970, 16, 319–328.

SULLIVAN, H. S. *The interpersonal theory of psychiatry.* New York: Norton, 1953.

THOMAS, W. I., and ZNANIECKI, F. *The Polish peasant in Europe and America.* New York: Dover, 1958.

THORNTON, D. A., and ARROWOOD, A. J. Self-evaluation, self-enhancement, and the locus of social comparison. *Journal of Experimental Social Psychology,* 1966, 2 (Supplement 1), 40–48.

VALINS, S. Cognitive effects of false heart-rate feedback. *Journal of Personality and Social Psychology,* 1966, 4, 400–408.

VALINS, S. The perception and labeling of bodily changes as determinants of emotional behavior. In P. Black (Ed.) *Physiological correlates of emotion.* New York: Academic Press, 1970. Pp. 229–243.

VALINS, S., and RAY, A. A. Effects of cognitive desensitization on avoidance behavior. *Journal of Personality and Social Psychology,* 1967, 7, 345–350.

WHEELER, L. Motivation as a determinant of upward comparison. *Journal of Experimental Social Psychology,* 1966, 2 (Supplement 1), 27–31.

WHEELER, L., SHAVER, K. G., JONES, R. A., GOETHALS, G. R., COOPER, J., ROBINSON, J. E., GRUDER, C. L., and BUTZINE, K. W. Factors determining choice of a comparison other. *Journal of Experimental Social Psychology,* 1969, 5, 219–232.

WORTHY, M., GARY, A. L., and KAHN, G. M. Self-disclosure as an exchange process. *Journal of Personality and Social Psychology,* 1969, 13, 59–63.

WRIGHTSMAN, L. S. Effects of waiting with others on changes in level of felt anxiety. *Journal of Abnormal and Social Psychology,* 1960, 61, 216–222.

WYLIE, R. C. *The self-concept: A critical survey of pertinent research literature.* Lincoln, Neb.: University of Nebraska Press, 1961.

ZANNA, M. P., GOETHALS, G. R., and HILL, J. F. Evaluating a sex-related ability: Social comparison with similar others and standard setters. *Journal of Experimental Social Psychology,* 1975, 11, 86–93.

ZILLER, R. C. Individuation and socialization. *Human Relations,* 1964, 17, 341–360.

ZILLER, R. C. *The social self.* New York: Pergamon Press, 1973.

ZIMBARDO, P. G. The human choice: Individuation, reason, and order versus deindividuation, impulse, and chaos. In W. J. Arnold and D. Levine (Eds.) *Nebraska symposium on motivation, 1969.* Lincoln, Neb.: University of Nebraska Press, 1970. Pp. 237–307.

CHAPTER 9

ADAMS, J. S. Toward an understanding of inequity. *Journal of Abnormal and Social Psychology,* 1963, 67, 442–436.

ADAMS, J. S. Inequity in social exchange. In L. Berkowitz (Ed.) *Advances in experimental social psychology.* Vol. 2. New York: Academic Press, 1965. Pp. 267–299.

ADAMS, J. S., and JACOBSEN, P. R. Effects of wage inequities on work quality. *Journal of Abnormal and Social Psychology*, 1964, 69, 19–25.

AUSTIN, W., and SUSMILCH, C. Comment on Lane and Messé's confusing clarification of equity theory. *Journal of Personality and Social Psychology*, 1974, 30, 400–404.

AUSTIN, W., and WALSTER, E. Participants' reactions to "equity with the world." *Journal of Experimental Social Psychology*, 1974, 10, 528–548.

BANDURA, A. Influence of models' reinforcement contingencies on the acquisition of imitative responses. *Journal of Personality and Social Psychology*, 1965, 1, 589–595.

BANDURA, A. Vicarious and self-reinforcement processes. In R. Glaser (Ed.) *The nature of reinforcement*. New York: Academic Press, 1971.

BANDURA, A., and PERLOFF, B. Relative efficacy of self-monitored and externally imposed reinforcement systems. *Journal of Personality and Social Psychology*, 1967, 7, 111–116.

BANDURA, A., ROSS, D., and ROSS, S. A. Imitation of film-mediated aggressive models. *Journal of Abnormal and Social Psychology*, 1963, 66, 3–11(a).

BANDURA, A., ROSS, D., and ROSS, S. A. Vicarious reinforcement and imitative learning. *Journal of Abnormal and Social Psychology*, 1963, 67, 601–607(b).

BANDURA, A., and WALTERS, R. *Social learning and personality development*. New York: Holt, Rinehart, and Winston, 1963.

BATES, J. E. Effects of a child's imitation versus nonimitation on adults' verbal and nonverbal positivity. *Journal of Personality and Social Psychology*, 1975, 31, 840–851.

BENTHAM, J. *An introduction to the principles of morals and legislation*. (First published 1789.) Oxford: Clarendon Press, 1879.

BERGER, S. M., and LAMBERT, W. W. Stimulus-response theory in contemporary social psychology. In G. Lindzey and E. Aronson (Eds.) *Handbook of social psychology*. (2nd ed.) Vol. 1. Reading, Mass.: Addison-Wesley, 1968. Pp. 81–178.

BLAU, P. M. Social exchange. In D. L. Sills (Ed.) *International encyclopedia of the social sciences*. Vol. 7. New York: Macmillian, 1968. Pp. 452–457.

COWAN, P. A., and WALTERS, R. H. Studies of reinforcement of aggression: I. Effects of scheduling. *Child Development*, 1963, 34, 543–552.

FESTINGER, L. *A theory of cognitive dissonance*. Stanford, Cal.: Stanford University Press, 1957.

FRIEDLAND, N., ARNOLD, S. E., and THIBAUT, J. W. Motivational bases in mixed-motive interactions: The effects of comparison levels. *Journal of Experimental Social Psychology*, 1974, 10, 188–199.

GERGEN, K. J. *The psychology of behavior exchange*. Reading, Mass.: Addison-Wesley, 1969.

HOMANS, G. C. Status among clerical workers. *Human Organizations*, 1953, 12, 5–10.

HOMANS, G. C. *Social behavior: Its elementary forms*. New York: Harcourt Brace, 1961.

JACQUES, E. *Equitable payment*. New York: Wiley, 1961.

KELLEY, H. H., and THIBAUT, J. W. Group problem solving. In G. Lindzey and E. Aronson (Eds.) *Handbook of social psychology.* (2nd ed.) Vol. 4. Reading, Mass.: Addison-Wesley, 1969. Pp. 1–101.

KELLEY, H. H., THIBAUT, J. W., RADLOFF, R., and MUNDY, D. The development of cooperation in the "minimal social situation." *Psychological Monographs,* 1962, 76, No. 19. Whole No. 538.

KUHN, D. Z., MADSEN, C. H., JR., and BECKER, W. C. Effects of exposure to an aggressive model and frustration on children's aggressive behavior. *Child Development,* 1967, 38, 739–746.

LANE, I. M., and MESSÉ, L. A. Distribution of insufficient, sufficient, and oversufficient rewards: A clarification of equity theory. *Journal of Personality and Social Psychology,* 1972, 21, 228–233.

LEVENTHAL, G. S., and MICHAELS, J. W. Extending the equity model: Perception of inputs and allocation of reward as a function of duration and quantity of performance. *Journal of Personality and Social Psychology,* 1969, 12, 303–309.

LEVENTHAL, G. S., WEISS, T., and LONG, G. Equity, reciprocity, and real—locating rewards in the dyad. *Journal of Personality and Social Psychology,* 1969, 13, 300–305.

LUCE, R. D., and RAIFFA, H. *Games and decisions.* New York: Wiley, 1957.

MESSÉ, L. A., and LANE, I. M. Rediscovering the need for multiple operations: A reply to Austin and Susmilch. *Journal of Personality and Social Psychology,* 1974, 30, 405–408.

MISCHEL, W., and GRUSEC, J. Determinants of the rehearsal and transmission of neutral and aversive behaviors. *Journal of Personality and Social Psychology,* 1966, 3, 197–205.

RABINOWITZ, L., KELLEY, H. M., and ROSENBLATT, R. M. Effects of different types of interdependence and response conditions in the minimal social situation. *Journal of Experimental Social Psychology,* 1966, 2, 169–197.

ROTTER, J. B. *Social learning and clinical psychology.* Englewood Cliffs, N. J.: Prentice-Hall, 1954.

SAHAKIAN, W. *Systematic social psychology.* New York: Chandler, 1974.

SCHOPLER, J. Social power. In L. Berkowitz (Ed.) *Advances in experimental social psychology.* Vol. 2. New York: Academic Press, 1965. Pp. 177–219.

SHAPIRO, E. G. Effect of expectations of future interaction on reward allocations in dyads: Equity or equality. *Journal of Personality and Social Psychology,* 1975, 31, 873–880.

SKINNER, B. F. *Science and human behavior.* New York: Macmillan, 1953.

SKINNER, B. F. *Beyond freedom and dignity.* New York: Knopf, 1971.

STOUFFER, S. A., SUCHMAN, E. A., DeVINNEY, L. C., STARR, S. A., and WILLIAMS, R. M., JR. *The American soldier: Adjustment during army life.* Vol. 1. Princeton, N.J.: Princeton University Press, 1949.

THIBAUT, J. W. An experimental study of the cohesiveness of underprivileged groups. *Human Relations,* 1950, 3, 251–278.

THIBAUT, J. W., and KELLEY, H. H. *The social psychology of groups.* New York: Wiley, 1959.

THORNDIKE, E. L. Animal intelligence: An experimental study of the associative process in animals. *Psychological Review*, 1898 Monograph Supplement No. 8.

WALSTER, E., BERSCHEID, E., and WALSTER, G. W. New directions in equity research. *Journal of Personality and Social Psychology*, 1973, 25, 151–176.

WALTERS, R. H., and WILLOWS, D. Imitation behavior of disturbed children following exposure to aggressive and nonaggressive models. *Child Development*, 1968, 39, 79–91.

WEINER, H. R., and DUBANOWSKI, R. A. Resistance to extinction as a function of self- or externally determined schedules of reinforcement. *Journal of Social Psychology*, 1975, 31, 905–910.

CHAPTER 10

ADERMAN, D. Elation, depression, and helping behavior. *Journal of Personality and Social Psychology*, 1972, 24, 91–101.

ADERMAN, D., and BERKOWITZ, L. Observational set, empathy, and helping. *Journal of Personality and Social Psychology*, 1970, 14, 141–148.

ADERMAN, D., BREHM, S. S., and KATZ, L. B. Empathic observation of an innocent victim: The just world revisited. *Journal of Personality and Social Psychology*, 1974, 29, 342–347.

ALTMAN, I., and TAYLOR, D. A. *Social penetration processes: The development of interpersonal relationships.* New York: Holt, 1973.

ARONSON, E. Some antecedents of interpersonal attraction. In W. J. Arnold and D. Levine (Eds.) *Nebraska Symposium on Motivation, 1969.* Lincoln, Neb.: University of Nebraska Press, 1970. Pp. 143–178.

ARONSON, E., and LINDER, D. Gain and loss of esteem as determinants of interpersonal attraction. *Journal of Experimental Social Psychology*, 1965, 1, 156–171.

ARONSON, E., and MILLS, J. The effect of severity of initiation on liking for a group. *Journal of Abnormal and Social Psychology*, 1959, 59, 177–181.

ARONSON, E., WILLERMAN, B., and FLOYD, J. The effect of a pratfall on increasing interpersonal attractiveness. *Psychonomic Science*, 1966, 4, 227–228.

BALES, R. F. Task roles and social roles in problem solving groups. In E. E. Maccoby, T. M. Newcomb, and E. L. Hartley (Eds.) *Readings in social psychology.* (3rd ed.) New York: Holt, Rinehart, and Winston, 1958. Pp. 437–447.

BERKOWITZ, L. Social norms, feelings, and other factors affecting helping and altruism. In L. Berkowitz (Ed.) *Advances in experimental social psychology.* Vol. 6. New York: Academic Press, 1972. Pp. 63–108.

BERKOWITZ, L., and DANIELS, L. Responsibility and dependency. *Journal of Abnormal and Social Psychology*, 1963, 66, 429–436.

BERKOWITZ, L., KLANDERMAN, S. B., and HARRIS, R. Effects of experimenter awareness and sex of subject and experimenter on reactions to dependency relationships. *Sociometry*, 1964, 27, 327–337.

BERSCHEID, E., DION, K. K., WALSTER, E. H., and WALSTER, G. W. Physical attractiveness and dating choice: A test of the matching hypothesis. *Journal of Experimental Social Psychology*, 1971, 7, 173–189.

BERSCHEID, E., and WALSTER, E. H. When does a harm-doer compensate a victim? *Journal of Personality and Social Psychology*, 1967, 6, 435–441.

BERSCHEID, E., and WALSTER, E. H. *Interpersonal attraction*. Reading, Mass.: Addison-Wesley, 1969.

BERSCHEID, E., and WALSTER, E. H. Physical attractiveness. In L. Berkowitz (Ed.) *Advances in experimental social psychology*. Vol. 7. New York: Academic Press, 1974. Pp. 157–215(a).

BERSCHEID, E., and WALSTER, E. H. A little bit about love. In T. L. Huston (Ed.) *Foundations of interpersonal attraction*. New York: Academic Press, 1974. Pp. 356–382(b).

BERSCHEID, E., WALSTER E. H., and BARCLAY, A. Effect of time on tendency to compensate a victim. *Psychological Reports*, 1969, 25, 431–436.

BICKMAN, L. The effect of another bystander's ability to help on bystander intervention in an emergency. *Journal of Experimental Social Psychology*, 1971, 7, 376–379.

BREHM, J. W., and COLE, A. H. Effect of a favor which reduces freedom. *Journal of Personality and Social Psychology*, 1966, 3, 420–426.

BREHM, J. W., GATZ, M., GOETHALS, G., McCRIMMON, J., and WARD, L. Psychological arousal and interpersonal attraction. Unpublished manuscript, Duke University, 1970.

BRISLIN, R. W., and LEWIS, S. A. Dating and physical attractiveness: Replication. *Psychological Reports*, 1968, 22, 976.

BRYAN, J. H., and TEST, M. A. Models and helping: Naturalistic studies in aiding behavior. *Journal of Personality and Social Psychology*, 1967, 6, 400–407.

BYRNE, D. Interpersonal attraction and attitude similarity. *Journal of Abnormal and Social Psychology*, 1961, 62, 713–715.

BYRNE, D. Attitudes and attraction. In L. Berkowitz (Ed.) *Advances in experimental social psychology*. Vol. 4. New York: Academic Press, 1969. Pp. 35–89.

BYRNE, D. *The attraction paradigm*. New York: Academic Press, 1971.

BYRNE, D., LONDON, O., and REEVES, K. The effects of physical attractiveness, sex, and attitude similarity on interpersonal attraction. *Journal of Personality*, 1968, 36, 259–271.

BYRNE, D., and NELSON, D. Attraction as a linear function of proportion of positive reinforcements. *Journal of Personality and Social Psychology*, 1965, 1, 659–663.

CARLSMITH, J. M., and GROSS, A. E. Some effects of guilt on compliance. *Journal of Personality and Social Psychology*, 1969, 11, 232–239.

CLARK, R. D., III. Effects of sex and race on helping behavior in a non-reactive setting. *Representative Research in Social Psychology*, 1974, 5, 1–6.

CLARK, R. D., III, and WORD, L. E. Where is the apathetic bystander? Situational characteristics of the emergency. *Journal of Personality and Social Psychology*, 1974, 29, 279–287.

CLORE, G. L., WIGGINS, N. H., and ITKIN, S. Gain and loss in attraction:

Attributions from nonverbal behavior. *Journal of Personality and Social Psychology*, 1975, 31, 706–712.

DARLEY, J. M., JR., and BATSON, C. D. "From Jerusalem to Jericho": A study of situational and dispositional variables in helping behavior. *Journal of Personality and Social Psychology*, 1973, 27, 100–108.

DARLEY, J. M., JR., and BERSCHEID, E. Increased liking caused by the anticipation of personal contact. *Human Relations*, 1967, 20, 29–40.

DARLEY, J. M., JR., and LATANÉ, B. Bystander intervention in emergencies: Diffusion of responsibility. *Journal of Personality and Social Psychology*, 1968, 8, 377–383.

DERMER, M., and THIEL, D. L. When beauty may fail. *Journal of Personality and Social Psychology*, 1975, 31, 1168–1176.

DEUTSCH, M., and COLLINS, M. E. *Interracial housing: A psychological evaluation of a social experiment.* Minneapolis, Minn.: University of Minnesota Press, 1951.

DION, K. K., BERSCHEID, E., and WALSTER, E. H. What is beautiful is good. *Journal of Personality and Social Psychology*, 1972, 24, 285–290.

ELDER, G. H., JR. Appearance and education in marriage mobility. *American Sociological Review*, 1969, 34, 519–533.

FESTINGER, L., SCHACHTER, S., and BACK, K. *Social pressures in informal groups: A study of human factors in housing.* New York: Harper, 1950.

FREEDMAN, J. L., CARLSMITH, J. M., and SEARS, D. O. *Social psychology.* (2nd ed.) Englewood Cliffs, N.J.: Prentice-Hall, 1974.

FREEDMAN, J. L. Transgression, compliance, and guilt. In J. R. Macaulay and L. Berkowitz (Eds.) *Altruism and helping behavior.* New York: Academic Press, 1970. Pp. 155–161.

FREEDMAN, J. L., CARLSMITH, J. M., and SUOMI, S. The effect of familiarity on liking. Unpublished manuscript, Stanford University, 1969.

FREEDMAN, J. L., WALLINGTON, S. A., and BLESS, E. Compliance without pressure: The effect of guilt. *Journal of Personality and Social Psychology*, 1967, 7, 117–124.

FROMAN, R. *Street poems.* New York: McCall, 1971.

GERARD, H. B., and GREENBAUM, C. W. Attitudes toward an agent of uncertainty reduction. *Journal of Personality*, 1962, 30, 485–495.

GERARD, H. B., and MATTHEWSON, G. C. The effects of severity of initiation on liking for a group: A replication. *Journal of Experimental Social Psychology*, 1966, 2, 278–287.

GERGEN, K. J., ELLSWORTH, P., MASLACH, C., and SEIPEL, M. Obligation, donor resources, and reactions to aid in three cultures. *Journal of Personality and Social Psychology*, 1975, 31, 390–400.

GERGEN, K. J., and GERGEN, M. International assistance from a psychological perspective. *1971 yearbook of world affairs.* Vol. 25. London: Institute of World Affairs, 1971.

GIBB, C. A. Leadership. In G. Lindzey and E. Aronson (Eds.) *Handbook of social psychology.* (2nd ed.) Vol. 4. Reading, Mass.: Addison-Wesley, 1969. Pp. 205–282.

GOFFMAN, E. On cooling the mark out: Some aspects of adaptation to failure. *Psychiatry*, 1952, 15, 451–463.

GOLIGHTLY, C., and BYRNE, D. Attitude statements as positive and negative reinforcements. *Science*, 1964, 146, 798–799.

GORMLY, J. A comparison of predictions from consistency and affect theories for arousal during interpersonal disagreement. *Journal of Personality and Social Psychology*, 1974, 30, 685–663.

GOULDNER, A. The norm of reciprocity: A preliminary statement. *American Sociological Review*, 1960, 25, 161–178.

HALPIN, A. W. *Theory and research in administration.* New York: Macmillan, 1966.

HOMANS, G. C. *Social behavior: Its elementary forms.* New York: Harcourt, Brace, 1961.

HORNSTEIN, H. A., MASOR, H. N., SOLE, K., and HEILMAN, M. Effects of sentiment and completion of a helping act on observer helping: A case for socially mediated Zeigarnik effects. *Journal of Personality and Social Psychology*, 1971, 17, 107–112.

HUSTON, T. L. Ambiguity of acceptance, social desirability, and dating choice. *Journal of Experimental Social Psychology*, 1973, 9, 32–42.

HUSTON, T. L. (Ed.) *Foundations of interpersonal attraction.* New York: Academic Press, 1974.

JONES, E. E. *Ingratiation: A social-psychological analysis.* New York: Appleton-Century-Crofts, 1964.

KREBS, D. L. Altruism—an examination of the concept and a review of the literature. *Psychological Bulletin*, 1970, 73, 258–302.

LATANÉ, B., and DARLEY, J. M., JR. *The unresponsive bystander: Why doesn't he help?* New York: Appleton-Century-Crofts, 1970.

LEEDS, R. Altruism and the norm of giving. Merrill-Palmer Quarterly, 1963, 9, 229–240.

LERNER, M. J. The desire for justice and reactions to victims. In J. R. Macaulay and L. Berkowitz (Eds.) *Altruism and helping behavior.* New York: Academic Press, 1970. Pp. 205–229.

LERNER, M. J., and MATTHEWS, G. Reactions to the suffering of others under conditions of indirect responsibility. *Journal of Personality and Social Psychology*, 1967, 5, 319–325.

LERNER, M. J., and SIMMONS, C. H. Observers' reaction to the "innocent victim": Compassion or rejection? *Journal of Personality and Social Psychology*, 1966, 4, 203–210.

LEVINGER, G., and SNOEK, J. D. *Attraction in relationship: A new look at interpersonal attraction.* Morristown, N.J.: General Learning Press, 1972.

LITTLE, K. Personal space. *Journal of Experimental Social Psychology*, 1965, 1, 237–247.

MACAULAY, J. R. A shill for charity. In J. R. Macaulay and L. Berkowitz (Eds.) *Altruism and helping behavior.* New York: Academic Press, 1970. Pp. 43–59.

MACAULAY, J. R., and BERKOWITZ, L. (Eds.) *Altruism and helping behavior.* New York: Academic Press, 1970.

METTEE, D. R. The true discerner as a potent source of positive affect. *Journal of Experimental Social Psychology*, 1971, 7, 292–303.

METTEE, D. R., TAYLOR, S. E., and FRIEDMAN, H. Affect conversion and the gain-loss liking effect. *Sociometry*, 1973, 36, 494–513.

MORENO, J. L. *Who shall survive?* Washington, D.C. Nervous and Mental Diseases Monograph, No. 58, 1934.

MURSTEIN, B. I. (Ed.) *Theories of attraction and love.* New York: Springer, 1971.

NEWCOMB, T. M. *The acquaintance process.* New York: Holt, Rinehart, and Winston, 1961.

NOVAK, D., and LERNER, M. J. Rejection as a consequence of perceived similarity. *Journal of Personality and Social Psychology*, 1968, 9, 147–152.

PILIAVIN, I. M., RODIN, J., and PILIAVIN, J. A. Good samaritanism: An underground phenomenon? *Journal of Personality and Social Psychology*, 1969, 13, 289–299.

PILIAVIN, J. A., and PILIAVIN, I. M. Effects of blood on reactions to a victim. *Journal of Personality and Social Psychology*, 1972, 23, 353–361.

PORIER, G. W., and LOTT, A. J. Galvanic skin responses and prejudice. *Journal of Personality and Social Psychology*, 1967, 5, 253–259.

PRUITT, D. G. Reciprocity and credit building in a laboratory dyad. *Journal of Personality and Social Psychology*, 1968, 8, 143–147.

RAWLINGS, E. I. Reactive guilt and anticipatory guilt in altruistic behavior. In J. R. Macaulay and L. Berkowitz (Eds.) *Altruism and helping behavior.* New York: Academic Press, 1970. Pp. 163–177.

ROSENFELD, H. Effect of an approval-seeking induction on interpersonal proximity. *Psychological Reports*, 1965, 17, 120–122.

ROSENHAN, D. L. Learning theory and prosocial behavior. *Journal of Social Issues*, 1972, 28, 151–163.

ROSENHAN, D. L., UNDERWOOD, B., and MOORE, B. Affect moderates self-gratification and altruism. *Journal of Personality and Social Psychology*, 1974, 30, 546–552.

ROSENTHAL, A. M. *Thirty-eight witnesses.* New York: McGraw-Hill, 1964.

ROTTER, J. B. *Social learning and clinical psychology.* Englewood Cliffs, N.J.: Prentice-Hall, 1954.

RUBIN, Z. Measurement of romantic love. *Journal of Personality and Social Psychology*, 1970, 16, 265–273.

RUBIN, Z. *Liking and loving: An invitation to social psychology.* New York: Holt, 1973.

RUBIN, Z. From liking to loving: Patterns of attraction in dating relationships. In T. L. Huston (Ed.) *Foundations of interpersonal attraction.* New York: Academic Press, 1974. Pp. 383–402.

SAEGERT, S., SWAP, W., and ZAJONC, R. B. Exposure, context, and interpersonal attraction. *Journal of Personality and Social Psychology*, 1973, 25, 234–242.

SCHACHTER, S. The interaction of cognitive and physiological determinants of emotional state. In L. Berkowitz (Ed.) *Advances in experimental social psychology.* Vol. 1. New York: Academic Press, 1964. Pp. 49–80.

SCHOPLER, J., and THOMPSON, V. D. The role of attribution processes in mediating the amount of reciprocity for a favor. *Journal of Personality and Social Psychology*, 1968, 10, 243–250.

SCHROEDER, D. A., and LINDER, D. Effects of actor's causal role, outcome severity, and knowledge of prior accidents upon attributions of responsibility. *Journal of Experimental Social Psychology*, 1976, 12, 340–356.

SCHWARTZ, S. Words, deeds, and the perception of consequences and responsibility in action situations. *Journal of Personality and Social Psychology*, 1968, 10, 232–242.

SCHWARTZ, S. Moral decision making and behavior. In J. R. Macaulay and L. Berkowitz (Eds.) *Altruism and helping behavior*. New York: Academic Press, 1970. Pp. 127–141.

SCHWARTZ, S., and CLAUSEN, G. T. Responsibility, norms, and helping in an emergency. *Journal of Personality and Social Psychology*, 1970, 16, 299–310.

SHAVER, K. G. Defensive attribution: Effects of severity and relevance on the responsibility assigned for an accident. *Journal of Personality and Social Psychology*, 1970, 14, 101–113.

SHERIF, M., HARVEY, O. J., WHITE, B. J., HOOD, W. E., and SHERIF, C. W. *Intergroup conflict and cooperation: The Robber's Cave experiment.* Norman, Oklahoma: University of Oklahoma Book Exchange, 1961.

SOLE, K., MARTON, J., and HORNSTEIN, H. A. Opinion similarity and helping: Three field experiments investigating the bases of promotive tension. *Journal of Experimental Social Psychology*, 1975, 11, 1–13.

SPENCE, J. T., and HELMREICH, R. Who likes competent women? Competence, sex-role congruence of interests, and subjects' attitudes toward women as determinants of interpersonal attraction. *Journal of Applied Social Psychology*, 1972, 2, 197–213.

STAUB, E. Instigation to goodness: The role of social norms and interpersonal influence. *Journal of Social Issues*, 1972, 28, 131–150.

STAUB, E., and SHERK, L. Need approval, children's sharing behavior, and reciprocity in sharing. *Child Development*, 1970, 41, 243–253.

STOGDILL, R. M. Validity of leader behavior descriptions. *Personnel Psychology*, 1969, 22, 153–158.

STOTLAND, E., and HILLMER, M. L., JR. Identification, authoritarian defensiveness, and self-esteem. *Journal of Abnormal and Social Psychology*, 1962, 64, 334–342.

SWENSEN, C. H. *Introduction to interpersonal relations*. Glenview, Ill.: Scott, Foresman, 1973.

SYKES, G. M., and MATZA, D. Techniques of neutralization: A theory of delinquency. *American Sociological Review*, 1957, 22, 664–670.

TESSER, A., and BRODIE, M. A note on the evaluation of a "computer date." *Psychonomic Science*, 1971, 23, 300.

THIBAUT, J. W., and KELLEY, H. H. *The social psychology of groups*. New York: Wiley, 1959.

WAGNER, C., and WHEELER, L. Model, need, and cost effects in helping behavior. *Journal of Personality and Social Psychology*, 1969, 12, 111–116.

WALSTER, E., and BERSCHEID, E. Adrenaline makes the heart grow fonder. *Psychology Today*, 1971, 5(1), 46–50.

WALSTER, E. H., BERSCHEID, E., and WALSTER, G. W. New directions in equity research. *Journal of Personality and Social Psychology*, 1973, 25, 151–176.

WALSTER, E. H., and PRESTHOLDT, P. The effect of misjudging another: Overcompensation or dissonance reduction? *Journal of Experimental Social Psychology*, 1966, 2, 85–97.

West, S. G., Whitney, G., and Schmedler, R. Helping a motorist in distress: The effects of sex, race, and neighborhood. *Journal of Personality and Social Psychology,* 1975, 31, 691–698.

Winch, R. F. *Mate-selection: A study of complimentary needs.* New York: Harper & Row, 1958.

Wispé, L. G. (Ed.) Positive forms of social behavior. *Journal of Social Issues,* 1972, 28, No. 3.

Wispé, L. G., and Freshley, H. B. Race, sex, and sympathetic helping behavior: The broken bag caper. *Journal of Personality and Social Psychology,* 1971, 17, 59–65.

Wrightsman, L. S., and Cook, S. W. Factor analysis and attitude change. Paper presented at the meeting of the Southeastern Psychological Association, Atlanta, Ga., 1965.

CHAPTER 11

Altman, I. *The environment and social behavior.* Monterey, Cal.: Brooks/Cole, 1975.

Apfelbaum, E. On conflicts and bargaining. In L. Berkowitz (Ed.) *Advances in experimental social psychology.* Vol. 7. New York: Academic Press, 1974. Pp. 103–156.

Ardrey, R. *The territorial imperative.* New York: Atheneum, 1966.

Atkinson, J. W. (Ed.) *Motives in fantasy, action, and society.* Princeton, N.J.: Van Nostrand, 1958.

Atkinson, J. W. *An introduction to motivation.* Princeton, N.J.: Van Nostrand, 1964.

Atkinson, J. W., and Feather, N. T. *A theory of achievement motivation.* New York: Wiley, 1966.

Atkinson, J. W., and Litwin, G. H. Achievement motive and test anxiety conceived as a motive to approach success and a motive to avoid failure. *Journal of Abnormal and Social Psychology,* 1960, 60, 52–63.

Bandura, A. *Aggression: A social learning analysis.* Englewood Cliffs, N.J.: Prentice-Hall, 1973.

Bandura, A., Ross, D., and Ross, S. A. Transmission of aggression through imitation of aggressive models. *Journal of Abnormal and Social Psychology,* 1961, 63, 575–582.

Bandura, A., Ross, D., and Ross, S. A. Imitation of film-mediated aggressive models. *Journal of Abnormal and Social Psychology,* 1963, 66, 3–11.

Berkowitz, L. *Aggression: A social psychological analysis.* New York: McGraw-Hill, 1962.

Berkowitz, L. The concept of aggressive drive: Some additional considerations. In L. Berkowitz (Ed.) *Advances in experimental social psychology.* Vol. 2. New York: Academic Press, 1965. Pp. 301–329.

Berkowitz, L. (Ed.) *Roots of aggression: A re-examination of the frustration-aggression hypothesis.* New York: Atherton Press, 1969.

BERKOWITZ, L. *A survey of social psychology.* New York: Holt, Rinehart, and Winston, 1975.

BERKOWITZ, L., and GEEN, R. G. Stimulus qualities of the target of aggression: A further study. *Journal of Personality and Social Psychology,* 1967, 5, 364–368.

BERKOWITZ, L., and LEPAGE, A. Weapons as aggression eliciting stimuli. *Journal of Personality and Social Psychology,* 1967, 7, 202–207.

BROWN, R. *Social psychology.* Glencoe, Ill.: Free Press, 1965.

BURNSTEIN, E., and WORCHEL, P. Arbitrariness of frustration and its consequences in aggression in a social situation. *Journal of Personality,* 1962, 30, 528–541.

BUSS, A. H. *The psychology of aggression.* New York: Wiley, 1961.

CATER, D., and STRICKLAND, S. *TV violence and the child: the evolution and fate of the Surgeon General's report.* New York: Russell Sage Foundation, 1975.

CHAFFEE, S. H., and MCLEOD, J. M. Adolescents, parents and television violence. Paper presented at the meeting of the American Psychological Association, Washington, D.C., 1971.

CLINE, V. B., CROFT, R. G., and COURIER, S. Desensitization of children to television violence. *Journal of Personality and Social Psychology,* 1973, 27, 360–365.

COOPERSMITH, S. *The antecedents of self-esteem.* San Francisco: Freeman, 1967.

DEUTSCH, M. The effect of motivational orientation upon threat and suspicion. *Human Relations,* 1960, 13, 122–139.

DEUTSCH, M. Socially relevant science: reflections on some studies of interpersonal conflict. *American Psychologist,* 1969, 24, 1076–1092.

DEUTSCH, M., and KRAUSS, R. M. The effect of threat on interpersonal bargaining. *Journal of Abnormal and Social Psychology,* 1960, 61, 181–189.

DEUTSCH, M., and KRAUSS, R. M. Studies of interpersonal bargaining. *Journal of Conflict Resolution,* 1962, 6, 52–76.

DOLLARD, J., DOOB, L. W., MILLER, N. E., MOWRER, O. H., and SEARS, R. R. *Frustration and aggression.* New Haven, Conn.: Yale University Press, 1939.

ENZLE, M. E., HANSEN, R. D., and LOWE, C. A. Causal attribution in the mixed-motive game: Effects of facilitory and inhibitory environmental forces. *Journal of Personality and Social Psychology,* 1975, 31, 50–54.

FEATHER, N. T. Valence of outcome and expectation of success in relation to task difficulty and perceived locus of control. *Journal of Personality and Social Psychology,* 1967, 7, 372–386.

FEATHER, N. T., and RAPHELSON, A. C. Fear of success in Australian and American student groups: Motive or sex-role stereotype? *Journal of Personality,* 1974, 42, 190–201.

FESHBACH, S., and SINGER, R. *Television and aggression.* San Francisco: Jossey-Bass, 1971.

FREEDMAN, J. *Crowding and behavior.* New York: Viking Press, 1975.

FREUD, S. *A general introduction to psychoanalysis.* New York: Boni and Liveright, 1920.

FREUD, S. *New introductory lectures on psychoanalysis.* New York: Norton, 1933.

FREUD, S. Why war? In J. Strachey (Ed.) *Collected papers*. Vol. 5. London: Hogarth Press, 1950. Pp. 273–287.

FROMM, E. The Erich Fromm theory of aggression. In S. Milgram (Ed.) *Psychology in Today's World*. Boston: Little, Brown, 1975. Pp. 136–142.

GALLO, P. S., and McCLINTOCK, C. G. Cooperative and competitive behavior in mixed-motive games. *Journal of Conflict Resolution*, 1965, 9, 68–78.

GEEN, R. G., and RAKOSKY, J. J. Interpretations of observed aggression and their effect on GSR. *Journal of Experimental Research in Personality*, 1973, 6, 289–292.

GERGEN, K. J. *The psychology of behavior exchange*. Reading, Mass.: Addison-Wesley, 1969.

GORANSON, R. E. Media violence and aggressive behavior: a review of experimental research. In L. Berkowitz (Ed.) *Advances in experimental social psychology*. Vol. 5. New York: Academic Press, 1970. Pp. 1–31.

GUMPERT, P., DEUTSCH, M., and EPSTEIN, Y. Effect of incentive magnitude on cooperation in the prisoner's dilemma game. *Journal of Personality and Social Psychology*, 1969, 11, 66–69.

HEIDER, F. *The psychology of interpersonal relations*. New York: Wiley, 1958.

HICKS, D. J. Short- and long-term retention of affectively varied modeled behavior. *Psychonomic Science*, 1968, 11, 369–370.

HORNER, M. Toward an understanding of achievement-related conflicts in women. *Journal of Social Issues*, 1972, 28, 157–175.

HOWITT, D., and CUMBERBATCH, G. *Mass media violence and society*. London: Paul Elek, 1975.

JOHNSON, R. N. *Aggression in man and animals*. Philadelphia: W. B. Saunders, 1972.

JONES, E. E., and GERARD, H. B. *Foundations of social psychology*. New York: Wiley, 1967.

KARABENICK, S. A. Valence of success and failure as a function of achievement motives and locus of control. *Journal of Personality and Social Psychology*, 1972, 21, 101–110.

KAUFMANN, H. *Aggression and altruism*. New York: Holt, Rinehart, and Winston, 1970.

KELLEY, C. M. *Uniform crime reports for the United States: 1974*. Washington, D.C.: U.S. Government Printing Office, 1975.

KELLEY, H. H., and STAHELSKI, A. The inference of intention from moves in the prisoner's dilemma game. *Journal of Experimental Social Psychology*, 1970, 6, 409–419.

KLOPFER, P. H. *Habitats and territories*. New York: Basic Books, 1969.

LAGERSPETZ, K., and NURMI, R. An experiment on the frustration-aggression hypothesis. Report of the Psychological Institute, University of Turku, Finland, 1964. No. 10.

LARSEN, O. N. (Ed.) *Violence and the mass media*. New York: Harper & Row, 1968.

LEYENS, J., CAMINO, L., PARKE, R., and BERKOWITZ, L. Effects of movie violence on aggression in a field setting as a function of group dominance and cohesion. *Journal of Personality and Social Psychology*, 1975, 32, 361–367.

LIEBERT, R. M., NEALE, J. M., and DAVIDSON, E. S. *The early window: The effects of television on children and youth.* New York: Pergamon Press, 1973.

LORENZ, K. *On aggression.* New York: Harcourt, Brace and World, 1966.

LUCE, R. D., and RAIFFA, H. *Games and decisions.* New York: Wiley, 1957.

MAHONE, C. H. Fear of failure in unrealistic vocational aspiration. *Journal of Abnormal and Social Psychology*, 1960, 60, 253–261.

MANNING, S. A., and TAYLOR, D. A. Effects of viewed violence and aggression: Stimulation and catharsis. *Journal of Personality and Social Psychology*, 1975, 31, 180–188.

MARLOWE, D., GERGEN, K. J., and DOOB, A. N. Opponent's personality, expectation of social interaction and interpersonal bargaining. *Journal of Personality and Social Psychology*, 1966, 3, 206–213.

MCCLELLAND, D. C. *The achieving society.* Princeton, N.J.: Von Nostrand, 1961.

MCCLELLAND, D. C., ATKINSON, J. W., CLARK, R. A., and LOWELL, E. L. *The achievement motive.* New York: Appleton-Century-Crofts, 1953.

MEHRABIAN, A. Measures of achieving tendency. *Educational and Psychological Measurement*, 1969, 29, 445–451.

MEYER, T. P. Effects of viewing justified and unjustified real film violence on aggressive behavior. *Journal of Personality and Social Psychology*, 1972, 23, 21–29.

MILLER, N. E. The frustration-aggression hypotheses. *Psychological Review*, 1941, 48, 337–342.

MONAHAN, L., KUHN, M., and SHAVER, P. Intrapsychic vs. cultural explanations of the "fear of success" motive. *Journal of Personality and Social Psychology*, 1974, 29, 60–64.

MONTAGU, M. F. A. (Ed.) *Man and aggression.* London: Oxford University Press, 1968.

MORRIS, D. *The naked ape.* New York: McGraw-Hill, 1967.

MORRIS, J. L. Propensity for risk taking as a determinant of vocational choice: An extension of the theory of achievement motivation. *Journal of Personality and Social Psychology*, 1966, 3, 328–335.

MOYER, K. E. Kinds of aggression and their physiological basis. Report No. 67-12. Department of Psychology, Carnegie-Mellon University, Pittsburgh, Pa., 1967.

MULVIHILL, D. J., and TUMIN, M. M. (Eds.) *Crimes of violence.* Vol. II: Staff report to the U.S. National Commission on the Causes and Prevention of Violence. Washington, D.C.: U.S. Government Printing Office, 1969.

MURRAY, H. A. *Explorations in personality.* New York: Oxford University Press, 1938.

NEMETH, C. A critical analysis of research utilizing the Prisoner's Dilemma paradigm for the study of bargaining. In L. Berkowitz (Ed.) *Advances in experimental social psychology.* Vol. 6. New York: Academic Press, 1972. Pp. 203–234.

OSKAMP, S. Effects of programmed strategies on cooperation in the Prisoner's Dilemma and other mixed-motive games. In L. S. Wrightsman, J. O'Conner, and N. Baker (Eds.) *Cooperation and competition: Readings on mixed-motive games.* Monterey, Cal.: Brooks/Cole, 1972. Pp. 147–189.

OSKAMP, S., and KLEINKE, C. Amount of reward as a variable in the Prisoner's Dilemma game. *Journal of Personality and Social Psychology*, 1970, 16, 133–140.

RADLOW, R., WEIDNER, M. F., and HURST, P. M. The effect of incentive magnitude and "motivational orientation" upon choice behavior in a two-person non-zero-sum game. *Journal of Social Psychology*, 1968, 74, 199–208.

RAPOPORT, A., CHAMMAH, A., DWYER, J., and GYR, J. Three-person and non-zero-sum non-negotiable games. *Behavioral Science*, 1962, 7, 39–58.

ROBBINS, L., and ROBBINS, E. Comment on: "Toward an understanding of achievement-related conflicts in women." *Journal of Social Issues*, 1973, 29, 133–137.

SCHACHTER, S. The interaction of cognitive and physiological determinants of emotional state. In L. Berkowitz (Ed.) *Advances in experimental social psychology*. Vol. 1. New York: Academic Press, 1964. Pp. 49–80.

SCOTT, J. P. Agonistic behavior of mice and rats: A review. *American Zoologist*, 1966, 6, 683–701.

SERMAT, V. Cooperative behavior and mixed motive games. *Journal of Social Psychology*, 1964, 62, 217–239.

SHURE, G. H., MEEKER, R. J., and HANSFORD, E. A. The effectiveness of pacifist strategies in bargaining games. *Journal of Conflict Resolution*, 1965, 9, 106–117.

SKINNER, B. F. *Beyond freedom and dignity*. New York: Knopf, 1971.

SMITH, W. P., and ANDERSON, A. J. Threats, communication, and bargaining. *Journal of Personality and Social Psychology*, 1975, 32, 76–82.

TANNENBAUM, P. H., and ZILLMAN, D. Emotional arousal in the facilitation of aggression through communication. In L. Berkowitz (Ed.) *Advances in experimental social psychology*. Vol. 8. New York: Academic Press, 1975. Pp. 149–192.

TERHUNE, K. W. The effects of personality in cooperation and conflict. In P. Swingle (Ed.) *The structure of conflict*. New York: Academic Press, 1970. Pp. 193–234.

THIBAUT, J. W., and KELLEY, H. H. *The social psychology of groups*. New York: Wiley, 1959.

TROPE, Y. Seeking information about one's own ability as a determinant of choice among tasks. *Journal of Personality and Social Psychology*, 1975, 32, 1004–1013.

ULRICH, R. E., WOLFF, M., and AZRIN, N. H. Shock as an elicitor of intra- and interspecies fighting behavior. *Animal Behavior*, 1964, 12, 145.

VINACKE, W. E. Variables in experimental games: toward a field theory. *Psychological Bulletin*, 1969, 71, 293–318.

WEBER, M. *The Protestant ethic and the spirit of capitalism*. New York: Scribner's, 1930.

WEINER, B. *Theories of motivation: From mechanism to cognition*. New York: Markham, 1972.

WEINER, B. *Achievement motivation and attribution theory*. Morristown, N.J.: General Learning Press, 1974.

WEINER, B., FRIEZE, I., KUKLA, A., REED, L., REST, S., and ROSENBAUM, R. M. Perceiving the causes of success and failure. In E. E. Jones, D. E. Kanouse, H. H. Kelley, R. E. Nisbett, S. Valins, and B. Weiner (Eds.)

Attribution: Perceiving the causes of behavior. Morristown, N.J.: General Learning Press, 1972. Pp. 95–120.

WEINER, B., and KUKLA, A. An attributional analysis of achievement motivation. *Journal of Personality and Social Psychology*, 1970, 15, 1–20.

WINTERBOTTOM, M. R. The relation of childhood independence to achievement motivation. Unpublished doctoral dissertation, University of Michigan, 1953.

ZUCKERMAN, M., and WHEELER, L. To dispel fantasy about the fantasy-based measure of fear of success. *Psychological Bulletin*, 1975, 82, 932–946.

CHAPTER 12

ADAIR, J. G. Demand characteristics or conformity?: Suspiciousness of deception and experimenter bias in conformity research. *Canadian Journal of Behavioural Science*, 1972, 4, 238–248.

ALLEN, V. L. Situational factors in conformity. In L. Berkowitz (Ed.) *Advances in experimental social psychology.* Vol. 2. New York: Academic Press, 1965. Pp. 133–175.

ALLEN, V. L., and LEVINE, J. M. Social support, dissent, and conformity. *Sociometry*, 1968, 31, 138–149.

APFELBAUM, E. On conflicts and bargaining. In L. Berkowitz (Ed.) *Advances in experimental social psychology.* Vol. 7. New York: Academic Press, 1974. Pp. 103–156.

ASCH, S. E. Effects of group pressure upon the modification and distortion of judgments. In H. Guetzkow (Ed.) *Groups, leadership, and men.* Pittsburgh, Pa.: Carnegie Press, 1951.

CARTWRIGHT, D. A field theoretical conception of power. In D. Cartwright (Ed.) *Studies in social power.* Ann Arbor, Mich.: Institute for Social Research, 1959. Pp. 183–220.

CHRISTIE, R., and GEIS, F. L. (Eds.) *Studies in Machiavellianism.* New York: Academic Press, 1970.

CRUTCHFIELD, R. S. Conformity and character. *American Psychologist*, 1955, 10, 191–198.

DAHL, R. A. The concept of power. *Behavioral Science*, 1957, 2, 201–218.

DEUTSCH, M., and GERARD, H. B. A study of normative and informational social influences on individual judgments. *Journal of Abnormal and Social Psychology*, 1955, 51, 629–636.

EXLINE, R., THIBAUT, J. W., HICKEY, C. B., and GUMPERT, P. Visual interaction in relation to Machiavellianism and an unethical act. In R. Christie and F. L. Geis (Eds.) *Studies in Machiavellianism.* New York: Academic Press, 1970. Pp. 53–75.

FESTINGER, L. Informal social communication. *Psychological Review*, 1950, 57, 271–282.

FESTINGER, L. *A theory of cognitive dissonance.* Stanford, Cal.: Stanford University Press, 1957.

FRENCH, J. R. P., JR., and RAVEN, B. The bases of social power. In D. Cartwright (Ed.) *Studies in social power.* Ann Arbor, Mich.: Institute for Social Research, 1959. Pp. 150–167.

GAMSON, W. A. *Power and discontent.* Homewood, Ill.: Dorsey Press, 1968.

GERARD, H. B., CONOLLEY, E. S., and WILHELMY, R. A. Conformity and group size. *Journal of Personality and Social Psychology*, 1968, 8, 79–82.

GODWIN, W. F., and RESTLE, F. The road to agreement: subgroup pressures in small group consensus processes. *Journal of Personality and Social Psychology*, 1974, 30, 500–509.

GRAHAM, D. Experimental studies of social influence in simple judgment situations. *Journal of Social Psychology*, 1962, 56, 245–269.

JACOBS, R. C., and CAMPBELL, D. T. The perpetuation of an arbitrary tradition through several generations of a laboratory microculture. *Journal of Abnormal Social Psychology*, 1961, 62, 649–658.

JAHODA, M. Conformity and independence—a psychological analysis. *Human Relations*, 1959, 12, 99–120.

JONES, E. E., and GERARD, H. B. *Foundations of social psychology.* New York: Wiley, 1967.

KELLEY, H. H. Two functions of reference groups. In G. E. Swanson, T. M. Newcomb, and E. L. Hartley (Eds.) *Readings in social psychology.* (2nd ed.) New York: Holt, Rinehart, and Winston, 1952. Pp. 410–414.

KELMAN, H. C. Processes of opinion change. *Public Opinion Quarterly*, 1961, 25, 57–78.

KIESLER, C. A., and KIESLER, S. B. *Conformity.* Reading, Mass.: Addison-Wesley, 1969.

LEWIN, K. Environmental forces. In C. Murchison (Ed.) *A handbook of child psychology.* (2nd ed.) Worcester, Mass.: Clark University Press, 1933.

LEWIN, K. *Field theory of learning.* Yearbook of the National Society for the Study of Education, 1942, Vol. 41, P. 2, 215–242.

LEWIN, K. Behavior and development as a function of the total situation. In L. Carmichael (Ed.) *Manual of child psychology.* (2nd ed.) New York: Wiley, 1946.

LEWIN, K. *Field theory in social science.* New York: Harper, 1951.

MACHIAVELLI, N. The prince. Translated by W. K. Marriott. In R. M. Hutchins (Ed.) *Great Books of the Western World.* Chicago: Encyclopedia Britannica, Inc., 1952. Vol. 23. Pp. 3–37. (Originally published 1532.)

MARCH, J. G. Measurement concepts in the theory of influence. *Journal of Politics*, 1957, 19, 202–226.

MILGRAM, S. Behavioral study of obedience. *Journal of Abnormal and Social Psychology*, 1963, 67, 371–378.

MILGRAM, S. Some conditions of obedience and disobedience to authority. *Human Relations*, 1965, 18, 57–76.

MILLER, N. E. Experimental studies of conflict. In J. McV. Hunt (Ed.) *Personality and the behavior disorders.* Vol. 1. New York: Ronald Press, 1944. Pp. 431–465.

MOSCOVICI, S., and FAUCHEAUX, C. Social influence, conformity bias, and the study of active minorities. In L. Berkowitz (Ed.) *Advances in experimental social psychology.* Vol. 6. New York: Academic Press, 1972. Pp. 150–202.

MOSCOVICI, S., and NEMETH, C. Social influence: II. Minority influence. In C. Nemeth (Ed.) *Social psychology: classic and contemporary integrations.* Chicago: Rand McNally, 1974.

NATIONAL OPINION RESEARCH CORPORATION. In Christie, R. and Geis, F. L. (Eds.) *Studies in Machiavellianism.* New York: Academic Press, 1970.

NEWCOMB, T. M. *Personality and social change.* New York: Dryden, 1943.

NIEBURG, H. L. *Political violence: The behavioral process.* New York: St. Martin's Press, 1969.

NOSANCHUCK, T. A., and LIGHTSTONE, J. Canned laughter and public and private conformity. *Journal of Personality and Social Psychology,* 1974, 29, 153–156.

ROSENBERG, L. A. Group size, prior experience and conformity. *Journal of Abnormal and Social Psychology,* 1961, 63, 436–437.

SCHOPLER, J. Social power. In L. Berkowitz (Ed.) *Advances in experimental social psychology.* Vol. 2. New York: Academic Press, 1965. Pp. 177–219.

SHERIF, M. *The psychology of social norms.* New York: Harper & Row, 1936.

SIEGEL, A. E., and SIEGEL, S. Reference groups, membership groups, and attitude change. *Journal of Abnormal and Social Psychology,* 1957, 55, 360–364.

STRICKER, L. J., MESSICK, S., and JACKSON, D. N. Conformity, anticonformity, and independence: Their dimensionality and generality. *Journal of Personality and Social Psychology,* 1970, 16, 495–507.

THIBAUT, J. W., and KELLEY, H. H. *The social psychology of groups.* New York: Wiley, 1959.

WHEELER, L. *Interpersonal influence.* Boston: Allyn and Bacon, 1970.

WILLIS, R. H. Conformity, independence, and anticonformity. *Human Relations,* 1965, 18, 373–388.

WRIGHTSMAN, L. S., and COOK, S. W. Factor analysis and attitude change. Paper presented at the meeting of the Southeastern Psychological Association, Atlanta, 1965.

CHAPTER 13

ARONSON, E., and MILLS, J. The effect of severity of initiation on liking for a group. *Journal of Abnormal and Social Psychology,* 1959, 59, 177–181.

BALES, R. F. *Interaction process analysis.* Cambridge, Mass.: Addison-Wesley, 1950.

BALES, R. F. How people interact in conferences. *Scientific American,* 1955, 192, 31–35.

BALES, R. F. *Personality and interpersonal behavior.* New York: Holt, Rinehart, and Winston, 1970.

BAVELAS, A. Communication patterns in task-oriented groups. *Journal of the Accoustical Society of America,* 1950, 22, 725–730.

BEM, D., WALLACH, M. A., and KOGAN, N. Group decision making under risk of aversive consequences. *Journal of Personality and Social Psychology,* 1965, 1, 453–460.

BORGATTA, E. F. A systematic study of interaction process scores, peer and self-assessments, personality and other variables. *Genetic Psychology Monographs*, 1962, 65, 219–291.

BROWN, R. *Social psychology*. Glencoe, Ill.: Free Press, 1965.

CAPLOW, T. *Two against one: Coalitions in triads*. Englewood Cliffs, N.J.: Prentice-Hall, 1968.

CARTWRIGHT, D. Risk-taking by individuals and groups: An assessment of research employing choice dilemmas. *Journal of Personality and Social Psychology*, 1971, 20, 361–378.

CARTWRIGHT, D., and ZANDER, A. (Eds.) *Group dynamics: Research and theory*. (3rd ed.) New York: Harper & Row, 1968.

CATTELL, R. B., and STICE, G. F. Four formulae for selecting leaders on the basis of personality. *Human Relations*, 1954, 7, 493–507.

COLLINS, B. E., and RAVEN, B. H. Group structure: attraction, coalitions, communication and power. In G. Lindzey and E. Aronson (Eds.) *Handbook of social psychology* (2nd ed.) Vol. 4. Reading, Mass.: Addison-Wesley, 1969. Pp. 102–204.

FESTINGER, L. Informal social communication. *Psychological Review*, 1950, 57, 271–282.

FESTINGER, L., RIECKEN, H. W., and SCHACHTER, S. *When prophecy fails*. Minneapolis, Minn.: University of Minnesota Press, 1956.

FESTINGER, L., SCHACHTER, S., and BACK, K. *Social pressures in informal groups: A study of human factors in housing*. New York: Harper, 1950.

FIEDLER, F. E. The influence of leader-key man relations on combat crew effectiveness. *Journal of Abnormal and Social Psychology*, 1955, 51, 227–235.

FIEDLER, F. E. A contingency model of leadership effectiveness. In L. Berkowitz (Ed.) *Advances in experimental social psychology*. Vol. 1. New York: Academic Press, 1964. Pp. 149–190.

FIEDLER, F. E. Validation and extension of the contingency model of leadership effectiveness: A review of empirical findings. *Psychological Bulletin*, 1971, 76, 128–148.

FISHBEIN, M., LANDY, E., and HATCH, G. Some determinants of an individual's esteem for his least preferred co-worker: An attitudinal analysis. *Human Relations*, 1969, 22, 173–188.

FRENCH, J. R. P., and RAVEN, B. The bases of social power. In D. Cartwright (Ed.) *Studies in social power*. Ann Arbor, Mich.: Institute for Social Research, 1959. Pp. 150–167.

GERARD, H. B., and MATTHEWSON, G. C. The effects of severity of initiation on liking for a group: A replication. *Journal of Experimental Social Psychology*, 1966, 2, 278–287.

GIBB, C. A. Leadership. In G. Lindzey and E. Aronson (Eds.) *Handbook of social psychology* (2nd ed.) Vol. 4. Reading, Mass.: Addison-Wesley, 1969. Pp. 205–282.

GRAEN, G., ALVARES, K., ORRIS, J. B., and MARTELLE, J. A. Contingency model of leadership effectiveness: Antecedent and evidential results. *Psychological Bulletin*, 1970, 74, 284–295.

GREENWOOD, J. M., and McNAMARA, W. J. Leadership styles of structure and consideration and managerial effectiveness. *Personnel Psychology*, 1969, 22, 141–152.

HALPIN, A. W. Studies in air crew composition: III. In the combat leader behavior of B-29 aircraft commanders. Washington, D.C.: Human Factors Operations Research Laboratory, Bolling Air Force Base, September, 1953.

HALPIN, A. W. *Theory and research in administration.* New York: Macmillan, 1966.

HALPIN, A. W., and WINER, B. J. The leadership behavior of the airplane commander. Columbus: Ohio State University Research Foundation, 1952. (mimeograph)

HEMPHILL, J. K. Leader behavior description. Columbus: Ohio State University Personnel Research Board, 1950.

HEMPHILL, J. K. Leadership behavior associated with the administrative reputation of college departments. *Journal of Educational Psychology*, 1955, 46, 385–401.

JANIS, I. L. *Victims of groupthink: A psychological study of foreign policy decisions and fiascoes.* Boston: Houghton Mifflin, 1972.

LATANÉ, B., and DARLEY, J. M., JR. *The unresponsive bystander: Why doesn't he help?* New York: Appleton-Century-Crofts, 1970.

LEAVITT, H. J. Some effects of certain communication patterns on group performance. *Journal of Abnormal and Social Psychology*, 1951, 46, 38–50.

MANN, R. D. *Interpersonal styles and group development.* New York: Wiley, 1967.

MORENO, J. L. *Who shall survive?* Washington, D.C.: Nervous and Mental Diseases Monograph, No. 58, 1934.

MOSCOVICI, S., and ZAVALLONI, M. The group as a polarizer of attitudes. *Journal of Personality and Social Psychology*, 1969, 12, 125–135.

PRUITT, D. G. Choice shifts in group discussion: an introductory review. *Journal of Personality and Social Psychology*, 1971, 20, 339–360.

SCHACHTER, S. Deviation, rejection, and communication. *Journal of Abnormal and Social Psychology*, 1951, 46, 190–207.

SCHACHTER, S. *The psychology of affiliation.* Stanford, Cal.: Stanford University Press, 1959.

SHERIF, M. *The psychology of social norms.* New York: Harper & Row, 1936.

SHERIF, M. *In common predicament: Social psychology of intergroup conflict and cooperation.* Boston: Houghton Mifflin, 1966.

SMELSER, N. J. *Theory of collective behavior.* New York: Free Press, 1963.

STEINER, I. D. Whatever happened to the group in social psychology? *Journal of Experimental Social Psychology*, 1974, 10, 93–108.

STONER, J. A. F. A comparison of individual and group decisions including risk. Unpublished masters thesis, School of Industrial Management, Massachusetts Institute of Technology, 1961.

THIBAUT, J. W., and KELLEY, H. H. *The social psychology of groups.* New York: Wiley, 1959.

TOCH, H. *The social psychology of social movements.* New York: Bobbs-Merrill, 1965.

WALLACH, M. A., and KOGAN, N. Sex differences and judgment processes. *Journal of Personality*, 1959, 27, 555–564.

WALLACH, M. A., KOGAN, N., and BURT, R. Group risk taking and field dependence-independence of group members. *Sociometry*, 1967, 30, 323–339.

EPILOGUE

BACK, K. (Ed.) Population policy and the person. *Journal of Social Issues*, 1974, 30, No. 4.

DION, K. L., BARON, R. S., and MILLER, N. Why do groups make riskier decisions than individuals? In L. Berkowitz (Ed.) *Advances in experimental social psychology*. Vol. 5. New York: Academic Press, 1970. Pp. 305–377.

FREEDMAN, J. L. *Crowding and human behavior*. New York: Viking Press, 1975.

FRIED, S., GUMPPER, D., and ALLEN, J. Ten years of social psychology. Is there a growing commitment to field research? *American Psychologist*, 1973, 28, 155–156.

GERARD, H. B., and MILLER, N. *School desegregation*. New York: Plenum, 1975.

HELMREICH, R. Applied social psychology: The unfulfilled promise. *Personality and Social Psychology Bulletin*, 1975, 1, 548–560.

HIGBEE, K. L., and WELLS, M. G. Some research trends in social psychology during the 1960's. *American Psychologist*, 1972, 27, 963–966.

KELMAN, H. C. *A time to speak: On human values and social research*. San Francisco: Jossey-Bass, 1968.

KRUGLANSKI, A. W. Theory, experiment, and the shifting publication scene in personality and social psychology. *Personality and Social Psychology Bulletin*, 1975, 1, 489–492.

LEWIN, K. Field theory and experiment in social psychology. In D. Cartwright (Ed.) *Field theory in social science: Selected theoretical papers*. New York: Harper & Row, 1951. Pp. 130–154.

LIPSEY, M. W. Research and relevance: A survey of graduate students and faculty in psychology. *American Psychologist*, 1974, 29, 541–553.

MARROW, A. J. *The practical theorist: The life and work of Kurt Lewin*. New York: Basic Books, 1969.

McGUIRE, W. J. The *yin* and *yang* of progress in social psychology: Seven Koan. *Journal of Personality and Social Psychology*, 1973, 26, 446–456.

MILLER, G. R. Jurors' responses to videotaped trial materials: Some recent findings. *Personality and Social Psychology Bulletin*, 1975, 1, 561–569.

NELSON, C. E., and KANNENBERG, P. H. Social psychology in crisis: A study of the references in the *Handbook of social psychology* (2nd ed.). *Personality and Social Psychology Bulletin*, 1976, 2, 14–21.

RING, K. Experimental social psychology: Some sober questions about some frivolous values. *Journal of Experimental Social Psychology*, 1967, 3, 113–123.

SHAVER, K. G., GILBERT, M. A., and WILLIAMS, M. C. Social psychology, criminal justice, and the principle of discretion: A selective review. *Personality and Social Psychology Bulletin*, 1975, 1, 471–484.

SMITH, M. B. Is experimental social psychology advancing? *Journal of Experimental Social Psychology*, 1972, 8, 86–96.

STOKOLS, D. On the distinction between density and crowding: Some implications for future research. *Psychological Review*, 1972, 79, 275–277.

WEINER, B. *Achievement motivation and attribution theory.* Morristown, N.J.: General Learning Press, 1974.

WILSON, W. C., and GOLDSTEIN, M. J. (Eds.) Pornography: Attitudes, use, and effects. *Journal of Social Issues,* 1973, 29, No. 3.

ZALKIND, S. S. (Ed.) Civil liberties. *Journal of Social Issues,* 1975, 31, No. 2.

Author Index

Subject Index

Guilt and altruism, 385–388

Hawthorne effect, 10. *See also*
    Awareness of being tested
Hedonistic calculus, 345, 548
Helping behavior, 56–58. *See also*
    Altruism
Horizontal structure of an attitude,
    219–220, 225, 548
Hostility
  as a reason for aggression, 454
  and deindividuation, 335–338
  in racial attitudes, 178
Hydraulic models, of aggression, 448–
    450
Hypothesis
  generation, 29, 61–63
  and implicit theory of social
    psychology, 29, 534
  testing, 62–63

I, 306–307, 548
Ideal self, 327, 548
Identification, 548
  in attitude change, 267–268
  and functions of attitudes, 269
  and social influence, 473–475
Illusions
  of free choice, 243
  of invulnerability, 523
  of unanimity, 523
Imitation, 369
  in aggression, 348–350, 453–455
  informational value of reinforcement,
    350–351
  in social learning theory, 347–348
Implicit personality theory, 141–149, 164
  definition of, 141
  measurement of, 141–149
    correlational methods, 142–146
    peer-nomination method, 147–148
    trait implication method, 146–147
Implicit theory of social psychology,
    14–19, 21, 29, 92, 192
Impression formation
  and attribution, 153–164
  central traits in, 106–107
  information integration theory of,
    149–153
  primacy effects, 105–106
  prior entry effect, 104
Incentive theory of attitude change, 3,

    250, 256–257, 259, 549
Independence
  from group pressure, 484, 549
  training and achievement motivation,
    440–442
Independent variable
  definition of, 63, 549
  operationalization of, 70–71
Index numbers, 48, 549
Individual differences, related to
  achievement motivation, 443–445
  aggression, 452
  competition, 423, 428, 435–445
  conformity, 489
  leadership, 509, 514–515
  self-esteem and self-concept, 328–330
Inequity, 370. *See also* Equity theory
  definition of, 364
  resolution of, 365
Information dependence, 181–182
Information-integration theory, 149–153,
    164, 549
Information-processing
  in attitude organization, 222–225, 549
  in attribution, 158
  in perception, 95
Informational social influence, 473–475,
    485–487, 549
Informed consent principle, 296, 549
Ingratiation, 235
Initiation, severity of and liking, 255,
    409–410, 516
Inoculation, 281–284, 549
Inputs, in equity theory, 363–369
Instigation to aggression, 448–459
Instinct
  and aggression, 448–450
  as explanation for social behavior, 6
  and territoriality, 449–450
Instrumental function
  of aggression, 454
  of attitudes, 269, 549
  of groups, 517–518
Insufficient justification. *See also*
    Attitude change; Role playing
  and attitude change, 249–261
  explanations of, 249–261
  principle of, 243–244, 549
Intelligence tests, 32–33, 83, 315
Intention
  in attribution theory, 154–158
  behavioral, 193, 223–224, 542